ULSTER SINCE 1600

Ulster Since 1600

Politics, Economy, and Society

Edited by
LIAM KENNEDY
and
PHILIP OLLERENSHAW

OXFORD
UNIVERSITY PRESS

Great Clarendon Street, Oxford, OX2 6DP,
United Kingdom

Oxford University Press is a department of the University of Oxford.
It furthers the University's objective of excellence in research, scholarship,
and education by publishing worldwide. Oxford is a registered trade mark of
Oxford University Press in the UK and in certain other countries

© Oxford University Press 2013

The moral rights of the authors have been asserted

First Edition published in 2013

Impression: 1

All rights reserved. No part of this publication may be reproduced, stored in
a retrieval system, or transmitted, in any form or by any means, without the
prior permission in writing of Oxford University Press, or as expressly permitted
by law, by licence or under terms agreed with the appropriate reprographics
rights organization. Enquiries concerning reproduction outside the scope of the
above should be sent to the Rights Department, Oxford University Press, at the
address above

You must not circulate this work in any other form
and you must impose this same condition on any acquirer

British Library Cataloguing in Publication Data

Data available

ISBN 978–0–19–958311–9

Printed in Great Britain by
MPG Books Group, Bodmin and King's Lynn

To the memory of J. M. Goldstrom, historian and trade unionist, 1929–2009.

Preface

In many respects the most distinctive of the Irish provinces, Ulster has been 'manufacturing history' at a pace that has often left historians and social scientists short of breath. From the plantations of the early seventeenth century to partition in the early 1920s, and beyond to the 'Troubles' of recent memory, there is no doubt that the northern province has occupied a central place in the historiography of modern Ireland. This is most obvious in relation to political history, arguably the primary colour in the Irish history spectrum, but economic, social, cultural, and demographic hues are also richly present. As Ireland's only industrial region, Ulster finds its place within a broader European experience. Ethnic and religious differences, by no means confined to Ireland, drew blood but they were not always the lethal forces sometimes implied by present-minded narratives.

The location of Ulster (see Map 1) needs to be borne firmly in mind. The east Ulster shoreline is situated close to the north of England and the west of Scotland. The watery highways allowed migration of people, technologies, and ideologies with relative ease. This particular social and geographic setting facilitated the formation of multiple identities, ideological differences, as well as economic and social modernization. In the case of industrialization, to take a prime example, the Belfast region had much more in common with Liverpool, Manchester, and Glasgow than with the rest of the island.

The coverage of Ulster in the historiography is unbalanced, not only in relation to time periods—the later twentieth century being the subject of a flood-tide of books, articles, and other media coverage—but in terms of subject matter as well. The magnetizing effect of the Troubles has attracted a disproportionate interest in political violence, paramilitary organizations, and abuses of state power. Yet to view the last four hundred years in the North through the prism of recent bloody events is to impoverish and distort our understanding of the lived experience of people in Ulster. This book aims to accord due recognition to the different phases of Ulster's history. Sometimes implicitly, other times explicitly, the book seeks to identify the constraints and opportunities—operating at local, regional, national, and international levels—that conditioned people's behaviour, be it in the political, social, economic, or cultural spheres. Change was of course a constant and its explication is of vital concern to the authors.

There are many people to be acknowledged, with much gratitude on our part, in the making of *Ulster Since 1600*. In particular, we benefited from helpful comments on population matters from Bill Macafee and Bruce Campbell and from Jim Mallory on Ulster prehistory. We offer a special word of gratitude to the staff at Oxford University Press. Stephanie Ireland has been an enthusiastic supporter, as well as an efficient and patient editor. Emma Barber and Emma Tuck were enormously helpful during the later stages of the editing process and we are much indebted to them both. The three anonymous reviewers appointed by OUP wrote constructive and helpful reports for which we are very grateful.

The volume is dedicated to the memory of the late Max (J. M.) Goldstrom. Max was a friend and fellow-historian for many years. He narrowly escaped the Holocaust, in which the rest of his family was consumed. As a 10-year-old child he was placed on a refugee train—the Kindertransport—which brought him to the safety of Britain just before the outbreak of the Second World War. Appointed to an assistant lectureship in history in Queen's University, Belfast in 1964, he and his wife Lorna made Belfast their home until his death in 2009. His creative achievements included early insightful contributions to Irish economic and social history, teaching generations of students in his own inimitable style, as well as service to the wider academic community through his active involvement in the Association of University Teachers at local and national level. He was one of the first in Britain and Ireland to notice the potential for digitizing historical sources, pioneering the use of OCR (optical character recognition) technology at Queen's. As such, he is the father of historical data digitization in Ireland. An appreciation of his life and work was published in *The Times*, 19 August 2009.

As the editors of other collective volumes will no doubt appreciate, it is a relief as well as a joy to have reached the final stage of a publishing venture and we offer our sincere thanks to all the contributors, not only for writing their chapters, but also for dealing with editorial demands over the last three years. There is still much research to be undertaken into the history of modern Ulster. In the meantime, we hope that readers find in this book helpful surveys of important themes, as well as material that is new and opinions with which to take issue.

Liam Kennedy and Philip Ollerenshaw

Contents

List of Maps and Illustration	xi
List of Tables	xii
List of Abbreviations	xiv
List of Contributors	xvi

	Introduction: Ulster since 1600 Liam Kennedy and Philip Ollerenshaw	1
1.	The Early Modern Economy, 1600–1780 Raymond Gillespie	12
2.	Politics and Society, 1600–1800 Thomas Bartlett	27
3.	Women in Ulster, 1600–1800 Mary O'Dowd	43
4.	People and Population Change, 1600–1914 Liam Kennedy, Kerby A. Miller, and Brian Gurrin	58
5.	Religion and Society, 1600–1914 S. J. Connolly	74
6.	Crime, Policing, and the Law, 1600–1900 Neal Garnham	90
7.	Popular Culture, 1600–1914 S. J. Connolly and Andrew R. Holmes	106
8.	Urban Ulster since 1600 R. J. Morris	121
9.	Migration and Emigration, 1600–1945 Donald M. MacRaild and Malcolm Smith	140
10.	The Rural Economy, 1780–1914 Liam Kennedy and Peter M. Solar	160
11.	Business and Finance, 1780–1945 Philip Ollerenshaw	177
12.	Labour and Society, 1780–1945 John Lynch	195
13.	Education since the Late Eighteenth Century N. C. Fleming	211
14.	Politics and Society, 1800–1960 James Loughlin	228

15. Gender, Family, and Sexuality, 1800–2000   245
    Diane Urquhart
16. Sport in the Nineteenth and Twentieth Centuries   260
    Alan Bairner
17. Agriculture and Rural Policy since 1914   275
    Alan Greer
18. Business and Labour since 1945   291
    Graham Brownlow
19. Social Policy and Social Change since 1914   308
    Peter Martin
20. Politics since 1960   325
    Graham Walker

Index   341

List of Maps and Illustration

MAPS

Map 1. The province of Ulster—towns	xvii
Map 2. The province of Ulster—physical features	xviii
Map 9.1. Migration: Ulster-born people in England and Wales in 1881, shown by Registration District	148
Map 9.2. Migration: Ulster-born people in England and Wales in 1881, shown by Registration District and distinguishing by county of origin	149
Map 11.1. Canals and navigations in Ireland, 1715–1876	185
Map 11.2. Railways in Ireland, 1834–1890	186

FIGURE

Figure 4.1. The population of the province of Ulster (000s), 1600–1911	59

List of Tables

4.1.	Age at marriage (AAM) for females and males in Ulster, 1841 and 1911	65
4.2.	Permanent celibacy among females and males in Ulster, 1841 and 1911: the proportion single in the age group 45–54 years	68
4.3.	The Protestant share of the Ulster population at various intervals between 1630 and 1911	71
6.1.	Density of policing in the four provinces of Ireland, 1832–52	94
6.2.	Reported homicides by province, 1866–92	98
6.3.	Indictable offences before the courts by province per 10,000 population, 1884–90	99
6.4.	Relative rates of prosecution for all criminal offences in Ulster counties and police districts, 1884–90	99
8.1.	Urban hierarchy of Ulster, 1659	124
8.2.	Urban hierarchy of Ulster, 1901	128
9.1.	Post-Famine emigration by Province	151
9.2.	Emigration from Ulster by county and as a share of county population, 1851–1911	151
9.3.	Scots-born and English-born residents of Belfast, 1841–1911	152
10.1.	Occupation of the land, by holding size (cumulative percentages) for the years 1854 and 1873	162
10.2.	Ulster's share of Irish agricultural exports: selected commodities, 1783–87	166
10.3.	An agricultural price index, based on Belfast market prices, selected years 1785–1913	174
11.1.	Percentage of gross UK tonnage launched in selected shipbuilding regions, 1880–1938	183
12.1.	Weekly wages of engineering workers, October 1905	201
12.2.	Distribution of the insured workforce in inter-war Northern Ireland	209
17.1.	Minimum tillage quotas 1940–49 (%)	284
18.1.	European growth, 1890–1992: average annual growth rates	292
18.2.	GDP per capita in Northern Ireland compared to the UK average, 1926–2000	292
18.3.	Comparative unemployment rates for Northern Ireland and the UK, 1950–2009	292
18.4.	Annual average percentage growth of net manufacturing output, 1948–70	293

18.5	Unemployment as a proportion of the civil labour force (expressed as a multiple of the average UK ratio), 1947–75	293
18.6	Index of identifiable public expenditure per head in the UK, minus social protection and agriculture (UK = 100), 2002–8	304
19.1	Death rates per 1000 population in Northern Ireland, England and Wales, Scotland, and Southern Ireland, 1922–99	312
19.2	Infant mortality per 1000 live births in Northern Ireland, England and Wales, Scotland, and Southern Ireland, 1922–80	312
19.3	Death rates per 1000 of population from tuberculosis in Northern Ireland, England and Wales, Scotland, and Southern Ireland, 1926–60	313
19.4	Deaths from heart disease per 1000 of population in Northern Ireland, England and Wales, Scotland, and Southern Ireland, 1926–80	313
19.5	Deaths from cancer per 1000 population in Northern Ireland, England and Wales, Scotland, and Southern Ireland, 1926–80	313
19.6	Life expectancy in Northern Ireland by selected ages and gender, 1910–99	314
19.7	Twelve-monthly average unemployment of insured workers in all industries in Great Britain and Northern Ireland, 1923–80	314
19.8	Unfit dwellings in Northern Ireland, 1974–97	320

List of Abbreviations

B.P.P.	British Parliamentary Papers
CAB	Cabinet [Papers]
CAP	Common Agricultural Policy
CSPI	Calendar of State Papers, Ireland
DARD	Department of Agriculture and Rural Development
DATI	Department of Agriculture and Technical Instruction
DETI	Department of Enterprise, Trade and Investment
DUP	Democratic Unionist Party
ERM	Exchange Rate Mechanism
FEA	Fair Employment Agency
FEC	Fair Employment Commission
GAA	Gaelic Athletic Association
GFA	Good Friday Agreement
H&WP	Harland & Wolff Papers
ICAI	Institute of Chartered Accountants in Ireland
IFA	Irish Farmers' Association
IFA	Irish Football Association
INV	Irish National Volunteers
IRA	Irish Republican Army
IREP	the Independent Review of Economic Policy
ITUC	Irish Trade Union Congress
LGD	Local Government District
PPA	Party Processions Act
NAUL	National Amalgamated Union of Labour
NIC	Northern Ireland Committee
NICRA	Northern Ireland Civil Rights Association
NIFPA	Northern Ireland Family Planning Association
NIHC	Northern Ireland House of Commons Debates
NIHE	Northern Ireland Housing Executive
NIHT	Northern Ireland Housing Trust
NILP	Northern Ireland Labour Party
NIO	Northern Ireland Office
NMSC	North/South Ministerial Council
OSMI	Ordnance Survey Memoirs, Ireland
PIRA	Provisional Irish Republican Army
PRONI	Public Record Office of Northern Ireland
PSNI	Police Service of Northern Ireland
RIC	Royal Irish Constabulary
RM	Resident Magistrate
RUC	Royal Ulster Constabulary
SDLP	Social Democratic and Labour Party
UDA	Ulster Defence Association
UDF	Ulster Defence Force

UEC	United Education Committee
UFU	Ulster Farmers' Union
UULA	Ulster Unionist Labour Association
UUP	Ulster Unionist Party
UUUC	United Ulster Unionist Council
UVF	Ulster Volunteer Force
UWC	Ulster Workers' Council

List of Contributors

Alan Bairner, Professor of Sport and Social Theory, Loughborough University

Thomas Bartlett, Professor of Irish History, University of Aberdeen

Graham Brownlow, Lecturer in Economics, Queen's University, Belfast

S. J. Connolly, Professor of Irish History, Queen's University, Belfast

N. C. Fleming, Senior Lecturer in History, University of Worcester

Neal Garnham, Senior Lecturer in History, University of Ulster

Raymond Gillespie, Professor of History, National University of Ireland, Maynooth

Alan Greer, Reader in Politics and Public Policy, University of the West of England, Bristol

Brian Gurrin, NUI Centennial Post-Doctoral Fellow in Irish Studies, National University of Ireland, Maynooth

Andrew R. Holmes, Lecturer in Modern Irish History, Queen's University, Belfast

Liam Kennedy, Professor Emeritus of Economic History, Queen's University, Belfast

James Loughlin, Reader in History, University of Ulster

John Lynch, Consultant Historian

Donald M. MacRaild, Research Professor in History, Northumbria University

Peter Martin, Visiting Research Fellow in the School of History and Anthropology, Queen's University, Belfast

Kerby A. Miller, Curators' Professor of History, University of Missouri, Columbia

R. J. Morris, Professor Emeritus of Economic and Social History, University of Edinburgh

Mary O'Dowd, Professor of Gender History, Queen's University, Belfast

Philip Ollerenshaw, Reader in History, University of the West of England, Bristol

Malcolm Smith, Senior Lecturer in Social Anthropology, University of Durham

Peter M. Solar, Professor of Economics, Vesalius College, Vrije Universiteit Brussel

Diane Urquhart, Senior Lecturer in Modern Irish History, University of Liverpool

Graham Walker, Professor of Political History, Queen's University, Belfast

Map 1. The province of Ulster—towns.

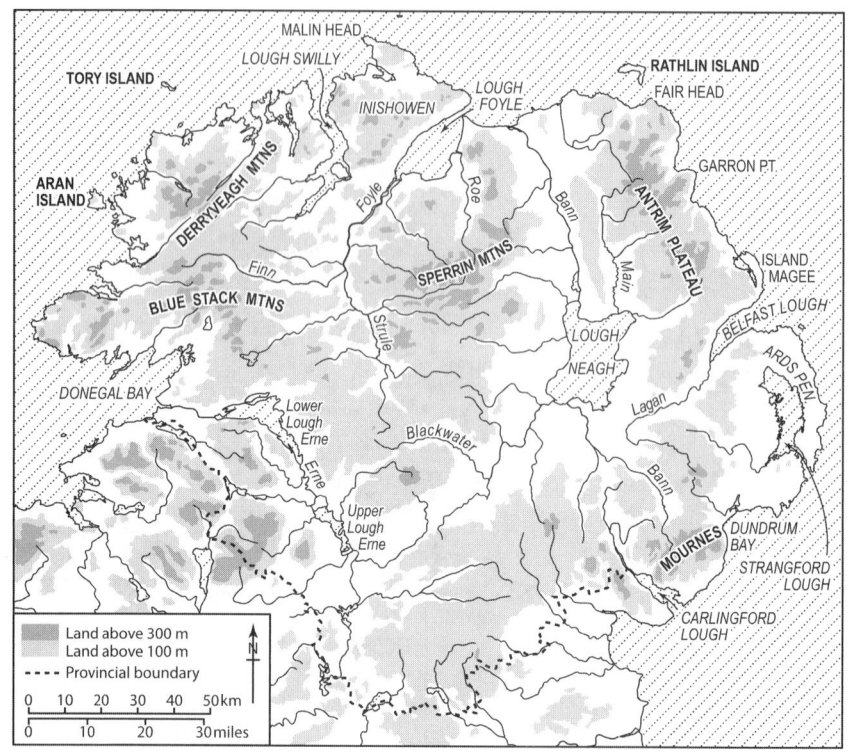

Map 2. The province of Ulster—physical features.

Introduction: Ulster since 1600

Liam Kennedy and Philip Ollerenshaw

To contemporary audiences, the terms Ulster, Northern Ireland, 'the North', are associated with images of communal conflict, sectarianism, and peace processes of indefinite duration. Traced over the last four centuries, however, the history of Ulster is much richer in its social, economic, and cultural variety, and also more peaceful, than these popular images would imply. As A. T. Q. Stewart reminds us: 'Before 1969, there was so little violent crime in Northern Ireland that a murder was a sensation to be talked about for years'.[1] This collaborative volume surveys the history of the province from 1600 to the present, in all its complexities, ambiguities, and contrariness. Its collective gaze takes in the variety of political, social, economic, and cultural forces that shaped society in the northern province of Ireland. The outcome is a set of interweaving narratives that are rich in human drama and the complexities of life in an ethnically divided society.

Ulster is a place apart, it has been said.[2] The nine-county province comprises about a quarter of the land area of Ireland and its north-east corner may have been the first part of the island to experience human settlement. Scholars have drawn on archaeological, anthropological, and geographical evidence to construct what Estyn Evans called 'the personality of Ulster'. Evans emphasized that the personality of the province long predated the seventeenth-century Plantations and that the 'differences between north and south at all periods seem to rest as much on the different sources of incoming peoples and cultures as on the environmental contrasts in Ireland itself'.[3] East Ulster's long-standing connections with Scotland were of fundamental importance in this respect and the region's Scottish ties were immeasurably strengthened with the Plantation. After the early 1700s, Scottish influence on the social, economic, and cultural life of the province was 'marked, though never dominant'.[4] Immigration gave Ulster a distinctive ethnic and religious mix, although the arrival in substantial numbers of Scottish Presbyterians should not be allowed to obscure the settlement of Scottish Catholics in the sixteenth and

---

[1] A. T. Q. Stewart, *The Narrow Ground: The Roots of Conflict in Ulster* (London, 1989), 2.
[2] The title of a book by the distinguished writer, Dervla Murphy, written in the 1970s at the height of the 'Troubles' in Northern Ireland. See D. Murphy, *A Place Apart* (London, 1979).
[3] E. E. Evans, 'The personality of Ulster', *Transactions of the Institute of British Geographers*, 51 (November 1970), 9.
[4] J. C. Beckett, 'Foreword', in C. Brady, M. O'Dowd, and B. Walker (eds), *Ulster: An Illustrated History* (London, 1989), 6.

seventeenth centuries as well as Catholics and Anglicans from England.[5] Rivalry and discrimination between different groups were generated by immigration and these encounters also led to emigration from Ulster as, for example, in the transatlantic movement of Irish Presbyterians in the early eighteenth century.[6]

This volume does not address directly the question whether Ireland was composed of one nation or two (although the existence of different ethnic groups is taken as read), but it is worth noting that on many occasions, northern unionists have been excluded by Irish nationalists in the definition of the nation while on other occasions unionists have excluded themselves.[7] Turning to the economic sphere, Ulster's trajectory was in important respects distinctive. In 1600 Ulster was a thinly populated, economically backward province; by 1900, despite the absence of coal and iron, the Belfast region had emerged as a significant industrial and commercial centre by UK and European standards. Its economic transformation is an exemplar of export-led growth, based first on proto-industry and later modern industrialization. Less favourably, the society incubated and perpetuated forms of politico-religious conflict that have generally outlived similar tendencies found elsewhere in western Europe.

In other respects, Ulster was part and parcel of a patchwork of regions that constituted the British and Irish Isles. As Sidney Pollard noted, industrialization in Britain and continental Europe was more of a regional than a national phenomenon, and Ulster certainly fits the generalization.[8] More generally, the province was subject to many of those wider forces making for social change in relation to religion, language, the status of women, and the living standards of the people. In social, economic, and cultural matters, Ulster opened outwards towards Britain and western Europe, be it in relation to music-hall entertainment or machine technology, notions of respectability or sexual *mores*, intellectual ideas or imported raw materials. While creating its own traditions in fields as diverse as Enlightenment thinking, Darwinian science, or landlord-tenant relations, it also resonated with historical forces within and beyond Ireland. It faced westwards as well as eastwards, and participated in the traffic in goods, ideas, and people within the framework of the Atlantic economy and the Atlantic world. Moreover, the influence of the British Empire should not be underestimated. Ireland has been described as both 'colonial' and 'imperial' and this description also necessarily applies to Ulster.[9] The evolution of society in Ulster and its vicissitudes are best comprehended, therefore, in terms of intersecting frames or levels, those of the region, the island of Ireland, the archipelago of British and Irish islands, the British Empire/Commonwealth, and the western world. These diverse influences, of varying strength and duration, acted and reacted on a society that was open to outside influences, not least because of its extensive diaspora.

[5] *Ulster: An Illustrated History*, Editors' Introduction, 11.
[6] Evans, 'Personality of Ulster', 16.
[7] J. Bowman, *De Valera and the Ulster Question, 1917–1973* (Oxford, 1982), 20–5.
[8] S. Pollard, *Peaceful Conquest* (Oxford, 1981), 111–23.
[9] K. Jeffery, 'Introduction', in idem (ed.), *'An Irish Empire'? Aspects of Ireland and the British Empire* (Manchester, 1996), 1.

Several chapters in this volume begin with the Ulster Plantation and go on to examine economic, social, political, gender, religious and cultural, demographic and urban themes, in the seventeenth and eighteenth centuries and sometimes beyond. Conflict between native and newcomer, legal and social transformation, improving literacy and changing patterns of popular culture, commercialization and urbanization, are some of the central concerns of these essays. They are followed by a series of essays that pursue these and other topics, including developments in the rural economy, industrialization and the rise of Belfast, the experience of urban labour, sectarianism in its different settings, the provision of education, and the evolution of sport in Ulster. The final group of essays continues the exploration of political, economic, and social change, beginning just before partition and extending into the early twenty-first century. Devolution, problems of economic adjustment, de-industrialization and unemployment, the outbreak and course of the Troubles, the changing nature of family life, and the increasing role of the state in rural, industrial, social, and educational policies feature prominently here. The volume concludes with an assessment of the 1998 Good Friday Agreement and the political prospects for Northern Ireland.

The opening chapter by Gillespie begins with the Plantation of Ulster and draws to a close in the later eighteenth century. Its subject matter is a number of 'interconnected revolutions'. With the Plantation land passed from an old to a new elite and fundamental changes in social organization followed. The spread of commercialization, although uneven, led to a more integrated economy, under common law. New towns, markets, and fairs (sometimes under landlord patronage), and an increasing export orientation were all features of the seventeenth and eighteenth centuries. A key feature was the growth of an export-oriented linen industry. Belfast expanded from a tiny settlement in 1600 to some 2000 houses by 1725. Derry, too, grew at an impressive rate. Migration from Scotland and England altered the ethnic balance in Ulster; the dispossession of native landholders served to perpetuate a sense of grievance on the part of the Gaelic Irish. At the same time, the seventeenth and eighteenth centuries provide ample evidence of the fragility of economic progress. War, plague, poor harvests, and trade depression in Ulster, no less than in other commercializing regions of Europe, could and did take their toll on life, living standards, and wealth accumulation.

The history of Ulster from 1603, as Bartlett reminds us, was part of the history of Scotland and England as well as of Ireland, and this 'tripartite identity would distinguish it from the other three provinces'. Tyrone's rebellion (1594–1603) was the most serious challenge to the British state in Ireland up to that time. The sharp decline in land held by the native Irish was an important result of the Plantation, and Bartlett explains not only the origins of the 1641 rebellion but also how that rebellion turned into a massacre of settlers in a manner unintended by its originators. The 1641 rebellion in Ulster ushered in two decades of 'massacre and mayhem', including famine and wholesale land confiscations. The province's Catholics were the big losers from the Williamite wars (1689–91). During the eighteenth century, growing prosperity and large-scale emigration of Presbyterians to the New World reduced the potential for unrest.

From the 1770s developments first in the American colonies and then in Europe had a direct impact on Ulster politics and society. New groups such as the United Irishmen (1791) and the Orange Order (1795) had both short- and long-term significance for the province. Bartlett concludes that just as the Ulster Plantation had followed the defeat of Tyrone's rebellion, so the 1798 rebellion 'made the Act of Union possible'.

Women were the less visible actors in these various historical episodes. The Flight of the Earls in 1607, to take one example, features prominently in the historiography of seventeenth-century Ireland but few have wondered how many women moved with their men in that famous flight. Some have entertained the belief that early-modern Gaelic society was a haven for women who enjoyed extensive rights in relation to their menfolk. However, in aristocratic Gaelic society, as Mary O'Dowd shows, women were used ruthlessly as pawns in a political game. The status of women at the lower levels of that society also seems to have been low. Surprisingly, perhaps, some such as widows gained in terms of property rights under the Plantation. The new society being fashioned by sword and law in the seventeenth century remained patriarchal of course but in different ways. Economic change, particularly the development of proto-industry in the eighteenth century, opened up opportunities for women. There were advances in literacy, and some non-conformist congregations even saw a role for women in preaching and related religious activity, but, in a telling conclusion, O'Dowd relates that women did not feature at all as political figures in the public sphere before 1800.

The seventeenth-century plantations and movements of people into Ulster gave rise to a complex society in terms of ethnicity, politics, and religion. These upheavals shaped its demography, although the original identities proved more malleable than is sometimes assumed, both in the short and the long run.[10] Kennedy, Miller, and Gurrin show how a thinly populated region in 1600 had come to hold a disproportionate share of the island's population two centuries later, as the economic and demographic 'centre of gravity of the island' moved northwards. Religious demography, seemingly inevitably, formed an important part of the story. The authors go on to unfold a new explanation of Ulster's and, by implication, Ireland's population explosion, before considering its nemesis in the catastrophic famine of 1846–50. The years between the Famine and the Great War were marked by lesser shocks and some demographic surprises. More generally, the chapter underlines the point that the 'historic' province of Ulster was not a homogenous entity but rather one in which sub-regions and localities could have widely varying social structures and identities.

The Reformation constitutes one of the great, if ragged, dividing lines in modern European history. Although affecting Ireland later than many European societies, it was clear by the 1630s that the distinction between natives and colonists, between Protestants and Catholics, had assumed an enduring quality. A significant division

---

[10] L. Kennedy, K. A. Miller, and B. Gurrin, 'The Planter and the Gael: Explorations in Irish Ethnic History', in K. White (ed.), *The Imaginary of the Stranger* (Letterkenny, forthcoming 2012).

opened up within Protestantism soon afterwards, which ran along ethnic as well as religious lines. By 1700 more than half the Protestants of Ulster were Presbyterian, and in ethnic terms were primarily of Scottish origin. Religious persecution was a commonplace within Catholic and Protestant societies in Europe, and Ireland was no exception. Connolly traces a range of reform tendencies within the major churches, as religious leaders and elders sought to impose greater discipline on recalcitrant clergymen and their sometimes unruly congregations. In terms of Catholicism, this culminated in the Devotional Revolution of the second half of the nineteenth century. Evangelical fervour marked the Anglican tradition from the late eighteenth century onwards, while Presbyterianism found itself subject to periodic secessions on the grounds of theological orthodoxy. If anything, these revivals sharpened religious animosities in nineteenth-century Ireland.

The legal developments of the early seventeenth century not only affected the structure of landholding, they also introduced changes to the criminal code. The court system was severely affected by the 1641 rebellion and Williamite wars. Garnham explores these legal changes and emphasizes that the spread of both the common law and the courts did not imply acceptance of them. 'Patronage, politics, and religious persuasion' affected expectation of the law. Although Ulster was left unaffected by the establishment of a modern police force in Dublin in 1786, the centrally-controlled Irish constabulary half a century later included all the provinces. As Garnham shows, eighteenth-century Ulster was not 'prodigiously violent' and was the least densely policed province in the 1840s. Sectarian conflict did play an important role in the nature of policing before 1914, not just in Belfast but in smaller towns and in rural areas too, and there were very considerable local variations in crime within the province. Overall, however, Ulster people 'were not a great deal more respectful of the law' than those elsewhere in Ireland, with alleged criminals being frequently protected by 'a conspiracy of silence'.

With regard to popular culture, a term which covers such a wide range of human activity that it is difficult to separate what it connotes from so much else that goes on in society, Connolly and Holmes see Ulster as conforming to a broadly European pattern. From the early modern period onwards there was a progressive withdrawal of elite support for sports and pastimes, extending also to language, modes of speaking, believing, and behaving, as practised and enjoyed by the mass of the people. In Ulster, as indeed in other border regions of Europe, this process was complicated by the diversity of its ethnic groups. These processes were by no means unilinear in time, and in the nineteenth century one is struck by the numbers of upper-class enthusiasts engaged in cultural revival activities, be it in relation to archaeology, language, folklore, or history. Connolly and Holmes counsel against the simple notion that the suppression of the more boisterous popular customs associated with wakes, marriages, drinking, party processions, blood sports, and other occasions of sociability, can be explained simply in terms of social control exercised by the upper classes and the clergy. Economic and social change, including in particular the advent of industrialization and new work disciplines, served to induce widespread re-evaluations of lifestyles. Many people were also alive to the emerging opportunities afforded by literacy, language change, and self-discipline.

In important ways, opportunities were also offered by urbanization in Ulster, a process that is analysed by Morris across a span of four centuries. During the Ulster Plantation, towns, both small and larger, were 'central to the project of domination, legitimacy, and economic development'. As with several other aspects of the Plantation, however, the results did not always mirror original intentions. Morris, like Gillespie, underlines the importance of the linen industry to urban growth, although many other factors were also at work. Derry headed the urban hierarchy in 1659, but had fallen well behind Belfast by 1831. By the latter date, the small town with a market and under 2000 inhabitants was common. Cavan, Fermanagh, and Donegal, in the south and west of the province had the lowest levels of urbanization. By the early twentieth century, industrialization had brought further changes to the Ulster urban hierarchy—but this was typical of the European experience. Morris also reminds us that Ulster failed to create a consensus as far as the urban order was concerned, with residential segregation and sporadic community violence on a large scale. After partition, the new devolved government showed little interest in slum clearance or in reducing overcrowding, and 'there was none of the innovative housing development of Liverpool, Leeds, or Vienna'. A range of health and welfare indicators pointed to deprivation in many of Ulster's urban centres. The violence from the 1960s not only divided urban communities further, 'the barricade and checkpoint became major ways of challenging or asserting state authority'. Following the Good Friday Agreement in 1998, reconciliation projects would become a much more common feature of Northern Ireland's towns and cities in the twenty-first century. Related to the rate and extent of urbanization is the movement of people into, out of, and within Ulster.

Few regions have been so defined by population movements. In the seventeenth century Ulster was a province of aggressive inward migration. In the succeeding three centuries, as MacRaild and Smith demonstrate, it was a region of net outward migration. Indeed there is a paradox here. The descendants of the Scottish and English newcomers laid the basis for commercial enterprises, both in the rural and urban sectors, which made east Ulster the most economically advanced region in Ireland. Yet Ulster continued to send thousands—in some decades, tens of thousands—of migrants across the Atlantic to North America. Presbyterians, of Scottish descent, dominated these outflows. From the later eighteenth century onwards many migrants found their way to Britain and to Scotland in particular. Ulster–Scotland links, which stretched back into early historical times, were deepened by reverse migration in the nineteenth century. Thus, one of the largest concentrations of Scots outside of Scotland, according to MacRaild and Smith, was to be found in Belfast. As with so much else, industry and industrialization animated these cross-channel movements. More generally, movements of people in recent centuries can be related to Ulster's positioning within a British and an Atlantic world that was experiencing unprecedented economic, social, and demographic change.

Environmental features such as soil, climate, and location distinguished Ulster from other regions in Ireland, and had implications for the kinds of farming pursued in this, the most northerly province. Mixed farming predominated during the eighteenth and nineteenth centuries. In the later nineteenth century, under conditions of European-wide agricultural depression, a shift towards livestock production gathered momentum. What is especially distinctive about the Ulster rural economy, however, was the interpenetration of rural industry and agriculture. These twin economic bases of commercial linen and food production helped cushion northern households against the inevitable fluctuations in prices and incomes associated with the developing market economy. Even the massive famines of the 1740s and the 1840s had a lesser impact in Ulster. By the eve of the Great War, the complex social structure of rural Ulster circa 1800—composed of landlords, middlemen, tenant farmers of varying size and wealth, farmer-weavers, cottier-weavers, and labourers—had given rise to a very different social formation. The major forces for change, according to Kennedy and Solar, may be found in factory-based industrialization, changes in international food markets, and the effectiveness of modern agrarian radicalism.

The uneven and fragile nature of regional economic growth outlined earlier by Gillespie is further discussed by Ollerenshaw. For the period between the later eighteenth century and the end of the Second World War, Ulster experienced not only its most rapid rates of industrialization but also (after 1920) its most severe structural economic problems. In important respects these problems have endured to the present day. In Ulster, as in some other industrializing regions such as northwest England and the west of Scotland, linen and cotton were crucial to the development of factory-based industry which in turn led to major changes in industrial location within Ulster itself. Belfast emerged as a major UK centre of industry, trade, and finance with some large, globally connected enterprises and a whole host of small- and medium-sized firms in both manufacturing and services. The Belfast Chamber of Commerce, founded in 1783, was the most important business association in the province and became militantly unionist a century later. The regional economic base, and the wider UK economy of which it was a constituent part, faced unprecedented challenges between the wars as high unemployment and relatively low incomes presented the new devolved government in Belfast with a range of difficulties, most of which it was impossible to overcome.

The object of economic activity is to enhance the material welfare of those who work in fields, factories, offices, workshops, and other places but, as Lynch indicates, in industrializing Ulster work relationships were also embedded in power relationships linking different social classes. These relations of production gave rise to varying degrees of tension between the owners of capital and labour, centring on wage payments, conditions of work, health, and safety. He is also careful to point out that divisions within the emerging working classes, in Ulster as elsewhere, can be as important as those between social classes, the major dividing line being between skilled and unskilled work. There were further cross-currents. Communal, sectarian, and later national differences complicated issues of working-class solidarity, trade union organization, and the emergence of a labour movement. Despite these cross-cutting loyalties, workers in Belfast developed a significant trade union membership. The dockers' strike of 1907, which spread to include sections of the police, was a high point in cooperation between workers from different politico-religious backgrounds, while the large-scale expulsion of mainly Catholic workers from their workplaces in Belfast in 1920 indicated just how fragile any such accommodations might be.

Modernizing and democratizing societies require mass literacy. The nineteenth century was an age of state initiatives for the education of the people. By 1900, Ireland had levels of basic literacy and numeracy that were comparable to those of leading societies elsewhere in the world. In that sense the national school system, as outlined by Fleming, was a resounding success. There were also limited advances in relation to secondary and university education but, as Fleming also recounts, education was a continuing site of conflict between the British state (and later on the statelet of Northern Ireland) and the major denominations. The churches were also in conflict with each other over access to young minds. Each sought as monopolistic a position as possible in relation to the doctrinal and ideological formation of its adherents. Segregation or 'benign apartheid' was, and still is, the order of the day. To use D. H. Akenson's resonant phrase, this meant that 'education and enmity' co-existed at the very heart of the already divided society of Northern Ireland.[11]

Politically and constitutionally, the Act of Union was the great legislative landmark in Ireland between 1800 and 1920. It provided as much of a focus for those who supported it as for those who were opposed and indeed the key political division in modern Ulster is that between unionist and nationalist. Loughlin's chapter examines post-1800 politics, presenting examples of interdenominational cooperation but also increasing polarization. The massacre of Protestants in 1641 and in 1798 had a long-lasting impact on Ulster's Protestant population. Despite the significance of localism in politics, clearer electoral demarcation between Catholic and Protestant was a feature of the nineteenth century. Catholic Emancipation in 1829, the growth of nationalism, the resurgence of the Orange Order, and the widely held Protestant belief that the Union underpinned economic progress all contributed to this. This polarization became especially obvious after Gladstone's conversion to Home Rule in 1885. The militarization of the unionist-nationalist conflict between 1912 and 1914, and the concentration of unionists in the northeast, pointed towards partition, as did the results of the 1918 General Election. However, as Loughlin notes, more traditional nationalism did survive in the northeast despite the challenge from an invigorated Sinn Fein. From the 1920s, the abolition of proportional representation for elections in Northern Ireland and the unwillingness of Westminster to intervene in Northern Ireland's domestic affairs led to the accumulation of unaddressed grievances which in the 1960s found effective expression in the civil rights campaign, and gave rise to unprecedented challenges to the government of Northern Ireland.

The family is often seen as the basic unit of society. As Urquhart argues, it shapes decisions affecting women in particularly powerful ways. She also suggests there

---

[11] D. H. Akenson, *Education and Enmity: The Control of Schooling in Northern Ireland, 1920–50* (Newton Abbot, 1973).

were distinctive elements to the demography of the northern counties, when analysed in gender terms. Gender ratios were skewed in favour of women in east Ulster, marriage rates were higher than in other Irish regions, while high rates of marital fertility, infant mortality, and maternal mortality persisted into the twentieth century. All may be related, in varying ways, to economic structure and high rates of female participation in the labour force. High rates of illegitimate births, relative to the low levels experienced in more Catholic-dominated areas of the island, gave rise to much polemical interest. Denominational differences in legitimate fertility were more pronounced, however, particularly from the Second World War onwards. Catholic fertility was two-thirds higher in 1971 as compared to Protestant fertility, although the two have tended to converge since then. The strident opposition of the Catholic Church to contraception slowed rather than blocked wider social trends towards reduced family sizes and enhanced status for women.

The interplay of politics and sport is a central theme of Bairner's chapter which focuses on the period since the late eighteenth century, taking in so-called 'foreign' games such as cricket, football, hockey, and rugby, as well as Gaelic games. He emphasizes the relative importance of the military and of rural society in the development of games and also notes the differential impact of partition on the organization or reorganization of various sports. In general, however, the consequences of new state formation for sport in the province were 'immediate, direct, and persistent'. Sport was both a way to escape political and social hardship and a key factor 'in the construction and reproduction of competing identities'. Some games had clear provincial elements in their organization; for example, the Ulster Branch of the Irish Rugby Football Union established in 1879, and the Ulster Council of the Gaelic Athletic Association in 1903. Representation at international, including Olympic, level has posed problems for individual sportsmen and women. Also symptomatic of the difficulties arising from representation and identity in the twenty-first century have been the debates surrounding a possible 'national' sports stadium in Northern Ireland.

Agriculture also had its difficulties, albeit of a very different kind. The long-term tendency in the modern period was decline, as reflected both in falling employment and a diminishing share of gross regional output. This mirrors the kinds of sectoral changes taking place within other industrial and post-industrial regions. The United Kingdom was relatively late in going down the road of protectionism and state support for farming, but from 1932 onwards these formed the basis of rural policy. Though fiercely individualistic and independent, the irony is that Ulster (and European) farmers were more than happy to become dependent on state subsidies and protection. The financial weakness of the Northern Ireland state, which affected all areas of economic and social expenditure, meant there was little room for distinctive Stormont initiatives. Real power resided at Westminster. As charted by Greer, the burden of support was transferred to Westminster initially and later to the European Union. Under the impact of managed competitive forces, the mixed farming regime sketched by Kennedy and Solar for earlier periods gave way to a reorientation in favour of livestock production and part-time farming.

Agriculture remained the single most important employer in Northern Ireland until well into the twentieth century, but manufacturing remained crucial to the region's economic viability. The economic performance of the region since 1945 is considered by Brownlow in its broader UK and European context. He explores the problems of 'peripherality' faced by the region in its efforts to achieve growth. In the second half of the twentieth century, unemployment was considerably higher, and incomes per head generally much lower, than the UK average. The region never achieved full employment and missed out on the 'golden age' of economic growth in western Europe between 1950 and 1973. The 1970s was a particularly disappointing decade and the economic fragility discussed in earlier chapters is reaffirmed for the later twentieth century. Brownlow considers it 'implausible' to attribute Northern Ireland's relatively poor performance to the 'Troubles' and looks instead to institutions, innovation, entrepreneurship, and productivity. Above all, the region's dependence on the public sector in the later twentieth and early twenty-first centuries stands out. De-industrialization and the growing importance of the public sector were reflected in the region's trade union membership and pattern of industrial relations.

Turning from economic to social policy, Martin argues there was no consensus within government, right from the beginning, on the role of the state in Northern Ireland. This ambiguity might be traced back to the differences between Liberal and Conservative groups within the Ulster Unionist alliance, as this developed in the later nineteenth century. This, together with the multiplicity of local authorities in Northern Ireland, could lead to inertia and also to important regional variations in service provision. In Northern Ireland, as in Britain, severe economic depression followed by the Second World War, led to unprecedented interest in social reform, including the belated establishment of the Ministry of Health and Local Government in 1944. The introduction of the National Health Service in Northern Ireland was, in Martin's words, 'an exercise in transplantation rather than re-imagination'. Controversial areas of public policy included the allocation of local authority housing, which became central to the civil rights campaign of the 1960s. The imposition of direct rule in 1972 had significant implications for health, housing, and employment policies. With regard to other indicators, such as consumer spending, there was considerable convergence between Northern Ireland and Britain so that by the early twenty-first century, levels of ownership of goods such as computers, microwaves, and satellite and cable television, matched those in Britain.

In the 1960s, as Walker's chapter shows, the lack of consensus on the legitimacy of the state in Northern Ireland, combined with the neglect of grievances by both the Westminster and Belfast governments, led to widespread disorder during the premiership of Terence O'Neill (1963–69). Though the descent into violence between 1968 and 1972 was by no means inevitable, the period saw the formation of a significant number of new political parties (including the Democratic Unionist Party, Social Democratic and Labour Party, and the Alliance Party), as well as the creation of loyalist and republican paramilitary groups such as the Ulster Defence Association and the Provisional Irish Republican Army. The prorogation of the

Northern Ireland Parliament in 1972 ushered in Direct Rule, and one consequence was the growing power of the Northern Ireland Office which increased the 'democratic deficit' for many years thereafter. The decision by Sinn Fein to contest elections, following the dramatic increase in support after the 1980–81 hunger strikes, was a key factor in Northern Ireland politics. Throughout the 1980s and most of the 1990s, the search for a cross-community settlement continued, but not until after the 1998 Good Friday Agreement was a relatively successful formula found. This has brought what Walker calls 'creeping normalization' to Northern Ireland, with devolved government, north-south bodies, and British-Irish cooperation. In the early twenty-first century, the spectacle of the DUP sharing government with Sinn Fein demonstrated just how far Northern Ireland politics had travelled since the height of the Troubles and widespread bloodshed some thirty years before.[12]

---

[12] At the symbolic level, and also indicating a degree of closure in relation to the Troubles, there was the public handshake of Queen Elizabeth II and Martin McGuinness of Sinn Fein in June 2012 during the course of the Queen's visit to Northern Ireland as part of her Diamond Jubilee celebrations.

1

The Early Modern Economy, 1600–1780

Raymond Gillespie

Over the seventeenth and eighteenth centuries the province of Ulster was transformed from a poor, sparsely populated, peripheral region to one that lay at the core of the Irish economy. That process did not proceed in a smooth, uninterrupted way. It is possible to identify at least three cycles of growth punctuated by sometimes deep recessions. The first phase was initiated by population increase in the early seventeenth century, resulting from colonization, and was brought to an end by a deep recession in the late 1630s that was transformed into depression by the wars of the 1640s. In the early 1660s the economic cycle began to move upwards, and growth proceeded apace until the recessionary decades of the early eighteenth century which, in turn, gave way to recovery from the middle of the century that forged forward into the 1790s. Just as the pace of growth was uneven, so the cycles of change were not smooth. Years of war, bad weather, harvest failure, and cattle disease, notably in the late 1620s, the early 1670s, and the early 1690s, served to interrupt the broad patterns of change.

Within this pattern of fluctuating fortunes there was a second set of forces at work that were less visible, but no less vital, to the economic transformation of early modern Ulster. These can best be characterized as structural forces that created the conditions necessary for economic modernization. In 1600, Ulster was part of a world in which lordship over men was the dominant social framework, in contrast to the society of the Anglo-Irish Pale where lordship over land was the main organizing social principle. The principal form of exchange in Ulster was not the market but a socially embedded network of duties that were paid by lesser lords to greater ones.[1] Land was organized not in great estates, as was the case in the eighteenth century, but in family units gathered together under the protection of regional lords. In return for traditionally sanctioned payments, these lords provided services such as military protection and arbitration in disputes. This was a world in which status was not determined by wealth but controlled by genealogy, the ability to command lesser families, and by accumulating cultural capital in the form of literary patronage. Thus the bardic poem was an important political as well as a literary device. The strength of this patronage system varied across Ulster. It is

---

[1] For sixteenth-century examples see M. Dillon (ed.), 'Ceart Uí Néill', *Studia Celtica*, 1 (1966), 1–18; S. Ó Dufaigh (ed.), 'Cíos Mhic Mhathghamhna', *Clogher Record*, 4 (1962), 125–34.

noticeable that in the sixteenth century, the O'Donnells of west Ulster were greater patrons of bardic poets, with some fifty-two surviving poems, as opposed to just twenty-two for the apparently more politically significant O'Neills.[2] It was also a system that, even without outside involvement, was changing in the late sixteenth century. Internecine warfare between the dynastic branches of the O'Neills and the rise in the number of Scots mercenaries, or gallowglasses, in Ulster were forcing social changes within that lordship.[3] Despite those pressures, this system with its traditional duties and renders, proved resilient to political change and, although it ultimately dissolved under the pressures of commercialization, some traces of the attitudes associated with it can be traced into the late seventeenth century.[4] According to Oliver Plunkett, the Catholic archbishop of Armagh, in the 1670s the native Irish, though now tenants to new landlords, continued to recognize their old lords and contributed to their upkeep, having 'great affection' for the old families.[5]

THE PROBLEMS OF PLANTATION

For the inhabitants of early modern Ulster, the moment when it became clear that their economic structures were about to undergo a transformation came towards the end of the first decade of the seventeenth century. The end of the Nine Years War in 1603 paved the way for some changes to the social framework of the province by introducing a common law framework to replace older customary rules, and by creating a set of land grants from the crown that defined property rights in a more careful way than hitherto. The persistence of the older elite after 1603 made these changes difficult to enforce. In 1607 this situation was transformed by the 'Flight of the Earls', in which the main lords of west Ulster left the province, initiating a series of changes that have been collectively described as the Plantation of Ulster. Unlike most early seventeenth-century plantations, that in Ulster was a sophisticated affair, involving not just a reassignment of lands but also a restructuring of the social order. This was most obvious in the allocation of the confiscated lands of the earls—the escheated counties—to new settlers, or undertakers, who undertook to settle the lands in blocks of between 1000 and 2000 acres. In east Ulster, which was not part of the plantation scheme, much larger estates were created, shaping a very different social structure between the two regions within the province. The grid of estates that was created was the lasting legacy of the seventeenth-century settlement, persisting long after most of the other results of the plantation process had collapsed under the weight of the rising of 1641.

---

[2] <http://www.dias.ie> (3 September 2010). The contrast is even more stark than this since the O'Neill poem count includes poems for minor branches.
[3] N. Canny, 'Hugh O'Neill and the Changing Face of Gaelic Ulster', *Studia Hibernica,* 10 (1970), 7–35.
[4] H. Morgan, 'The End of Gaelic Ulster: A Thematic Interpretation of Events Between 1534 and 1610', *Irish Historical Studies,* 26 (1988), 8–32.
[5] J. Hanly (ed.), *The Letters of Saint Oliver Plunkett, 1625–1681* (Dublin, 1979), 74.

Forty per cent of the escheated counties were allocated between Scottish and English undertakers, 14 per cent to the native Irish, and 13 per cent to servitors, mainly ex-soldiers and government servants who were held to be the backbone of the settlement. One-tenth of the escheated lands were granted to the London companies in County Londonderry, with the remainder allocated between the Church, Trinity College, Dublin, and the newly founded royal schools. Undertakers were required to build castles, introduce settlers, construct towns, and create markets. Of greater significance than the simple requirement to introduce settlers were the terms on which they were to be settled.

The revised conditions of the Ulster plantation in 1610 stipulated that an estate was to be divided among settlers in specified numbers of freeholds, leaseholds, and tenancies at will, thus attempting to regulate not only landholding but social structures and relationships.[6] The planners focused on institutions that would create societies rather than isolated estates. The social significance of the markets that the undertakers were required to create is a case in point. As a tract on Ireland in the early 1640s described the process of establishing markets, 'they have placed markets and fairs throughout the land whereby the diligent may make use of their labours and whereby the commerce and intercourse would advantage and incorporate the people'.[7] Similar comments were made in more official contexts. A market created at Dundrum, County Down, in 1629 was to be 'for the public good of the inhabitants residing at or near Dundrum and with the intention that they may have free trade and commerce among themselves and with other liege subjects… by which the rude and country people of that region may be led to a more humane and civil mode of life and the more easily procure a provision of all necessaries'.[8] Perhaps the matter was put most pithily by William Parsons in 1622 when he described markets and fairs as 'commonwealth meetings'.[9] Creating markets as part of the plantation scheme had a logic far beyond the economic and lay at the core of the forming of a new type of society, British in outlook, and legal in its articulation. The rise of a commercial economy was clearly part of a wider social process.

Seen as a planning exercise the Ulster plantation was a significant achievement for an early modern administration. As was common in these situations, problems rapidly emerged in the execution of the scheme. Difficulties became apparent at two levels. First, at the level of the undertakers themselves the sort of people who had been envisioned for the task did not wish to participate. Some grantees who were courtiers rapidly sold their grants to others. Those who were prepared to become part of the long-term future of Ulster tended to fall into two groups: either those who had failed in England or Scotland and looked to Ulster to restore their fortunes, or those from England or Scotland who were deeply ambitious but whose resources did not allow them to realize those ambitions at home. These two groups combined into a social elite that lacked either capital or the social authority to

---

[6] T. W. Moody (ed.), 'The Revised Articles of the Ulster Plantation, 1610', *Bulletin of the Institute of Historical Research*, 12 (1935), 181.
[7] British Library, London, Add MS 4777, f. 66v.
[8] J. Morrin, *Calendar of the Patent and Close Rolls of Chancery in Ireland, Charles I* (Dublin, 1864), 452.
[9] V. Treadwell (ed.), *The Irish Commission of 1622* (Dublin, 2007), 760.

fulfill the role that they had been intended to play. As Lord Deputy Chichester commented in 1610, the settlers for the Ulster plantation were a disappointing lot, 'those from England are, for the most part plain country gentlemen... If they have any money they keep it close, for hitherto they have disbursed but little.... The Scottish come with greater part and better accompanied but it may be with less money in their purses.'[10] Short of capital, some landlords made long leases with low rents but high entry fines, which created a financial prison of debt from which few could escape, and which would have long-term consequences for many.[11]

Secondly, at the level of the settlers there were even more difficult problems. Settlers did not materialize in the numbers that were anticipated and by c.1630, the male settler population of Ulster may only have been about 15,000.[12] This was dwarfed by the native Irish population. Evidence here is thin but a unique documentary survival for Donegal in the mid-1620s suggests that there the natives outnumbered the settlers by some three to one.[13] More fragmentary evidence extracted from the undertakers' certificates of the state of their lands furnished to the commissioners in 1622 indicates a varied pattern. In the Londonderry settlement, the balance between native and newcomer was the same as it was in Donegal. In Tyrone the position was more closely balanced with native families outnumbering settlers by only 1.7:1 on undertakers' estates while in the well-settled baronies of Fews and O'Neill, and in Armagh, settler families outnumbered those of the natives by three to one.[14] Not only was the size of the settler population rather smaller than expected, but its distribution was erratic. By the 1630s, it was heavily clustered around the major ports and their hinterlands. In particular, settlers concentrated in east Ulster, outside the official area of the plantation but closest to Scotland and England. This created a plentiful supply of labour on the lands of south Antrim, north Down, and along the Lagan Valley corridor into north Armagh. Again the Laggan, in the hinterland of Derry, was well settled.[15] In other, more marginal, areas in the west of the province, native Irish dominated. By 1660 some 20 per cent of townlands in the core of Ulster in north Armagh and east Londonderry had no Irish while at the edge of the province only between 5 and 10 per cent can be so described.[16] Some caution needs to be exercised in interpreting such figures since they clearly include the effects of war and dislocation in the 1640s and 1650s but the general pattern appears to be clear.

Modest though these demographic changes may seem, they took place in the context of a low population base and were enough to increase the labour supply of

---

[10] *Calendar of State Papers Relating to Ireland, 1608–10*, 525–6.
[11] P. Roebuck, 'Landlord Indebtedness in Ulster in the Seventeenth and Eighteenth Centuries', in J. M. Goldstrom and L. A. Clarkson (eds), *Irish Population, Economy and Society* (Oxford, 1982), 135–55.
[12] P. Robinson, *The Plantation of Ulster* (Dublin, 1985), 104.
[13] British Library, London, Add MS 3827, f. 63.
[14] Treadwell (ed.), *The Irish Commission of 1622*, 540–9, 567–87, 624–33.
[15] Robinson, *Plantation of Ulster*, 93–4.
[16] W. J. Smyth, *Map-making, Landscapes and Memory: A Geography of Colonial and Early Modern Ireland* (Cork, 2006), 350.

Ulster sufficiently to boost output significantly. At the same time, breakup of the lordship system allowed much of this additional output to be exchanged in the market place. However a low, relatively poor, population had little consuming power and thus much of this additional output found its way into the export market. The customs yield of Carrickfergus, for example, increased almost sevenfold between 1616 and 1635, and while the yield from the smaller ports of east Ulster grew less strongly, it was nevertheless significant.[17] The impact of this growth in trade also fed into the growth of port towns of Ulster. Belfast, for instance, did not exist in 1600, yet by 1640 its population lay between 400 and 500 souls and Derry probably had some 1500 people.[18] It is difficult to be specific about the nature of this trade since port books have not survived but the indications are that raw materials, such as live cattle, timber, and linen yarn, formed the mainstay of Ulster exports. While output had been increased, the structure of the economy was much as it had been in the late sixteenth century.[19]

The emergence of this increasingly commercialized world, underpinned by a system of common law, presented problems of adjustment for the surviving native Irish population of Ulster. Many who failed to adapt to the more commercialized world of buying and selling and setting market rents, fell into debt and were forced to sell their grants. In Armagh, for instance, the percentage of land held by native Irish fell from about 25 per cent at the plantation to about 19 per cent in 1641, and in Cavan the fall was from 20 per cent to 16 per cent over the same period.[20] At a lower social level the dramatic economic growth that characterized Ulster after the plantation meant that there was a growing number of settlers, and the demand for high quality land increased. This inevitably reshaped the patterns of settlement on many estates with a greater measure of segregation on some of them.[21] Such patterns of segregation combined with Catholic revitalization after 1622 suggests that the levels of assimilation that probably existed in the first two decades of the plantation may have shaded into accommodation in the 1630s.

DESTROYING THE OLD ORDER

In late 1639 and throughout 1640, a series of events conspired to transform the nature of Ulster society. Political instability in Scotland and Ireland in 1639 and 1640 combined with a series of bad harvest failures. The impact of these failures was exacerbated by the quartering of an Irish army, intended for service against the Covenanters in

---

[17] D. Woodward, 'Irish Trade and Customs Statistics, 1614–1641', *Irish Economic and Social History*, 26 (1999), 58–64.
[18] R. Gillespie, *Early Belfast: The Origins and Growth of an Ulster Town to 1750* (Belfast, 2007), 71.
[19] R. Gillespie, *The Transformation of the Irish Economy, 1550–1700* (Dundalk, 1998), 32–4.
[20] R. Gillespie, 'The End of an Era', in C. Brady and R. Gillespie (eds), *Natives and Newcomers: Essays on the Making of Irish Colonial Society, 1534–1641* (Dublin, 1986), 195.
[21] Robinson, *Plantation of Ulster*, 102–3.

Scotland, on east Ulster. This volatile situation was made worse by attempts by the Dublin administration to impose political and religious conformity on Ulster by compelling the swearing of a 'Black Oath' by the inhabitants of Ulster, who were considered to have political sympathies with the Scottish insurgents. The economic cost of this was clear. Ulster's share of the customs yield halved between 1632 and 1639. This mixture of religious tensions, political instability, and economic crisis formed the background for the outbreak of widespread violence in the province, first in the Covenanter disturbances of 1640 and then in a wider insurrection at the end of 1641. Whatever the political and religious implications of this, the economic consequences were catastrophic. The collapse of trade that followed the insurgency quickly transformed a harvest crisis into a monetary one. Ulster's money supply was dependant on a favourable balance of trade, and as this moved into deficit the volume of specie fell and fixed payments, such as rent, could not be made. Markets ground to a halt and a trade crisis turned into a monetary collapse. This was clearest in towns. Belfast, for instance granted freedom to only two men in 1642 as opposed to nineteen in 1641, indicating a considerable slowdown in economic activity.[22] At the same time, the costs of war rose with Ulster landlords raising and paying for some 8500 foot and 740 horse under royal commissions in late 1641 and early 1642.

The demographic shock of the war was immense. In the early weeks of the rising, a significant proportion of the settler population had been murdered. While later polemicists exaggerated this figure, it may have been between 10 and 20 per cent of the settler population in Armagh.[23] The proportion was probably lower in other parts of the province since tensions were particularly acute in Armagh in comparison to other areas. In addition there was considerable dislocation of population. Comparison of surnames from the muster rolls of the 1630s and the hearth money rolls of the 1660s suggests that in some parts of the country between 50 and 80 per cent of the pre-1641 population may have left their homes.[24] To this must be added the more unquantifiable, but equally real, tensions, fears, and polarization that spread through Ulster in the early 1640s that had the effect of undermining confidence and retarding any prospect of a recovery.[25]

The war that followed the rising of 1641 was prosecuted erratically, and characterized by sporadic raiding rather than large-scale military action. By the end of 1642, the Ulster economy may have stabilized but it had done so at a level far below that of 1641. In Belfast, admissions to freedom rose in 1643 over the abysmal levels of 1642, indicating more people being prepared to work in the town, but the increase was marginal. The existence in Ulster of a Presbyterian, Scottish-controlled army paid by parliament meant that attempts to reach an accommodation between the King and his Ulster subjects, which resulted in the peace of 1643

---

[22] R. M. Young (ed.), *The Town Book of the Corporation of Belfast* (Belfast, 1896), 249–51.
[23] H. Simms, 'Violence in County Armagh, 1641', in Brian Mac Cuarta (ed.), *Ulster, 1641* (Belfast, 1993), 137.
[24] W. Macafee and V. Morgan, 'Population in Ulster, 1660–1760', in P. Roebuck (ed.), *Plantation to Partition: Essays in Ulster History in Honour of J. L. McCracken* (Belfast, 1981), 47.
[25] R. Gillespie, 'Destabilising Ulster, 1641–2', in Mac Cuarta (ed.), *Ulster 1641*, 107–22.

in the rest of Ireland, were to be doomed in Ulster. Tensions between this force and the existing British settlers also created uncertainties. Nevertheless there are some signs of improving economic activity, albeit at a very low level, by the later 1640s. Belfast, for instance, which had been relatively little affected by the war, in contrast to Derry which withstood a siege, saw the numbers of freemen admitted over the 1640s rise from fifteen in 1644 to thirty in 1647. As the political and military conditions deteriorated into 1649, the numbers admitted fell back to three. All this was a long way short of the numbers admitted in the 1630s but it does suggest some improving activity through the late 1640s. By the mid-1650s, however, the full extent of the political and economic crisis of the 1640s had become all too obvious. The yield in tithes in the economic core of Armagh and Down had fallen by between 30 and 32 per cent, although in County Antrim the fall was only a quarter.[26] Much of the detail of what this meant for the rural economy is unknown but among the most significant losers from the disruption were the larger Ulster landlords, especially those of east Ulster. In the early seventeenth century, at least some of the larger landowners had used the volatile conditions to establish themselves as powerful figures, limiting royal control over their properties.[27] While this may have been feasible in the short term, the economics of their dominance of local society was unstable, and with the crisis of the 1650s their power base crumbled. This followed ten rent-less years in the 1640s, substantial fines for their support of the King, as well as the assessment, resulting in bankruptcy and land sales on the part of many families. This in turn led to the rise of a new group of landowners who would dominate eighteenth-century Ulster.[28]

The latter part of the 1650s appears to have witnessed some measure of economic recovery in parts of Ulster. The aftermath of war created opportunities for migrants who were prepared to settle in Ulster. By 1659 the adult male settler population of Ulster was probably about 20,000.[29] This represents a very significant increase on the estimate of 15,000 in 1630 and, allowing for the effects of massacre and dislocation as a result of war, it was a remarkable increase. In the case of Belfast, the emergence of a relatively stable merchant community, dominated by a number of powerful families such as the McCartney and Knox families, dates from the 1650s and their impact can be seen in the following decade with a significant rise in merchant apprentices as opposed to individual merchants from elsewhere becoming freemen of the town.[30] In Derry, there was a surge of both marriages and baptisms in the late 1650s suggesting that young immigrants were setting up households in the city.[31]

---

[26] Representative Church Body Library, Dublin, GS 2/7/3/27; T. G. F. Paterson (ed.), 'Cromwellian Inquisitions as to Parishes in County Armagh in 1657', *Ulster Journal of Archaeology*, 3rd ser., 2 (1939), 212–49.

[27] R. Gillespie, *Colonial Ulster: The Settlement of East Ulster, 1600–1641* (Cork, 1985), 84–113.

[28] R. Gillespie, 'Landed Society and the Interregnum in Ireland and Scotland', in R. Mitchison and P. Roebuck (eds), *Economy and Society in Scotland and Ireland, 1500–1939* (Edinburgh, 1988), 38–47.

[29] Robinson, *Plantation of Ulster*, 105.

[30] J. Agnew, *Belfast Merchant Families in the Seventeenth Century* (Dublin 1996), 10–13.

[31] C. Thomas, 'Family Formation in a Colonial City: Londonderry, 1650–1750', *Proceedings of the Royal Irish Academy*, 100 (2000), 92.

RESTRUCTURING ULSTER

The restoration of Charles II brought the political instability of the 1640s and 1650s to an end and provided a context for economic improvement in the years after 1660. It would be wrong to overestimate the speed and strength of recovery. In 1670 the half-yearly value of the rent of the Countess of Huntington's land in Fermanagh and Tyrone had not yet reached the level at which it stood in 1641.[32] Again on the Brownlow estate in the economic core of the Lagan Valley, the 1677 rental was less than 90 per cent of the 1641 total.[33] Yet it is possible to be too pessimistic about the economic state of Ulster in the years after 1660. It is true that there were years of economic crisis. The first and second Dutch wars of the 1660s undoubtedly retarded recovery as did the severe harvest failures in 1672, 1674–75, and 1682. Against this there are indications of a rise in the standard of living. By the 1680s, for instance, tobacco had become an established part of the Ulster trade and by the middle of that decade, five Ulster ports accounted for some 20 per cent of Irish tobacco imports, the largest share moving through Belfast and Derry.[34] Evidence of prosperity is also to be found at the level of individuals. Andrew Rowan, the Church of Ireland incumbent of Clogh, in County Antrim, for instance recorded the purchase of a series of luxury goods through the 1670s and 1680s in his notebook. These included sugar, tobacco, white bread, silk, silk buttons, plate, and a clock. While some of these could be acquired through the network of pedlars that stretched across Ulster, others had to come from the larger towns where substantial merchants carried on trade.[35] The import trade of Belfast also hints at the growth of a luxury goods market both inside and outside the town, including silk, tobacco, glass, and sugar.[36]

What fed this apparent prosperity was a trade boom after 1660. This is most obvious in the expansion of the port towns. Belfast, for instance, expanded rapidly from some 530 houses in 1663 to 2000 in 1725. On the strength of this the towns in its wake, such as Lisburn and Lurgan, grew dramatically with Belfast merchants using them as feeders for their export trade. By 1690 some could regard it, wrongly, as the second largest port in Ireland.[37] Derry likewise saw its population grow from perhaps about 1000 in the 1660s to close on 3000 by the early eighteenth century.[38] Here too the effect was felt in the towns in its hinterland, not least in Strabane.[39]

---

[32] Huntington Library, San Marino, HAM 76.
[33] R. Gillespie (ed.), *Settlement and Survival on an Ulster Estate: The Brownlow Lease Book* (Belfast, 1988), lix.
[34] British Library, Add MS 4759.
[35] R. Gillespie, 'The World of Andrew Rowan', in B. Collins, P. Ollerenshaw, and T. Parkhill (eds), *Industry, Trade and People in Ireland, 1650–1950: Essays in Honour of W. H. Crawford* (Belfast, 2005), 10–30.
[36] Gillespie, *Early Belfast*, 115–16.
[37] Ibid., 115–16, 117–18, 147.
[38] A. Thomas, *Derry-Londonderry* (Irish Historic Towns Atlas, 15) (Dublin, 2005), 10.
[39] W. Roulston, *Restoration Strabane, 1660–1714* (Dublin, 2007), 30–4.

The trade boom of Restoration Ulster was not simply the result of normal economic cycles. It was created by a fundamental restructuring of the Ulster economy in response to a number of external stimuli. Whereas the mainstays of the early seventeenth-century export trade had been in raw, unprocessed goods, the late seventeenth-century economy developed on the back of processed beef, butter, and cheese rather than live cattle. Some non-renewable natural resources, such as the woodlands of the Lagan Valley and the Lough Neagh basin, had been cut out by 1660 and this necessitated a shift away from timber in the trade of some Ulster ports. Legislative changes, most especially the Cattle Acts of 1663 and 1665, may have encouraged the shift from raw materials, but it is clear that the move was taking place before these acts were passed. Changes in the pattern of exports were the result of Ulster merchants, many of whom had migrated to the province in the 1650s, moving into new and more profitable markets, especially those of continental Europe and, to a lesser extent, North America. France, Flanders, and Spain took a great deal of Belfast's butter and barrelled beef that previously had been sent to Scotland or England, and in doing so created a diversified trade with considerable value added.

The prosperity provided by this trade boom was not automatic. There were several factors at work that might have retarded the translation of a trade boom into a rise in per capita income. Increasing and more regular government taxation with the introduction of the hearth tax in the 1660s was one factor that could have borne down on the rural population. The Restoration land settlement had a very limited impact on Ulster. Large landowners in the east of the province, such as the Catholic Earl of Antrim, had contacts at court and a respectable royalist track record that saw them favourably treated. Further west in the province in the plantation counties Protestants also with royalist credentials held on to their lands. Nevertheless the uncertainty that the land settlement created undoubtedly had an impact on confidence. More serious was the dramatic rise in population experienced by many areas of Ulster in the years after 1660s that threatened to swamp any improvement in per capita income. Contemporaries were certainly aware of the possibility of a rise in poverty in the economic core of Ulster and began to develop local institutional responses to it.[40] In some minds, this risk of increased poverty was linked to the non-payment of rent. Landlords responded by introducing 'projects' on to their estates that would provide employment and create wealth. The most significant of these projects was the weaving of linen. At Lurgan, in the Lagan Valley, the landlord, Arthur Brownlow, created a linen market by buying up all the woven cloth offered for sale, presumably using his contacts to sell this elsewhere. This was an initiative taken up by others such as the Earl of Abercorn at Strabane in the 1690s and the promotion of linen manufacture at Lisburn with the arrival of Huguenots in the 1680s.[41] In such

---

[40] D. Dickson, 'In Search of the Old Irish Poor Law', in Mitchison and Roebuck (eds), *Economy and Society in Scotland and Ireland*, 151–2.

[41] Gillespie, *Settlement and Survival*, xxxiii–xxxix; W. H. Crawford, *The Impact of the Domestic Linen Industry in Ulster* (Belfast, 2005), 8–22; Roulston, *Restoration Strabane*, 33–4.

ways, landlords provided a cushion for the most vulnerable tenants at a time of rising population and ensured the payment of their rent.

The economic growth of the late seventeenth century was based mainly on increased volume rather than increasing prices for cattle products, which in Europe tended to fall. The fall in output volumes after the harvest crisis and cattle plague of 1687 provided a trigger for rural discontent. That discontent coincided with the emerging political crisis as the Catholic James II, who had come to the throne in 1685, was steered into an increasingly more radical political path by his Irish Lord Lieutenant, the Earl of Tyrconnell. The recall of urban charters, including that of Belfast, and the packing of urban corporations with Catholics, caused deep unease in Ulster and a flight of people and capital from the region. It was not until 1689 when James, by then in Ireland having been deposed from the throne of England, summoned a parliament and threatened to attaint Ulster landlords. This proved a step too far for Ulster Protestants who had generally remained loyal to that point. James met serious resistance at Derry in 1689 and in 1690 a Williamite force landed in Ulster, marched south and defeated the King at the Boyne.[42]

THE LONG DECLINE

The end of the war of the 1690s invites comparison with the end of the wars of the 1640s and 1650s. Compared with the dislocation of the 1640s and 1650s the Williamite war was a less traumatic affair. War had not taken the same demographic toll in massacre and plague that the 1640s and 1650s had. The effect of the 1689–90 war was highly regional. Areas in which the army had been active in the 1680s, such as Blaris in County Antrim, could show considerable disruption with increased mortality rates as soldiers brought disease and disruption.[43] The marks of the siege of Derry city in 1688 were still to be seen in the urban fabric into the eighteenth century, and Newry, in the direct line of march of the Williamite force, had been flattened. However, many other areas had been hardly affected at all by war. As a result Ulster made a quick recovery. This was aided by a series of very bad harvests in Scotland in the 1690s which served as a push factor for those considering migration to Ulster.[44] How many did migrate to Ulster, where harvest conditions were much better, in search of cheap land is unclear. A great deal of the settlement may have been concentrated in the undeveloped western part of the province where a doubling of the population may have taken place.[45] This Scottish migration decisively shifted the ethnic balance in Ulster. One contemporary noted that before the 1690s, notwithstanding the plantation, most tenants in Ulster had been Catholic whereas after, 'Scottish men came over into the north with their

---

[42] R. Gillespie, 'The Irish Protestants and James II', *Irish Historical Studies*, 28 (1992–3), 124–33.
[43] V. Morgan, 'A Case Study of Population Change Over Two Centuries: Blaris, Lisburn 1661–1848', *Irish Economic and Social History,* 3 (1976), 12–13.
[44] M. Flinn (ed.), *Scottish Population History from the Seventeenth Century to the 1930s* (Cambridge, 1977), 164–86.
[45] Macafee and Morgan, 'Population in Ulster', 58–9.

families and effects and settled there so that they are now at this present the greater proportion of the inhabitants of Ulster'.[46] The influence of a newly reorganized Presbyterian church expanded rapidly, pushing deep along the Foyle Valley and into central Ulster.[47] In this case, capital appears to have followed people and with the post-revolution demographic recovery came a short-lived surge in investment and building.

This rapid recovery from war did not last. In the years after 1710, the Ulster economy went into a severe and prolonged recession. Population growth collapsed to almost zero. The immigration that had characterized the demographic environment up to 1710 was replaced by emigration, particularly to North America. Bad harvests, trade disruption, and rent increases all contributed to the rise of emigration. During the crisis of 1717–19, some six or seven thousand left for America and even more did so in the crisis of 1727–29. In more normal years, a thousand might cross the Atlantic each year and after 1730 the pace of migration quickened noticeably.[48] More striking from a demographic perspective is the collapse of the marriage rate in at least some parishes. In the case of Blaris the average number of marriages per annum fell from 25.8 in the decade 1691 to 1700 to just seven in the decade 1731–40.[49] Clearly this had significant demographic implications, but it was also a measure of the confidence of a population in the future, and by that measure future expectations in Ulster were at a very low ebb indeed in the middle of the eighteenth century. Almost everywhere there were signs of general economic stagnation. The trade of the major ports stagnated and in some cases declined. The tonnage of vessels using the port of Derry hardly changed between 1720 and 1750.[50] By 1720 fewer ships were passing through the port of Belfast than had been the case in 1710, and even when matters recovered in the following decade Belfast's relative trading position in Irish terms had declined appreciably.[51]

The reasons for this decline were more complex than they appeared to most contemporaries, who were often inclined to attribute the recession to the political machinations of the London government in Ireland. Currency instability, such as the Wood's halfpence crisis of the 1720s which saw Derry merchants banding together to refuse the debased coinage, was blamed on a government desire to exploit Ireland as a colony rather than a distinct polity. Political factors appear to have been relatively muted in this long recession. More important was a long series of harvest failures in the years before the mid-1750s. In Derry, the surplus of burials

---

[46] J. T. Gilbert (ed.), *A Jacobite Narrative of the Wars in Ireland* (Dublin 1892), 55–6.

[47] A. Gailey, 'The Scots Element in North Irish Popular Culture', in *Ethnologia Europea*, 8 (1975), 6–7; R. Gillespie,'The Presbyterian Revolution in Ulster, 1660–90', in W. J. Shiels and D. Wood (eds), *The Churches, Ireland and the Irish,* Studies in Church History, 25 (Oxford, 1988), 159–70.

[48] K. Miller, *Emigrants and Exiles: Ireland and the Irish Exodus to North America* (Oxford, 1985), 139–40, 152–5.

[49] Morgan, 'A Case Study of Population Change Over Two Centuries', 13.

[50] R. Gavin, W. Kelly, and D. O'Reilly, *Atlantic Gateway: The Port and City of Londonderry Since 1700* (Dublin, 2009), 12.

[51] Gillespie, *Early Belfast*, 128–9.

over baptisms increased dramatically after 1710, reflecting a higher death rate.[52] Perhaps most dramatic was the 'great frost' of 1739 followed by the famine of 1740 which seems to have been very severe indeed. Burials at Blaris, for instance, show a very marked spike for those years and there was a corresponding fall in baptisms within a year, suggesting considerable local disruption.[53] A run of poor harvests culminated in a particularly bad winter and disastrous harvest. In 1756–57 a harvest crisis saw a doubling of burials in Belfast with an even greater increase in the numbers of the poor falling victim to famine. From this crisis, ideas emerged about the establishment of a poor house in the town and the Belfast Charitable Society, subsequently incorporated by act of parliament in 1774, was founded as a direct result of this crisis.[54] The effects were, of course, regional. The north-west of Ulster was less affected by this crisis than the east of the province, allowing the consolidation of linen weaving there at a time when it was in recession elsewhere.[55]

Harvest crises were not the only forces at work in shaping the early eighteenth-century economy. War dislocated the patterns of continental trade, so carefully constructed in the late seventeenth century, and created commercial problems that exacerbated the natural ones. The outbreak of European war in 1702 disrupted trade, resulting in a dramatic slowing down of markets within Ulster. Some respite from this immediate problem was provided by bad harvests and cattle disease in France in the early 1710s, which increased demand for imports. The settlement that followed the peace of Utrecht in 1713 should have improved Ulster's access to European markets, but financial crises in England, which disrupted the linen markets, together with bad domestic harvests, retarded economic recovery. By the 1730s Ulster merchants were increasingly looking to North America with the passenger and flax seed trades increasing.[56] Not all the province was equally affected by commercial problems. The best guess at population in the early eighteenth century suggests that in the west of Ulster, in areas such as Donegal and Fermanagh, population may have stagnated whereas in the more commercially orientated county of Antrim it may have fallen.[57] At least some of the more remote parts of Ulster may have been protected from the worst of the commercial crises because they were poorly integrated into the commercial economy. Marginal areas, such as Magilligan in north County Londonderry, developed only a small commercial sector, including illicit distillation and a trade in rabbit skins, to pay the rent but in essence these remote areas remained subsistence economies.[58]

---

[52] Thomas, 'Family Formation in a Colonial City', 92.
[53] Morgan, 'A Case Study of Population Change Over Two Centuries', 8, 11.
[54] R. Gillespie and A. O'Keeffe (eds), *Register of the Parish of Shankill, Belfast, 1745–1761* (Dublin, 2006), 32–7.
[55] G. Kirkham, '"No More To Be Got Off The Cat But The Skin": Management, Landholding and Economic Change on the Murray of Broughton Estate, 1670–1755', in W. Nolan, L. Ronayne, and M. Dunlevy (eds), *Donegal: History and Society* (Dublin, 1995), 369–70.
[56] R. MacMaster, *Scotch-Irish Merchants in Colonial America* (Belfast, 2009).
[57] D. Dickson, S. Daultrey, and C. Ó Grada, 'Hearth Tax, Household Size and Irish Population Change, 1672–1821', *Proceedings of the Royal Irish Academy,* 82 (1982), 177.
[58] G. Kirkham, 'Economic Diversification in a Marginal Economy: A Case Study', in Roebuck (ed.), *Plantation to Partition,* 64–81.

RECOVERY

Identifying the point at which the Ulster economy turned in the mid-eighteenth century is difficult. It clearly varied within the province, but as a whole it seems that the economy began to grow more strongly from the early 1750s. After almost fifty years of showing little growth, population as measured by the yield of the hearth tax began to grow more strongly. In the last half of the eighteenth century Ulster showed growth rates of between 1.8 and 2.2 per cent per annum, the strongest in Ireland. There were, of course significant regional variations. In the eastern part of the province, particularly Antrim, Down, and Londonderry, population growth rates were markedly lower than in the western part of the province.[59] In part this represents a 'catch up' effect as some of the more isolated parts of Ulster were drawn into the more commercialized economy. As early as the 1760s, the signs of a more commercialized economy were marked in south Ulster. There were, for instance, increasing complaints about a scarcity of specie suggesting increasing cash transactions.[60] Even in the core of Ulster, marginal lands were being reclaimed to accommodate a growing population and an extensive road-building programme was integrating previously isolated areas into the main trading regions of central and east Ulster. The construction of the Newry canal between 1731 and 1742 further linked Ulster to Dublin allowing goods from the capital to be brought into Lough Neagh and shipped to all the counties bordering the lough.

What supported this demographic recovery was the resurgence of the linen trade which had consolidated itself in the early years of the eighteenth century. By the 1750s it flourished in the areas of highest population growth. Some of the variables in this resurgence were technological. Improvements in bleaching techniques, for instance, ensured that the output of a bleachgreen could rise tenfold during the late eighteenth century. Again, the expansion of Dublin in the late eighteenth century generated capital that was utilized by drapers and bleachers in the Ulster linen trade. They used the Dublin linen hall as an outlet for their wares in preference to the local ports of Ulster, since their main market for fine linens was in England. More important was the influence of landlords in the development of the trade. This might be direct influence, such as the establishment of markets to allow goods such as linen to be sold on their estates. In addition to the construction of villages such as Hillsborough, Cookstown, and Greyabbey as manufacturing centres, the building of linen halls in Ulster towns was often due to landlord initiatives.[61] What may well have been of greater significance was the willingness of landlords to make direct leases to tenants. In the early part of the eighteenth century many Ulster landlords, in an attempt to secure the income from their lands in depressed times, had leased large tracts of lands to middlemen who then sublet to smaller tenants, taking profit in the difference between his rents and the head rent.

---

[59] Dickson, Daultrey, and Ó Grada, 'Hearth Tax', 170, 172.
[60] W. H. Crawford, 'Economy and Society in South Ulster in the Eighteenth Century', *Clogher Record*, 8 (1972–6), 249–50.
[61] Crawford, *Impact of the Domestic Linen Industry*, 66–8.

With signs of economic recovery, landlords began to take former subtenants as main tenants to maximize their income. As a result holdings became smaller and tenants as well as cottiers looked towards the linen trade to supplement their farming income.[62] Survival at the lower end of this social scale was made possible by increasing specialization. Drapers or bleachers, for instance, might well advance capital to weavers to allow them to enter the trade, and in so doing they created networks which might be important as ways in which political or religious information could flow. By the 1780s much of the weaving business had concentrated in the 'linen triangle' between Belfast, Armagh, and Dungannon, with these towns emerging as the main brown linen markets by 1782.[63]

The effects of the rise of the linen trade were widespread. The network of weavers, drapers, and bleachers all served to integrate the components of the Ulster economy in a much tighter way than hitherto. It also served to integrate the periphery of Ulster more firmly into the core. The demand for flax in the weaving area of the 'linen triangle' could not be satisfied from within that area. Thus these areas became increasingly dependent on the west of the province to supply the raw materials needed. By the 1780s Sligo had become part of the Ulster economy through this mechanism. On the other hand the rise of handloom weavers within the 'linen triangle' proved to be socially deeply divisive. Population densities within this area rose steeply leading to tensions and competition for even small holdings of land. The fracture lines within this area are visible from the mid-1780s. In Armagh, disputes manifested themselves in the formation of agrarian secret societies of which the most important became known as the 'Defenders'. In its initial form much of this unrest manifested itself as market brawls but by the end of the 1780s, the local disputes had become enmeshed in much wider political turmoil that was to have repercussions in Ulster throughout the 1790s.[64]

CONCLUSION

Between 1600 and 1780 the province of Ulster had undergone a series of interconnected revolutions. Perhaps most obviously the ownership of land has passed from one elite to another. Less obviously, but more importantly, the form of social organization had also been transformed. Ulster had moved away from a society constructed around fragmented, semi-independent lordships that were organized on the basis of customary rules, and in which the economic surplus was redistributed through a set of socially embedded duties and exactions. By the 1780s the province had become a much more integrated market economy, albeit one with profound social and religious divisions. The common law rather than custom provided the framework for the workings of day-to-day life and the law of property

---

[62] Ibid., 80–3.
[63] W. H. Crawford and B. Trainor, *Aspects of Irish Social History, 1750–1800* (Belfast, 1969), plate vii.
[64] For this see D. W. Miller (ed.), *Peep O'Day Boys and Defenders* (Belfast, 1990); Crawford, *Impact of the Domestic Linen Industry*, 105–15.

framed a good deal of economic activity. Although the degree of commercialization varied regionally, markets everywhere had become more important in the redistribution of the economic surplus, and overseas trade was an increasingly important determinant of expansion or contraction of economic life. The market, however, had not completely triumphed. Relations between landlords and tenants still contained a strong paternalistic tinge and landlords often behaved in ways that were more in line with maximizing status than economic gain. In this process the plantation of Ulster may have provided an important initial stimulus but it would not determine the outcome of the forces it set into play. The evolution of modern Ulster was a slow and painful journey from the world of status to that of contract. The diversification of the economy with the introduction of domestic industry, especially linen weaving, from the closing decades of the seventeenth century, was a particularly significant feature of the modernization of the Ulster economy. While population growth and internal colonization spread economic development, the region's economy remained susceptible to severe disruption and dislocation as a result of war and harvest crises. Ultimately the forces of economic and social improvement created a recognizably modern world by 1780 with all the problems that that entailed and these remained to be solved in the following century.

FURTHER READING

W. H. Crawford, 'Landlord and Tenant Relations in Ulster, 1609–1820', *Irish Economic and Social History*, 2 (1975), 5–21.

W. H. Crawford, 'The Political Economy of Linen', in C. Brady, M. O'Dowd, and B. Walker (eds), *Ulster: An Illustrated History* (London, 1989), 134–57.

W. H. Crawford, *The Management of a Major Ulster Estate in the Late Eighteenth Century* (Dublin, 2001).

M. Dowling, *Tenant Right and Agrarian Society in Ulster, 1600–1870* (Dublin, 1999).

R. Gillespie, 'Continuity and Change: Ulster in the Seventeenth Century', in Brady, O'Dowd, and Walker (eds), *Ulster: An Illustrated History* (London, 1989), 104–33.

R. Gillespie, *Early Belfast: The Origins and Growth of an Ulster Town to 1750* (Belfast, 2007).

P. Robinson, *The Plantation of Ulster* (Dublin, 1985).

2

Politics and Society, 1600–1800

Thomas Bartlett

In his foreword to the pioneering *Ulster: An Illustrated History*, J. C. Beckett remarked: 'The history of Ulster is part of the history of Ireland from which it cannot be wholly separated without distortion. But it has some distinctive characteristics that justify our treating it separately, though not of course in isolation, from the history of Ireland as a whole.' These characteristics, Beckett believed, owed much to the surrender of Hugh O'Neill, Earl of Tyrone, in March 1603 and the consequent end of the Gaelic order in Ulster, which meant that the province was finally brought fully under royal control. That this occurred at precisely the time of the Anglo-Scottish union of crowns, when James VI of Scotland became James I of England in succession to Elizabeth I, was also highly significant, for this junction led inexorably to a 'marked though never dominant' Scottish influence in the political, social, cultural, and economic life of the province.[1] In other words, after 1603 the history of Ulster could not be other than part of the history of Scotland and of England, as well as of Ireland, and this tripartite identity would distinguish it from the other three provinces. Beckett's remarks have especial relevance for the period under review.

THE ULSTER PLANTATION

In September 1607 alarmed and probably depressed by developments since 1603, Tyrone, along with his former allies and some eighty followers, took ship for Spain. The 'Flight of the Earls' as it was known—for the Earl of Tyrconnell, a fellow rebel from the 1590s, had gone with him—was taken as proof that Tyrone and his friends had been plotting treason, and his lands and theirs were declared confiscate to the crown. In a clear breach of faith, those lesser Gaelic lords who had been urged by the crown to encroach on Tyrone's territory now had their claims denied, and the way was open for a thoroughgoing plantation of six of the nine counties of Ulster.[2]

---

[1] C. Brady, M. O'Dowd, and B. Walker (eds), *Ulster: An Illustrated History* (London, 1989), 6.
[2] N. Canny, *Making Ireland British 1580–1650* (Oxford, 2001), is the best modern guide to these events.

In a marked departure from previous practice where plantations elsewhere in Ireland were concerned, there was to be a very strong Scottish involvement in the proposed scheme for Ulster, with just over half the main undertakers listed as being of Scottish origin. Now, Scottish interest in Ulster was no new thing: in the late sixteenth century, Scottish landowners and crown officials had constantly sought to extend their influence in the province, and some had even regarded Ulster as potentially a Scottish colony, but they had generally been resisted by Elizabeth I and her officials in Dublin Castle. More recently Sir Hugh Montgomery and Sir James Hamilton, two Scottish magnates, had purchased (swindled, might be more accurate) extensive lands in Antrim and Down from Gaelic chieftains in prison and in financial difficulties, and had brought over Scottish tenants to settle there. However, the decisive shift in the English government's stance occurred because James I, a Scot, unlike Elizabeth, was enthusiastic about Scottish involvement in Ulster (he may even have coined the word 'British' to describe the proposed Scottish and English settlements there), and hence allocating over 80,000 acres to Scottish undertakers was undoubtedly a sure way to win the King's approval for the scheme.[3]

The Ulster plantation proved to be no overnight success story: settlers—Scottish or English—were hard to find and just as hard to retain, and there was a significant failure on the part of the original undertakers to stay the course. Within twenty years, some 50 per cent of the original Scottish undertakers had sold up—usually to English undertakers—and moved on. Nonetheless, between 1610 and 1630 there was a sizeable Scottish migration, perhaps 7000 males and females, to the north-east of Ulster—County Down, south County Antrim, and the 'Route' area of north Antrim and as many again to the Foyle basin better known as 'the Laggan', an area centred on Londonderry (as Derry had been christened in honour of the London companies' involvement), but including areas of east Donegal and north Tyrone. Added to the estimated 10,000 English settlers who arrived down to the early 1630s in the planted areas, this produced a grand total of around 24,000 'British' newcomers to Ulster.[4]

What of the native Irish under the Plantation of Ulster? Initially it appears that the land awarded to the native Irish (about 20 per cent of that available) was little different in quality from that allocated to other grantees. Maps and surveys of the plantation were primitive or non-existent and it would not have been always possible to distinguish good quality land from indifferent. Within thirty years, however, the quantity of land held by the native Irish had sharply declined and its quality had noticeably deteriorated. The explanation for this significant development, to a large extent, is that those native Irish who ran into financial difficulties were not allowed to sell their holdings to fellow Irish but instead were forced to sell to Scots or English settlers. As a result, by 1640 there was a large increase in the land held by newcomers and a corresponding decline in Gaelic Irish landowning. Moreover, by 1640 Gaelic Irish settlement was concentrated above the 150-metre

---

[3] Canny, *Making Ireland British*, 188–211.   [4] Ibid., 211.

contour line and away from the more prosperous river valleys, with political consequences that were soon to be revealed.⁵ There was no shortage of combustible materials in Ulster, and in October 1641 there was an explosion.

THE 1641 REBELLION

On the night of 22 October 1641, Sir Phelim O'Neill, one of those native Irish leaders who had initially done well under the Ulster Plantation but who had since become mired in debt, along with some followers, entered Charlemont Fort, County Armagh, and invited himself to dinner with Toby, Lord Caulfeild, the governor of the fort.⁶ Once inside, O'Neill and his servants quickly overpowered the guards, and seized the fort. Some miles away, at roughly the same time, a party of Donnellys occupied Dungannon Castle, County Tyrone, and over the next twenty-four hours, other forts fell into the hands of native Irish rebels: the O'Quinns captured Mountjoy Castle in Tyrone, the O'Hanlons were in command of strong points around Tanderagee, County Armagh, the Magennises and MacCartans took Newry, County Down, and the MacMahons seized Castleblayney and Carrickmacross, County Monaghan. Within two weeks, Gaelic Irish rebels were in control of all of Ulster apart from Derry, Enniskillen, and much of counties Down and Antrim, and they had advanced south to lay siege to Drogheda. In early December, the Old English, as the Catholic descendants of medieval settlers elsewhere in Ireland were known, threw in their lot with the Ulster rebels and plans were quickly afoot for an all-Ireland forum for Old English and native Irish, duly established at Kilkenny in October 1642.

However, long before then, the rising had turned into something entirely different from that envisaged by Sir Phelim O'Neill and his co-conspirators. It was not just that plans to capture Dublin Castle in the first hours of the rising had gone awry, although this was undoubtedly a major setback. Nor was it that, despite rebel successes in Ulster, enough defensible positions and seaports still remained in settler hands to ensure that the rebellion there would rapidly meet with resistance. Worse than either of these, the rebellion, conceived as a forceful demonstration to Charles I and the English parliament of the collective strength of the Gaelic Irish lords, in its execution had quickly turned into a pitiless onslaught by the native Irish on the settler population of Ulster and elsewhere. In the days and weeks following the relatively courteous capture of Lord Caulfeild at Charlemont Fort, wholesale looting of the settlers' possessions took place everywhere, with thousands of men and women in the Plantation area expelled naked from their homes and a substantial, though ultimately unknowable, number slain in cold blood. Many more perished in the freezing weather as they made their way to sanctuary in

---

⁵ Ibid., 243–300.
⁶ The literature on the 1641 rebellion is now extensive: for a guide and an interpretation see ibid., 461–534.

Dublin or Belfast. Tellingly, Caulfeild himself was murdered a few months later while being transferred into O'Neill's custody.[7]

The origins of the rebellion lie in England, Scotland, and Ulster. During the reign of Charles I, relations between the King and his parliament had deteriorated markedly with Charles increasingly viewed as variously a monarch who aimed at personal rule, or as a secret Catholic, hell-bent on bringing England back to Rome. His governor in Ireland, Thomas Wentworth, Earl of Strafford, Lord Deputy of Ireland, 1631–40, by far the King's most formidable servant, seemed tailor-made for the first of these tasks, while the Archbishop of Canterbury, William Laud, appeared to be Charles's willing accomplice in the second. Laud had not hesitated to call on Wentworth to enforce the thirty-nine articles of the 1634 Westminster Confession of Faith (hateful to Presbyterians) in Ulster, and he had approved Wentworth's drive to enjoin an oath of loyalty and obedience on Church of Ireland ministers in Ulster, many of whom were in fact 'closet' Presbyterians. A refusal to take the so-called 'Black Oath' led many of them to flee to Scotland where they added their weight to the more forceful opposition that was being planned there to Charles's and Laud's religious policies.

In Scotland, the attempt to enforce religious uniformity had quickly met with armed resistance from Presbyterians, convinced that royal policy in this respect was tantamount to re-Catholicizing the country. A covenant to resist was drawn up by those unalterably opposed to Charles's religious policy and an army was formed to give teeth to their opposition. Matters rapidly spiralled out of Charles's control. The royal army sent to coerce the Scots melted away as it marched to the north of England, while the Scottish Covenanters, now largely unchallenged, moved rapidly south.[8] Desperate for men and money to prosecute the war, Charles had little option but to turn to his despised and hitherto largely ignored English parliament. However, the House of Commons had its own priorities, and none of them included helping the King out of his difficulties. Substantial constitutional changes were instead sought, especially in such matters as the regular summoning of parliament, the implementation of a more robust anti-Catholic religious policy, and guarantees on the appointment and accountability of the King's servants. Squeezed on two fronts—Scots to the north, and 'Puritan' opponents in his parliament—Charles's rule began to unravel.

A vital player in the unfolding crisis of the Stuart monarchy was Sir John Clotworthy who served as a link between Charles's Ulster, Scottish, and English opponents. Born in County Antrim, of Devon stock, Clotworthy was a firm Presbyterian—indeed he had been a patron of Presbyterian clergy in east Ulster—and he had travelled to Scotland to publicize the iniquities of Wentworth's 'Black Oath' in Ulster and to make contact with the Covenanters. In addition, Clotworthy was brother-in-law to the King's most determined opponent in England, John

---

[7] Details of the murders, robberies, and other crimes are to be found in the Depositions of 1641 which have now been digitized and are available via the Trinity College Dublin website.

[8] A. MacInnes, *The British Revolution, 1629–60* (London, 2004).

Pym, and he appears to have played a key role in orchestrating the Ulster-Scottish-English opposition to Charles.[9] Certainly, when Charles looked to Wentworth as the only man to manage the crisis in his interest, it was Clotworthy who moved to quash this plan. Wentworth was accused of treason, put on trial, found guilty (largely on Irish evidence brought forward by Clotworthy), and executed in April 1641. A further blow to Charles came when Wentworth's Irish army, which had contained a substantial Catholic contingent, was ordered to disband at Belfast, where it had assembled prior to embarkation for the war in Scotland.

Leaders among both the Old English and the Gaelic Irish of Ulster observed these developments in Britain closely and with growing alarm. The Old English, already outraged by Wentworth's financial exploitation of their abject loyalty to Charles and by his plans for a plantation of their lands in Connacht, faced a cruel dilemma. The King clearly did not value their fidelity, only their finances, but his wife, Henrietta Maria, was a Catholic and hence, presumably, approachable as a co-religionist, and there remained a slim chance that Charles might be persuaded to turn to them in his hour of need. No such comforting notion could be entertained of his opponents, the Puritans, or the 'malignant party', as the Old English termed them, for their anti-Catholicism was well known. Worse, it was possible, although unlikely, that Charles and the parliamentary opposition led by Pym might cut a deal based on royal concessions to them. There was every reason to fear that any such arrangement would fatally undermine Old English interests outside Ulster. In short, if Charles triumphed, the outlook seemed bleak; if his opponents were victorious, the future was bleaker still. Consequently, and perhaps against their better judgement, some prominent Old English leaders began to listen to urgent whispers from such figureheads of Gaelic Ulster as Sir Phelim O'Neill, Sir Philip McHugh O'Reilly, and Conor Lord Maguire.

For men such as these, Ulster loyalists who had been rewarded for their role in the downfall of Tyrone in 1603, who had profited—at least initially—from the Ulster Plantation, and who had on the surface integrated well into the new dispensation installed following the Flight of the Earls (all three, for example, were Members of Parliament), there was another lesson to be learned from the deepening crisis across the water. Put simply, the Scots Covenanters had shown how to make an effective protest against Stuart despotism. Faced with unacceptable changes in religion, the Scots had mobilized, bound themselves by covenant, and had taken arms against the King. They had achieved, by any standards, a brilliant success: the hated religious policy was abandoned, and King Charles, faced with an invasion, had been humiliatingly forced to buy off the Scottish army as it moved south. This was a most impressive demonstration of the Scots' military strength and political unity, and it seems clear that this was the model that the Ulster leaders had in mind when they embarked on their conspiracy. In essence, their plan was as follows: first, seize the Ulster forts along with Dublin Castle; second, mobilize a new army from

---

[9] See the entry for Clotworthy by R. Gillespie, in J. McGuire and J. Quinn (eds), *Dictionary of Irish Biography*, Vol. 2 (Cambridge, 2009), 601–2.

the remnants of Wentworth's disbanded force; third, claim authorization from Charles I to rebel, so to speak, on his behalf; fourth, attract support from abroad (Cardinal Richelieu, Louis XIII's minister, was apparently kept informed of the conspiracy); and finally, draw in the Old English lords elsewhere in Ireland. At this point, having demonstrated their strength, unity, and purpose, Charles would have no option but to negotiate with them, and he might even call on them for help in his struggles with the Scots and his disaffected English subjects. In the event, as we have seen, the Ulster rising of 22–23 October 1641 moved immediately beyond these limited goals to become the first popular uprising in Irish history, one that the leaders of the conspiracy were by no means able, at least initially, to control.

Contrary to what the rebel leaders had planned, the rebellion plunged not just Ulster, but all Ireland into a twenty-year nightmare of massacre and mayhem, including man-made famine and wholesale confiscation, and it would help pitch the three Stuart kingdoms into multiple civil wars the outcome of which would profoundly alter all of them.

WAR IN THE 1640s AND ITS AFTERMATH

During the 1640s, no fewer than three armies operated in Ulster.[10] The first, formed in the immediate aftermath of the rising, originated in the Laggan area of east Donegal, whence it took its name. This Laggan army was commanded by brothers Sir Robert and Sir William Stewart and operated around Derry and Coleraine. However, it combined with other regiments raised by, among others, Sir Ralph Gore in south Donegal, and Sir William Cole in Enniskillen, County Fermanagh. The Laggan army was composed almost entirely of British settlers, many of whom had seen military service, and at its peak might have numbered 8000 men. When equipped with guns and ammunition supplied by Dublin Castle in the spring of 1642, this military formation proved altogether formidable—'one of the most remarkable armed forces in history', enthused its nineteenth-century historian.[11] Ably led by Sir Robert Stewart, a veteran of the continental wars, its mobility and utter ruthlessness struck terror into the Gaelic Irish during its nine years of campaigning in the north-west of Ulster.

Opposed to the Laggan army was the Ulster army, as it later became known. This was led initially by one of the chief conspirators, Sir Phelim O'Neill, and consisted almost entirely of Gaelic Irish. It lacked just about everything that seventeenth-century armies required—training, discipline, muskets, munitions, and artillery—and while it sought to make up for these deficiencies with a raw courage which readily revealed itself in headlong charges, this was scarcely sufficient. It proved inept at attempted sieges such as those at Coleraine, County Londonderry,

---

[10] See K. McKenny, *The Laggan Army in Ireland 1640–1685* (Dublin, 2005); and J. Casway, *Owen Roe O'Neill and the Struggle for Catholic Ireland* (Philadelphia, 1984).
[11] Lord Ernest Hamilton, quoted in McKenny, *Laggan Army*, 20.

or at Drogheda, County Louth, and its performance in the field was poor: in June 1642, near Raphoe, County Donegal, a force of Ulster Irish under the command of Sir Phelim O'Neill was routed by the numerically inferior men of the Laggan army. To the victors' glee, Sir Phelim's trunk was captured, allegedly containing the crown with which he was to be made Prince of Ulster. A turning point in the Ulster army's fortunes came in July 1642 when Owen Roe O'Neill, a nephew of Tyrone and a forty-year veteran of the Spanish service, came ashore at Doe Castle in County Donegal and took over command from the hapless Sir Phelim. Owen Roe immediately set about training and disciplining his men, but it took time before any improvements were apparent. The Ulster army's calamitous defeat at Clones, County Monaghan in June 1643 at the hands of Sir Robert Stewart was to reveal yet again just how much remained to turn it into an effective fighting force.

A few months before the arrival of Owen Roe O'Neill from the Spanish Netherlands, yet another army, a Scottish one of some 2000 men headed by Major General Robert Monro (a veteran of the Swedish service), and paid for by the English parliament, landed at Carrickfergus, County Antrim, and quickly set about defending (and extending) the Scots' colony in Antrim and Down. In June 1642, Monro organized the first meeting of a presbytery in Ulster, serving notice that his army was first and foremost a Scottish covenanting force and revealing his determination to embed Presbyterianism wherever he had the power. It is from the arrival of Monro's army that the history of Presbyterianism in Ulster rightly begins, and its diffusion later was to be largely coterminous with the areas that came under Monro's control. Quickly taking the offensive, Monro's army embarked on two short campaigns in the summer of 1642 that established its dominance in east Ulster. By the beginning of 1643, Monro's campaigns, along with those of the Laggan army to the west, had the Gaelic Irish rebels in retreat everywhere throughout the province. Ironically, by September 1643, Charlemont Fort, the first success of the rebels, was the only place of note in Ulster still in their hands.

The various campaigns undertaken by these three armies in Ulster need not detain us. Given the sectarian furies unleashed by the explosion of October 1641, it can come as no surprise that the massacre of civilians, the slaughter of prisoners, and the wanton destruction of property were routine. As a result of the atrocities of 1641 (however exaggerated), there was a burning desire for revenge on the part of the British settlers and a flat refusal to recognize enemy combatants, even in some instances their womenfolk, as fellow-humans (they were all rather 'the progeny of the Babylonish whore').[12] In addition, each army was beset with supply problems, and a starving, ill-disciplined soldiery—English, Irish, or Scottish—was unlikely to be moved to pity by the plight of the unfortunates who had their cattle run off, their food seized, and their dwellings pulled down. Lastly, the nature of the warfare in 1640s Ulster meant that excesses were inevitable, for large set-piece

---

[12] D. Harcourt, *A New Remonstrance from Ireland Containing an Exact Declaration of the Cruelties... Exercised by the Popish Rebels...* (London, 1643).

battles were generally avoided. Rather, there was an emphasis on punitive columns that sallied out to waste and destroy enemy territory and property, and thus break the enemy's capacity to resist. It was all too predictable then that when a garrison of (mostly) Scottish settlers surrendered at Augher in November 1641, they were promptly slaughtered by the rebels.[13] Similarly when Captain Daniel Bartlet, 'a noble and forward gentleman' seized one of O'Neill's forts in April 1642, he and his men killed all they found there, men, women, and children, 'making such a slaughter as hath not been seen since the rebellion'.[14] And when Monro captured Newry, he had some sixty rebel soldiers shot to death or hanged, and there was a report that sixteen women with them were stripped and flung into the river.[15]

Most probably, facile triumphs such as these led Monro into making a grave error of judgement. Emboldened by numerous victories over the rebels ('these bragging impostures who are not able to defend their own country from a handful of us', in his view),[16] in June 1646 he set out to destroy Owen Roe O'Neill and his newly trained Ulster army. On receiving news that O'Neill's forces were to quarter at Benburb, County Tyrone, Monro's men, some 5000 strong, marched to oppose them. Monro was cautious as he approached the Ulster army but, as he later explained, his men would not be patient: 'All our army, foot and horse, did earnestly covet fighting which was impossible for me to gainstand [=resist] without being reproached for cowardice'. Their impetuosity was to cost Monro and his men dearly, for they were routed with many killed and taken prisoner, and he himself narrowly escaped capture. Still, there was some consolation for Monro: because the Ulster army 'loved the spoyle better than to prosecute the victory' he claimed that it had not pursued his defeated army. And there was further comfort, he noted piously, in that 'being now humbled before God we increase in courage and resolution'.[17]

The war in Ulster was complicated by its relationship to the English and Scottish wars, and to the war fought by the Confederate Catholics of Kilkenny, for there were British settlers who were loyal to Charles and there were those who sided with parliament.[18] Even the Laggan army was torn, for Sir William Stewart, a Presbyterian, favoured parliament, especially after the Scottish Covenanters declared against Charles in September 1643, while his brother Sir Robert remained a royalist at heart. At the same time, resistance in Ulster on each side, royalist and parliamentarian, to the truce that was concluded in September 1643 between royalist forces

---

[13] McKenny, *Laggan Army*, 41–2.
[14] S. Johnson, *Exceeding Good Newes from the Neweries in Ireland*... (London, 1642).
[15] Anon., *A true relation of the proceedings of the Scottish armie now in Ireland by three letters*.... (London, 1642). For the fate of the women, see R. Pike, *A True Relation of the Scots and English Forces in the North of Ireland* (London, 1642). This pamphlet was ordered to be burned by the common hangman because it allegedly contained false news.
[16] Anon., *A Full Relation of the Late Expedition of... Lord Monroe, Major-General of All the Protestant Forces in Ulster*... (London, 1644).
[17] *A Letter from General Major Monro Concerning... Ireland* (London, 27 June 1646).
[18] T. Ó hAnnracháin, *Catholic Reformation in Ireland, the Mission of Rinuccini 1645–49* (Oxford, 2002), *passim*.

under Ormond and the Confederate Catholics, papered over these divisions. The Cessation—or 'so great a masterpiece of the devil', as opponents dismissed it[19]— was widely ignored in Ulster and the war continued there.[20] However, when the Scottish Covenanters (or Presbyterians) declared for Charles in the second civil war, matters became immeasurably more complicated and defy easy explanation. The Presbyterian Monro, for example, a parliamentary hero in the 1640s, found himself imprisoned by parliament in the 1650s, and when in March 1649 Sir Charles Coote, the homicidal commander of parliamentary forces was besieged in Derry by Sir Robert Stewart, the royalist commander of the Laggan army, bewilderingly, it was none other than Owen Roe O'Neill who came to his rescue.[21]

The chaos caused by Charles's execution in January 1649 was brought to a bloody end by the ruthless campaigns waged by Oliver Cromwell and the New Model Army, first against royalists and Presbyterians in Scotland, then against royalists and Catholics in Ireland, and lastly against those in England who declared allegiance to Charles II. Ulster was spared a visit by Cromwell but that made little difference to the already collapsing fortunes of the Gaelic Irish. Owen Roe O'Neill died of natural causes in November 1649, and Heber MacMahon, Catholic bishop of Clogher, replaced him as leader of the Ulster forces, seeing off an attempt by Sir Phelim O'Neill to retake command. In June 1650, a parliamentary force under Coote almost annihilated the Ulster army under MacMahon at Scarrifhollis, near Letterkenny, County Donegal. MacMahon was later hanged in Enniskillen, County Fermanagh. In August 1650, Charlemont Fort surrendered to parliamentary forces and in March 1653, Sir Phelim O'Neill, who had been waging a guerrilla campaign in Armagh, was captured and subsequently executed. The formal end of the war in Ulster came with the surrender of Sir Philip MacHugh O'Reilly in April 1653. Because he had treated Protestants fairly during the1640s, his life was spared and he was allowed to enter Spanish service. The Ulster rebellion of 1641 was finally over.

The restoration of the monarchy in 1660 brought a guarantee of Protestant land titles, and the re-establishment of the Church of Ireland at the same time brought further reassurance that political, social, and religious authority would reside with them. Admittedly, the accession to the throne in 1685 of James II, a professed Catholic, would re-awaken latent memories of the 1641 massacres and would eventually propel Protestant Ulster into resistance. Nonetheless, by the 1680s a Protestant or Anglican ascendancy was in place (almost all the great landowners in Ulster were Anglicans, rather than Presbyterian), and by and large Protestants of the Church of Ireland would remain the governing elite in Ulster for the future.

What of the Presbyterians? Monro's campaigns had made east Ulster in fact what it had been notionally, a Scottish colony, and his marches into Cavan and Monaghan had established a strong Scottish and Presbyterian presence there as well. It was from the 1650s that Belfast, hitherto almost unknown and overshadowed

---

[19] Col. L. Crawford, *Ireland's Ingratitude to the Parliament of England*... (London, 1643), 12.
[20] McKenny, *Laggan Army*, 74–100.
[21] See R. Armstrong, *Protestant War: The 'British' of Ireland and the Wars of the Three Kingdoms* (Manchester, 2005), 221–2.

by Carrickfergus, began its rise to prominence. This was amusingly demonstrated when in 1649 the Presbytery of Belfast issued a sharp criticism of the English parliament's execution of Charles and its religious policy. Such temerity from a hitherto obscure (and newly minted) body drew a withering rebuke from none other that the poet (and parliamentary apologist) John Milton: 'we must...ask who this Presbytery at Belfast is that take upon them[selves] the magisteriall to examine and condemn the proceedings of the parliament of England'.[22] It was the first time, but assuredly not the last, that Belfast, that 'barbarous nook of Ireland', as Milton described it, would presume to admonish London.

While Monro and his Covenanters were strengthening their hold on east Ulster, the Laggan army had likewise been instrumental in consolidating the Scottish presence in west Ulster, notably in east Donegal, the Foyle basin generally, and as far south as Fermanagh. How this was done remains unclear, but there were frequent allegations that the Laggan army had quickly become a Scottish army, with English settlers regularly denied military commissions. Moreover, those Scots in command, as one complaint had it, have 'so oppressed the poor English by settling garrisons among them, quartering upon those that live there and absolutely disposing of all Englishmen's lands at their meer will and pleasure that the poore English are quite undone'.[23] Whatever the truth of the matter, by the early 1650s the Scots were dominant in east and west Ulster, with the English holding the middle ground, and the Gaelic Irish strong in peripheral areas and on mountainous ground. This settlement pattern, with local variations, remained relatively stable until well into the nineteenth century and beyond.

The Scottish presence in east and west Ulster was reinforced in the decades after 1650 as additional Scots settlers flocked into those areas. This was a movement of people that was especially striking in terms of numbers in the 1690s and one that can be regarded as constituting the real Ulster plantation. But while the Scots would work the land as tenant farmers, the English would continue to dominate among the landed classes because, as noted above, large landowners in Ulster adhered overwhelmingly to the Church of Ireland rather than to Presbyterianism. A division between occupancy and ownership had opened up that, as elsewhere in Ireland, would lead to conflict in the future.

ULSTER AND THE WILLIAMITE WAR

In a short account of his flight from Ireland published in London in 1689, an anonymous Anglican 'clergyman' reflected gloomily that 'at least once in forty years there breaks forth there the same cruel and bloody rebellion'.[24] Many of his

---

[22] [J. Milton], *A Necessary Examination of a Dangerous Design and Practice Against...England, by the Presbytery at Belfast...* (London, 1649), 5.
[23] *An Answer to a Most Pernicious and Factious Petition Framed Against the Scots in Ireland* (London, 1647).
[24] *A Short View of the Methods Made Use of in Ireland for the Subversion...of the Protestant Religion and Interest in That Kingdom* (London, 1689), 1.

co-religionists agreed with him. Admittedly, the reign of Charles II (1660–85) had been fraught for Irish Anglicans and Presbyterians, for this was when 'the papists were too much countenanced and indulg'd', but all that paled into insignificance compared to the actions of the new king. Irish Catholics were reportedly delighted at Charles's death and James's accession. One writer commented that Irish Catholics spent days celebrating with 'the beating of drums, playing upon the bag-pipes and other musical instruments, in drinking and serenading in the night time'.[25] James's chosen instrument in Ireland, Richard Talbot, Earl of Tyrconnell, a long-standing Catholic champion, struck 'unspeakable terrour' along with 'consternation, dismal apprehension and panick fears' into Protestant hearts.[26] Tyrconnell's oaths about 'damn'd hereticks' did nothing to calm matters, while his actions in filling the Irish army with Catholics and thus 'metamorphosing mantles into redcoats, brogues into jackboots and cowboys into captains' seemed a key part of some devilish plan. Inevitably, a letter was discovered that revealed that a wholesale massacre of Protestants was at an advanced state of planning. As 'G.P.', the author of a pamphlet on the plight of Irish Protestants under James observed: 'It is as incredible to comprehend as it is impossible to express what operation this [letter] had on the minds of all Protestants'. Protestants in Ulster—Church of Ireland or Presbyterian, it mattered not—'upon this alarm began to stand upon their guard and to keep strong wards and watches', resolving neither to fly nor be surprised.[27] Some did flee their homes—like 'the Jews out of Egypt', it was noted—and by 1688 increasingly the only option seemed to be fight or flight.

The birth of a son to Mary of Modena, James's queen, in June 1688 brought matters to a head: 'T'would require a volume to describe the...various scenes of joy which they [Catholic Irish] shew'd upon this occasion'.[28] However, Protestants in the Stuart kingdoms were not so pleased: an elderly Catholic king could perhaps be endured, for his Protestant daughter would succeed in a few years, but a Catholic dynasty could not. Within months, William of Orange, the Protestant champion, had easily ousted James II, his father-in-law, from his throne. The latter eventually made his way to Ireland, landing at Kinsale, County Cork in March 1689, and the war was on.[29]

In Ulster, Protestant associations were quickly formed in Antrim and Down, declared for William and pledged themselves to resist Tyrconnell. An early setback for them occurred at Dromore, County Down, in March 1689 when a mixed Protestant and Presbyterian force was routed by soldiers loyal to James. Elsewhere in Ulster, however, matters were more favourable to the Williamites. At Derry, the gates were shut against a royal regiment in December 1688, and in April 1689 James himself was refused entry. He promptly besieged the city, but

---

[25] *A Full and Impartial Account of All the Secret Consults... of the Romish Party in Ireland* (London, 1689), 45.
[26] Ibid., 67–8.
[27] G. P., *An Apology for the Protestants of Ireland...* (London, 1689). A mantle was an all-enveloping cloak. Since Tudor times it had been a trademark garment of the Gaelic Irish.
[28] *A Full and Impartial Account of All the Secret Consults...*, 45.
[29] See R. Doherty, *The Williamite War in Ireland, 1688–91* (Dublin, 1998).

in such an incompetent manner that it was often not clear who was besieging whom. A Williamite naval force eventually came to Derry's relief in July 1689. A French observer remarked aptly that it had been '*un siège tout extraordinaire*'.[30] Nonetheless, James's failure was a huge morale boost for the Williamites: it was 'the saving of Ireland', commented one writer.[31] Meanwhile in south-west Ulster, a force on the model of the Laggan army of the 1640s was reconstituted in Enniskillen, and it won early victories over the Jacobites, as James's followers were known, at Belleek and Newtownbutler, County Fermanagh, in May and July 1689, respectively.

Ulster was the Williamite heartland of Ireland, and Carrickfergus was the first port captured by William's trusted commander, the 73-year-old Duke de Schomberg. The Jacobite garrison with its womenfolk was permitted to depart on terms but, in a grim reprise of the scenes of 1641, it was assailed by 'country people' who attempted to steal from them what they could, often with unfortunate results. As one observer recorded:

> Women likewise falling upon their trulls (=sluts) unrigg'd them of everything they had on…. I saw one of the townswomen come up to one Eveling (=Evelyn/Éibhlín) crying out you whore, this is my gown off with it; another cryed this is my petticoat off with it, a third with open mouth swore the smock was hers and a little girl cried the hood upon her head was hers. They fell to it who should get off their own first, that to tearing they went so that gown, petticoat, smock and hoods and all were not worth two pence by the time they had got them off.

With some satisfaction, the author noted that the bedraggled garrison and their companions 'would have nothing left but their lives' by the time they reached Lisburn.[32]

Schomberg's subsequent march to Dublin faltered at Dundalk, County Louth and the war dragged on into 1690. A reluctant William was forced to journey to Ireland to take personal command of his forces, and he was successful at the River Boyne in July. Schomberg was a noted casualty at that battle. Even though the Jacobite army remained largely intact after the defeat at the Boyne, James accepted that the war was over for him. The English dimension of the conflict had concluded: William would be King of England. The Irish dimension to the war ended, with due allowance for some subsequent guerrilla action, at Aughrim, County Galway in July 1691 where the Jacobite army was cut to pieces. Its French commander, Saint-Ruth, fell in the battle. The defeated remnants of the Jacobites later took ship for France. The Williamite war was finally over.[33]

---

[30] [Jean de la Brune?] *Histoire de la Revolution d'Irlande Arriveé Sous Guillaume III* (Amsterdam, 1691).
[31] *Ireland Preserv'd and the Protestant Interest Defended in the Year 1689* (London, 1707).
[32] *Great News from the Duke of Schomberg's army… with a Journal of the Whole Siege of Carrickfergus* (London, 1689).
[33] See J. Childs, *The Williamite Wars in Ireland 1688–91* (London, 2007).

CONFLICT IN THE EIGHTEENTH CENTURY

As with the wars of the 1640s, Catholics everywhere in Ireland were the principal losers in this conflict: as rebels (however much they disputed that designation) they would suffer a further loss of land, and many of their swordsmen, clerics, and potential leaders had little option but to serve, trade, practice, or work abroad.[34] New and stringent Penal Laws were enacted against those who remained. The Catholics of Ulster, already the least prosperous on the island, were completely cast down after 1690. A government report in 1731 into the state of Catholicism throughout Ireland confirmed that members of that religion were worst off in Ulster.[35] It would be many decades before Catholics would exhibit signs of progress, or assertiveness. In the meantime, Catholics avoided drawing attention to themselves, shunned controversy, and brooded over the wrongs inflicted upon them.

Matters were altogether different for members of the Church of Ireland. As the victors in the war, they were now confirmed as the governing class and would command most political and social authority in Ulster and elsewhere. Presbyterians might legitimately have expected to be similarly recognized and rewarded, but it was not to be.[36] As noted, they had been early and enthusiastic adherents of William of Orange and had been among the first openly to resist James II. In June 1690 William had increased the small *regium donum*, or subsidy, paid to their ministers in gratitude. And yet, with the war won and the Catholic menace seen off, apparently forever, there had been a swift and marked change in attitude, not on the part of William III, but rather among members of the Established Church in Ireland. There were fears voiced at Presbyterian expansion at the expense of the Established Church, and some Anglicans were heard to murmur that, with the Catholics now vanquished, Presbyterians might yet constitute as grave, or even a graver, threat to the Church of Ireland and the establishment. The wartime partnership of Anglican and Dissenter was swiftly forgotten, and a number of Penal Laws, not as stringent as those against Catholics, but still galling, were enacted that sought to restrict public and political office to those within the Anglican communion. One result of this policy of exclusion was that the Irish parliament throughout the eighteenth century would be overwhelmingly Anglican in composition, with only a handful of Ulster Presbyterians having a seat in it.[37] It would be a similar story at local government level where Presbyterians found themselves generally excluded as well. This raises two questions: why did Presbyterians in Ulster apparently accept their second-class status for most of the eighteenth century, and why did they reject it by the century's end?

The answers to these questions are not at all straightforward. It may be conceded that there were in fact protests. In the 1760s, the 'Oak Boys' staged a minor revolt

---

[34] See O. P. Rafferty, *Catholicism in Ulster 1603–1983: An Interpretative History* (Dublin, 1984), Ch. 2.
[35] Rafferty, *Catholicism in Ulster*, 73.
[36] I. McBride, *Scripture Politics: Ulster Presbyterians and Irish Radicalism in the Late Eighteenth Century* (Oxford, 1998).
[37] T. Bartlett, *The Fall and Rise of the Irish Nation: The Catholic Question, 1690–1830* (Dublin, 1992), 30–3.

in south Ulster against county charges and local fees, and a decade later the 'Hearts of Steel' demonstrated on the Donegall estates in County Antrim over leasing practices. Both disturbances were significant in that they revealed a predominantly Presbyterian tenantry in these areas that was quite prepared to resist injustice and challenge unfair rents.[38] Still, the puzzle remains as to why there were not more serious outbreaks of trouble before the 1760s. One reason may lie in the very large number of Presbyterians (at least 100,000) that emigrated from Ulster between 1700 and 1780 to the British colonies in North America. Emigration, by siphoning off so many potential troublemakers, helped reduce the amount of combustible material in Ulster. Many of those who departed claimed that they had done so because they were oppressed by (Church of Ireland) landlords, and because they resented having to make payments such as tithe and other fees to a church that they regarded as little different from the Church of Rome. Had they stayed they might have posed a threat to the Anglican establishment.

Another reason for the Dissenters' apparent acquiescence in their inferior status was that their attention and energy were otherwise engaged. Compared to matters theological—for the Presbyterians had developed what one historian has described as a 'fissiparous culture of controversy'[39]—parliamentary issues held little attraction. Dissenting energies were drawn to divisions between 'New Light' and 'Old Light', or between 'Subscribing' or 'non-Subscribing', and there were even disputes imported from Scotland that had no local relevance.[40] In addition, we may remember that Presbyterians had their own form of ecclesiastical government, with its presbyteries and church courts. These were not subject to government interference, nor was there any prohibition on Presbyterians journeying to the 'mother country', Scotland, for their education. In short, Presbyterians could enjoy a 'distinct moral existence'[41] outside and beyond the control of the Anglican establishment.

In addition, by the middle of the eighteenth century, Ulster had become relatively prosperous. Once the poorest of the four provinces, Ulster was on track to dominate the Irish economy. Linen manufacture, based in mid-Ulster but with links to all the Ulster counties, and beyond to Sligo and Leitrim, was thriving, and economic concerns with manufacturing, trade, and commerce, rather than with politics were dominant. How else to explain why Presbyterian Belfast, by 1750 the capital of Presbyterian Ulster, gamely accepted that its representation in the Irish parliament was entirely in the hands of the Church of Ireland Donegall family? The town had then a population of 8549 people of whom only sixty people belonged to the Church of Ireland.[42] Such a situation could hardly last.

---

[38] J. Smyth, *The Men of No Property: Irish Rebels and Popular Politics in the Late Eighteenth Century*. (London, 1992), 33–5; J. S. Donnelly Jr, 'Hearts of Oak, Hearts of Steel', *Studia Hibernica*, 21 (1981), 7–73.

[39] McBride, *Scripture Politics*, 7.

[40] 'New Lights' were more intellectually rigorous and innovative in their theology, while 'Old Lights' tended to be more fundamentalist and conservative. Similar distinctions may be found among those who subscribed, or refused to subscribe, to the Westminster Confession of Faith (1646). See McBride, *Scripture Politics*, 6–8.

[41] Quoted in ibid., 6.   [42] Ibid., 64.

The breakdown, when it came, was ignited by events abroad, first in the American bid for independence, and then with the French Revolution and the setting up of another republic. Strong familial and trading links with North America led the Presbyterians of Ulster to support their struggle, many seeing it as a war of Dissent against Anglicanism in the colonies. With the formation in 1778 of the Volunteers, a disproportionately Presbyterian and Ulster body, an attack was launched first on the constitutional links between Ireland and England, and then on the relationship between the Irish people and the Irish parliament. The first succeeded in its own terms, the second, the movement to reform parliament, ran into sand by 1785, largely because there was no agreement as to whether 'the Irish people' included the Roman Catholics.

Fresh momentum came with the outbreak of revolution in France. In October 1791, the Society of United Irishmen was set up in Belfast. Despite its grand title, it was initially little more than a Presbyterian Committee on the model of the rather successful Catholic Committee that had for some years lobbied on behalf of Irish Catholics. Events in France now united Old Light and New Light Presbyterians. Those who were traditional and fundamentalist saw the overthrow of Louis XVI and the Catholic Church in France as presaging the downfall of international Catholicism, even as the fulfilment of a biblical prophecy: while those who were more experimental—the New Light—saw fresh opportunities for republican government in Ireland and elsewhere. In a momentous departure from the practice of centuries, both were to varying degrees prepared to enlist the aid of Irish Catholics in their quest for political reform. If French Catholics could embrace liberty and republicanism and renounce priestcraft and superstition, then why could Irish Catholics not do the same, as Theobald Wolfe Tone boldly argued in his 1791 pamphlet directed to the northern Dissenters.[43]

This plan encountered fierce resistance both from Dublin Castle and, on the ground in Ulster, from Anglican landlords and their Church of Ireland tenantry. The formation of the Orange Order in Armagh in 1795 served notice that not all were prepared to abandon what had seemed the lessons of Irish history and to embrace new alliances. The emergence of the Catholic Defender movement in south Ulster equally challenged the non-sectarian message of the United Irishmen. Sectarian violence between Catholic and Protestant became routine, and by the mid-1790s Ulster was on the verge of an uprising. As is well known, the rising when it came in 1798 was largely confined to Antrim and Down and was easily suppressed: Presbyterian rebels were largely put down by Anglican and Catholic soldiers. In County Down, 'General' Henry Monro, a distant relative of the Scottish commander of the 1640s in east Ulster, was executed for his part in the rebellion, and many other leaders were transported or exiled. Just as the Ulster Plantation had followed the Tyrone Rebellion, so too the 1798 Rebellion made the Act of Union possible. As in 1603, so in 1798, the political scene had been transformed by war.

---

[43] A Northern Whig [Theobald Wolfe Tone], *An Argument on Behalf of the Catholics of Ireland* (Dublin, 1791). See, in general, A. T. Q. Stewart, *The Summer Soliders: The 1798 Rebellion in Antrim and Down* (Belfast, 1995).

FURTHER READING

N. Canny, *Making Ireland British, 1580–1650* (Oxford, 2001).
J. Childs, *The Williamite Wars in Ireland, 1688–91* (London, 2007).
R. Gillespie, *Colonial Ulster: The Settlement of East Ulster, 1600–1641* (Cork, 1985).
P. Griffin, *The People with No Name: Ireland's Ulster Scots, America's Scots Irish and the Creation of a British Atlantic World, 1689–1764* (Liverpool, 2001).
P. Higgins, *A Nation of Politicians: Gender, Patriotism and Political Culture in Late Eighteenth Century Ireland* (Madison, 2010).
I. McBride, *Scripture Politics: Ulster Presbyterians and Irish Radicalism in the Late Eighteenth Century* (Oxford, 1998).
K. McKenny, *The Laggan Army in Ireland, 1640–1685* (Dublin, 2005).
A. T. Q. Stewart, *The Summer Soldiers: The 1798 Rebellion in Antrim and Down* (Belfast, 1995).

3

Women in Ulster, 1600–1800

Mary O'Dowd

THE FLIGHT OF THE EARLS: WOMEN AND A TRANSITIONAL SOCIETY

When Hugh O'Neill, Earl of Tyrone, Rory O'Donnell, Earl of Tyrconnell, and Cuchonnacht Maguire boarded ship at Rathmullan in September 1607, they were accompanied by a group of about forty kinsfolk and followers, among whom were six women. These were Tyrone's wife, Catherine McGuinness, Tyrconnell's sister, Nuala O'Donnell, his sister-in-law, Rosa O'Doherty, and three maidservants. The latter included a wet nurse for Tyrconnell's son, Hugh, who was less than a year old. The maidservants would also have helped to care for the other children on board. Among these were Tyrone's three sons, two of whom were under the age of seven, as well as Hugh, the son of Cathbar O'Donnell, and Rosa O'Doherty, who was just over 2 years old.[1]

From the perspective of a historian of women, there are two notable aspects to the famous 'Flight of the Earls'. Firstly, the presence of so few women on board resonates with the military nature of Gaelic society and the relatively low status of women in it. Secondly, the men who led the group were clearly concerned to take their sons and heirs with them. Some weeks before the departure, the Earl of Tyrone had travelled to County Louth to collect one of his sons who was living with his foster family, the Moores.[2] Tyrone was also, reportedly, very upset that he could not locate his younger son, Con, in time and had to leave without him.[3] Similarly, Tyrconnell was anxious that his infant son Hugh accompany him to the Continent, and he boarded the ship at Lough Swilly without the boy's mother, Bridget, who never saw either her son or her husband again. Tyrconnell's brother, Cathbar was also caught up in the panic to ensure that sons and heirs be

---

[1] *Calendar of State Papers, Ireland, 1606–8*, 435–6; B. Jennings, *Wild Geese in Spanish Flanders* (Dublin, 1964), 483–4; J. McCavitt, *The Flight of the Earls* (Dublin, 2002), 97–8; C. Mooney, 'A Noble Shipload', *Irish Sword*, 2 (1954–6), 195–204. Apart from the O'Neill and O'Donnell children, a grandson and a grandnephew of O'Neill's were also on board as were two sons of his steward, Ever McConnell. See P. Walsh (ed.), *The Flight of the Earls by Tadhg Ó Cianáin* (Dublin, 1916), 16.
[2] McCavitt, *Flight of the Earls*, 95; *CSPI*, 1606–8, 463.
[3] *CSPI*, 1606–8, 261.

included in the passenger list, as he allegedly 'violently seized' his young son from his foster parents as they travelled along the road to where he had arranged to meet them.[4]

The men's concern to bring their sons to Europe was motivated by more than anxiety about the children's safety. There was also recognition that the sons represented the future lineage of their respective families. None of the contemporary accounts of the flight indicate that there was any attempt made to include daughters in the departing group. Among those left behind to fend for themselves was Róise, daughter of Hugh O'Neill, who had been used in a ruthless fashion by her father in the labyrinthine network of marriage alliances that he had formed before and during the wars of the 1590s. Róise was first married to O'Neill's ally in the war, Hugh Roe O'Donnell. O'Donnell ended the marriage in 1598, allegedly because Róise had not produced children. Some years later she was married to another supporter of her father's, Donal Ballagh O'Cahan. The latter sent Róise back to her father early in 1607 on the grounds that their marriage was illegal and that he was still married to his first wife, Mary O'Donnell, a former sister-in-law of Róise. There were also, however, political reasons for the ending of the marriage as it coincided with the attempt by the Dublin administration to persuade O'Cahan to assert his independence from Tyrone. Róise, once again, was a victim of her father's political circumstances.[5]

Róise's fate after the departure of her father to the Continent in 1607 is not known but her use as a pawn in the political alliances of her family was a common experience of women in aristocratic Irish families. Despite the popular perception of Gaelic Ireland as a society that encouraged independence in women, in reality women's lives were circumscribed and controlled by the men in their families. As in Róise's case, marriages often formed part of a political alliance between two lordships. Catherine McGuinness, for example, was the Earl of Tyrone's fourth wife, and he had married his second and third wives while his first wife was still alive.[6]

It is likely that Catherine McGuinness and Rosa O'Doherty had little choice but to follow their husbands to Europe. They would have had no financial resources of their own if they had stayed behind. In 1604 Catherine McGuinness had complained of the 'many violences' that her husband 'had done to her in his drunkenness, and that she was weary of her unquiet life'. She had asked the Dublin administration for the means to leave him.[7] The government was, however, more interested in the access that McGuinness had to her husband than they were in supporting a woman with no income of her own. McGuinness was clearly a

---

[4] McCavitt, *Flight of the Earls*, 93–5; J. Casway, 'Rosa O Dogherty: A Gaelic Woman', *Seanchas Ardmhacha*, 10, 1 (1980–1), 47.

[5] J. Casway, 'The Decline and Fate of Dónal Ballagh O'Cahan and his Family', in M. Ó Siochrú (ed.), *Kingdoms in Crisis: Ireland in the 1640s* (Dublin, 2001), 44–62; P. Walsh, *The Will and Family of Hugh O'Neill: Earl of Tyrone. With an Appendix of Genealogies* (Dublin, 1930), 36–8.

[6] Walsh, *The Will and Family of Hugh O'Neill*, 16–28; Hugh O'Neill, 2nd Earl of Tyrone; entry by N. Canny, *Oxford Dictionary of National Biography*.

[7] *CSPI*, 1603–6, 409.

reluctant participant in the famous flight of her husband. At one stage in the long journey to the boat in Rathmullan, she 'slipped down from her horse, and weeping, said she could go no further; whereupon the earl drew his sword, and swore a great oath that he would kill her in the place, if she would not pass on with him, and put on a more cheerful countenance'.[8]

Tyrconnell's wife, Bridget Fitzgerald, was left without any income when her husband fled Ireland, and she quickly discovered how difficult the position of a separated woman was in Gaelic Ireland. The tenants on her husband's estates in Donegal had little respect for her as an abandoned wife. As the Lord Deputy Sir Arthur Chichester reported to London in 1607, she had been left without an income, and 'the tenants would not live under her, she being a lady, and, in their opinion, not able to defend them'.[9] The countess survived by moving to live in England where she enjoyed the patronage of the family of her mother, a daughter of Charles Howard, Earl of Nottingham, a member of the English privy council.[10]

The Countess of Tyrconnell, perhaps more than the tenants on her husband's lands, must have been aware that she was living in a time of transition, and that Gaelic laws and customs were giving way gradually to English common law and assize courts. While the erosion of Gaelic society was mourned by the *filidh* as the end of the civilized world, it would be difficult to argue that it was a disaster for the legal status of women. Women's right to own or control property, for example, in Gaelic society was very limited. In the strict interpretation of Gaelic custom, family land was divided among all the male heirs of the extended family going back over several generations. If a man died without sons, his claim to a share in the family property passed to his brothers or nephews or to other male relatives. By contrast, under English common law, a daughter could inherit her father's estate if he had no sons.[11]

The notion of a marriage dowry existed in both Irish and English legal systems but there were significant differences in its purpose. In English society, a dowry was considered as a starting point for the marriage. A woman could bring cash or kind, often in the form of cooking utensils or household goods, as well as stock for the farm. In wealthier families the dowry consisted of cash or property. If the woman was widowed, she was entitled, as a minimum, to a third of her husband's estate for

---

[8] McCavitt, *Flight of the Earls*, 95.
[9] C. P. Meehan, *The Fate and Fortune of Hugh O'Neill, Earl of Tyrone, and Rory O'Donel, Earl of Tyrconnel* (Dublin, 1868), 246.
[10] M. Kerney Walsh, *'Destruction by Peace'; Hugh O'Neill after Kinsale* (Monaghan, 1986), 29–20; Meehan, *The Fate and Fortune of Hugh O'Neill and Rory O'Donell*, 236–41, 246.
[11] If there was more than one daughter, the land was shared between them as co-heiresses. See K. W. Nicholls, 'Some Documents on Irish Law and Custom in the Sixteenth Century', *Analecta Hibernica*, 26 (1970), 103–29; M. O'Dowd, *A History of Women in Ireland, 1500–1800* (Harlow, 2005), 73–113; 'Women and the Irish Chancery Court in the late Sixteenth and early Seventeenth Centuries', *Irish Historical Studies*, 31 (1999), 470–87; 'Property, Work and Home: Women and the Economy, c.1170–1850', in A. Bourke *et al.* (eds), *Field Day Anthology of Irish Writing*, Vol. 5 (Cork, 2001), 464–91; K. W. Nicholls, 'Irish Women and Property in the Sixteenth Century', in M. MacCurtain and M. O'Dowd (eds), *Women in Early Modern Ireland* (Edinburgh, 1991), 17–31.

her lifetime. In Gaelic society, however, a widow was only entitled to receive back the dowry that she brought to the marriage or its equivalent in cash or kind. The dowry thus represented not only what the woman brought to the marriage but also what she would get if widowed.[12] One of the advantages of the Gaelic system of dowry from the wife's point of view was that it was identified as her property. Thus, when Hugh O'Donnell, Lord of Tyrconnell, married the Scottish woman, Fiona MacDonnell (Iníon Dubh) in the 1570s, she brought to the marriage a troop of Scottish soldiers that she appears to have commanded and used for her own purposes. The Irish type of dowry allowed Fiona to play an important role in the development of the power base of her son, Hugh Roe.[13] More usually, however, the dowry consisted of household goods or cattle which gave women no political or military control.[14]

English law, therefore, allocated single women and widows more specific rights to property and material wealth than Gaelic customary law. The operation of the new land laws on women's inheritance was in evidence in the province when the plans for the plantation were announced in 1609. Among the native Irish or 'deserving' Irish who were given grants of land in the scheme were heiresses and widows.[15] Somewhat surprisingly, one of the widows whose legal claims were recognized by the plantation planners was Fiona MacDonnell.[16] Another woman who benefited from the new laws on widow's entitlements was Catherine O'Neill who was granted an extensive estate in County Tyrone with the remainder (i.e. the holder of the land after Catherine's death) to her young son, Phelim, who subsequently became one of the leaders of the rebellion in 1641.[17]

There were no English or Scottish women among the initial grantees of plantation lands. The first generation of undertakers and servitors were all men, but by the time of the 1622 survey of the scheme, a number of widows were listed as in charge of estates and participating eagerly in the plantation project.[18] They included Lady Coach, widow of Sir Thomas Coach, who by 1622 was recorded as having built a house and a bawn near Lough Swilly in County Donegal where she was living with her 'family'.[19]

The only detailed description that we have of the role of a woman on a planter estate is an early eighteenth century account of Elizabeth Montgomery whose husband settled in the Ards peninsula in the early seventeenth century. While Lady Montgomery was not a widow, her husband 'was by business much and often kept from home'.[20] During his absence, she ran the estate and took responsibility for

---

[12] O'Dowd, *Women in Ireland, 1500–1800*, 76–7, 98–9.
[13] D. McGettigan, *Red Hugh O'Donnell and the Nine Years War* (Dublin, 2005), 35–9, 41, 46, 47, 53–5, 63, 89–90, 98, 102.
[14] O'Dowd, *Women in Ireland, 1500–1800*, 98–100.
[15] G. Hill, *An Historical Account of the Plantation in Ulster* (Belfast, 1877), 130–1, 322, 340.
[16] Ibid., 328.   [17] Ibid., 318–19.   [18] Ibid., 585.
[19] V. Treadwell (ed.), *The Irish Commission of 1622: An Investigation of the Irish Administration 1615–1622 and its Consequence 1623–1624* (Dublin, 2006), 615.
[20] G. Hill (ed.), *The Montgomery Manuscripts (1603–1706)* (Belfast, 1869), 62–6, as reprinted in *Field Day Anthology of Irish Writing*, Vol. 5, 493–4.

overseeing the building and decorating of the family home.²¹ Lady Montgomery also encouraged British tenants to settle on the land, offering them grass for their stock and 'an house and garden-plot to live on, and some land for flax and potatoes,...' and, according to the family chronicler, 'this was but part of her good management, for she set up and encouraged linen and woollen manafactory, which soon brought down the prices of ye breakens [tartans] and narrow cloths of both sorts'.²²

This depiction, albeit benign, of the assistance and encouragement that Elizabeth Montgomery gave to the tenants on the estate is in stark contrast to the report of Bridget Fitzgerald being shunned by the tenants on her husband's lands in Tyrconnell. In Gaelic society, the landlord was expected to take on a military (and manly) role of defending his tenants rather than supervising the distribution of tenancies and the crops that were grown on the property. In England and Scotland, the figure of the woman estate manager was not uncommon, but she was a new phenomenon in the Ulster rural landscape of the seventeenth century. As such, she was a visible sign of the changing nature of society. The female landholder or manager in the form of the heiress, the widow, and the married woman, thus represented new roles and images for elite women in seventeenth-century Ulster.

A PATRIARCHAL SOCIETY?

It is important, of course, not to exaggerate the extent of the change in women's legal status in the early decades of seventeenth-century Ulster. Patriarchy was embedded in English common law and early modern Ulster was a strongly patriarchal society. On marriage, most women ceased to have an independent legal existence and were represented by their husbands in legal and financial proceedings. The transition to English landed inheritance practices also meant that primogeniture prevailed in landed families with most of the estate being inherited by the eldest son.²³

From the 1660s, patriarchy was reinforced by the introduction of the marriage or family settlement which enabled a father to continue to control the distribution of wealth within his family after his death.²⁴ The bulk of a landed estate was reserved for the eldest son while younger sons might be given cash legacies to finance their education, and daughters were given a specified sum of money for their marriage portion. If the settlement was made as part of the negotiations for a marriage, it would also specify the amount (the jointure) that the husband would give his wife in the event of his death. Use of a strict settlement could also enable families to override the claim of an heiress to her father's estate if the land was entailed to male

---

[21] Ibid. [22] Ibid.
[23] O'Dowd, *A History of Women in Ireland, 1500–1800*, 73–113.
[24] See D. Wilson, *Women, Marriage and Property in Wealthy Landed Families in Ireland, 1750–1850* (Manchester, 2009), 39–86.

heirs only. Thus if a man died without sons, his property would pass to his nephew, brother, or other male relative. Malcomson cites the example of Acheson Moore who had property in County Tyrone and nominated a distant male relative (his mother was a sister of his heir's great-grandmother) as his heir rather than leave his estate to his daughters.[25]

The harshness of the law was often, however, diluted by the affection of husbands for their wives and their concern for the care of their children following their deaths. A loving husband could use a written will to bequeath to his widow considerable control over his estate and children, appointing her as sole or joint executor and instructing his children to abide by the choice of spouse as determined by their mother.[26] By the late seventeenth century, it was not uncommon for fathers to leave either money or land to a daughter with the stipulation that it was for her 'sole and separate use...not withstanding her coverture', i.e. her legal status as a married woman.[27]

While owners of large estates maintained the principle of primogeniture in their inheritance practices, smaller landowners and tenant farmers often distributed their goods and property more equitably. This was particularly the case with tenant farmers in rural Ulster who had a small inheritance of goods and cash to leave to their wives and children.[28]

The wills of small landowners and tenant farmers reflect the fact that partnership and cooperation were the prevailing characteristics in most marriages as the demands of the rural economy depended on the work of all members of the family. Although the first generation of settlers in seventeenth-century Ulster maintained the pastoral economy of Gaelic society, by the early eighteenth century, the cultivation of flax and the production of linen yarn or cloth was the principal means by which many rural families survived. The different labour tasks involved from the sowing of the flax seeds to the spinning of the yarn were divided between men, women, and children in the family.[29] In households where no weaving was done, the women's work as spinners of the yarn brought much-needed cash income into the household.

Young unmarried daughters might also be hired out for six months of the year to other households in need of additional spinners. The women were paid partly in kind and partly in cash which was sent directly to their parental home.[30] Thus the

---

[25] A. P. W. Malcomson, *The Pursuit of an Heiress: Aristocratic Marriage in Ireland 1740–1840* (Belfast, 2006), 19–20.

[26] O'Dowd, *History of Women in Ireland*, 93–105; Wilson, *Women, Marriage and Property in Wealthy Landed Families*, 43–5, 60–1.

[27] Ibid., 70. See also 69–71, 127–31.

[28] PRONI, T/581/4, 339; T/581/8; T/403/1.

[29] See, for example, the printed engravings by W. Hincks, 'Illustrations of the Irish Linen Industry in 1783', *Ulster Folk Life*, 23 (1977), 1–32.

[30] M. O'Dowd, 'Women and Paid Work in Ireland, 1500–1800', in B. Whelan (ed.), *Women and Paid Work in Ireland* (Dublin, 2000), 13–29; W. H. Crawford, 'Women in the Domestic Linen Industry', in M. MacCurtain and M. O'Dowd (eds), *Women in Early Modern Ireland* (Edinburgh, 1991), 255–64.

young spinners, living away from home, continued to contribute to the family economy. In the 1750s, for example, Molly O'Neill was hired regularly for a half year's work on the Orr family farm in County Tyrone. Molly's wages were paid in instalments, and the farm account book reveals that in her first year of employment, her mother was paid 7s 7d from her daughter's wages. In subsequent years, O'Neill continued to contribute to her family's income with cash and agricultural produce being sent directly to her relatives. O'Neill also, however, had a small cash income of her own which she used to buy items of clothing at the fair in Kilkeel.[31] Despite the fact that most of her wage went directly to her parents, the spinner and farm servant had, therefore, a certain amount of financial independence.

Most young girls spent only a short period of time in service before they married. On the Brownlow estate in County Down, the average term of employment was one to two years, the majority leaving, according to the household accounts 'at her own desire'.[32] For most young women, therefore, domestic service was a brief interlude, usually in their teenage years, prior to setting up their own homes and starting a family. Some women inevitably stayed longer and household account books document rather poignantly the lives of women who spent all their adulthood in service. For the most fortunate, service in a big estate house provided one of the few career structures for women in which promotion and a rise in income was possible. Through the Brownlow estate records, it is possible to trace the careers of women like Peggy Watson who was first employed in the 1770s as a nursery maid at an annual wage of 4 guineas. Watson subsequently became a housemaid and in 1785 was promoted to the position of Mrs Brownlow's maid with a salary of 8 guineas. As a lady's maid, Watson not only received an augmented income but would also have had a higher status in the household than the more lowly nursery or housemaid.[33]

The burgeoning economy of eighteenth-century Ulster, fuelled by the production of linen cloth, fostered urban growth which in turn opened up new economic opportunities for single, married, and widowed women. The surviving correspondence and wills of merchants and businessmen document the extent to which husbands as well as wives contributed to the family income. We can document the story of one such couple, Elizabeth and Robert Shipboy, who managed a shop in Coleraine in the 1770s as a joint enterprise. Robert was in charge of the main clothing business while Elizabeth advertised a mantua or gown-making service. When Robert died, Elizabeth ran the Coleraine shop on her own for a number of years, but in 1793 she sold up and moved to Belfast where she joined with her son James to establish a millinery and carpet business in High Street.[34] From then until her death two years later, Elizabeth and James appear to have been partners in the

---

[31] PRONI, T/3301, 9, 13, 18, 21.
[32] O'Dowd, 'Women and Paid Work in Ireland', 16–19.
[33] PRONI, D/1928/A/1/8, 13, 34, 121.
[34] *Belfast News Letter*, 19–22 February 1788, 12–16 June 1789, 3–6 August 1790, 3–6 July 1792, 28 December 1792, 1 January 1793, 20–23 June 1794, 1–5 June 1795; PRONI, D/530/14; 22/6, 7. See also T. H. Mullan, *Coleraine in Georgian Times* (Belfast, 1877), 92–3.

business. They signed receipts for money jointly and individually. They advertised, however, under the name 'Elizabeth and James Shipboy' and it is clear that Elizabeth remained the senior partner until her death.[35] She was also sufficiently well-known to merit a brief obituary notice in the *Belfast News Letter*.[36]

The growth in commercial life of towns in Ulster opened up economic opportunities not just for married and widowed women but for single women too. Unmarried women set up small businesses which required little capital other than their own domestic skills such as dressmaking or food production. The best-known enterprise run by two single women was a small muslin business managed by Mary Ann and Margaret McCracken from the mid-1790s through to 1815.[37] While some single women may have been dependent on their business for their survival, Mary Ann McCracken wrote that she persuaded her sister to start the business 'so that she might have a little money to use as she pleased'.[38] Like Molly O'Neill and other servant girls, McCracken appreciated the independence that a 'little money' could bring to her life.

The McCracken business ended in 1815, by which time the domestic linen industry was in decline. The move to mills and large-scale production did not end women's domestic production, but it did, nonetheless, limit the ability of women to contribute to the family economy through spinning in their own homes. The erosion of the income to be earned from spinning also plunged many households into poverty.[39]

Medieval historian Judith Bennett has rightly cautioned against idealizing the marital partnership involved in the pre-modern economy.[40] Nonetheless, the changing economy of eighteenth-century Ulster helped to soften if not undermine patriarchal control in the family. Urban expansion also facilitated women's agency, giving entrepreneurs such as Elizabeth Shipboy the possibility of developing their business acumen and of receiving public recognition for doing so. The new economic opportunities also enabled women such as Mary Ann McCracken to have some financial independence, however limited.

RELIGION: A MEANS TO A PUBLIC LIFE?

If economic development facilitated women's agency, to what extent was this helped or hindered by attitudes to women supported by the prevailing church authorities and religious practice? By far the most visible presence in the histor-

---

[35] O'Dowd, *History of Women in Ireland, 1500–1800*, 114–17; PRONI, D/530/22/19.
[36] Will of Elizabeth Shipboy, undated, PRONI, D/530/13; obituary in *Belfast News Letter*, 4 June 1795.
[37] *Merchants in Plenty: Joseph Smyth's Belfast Directories of 1807 and 1808* (Belfast, 1991), 11–38.
[38] M. McNeill, *The Life and Times of Mary Ann McCracken, 1770–1866: A Belfast Panorama* (Dublin, 1960), 41, 57, 112, 114, 130–4, 245.
[39] M. E. Daly, *Women and Work in Ireland* (Dundalk, 1997), 9–11.
[40] J. M. Bennett, 'Medieval Women, Modern Women: Across the Great Divide', in A. Shapiro (ed.), *Feminists Revision History* (New Brunswick, 1994), 47–72.

ical record is women from dissenting communities: Presbyterians, Quakers, and, later, Methodists. Unlike Catholicism, Protestantism encouraged women to learn how to read, if not to write. While Roman Catholicism and the Church of Ireland emphasized the authority and leadership of the ordained minister in religious services, dissenters in the Presbyterian and Quaker communities fostered greater lay involvement in church organization, which made them more accessible to women. The persecution of Presbyterian ministers in the early decades of the seventeenth century also facilitated a role for women in the fledgling church as they provided accommodation for ministers and, in the absence of a church building, gathered together in their own houses for prayer meetings.[41] In the late 1630s, Henry Leslie, Bishop of Down and Connor became so frustrated with the influence of Presbyterianism on women in Ulster that he referred to it as the 'feminine heresie'. Leslie's condemnation of Presbyterianism indirectly reveals its attraction for women:

> ...it is naturall unto the daughters of Eve to desire knowledge and those men [i.e. Presbyterian ministers] puff them up with an opinion of science, enabling them to prattle of matters of divinity which they and their teachers understand much alike; insomuch that albeit St. Paul hath forbidden women to speake in the church, yet they speak of church-matters more than comes to their share.[42]

Leslie also believed that Presbyterianism propagated greater equality between the sexes and gave women unnatural ideas about their role in the household:

> [Presbyterian ministers] allow them to be at least quarter-masters with their husbands...I have not observed that faction to prevaile but where husbands have learned to obey their wives...[43]

The popular image of early modern Ulster Presbyterianism is one of a community in which the minister and elders maintained strict control over the congregation, particularly in the area of sexual morality. The earliest session minutes indicate that sex outside marriage was condemned and punished by public shaming of the offenders. Later in the eighteenth century, as Presbyterianism expanded and divided, it is possible to distinguish different levels of intensity with which sexual offences were condemned in local communities. It is also worth noting that while all sessions, regardless of their denominational affiliation, condemned premarital fornication, the laity continued throughout the eighteenth century to engage in it. As historians Donald Akenson and Paul Gray have pointed out, some Presbyterian communities tolerated premarital sex as long as the couple married afterwards. Gray's quantitative analysis of baptismal and marriage registers in late eighteenth-century Carnmoney indicates that there was a relatively high number of pregnant brides (ranging from 13 per cent in the 1770s to 19 per cent in the

---

[41] O'Dowd, *A History of Women in Ireland*, 169–74.
[42] Cited in J. Seaton Reid, *History of the Presbyterian Church in Ireland: Comprising the Civil History of the Province of Ulster...* (2 Vols, Belfast, 1867), I, 193.
[43] Ibid.

1780s and 1790s), but at the same time, the number of births outside marriage was surprisingly low (0.8–1.3 per cent).[44] In other words, premarital sex and pregnancy was usually followed by marriage.

From the perspective of the historian of women, the strict, almost prurient image of the kirk session should be balanced against the notion that it gave women a public venue in which to complain about sexual abuse, as well as a voice to ask for maintenance for illegitimate children. In a telling confirmation of the use of the session as a means of dealing with sexual abuse, a Catholic mother, Alice Maguire, reported to the Seceder session in Cahans in 1767 that she suspected that a married man, John Makee, had 'debauched' her daughter whom he had hired as a servant. She requested that the session compel Makee to confess his 'faulty conduct' and to leave her daughter alone. The session was sympathetic to Alice's pleas because, as they pointed out to Makee, it was unlikely that a Catholic woman would come to the sessions to make such a charge if it was untrue.[45]

Another dissenting community that provided a public space for women was the Society of Friends. By the 1790s, Quaker communities in Ulster were holding regular 'women's meetings' at which the women in the congregation met to discuss specific issues that had been delegated to them by the 'men's meetings'. In particular, the arrangements for marriage were deemed to be women's business. Members of the women's meetings undertook to visit the home of the future bride to ensure that she had the consent of her parents and that she was in the right frame of mind to marry.[46] The agenda for the women's meetings was to a certain extent controlled by the men in the community, but the meetings, nonetheless, gave women a regular input into the affairs of the Society.

When John Wesley began his visits to Ireland in the 1740s, he identified women in the Church of Ireland as being particularly useful as advocates for his particular brand of Protestantism. Women provided a support network for early Methodism as they made their homes available for services and supplied lodgings for itinerant preachers. Wesley also encouraged women to form classes in which small groups of believers met privately to read the scriptures and to share the contents of spiritual diaries in which men and women wrote about their daily religious thoughts and prayers.[47] Wesley was also supportive of the notion of women preachers. The best-known female Methodist preacher in Ireland was Alice Cambridge who

---

[44] P. Gray, 'A Social History of Illegitimacy in Ireland' (PhD thesis, Queen's University, Belfast, 2000), 97–145; D. H. Akenson, *Small Differences: Irish Catholics and Irish Protestants 1815–1922: An International Perspective* (Kingston, Ontario, 1988), 28–38; idem, *Between Two Revolutions: Islandmagee, County Antrim 1798–1920* (Dublin, 1979), 122–3. See also A. R. Holmes, *The Shaping of Ulster Presbyterian Belief and Practice, 1770–1840* (Oxford, 2006), 225–7.

[45] Cahans session book, 1751–1802, entry dated 17 July 1767 (Presbyterian Historical Society, Belfast).

[46] P. Kilroy, 'Quaker Women in Ireland, 1660–1740', *Irish Journal of Feminist Studies*, 2 (1997), 1–17; R. L. Greaves, *God's Other Children: Protestant Nonconformists and the Emergence of Denominational Churches in Ireland, 1660–1700* (Stanford, 1997), 343–8; Minutes of the Lisburn Women's Meetings, 1793–1800 (PRONI, Microfilm 16/16).

[47] D. Hempton and M. Hill, 'Women and Protestant Minorities in Eighteenth-Century Ireland', in MacCurtain and O'Dowd (eds.), *Women in Early Modern Ireland*, 197–211.

conducted a very successful tour of Ulster provincial towns in the first decade of the nineteenth century.⁴⁸ Despite Wesley's encouragement of women preachers, however, the 1802 conference of the church proclaimed its disapproval that women 'should preach or should exhort in public'.⁴⁹

The absence of a large, literate, Catholic middle or upper class in early modern Ulster means that the voices of Catholic women are either invisible or difficult to identify in the historical record. In other parts of Ireland, small communities of female religious were formed in many Irish towns from the mid-eighteenth century onwards. This was not, however, a development that occurred in Ulster towns and it was not until the second half of the nineteenth century that the figure of the nun became a more common sight in the Ulster urban landscape.

Analysts of patriarchal societies write of the spaces or 'wriggle room' that women create in order to undermine or dilute the strict enforcement of male patriarchal control. In early modern Ulster, it was the dissenting communities that provided women with the most 'wriggle room' as they learnt to read, write, and have a public voice, however, muted. By the 1790s, too, there are indications that women in the wider Protestant community were actively engaged in widening the boundaries of the public sphere for women through their participation in philanthropic projects. In Belfast, for example, middle-class women like Martha McTier organized small charity schools and societies such as the Humane Female Society for the Relief of Laying-in Women which established the Belfast Lying-in Hospital.⁵⁰ Another development that is also perceptible by the 1790s is that women were increasingly making use of their literacy skills to read not just religious texts but also more widely.

AN EDUCATIONAL REVOLUTION?

Figures for literacy rates in early modern Ireland are scarce and difficult to interpret.⁵¹ Nevertheless, we can point to developments that suggest that more women were literate by the last quarter of the eighteenth century than was the case in 1700. First, we can document through newspaper advertisements the establishment of an increasing number of schools for girls in Belfast and other provincial towns. Many of the schools advertised a similar curriculum that was a mixture of lessons on social skills such as dancing, drawing, and embroidery as well as more academic subjects such as writing classes, arithmetic, and geography. While most of the pupils were drawn from the burgeoning middle-class merchant and business

---

⁴⁸ C. H. Crookshank, *Memorable Women of Irish Methodism in the Last Century* (London, 1882), 191–203.
⁴⁹ Hempton and Hill, 'Women and Protestant Minorities in Eighteenth-Century Ireland', 202.
⁵⁰ J. Agnew (ed.), *The Drennan-McTier Letters, 1776–1819* (3 Vols, Dublin, 1998–9), 115–16, 121, 193, 219, 354, 722.
⁵¹ The earliest and most detailed figures on literacy date to 1841. See N. Ó Ciosáin, *Print and Popular Culture in Ireland, 1750–1850* (Basingstoke, 1997), 31–2.

families living in the linen towns of east Ulster, some teachers also organized evening classes for pupils who were working during the day.[52]

We can also identify an increase in women's literacy through the number of books published in Belfast which were directed at a female readership. In particular, there was a thriving market in books for teaching girls or that could be used to instruct both girls and boys. Among these was Sarah Fielding's *The Governess, or Little Female Academy…for the Entertainment and Instruction of Young Ladies in Their Education* (12th edition, Belfast, 1779), a very popular text used by teachers of girls in England and elsewhere in Ireland.[53] Another well-liked book was *The Young Gentleman and Ladies Monitor, Being a Collection of Select Pieces From Our Best Modern Writers* (Belfast, 1788, 1794, 1796) which was used in the newly opened Belfast Academy but clearly could also be used to teach 'young ladies'. David Manson taught both sexes in his much-admired school in Belfast and published two books which explicitly assumed that the reader was interested in teaching girls as well as boys.[54]

Another text directed at a female readership that was read in northern towns in the late eighteenth century was the periodical, *The New Magazine* which appeared for two years from 1799 to 1800 and was edited by James Delap.[55] A subscription list published in 1799 indicates that the journal had a significant readership in the province. At least 100 of the 275 issues (36 per cent) were ordered from Ulster-based subscribers. The editor of the *New Magazine* noted in his first issue that he would endeavour to 'make this compilation agreeable to men of sense yet to my fair countrywomen, it will be found peculiarly adapted'. Each issue of the journal contained articles that were specifically targeted at a female readership, including a series of very positive profiles of English women authors who had written about girls' education. In addition, the *New Magazine* regularly reviewed books for children, especially school books or books which could be used to teach children at home. The editor was clearly hoping that his journal would appeal not just to female school teachers but also to literate mothers anxious to teach their children in the most up-to-date fashion.

Other indicators of increased literacy among girls from middling and upper class families are the references to reading in the private correspondence of women. Martha McTier's letters to her brother testify to her wide intellectual interests as she wrote enthusiastically about the books she was reading on contemporary politics and political ideas, philosophy, religion, and history. Later in life, when McTier was caring for her brother's young son, Tom, she began also to read books on the education of children.[56]

---

[52] *Belfast News Letter* online index <http://www.ucs.louisiana.edu/bnl/>; L. Wylie's online edition of Belfast trade directories at <http://www.lennonwylie.co.uk/1819_IndexandHistory.htm>.

[53] There were three Dublin editions: 1749, 1752, 1791, and a Cork edition, 1769.

[54] P. J. Kane, 'The Life and Works of David Manson: A Belfast School-Teacher, 1726–1792' (unpublished M.Ed. Thesis, Queen's University, Belfast, 1984), 27–46.

[55] For the identification of Delap as editor see A. Markey, 'Irish Children's Fiction, 1727–1820', in *Irish University Review* (Spring/Summer, 2011), 123.

[56] Agnew (ed.), *The Drennan-McTier Letters, 1776–1819*. See also Maria Luddy, 'Martha McTier and William Drennan: A "Domestic History"', in ibid., Vol. 1, xix–li; Catherine Kennedy, '"Womanish Epistles?" Martha McTier, Female Epistolarity and Late Eighteenth-Century Irish Radicalism', *Women's History Review*, 13 (2004), 649–67.

The transition to wider literacy skills for women in this middling and upper class section of Ulster Presbyterian society can also be traced through the Tennent family archive. In the 1790s and first decade of the nineteenth century, Anne Tennent, wife of the Presbyterian minister, John Tennent, regularly appealed to her son, William to send her books from Belfast. The fact that such requests were always relayed to William through his father's correspondence with him suggests that Anne was not a fluent writer. Anne's son, William Tennent sent all his daughters to school and in the early decades of the nineteenth century his daughter Eliza was not just attending lectures and classes in the newly opened Belfast Academy but also keeping extensive notes on what she had learned. Like her grandmother, Eliza read widely but unlike her grandmother, she wrote about what she had read and maintained a regular correspondence with her father and other members of her family. The papers of Eliza Tennent are striking evidence of the new image of the educated woman who began to appear in Ulster by the 1820s.[57]

A POLITICAL WOMAN?

If it is possible to detect advances in women's education and educational opportunities what of women's political role? Clearly, no woman had direct access to political power in early modern Ulster. There were no female Gaelic chieftainesses nor did any woman hold public office or have the right to vote personally in parliamentary elections. A small number of elite women had access to the political process through their control of the parliamentary representative attached to their family property. The most notable example of this in Ulster, however, dates to the post-Union period when the Marchioness of Downshire managed the parliamentary seat on her family's estate during the minority of her son.[58]

Most women's access to political life was more indirect. The war conditions of the seventeenth century drew women willingly and, in many cases, unwillingly, into the political conflict. Rosa O'Doherty, for example, seems to have acted as a messenger and go-between for her second husband, Owen Roe O'Neill, who was commander of the confederate troops in the 1640s.[59] Women were also involved in the riots and group actions that constituted the 'massacres' of 1641.[60]

Later, in the 1790s, women provided nursing services and safe houses for men in the Defender and United Irishmen organizations. There was a United Irishwomen's organization but it does not appear to have been very active, and may have been

---

[57] The Tennent Papers are in PRONI (D1748). The papers of Eliza Tennent are in D1748/H. For Anne Tennent's requests for books see, for example, D1748/B/1.

[58] P. Jupp, *British and Irish Elections, 1784–1831* (Newton Abbot, 1973); J. Lewis, *Sacred to Female Patriotism: Gender, Class, and Politics in Late Georgian Britain* (London, 2003), 16–17, 21–2, 56, 154–5.

[59] J. Casway, 'Rosa O Dogherty', 53–62.

[60] M. O'Dowd, 'Women and War in Ireland in the 1640s', in O'Dowd and MacCurtain (eds.), *Women in Early Modern Ireland,* 91–111.

mainly a means of swearing women to secrecy about the affairs of the organization, particularly in the late 1790s when it was preparing for rebellion.[61]

The emergence of radical politics in the last quarter of the eighteenth century did, however, arouse the political interest of women, particularly in Belfast. Martha McTier followed political affairs in the city with great interest and clearly supported the involvement of both her brother and her husband in the early years of the United Irishmen. In a similar fashion, Mary Anne McCracken sympathized with her brother's republican beliefs.[62]

Drennan and McTier were familiar with the work of Mary Wollstonecraft and shared her views on the status of women.[63] Late one night in March 1797 in a letter to her brother, then in prison in Dublin, Mary Anne McCracken expressed her opinion on the status of women using the language of political radicalism. She wrote of 'the slavery of women' and expressed the hope that 'the female part of creation as well as the male' would soon 'throw off the fetters with which they have been so long mentally bound'.[64] These were views, however, written in private correspondence and neither McCracken nor McTier publicly challenged the gender inequalities of their time. It is a telling indication of women's public profile in the late eighteenth century that both women would have been better known in Belfast for their charity and philanthropic work than for their political views. In 1800, the figure of the politically active woman was not yet visible in Ulster.

CONCLUSION

As is often the case in women's history, it is difficult to generalize about the impact on women of the transformation of Ulster society from 1607 to 1800. Changes in the law and the economy as well as the introduction of new forms of religious practice undoubtedly opened up new opportunities for women. The main beneficiaries of these changes were, however, women in the middling and upper classes and particularly those in the Protestant community. At the lower levels of society, change was less obvious and frequently detrimental to women's status. While poor women could participate in the expanding economy of the middle decades of the eighteenth century, the quality of many women's lives was adversely affected by the decline in the domestic linen industry and the ending of their access to cash through spinning. Perhaps the most important aspect of the changes that occurred in women's lives during this period was that the possibility of change was identified. Access to literacy and the world of books, economic wealth, and new positions

---

[61] M. O'Dowd, 'The Political Writings and Public Voices of Women, c. 1500–1850', in *Field Day Anthology of Irish Writing*, Vol. 5, 11.

[62] Kennedy, '"Womanish Epistles?"', 649–67.

[63] Ibid., 661. For interest in Wollstonecraft's work in Belfast see J. Gray, 'Mary Anne McCracken: Belfast Revolutionary and Pioneer of Feminism', in D. Keogh and N. Furlong (eds), *The Women of 1798* (Dublin, 1998), 47–63.

[64] *Field Day Anthology of Irish Writing*, Vol. 5, 54–5.

of employment and participation in public affairs may have only benefited a minority of women by 1800, but these were also the areas in which women were to make the most strides in the subsequent century.

FURTHER READING

M. E. Daly, *Women and Work in Ireland* (Dundalk, 1997).
M. MacCurtain and M. O'Dowd (eds.), *Women in Early Modern Ireland* (Edinburgh, 1991).
M. O'Dowd, 'The Political Writings and Public Voices of Women, *c.* 1500–1850', in A. Bourke (ed.), *Field Day Anthology of Irish Writing*, Vol. 5 (Cork, 2002).
M. O'Dowd, *A History of Women in Ireland, 1500–1800* (Harlow, 2005).
B. Whelan (ed.), *Women and Paid Work in Ireland* (Dublin, 2000).
D. Wilson, *Women, Marriage and Property in Wealthy Landed Families in Ireland, 1750–1850* (Manchester, 2009).

4

People and Population Change, 1600–1914

Liam Kennedy, Kerby A. Miller, and Brian Gurrin

INTRODUCTION

Ulster in 1600 was a thinly populated, war-torn province with a population of probably no more than 200,000 people. This represents a mere 10 per cent or less of its peak population on the eve of the Great Famine. At a guess, the population of the whole island was in the region of one million.[1] The economies of the Ulster Gaelic lordships were based on primitive livestock production, with tillage crops as a minor adjunct. Trade was limited, as was urban development. These conditions made for low population densities. Crown-controlled, military enclaves at Carrickfergus and Newry, and religious centres at Downpatrick, Armagh, and Derry only mildly modify this portrayal of an essentially rural landscape and society. Ulster lagged well behind Leinster and Munster in terms of population density, urbanization, and wealth. Yet, in a remarkable transformation, by the end of our period Ulster had surpassed the other provinces of Ireland in terms of economic development and population growth. Between the early 1600s and 1841 the population of the province expanded tenfold. In 1911 Ulster held more than a third of the people of the island. In effect, the economic and demographic centre of gravity of the island had shifted northwards.[2]

POPULATION CHANGE

All population estimates before the first completed census of Ireland in 1821 are fraught with uncertainty. For the pre-census period, for particular subperiods, we can only sketch the direction of change with any certainty. Taking the seventeenth century as a whole, for instance, it is clear that Ulster gained in population. These gains were achieved despite military and political upheavals, and despite also a massive setback to population due to war, famine, and disease between 1641 and 1652.[3] An outbreak of

---

[1] T. W. Moody, F. X. Martin, and F. J. Byrne, (eds), *A New History of Ireland*, III: *Early Modern Ireland, 1534–1691* (Oxford, 1976). On demographic trends see N. Canny's review of this volume: 'Early Modern Ireland: An Appraisal Appraised', *Irish Economic and Social History*, 4 (1977), 63–5.

[2] This rising share of the island's population did not proceed in a steady, cumulative fashion. The major relative gains were concentrated in two periods: 1600–1732, a period dominated by the plantations and inward migration, and the much later period of 1851–1911 when industrialization was proceeding at a rapid pace.

[3] P. Lenihan, 'War and Population, 1649–52', *Irish Economic and Social History*, 24 (1997), 1–21.

bubonic plague, amplified by the misfortunes of war and malnutrition, proved to be especially lethal during the years 1649–52. This was the first of the Three Great Famines of early-modern and modern Irish society. These overshadowed all other subsistence crises in recent centuries and, curiously, broke out at hundred-year intervals. The others were the great frost and famine of 1740–41 and the better-known potato famine of 1846–50. In each of these island-wide calamities in the region of 15 per cent of the people may have perished. Only one of the three was associated with warfare or ideological purges, which contrasts with many famines in the modern world.

The expansion of population in Ulster after the early 1650s relied heavily on inward migration. Settlers and newcomers arrived in three waves, the first accompanying the plantation of Ulster in the years after 1608. The second followed the uprisings of 1641 and the Cromwellian re-conquest of Ireland. The third and largest influx came in the final decade of the seventeenth century as poor Scottish farmers and labourers fled famine and streamed into the north of Ireland during the 'ill years' of the 1690s in Scotland.[4] But population growth in the longer term was by no means dependent on inward migration. From being a land of immigration and settlement in the seventeenth century, Ulster became a land of emigration after the 1710s. Nonetheless, natural increase—the excess of births over deaths—was sufficient to ensure vigorous population increase. Figure 4.1 presents some

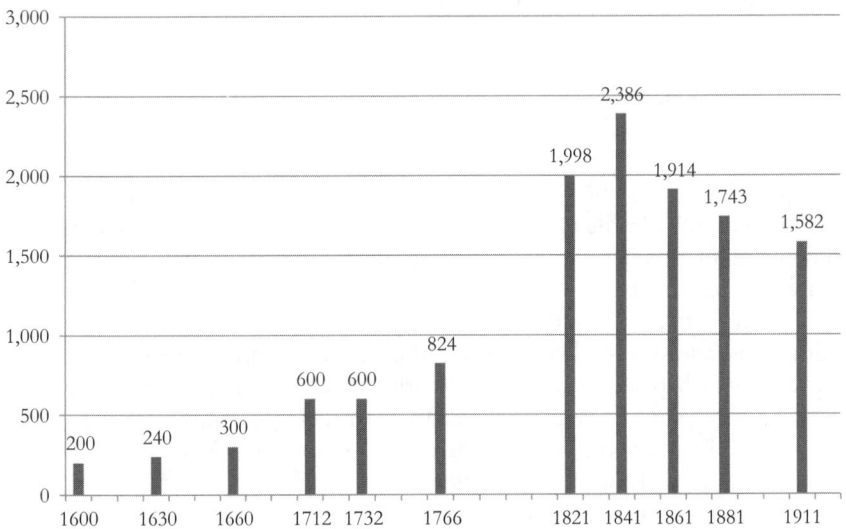

Figure 4.1. The population of the province of Ulster (000s), 1600–1911.

Sources: Population figures for the nineteenth century are from the Census of Ireland. The earlier *estimates* of population are derived from a variety of sources: W. Macafee, 'The Movement of British Settlers into Ulster during the Seventeenth Century', *Familia: Ulster Genealogical Review*, 2 (1992), 94–111; P. Robinson, *The Plantation of Ulster: British Settlement in an Irish Landscape, 1600–1670* (Dublin, 1984); *A Census of Ireland, circa 1659: With Essential Materials from the Poll Money Ordinances 1660–1661*, edited by S. Pender, with a new introduction by W. J. Smyth (Dublin, 2002); D. Bindon, *An Abstract of the Number of Protestant and Popish Families in the Several Counties and Provinces of Ireland* (Dublin, 1736); D. Dickson *et al.*, 'Hearth Tax, Household Size and Irish Population Change, 1672–1821' (1982), 155; B. Gurrin, K. A. Miller, and L. Kennedy, *Catholics and Protestants in Eighteenth-Century Ireland: The Religious Censuses of the 1760s* (Dublin, forthcoming, 2013).

[4] K. Cullen, *Famine in Scotland: The Ill Years of the 1690s* (Edinburgh, 2010).

tentative estimates of population levels for the period 1600–1766, while from 1821 onwards we are on rather firmer statistical ground by virtue of reliance on the official decennial censuses.[5]

In broad terms, Figure 4.1 shows growth in population during the seventeenth century, particularly in the second half of that century. The growth in population was spectacular after 1732 or, more accurately, after the great famine of 1740–41. By 1821 the people of Ulster numbered some two millions, and by the eve of the next great famine in 1845 the total had climbed to two and a half million. By then the population of Ireland had peaked at 8.4 million, a level never reached before or since. In the century before the 'hungry 1840s', Ireland had the fastest growth of population of any European country, with the possible exception of thinly populated Finland.[6] According to estimates by Dickson *et al.*, Ulster in turn was top of the provincial growth league in later eighteenth-century Ireland (1753–91),[7] thereby placing the region at the outer rim of the European experience. The challenge, therefore, is to understand how this population explosion come about and the factors detonating it.

The larger, international context must form an important part of any interpretation. Sustained population growth in Ireland and Ulster, evident from the 1740s onwards, was part of a pan-European phenomenon. This suggests general as well as specific forces at play. These might include climatic change, resulting in more bountiful harvests, and a natural decline in the virulence and prevalence of epidemic diseases. Both factors would lead to a decline in deaths and to greater longevity. Improvements in food supply due to greater commercialization, improvements in transport, and the greater integration of food markets, as was evident in parts of Europe and including eighteenth-century Ulster, would also help.[8]

In principle, population increase could come about as a result of a fall in the death rate or a rise in the birth rate, or a combination of the two. The only other component of population change—migration—was generally unimportant in eighteenth-century Europe. Indeed in the Ulster case, net migration, to North America in particular, served to moderate population increase, hence the conundrum to be resolved is all the greater. The dearth of empirical source materials (representative baptism, marriage, and burial registers) makes the challenge all the greater: seventeenth- and eighteenth-century Irish demographic history is in large part an exercise in controlled conjectures, with a dash of imagination.

The more settled political conditions of the eighteenth century meant that major military conflicts were absent from Ulster society, the one partial exception being the Antrim and Down risings of 1798. So, as compared to the preceding century, there was no heavy excess mortality due to warfare serving to reduce

---

[5] The eighteenth-century figures are likely to err in the direction of being underestimates.

[6] J. Mokyr and C. Ó Gráda, 'New Developments in Irish Population History, 1700–1850', *Economic History Review*, 37 (1984), 473–88.

[7] D. Dickson, C. Ó Gráda, and S. Daultrey, 'Hearth Tax, Household Size and Irish Population Change, 1672–1821', *Proceedings of the Royal Irish Academy*, 82C (1982), 170.

[8] K. G. Persson, *Grain Markets in Europe, 1500–1900: Integration and Deregulation* (Cambridge, 2000).

population. On the other hand, there is little reason to believe that advances in medical care had any significant impact on mortality. The County Infirmary Bill of 1765–66 made provision for county infirmaries, with nine of these allocated to Ulster.[9] But these catered for small numbers of people, and mainly for better-off Anglicans rather than the common people. Belfast did not get a maternity hospital until 1794. A fever hospital was opened a few years later, in 1797.[10] Macafee, on the basis of a small number of local studies, suggests that a decline in child mortality from the mid-eighteenth century may have triggered an increase in nuptiality and hence rising fertility later on.[11] Why this might have been so is not clear. In truth, we know little about the course of mortality in eighteenth-century Ireland, other than that mortality was high in the first half of the century: the 1720s witnessed economic and climatic setbacks, with an associated rise in mortality; then there was the somewhat neglected famine of 1740–41, the second of the mortality disasters mentioned earlier.[12] Viewed in regional perspective, Ulster was less badly affected by comparison with other regions of Ireland. The years 1774–75 were also years of crisis in Ulster, though to a lesser extent than in 1740–41. Mortality seems to have fallen in the second half of the century, in large part due to the pan-European reasons mentioned earlier.

A rise in the birth rate may well be the major component of population change. An increase in births could be due to earlier marriage, thereby increasing the length of years over which children could be conceived. Similarly, an increase in the marriage rate—the extent to which people marry varies historically—would also serve to increase the birth rate. In addition, it is possible that marital fertility, independent of these two other forces, could have risen in the later eighteenth century. It may be helpful at this point to take a quick sideways glance at the neighbouring island. The work of Wrigley and the Cambridge Group for the Study of Population and Social Structure places the main explanatory weight for the eighteenth century on an increase in the birth rate rather than a decline in the death rate.[13] Remarkably, K. H. Connell, the father of Irish population history, had anticipated this emphasis on fertility a generation earlier.[14] But was Connell right and does the English story fit the Irish case?

A new model of fertility change, hinging on resource endowments, property rights, innovation, and economic change, might run as follows. On the endowment side, mid-eighteenth century Ulster and Ireland generally had significant areas of marginal land available for reclamation and colonization by young families,

---

[9] A. Sneddon, 'State Intervention and Provincial Health Care: The County Infirmary system in Late Eighteenth-Century Ulster', paper read to the annual conference of the Irish Economic & Social History Society, November, 2011.
[10] Ibid.
[11] W. Macafee, 'The Pre-Famine Population of Ireland: A Reconsideration', in B. Collins, P. Ollerenshaw, and T. Parkhill (eds), *Industry, Trade and People in Ireland, 1650–1950* (Belfast, 2005), 77.
[12] D. Dickson, *Artic Ireland* (Belfast, 1997).
[13] E. A. Wrigley, 'The Growth of Population in Eighteenth-Century England: A Conundrum Resolved', *Past and Present*, 98 (1983), 131. For the more detailed study see Wrigley *et al.*, *English Population History from Family Reconstitution, 1580–1837* (Cambridge, 1997).
[14] K. H. Connell, *The Population of Ireland, 1750–1845* (Oxford, 1950).

while the extensive bogs supplied cheap fuel. Conditions in some localities must have approximated those of a semi-open 'frontier', for a few generations at least. The landlord-middleman-tenant arrangements constituted a property rights system in which control over lettings, and sublettings, was weak by comparison with Scottish landlords, for instance.[15] The physical endowment of land and the historical inheritance of weak property rights combined to facilitate the creation of new households, that is, other conditions permitting.

An agricultural innovation that was to have profound implications for the rural economy was the widespread adoption of the potato as a food crop, alongside oatmeal which was the other staple foodstuff. The potato helped improve the security of the food supply in most years. Ulster maintained a dual-crop economy, and harvest failures affecting oats and potatoes fortunately tended not to be synchronized.[16] The potato, as a crop in a rotation system, also facilitated the reclamation of wasteland, which was important both in relation to rough upland and boggy lowland areas of Ulster. As well as increasing the supply of land, it also economized on existing farmland. An acre of potatoes could produce far more sustenance than an acre of oats, the other staple food in Ulster. So the potato could be seen as a technological innovation that increased the productivity of land. Thus as the threshold size for a viable landholding declined, this facilitated the subdivision of existing farms and the formation of new households. But the influences of the apparently miracle food of the potato may have extended even further. The potato was a highly nutritious food, providing the carbohydrates, most of the proteins, minerals, and vitamins humans needed, with beneficial effects for physique and bodily strength. Ó Gráda has shown that the heights of Irish men exceeded those of English men in the early 1800s, confirming the impressions of visitors to Ireland of a sturdy people.[17] The Halls, who toured Ireland in 1840, reported from County Limerick that 'the women of all ranks throughout the county are remarkably beautiful in form and feature'.[18] More speculatively, the potato diet may have had a direct influence on fertility. It may, for instance, have improved fecundity (the capacity to produce children) and fecundability (the probability of conception within a given time period) among women, although of course we have no historical evidence on either. Equally speculatively, it may have shortened the breast-feeding period of lactating mothers. This intriguing possibility is suggested by some evidence from Finland, where a potato and cereal diet prevailed, as in Ulster.[19] A potato and milk mash may have allowed earlier weaning, thereby reducing the

---

[15] On the power of Scottish landlords see W. H. Crawford, 'Ulster as a Mirror of the Two Societies,' in T. M. Devine and D. Dickson (eds.), *Ireland and Scotland, 1600–1850: Parallels and Contrasts in Economic and Social Development* (Edinburgh, 1983), 60–9.

[16] P. M. Solar, 'Harvest Fluctuations in Pre-Famine Ireland: Evidence from Belfast and Waterford Newspapers', *Agricultural History Review*, 37 (1989), 157–65.

[17] C. Ó Gráda, *Black '47 and Beyond: The Great Irish Famine in History, Economy and Memory* (Princeton, 2000), 24-34.

[18] Mr and Mrs S. C. Hall, *Ireland: its Scenery and Character, etc* (new edition, London, Vol. 1, 1850), 339.

[19] B. Moring, 'Motherhood, Milk, and Money: Infant Mortality in Pre-Industrial Finland', *Social History of Medicine*, 2 (1998), 177–96. Potatoes may have reduced infant and child mortality, as well, as they seem to have been especially palatable to young children.

woman's sterile period, and thus shortening the interval between births. Morgan's detailed work on Coleraine for the period 1769–1847 suggests birth intervals of thirty months, while Eversley's study of Irish Quakers in the eighteenth century also indicates birth intervals of thirty months, but two to four months shorter than their English counterparts.[20] So perhaps the potato diet did influence fertility directly in one or more ways.

Then there is the changing economic environment, the fourth and most dynamic element in the explanatory sketch. The spread of the household-based linen industry from the early eighteenth century onwards, created part-time employment for tens of thousands of men, women, and children across Ulster. It supplemented earnings from small-scale farming, and could be fitted into the slack seasons in the farming year. Driving this expanding industry, cyclical fluctuations notwithstanding, was rising demand for Irish linens in Britain and the British colonies, which in turn was reflected in rising prices and incomes for producers in Ulster.[21] By the later eighteenth century, it became possible for linen weavers to make a living primarily from linen. The sector provided opportunities for sons to become independent producers at an earlier stage of the life cycle than would have been possible under purely farming conditions. The demographic implications are clear enough. Bearing in mind that Ireland formed part of the wider West European demographic system in which economic independence was a prerequisite for marriage, earnings from handloom weaving and spinning eased the barriers to marriage and the setting up of new households.[22] Six of the nine Ulster counties in 1841 had population densities of 400 or more persons per square mile of arable land, well above the Ireland average of 335.[23] To take the outstanding example, in County Armagh where cottage industry was heavily concentrated, the density of population in 1841 was 511 persons per square mile, the highest for any of the Irish counties. Or to take a micro example, in the townland of Lisummon in the same county, where many of the households combined linen weaving and small scale farming, population increased by one-third in the space of two decades (1820–41).[24] What we are seeing, therefore, is how the creation of new livelihoods, due to an expanding market for linen manufactures, was being translated in the demographic sphere into more marriages, more households, and more births.

Changing market conditions affected not only linen textiles but agriculture as well. Together, these two closely intertwined sectors dominated the pre-industrial economy of Ulster. Rising prices for grain, evident from the 1760s, made tillage farming more attractive. This was particularly true during the quarter-century of

---

[20] V. Morgan, 'The Church of Ireland Registers of St. Patrick's Coleraine, as a Source for the Study of a Local Pre-Famine Population', *Ulster Folklife*, 19 (1973), 63.

[21] W. H. Crawford, *Domestic Industry in Ireland* (Dublin, 1972).

[22] D. W. Miller, 'The Armagh Troubles, 1784–1795', in J. S. Donnelly and S. Clark (eds), *Irish Peasants: Violence and Political Unrest, 1780–1914* (Madison, 1983), 155–91.

[23] *Census of Ireland 1841: Report* (Online Historical Population Reports: <http://www.histpop.org>, accessed 10 November 2011).

[24] M. Goss, 'Rural Change in the Co. Armagh Townland of Lissummon', *Journal of the Poyntzpass and District Local History*, 1 (1987), 62–4.

the French Wars (1793–1815), when the price of oats doubled in some years under the pressure of wartime demand and poor harvests.[25] Grain production, as was also true of flax cultivation, was much more labour intensive than livestock farming, so the demand for labour intensified in the later eighteenth and the early nineteenth centuries. This was the classic period of population expansion. Moreover, a switch to tillage farming could accommodate greater numbers of small farms in a way that livestock farming could not, so the dilemma facing the pater familias in command of a landholding—accommodate more than one son by means of subdivision or resist fragmentation of the farm—became less acute.

To sum up, it would seem that a historically specific conjuncture of land endowments, social institutions (the structure of property rights in particular), crop innovation, and changes in market conditions underpinned the explosion in population numbers. Knowing the precise mechanics of the model, however, would require much more empirical information than we currently possess. There is a debate, for instance, as to whether reliance on the potato was as much in response to population pressure as a cause of population growth.[26] We have only limited knowledge for the average age at marriage of Irish women before the 1740s. We may dismiss wild stories of Irish women marrying soon after puberty. Less dramatically, however, Eversley found that Quaker women in Ireland married several years earlier than English Quaker women in the period 1650–1749. Reviewing other strands of the meagre evidence, Macafee concluded that Irish marriage ages were younger than in other European countries for the later eighteenth century: 'at least two to five years below the average marriage age for women in France, Germany, Belgium and Scandinavia'.[27] This might suggest a high-pressure demographic system in Ireland before the famine of the 1740s; that is, a relatively young age at marriage, high fertility but also high mortality (including high child mortality). As mortality crises lessened after the 1740s, this latent or intrinsic fertility—without any radical changes in marriage ages of the kind posited by Connell—could have released a head of pressure that saw population levels rise and rise within an environment that was increasingly accommodating of population increase. The latter included pre-existing resource endowments and a rapidly rising demand for labour in the linen textiles and agricultural sectors. If true, this would also mean that the adoption of the potato, the colonization of wasteland, and the subdivision of holdings were responses to population pressure. This interpretation would fit a Boserup-style model of agrarian change in which the pressure of mounting population, instead of leading to a Malthusian crisis, leads towards the more intensive use of land resources, thereby increasing the food supply.[28] If one did not wish to go quite this far, one could visualize a matrix of forces interacting through time, in which

---

[25] L. Kennedy and P. M. Solar, *Irish Agriculture: A Price History, from the Mid-Eighteenth Century to the Eve of the First World War* (Dublin, 2007), 58.

[26] L. M. Cullen, 'Irish History without the Potato', *Past & Present*, 40 (1968), 72–83; J. Mokyr, 'Irish History with the Potato', *Irish Economic and Social History*, 8 (1981), 8–29.

[27] Macafee, 'Pre-Famine Population of Ireland', 80.

[28] E. Boserup, *The Conditions of Agricultural Growth: The Economics of Agrarian Change under Population Pressure* (London, 1965).

Table 4.1. Age at marriage (AAM) for females and males in Ulster, 1841 and 1911

Counties & Belfast	AAM female 1841	AAM female 1911	AAM male 1841	AAM male 1911
Antrim	26.4	27.5	28.6	30.1
Armagh	26.2	27.9	28.9	31.1
Belfast	25.4	26.9	26.6	28.8
Cavan	25.6	30.3	29.1	35.3
Donegal	25.9	29.4	28.9	34.2
Down	26.4	27.6	28.8	30.4
Fermanagh	26.1	28.6	29.2	33.7
Londonderry	26.9	28.4	28.1	31.7
Monaghan	27.0	28.8	29.8	34.0
Tyrone	26.4	28.6	29.1	32.5

Source: Singulate mean age at marrriage (SMAM) calculated from the Census of Ireland, 1841 and 1911.

causal relationships were two-way as between population growth on the one hand and potato cultivation, land reclamation, and subdivision of holdings (with possible interrelationships between these three) on the other.[29] Either scenario might be seen as nesting within the larger system sketched above, that of land endowments, weak property rights, crop innovation, and market changes that favoured labour-intensive products in the agricultural and proto-industrial sectors of the Ulster economy.

A pre-industrial economic environment could not accommodate population growth rates of up to 2 per cent per annum indefinitely (implying a doubling of population every 35 years). The Boserup thesis is perhaps too optimistic for the rural economy in the long run. Emigration turned into a broadening stream after Waterloo, and then into a torrent in the late 1840s.[30] Demographic adjustments to deflation, economic depression, and the decline of rural industry took other forms as well. Although the evidence is not entirely conclusive, it seems that age at marriage rose in the pre-Famine decades, which would indicate a more sober assessment of the possibility of forming new and economically viable households at an early age. By 1841, the age at marriage for women had risen to 26 years in most of the Ulster counties, though in Monaghan, in outer Ulster, it was already as high as 27 years.[31] The youngest marriages were contracted in the industrializing town of Belfast but even here the average was 25–26 years of age. The oldest ages at marriage for men were to be found once again in Monaghan (29.8 years), and the

---

[29] For example, the earlier suggestion of a direct impact on fertility, due to the more widespread incorporation of the potato into people's diets, suggests an exogenous role for potatoes in *promoting* population growth, but this is consistent also with the adoption of the potato as a *response* to population pressure. The relationship may thus be conceived as a two-way one.
[30] D. H. Akenson, *Ireland, Sweden and the Great European Migration, 1815–1914* (Liverpool, 2011).
[31] Source as for Table 4.1.

youngest (26.6 years) in the town of Belfast. The Monaghan findings suggest a local society under economic stress, related no doubt to the small size of farms in the county, an infertile soil, and the withering away of rural textiles as the linen industry was reoriented towards Belfast and the Lagan Valley. As a general comment one can say that, by the eve of the Great Famine of the 1840s, age at marriage was in line with other West European societies, which seems not to have been the case a half century earlier.

Delayed marriage, in the context of a non-contraceptive society, meant fewer children and hence slower population growth, as had been advocated by Malthus in his famous policy prescription of 'preventive checks'.[32] This is precisely what we see in Ireland and in Ulster between the census dates of 1821 and 1841, and indeed thereafter. Population in Ulster increased by 19 per cent, an annual growth rate of less than 1 per cent (0.9 per cent), in this period, much the same as for Ireland generally, and signifying a marked deceleration in population growth. The cataclysm of the Great Famine ravaged Ulster, though not to the same extent as in the western counties of the island. While the numbers of people living in Ulster fell by 16 per cent during the Famine decade—not very different from the countrywide decline of 20 per cent—the big difference is that excess mortality in Ulster was less severe than in the west and the south of the island. O'Rourke and Ó Gráda estimate a famine-related death rate of 7.7 per cent for Ulster and the much higher rate of 12.2 per cent for Ireland as a whole.[33]

Whether the Famine initiated changes in demographic behaviour is doubtful, but it certainly accelerated changes already in train: a tendency towards later age at marriage for men and women, a rise in non-marriage (or permanent celibacy) among men and women, and streams of emigration that affected all localities and the poorest social classes. By 1911 women typically approached the matrimonial ceremony in their late twenties, while men were a few years older, in their early thirties. Belfast is an exception, by virtue of its urban, industrial character. The late age at marriage of men in the outer Ulster counties conjures up images of the poet, Patrick Kavanagh's depiction of his native parish of Inniskeen, County Monaghan, a few decades later.[34] Yet for all that has been said about the slow march to the altar in post-Famine Irish society, the changes apparent in much of Ulster society were not that dramatic when viewed over a period of seven decades.

Non-marriage or permanent celibacy was a different matter. Permanent celibacy is conventionally measured as the proportion of women or men in the age group 45 to 54 years who had never married. Most of these, we may presume, would never marry. What is perhaps surprising is that non-marriage was already fairly high among women in counties Antrim, Down, and Londonderry even before the

---

[32] T. R. Malthus, *An Essay on the Principle of Population* (introduction by D. Winch, Cambridge, 1992). The first version of the Essay was published in 1798.

[33] C. Ó Gráda and K. O'Rourke, 'Mass Migration as Disaster Relief: Lessons from the Great Famine', *European Review of Economic History*, 1 (1997), 14.

[34] P. Kavanagh, *The Green Fool* (London, 1971); Kavanagh, *Tarry Flynn* (London, 1972).

Famine, suggesting that social conditions were already putting a break on marriage prospects. Interestingly this was less true for men, where virtually universal marriage seems to have prevailed. The most striking example was that of County Cavan where 92 per cent of older men had married. If one takes into account a homosexual minority, the physically handicapped, and the mentally unwell, all of whom are present in any normal population, this is as close to universal marriage as one is likely to get.

But it is the surge in celibacy in the second half of the nineteenth century that really impresses. In County Monaghan, for instance, for every single older woman in 1841 there were almost three by the eve of the First World War. Standing next to these women, in the same age category (45–54 years) and in the same county in 1911, were even larger numbers of unmarried men. So much deeper forces than a gender imbalance were at play. Limited economic opportunities, rising expectations of material comfort, as well as a rigid class structure may well be relevant.[35] Even in Belfast there was an elevated non-marriage rate among females, though the gender imbalance in the workforce may form part of the explanation. Belfast men by contrast seem to have enjoyed a buyer's market. In the international marriage stakes, rural Ulster (and rural Ireland more generally) was something of a demographic freak. Thus in the 1930s in Northern Ireland (six of the Ulster counties), 25 per cent of women and 22 per cent of men aged 45 years or over were not married. The comparable figures for England and Wales were 16 per cent and 10 per cent respectively; for France they were 10 per cent and 8 per cent; for Spain 12 per cent and 8 per cent; and for Italy 12 per cent and 9 per cent.[36] The proportions unmarried in the Irish Free State were not very different from those found in Northern Ireland (though male celibacy was higher, probably reflecting the country's more rural character). Non-marriage bore both an Ulster and an Irish face (see Table 4.2).

ETHNIC, RELIGIOUS, AND POLITICAL DEMOGRAPHY

The general population history of Ulster and Ireland is nothing if not dramatic. But there are other dimensions to sex, survival, and reproductive behaviour among the peoples of Ulster that are equally compelling. Foremost among these are the interconnections between religion, politics, and demography. The demographic relationships between Ulster's Protestants and Catholics have been a contentious issue since the Plantation's origins in the early 1600s, and it is arguable that Ireland's and Ulster's partition in 1920 represented its political resolution. However, it would be a mistake simply to project the patterns of Ulster's religious demography backwards from the early twentieth to the early seventeenth century, or to regard the

---

[35] R. E. Kennedy, *The Irish: Emigration, Marriage and Fertility* (London, 1973); T. Guinnane, *The Vanishing Irish: Households, Migration and the Rural Economy in Ireland, 1850–1914* (Princeton, 1997).
[36] Kennedy, *The Irish*, 142.

Table 4.2. Permanent celibacy among females and males in Ulster, 1841 and 1911: the proportion single in the age group 45–54 years

Counties & Belfast	Female celibacy 1841 %	Female celibacy 1911 %	Male celibacy 1841 %	Male celibacy 1911 %
Antrim	17	30	11	26
Armagh	13	28	11	28
Belfast	11	21	8	13
Cavan	10	23	8	33
Donegal	13	29	10	33
Down	18	29	13	24
Fermanagh	14	29	10	34
Londonderry	17	30	10	24
Monaghan	11	30	9	35
Tyrone	14	31	11	36

Source: calculated from the Census of Ireland, 1841 and 1911.

configurations that prevailed in 1920 as somehow natural or inevitable. This is because: first, the demographic relationships among Ulster's largest ethno-religious communities were by no means the same; second, because the changes that occurred between the early 1600s and early 1900s, particularly at local and regional levels, were often very considerable; and third, even though hindsight usually identifies only 'two traditions', those of Protestant and Catholic, in Ulster it was often the differences between the demographic experience of the Anglican and Presbyterian communities that were most striking. Furthermore, the area of the 'historic' province of Ulster was by no means a homogenous entity, either before or after the seventeenth century, and is better understood as a mosaic of regions and subregions with different ethnic, economic, political, and hence demographic characteristics.

We also need to be mindful of the limitations of the source materials. Most of our pre-census information on ethnic or religious affiliation comes from a variety of sources, uneven in quality and geographical coverage. These include the Plantation surveys of the early 1600s, the Poll Tax records of *c.*1660, the hearth-tax schedules of 1732, 1740, and 1764–65, as well as occasional religious counts undertaken by the bishops and clergy of the Church of Ireland, most notably that of 1766. Moreover, the statutory censuses did not take note of religious affiliation until 1861, though there is the very useful religious enquiry of 1834 which was authorized by parliament.[37] There is a further set of complications, which in their way are revealing of the richness and complexity of social life in the northern counties. The religious and ethnic boundaries separating the various denominations were more permeable than is often assumed.[38] So despite the high levels of

---

[37] *First Report of the Commissioners of Public Instruction, Ireland*, British Parliamentary Papers, 33, 1835.
[38] L. Kennedy, K. A. Miller, and B. Gurrin, 'The Planter and the Gael: Explorations in Irish Ethnic History', in K. White (ed.), *The Imaginary of the Stranger* (Letterkenny, forthcoming 2012).

social and spatial segregation between Protestants and Catholics, as also between Anglicans and Presbyterians, that apparently prevailed in most of Ulster from early on, intermarriages and conversions certainly occurred. In the 1600s and 1700s, Ulster Catholics were under great legal and economic pressure to convert to Protestantism—especially, but not inevitably, to the Established Church. As early as the 1640s, for instance, a 'remarkable' number of the members of the Presbyterian congregation in Templepatrick, County Antrim, had 'Celtic names' (for example, McGuckin, O'Donally); and a century later a substantial minority of Protestant householders in Kilrea and Tamlaght O'Crilly parishes, County Londonderry, had native Irish surnames such as O'Deegan and O'Cain.[39] Conversely, and despite the disadvantages thereby incurred, the offspring of British settlers not infrequently converted to Catholicism, especially in rural, Protestant-minority districts. Thus, the Church of Ireland clergy who described their parishes to William Shaw Mason c.1813–18, often lamented the frequency of formal and 'unhallowed unions' between local Protestants and Catholics; and Macafee's surname analysis of the inhabitants of Killelagh parish, County Londonderry, indicates that by 1831, a minority of people of British or 'settler' descent were no longer Protestants.[40] Likewise, mobility between Anglican and Presbyterian (and other Protestant) congregations appears to have been common, and clergymen of both faiths often commented ruefully on their parishioners' susceptibility to denominational rivals.[41]

The Protestant presence, at least in any numbers, may be traced back to the Plantation of Ulster, although paradoxically most early British incomers were drawn to the privately-settled counties of Antrim and Down which lay westwards of and adjacent to the Scottish Lowlands. By 1622 two further major areas of British settlement were apparent: a principally English settlement in mid-Ulster, extending from Belfast through the Lagan Valley corridor into the areas south and west of Lough Neagh, particularly in north Armagh, east Tyrone, and the Clogher Valley; and a predominantly Scottish concentration in north-west Ulster's Foyle Valley, in and adjacent to the towns of Londonderry and Strabane.[42] Fresh waves of migrants carried the British and largely Protestant numbers to 40–50,000 by 1630.[43] At a rough guess, these might have accounted

---

[39] W. T. Latimer, 'The Old Session-Book of Templepatrick Presbyterian Church, Co. Antrim: Part II', *Journal of the Royal Society of Antiquaries of Ireland*, 5th ser., 11 (1901), 165; J. W. Kernohan, *The Parishes of Kilrea and Tamlaght O'Crilly* (Coleraine, 1912), 28; W. S. Mason, *A Statistical Account, or Parochial Survey of Ireland*, Vol. 3 (Dublin, 1819), 27–8 (Ardclinis and Laid, Co. Antrim); Rev. S. Butler, 'Statistical Account of the Parish of Tamlaghtard… Co. Derry [1823–4]' (PRONI, T.3239/1); W. B. Steele, *The Parish of Devenish* (Enniskillen, 1937), 156–7; W. Macafee, 'The Colonization of the Maghera Region of South Derry during the Seventeenth and Eighteenth Centuries', *Ulster Folklife*, 23 (1977), 90–1.

[40] Macafee, 'Colonization of the Maghera Region', 90–1. We estimate this proportion as about one-fifth.

[41] For example, S. Burdy, *The Life of Philip Skelton* (Oxford, 1914 repr. [1792]), 154–6; W. T. Latimer, *A History of the Irish Presbyterians* (Belfast, 1902 edn), 401–4, 490–1, 509; J. H. Gebbie, *Ardstraw (Newtownstewart): Historical Survey of a Parish, 1600–1900* (Omagh, 1968), 99–100; and N. Yates, *The Religious Condition of Ireland, 1700–1850* (Oxford, 2006), 293, 295–6.

[42] P. S. Robinson, *The Plantation of Ulster: British Settlement in an Irish Landscape, 1660–1760* (Dublin, 1984), *passim*.

[43] W. A. Macafee, 'The Movement of British Settlers into Ulster during the Seventeenth Century', *Familia: Ulster Genealogical Review*, 2/8 (1992), 95.

for 15 per cent of the overall population. The massacres of Protestants in 1641 and further wartime disruptions set back the colonial settlement schemes, but following the Cromwellian conquest of Ireland there were major influxes of Scottish and, to a lesser extent, English settlers after mid-century. By 1660, on the evidence of the Poll Tax returns, people of British origin—Protestant in the main—constituted a large minority, of perhaps 35 per cent of the population.[44] Further large-scale movements following the end of the Williamite wars in 1691, brought thousands of Scots into Ulster. This third wave of newcomers, including many famine refugees, tilted the ethnic and religious balance in favour of people of British origin or recent ancestry, and also confirmed the numerical dominance of Presbyterians within the Protestants of Ulster.

Thus in the century after 1610, and despite some setbacks, the British and Protestant penetration of Ulster had advanced to the point where the newcomers formed a majority in the province as a whole (see the estimates in Table 4.3). The early eighteenth century was perhaps the highpoint of Protestant expansion; that is, before Presbyterian emigration assumed serious proportions. The progress of Protestantism and its adherents was uneven, however. The strongholds were in Antrim and Down, and north Armagh, but in the more thinly populated counties of outer Ulster, Catholics remained in a majority. The next long phase in changing religious balances extended from the opening decades of the eighteenth century to the eve of the Great Famine. The trend towards Protestant demographic dominance was first arrested (1732–66) and then reversed (1766–1831), the period as a whole being characterized by a recovery in Catholic demographic power.[45] Even in the years between 1732 and 1766, Catholic population growth rates exceeded those of Protestants in many parts of Ulster,[46] though it is not clear, in view of the fragility of the estimates, if this Catholic resurgence meant more rapid growth rates relative to Protestants at the level of the province as a whole. In the next period, that of 1766–1831, there is little doubt. The Catholic population expanded more rapidly than the Protestant population of the province, probably right up to the eve of the Famine, and as a consequence the Protestant share of population drifted downwards to less than 50 per cent of the total.

The intriguing aspect of these faltering Protestant growth rates, particularly between 1766 and 1831, is that most of the difference was accounted for by the slow growth of Presbyterian numbers. This in turn reflected the disproportionate numbers of Presbyterians emigrating from the province. To take a fairly extreme

---

[44] However, the data for counties Tyrone and Cavan are missing, so a proportion of one-third or so may be nearer the mark.

[45] These changes are discussed more fully, at a county and sometimes parish level, in B. Gurrin, K. A. Miller, and L. Kennedy, *Catholics and Protestants in Eighteenth-Century Ireland: The Religious Censuses of the 1760s* (Dublin, forthcoming 2013).

[46] In County Fermanagh, for instance, the Catholic growth rate at 0.87 per cent per annum (for the period 1732–66) was more than twice that of Protestants whose annual growth rate was only 0.35 per cent, according to the authors' calculations. This was for the period 1732–66 and, it may be noted, the Catholic growth rate in Fermanagh was also higher in the next period (1766–1831). The weakening of the Protestant position could also be due to conversions to Catholicism, probably through intermarriage, in Catholic-dominated areas. A similar but reverse process is likely to have operated in Protestant-dominated areas in the east of the province.

Table 4.3. The Protestant share of the Ulster population at various intervals between 1630 and 1911

1630	1660	1732	1766	1831	1861	1881	1911
15–17%	30–40%	50–60%	50–55%	47%	50%	52%	56%

Sources: as for Table 4.1.

example, that of the parish of Moira in northwest County Down: the Presbyterian share of the local Protestant population halved from 50 per cent to 24 per cent between 1766 and 1831, whereas the Anglican proportions soared at the expense of both Moira's Presbyterian and Catholic communities. In the more westerly counties of Tyrone and Donegal, there was an absolute as well as a relative decline in Presbyterian numbers in some localities. Socio-economic differences between Presbyterians and Anglicans (as more generally between Catholics and Protestants) may help explain these disparities. Conversions to the Established Church also form part of the story, although how quantitatively important this was must await further research. Likewise, although it is difficult to separate social and political motives, overt political pressures in the late 1790s, and a broadly politicized alienation from the post-Union 'establishment', appear to have informed much late eighteenth- and early nineteenth-century Presbyterian emigration to an idealized American republic.[47]

The Great Famine reversed the trend towards an increasingly larger Catholic share of population. While there is no doubt that some lower-class Protestants suffered terribly during the Famine, particularly in counties like Cavan and Monaghan where the failure of rural industry preceded the failure of the potato crop, it is nonetheless the case that Ulster Catholics bore the heavier burden, although on the basis of poverty and location rather than theology.[48] The Famine also served to generalize emigration to the more remote Catholic, and sometimes Gaelic-speaking communities of Ulster, a reminder, if one is needed, that the 'historic' province of Ulster was not a single entity. In the Census of Ireland for 1861 we find, against a backdrop of falling population, that the religious see-saw had by then tilted back towards equality (Table 4.3).

The demographic balance tipped more decisively in favour of Protestants in the late Victorian and Edwardian periods. The Catholic share of population underwent a substantial fall from 50 per cent in 1881 to 44 per cent in 1911. The share of the Church of Ireland actually rose from 20 per cent to 23 per cent over the same period, while Presbyterians maintained their share at 26–27 per cent. Anglicans and Presbyterians, who in earlier generations had often viewed each other with hostility, cooperated more closely from the 1880s within a pan-unionist

---

[47] K. A. Miller, 'Forging "the Protestant Way of Life": Class Conflict and the Origins of Unionist Hegemony', in Miller, *Ireland and Irish America: Culture, Class and Transatlantic Migration* (Dublin, 2008), 190–4.
[48] C. Kinealy and T. Parkhill (eds), *The Famine in Ulster* (Belfast, 1996).

alliance in favour of the Union and in opposition to the nationalist, mainly Catholic demand for Home Rule. The decisive factor driving these demographic changes was the spectacular growth of Belfast and the manner in which it provided livelihoods for short-distance migrants from the predominantly Protestant counties of Antrim and Down.

But the striking fact is that outside of the industrialized Lagan Valley, rural depopulation was on much the same scale as in other regions of Ireland. The socioeconomic causes of this decline were much the same in Ulster as in rural Ireland more generally: the increasing commercialization of farming and a shift towards less labour-intensive livestock farming; the associated consolidation of farms; the decline in handicraft industry as modern textile and engineering firms mushroomed in the Belfast region; the role of cheaper shipping and rail networks in facilitating the import of mass-produced goods from Britain and America, in the process making local producers redundant; the shift among farmers from partible to impartible inheritance and the monetization of marriage through the dowry system. These were the push factors making for rural exodus but clearly also rising expectations regarding acceptable living standards were at least, if not more, important.

Viewed in religious demographic terms, and again excluding from consideration 'Ireland's only industrial city', the population decline experienced by Ulster Catholics was only a little greater than that affecting Ulster Protestants. Indeed in counties Cavan and Monaghan, the contraction in Protestant numbers was greater than that for Catholics.[49] What this tells us is that industrialization rather than the Great Famine was the principal determinant of the shifting religious (and political) demographic balance. It also suggests, as do the varying trends in population numbers as between the three major religious groupings in different time periods, that there was no inevitable pathway from Plantation to Partition.

Industrialization and urbanization were also central to a further set of changes, as yet only present in embryonic form on the eve of the First World War, but of considerable import for society and politics in twentieth-century Northern Ireland. It is that Belfast was a participant, albeit a slow and somewhat reluctant one, in the West European fertility transition of the later nineteenth century. By 1911 small numbers of Protestants, typically those of higher socio-economic status, were deliberately restricting fertility within marriage.[50] Birth control practices gradually diffused to the larger Protestant population such that by 1971, Catholic marital fertility was two-thirds higher.[51] As religious and political affiliations in Ulster have been highly correlated since the Home Rule controversies of the 1880s, and remain so to this day, this divergence in fertility behaviour was replete with political as well

---

[49] Calculated from W. E. Vaughan and A. J. Fitzpatrick, *Irish Population Statistics, 1821–1911* (Dublin, 1978).

[50] L. Kennedy, L. Pozzi, and M. Manfredini, 'Marriage, Fertility, Social Class and Religion in an Irish Industrial City in 1911', *Popolazione e Storia*, 2 (2010), 83–110.

[51] C. Ó Gráda and B. Walsh, 'Fertility and Population in Ireland, North and South', *Population Studies*, 49 (1995), 266.

as social significance. The politics of demography mattered: in a deeply divided society an appreciation of the 'force of numbers' was never far from the communal consciousness.

FURTHER READING

D. H. Akenson, *Ireland, Sweden and the Great European Migration, 1815–1914* (Liverpool, 2011).
K. H. Connell, *The Population of Ireland, 1750–1845* (Oxford, 1950).
D. Dickson, C. Ó Gráda, and S. Daultrey, 'Hearth Tax, Household Size and Irish Population Change, 1672–1821', *Proceedings of the Royal Irish Academy*, 82C (1982).
B. Gurrin, K. A. Miller, and L. Kennedy, *Catholics and Protestants in Eighteenth-Century Ireland: The Religious Censuses of the 1760s* (Dublin, forthcoming, 2013).
W. Macafee, 'The Pre-Famine Population of Ireland: A Reconsideration', in B. Collins, P. Ollerenshaw, and T. Parkhill (eds), *Industry, Trade and People in Ireland, 1650–1950* (Belfast, 2005), 69–86.
J. Mokyr and C. Ó Gráda, 'New Developments in Irish Population History, 1700–1850', *Economic History Review*, 37 (1984), 473–88.

5

Religion and Society, 1600–1914

S. J. Connolly[1]

CONFESSIONALIZATION AND CIVIL WAR

Ulster at the beginning of the seventeenth century was a region just beginning to be touched by the great movements for religious change that over the previous eight decades had convulsed the greater part of Europe. Neither the Protestantism re-adopted by the English state under Elizabeth I, nor the reformed Catholicism of the Counter Reformation, had made much headway in the kingdom's most politically recalcitrant and culturally self-sufficient province. Conventional depictions of a late medieval church sunk in lethargy and corruption are misleading. Recent research suggests that Ulster dioceses were served by a well-distributed body of parish clergy, mostly trained by apprenticeship rather than at a university, but to all appearances reasonably conscientious in the discharge of their duties.[2] What they professed, however, was essentially a 'civic religion'.[3] Ecclesiastical office at all levels was largely in the hands of specific ecclesiastical families, often passing from father to son. Religious practice gave prominence to the cults of local saints. Marriage was primarily a contract between families, and penance an extension of the compensatory, as opposed to retributive, righting of wrongs that formed the basis of the Gaelic legal system.

The same tradition of a pragmatic reconciliation of the secular and the sacred shaped initial responses to the Reformation. Several Ulster bishops declared their acceptance of Henry VIII's assertion in 1536 of royal supremacy over the church, although those still alive were later equally willing to serve under the restored Catholic regime of Mary I (1553–58). As late as 1611 Brutus Babington, Protestant Bishop of Derry, reported that he had persuaded more than half of the clergy whom he found occupying churches in his new diocese to adopt the liturgy of the Church of England, aided by the recently published Irish language version of the

---

[1] I am grateful to Dr Andrew Holmes for his comments on an earlier version of this chapter.
[2] H. A. Jefferies, 'The Diocese of Dromore on the Eve of the Tudor Reformation', in L. Proudfoot (ed.), *Down: History and Society* (Dublin, 1997), 123–40.
[3] The phrase is from P. J. Corish, *The Catholic Community in Ireland in the Seventeenth and Eighteenth Centuries* (Dublin, 1981), 5. For a general account see S. J. Connolly, *Contested Island: Ireland 1460–1630* (Oxford, 2007), 51–8.

Book of Common Prayer.[4] Already by this time, however, the prospects for a gradually developing native Reformation were rapidly disappearing. One reason was the improving circumstances of the Church of Ireland, permitting the progressive replacement of a locally recruited reading clergy, trusted only to deliver the set words of the prescribed service each Sunday, with graduate ministers competent to expound a complex, bible-based theology but recruited mainly in England and Scotland.[5] Meanwhile, the Catholic Church in Ulster, seriously disrupted by the violence of the years 1595–1603, was also beginning to reorganize. Commencing with the provincial synod held at Drogheda in 1614, a new generation of ecclesiastics began the task of constructing a clear system of diocesan and parochial administration. By the early 1630s, most dioceses had a resident bishop. The restoration of ecclesiastical discipline stemmed the drift of native clergy into the service of what was in any case an increasingly inhospitable Church of Ireland. In addition reformers devoted much energy to discouraging Catholics from turning to the Protestant clergy for baptisms or marriages, and to prohibiting marriage to non-Catholics. By the 1630s what was to be the enduring line of division between Protestant settler and Catholic native had been clearly drawn.[6]

At the same time that it sought to construct unambiguous confessional boundaries, the new leadership of the Ulster Catholic church, trained on the Continent, embarked on the first stages of what was to be a radical restructuring of popular religion. Their reform programme followed the principles laid down at the Council of Trent, convened in 1545 to devise a European-wide strategy for rolling back the Protestant heresy. Purpose-built mass houses began to appear from the mid-1620s, replacing the parish churches appropriated or demolished by the Protestant establishment. Ecclesiastical regulations emphasized the importance of religious instruction through the catechism, and insisted on the central role in religious life of the clergy and the parish church. Pilgrimages were to be supervised and regulated, and relics and other sacred objects kept solely in clerical hands. Marriage and baptism were to be celebrated as sacraments rather than as public demonstrations of the creation or confirmation of social bonds, and funerals were to be occasions for devotion rather than festivity. However, the new regime, with its emphasis on obedience to episcopal authority, regular performance of pastoral duties, and closer supervision of the conduct of the clergy, was not always to the taste of the locally trained priests who served in the majority of Ulster parishes. The novel insistence on clerical celibacy, in particular, remained a source of recurrent conflict. Against this background, progress in disseminating the beliefs and routines of Counter-Reformation Catholicism within Ulster was to be gradual and uneven.

In settling as it did into the role of a colonial church, the Church of Ireland had to cater for two rather different religious traditions. Scots, making up a majority of the migrants now flooding into Ulster, came from a religious culture that had been

---

[4] Babington to Salisbury, 20 January 1611, in *CSPI 1611–1614*, 4.
[5] A. Ford, *The Protestant Reformation in Ireland 1590–1641* (Dublin, 1997), Ch. 7.
[6] B. MacCuarta, *Catholic Revival in the North of Ireland 1603–1641* (Dublin, 2007), 42–51. See also O. Rafferty, *Catholicism in Ulster 1603–1983* (Dublin, 1994), Ch. 1.

more thoroughly purged than English Protestantism of lingering ceremonial elements, and in which the claims of episcopacy continued to be contested. In Ulster they encountered bishops who, whether guided by their own private theological preferences or by the shortage of other qualified clergy, were ready to turn a blind eye to ministers who omitted uncongenial parts of the prescribed liturgy, or introduced a system of parochial discipline involving lay elders on the model of the Scottish kirk session. Some were apparently willing even to fudge the issue of episcopal ordination. The most dramatic manifestation of the distinctive religious culture that thus took shape in areas of Scottish settlement was a series of giant revivalist meetings that commenced in 1625 at Carrickfergus in County Antrim and spread over the next few years to neighbouring counties. Crowds of 1000 or more assembled for two or three days of sermons, before joining in communion, taken not kneeling or even standing, but seated together at long tables.[7]

In the mid-1630s, this quiet toleration of diversity within Ulster Protestantism came decisively to an end. Thomas Wentworth, appointed Lord Deputy in 1633, immediately extended to Ireland the campaign initiated by Archbishop Laud of Canterbury to restore the established church to its original position as a middle way between the corruptions of popery and the excesses of Calvin's Geneva. His chief instrument was his own chaplain John Bramhall, promoted in 1634 to the bishopric of Derry. One part of the reform programme was to restore the endowments of the church, by recovering assets improperly transferred to lay hands and forcing new terms on holders of lucrative farms of tithes or other revenues. By 1640 Bramhall claimed to have increased ecclesiastical incomes in the province of Armagh by £14,500. But there was also a new drive for conformity. Bishops began to require congregations to adopt the full liturgy prescribed in the Book of Common Prayer, with clergy unwilling to comply being removed from their parishes, and some of their lay supporters called before a newly established disciplinary tribunal, the Court of High Commission.[8] When open revolt against Laud's religious policy commenced in Scotland from 1637 Wentworth increased the pressure on potential sympathizers in Ulster, quartering 1500 soldiers in the north-eastern counties and requiring adult males to take an oath declaring their sole obedience to the king.

The political crisis in England, followed by the rising of the Ulster Irish in October 1641, put a dramatic end to Wentworth's drive for Protestant uniformity. In June 1642, chaplains and elders from the army sent from Scotland to protect the settlers organized themselves into a presbytery. Their example encouraged local Scots to create their own congregations and to send to Scotland for ministers. By the end of the 1650s there were some eighty congregations grouped into five districts or 'meetings'. When the monarchy was restored in 1660 there was some discussion of a new established church that would accommodate different shades of Protestant opinion. In the event what were restored were the former episcopal structures, governed by Bram-

---

[7] M. J. Westerkamp, *Triumph of the Laity: Scots-Irish Piety and the Great Awakening 1625–1760* (New York, 1988), Ch. 1.
[8] J. McCafferty, *The Reconstruction of the Church of Ireland: Bishop Bramhall and the Laudian Reforms 1633–1641* (Cambridge, 2007).

hall, returning in vindictive triumph from a long exile, and by other survivors of the old Laudian regime. Sixty-one out of seventy ministers serving in Ulster parishes refused to accept episcopal ordination and were accordingly expelled from their parishes. Over the next three decades what now became Protestant dissenters faced sporadic harassment, on account both of their religious nonconformity and of their links to rebellious co-religionists in Scotland. By this time, however, the Presbyterian organizational system developed during the 1650s was too well established to be eradicated. Instead the restoration of episcopacy served only to create a rival ecclesiastical system, supported by a clear majority of the Protestant population of Ulster.

For the Catholic Church in Ulster the war years and their aftermath were particularly traumatic. Where elsewhere in Ireland the Confederate Catholics had supported a triumphantly restored Counter-Reformation church, the north and north-east had remained under Protestant control. Following the Cromwellian conquest priests were hunted with a relentless vigour without parallel either earlier or later; it is this period, rather than the so-called 'penal era' of the following century, that was recalled in later folkloric traditions of gatherings at a 'mass rock' concealed among mountains or bogs. In these adverse conditions popular Catholicism displayed a resilience that testified both to the effectiveness of Counter-Reformation pastoral methods and to the intensity of the process of confessionalization that had taken place since the days of Brutus Babington. Oliver Plunkett, sent to Armagh as archbishop in 1669 after many years in Rome, reported favourably on the general level of piety: 'the people are so devout that they will go three miles to hear mass, very often in the rain, and they will go twelve miles to receive confirmation'. The conduct of the clergy, on the other hand, remained a cause of serious concern. In Derry, the vicar apostolic in charge of the diocese had lived in public concubinage for thirty years. In Clogher the vicar general was a notorious drunkard in whose household two servant girls had become pregnant. In Raphoe, the clergy as a whole 'are very weak as regards doctrine and conduct of life; there is not a single man in it fit to be vicar general'.[9] As in the early seventeenth century the efforts by Plunkett and others to impose stricter standards of behaviour and performance met with widespread resistance. There was also conflict between secular and regular clergy, arising partly out of competition for the limited support that could be obtained from an impoverished laity, and partly from attempts to subject members of religious orders to episcopal authority. The tensions that resulted were dramatically revealed when several native Irish Franciscans became witnesses against Plunkett at the trial that led to his execution for treason in 1681.

ESTABLISHMENT AND DISSENT

The war of 1689–91 completed the redefinition of sectarian alignments that had taken place during the seventeenth century. Presbyterians in parts of Ulster had initially responded to James II's promise of religious toleration by withholding

---

[9] J. Hanly (ed.), *The Letters of Saint Oliver Plunkett 1625–81* (Dublin, 1979), 69, 74, 78, 226, 305–6.

tithes, seizing parish churches, and in some cases offering violence to ministers or their servants. Once it became clear that what was in prospect was a struggle to establish either Protestant or Catholic supremacy, this opportunistic support collapsed. Instead dissenters and Anglicans came together in support of William of Orange. The Protestant alliance that resulted, however, did not survive the military conflict. Even before the war had ended, recriminations had begun over the relative contribution of dissenter and churchman to the defence of Derry. During the 1690s bishops in Ulster began a renewed campaign of harassment, prosecuting dissenting schoolmasters for teaching without a licence and refusing to recognize marriages performed by Presbyterian clergymen. Hostility to dissenters was sharpened by the renewed surge of Scottish immigration in the late 1690s and early 1700s. Presbyterians now amounted to half or more of the Protestant population of Ireland, and substantially outnumbered Anglicans within Ulster. The example of Scotland, where Presbyterians had taken advantage of the political crisis of 1688–89 to displace episcopacy as the established church, further heightened the anxiety of churchmen. One response was the addition to the 1704 act to prevent the growth of popery of a clause requiring all holders of offices of trust or profit under the crown to qualify by taking communion in the Church of Ireland, the so-called sacramental test. After 1714 the coming to power in both kingdoms of a Whig administration largely put an end to harassment of Presbyterians by the church courts. But attempts by the London government to have parliament repeal the sacramental test proved unsuccessful, as even Whig members of the Church of Ireland made clear that they had no intention of sharing power with so formidable a body of religious rivals.

Ulster Presbyterians were alarming, not just because of their numbers, but because of their economic strength and organizational cohesion. By this time the great majority of the Scottish proprietors granted estates during the plantation had defected to the established church. However, the greater part of Ulster's commercial wealth was in Presbyterian hands. The main significance of the sacramental test was thus that it excluded Presbyterians from what would otherwise have been their dominant position in urban corporations. Observers also commented with alarm on the tight internal discipline maintained by ministers and elders through the kirk session. Already by the early eighteenth century, however, rising commercial prosperity, along with the intellectual influences of the early Enlightenment, had begun to erode this internal cohesion. In 1725, a group of ministers no longer willing to subscribe without reservation to the statement of orthodox Calvinist theology contained in the Westminster Confession of Faith withdrew into a separate Presbytery of Antrim. Over the next few decades the practice of subscription lapsed even within the main Presbyterian body, extending the division between what came to be known as Old Light and New Light parties. This fragmentation of what had been perceived as a monolithic rival, along with the commencement from 1717 of an outward flow of mainly Presbyterian migrants to the American colonies, did much to calm the fears of supporters of the established church and so reduce what had for a time been acute sectarian tensions within Ulster Protestantism.

Despite the fears of many of its supporters, then, the Church of Ireland entered the eighteenth century with its privileged position largely intact. Its Ulster province had additional advantages. A more numerous laity than were to be found elsewhere provided an antidote to demoralization, while the church continued to benefit from the generous re-endowment in lands that had formed part of the plantation. A return in 1791 found that of 355 glebe houses for the use of resident clergymen, 173 were in Ulster dioceses.[10] Privilege also brought disadvantages: the integration of senior appointments into a system of nakedly political patronage, the liberation of holders of legally enforceable tithes from the need to win the approval of a congregation, and the security of tenure enjoyed by all but the most delinquent incumbents. But appointment on political grounds did not always produce mere time-serving careerists. William King, appointed bishop of Derry in recognition of his services in defending the legitimacy of the Revolution of 1688, and subsequently promoted to Dublin, was a tireless campaigner for higher pastoral standards. Hugh Boulter, appointed to Armagh in 1724 specifically to strengthen the English interest in the aftermath of the heated constitutional dispute over Wood's halfpence, was likewise a committed churchman who used his influence with government to sponsor reform measures such as an act of 1728 intended to facilitate clerical residence and improve the maintenance of curates. At his death he left most of his personal fortune to be used for the augmentation of poor benefices and the purchase of glebe lands for the support of the clergy. In the same way William Nicolson of Derry (1718–27) and Francis Hutchinson of Down and Connor (1720–39) were installed in their respective dioceses as sound Whigs, but were also resident and hard working ecclesiastical administrators.[11] Where the lower clergy are concerned, meanwhile, even the censorious King, who in 1700 inspected the whole province of Armagh, reported that 'the clergy in the north were never more numerous, more industrious, and more learned than at this time... Except in one diocese I hardly found any liable to exception.' There were cases of non-residence, but a return from Clogher in the same year found that only three of twenty-two incumbents lived outside the diocese.[12]

Turning to popular Protestantism, developments during the eighteenth century testify to a continued lively interest in religious matters, and in particular to the appeal to large numbers of a vital and demanding religious message. Among Presbyterians discontent with the spread of New Light opinions in the Synod of Ulster led many to turn to two more strictly orthodox denominations imported from Scotland, the Seceders, active in Ulster from 1746, and the Reformed Presbyterians or Covenanters, present from 1757. By 1792, there were six Reformed

---

[10] *An Account of the Number of Parishes in Ireland* (B.P.P., 1806, 14), 277.
[11] F. G. James, *North Country Bishop: A Biography of William Nicolson* (New Haven, 1954); A. Sneddon, *Witchcraft and Whigs: The Life of Bishop Francis Hutchinson, 1660–1739* (Manchester, 2009).
[12] King to Sir Robert Southwell, 19 November 1700 TCD MS750/2/2, 17 ; Visitation of Clogher, 1700 (Representative Church Body Library, Dublin 61/6/3).

Presbyterian congregations, and no less than forty-six congregations of Seceders.[13] From 1746, John Cennick, a missionary for the Moravians, a revivalist sect of Central European origins, built up a network of over 200 societies, mainly in County Antrim, although most did not long survive his death in 1755. Another active evangelist, John Wesley, enjoyed more lasting success. By 1801 there were some 24,000 members enrolled in Methodist societies in Ireland, of whom about half were found in two areas of Ulster, a south-west region centred on Lough Erne, and the 'linen triangle' roughly bounded by Dungannon, Newry, and Lisburn. This concentration in areas of substantial English settlement, rather than in the Presbyterian dominated north-east, was understandable, given that Methodism had begun as an offshoot of the established church. But it is also significant, given the common perception of a spiritually moribund established church, that Wesley's missionary efforts received a cordial welcome from a good number of Ulster bishops and Anglican clergy.[14]

For Ulster Catholics, the defeat of James II brought a new wave of repression. The popery acts of 1704 and 1708, aimed at destroying the remnants of Catholic landed power, were of little relevance, since the relatively small number of Ulster proprietors to survive the plantation had been dispossessed in the 1650s. The Catholic clergy, however, faced a new onslaught, following acts of parliament requiring the expulsion of bishops and regular clergy, prohibiting Catholic schools, and allowing the remaining clergy to operate only if registered with the authorities. As in earlier decades local connections could undermine national policy objectives. In Belfast in 1708, for example, several Protestants came forward to give bail for an imprisoned priest, citing his services in protecting their lives and property during the brief period of Catholic ascendancy under James II.[15] But the disruption was, over several decades, real. As late as 1731 the bishop of Derry, replying to a nationwide enquiry initiated by the Irish parliament, reported that there were no Catholic schools in his diocese. '... sometimes a straggling schoolmaster sets up in some of the mountainous parts of some parishes, but upon being threatened, as they constantly are, with a warrant, or a presentment by the churchwardens, they generally think proper to withdraw'. In Clogher, the bishop, although known to the Protestant authorities, took the precaution of living under an assumed name, and 'disappears since these enquiries'.[16] Precise comparison is difficult, but it seems likely that at least sporadic enforcement of the laws continued longer in Ulster than in areas where Protestant manpower was more limited and the risks attached to provoking local Catholic resentment greater.

---

[13] I. McBride, *Scripture Politics: Ulster Presbyterians and Irish Radicalism in the Late Eighteenth Century* (Oxford, 1998), 41–83; A. R. Holmes, *The Shaping of Ulster Presbyterian Belief and Practice 1770–1840* (Oxford, 2006).

[14] D. Hempton and M. Hill, *Evangelical Protestantism in Ulster Society 1740–1890* (London, 1992), Ch. 1.

[15] W. P. Burke, *The Irish Priests in the Penal Times (1660–1760)* (Waterford, 1914), 281.

[16] 'Report on the State of Popery, 1731', *Archivium Hibernicum*, I (1912), 16–17. For a brief overview see Rafferty, *Catholicism in Ulster*, Ch. 2.

These difficult conditions had implications for the maintenance of internal discipline. Between 1707 and 1746 Rome gradually reconstructed the Irish episcopal hierarchy, in some cases appointing to bishoprics that had been vacant for thirty years or more. However the conditions under which the church had to operate, tolerated at best by a suspicious state, allowed little scope for effective supervision on the part either of the Vatican authorities or of local bishops. Against this background the survival of a functioning ecclesiastical system came to depend heavily on a pattern of dynastic succession that harnessed the authority of prominent local families. Between 1707 and 1747, three successive MacMahons served as bishops of Clogher, in each case being promoted from there to the archdiocese of Armagh. Thereafter two successive O'Reillies held the diocese until 1801. When Rome, in 1758, passed over local candidates and appointed Anthony Blake, from an Old English Connacht family, to Armagh, the results were disastrous. Blake was removed in 1782, after several years of bitter factional dispute, although how far his downfall was due to his outsider status, and how far to his own neglect of the diocese—opponents claimed that he resided in Connacht and came to Ulster only to collect exorbitant fees from his clergy—remains unclear.[17] Family ties were also important at parish level, with nephew frequently succeeding uncle. Later, in the changing circumstances of the early nineteenth century, bishops seeking to reassert their right to appoint and move parish clergy as they thought fit ran into serious difficulties, as priests defended what they had come to regard as their hereditary entitlement to occupy particular parishes, often with the support of powerful factions among the laity.[18]

A further constraint on the pastoral effectiveness of the Catholic clergy, lasting longer than penal legislation, was the limited financial support available from a generally poor population. The supply of priests, dependent on multiple small payments, was in fact comparatively healthy. Ulster dioceses in 1834–35 had an average of 2845 Catholics for every clergyman, compared to 2987 in the rest of Ireland. Since 1800, moreover, the number of parish priests and curates had risen by more than half, as compared to only a third in other dioceses, presumably reflecting the extent to which Catholics as well as Protestants benefitted from the superior prosperity of early nineteenth-century Ulster. Church building, on the other hand, required larger capital sums, and here Catholic Ulster emerges as clearly disadvantaged. In the 1830s, mass was still being celebrated in the open air in parts of counties Tyrone and Londonderry. In such circumstances there was little scope for elaborate religious ceremonial. As late as 1851 Paul Cullen, newly arrived from Rome as archbishop of Armagh, complained that 'the exterior ceremonies of religion are very neglected, and matters proceed as in the time of the persecutions'.[19] A survey of church attendance carried out during 1834 suggested that on a typical

---

[17] P. Whelan, 'Anthony Blake, Archbishop of Armagh 1758–1787', *Seanchas Ardmhacha*, 5 (1970), 289–323.

[18] Factional conflict in Clogher is documented in the diocesan archives, PRONI Dio(RC) 1. See in particular the account of the parish of Aughnamullen East in Dio(RC) 1/10B/3. See also S. Ó Dufaigh, 'James Murphy, Bishop of Clogher, 1801–24', *Seanchas Ardmhacha*, 6 (1968), 419–92.

[19] P. MacSuibhne (ed.), *Paul Cullen and his Contemporaries* (3 Vols, Naas, 1961–77), 75, 81.

Sunday not more than around 40 per cent of the Catholic population attended mass. These results may well have reflected a recent deterioration in levels of religious practice, as population outstripped the church accommodation available. But the scale of non-attendance confirms suspicion that, despite the undoubted progress made during the seventeenth century, the goals laid down more than two centuries earlier at Trent had never been fully realized.[20]

REVIVAL AND REFORM

By the time the Commissioners conducted their survey, however, major changes were under way. Diocesan records show a new generation of bishops, such as James Murphy in Clogher (1801–24) and Michael Blake in Dromore (1833–60), reasserting their authority and imposing a new disciplinary regime on the lower clergy.[21] They also renewed the campaign against unorthodox popular beliefs and practices. By the mid-1830s observers for the Ordnance Survey could report the widespread abandonment, under pressure from the Catholic clergy, of gatherings at holy wells, wake games, and other traditional practices. In their place bishops and priests took the first steps towards establishing a more varied repertoire of approved devotional practices. By 1834, for example, the town of Newry had three separate lay societies whose members committed themselves to attending confession and communion together once a month. Elsewhere too there were reports of new confraternities and sodalities, rosary societies, and book societies distributing approved religious literature. In Ulster, as elsewhere, the real transformation of popular religious practice, what has been referred to as the devotional revolution, was to come only in the period after 1850. But the foundations were clearly being laid in the previous two or three decades.

It would be easy to assume that the new vigour with which the Catholic clergy of the early nineteenth century approached their pastoral duties reflected their church's final liberation from the shackles of the penal laws. In fact, however, a revitalized Catholicism was only one manifestation of a general quickening of religious enthusiasm, crossing both denominational and national boundaries, that took place in the late eighteenth and early nineteenth centuries. Where Protestants were concerned, its most obvious manifestation was in the rising influence of evangelicalism, characterized by a central focus on the doctrine of the atonement, a return to bibliocentric theology, a commitment to religious and social activism, and, above all, a new emphasis on personal experience, sometimes though not always including the traumatic progress from despair to assurance summed up in the notion of conversion. In the Synod of Ulster in particular, rising evangelical influence transformed religious life in the first half of the nineteenth century. Reformers called for a more systematic routine of visitation and religious instruction,

---

[20] For the material in this and the next paragraph see S. J. Connolly, 'Catholicism in Ulster 1800–1850', in P. Roebuck (ed.), *Plantation to Partition: Essays in Ulster History* (Belfast, 1981), 157–71.

[21] Ó Dufaigh, 'James Murphy'; Letter book of Michael Blake, PRONI T3371.

and for a tightening of congregational discipline, enforced where necessary by the exclusion of offenders from communion. By the 1830s, observers noted the influence of Presbyterian as well as Catholic clergy in suppressing unorthodox practices, notably the holding of festive wakes over the bodies of the dead, and in curbing excessive drinking and disorderly popular amusements. There was also a renewed emphasis on theological orthodoxy. In 1835, following the withdrawal of a dissident minority to form the Remonstrant Synod, the Synod of Ulster restored the requirement that ministers subscribe to the Westminster Confession of Faith. This in turn paved the way for a union in 1840 with the Seceders to form the General Assembly of the Presbyterian Church in Ireland.[22]

A reaffirmation of orthodox doctrine might at first sight imply a retreat from reason in response to the multiple uncertainties of an age of social, political, and scientific transformation, a Protestant counterpart to the ultramontane dogmatism of the nineteenth-century Catholic Church. In fact the intellectual outlook of the evangelical mainstream of Ulster Presbyterianism in the mid-nineteenth century was confident and outward-looking. Its spokesmen based their arguments on the Common Sense philosophy developed in eighteenth-century Scotland, supporting their propositions by an empirical appeal to observable features of human consciousness. On this basis they could see science and theology as separate but mutually compatible fields of enquiry, and could accept the methods, though not the conclusions, of the new form of textual criticism being applied to the Christian scriptures. By the late nineteenth century, on the other hand, this apparently successful synthesis of faith and science had begun to be eroded, in part by new trends in philosophy and psychology, and in part by the rise of a popular evangelicalism unsympathetic to theological speculation. The result was an anti-intellectual reaction in sections of Ulster Presbyterianism, vividly exposed in 1927, when conservatives influenced by North American fundamentalism initiated the trial for heresy of the Union Theological College professor, J. E. Davey.[23]

Developments within Ulster Presbyterianism, where pastoral and moral reform were inextricably bound up with the rising influence of evangelicalism, must be set against the rather different course of events in the Church of Ireland. Here too evangelical commitment inspired individual clergymen to new levels of pastoral commitment. There were also active evangelical laymen. In particular a group of south Ulster landlords, led by the Earl of Farnham and the Earl of Roden, vigorously promoted moral and religious reform among their tenants. However, it was not until 1842 that the first evangelical was appointed to an Irish bishopric. Instead the improvement in pastoral standards that took place in the first half of the nineteenth century was primarily the work of churchmen of more traditional views. In Down and Connor, Richard Mant, bishop from 1823 until 1848, came into direct

---

[22] Holmes, *Shaping of Ulster Presbyterian Belief and Practice*.
[23] A. R. Holmes, 'Biblical Authority and the Impact of Higher Criticism in Irish Presbyterianism, ca. 1850–1930', *Church History*, 75 (2006), 343–73; idem, 'Presbyterians and Science in the North of Ireland before 1874', *British Journal for the History of Science*, 41 (2008).

conflict with evangelicals in his diocese over his commitment to the use of the surplice, the observance of holy days, and other high church practices. Yet he was also an energetic upholder of pastoral standards, and a particularly active builder of new churches.[24] Across Ulster as a whole statistics on clerical residence testify to the unspectacular but steady improvements being achieved. Already by 1806, at a time when only 56 per cent of incumbents in Ireland as a whole were resident in their benefices, the only Ulster dioceses in which the proportion was below 70 per cent were Clogher (63 per cent) and Kilmore (56 per cent). By 1832 the proportion had risen to 71 per cent in Clogher and to 85 per cent in Kilmore, while in all but one of the other four dioceses what had already been a comparatively favourable position had also further improved.[25]

Neither the efforts of conservative reformers like Mant, nor the labours of committed evangelicals, however, were sufficient to preserve the status of the Church of Ireland in a changing political world. The Act of Union had joined the churches of England and Ireland into one religious establishment, which 'shall be deemed and taken to be an essential and fundamental part of the union'.[26] In practice the two groups of churchmen continued to manage their own affairs. And as successive British governments came to see concessions to the Catholic majority in Ireland as the best means of stabilizing government there, the theoretical amalgamation of the two establishments provided little protection. The Church Temporalities Act of 1833 reduced the Ulster dioceses by three, amalgamating Raphoe with Derry, Clogher with Armagh, and Dromore with Down and Connor. An act of 1838 converted tithe into a rent charge paid by landlords rather than by the agricultural population as a whole. Disestablishment in 1870 stripped the church of its political privileges in Ireland, though not in England or Wales. The act was a serious blow to an institution that saw itself as the true heir to the work of St Patrick. It was the wife of an Ulster bishop, William Alexander of Derry, who lamented that 'dimly dawns the new year on a churchless nation'. On the other hand, disestablishment, along with the bonds created by a shared evangelical commitment, helped to reduce long standing divisions between Anglicans and Presbyterians, opening the way to closer cooperation against the threat that both perceived from the growing strength of Irish Catholic nationalism in the last quarter of the nineteenth century.

The drive for reform and renewal among both Catholic and Protestant denominations was a development seen across Great Britain and Ireland in the first half of the nineteenth century. What distinguished Ireland, including Ulster, was the strength of the popular response. Among Presbyterians in County Antrim and elsewhere, investigators for the Ordnance Survey in the 1830s reported not just the decline, under clerical pressure, of traditional amusements and social gatherings, but a new religious seriousness. In some cases, the abandoned pastimes had been

---

[24] N. Yates, *The Religious Condition of Ireland 1770–1850* (Oxford, 2006), 96–9, 284–9.

[25] D. H. Akenson, *The Church of Ireland: Ecclesiastical Reform and Revolution 1800–1885* (New Haven, 1971), 128–9.

[26] *Irish Statutes*, 40 Geo. III, *c.* 38, article 5.

replaced by singing schools dedicated to sacred music. In 1859 prayer meetings inspired by news of a religious revival in the United States developed into a massive display of popular enthusiasm, affecting all Protestant denominations but strongest among Presbyterians. Huge crowds attended sermons and gatherings for prayer, and thousands passed through an emotionally draining conversion experience.[27] By this time too the religious practice of Ulster Catholics was being transformed. A smaller population and a rise in average incomes provided the material basis for a dramatic expansion in ecclesiastical resources. By the 1870s the number of Catholics for each parish priest or curate was half what it had been four decades earlier, and there had also been a marked growth in the number of members of both male and female religious orders. Visitation records from the archdiocese of Armagh confirm that it was during the 1850s and 1860s that the decisive changes took place in popular religious behaviour. New devotional practices such as Benediction and the Stations of the Cross became regular occurrences, altar furniture and vestments became more elaborate, and the spread of lay sodalities and confraternities disseminated the habit of frequent confession and communion among both men and women.[28]

In the task of promulgating these new standards of religious practice the development of Belfast posed, for Catholics and Protestants alike, a particular challenge. As in other major centres of early British industrialization the explosion of population—from around 20,000 in 1800 to just under 100,000 fifty years later—left all denominations struggling to cope, while the often traumatic transfer to a new environment stripped migrants from the countryside of the connections that had formerly sustained religious practice. In 1836 a minister claimed that of 2000 Presbyterians inhabiting the industrial suburb of Ballymacarrett, 1500 had no connection with any church.[29] The occasion, however, was the opening of a new Presbyterian place of worship, one of several built during the 1830s in working-class districts of the expanding town. The Church of Ireland also responded to the challenge. Christ Church, opened in 1833, offered 1000 free seats in the heart of the poor residential district that had grown up to the west of the town centre. Its curate, Thomas Drew, a dynamic preacher and energetic organizer, quickly built up a large congregation.[30] Elsewhere too a study of membership lists for thirteen Protestant congregations of different denominations for the late nineteenth and early twentieth centuries confirms that energetic pastoral work bore significant fruit. It was true that in most congregations the middle classes were over-represented in comparison to their share of population, and the unskilled under-represented. But Belfast church-goers came from all social levels, with a strong representation in most places of worship of the skilled working class.[31]

---

[27] M. Hill, 'Ulster Awakened: The '59 Revival Reconsidered', *Journal of Ecclesiastical History*, 41 (1990), 443–62.
[28] A. McKinney, 'Joseph Dixon and the Archdiocese of Armagh, 1852–1866' (Ph.D. thesis, Queen's University, Belfast, 2008).
[29] *Belfast News Letter*, 10 June 1836.
[30] Hempton and Hill, *Evangelical Protestantism*, 111–12.
[31] D. Huddleston, 'Religion and Social Class: Church Membership in Belfast c.1870–1930' (M.Phil., Queen's University, Belfast, 1998).

The fortunes of Catholicism in Belfast were somewhat different. Church attendance in the early nineteenth century was in fact higher than in the Ulster countryside: one informed estimate, in 1824, was that 8250 Catholics out of a population then estimated at 13,200 attended mass, while the Commissioners of Public Instruction, ten years later, put the figure at 9500 out of 20,000.[32] This would suggest that many early migrants to this less-than-welcoming city found in their church a source of reassurance and the basis of a social network. Over the next few decades, however, conditions deteriorated sharply. By 1863 it was claimed that 'not more than one out of every three actually hears mass on Sundays'.[33] Responsibility for this state of affairs, by now an anomaly in comparison to the much expanded Catholic establishment elsewhere in Ireland, lay with the bishop, Cornelius Denvir. A scholar rather than a zealot, he came under increasing attack from the 1850s for his failure, inspired by what colleagues saw as timidity in the face of the Protestant establishment, to build new churches or increase the number of priests serving in the town. By 1865, however, Denvir had been forced to resign. His successor, Patrick Dorrian, quickly expanded the number of clergy, introduced the Christian Brothers and other religious orders, and began a programme of church building. A papal jubilee in May 1865, at the very start of Dorrian's episcopate, confirmed the poor state of pastoral services in the diocese, but also the enthusiasm among the laity for the new regime now offered. 'All have gone to confession', the bishop reported, 'except two or three Freemasons and some very few in the lower ranks.... The greater part of the penitents were persons who had been absent for years and many never at confession before.'[34] The next four decades saw an extensive programme of church building, and a sevenfold increase in the number of parish clergy, permitting Belfast Catholics to develop the same high levels of religious practice exhibited by their co-religionists elsewhere in Ireland.[35]

Alongside a more active pastoral role for the Catholic Church, and a more ostentatious pattern of popular devotion, went a greater willingness to assert the claims of Catholics to a role in Irish public life. In 1896 Henry Henry, Bishop of Down and Connor, set up a Catholic Association. Henry's supporters were from the small Belfast Catholic middle class, and their aims were conservative: to secure Catholic representation within the recently expanded system of municipal wards, and so guarantee a share of patronage and local influence. For a time it seemed as if such assimilationist tactics could bear fruit. When the former Queen's College became a university in 1908, four Catholics were appointed to its governing senate.

---

[32] *First Report of the Commissioners of Public Instruction, Ireland* (B.P.P., 1835, 33), 216–17; A. Macaulay, *William Crolly, Archbishop of Armagh 1835–49* (Dublin, 1994), 117.

[33] Joseph Dixon to Tobias Kirby, 31 October 1863 (Irish College, Rome, Kirby Papers, 1863/280).

[34] For a fuller account, see S. J. Connolly, 'Paul Cullen's Other Capital: Belfast and the Devotional Revolution', in D. Keogh (ed.), *Paul Cullen and his World* (Dublin, 2011), 289–307.

[35] A. C. Hepburn, *A Past Apart: Studies in the History of Catholic Belfast 1850–1950* (Belfast, 1996), 128–30.

Subsequent lobbying secured the establishment of a lectureship in scholastic philosophy, making it possible for Catholic clerical students to attend the university before proceeding to the seminary at Maynooth to complete their training. Meanwhile Dr Peter O'Connell, senior surgeon at the Mater Hospital, became one of the university's four lecturers in clinical medicine. O'Connell, a close ally of Henry, also served as High Sheriff of Belfast in 1907 and was knighted the following year for his services to medicine. By the time of his elevation, however, a new political leader, Joseph Devlin, had used two grassroots movements, the United Irish League and the Ancient Order of Hibernians, to overthrow Bishop Henry's Catholic Association and bring Catholic Belfast into line with the Home Rule movement in the island as a whole. Within a further four years the introduction of the third Home Rule Bill was to put a decisive end to any possibility of mutual accommodation within the city.[36]

The religious structure of Ulster society at the beginning of the twentieth century was still largely determined by the defeats and victories of three centuries earlier. In the peripheral, and generally poorer, counties of Cavan, Donegal, and Monaghan, Catholics made up three-quarters or more of the population; in the east Ulster heartland of Antrim and Down they accounted for less than one third; in the southern and central Ulster counties, Armagh, Fermanagh, Londonderry, and Tyrone, the balance between the descendants of the pre-plantation natives and of the English and Scottish settlers was close to equal. Catholics everywhere in Ulster were concentrated at the bottom of the scale: among small farmers and landless labourers in the countryside, unskilled or semi-skilled workers in the towns. The small Catholic middle class consisted largely of doctors, lawyers, shopkeepers, and publicans, providers of services to their own community in a religiously segregated society.[37] The long standing political and religious rivalry between Church of Ireland and Presbyterian was much reduced, though not wholly banished.[38] But the social divisions inherited from two contrasting migrant streams remained, with Presbyterians better represented among skilled workers, as well as among holders of commercial and industrial capital, and among larger farmers in the countryside.[39] Between 1898 and 1904 Belfast acquired an Anglican cathedral to match the city status conferred ten years earlier. But the Church of Ireland remained woefully underfunded. In 1898 there were only 21,000 church places for the city's 92,000 nominal episcopalians.

---

[36] A. C. Hepburn, *Catholic Belfast and Nationalist Ireland in the Era of Joe Devlin 1871–1934* (Oxford, 2008), 49–74; obituary of O'Connell, *British Medical Journal*, 19 November 1927.

[37] Hepburn, *A Past Apart*, Chs 3–6; idem, *Catholic Belfast*, Ch. 2.

[38] For continued Presbyterian complaints of undue favour shown to members of the former established church see R. McMinn, 'Presbyterians and Politics in Ulster, 1871–1906', *Studia Hibernica*, 21 (1981), 127–46.

[39] On the greater economic dynamism of the Scots, reflecting the higher proportion of capital-holding independent settlers, as opposed to sponsored migrants, see L. M. Cullen, *The Emergence of Modern Ireland 1600–1900* (London, 1981), 55–6. For socio-economic differences in the nineteenth century see McMinn, 'Presbyterians and Politics', 129–32; B. M. Walker, *Ulster Politics: The Formative Years, 1868–76* (Belfast, 1989), 17–19; Hepburn, *A Past Apart*, 80–2.

An increase in the number of clergy between 1911 and 1914 was achieved only through the extraordinary expedient of collections being taken up in Dublin and other southern dioceses to subsidize the Church of Ireland in the island's largest and wealthiest city.[40]

A more recent historical legacy, dating from the mid-nineteenth century, was the high levels of church attendance among both Catholics and Protestants, setting Ulster, like the rest of Ireland, increasingly apart from other parts of western Europe. Levels of popular devotion in Belfast were particularly striking at a time when industrial cities in general had seen organized religion lose much of its hold over the working class population. Such high levels of popular piety were a monument to two generations of labour by evangelical pastors and ultramontane priests. But alongside this narrative of the flourishing of a revitalized popular religion, Catholic and Protestant, must be set its darker obverse. Lords Farnham and Roden may have sponsored projects for moral and religious improvement on their estates. But they were also champions of the Second Reformation, the major missionary effort aimed at the conversion of the Catholic population that contributed significantly to the rise of sectarian tensions in the 1820s and subsequently. In Belfast, Thomas Drew was a dynamic preacher and a dedicated agent of his church's mission to the working class. But he was also a vehement anti-Catholic controversialist, whose inflammatory preaching was identified as one major cause of the sectarian violence that erupted in the summer of 1857.[41] On the Catholic side, equally, the 'devotional revolution' of the mid-nineteenth century was inseparable from a new spirit of sectarian exclusiveness, evident in the demand for denominational education at every level and in a deep hostility towards marriage to non-Catholics, already evident long before the publication in 1908 of the pope's notorious decree *Ne Temere*.[42]

Such examples are a reminder of the extent to which continued high levels of religious practice were a by-product of the deep sectarian divisions that dominated Irish public life. Elsewhere in Europe growing estrangement from organized religion reflected the sense among radicals and class conscious workers that the churches were part of an unjust social and political order. In Ireland, by contrast, religious and political allegiances reinforced rather than undermined one another. Their overlap produced what was increasingly, in the context of a secularized western Europe, an exceptional popular piety. But it was a piety inextricably linked to bitter, and in the case of Ulster sometimes murderous, animosities.

---

[40] R. B. McDowell, *The Church of Ireland 1869–1969* (London, 1975), 78–9; A. Scholes, *The Church of Ireland and the Third Home Rule Bill* (Dublin, 2009), 24–5.

[41] J. Holmes, 'The Role of Open-Air Preaching in the Belfast Riots of 1857', *Proceedings of the Royal Irish Academy*, 102, C (2002), 47–66.

[42] For the enthusiastic use that was nevertheless made of the decree by unionist propagandists see Hepburn, *Catholic Belfast*, 129–31.

FURTHER READING

A. Ford, *The Protestant Reformation in Ireland 1590–1641* (Dublin, 1997).

D. Hempton and M. Hill, *Evangelical Protestantism in Ulster Society 1740–1890* (London, 1992).

A. R. Holmes, *The Shaping of Ulster Presbyterian Belief and Practice 1770–1840* (Oxford, 2006).

A. Macauley, *Patrick Dorrian, Bishop of Down and Connor* (Dublin, 1990).

B. MacCuarta, *Catholic Revival in the North of Ireland 1603–1641* (Dublin, 2007).

O. Rafferty, *Catholicism in Ulster 1603–1983* (Dublin, 1994).

6

Crime, Policing, and the Law, 1600–1900

Neal Garnham

THE CONTEXT

The defeat of the Earl of Tyrone in the Nine Years' War and the subsequent Treaty of Mellifont opened up the north of Ireland to many new influences. Especially once the scheme of plantation had been established, revisions would take place in the province's politics, economy, and social structures. Amongst these were fundamental changes in the system of law and its administration. In the wake of Gaelic defeat, departure, and decline, came the common law of England and the courts that oversaw its implementation. The new common law jurisdiction had profound effects on the systems of land tenure and civil justice. Systems of freehold and leasehold replaced Gaelic practices of inheritance and clientage, and royal courts replaced older Brehon structures for settling grievances.[1] While the impact of these changes on the system of landholding has long been recognized by historians, the accompanying shifts in the criminal code and its administration have been less well explored. Assize courts, the main criminal courts throughout our period, had been held in at least four Ulster counties, Down, Antrim, Monaghan, and Cavan, in the 1590s. However it was really only from 1603 that the province more widely began to receive visits from judges equipped with royal commissions to try felons and other criminals.[2] According to Raymond Gillespie, by the 1620s an Irish term for 'assizes' had been coined, suggesting recognition of the courts' existence, though not necessarily their legitimacy, at most social levels.[3] At a lower legal level the establishment of the manorial system in Ulster led to the creation of a system of courts dependent upon seigneurial rights. The court leet, overseen by a landlord-appointed seneschal, seems to have been a relatively widespread local institution by the 1630s.[4]

---

[1] N. Canny, 'Hugh O'Neill, Earl of Tyrone, and the Changing Face of Gaelic Ulster', *Studia Hibernica*, 10 (1970), 7–35; H. Morgan, 'The End of Gaelic Ulster? A Thematic Interpretation of Events between 1534 and 1610', *Irish Historical Studies*, 27 (1988), 8–32; J. McCavitt, *The Flight of the Earls* (Dublin, 2002), 66–8.

[2] J. McCavitt, '"Good Planets in Their Several Spheares": The Establishment of the Assize Circuits in Early Seventeenth Century Ireland', *Irish Jurist* (new series), 24 (1989), 248–78.

[3] R. Gillespie, *Seventeenth-Century Ireland: Making Ireland Modern* (Dublin, 2006), 25.

[4] R. Gillespie, *Colonial Ulster: The Settlement of East Ulster 1600–1641* (Cork, 1985), 156–8;. J. Wilkinson, *A Treatise Collected Out of the Statutes of This Kingdom, and According to Common Experience of the Laws, Concerning the Office and Authorities of Coroners and Sheriffs, Together With an Easy and Plain Method For the Keeping of a Court Leet, Court Baron, and Hundred Court etc* (Dublin, 1734). This, and several later such manuals on the court leet, were all reprints of earlier English originals.

The establishment of these institutions acts as the best available marker for the advancement of the common law in Ulster. It might also be argued that this advance marked out the emergence of a truly colonial government in Ireland.[5]

The early history of the courts in Ulster was somewhat disjointed. The outbreak of war in Ulster from 1641 unsurprisingly led to a collapse of the system of Crown courts in the short term. What, if anything, took their place is uncertain. An attempt by the Lord Lieutenant to re-establish the Crown courts to allow for the 'due administration of justice in the province of Ulster' in 1650 seems to have come to nothing.[6] Under the Commonwealth, a judge was sent north in 1651 to try both civil and criminal cases. However it was not until 1655 that regular circuits of courts were re-established and the office of Justice of the Peace revived.[7]

At the Restoration, the courts were re-established on the old lines, from which in truth the Cromwellian regime had not diverged much in the first place. A particular focus in Ulster, however, seems to have been the legal persecution of Protestant dissenters.[8] Under James II the Irish judiciary, previously a Protestant monopoly, had a Catholic majority by 1687. Even in Ulster, where the gentry were overwhelmingly Protestant, Catholic magistrates were appointed in some numbers.[9] The Williamite war brought disruption to the courts once more, but the subsequent settlement established a system of common law courts that would remain largely unchanged for more than two centuries. While the central courts lay in the capital, in Ulster and the other provinces the leading criminal courts were the assizes, held twice a year and overseen by judges sent from Dublin. Courts of quarter session, convened under local magistrates, met four times a year and dealt with lesser offences. Manorial and borough courts were convened under various charters and licences, but may have dealt with comparatively little criminal business.[10]

The courts that administered the common law in Ulster were established shortly prior to the province's plantation. This was comparatively late in an Irish context. Subsequent conflicts disrupted their business, but they seem to have become key components in the governance of the province relatively quickly. From the Williamite settlement to the granting of Irish independence, the system remained largely unchanged. It was initially modelled on that of England, though it might be argued that the eventual outcomes in the two areas were very different.

---

[5] H. Pawlisch, *Sir John Davies and the Conquest of Ireland: A Study in Legal Imperialism* (Cambridge, 1985); Nicholas Canny, *Making Ireland British, 1580–1650* (Oxford, 2001), 172–5.

[6] Commission from the Lord Lieutenant of Ireland, 8 August 1650, *HMC Ormonde Manuscripts* (new series), I, 157.

[7] Parliamentary Commissioners at Dublin to Commissioners at Belfast, 12 November 1651 in R. Dunlop (ed.), *Ireland under the Commonwealth, Being a Selection of Documents Relating to the Government of Ireland from 1651–1659*, Vol. I (Manchester, 1913), 77–8; T. Barnard, *Cromwellian Ireland: English Government and Reform in Ireland, 1649–1660* (Oxford, 1975), 257–77.

[8] F. E. Ball, *The Judges in Ireland, 1221–1921*, Vol. 1 (New York, 1927), 282–3.

[9] J. G. Simms, *Jacobite Ireland, 1685–91* (London, 1969), 33; D. W. Miller, 'The Earl of Tyrconnell and James II's Irish Policy, 1665–1688', *Historical Journal*, 20 (1977), 802–23.

[10] J. L. McCracken, 'The Political Structure, 1714–60', in T. W. Moody and W. E. Vaughan (eds), *A New History of Ireland*, Vol.4: *Eighteenth Century Ireland, 1691–1800* (Oxford, 1986), 66–9.

By the opening of the twentieth century, although Ireland and England were united under a single parliament, they had differing systems of policing, contrasting levels and natures of crime, and criminal codes that were far from coincident.

POLICING

With the expansion of British settlement in Ulster came the established system of law enforcement. Initially sheriffs appointed by the Dublin administration in the name of the Crown were responsible for overseeing the enforcement of the law along with many other duties. What emerged during the seventeenth century was a system of parish and baronial constables in rural areas, and watch and ward in urban centres.[11] The ideal of the self-policing society on the English model, in which all male citizens served in turn to enforce the law, was introduced for the first time.

The evidence suggests that this system did not work particularly well in England where it had evolved. The same may have been the case in Ireland.[12] Busy citizens were uninterested in the inconvenience and danger that serving in these offices could entail. As a result unsuitable substitutes were employed, and the physically and morally unfit often appeared as constables.

When greater threats presented themselves, greater resources would be deployed. In 1667 the recently formed militia was used in Ulster to pursue 'a few tories at large'.[13] Such threats, which persisted well into the eighteenth century in the less accessible areas of the province, would eventually be dealt with by limited deployments of the army, as well as the offering of rewards, and the rounding up of those who harboured the bandits.[14] There may be some validity to the notion that those who operated outside the law in this way in the wake of the Cromwellian and Restoration settlements were acting as proto-nationalist guerrillas, but it is worth noting that in 1617 the leader of a large group of 'woodkerne' in counties Tyrone and Londonderry was killed by 'certain of the Irishry' employed by a local planter, and in 1668, a group of Tories out and on their keeping in Ulster were described as 'both English, Irish and Scotts'.[15]

It was not until the later eighteenth century that innovations came to be made in policing in Ireland. In 1773 and 1787 the Irish parliament passed legislation that sought to bolster the baronial constables, but with little success. In 1786

---

[11] See for example, R. M. Young (ed.), *The Town Book of the Corporation of Belfast* (Belfast, 1892), 70, 128, and 136.

[12] See however J. Sharpe, 'Enforcing the Law in the Seventeenth-Century English Village', in V. A. C. Gattrell, B. Lenman, and G. Parker (eds), *Crime and the Law: The Social History of Crime in Western Europe since 1500* (London, 1980), 107–8.

[13] Lord Lieutenant to Commissioners of the Militia, 7 January 1667, in *CSPI, 1666–69*, 270.

[14] S. J. Connolly, *Religion, Law, and Power: The Making of Protestant Ireland 1660–1760* (Oxford, 1992), 203–11.

[15] Lord Deputy, Dublin, to Sir Robert Winwood, 11 January 1617, in *CSPI, 1615–25,* 146; R. Leigh, Dublin to J. Williamson, 9 June 1668, TNA, SP 63/324/83.

arguably the first modern police force in the British and Irish Isles was established in Dublin.[16] These innovations had little impact in Ulster, and in fact Ulster MPs were prominent in the unsuccessful opposition to the 1787 Act.[17] In 1814 the Union parliament established the Peace Preservation Force to counter the widespread rural unrest that had emerged in the wake of a downturn in agriculture and growing opposition to tithes. Centrally organized but locally funded, the force was eventually deployed in sixteen counties across Ireland. Only one, Donegal, was in Ulster, and here it has been suggested that the force was used as much to control illicit distillation as it was to counter agrarian crime.[18] From 1822, legislation permitted each county to establish its own professional constabulary to replace the older parish and baronial forces. The Ulster counties were markedly slow in taking up the opportunity. County Down did not establish its force until 1825.[19] This reluctance to innovate was inspired perhaps both by a perception that change was unnecessary, but also by the costs that would be incurred.

In 1836 further legislation was passed to consolidate the police forces in Ireland, and the centrally controlled Irish Constabulary was created to replace the existing forces. The reaction from Ulster was not positive. Lord Roden, a County Down proprietor, had been prominent in the opposition to the legislation in the House of Lords, arguing that the measure undermined the authority of the local magistracy. Lord Londonderry dismissed the act as simply intended to placate the Irish political allies of the minority Whig administration. More precisely, it seems that this shift was seen by Ireland's Protestant political classes as 'just another sign of the ongoing assault on Protestant Ireland' by the London government. With its relatively large Protestant population, such measures were likely to have been felt more keenly in Ulster than elsewhere.[20]

As Table 6.1 shows, in the first half of the nineteenth century Ulster was the least densely policed of the provinces whether in relation to population or area. In 1832 the population of Leinster was more than two and a half times as heavily policed as Ulster, while in 1852 Munster was almost half as heavily policed again as Ulster. These figures may well be slightly skewed by the omission of the small urban police forces in the north in the city of Derry and the town of Belfast, but the contrasts are striking. It is likely that the comparative under-policing of Ulster was primarily due to the lesser incidence of agrarian conflict, but sectarian disturbances were prevalent and generally led to increased police numbers. The growing urban centre of Belfast experienced its first large-scale sectarian riot in July 1813. It is also worth noting that the application of much of the earlier policing legislation was often shunned because of both the costs it involved, and the fact that it removed power

---

[16] B. Henry, *Dublin Hanged: Crime, Law Enforcement and Punishment in Late-Eighteenth Century Dublin* (Dublin, 1994), 137–53.
[17] S. H. Palmer, *Police and Protest in England and Ireland, 1780–1850* (Cambridge, 1988), 113.
[18] G. Broeker, *Rural Disorder and Police Reform in Ireland, 1812–1836* (London, 1970), 71–126; Palmer, *Police and Protest*, 221–6.
[19] Palmer, *Police and Protest*, 247–8.
[20] Hansard (3rd series), HL Vol. 30, cols. 1002–7 and 888–9 (26 August 1835); S. Farrell, *Rituals and Riots: Sectarian Violence and Political Culture in Ulster, 1784–1886* (Lexington, 2000), 72.

Table 6.1. Density of policing in the four provinces of Ireland, 1832–52

	1832		1842		1852	
	Square miles per policeman	Inhabitants per policeman	Square miles per policeman	Inhabitants per policeman	Square miles per policeman	Inhabitants per policeman
Ulster	6.9	1890	5.5	1586	3.7	890
Munster	5.4	1281	3.6	928	2.6	525
Connaught	4.4	892	4.8	1030	3.2	487
Leinster	2.9	723	2.4	630	2.2	490

Source: Figures derived from Palmer, *Police and Protest*, 555–6, and W. E. Vaughan and A. J. Fitzpatrick (eds), *Irish Historical Statistics: Population, 1821–1971* (Dublin, 1978), 15–16.

from local hands. This could happen in the face of considerable law breaking. In 1816, the agent of the Abercorn estates in Donegal reported that after the capital conviction of a man for shooting at a magistrate, the prosecutor was subsequently murdered, and the houses of jurymen attacked. However, he still wished to 'keep clear of the Peace Preservation Bill' as 'we could not well bear the cost'.[21]

Sectarian conflict fundamentally affected the policing of Ulster in the second half of the nineteenth century, however. Belfast and Derry had both established borough police forces through specific legislation at the beginning of the century. The Belfast force failed to control sectarian rioting in the city in 1857 and 1864. Fuelled by what now seems to have been contrived allegations of sectarian bias in the force, an enquiry in 1865 recommended that the local police be disbanded and replaced by detachments of the centrally controlled Irish Constabulary.[22] In Derry, the force was confronted by similar disturbances in 1869 and 1883 and suffered the same fate in 1885.[23] These events were important as they saw the final shifts occur in the movement of the control of the policing of Ulster out of the province and into the hands of the Dublin administration. Policing in Ulster had begun in the seventeenth century as a locally controlled, Protestant-led initiative, with magistrates overseeing a system of constables. By the end of the nineteenth century, the entire province was policed by a force that was not only controlled from Dublin, but primarily recruited from other provinces, and whose rank and file were overwhelmingly Catholic.[24]

---

[21] J. Sinclair, Lifford, to [Earl of Abercorn], 20 July 1816, PRONI, D/632/A/172/7.

[22] B. Griffin, *The Bulkies: Police and Crime in Belfast, 1800–1865* (Dublin, 1997); *Report of the Commissioners of Enquiry Respecting the Magisterial and Police Arrangements and Establishments of the Borough of Belfast* (B.P.P., 1865, 28 [cd 3466]).

[23] *Report of Royal Commissioners of Enquiry Into Riots and Disturbances in the City of Londonderry* (B.P.P., 1870, 32 [cd5], 411ff.); *Report of Royal Commissioners of Enquiry Into Riots and Disturbances in the City of Londonderry in November 1883* (B.P.P., 1884, 37 [cd 3954], 515ff.). The history of the Londonderry Borough Police remains to be written, despite the survival of much relevant material.

[24] E. Malcolm, *The Irish Policeman, 1822–1922: A Life* (Dublin, 2006), 53 and 56. The officer corps of the force remained predominantly Protestant however: see W. J. Lowe, 'Irish Constabulary Officers, 1837–1922: Profile of a Professional Elite', *Irish Economic and Social History*, 32 (2005), 31–4.

CRIME

Attempting to gauge the nature and frequency of crimes in early modern Ireland is frustrating. The scant evidence available for the seventeenth century consists of anecdotal materials and fragmentary survivals. Gaol delivery rolls for seven assizes give a brief insight into the offences committed, which included killings but mainly thefts.[25] Amongst those acquitted at the Tyrone assize of March 1615 was Hugh McDonnell O'Neale, who had allegedly called King James 'but a verie poor fellow'.[26] The tallies of deaths, destruction, and pillaging that took place in the 1640s and 1689–91 could serve to distort our view of the century, and occasionally reports emerge that give contradictory views. A report by the Lord Deputy and Privy Council in 1623 that 'burglaries, robberies and outrages' were common against the Ulster planters, should perhaps be balanced by a letter of seven years earlier stating that the few outlaws who were preying on the northern settlers could be 'scattered without any great labour'.[27] At the very least Ulster, along with the rest of Ireland, seems to have avoided the worst excesses of the various witch crazes that swept across the rest of the British and Irish Isles in the seventeenth century.[28]

Marginally more information is available for the eighteenth century. Surviving indictment data for County Armagh give some insight into the business of the assizes. The commonest crime prosecuted was assault, although its legal definition made it clear that the offence was not necessarily one of violence. Murder, perhaps a more reliable measure of the nature of criminal violence, was prosecuted on average just over three times a year between 1735 and 1797. Although higher than comparable rates in the south of England, the suggestion is that Ulster was not a prodigiously violent place.[29] Crimes against property fluctuated greatly from year to year, but perhaps unsurprisingly, they seem to have been largely affected by the economic climate. In times of dearth, thefts rose, while in years of plenty, prosecutions declined.[30] The connection between famine and crime had been noted in the 1660s.[31] More fragmentary evidence from Tyrone supports the general trends noted for Armagh.[32] There also seems to be some evidence that attitudes amongst those in authority may have begun to harden in the last decade of the century, as political and sectarian tensions heightened. Grand juries, composed of twenty-three

---

[25] J. F. Ferguson, 'The Ulster Rolls of Gaol Delivery', *Ulster Journal of Archaeology* (1st series), I (1853), 260–70, and II (1854), 25–8.

[26] R. M. Young (ed.), *Historical Notices of Old Belfast and its Vicinity* (Belfast, 1896), 39.

[27] TNA, SP63/237/41, Lord Deputy and Council, Dublin to Privy Council, London, 22 July 1623; Lord Deputy, Dublin to Sir Robert Winwood, 25 October 1616 in *CSPI, 1615–25*, 140.

[28] R. Gillespie, 'Women and Crime in Seventeenth-Century Ireland', in M. MacCurtain and M. O'Dowd (eds), *Women in Early Modern Ireland* (Edinburgh, 1991), 43–52.

[29] N. Garnham, 'How Violent Was Eighteenth-Century Ireland?', *Irish Historical Studies* 30 (1997), 377–92.

[30] N. Garnham, *The Courts, Crime and the Criminal Law in Ireland, 1692–1760* (Dublin, 1996), 149–67.

[31] Sir G. Rawdon, Carrickfergus, to Viscount Conway and Killulta, 16 April 1669 in *CSPI, 1666–69*, 709–10.

[32] County Tyrone Assize Grand Jury Indictment Book, 1745–1809, PRONI, TYR/4/2/1. This document is extensively water and fire damaged in its later pages.

of the leading residents of the county, were charged at the biannual assizes with examining the bills of indictment around which prosecutions were formed. Examining the *prima facie* case, they decided if it would proceed to trial or not. In the 1740s the County Armagh grand jury returned only just over half of cases presented to it as 'true bills', and sent them for trial. By the 1790s the rate had risen to over 80 per cent. In County Monaghan in the 1790s, the grand jury sent almost 90 per cent of cases for trial.[33]

The imposition of martial law from March 1798 had much less to do with controlling ordinary crime than countering the political agitations of the United Irishmen. In the wake of the 1798 rising, Ulster seems to have experienced something of a continuing breakdown in law and order. Certainly the Dublin administration did not feel secure enough to repeal martial law until 1806, and the predominantly Protestant Yeomanry force was kept in place in Ulster until the 1820s.[34] In many areas of Ulster, but notably in County Armagh, politics, crime, and sectarianism had been merging from the 1780s. Driven by economic rivalries and feelings of political abandonment, Protestants in the county formed groups that raided Catholic homes, seizing firearms and destroying looms. These 'Peep o' Day Boys' would eventually be opposed by Catholic 'Defenders'. These groups would subsequently find themselves supplying recruits to the opposing sides in 1798. Beyond that conflict, especially in south Ulster, their adherents seemed to have been transformed into Ribbonmen and members of the Orange Order.[35] Sectarian conflict spread widely across Ireland, but was most intense in Ulster, where numbers of Protestants and Catholics were more evenly balanced. This would have broad-reaching repercussions for the criminal justice system in Ulster.

Having said this, levels of fatal violence in pre-famine Ulster may have been low. In 1841 the three Irish counties with the lowest levels of coroner's inquests per head of population included two from Ulster: Antrim and Donegal. The rate in Wicklow, which had the highest rate, was more than ten times that in Antrim.[36]

As far as levels of crime in the later nineteenth century are concerned, Ulster may have emerged as perhaps the least disorderly of the four Irish provinces. Vaughan has calculated that Ulster saw the lowest occurrence of 'serious crime' of the four provinces in the period 1851–80. Other than in the period of the Ulster Tenant League in the 1850s, the province also exhibited the lowest levels of reported 'agrarian outrages'. This seems likely to be connected to better landlord-tenant relations in Ulster, which was in turn reflected in lower rates of evictions.[37] However Vaughan's periodization excludes two phases which saw levels of crime in Ulster rise, as they did elsewhere in Ireland. The Great Famine (1845–49) forced many back on their

---

[33] Armagh Public Library, County Armagh Assize Indictment Books, 1735–97; County Monaghan Assize Grand Jury Payment and Indictment Book, 1794–1831, PRONI, MIC/309/1.

[34] A. Blackstock, *An Ascendancy Army: The Irish Yeomanry 1796–1834* (Dublin, 1998), 232–66.

[35] D. W. Miller, 'The Armagh Troubles, 1784–95', in S. Clark and J. S. Donnelly Jr (eds), *Irish Peasants: Violence and Political Unrest, 1780–1914* (Madison, 1983), 155–91.

[36] W. E. Vaughan, *Murder Trials in Ireland, 1836–1914* (Dublin, 2009), 22.

[37] W. E. Vaughan, *Landlords and Tenants in Mid-Victorian Ireland* (Oxford, 1994), 233–4, 236–7, and 281–4.

wits. Few were perhaps as desperate or resourceful as the man from Londonderry who, when he was sentenced to a short prison term in 1846 for a petty theft, threw a stone at the magistrate laying down the sentence in an attempt to secure his transportation out of Ireland, and thus avoid the deprivation and starvation that surrounded him.[38] The Land War (1879–82), though perhaps less vehemently fought in Ulster than elsewhere, saw the policing of Ulster placed under great strain, and opportunists seem to have taken advantage of the situation to embark on something of a crime spree.[39] Ulster did experience high levels of disturbances in some areas at other times, and it was also the scene of two of the most notorious and well-researched incidents of agrarian murder. A survey of material in the National Archives suggests that between 1835 and 1855, more than a dozen agrarian murders took place within a ten-mile radius of the south Armagh town of Crossmaglen. The area was regarded as being particularly disturbed by the authorities, although it was the eventual murder of Thomas Bateson, land agent to Lord Templeton and a relation of the MP for County Londonderry that seems to have engendered most official interest.[40] In 1860, James Murray, the agent on John George Adair's Derryveagh estate in Donegal, was done to death by persons unknown. His employer reacted to the failure of the courts to secure a conviction by evicting all those rumoured to have had a hand in the affair. It was an event that lived long in local memory.[41] Eighteen years later the same county saw the killing of the 72-year-old Earl of Leitrim, along with his driver and clerk. Again enquiries were met with a conspiracy of silence, although the alleged assassins were eventually commemorated in 1960 by the erection of a stone memorial to them.[42] The fact that between 1852 and 1914 there were no executions of criminals in counties Donegal and Fermanagh may be as much a testimony to the ineffectiveness of the police in securing convictions as to the law-abiding nature of their inhabitants.[43]

Statistics regarding homicides in general, derived from the papers of the Chief Secretaries Office, also suggest that Ulster experienced relatively low levels of violent crime in the second half of the nineteenth century (see Table 6.2). However, the province of Leinster had the lowest apparent occurrence of murder. More

---

[38] W. J. Lowe, 'The Irish Constabulary in the Great Famine', *Eire-Ireland*, 29 (1994), 47–67; *Londonderry Sentinel*, 14 October 1846.

[39] S. A. Ball, 'Policing the Land War: The Development of British Government Policy Towards Political and Agrarian Protest and Crime in Ireland, 1879–92' (unpublished Ph.D. thesis, University of London, 2000), 220–65; W. J. Lowe, 'The Constabulary Agitation of 1882', *Irish Historical Studies*, 31 (1998), 37–59.

[40] K. McMahon and T. McKeown, 'Agrarian Disturbances around Crossmaglen, 1835–55', *Seanchas Ardmacha*, 9 (1979), 302–32; 10 (1981), 149–75; 10 (1982), 380–416; 11 (1985), 342–61; 12 (1986), 213–51; 12 (1987), 194–250; 13 (1989), 167–229. Of the fourteen killings detailed at least one seems to have been related only tangentially to agrarian issues, and another may not have actually occurred. M. McMahon, *The Murder of Thomas Douglas Bateson, County Monaghan, 1851* (Dublin, 2006).

[41] W. E. Vaughan, *Sin, Sheep and Scotsmen: John George Adair and the Deryveagh Evictions, 1861* (Belfast, 1983).

[42] A. P. W. Malcolmson, *Virtues of a Wicked Earl: The Life and Legend of William Sydney Clement, 3rd Earl of Leitrim, 1806–1878* (Dublin, 2008).

[43] Vaughan, *Murder Trials*, 330.

Table 6.2. Reported homicides by province, 1866–92

	Homicides	Population (1881)	Homicides per 10,000 population
Ulster	556	1,743,075	3.19
Munster	702	1,331,115	5.27
Connaught	322	821,657	3.92
Leinster	354	1,278,989	2.77
Ireland	1934	5,174,836	3.74

Source: Derived from C. A. Conley, *Melancholy Accidents: The Meaning of Violence in Post-Famine Ireland* (Lanham, 1999), 142–3; Vaughan and Fitzpatrick (eds), *Irish Historical Statistics*, 16.

worrying perhaps are accusations that in Ulster, again as elsewhere in Ireland, there was a peculiar toleration of murder and a reluctance to both prosecute and convict in such cases.[44]

Returns made by the Constabulary regarding indictable offences tried in the courts in the 1880s show that levels of reported crime in Ulster fluctuated from year to year, although generally not enormously. The relationship between reported incidents of crime and actual perpetrations, as well as the general utility of criminal statistics, are widely debated topics, and it is perhaps best to say that they are at most indicative of trends.[45] The implication here is that Ulster experienced levels of crime below the national average. However, the province was more crime-ridden than predominantly rural Connaught. While Ulster may have had low levels of agrarian crime, incidents of theft, drunkenness, and assault took place much more frequently, but at levels that were still below the norm for Ireland as a whole.

Moreover these aggregate figures mask great variations between one area of the province and another. Over the same period covered in Table 6.3, the police district of Belfast experienced a prosecution rate more than three times as high as neighbouring County Antrim. Table 6.4 gives the relative frequencies of prosecutions in the Ulster sub-regions.

These figures defy simplistic explanations. It seems clear that Belfast, with its history of sectarian conflict, concentration of economic activity, and offer of urban anonymity to the individual, probably suffered higher levels of crime than elsewhere. However, whether the dearth of prosecutions in Donegal was due to a lack of crime, inadequate policing, or a popular reluctance to resort to the law, is uncertain. Although prosecution levels in predominantly Protestant Antrim and Down remained proportionately low, the high levels of prosecutions in counties Londonderry

---

[44] [Rev P. Skelton], *A Dissertation on the Constitution and Effects of a Petty Jury* (Dublin, 1737), 31–2; Rev. W. Henry, *An Earnest Address to the People of Ireland Against the Drinking of Spirituous Liquors* (Dublin, 1753), 1; John Stewart, Lifford, to Marquis of Abercorn, 22 August 1810, PRONI, D/623/A/143/56, Both Skelton and Henry held parishes in Ulster.

[45] A valuable discussion of the issues is available in V. A. C. Gatrell and T. B. Hadden, 'Nineteenth-Century Criminal Statistics and Their Interpretation', in E. A. Wrigley (ed.), *Nineteenth-Century Society: Essays in the Use of Statistical Methods for the Study of Social Data* (Cambridge, 1972), 82–103.

Table 6.3. Indictable offences before the courts by province per 10,000 population, 1884–90

	1884	1885	1886	1887	1888	1889	1890	1884–90
Ulster	326.6	313.5	311.2	329.7	347.3	358.3	394.7	340.2
Munster	463.9	441.3	408.6	332.9	405.8	410.8	496.5	422.8
Leinster	717.2	723.6	710.8	713.9	760.2	745.0	780.4	721.0
Connaught	328.3	304.7	287.6	303.9	293.5	320.5	355.8	313.5
Ireland	464.3	447.0	431.3	436.8	454.2	451.5	507.6	456.1

Source: Figures taken from *Criminal and Judicial Statistics for Ireland, 1885, 1887, 1889, and 1891* (B.P.P., 1886, 77 [cd 4796],17; B.P.P., 1888, 113 [cd 5495]; 17, B.P.P., 1890, 80 [cd 6122], 17–8; and B.P.P., 1890–91, 93 [cd 6511], 18). The figures from 1888 do not include offences tried under the Criminal Law and Procedure (Ireland) Act (1887). This was a coercion measure introduced by the Tory administration to counter organized agrarian protest. For the background see V. Crossman, *Politics, Law and Order in Nineteenth-Century Ireland* (Dublin, 1996), 163–4.

Table 6.4. Relative rates of prosecution for all criminal offences in Ulster counties and police districts, 1884–90

Sub-region	Annual average of prosecutions per 10,000 population
County Antrim	9
County Donegal	11
Carrickfergus Town	15
County Down	21
County Fermanagh	27
County Tyrone	28
County Monaghan	35
County Armagh	40
County Cavan	42
County Londonderry	47
Belfast Police District	55

Sources: As for Table 6.3. The town of Carrickfergus enjoyed county status in this period. The Belfast police district covered the majority of the urban centre in both counties Antrim and Down. Average figures are given to the nearest whole number.

and Armagh seem to suggest that a preponderance of Protestants was no guarantee of conformity with the law. Similarly there seems to be little general correlation between official figures for criminal prosecutions and relative poverty. Comparatively poor Donegal and Fermanagh experienced much lower levels of prosecutions than prosperous Armagh.

Ulster stands out in the nineteenth century for the low levels of agrarian crime committed there, compared to the other Irish provinces. Indeed the levels of reported crime at large in the north were generally lower than the average for Ireland as a whole. However, official statistics suggest that neither with regard to homicides nor crime at large was Ulster the most crime-free province. When compared to levels elsewhere in the United Kingdom, Ulster's crime levels also seem unremarkable.

Between 1884 and 1889 Ulster juries tried five cases per 10,000 inhabitants. In England and Wales, the rate was 4.6.[46]

THE LAW

By and large Ulster was subject to the same code of law as the rest of Ireland throughout our period, and like the court system, much of this was taken from English precedent. However, some pieces of legislation were enacted in the eighteenth century that were limited to Ulster in their competency, and events in Ulster would subsequently on occasion lead to the passing of legislation that would affect Ireland as a whole.

The Oakboy disturbances in Ulster in the 1760s probably played some part in the passing of the first Whiteboy Act in 1766, and agrarian agitation on the Donegall estates in Ulster spawned specific legislation designed to control the disturbances in the 1770s.[47] Political and sectarian disturbances in the north also played a part in the passing of the Insurrection Act in 1796. In the year from March 1796, most of Ulster was proclaimed under the Act, allowing arms to be seized, a curfew to be imposed, and substantial numbers of people to be arrested or simply ordered for transportation or naval service.[48] Other measures, inspired by Ulster's sectarian tensions, would emerge in the nineteenth century.

In 1849 a clash between Catholics and Protestant Orangemen on the 12 July at Dolly's Brae in County Down gave rise to more than a dozen deaths, a government enquiry, a bellicose Orange song, and the Party Processions Act of 1850.[49] Exactly eleven years later a sectarian clash in the north Armagh village of Derrymacash led to a further fatality, another enquiry, and another act of parliament: the Party Emblems Act. The first of these prevented individuals parading with banners, weapons, or music 'calculated to provoke animosity' under penalty of up to a month's imprisonment. The second prohibited the display of any such flags or emblems in a public place, under the threat of the like penalty.[50] Although these measures applied across Ireland and could be used to prevent both Catholic and

---

[46] The figures for England and Wales are taken from *Return of Judicial Statistics of England and Wales, 1885* (B.P.P., 1886, 72), 129. Comparisons of criminal statistics for Ireland and Britain are notoriously difficult. This example uses only cases tried before juries, not those dealt with summarily by magistrates. The more extensive powers given to Irish Resident Magistrates would suggest that these levels would have been considerably higher in Ireland.

[47] J. S. Donnelly Jr, 'Hearts of Oak, Hearts of Steel', *Studia Hibernica*, 21 (1981), 7–73; E. Magennis, 'A "Presbyterian Insurrection"? Reconsidering the Hearts of Oak Disturbances of July 1763', *Irish Historical Studies*, 31 (1998), 165–87.

[48] R. B. McDowell, *Ireland in the Age of Imperialism and Revolution 1760–1801* (Oxford, 1979), 553–6; *Parliamentary Register*, 16 (London, 1780), 12–121.

[49] C. Kinealy, 'A Right to March? The Conflict at Dolly's Brae', in D. G. Boyce and R. Swift (eds), *Problems and Perspectives in Irish History since 1800: Essays in Honour of Patrick Buckland* (Dublin, 2004), 54–78.

[50] N. P. Maddox '"A Melancholy Record": The Story of the Nineteenth Century Irish Party Processions Acts', *Irish Jurist* (new series), 39 (2004), 256–60.

Protestant displays, they had their origins, and were applied with the greatest frequency, in Ulster. They were in truth primarily designed to prevent the holding of provocative Protestant marches, usually organized by the Orange Order, and the display of Orange banners and flags.

Sectarianism in Ulster, or at least the perception of it, also coloured the law as it evolved regarding criminal procedure in Ireland. The case of the Queen v McKenna in 1869, in which the Catholic John McKenna was to be tried for the murder of a Protestant in County Monaghan, led to fundamental changes in the Irish jury system. Following allegations of the packing of the jury with Protestants, legislation was passed to regulate jury selection more carefully, and to allow occupiers of property as well as freeholders and larger tenants to serve.[51]

Sectarian tensions in nineteenth-century Ulster led to changes in the criminal law and procedure in Ireland. These changes were part of a growing divergence between the legal cultures of Britain and Ireland. Thus, arguably, actions taken by Ulster's Protestants with the intention of underlining what they saw as components of their British identity and heritage resulted in Ireland, at least in terms of legal developments, becoming a more identifiably separate entity.

ATTITUDES TO THE LAW AND CRIME

The extent to which the introduction of the common law and its attendant courts were welcomed in Ulster, and how far the law and its administration were seen as legitimate, are key questions. They are also exceedingly difficult to answer. Fynes Moryson had suggested in 1602 that the Gaelic population in Ulster seemed 'to thirst for justice'.[52] The subsequent claim in 1605 by the Lord Deputy that the inhabitants of Ulster would quickly realize the 'benefit and blessings' of living under the new code of law probably referred more to the civil jurisdiction than the criminal, as did Sir John Davies' claim that the Irish courts dealt with a 'multitude of causes', and Sir Thomas Phillips' suggestion that the Irish of Ulster were using the law to defend themselves against the 'wrongs of their chieftains'.[53] At least one modern historian, however, has highlighted how the native population of the north 'generally resorted to the common law' in dealing with all manner of crimes committed against them, and seems to suggest this was perhaps a mark of legitimacy.[54] The fact that in 1641 the Catholic insurgents armed themselves not just with

---

[51] J. P. McEldowney, 'The Case of the Queen versus McKenna (1869) and Jury Packing in Ireland', *Irish Jurist* (new series), 32 (1997), 339–53. Thomas O'Hagan, the author of the measure and the Irish Attorney General, was allegedly the only Irish law officer to sit in parliament in this period (see T. A. Jenkins (ed.), *The Parliamentary Diaries of Sir John Trelawny, 1858–1865* (London, 1990), 204).

[52] F. Moryson, *An Itinerary Containing His Ten Yeeres Travel Through the Twelve Dominions of Germany, Bohmerland, Sweitzerland, Netherland, Denmarke, Poland, Italy, Turky, France, England, Scotland and Ireland*, Vol. 3 (Glasgow, 1908), 213.

[53] Sir Arthur Chichester to Lord Salisbury, 3 July 1605, TNA, SP 63/217/47; Sir John Davies, *A Report of Cases and Matters in Law Resolved and Adjudged in the King's Courts in Ireland, 1604–12* (Dublin, 1762), 5; Sir Thomas Phillips to Lord Salisbury, 19 May 1605, TNA, SP 63/217/30.

[54] Gillespie, *Colonial Ulster*, 111.

weapons but with forged Royal warrants and commissions, implies that although 'the writ of English common law had not run long in Ulster', at least an awareness of legal form was widespread.[55]

In eighteenth-century Ulster, as in the rest of Ireland, the ideal of a disembodied and impartial administration of the law was rarely either desired or sought. It is clear that in the early modern period, patronage relationships played a leading role in the administration of justice, and this was desired by most parties. Such attitudes persisted into the nineteenth century, with landlords and proprietors seeking to protect their own tenants, while being happy to assist them in their struggles against others.[56]

After the Union the state sought actively to intrude in what had been the local world of the criminal law's management and enforcement. The objective was ostensibly to counter the partiality within the system, dominated as it was by Protestants. Many innovations were made, notably the introduction of state prosecution and paid magistrates, as well as the eventual centralizing of policing already mentioned. These changes removed the prerogative of prosecution from the victim and diminished the role of the local justice of the peace in both investigating and trying criminal cases. Public prosecution in a very limited number of cases had emerged from an early date in Ireland, but the establishment of Crown Solicitors in Ireland saw decisions regarding prosecutions as well as their management, shift from the individual to the paid employee of the state. In Ulster, public prosecutors seem to have been established in the wake of the 1798 rising, though the office then lapsed, only to be revived in the early 1830s.[57] 'Stipendiary magistrates' had first been introduced in the eighteenth century, but became more common from 1814, and were effectively replaced by a system of salaried 'Resident Magistrates' (RMs) from 1822. Appointments could initially be made only at the request of local elites, and unsurprisingly they were not common in Ulster. However, by 1837 there had been forty-seven Stipendiary Magistrates appointed across Ireland, ten of whom held office in Ulster. Between 1839 and 1841 sixteen new 'Stipendiaries' were established across the country. Five were appointed in Ulster, of whom two were installed specifically to oversee the implementation of the Party Processions Act.[58]

---

[55] R. Armstrong, *Protestant War: The 'British' of Ireland and the War of the Three Kingdoms* (Manchester, 2005), 18; N. Canny, 'What Really Happened in Ireland in 1641?', in J. H. Ohlmeyer (ed.), *Ireland from Independence to Occupation, 1641–1660* (Cambridge, 1995), 28–30.

[56] See, for example, John Hamilton to Marquis of Abercorn, 3 December 1771, PRONI, T2541/IA1/9/147, Ward to Ward, 23 October 1766, PRONI, D/2092/1//8/112; J. L. Foster, Dunleer, to Lord Oriel, Collon, 8 July 1826, PRONI, D/207/74/212.

[57] J. McEldowney, 'Crown Prosecutions in Nineteenth-Century Ireland', in D. Hay and F. Snyder (eds), *Policing and Prosecution in Britain, 1750–1850* (Oxford, 1989), 340–62; *Account of the Expenditure of Several Sums Issued by the Treasury of Ireland… for Criminal Prosecutions in the years 1801, 1802, 1803 and 1804 respectively* (B.P.P., 1805, 6, 510–11 [cd 119]). The two Crown solicitors on the North East circuit, which covered five Ulster counties, were paid in excess of £10,000 over these four years in fees and expenses. V. T. H. Delaney, *The Administration of Justice in Ireland* (Dublin, 1962), 47–8.

[58] P. Bonsall, *The Irish RMs: The Resident Magistrates in the British Administration in Ireland* (Dublin, 1997), 11–16; *Returns of the Names and Stations of All Persons Appointed Stipendiary Magistrates etc under the Irish Constabulary Bill etc*, (B.P.P., 1837, 46), 335–8; *Return Relating to Stipendiary Magistrates*, (B.P.P., 1844, 43), 513–14.

Work on the courts in other areas of Ireland in the pre-Famine period has stressed the frequency with which all classes took to using the courts of quarter session to pursue their grievances against their neighbours and even their betters.[59] In Ulster too this seems to have been the case. In 1837 Lord Caledon complained to the Chief Secretary about the large number of frivolous cases that were being brought before the County Tyrone courts.[60] Whether such a high level of business indicated an acceptance of the courts or any acknowledgement of their legitimacy is extremely debatable. Ulster's Catholic press frequently expressed their lack of confidence in a system they saw as inherently biased towards Protestants.[61] But such activity does at least testify to the extent to which the law and legal action had permeated Ulster society by the early nineteenth century.

CONCLUSION

The common law and the courts that administered it were late to be established in Ulster, but became widespread very quickly. This rapid spread and the apparently high level of business they dealt with, do not necessarily suggest that there was widespread acceptance of them however. In fact, the evidence suggests that amongst both Catholics and Protestants the acceptance of the rule of law was always qualified by other considerations. Patronage, politics, and religious persuasion perpetually coloured men's expectations of the law. Partly in an attempt to counter this, nineteenth-century Ulster, as well as the rest of Ireland, saw an unprecedented expansion of the central government role in the criminal justice system. This was not always done either successfully or subtly.[62] Moreover, it was not generally welcomed by Ulster's local elites, nor at least initially by the Protestant masses. At the same time there is little evidence to suggest that in the shorter term it ameliorated the position of Catholics to any great degree.

Sectarian tensions shaped and formed the law and policing in Ulster, perhaps to a greater extent than the agrarian conflicts which had such an impact on these elsewhere in Ireland. Agrarian protests across Ireland led to fundamental changes in Irish policing and Irish law, and ensured that these diverged considerably from the comparable bodies and practices in England. Ulster may have experienced less agrarian disorder than the other provinces, but it was replaced as a catalyst for legal and administrative change by conflict between the opposing religious and political groups in the province.

---

[59] R. McMahon, 'The Court of Petty Sessions and Society in Pre-Famine Galway', in R. Gillespie (ed.), *The Re-making of Modern Ireland* (Dublin, 2004), 101–37; D. McCabe, 'Social Order and the Ghost of Moral Economy in Pre-Famine Mayo', in R. Gillespie and G. Moran (eds), *A Various Country: Essays in Mayo History* (Dublin, 1987), 91–112.

[60] Lord Caledon to Lord Morpeth, 20 January 1837, PRONI, D/2433/C/12/2/120. See also, A. MaCartney, Dublin, to [Lord Oriel, Dunleer], 5 July 180, PRONI, D/562/4142A.

[61] See, for example, *Belfast Vindicator*, 22 May 1841; *Newry Examiner*, 30 December 1841, and *Dublin and London Magazine* I (November 1823), 419.

[62] D. S. Johnson, 'The Trials of Sam Gray: Monaghan Politics and Nineteenth-Century Irish Criminal Procedure', *Irish Jurist* (new series), 20 (1985), 109–34.

Despite the element of political rhetoric which liked to declare Ulster to be a notably loyal and law-abiding province, the statistics suggest this was not markedly so. Crime levels may well have been below the national average, but in some areas at least crimes of considerable brutality and notoriety could be committed with apparent impunity. In the mid-eighteenth century an Irish judge on circuit in Ulster chose to draw an equivalence between Protestantism, political loyalty, and a tendency to abide by the law.[63] By the mid-nineteenth century Ulster Protestants were doing this for themselves, and equating the Catholicism that dominated the other provinces with disloyalty and criminality. In the Ulster press, warnings were issued of the 'Romanist threat of resistance to the law', and the wish of the Catholic clergy to 'stand above the law'. Writing of the Land War, a Belfast journalist could refer without any self-consciousness to 'the traditionally loyal and law-abiding province' of Ulster. A Liberal Unionist MP for County Tyrone later reckoned Ulster's Protestants lived in districts 'unstained by crime' for they were 'loyal and law-abiding citizens'.[64] Yet in truth the evidence suggests that the population of the province of Ulster was not a great deal more respectful of the law than that elsewhere in Ireland. William Johnston, a small Protestant landed proprietor from County Down, managed to build an entire political career on his defiance of the 1850 Party Processions Act.[65] Ulster's Catholics, when the occasion allowed, seem to have been just as keen to pack juries with their co-religionists as Protestants were alleged to be.[66] It seems that acceptance of the law in Ulster was largely conditional for all parties.

FURTHER READING

S. Farrell, *Rituals and Riots: Sectarian Violence and Political Culture in Ulster, 1784–1886* (Lexington, 2000).

N. Garnham, *The Courts, Crime and the Criminal Law in Ireland, 1692–1760* (Dublin, 1996).

B. Griffin, *The Bulkies: Police and Crime in Belfast, 1800–1865* (Dublin, 1997).

D. S. Johnson, 'The Trials of Sam Gray: Monaghan Politics and Nineteenth-Century Irish Criminal Procedure', *Irish Jurist* (new series), 20 (1985), 109–34.

---

[63] *The Respective Charges Given to the Grand Jury of the County of Armagh at the General Assizes Held There, 23 July 1763 by the Then Going Judges of Assize Mr Justice Robinson and Mr Justice Tenison: on the Occasion of the Late Commotions in Several of the Northern Counties* (Dublin, 1763), 18. For the same assertion over a century later see the comments of Lord Justice Fitzgibbon in *Belfast News Letter*, 18 July 1882.

[64] *Belfast News Letter*, 1 August 1855, 8 April 1887, and 28 February 1888; *The Graphic*, 16 June 1892. The phrase was almost a cliché by the 1880s (see also *Belfast News Letter*, 12 July 1899 and 18 July 1882; *Aberdeen Weekly Journal*, 7 November 1883; *Glasgow Herald*, 15 May 1883; and *Dundee Courier and Argus*, 23 September 1893). For the phrase's rather sceptical use by the British Liberal and Irish Nationalist press see *Freeman's Journal*, 6 January 1888; *Bristol Mercury*, 27 February 1893; and *North-Eastern Daily Gazette*, 6 May 1882.

[65] A. McClelland, *William Johnston of Ballykilbeg* (Lurgan, 1990); Farrell, *Rituals and Riots*, 154–73.

[66] Vaughan, *Murder Trials*, 133–4.

J. McCavitt, '"Good Planets in Their Several Spheares": The Establishment of the Assize Circuits in Early Seventeenth-Century Ireland', *Irish Jurist* (new series), 24 (1989), 248–78.

J. P. McEldowney, 'The Case of the Queen versus McKenna (1869) and Jury Packing in Ireland', *Irish Jurist* (new series), 32 (1997), 339–53.

E. Magennis, 'A "Presbyterian Insurrection"? Reconsidering the Hearts of Oak Disturbances of July 1763', *Irish Historical Studies*, 31 (1998), 165–87.

7

Popular Culture, 1600–1914

S. J. Connolly and Andrew R. Holmes

CONTRASTING CULTURES

Early modern Ulster was, like other parts of pre-industrialized Europe, a society marked by important cultural distinctions: between the pastimes, customs, and beliefs of the elite and of the common people; between standardized national languages and local dialects; between the written and the spoken word. But it was also a society transformed by massive immigration. By the late 1660s around one-third of the province's inhabitants were British settlers, among whom Scots outnumbered English by around three to two. As demonstrated in Chapter 1, the balance between inhabitants of Irish and British descent was roughly even a few decades later. Contemporaries, even in the nineteenth century, regularly analysed their society in terms of the ethnic divisions resulting from this influx. An account of the County Antrim parish of Killead, written in 1838, presented it as a zone of cultural transition, where the traveller who headed south would note the disappearance of the Scottish accent and perceive 'in their orchards, gardens and taste for planting (particularly the elms in the hedgerows along the roadside), the characteristics of an English colony'.[1] In the same spirit, the Rector of Dungiven, County Londonderry, in 1813, contrasted the 'natural politeness and urbanity' of his 'Irish' parishioners with 'the rough and ungracious salutation but too common among the descendants of the Scotch'. More predictably, he saw a distinction between the steady methodical industry of the latter, and the improvident habits of their neighbours of native descent, who continued their attachment to 'the remains of barbarous tastes and habits derived from their ancestors'.[2] Traditional stereotypes must of course be treated with caution. But the central point remains. A history of mass migration meant that in Ulster, the familiar categories of elite and popular culture co-existed with other lines of division, ethnic in origin though often expressed in terms of religious allegiance, that partly reinforced, and partly cut across them.

---

[1] A. Day, and P. McWilliams (eds), *Ordnance Survey Memoirs of Ireland* (40 Vols, Belfast, 1990–8) [hereafter *OSMI*], 35:17.

[2] W. S. Mason, *A Statistical Account or Parochial Survey of Ireland* (3 Vols, Dublin, 1814–19), [hereafter Mason], 1, 314, 308.

That co-existence complicates what was in some respects a familiar story. The general pattern across western Europe, as outlined in Peter Burke's classic study *Popular Culture in Early Modern Europe* (1979), was for a progressive polarization, as members of the social and political elite withdrew their patronage from popular sports and entertainments, and denigrated or suppressed beliefs and practices in which their predecessors had been happy to participate.[3] It is a process clearly apparent in the linguistic history of Scottish Ulster.[4] Scottish aristocrats and gentlemen granted land in Ulster had initially spoken their own variety of English. In 1624 they had petitioned the Irish council to appoint a clerk capable of dealing with letters written in Scots. Within a few decades, however, the Ulster landed classes, regardless of ethnic origins, spoke and wrote to one another in standard English, and Scots had become the dialect of peasants and tradesmen. In the late eighteenth century, in a second phase of the process analysed by Burke, Scots had reappeared as a literary language, in the work of a new generation of poets. Robert Burns was a specific inspiration, but the broader context was the revival of interest in popular verse forms, traditions, and folklore that Burke has labelled the 'rediscovery of the people'. The elite re-appropriation of Scottish culture continued into the second half of the nineteenth century, including the formation of Burns Clubs in Belfast and its hinterland.[5]

About the internal cultural divisions of the native Irish population much less is known. The surviving sources are those of an intellectual elite, the poets, historians, and genealogists who served the dynastic needs of ruling households, and the judges who interpreted centuries-old and theoretically immutable legal texts. How far the common people partook of a popularized version of this elaborate and fiercely anti-egalitarian culture, and how far they turned instead to their own songs, stories, and traditions, remains unclear. There are, however, indications that by the late sixteenth century, the Gaelic lords even of Ulster were beginning to adopt elements of English dress and manners.[6] In other circumstances, it can be assumed, they would, like their counterparts in Highland Scotland and their Scottish settler neighbours, have come over time to be wholly absorbed into the culture of the metropolitan elite. Instead, military defeat in the period 1595–1603, and again following the civil wars of the middle and late seventeenth century, largely eliminated the native Irish ruling class.

The overthrow of the Gaelic aristocracy left the sophisticated Irish language culture it had patronized in a curious intermediate position. Its practitioners no longer constituted a privileged caste. Instead poets like Art MacCooey (1738?–73) of south Armagh now made a modest living as small farmers, artisans, or even labourers. No longer able to undergo an elaborate training in specialist bardic

---

[3] P. Burke, *Popular Culture in Early Modern Europe* (London, 1979).
[4] P. Robinson, 'The Scots Language in Seventeenth-Century Ulster', *Ulster Folklife*, 35 (1989), 86–99.
[5] F. Ferguson and A. R. Holmes (eds), *Revising Robert Burns and Ulster: Literature, Religion and Politics, c.1770–1920* (Dublin, 2009).
[6] H. Morgan, 'The End of Gaelic Ulster: A Thematic Interpretation of Events between 1534 and 1610', *Irish Historical Studies*, 26 (1988), 8–32.

schools, they wrote in vernacular Irish, and in a simpler and more accessible metre. Their poems dealt in part with the everyday life of the countryside, and with contemporary events such as the agitation of the Hearts of Oak. Some of the more colourful among them, in turn, became figures in popular folklore, remembered as wits, drinkers, or womanizers. At the same time, the literature they kept alive, through the copying and circulation of manuscripts, remained firmly a part of the learned tradition. MacCooey, for example, showed a familiarity with both Greek and Latin literature, as well as with classic Gaelic texts.[7] Against this background it is difficult to know how far his work can be taken as a reflection of the otherwise impenetrable world of the Irish-speaking population. In particular, poems lamenting the vanished Gaelic social order, and looking to a restoration of the exiled Stuarts, have been read in very different ways: as evidence of real and widespread popular disaffection, as largely rhetorical exercises on a traditional theme, or as reflecting the nostalgia of a specific group, the poets, for a lost world in which they had enjoyed a position of privilege and esteem.

This sophisticated literary culture, surviving across decades in an economically deprived and politically marginalized population, testifies to the deep roots and internal coherence of the tradition on which it rested. Yet MacCooey was himself acutely aware of the changes in language and manners taking place, in his own lifetime, within the society in which he lived. Already by the late seventeenth century the native Irish had largely abandoned the distinctive physical appearance—a hanging 'glib' of hair over their foreheads, and a mantle or large cloak—that had set them apart from the settler population. By MacCooey's time, their descendants—broadly to be identified with the Catholic population—were also becoming predominantly English speaking. Already by the 1770s only about 18 per cent of the children born in Armagh, a county where around half of the population were of Gaelic descent, would acquire a knowledge of Irish; by the 1830s the figure would be only 8 per cent. Irish was still the main language spoken in late eighteenth-century Donegal, and was significant in Cavan and Monaghan, but elsewhere it was clearly in retreat.[8] Its decline, in a process familiar in many parts of western Europe, opened the way to the development of a more positive attitude on the part of the social and political elite to what had been part of a despised plebeian culture. A Belfast newspaper in 1805 wrote in support of a sermon in Irish preached in one of the Presbyterian meeting houses, referring proudly to the 'pure stream' of the Celtic language spoken in Ireland, as opposed to the 'dialect' spoken in Scotland.[9] One consequence of this new enthusiasm among members of the

[7] T. Ó Fiaich, 'Art MacCooey and his Times', *Seanchas Árdmhacha*, 6 (1972), 217–50; A. J. Hughes, 'Gaelic Poets and Scribes of the South Armagh Hinterland in the Eighteenth and Nineteenth Centuries', in A. J. Hughes and W. Nolan (eds), *Armagh: History and Society* (Dublin, 2001), 505–57.

[8] G. Fitzgerald, 'Estimates for Baronies of Minimum Level of Irish-Speaking amongst Successive Decennial Cohorts: 1771–1781 to 1861–1871', *Proceedings of the Royal Irish Academy*, C, 84 (1984), 117–55. Fitzgerald's figures relate to individuals born in the decades specified who claimed a knowledge of Irish in censuses from 1851 onwards. In 1861, 49 per cent of the population of Armagh were Catholics. A return by hearth tax collectors in 1732 put the proportion at 35 per cent, but this is likely to have been a significant underestimate.

[9] *Belfast Commercial Chronicle*, 6 July 1805.

educated class was that a new generation of Gaelic poets and scholars found opportunities of employment as aids to antiquarians seeking to explore the Gaelic past. Others, more contentiously, served as teachers or translators for the Protestant missionary societies who in the same period began to look to the Irish language as a tool of evangelization.

PATTERNS OF WORK AND LEISURE

Any discussion of popular culture in early modern Ulster must thus take account of the background of English and Scottish settlement, and the ethnic and religious distinctions it created. At the same time it is also important to recognize the shared features. In particular Catholics, Presbyterians, and Anglicans alike participated in the irregular pattern of leisure and festivity characteristic of a pre-industrialized society: a sparse routine of frugal living and arduous labour punctuated by short bouts of sociability and feasting. The incumbent of the parish of Maghera, writing in 1814, offered a possibly idealized image of a shared calendar of high-days and holidays:

> As to customs, we have no controversy here, about regaling ourselves with the juice of the barley on St Patrick's day; eating pancakes on Shrove Tuesday; a goose at Michaelmas, and nuts and apples on Halloween: on Sunday before Easter, palm twigs; on the 17th of March, a green shamrock; and on the 12th July, orange lilies are worn. On Shrove-Tuesday, and a few days before it, the Roman Catholics usually marry, being prohibited to do so in Lent or Advent.[10]

Easter played a particularly important role in this festive cycle as it 'was one of the few "idle" or free days in the year for the mass of the people'.[11] On Cave Hill outside Belfast, 'the young and old of both sexes' gathered on the Monday and Tuesday for the traditional sport of rolling painted or dyed eggs down the sides of the hill, while 'tents are pitched and spirits and refreshments in great variety are exposed for sale'.[12] Elsewhere too there were assemblies for dancing and festivity, as well as for horseracing and cockfighting. The beginning of May was another shared festival. Denominational differences appeared where Catholics celebrated by the lighting of May Eve bonfires and celebrations round a decorated May bush, whereas Protestants erected May poles on May Day itself. An observer in Ballymoney, County Antrim, on the other hand, was astonished to see the practice of using branches from rowan trees as charms against witchcraft 'kept up by many intelligent persons, and particularly in a district where the great mass of the population are educated. Although the practice is more general amongst the Roman Catholics than any other sect, yet it is not confined exclusively to them.'[13]

---

[10] Mason, 1, 593.
[11] A. Gailey, 'Sources for the Historical Study of Easter as a Popular Holiday in Ulster', *Ulster Folklife*, 26 (1980), 68.
[12] *OSMI*, 2:112.   [13] *OSMI*, 16:19.

May Eve, the ancient Celtic festival of Bealtaine, was of significance as a turning point in the agricultural year, the beginning of summer, and a date on which rents fell due and labourers and servants commenced or ended their term of service. St John's Eve, marked by the lighting of bonfires, was another important landmark, marking the midsummer solstice. Harvest time too came to be associated with popular festivities. In eastern parts of Ulster, the 'churn' or harvest home was popular. The last sheaf was plaited and left in the field by the harvesters who then took it in turns to throw their sickles at the sheaf, and the person who severed it was made the 'harvest king'. He was then paraded to a feast of celebration where he took the seat at the right hand of the master of the harvest.[14] Harvest customs merged with those associated with Halloween. The incumbent of Maghera noted that 31 October 'being Holy Eve, or as the Scotch call it, "hallow-e'en", various tricks are played by the young people, who are anxious to know what husbands or wives they are to get; and some ridiculous and impious means are used, between joke and earnest, to dive into the secrets of futurity'.[15]

Fairs and markets provided other regular sites for sociability and the consumption of alcohol, becoming the focus of much accumulated popular customs. It was noted for Killdrumsherdan in County Cavan that attendance 'at fairs, wakes, weddings and markets are their favourite amusements, where mirth, jollity and dancing abound'.[16] One contemporary simply stated that fairs and markets in Ardclinis were now 'more attended for amusement than business', and resulted sometimes in broken heads.[17] Although many fairs had been long established, others were of a more recent date. The yearly fair at Wooden Bridge, Magilligan, in County Londonderry began in 1800 and attracted hundreds of young men and women to the so-called 'Bridge Dance'. They enjoyed themselves at drinking and dancing, and were 'well supplied with liquors, bread, fruit, gingerbread'. Tents were pitched for eating and drinking, but it was noted that 'None frequent these fairs but the Roman Catholics.'[18]

Festive gatherings of this kind, offering a brief release from an otherwise spartan and laborious daily round, were by their nature likely always to have been boisterous. By the early nineteenth century, however, contemporaries had begun to express growing concern about the level of drunkenness and disorder. Such criticism may in part reflect changes in expectations, due to the drifting apart of elite and popular culture, the growth of evangelicalism in Protestant Ulster, and possibly a new fear of popular disorder following the radical 1790s. Yet evidence of rising consumption of spirits at a national level, and of a marked rise in illicit distilling, especially in the north-west, suggests that popular festivities may in fact have become more frequent and riotous.[19] Brawling was another common feature of the explosive release associated with major festivals. From

---

[14] A. R. Holmes, *The Shaping of Ulster Presbyterian Belief and Practice, 1770–1840* (Oxford, 2006), 90–1.
[15] Mason, 1, 594. [16] *OSMI*, 40:36. [17] Mason, 3, 25. [18] *OSMI*, 11:125.
[19] E. Malcolm, 'The Rise of the Pub: A Study in the Disciplining of Popular Culture', in J. S. Donnelly Jr and K. A. Miller (eds), *Irish Popular Culture 1650–1850* (Dublin, 1998), 65.

the 1780s, this came frequently to take the form of sectarian clashes, occurring on festivals such as 17 March or 12 July, but also on other occasions, as in the clashes between Ribbonmen and Orangemen that took place on three successive fair days at Garvagh, County Londonderry, culminating in the celebrated 'battle' in 1813.[20] The use of firearms, on this and other occasions, reflected an abandonment of traditional restraints driven by religious and political antagonisms. But it would be unwise to discount entirely the element of recreational violence even in the more vicious of the encounters that took place in both town and countryside.

Religious observances also provided opportunity for social interaction and the expression of popular culture. Sunday services provided a regular meeting point for local communities and were an important occasion for display as members of all the churches dressed in their finest clothes.[21] In Presbyterian areas of east Ulster, the practice of retiring from the meeting-house in the interval in the middle of the service provided the occasion for the consumption of alcohol, facilitated by the frequent erection of vending stalls outside the meeting-house gate. An anonymous travel writer visited Broughshane on a Sunday morning in 1812 and observed that 'the people were coming out from worship, between sermons and not a few entering the public-houses; our inn was soon nearly full to the door, old and young merrily sacrificing to the "jolly god", in a manner which fully evinced, that they were "o'er all the ills of life victorious"'.[22] The same features characterized the biannual observance of the sacrament of the Lord's Supper in Presbyterian communities.[23] In areas of dispersed settlement such 'tween sermon' drinking was part of the Sabbath's function in providing 'one of the regular social meeting points in the pattern of rural life'.[24] The same pattern of behaviour was observed in the predominantly Catholic parish of Donaghmoyne in County Monaghan, where after church on Sunday 'they amuse themselves by meeting in large numbers on a road convenient to a public house generally, where they dance, or else by shooting and hunting, football, playing, leaping, throwing the stone. Drinking on that day prevails to a great extent.'[25] Another, distinctively Catholic, fusion of religious and social functions was to be seen in the case of the patterns celebrated at wells and other sites on the feast day of the saint to whom they were dedicated, in which prayer and penitential observance were followed by drinking, dancing and games in a carnival atmosphere.[26]

Another area of parallel or overlapping popular custom was the rites of passage associated with birth, marriage and death. At Maghera, 'Entertainments are given by

---

[20] A. McClelland, 'The Battle of Garvagh', *Ulster Folklife*, 19 (1973), 41–9.
[21] A. Day, '"Habits of the People": Traditional Life in Ireland, 1830–1840', as recorded in the Ordnance Survey Memoirs', *Ulster Folklife*, 30 (1984), 30.
[22] *Belfast Monthly Magazine*, 8 (1812), 368.
[23] Holmes, *Shaping*, 189–90.
[24] A. Gailey, 'Folk-Life Study and the Ordnance Survey Memoirs', in idem and D. Ó hÓgáin, (eds.), *Gold Under Furze: Studies in Folk Tradition* (Dublin, 1983), 153.
[25] *OSMI*, 40:109.
[26] D. Ó Giolláin, 'The Pattern', in Donnelly and Miller (eds), *Irish Popular Culture*, 201–21.

all descriptions of people here at christenings, weddings, wakes, and funerals'.[27] A parade to and from the marriage ceremony was common in many parts of Ulster. Usually referred to as the 'merry convoy', this was often accompanied by gunfire from well-wishers and represented a compelling mixture of festivity, danger, and excitement. A more sedate example may be found in the parish of Bovevagh, County Londonderry, where the 'bridal party march in rank and file to their place of worship and, after the ceremony, solace themselves with bread and butter, tea and whiskey. The Irish always go on foot, the Scotch endeavour to procure a car.'[28] This was a liminal event in which the friends of the couple brought the bride and groom to the place of marriage by means that indicated the transition from one sort of relationship to another. Moreover, there is a clear distinction between the practices of Presbyterians and the Catholics in terms of the financial ability to procure a carriage.

A variety of customs surrounded death and, again, combined both religious and worldly elements. For example, Catholic funerals were often accompanied by *caoineadh*, the so-called 'Irish cry' or keen, a much-noted observance and one that combined religious devotion, performance, and melodrama.[29] The experience of death is most associated with the wake, which, as an account from Maghera shows, took on distinctive characteristics depending on the religion of the deceased. 'The Irish wake here, as well as elsewhere, is a scene of mirth rather than sadness.' The body was laid out on the earth with a sheet and two candles while 'pipes, tobacco and snuff' were passed around. Whiskey drinking had, however, declined as it had been prohibited by the Catholic clergy because it was 'found to be the cause of riot and other improprieties'. The Presbyterian wake was 'conducted with profound silence and great decorum'. Refreshments were available in another room, though rarely taken, and Bible reading was a common feature. The wakes of members of the Church of Ireland differed little from those in other parts of Ireland though they are 'somewhat less expensive and more solemn than those of the south or west'.[30] The evident bias of the author in favour of the Protestant wakes overlooked the devotion of Catholics and the mixture of religion and worldliness amongst Protestants. An essential element of the wake was social interaction amongst neighbours, friends, family, and the occasional stranger. The night was passed in various ways—drinking and feasting, story-telling, practical jokes, and lengthy discussions.[31] The Presbyterian wake was intensely scripted and involved traditional forms and rituals, including readings from the Bible and psalm singing. Alongside the appropriate behaviour and religious devotion were business transactions, joking, pranks, and drunkenness. It is clear that the wake with its combination of both sacred and secular elements was an important occasion for small rural communities of whatever religious persuasion.

---

[27] Mason, 1, 595.   [28] *OSMI*, 25:26.
[29] P. Lysaght, '*Caoineadh Os Cionn Coirp*: The Lament for The Dead in Ireland', *Folk-Lore*, 108 (1997), 65–82.
[30] Mason, 1, 595–6.
[31] G. Ó Crualaoich, 'The "Merry Wake"', in Donnelly and Miller (eds), *Irish Popular Culture*, 173–200; Holmes, *Shaping*, 231–8.

To this cycle of holidays and festivals, many of them long established, there was added during the eighteenth century a significant new element, the rise of literacy levels and the emergence of a printed popular literature. A study of leases in rural north-west Ulster shows that the proportion of Protestant tenants signing by name rather than mark rose from 69 per cent in the period 1750–79 to 83 per cent by the early nineteenth century; among Catholics the increase was from 35 per cent to 64 per cent.[32] The new taste for reading inspired a growing trade in chapbooks, small cheaply produced volumes distributed by pedlars or sold in local shops. The content in many cases testified to an earnest desire for self-improvement, offering guides to polite conduct, manuals of arithmetic, and compendia of useful knowledge, as well as a wide range of religious texts. Criminal biography, a popular genre throughout the Europe of the period, included James Cosgrove's *Irish Rogues and Raparees*, a version of which was published in Belfast in 1776. What is most striking, however, is the presence among the texts known to have circulated in Ulster of material whose origin did not lie in the popular culture of any society: versions of classical texts such as the fables of Aesop, and cut down versions of medieval chivalric romances such as *Valentine and Orson*, and the *Seven Champions of Christendom*.[33] Here, with the advent of the commercialized production of materials for a mass audience, the question of how popular culture is to be defined takes on a new complexity. The observances of May Day, or the customs of the wake, may well have been modified over time by contact with, or pressure from, the authorities in church and state. But their origins clearly lay in the population among whom they were kept up. The chapbook, however, like the music hall performance or penny dreadful of the next century, was a cultural product for, but not of, the mass public to whom it was addressed.

POPULAR CULTURE UNDER ATTACK

In November 1799, the owners of the Belfast provision merchant business Cavan and Heron petitioned the Lord Lieutenant to suppress the races due to be held at Ballyhackamore, a few miles outside the town, later in the month. Otherwise they feared that their employees, 'coopers and butchers, cutters, salters and packers to the number of four hundred and upwards', would abandon their work and spend not just one week but two 'in disputation and drunkenness', while the firm's beef would rot, 'being a perishable commodity, and your memorialists so circumstanced that they cannot stop a day without being much inconvenienced'.[34] Their memorial was a striking early instance of the conflicts that arose as a new type of economic

---

[32] G. Kirkham, 'Literacy in North-West Ulster 1680–1860', in M. Daly and D. Dickson (eds), *The Origins of Popular Literacy in Ireland: Language Change and Educational Development 1700–1920* (Dublin, 1990), 73–96.

[33] J. R. R. Adams, *The Printed Word and the Common Man: Popular Culture in Ulster 1700–1900* (Belfast, 1987).

[34] Memorial of Cavan and Heron, 14 November 1799, National Archives of Ireland, Rebellion Papers 620/56/83.

enterprise found the traditional irregular pattern of work and leisure no longer adequate for its needs. The trend towards a stricter labour discipline was often linked to mechanization, making it necessary to coordinate the labour of workers with the expensive running of machinery. But even without mechanization, large-scale production, as in the case of Cavan and Heron, made it impossible to tolerate the casual habits of an earlier age. Already by 1840, before the coming of the powerloom, weavers in Belfast and elsewhere were being coerced into entering 'factories' or 'lock ups' where they could be subjected to the discipline of fixed hours and constant supervision.[35] Employees with more bargaining power, grouped in smaller workshops, could retain the old ways for longer. As late as 1838, the Presbyterian temperance advocate John Edgar complained that 'whole classes of tradesmen' in Belfast 'spend in idleness and dissipation the Monday and very frequently the Tuesday'.[36] For most, however, the fixed working day had by this time become all but inescapable.

The curtailment of leisure in the first half of the nineteenth century, and the consequent decline of traditional amusements, was not confined to the industrial population. For those engaged in agriculture, too, falling prices in the period following the Napoleonic Wars forced people to work longer hours while leaving less spare money for leisure activities. Investigators for the Ordnance Survey in the middle and late 1830s repeatedly commented on the reduced level of popular amusements. The Memoir of Ballymartin in south Antrim written in December 1838 noted that the taste of the local Presbyterian population 'for recreation has, owing to the pressure of the times and the want of the means of enjoying themselves, considerably declined of late years'.[37] There was also a tightening of control from above. In the years following the rebellion of 1798, traditional gatherings for amusement were for a time discouraged. The establishment of the county constabulary in 1822, and even more of the Irish constabulary in 1836, led to stricter controls on public houses and the suppression of public drunkenness, brawling, and other forms of public disorder. In Belfast, the town police, established in 1816, took on the same role as 'domestic missionary' as the police forces of other industrial towns, acting not just to pursue criminals and preserve public order, but to clear the streets of drunkards, prostitutes, and other nuisances, and to suppress or regulate public gatherings for amusement.[38] Legislation against 'party processions', in force in 1832 and again from 1850, curtailed what had become a central part of Ulster's festive calendar.

The clergy of all denominations were a further important influence. Internal reform within the Church of Ireland, and the rising influence of evangelicalism within the Protestant denominations in general, encouraged a new spirit of pastoral

---

[35] *Hand Loom Weavers Commissioners, Part 3* (B.P.P., 33, 1840), 633–5, 641, 666, 717–18.
[36] *Select Committee of Enquiry into Drunkenness* (B.P.P., 8, 1834), 71.
[37] *OSMI*, 2:9.
[38] B. Griffin, *The Bulkies: Police and Crime in Belfast 1800–1865* (Dublin, 1997). See R. D. Storch, 'The Policeman as Domestic Missionary: Urban Discipline and Popular Culture in Northern England, 1850–1880', *International Review of Social History*, 9 (1976), 481–509.

zeal, and a determination to improve popular morals.[39] On Devenish island in Fermanagh, 'the cruel amusement' of cock-fighting on Easter Monday had been ended 'owing to a strong sense of religion, strengthened by the spirit and necessity of industry'.[40] At Desertlyn in County Londonderry: 'They have not now any regular amusements: going to fairs, dancing, assembling at Easter have been almost totally given up, partly from the increased habits of industry and partly from the exertions of the clergy.'[41]

One area of particular concern to the Presbyterian clergy was the reform of the traditional wake. From the mid-1820s, church courts began to publish resolutions committing themselves to the reform. The arguments against these practices were a mix of religious, economic, and social concerns. Carntall congregation in County Tyrone produced a resolution in 1831 declaring that whiskey drinking at wakes was

> injurious to the temporal and spiritual welfare of society; it tends to harden the mind against all the solemnities of death and eternity; it is distressing to the afflicted feelings of the relatives of the deceased; it is a serious inconvenience to many families by subjecting them to an unnecessary expense; and it cannot possibly be productive of any good to the community.

Moreover, they considered 'the practice of assembling publicly at wakes' to be 'injurious to the morals of the people, and annoying to the relatives of the deceased'. Reform seems to have had a bigger impact upon the mood and decorum of the wake than on the consumption of alcohol, and it is important to appreciate the scale of the task facing reformers. Individuals risked losing face by declaring adherence to principles that were not generally held by the local community. Many Presbyterian ministers realized that reform would be a long-term undertaking and that a flexible approach was needed to deal with the sensibilities of rural communities. In a letter to the recently installed minister of Islandmagee in 1829, Henry Cooke stated that wakes ought to be discouraged but that if the local custom was for the minister to attend then he should do so. Once there, he should follow Cooke's example and refuse to take alcohol or 'dainties', and should seek to preach in the house. Cooke's practice was then to bring the corpse to the meeting-house where he could perform a religious service before the committal. 'Introduce no violent departure from old custom, except where it is sinful; but introduce improvement gently and rationally, and God will bless your labours. Substitute for the late hours of wakes something better as soon as you can; but even that do with caution, lest your good be evil spoken of.'[42]

The Catholic clergy continued to be hampered by lack of manpower and resources, but there too the early nineteenth century saw a drive to raise pastoral standards, as well as a more critical attitude to popular amusements.

---

[39] S. J. Connolly, *Priests and People in Pre-Famine Ireland 1780–1845* (2nd edn, Dublin, 2001); Connolly, *Religion and Society in Nineteenth-Century Ireland* (Dundalk, 1985); D. Hempton and M. Hill, 'Godliness and Good Citizenship: Evangelical Protestantism and Social Control in Ulster, 1790–1850', *Saothar*, 13 (1988), 68–80.
[40] Mason, 2, 195–6. [41] *OSMI*, 31:47. [42] Holmes, *Shaping*, 236–8.

The local priest at Magilligan succeeded in ending drunkenness at funerals, and in Termoneeny the funeral cry was 'now seldom heard'. Hymns had been introduced, 'and the change, although not so impressive and characteristic, is calculated to inspire a more religious train of ideas'.[43] The gatherings at Struel Wells in County Down, once not only tolerated but actively supported by local clergy, were likewise suppressed.[44] Even Lough Derg, long regarded as the premier centre of pilgrimage in Ireland before 1845, underwent significant changes between 1750 and 1850.[45] The observances became less demanding as reformers tried to bring them into line with Tridentine norms. The reformers reduced the duration of the pilgrimage, closed the purgatorial caves, taught the catechism, and placed a renewed emphasis on receiving the sacraments worthily. In addition, the Mass of the Dead was set aside along with naked public emersion, the superstitious use of pebbles, and the general mood of religious enthusiasm.

The image of a vibrant, unruly popular culture undermined and constrained by the combined forces of economic change, political repression, and a newly censorious religious establishment is a familiar one, closely mirroring the analysis offered for Great Britain by the social historians of the 1960s and 1970s.[46] More recent research, however, has substituted a more complex narrative that recognizes continuity and adaptation as well as suppression, and that acknowledges the agency of plebeian populations in the reshaping of their own culture in the face of changing circumstances.[47] To see a decline in heavy drinking or in support for blood sports as evidence solely of 'social control' exercised from above is to make the arbitrary assumption that those involved were incapable of developing their own aspirations to a more humane and orderly existence for themselves and their children.[48] In the same way, reports in the 1830s that Presbyterians in County Antrim had abandoned dances and other formerly popular social gatherings in favour of singing schools devoted to sacred music must be recognized as testimony, not just of the repressive efforts of evangelical ministers, but to a shift in popular religious sensibilities and recreational tastes.

Perhaps the clearest indication of the changes that took place in popular preferences and aspirations was the emergence in the late eighteenth century of reading societies and book clubs. Many were initially associated with political radicalism, but by the early nineteenth century they had become centres for the discussion of

---

[43] *OSMI*, 6:126. [44] Connolly, *Priests and People*, 146, 147, 149.

[45] J. S. Donnelly, 'Lough Derg: The Making of the Modern Pilgrimage', in W. Nolan, L. Ronayne, and M. Dunlevy (eds), *Donegal: History & Society. Interdisciplinary Essays on the History of an Irish County* (Dublin, 1995), 491–508.

[46] This literature is surveyed in J. Sharpe, 'Popular Culture in the Early Modern West', in M. Bentley (ed.), *Companion to Historiography* (London, 1997), 361–76.

[47] J. M. Colby and A. W. Purdue, *The Civilisation of the Crowd: Popular Culture in England, 1750–1900* (rev. edn, Stroud, 1999); T. Harris (ed.), *Popular Culture in England, c. 1500–1850* (Basingstoke, 1995).

[48] F. M. L. Thompson, 'Social Control in Victorian Britain', *Economic History Review*, 34 (1981), 189–208.

useful knowledge and religious seriousness.⁴⁹ In Articlave, County Londonderry, for example, a reading society was established in 1825 by young men seeking improvement of themselves and 'others less favourably circumstanced'. The society quickly flourished owing to the exclusion of discussion of religious or political topics. There was concern amongst some that this society took attention away from reading the Bible, but 'with greater propriety might it be said that the time spent reading our books would be spent in the *alehouse*, the *country dance* or perhaps at the *card table*'. Out of the 450 volumes in the library, there was plenty for the farmer, mechanic, astronomer, and geologist, who could be induced by no earthly power 'to quit such a mental feast and join the *heart-sickening, soul-destroying* revel…of a country alehouse carouse'.⁵⁰ Another noticeable instance of a change in personal standards of behaviour was the extension of the temperance movement amongst upper-working class and middle-class Catholics and Protestants.⁵¹ Alcohol by no means disappeared from popular culture, but traditional habits were now in contest with impulses towards new ideals of self-discipline and respectability whose origins lay, not just in the influence of philanthropists and reformers, but within popular culture itself.

One further change in popular culture that was well under way by the 1830s was a marked reduction in the province's linguistic diversity. The Scottish element in rural Presbyterian speech was to remain clear, but its features were being softened. Whereas the inhabitants of Dunaghy, County Antrim, spoke English 'with a mixture of Scotch', producing 'a disagreeable jargon', the broad Scotch of the inhabitants of Anahilt, in neighbouring County Down, was giving way to a milder accent owing to 'the intercourse created by increasing trade, and good roads'.⁵² Meanwhile Irish was in steep decline. The Rector of Dungiven noted in 1813 that although the people of the mountains spoke a 'very pure dialect' of Irish, all of the men and many women spoke English 'which the necessity of transacting business in the low lands, obliges them to adopt'.⁵³ Where one in five Ulster children born in the 1770s acquired a knowledge of the language as they grew up, the same was true of only one in twelve of those born in the 1830s. How far those of English or Scottish descent who modified their speech did so consciously is not clear. A manual advising inhabitants of Belfast how to rid their speech of tell-tale provincialisms appeared in 1860, but it is likely to have been aimed at a middle or lower middle-class readership.⁵⁴ What is almost certainly true, however, is that those who made the transition from Irish to English, or made sure that the latter only was transmitted to their children, did so in the belief that they were adopting the language of opportunity.

---

⁴⁹ J. R. R. Adams, 'Reading Societies in Ulster', *Ulster Folklife*, 26 (1980), 55–64; Holmes, *Shaping*, 279–81.
⁵⁰ *OSMI*, 11:67–8.
⁵¹ E. Malcolm, *'Ireland Sober, Ireland Free': Drink and Temperance in Nineteenth-Century Ireland* (Dublin, 1986).
⁵² Mason, 1, 259; 2, 16.   ⁵³ Mason, 1, 320.
⁵⁴ D. Patterson, *The Provincialisms of Belfast and the Surrounding Districts Pointed Out and Corrected: To Which is added an Essay on Mutual Improvement Societies* (Belfast, 1860).

CONTINUITY AND CHANGE

Alongside the changes arising both from outside and within popular culture, it is also necessary to acknowledge the continuities. In particular it is important to note the persistence of the rural character of the Ulster population. In 1881 less than a quarter of the population of Ulster lived in settlements of over 2000 individuals. Neal Garnham has noted that this fact, in conjunction with others, helps explain the persistence of blood sports in Ulster despite the efforts made to eradicate behaviour now seen as brutalizing and unacceptably cruel.[55] Similar themes can be seen in the adaptation of calendrical customs to the new moral order.[56] Traditional harvest pastimes such as the churn were replaced by harvest thanksgiving services in Presbyterian congregations. Decorations of fruit, vegetables, and elaborate straw work were retained but placed within the confines of a church building and under the superintendence of religious professionals. The paraphernalia associated with Christmas was another adaptation to the new century. Traditionally against the observance of the festivals of the Christian year, Presbyterians in the late nineteenth century gradually began to hold religious services on Christmas Day, at the same time as the festival itself was becoming increasingly commercialized.

Even in the more disruptive context of Belfast's expansion from medium-sized commercial centre to industrial giant, adaptation was as important as suppression or decline. The gatherings on Cave Hill on Easter Monday, the most important date in the festive calendar, continued into the 1850s, despite sporadic attempts at obstruction by reformers and local landowners. Their decline thereafter was due to the rise of an alternative attraction, the public pleasure gardens created on the flat expanse of reclaimed land, created by recent harbour improvements, known as the Queen's Island, where visitors paying a penny admission, and another penny for the ferry, could enjoy a small zoo, an amusement arcade, and other facilities. The pleasure gardens disappeared after 1880, as Harland and Wolff's shipyard took over the Island, but already before then their attractions had given way to other venues. On 14 April 1879 eight ferries were deployed to carry visitors to what was to be the last Easter Monday on the Island. However these, a newspaper suggested, were mainly country folk attracted by its former reputation. For the people of Belfast themselves, with factories and warehouses closed and shops open only up to noon, there was a range of alternative venues: two pantomimes at the Theatre Royal, a circus in the Ulster Hall, and a special programme at the Alhambra music hall. Out of doors the largest crowds assembled at the Botanic Gardens, to watch races and acrobatic displays, as well as 'boxing, fencing, broadsword and bayonet exercises' provided by soldiers from the local regiment.[57]

---

[55] N. Garnham, 'The Survival of Popular Bloodsports in Victorian Ulster', *Proceedings of the Royal Irish Academy*, C, 107 (2007), 107–26.

[56] P. S. Robinson, 'Harvest, Halloween, and Hogmanay: Acculturation in Some Calendar Customs of the Ulster Scots', in J. Santino (ed.), *Halloween and Other Festivals of Death and Life* (Knoxville, Tenn., 1994), 3–23.

[57] *Belfast News Letter*, 15 April 1879.

From one perspective, of course, the evolution of Easter Monday represented a domestication, even a neutering, of popular culture. What had been a boisterous plebeian festival had become a matter of attendance, as passive spectators, at commercialized entertainment; or admission, on condition of good behaviour and under the watchful eye of park keepers, to the carefully laid out lawns and flower beds of the Botanic Gardens or the city's gradually increasing number of public parks. But this was a development rooted in the changing circumstances of the working classes themselves. The old festive calendar, with its brief periods of explosive release, had represented the safety valve that sustained a regime of long hours of labour for sparse reward. By the last quarter of the century, factory legislation, although formally applying only to women and juveniles, had in practice reduced the hours worked by male factory operatives from fourteen to twelve, with a Saturday half-holiday. By the end of the century most workers also received a week's paid holiday.[58] As a result sea-side towns like Portrush and Donaghadee, already popular through the cheap day excursions offered by the railways from the 1840s onwards, were now able to reach a new level of development as holiday resorts for the urban working class.

The other key development was the rise from the 1850s of working class spending power. In Belfast in particular, the growth of shipbuilding created an elite of skilled workers. Wages for the unskilled were by contrast low by the standards of the United Kingdom as a whole, but the employment provided for women and children in the linen mills ensured relatively good family incomes. It was against this background of increased leisure and modest prosperity that new venues for entertainment developed. The small, gloomy drinking dens so often condemned by temperance reformers gave way to the public house, with its bright lighting reflected in mirrors and polished mahogany, a place where alcohol was still central but new standards of behaviour nevertheless applied.[59] As early as the 1830s some larger establishments had operated as 'singing saloons', offering music and other forms of entertainment. In 1873 Belfast got its first music hall, with the opening of the Alhambra Theatre, whose programme soon included stars of the English musical hall circuit, such as Harry Lauder, as well as home-based performers offering material tailored to local tastes. Music halls also provided the initial venue for what was at first the novelty of cinematography, seen for the first time in Belfast in 1896. In 1908, however, Belfast became the site of the first full-time cinema in Ireland, located in St George's Hall, High Street.[60]

The commercialization of leisure time was also reflected in the emergence of spectator sports. The Gaelic Athletic Association, after some false starts, made some progress in Ulster from 1898 onwards. However, its spread was inhibited both by its associations with political nationalism and by strong local opposition

---

[58] D. L. Armstrong, 'Social and Economic Conditions in the Belfast Linen Industry, 1850–1900', *Irish Historical Studies*, 7 (1951), 235–69.
[59] J. Gray, 'Popular Entertainments', in J. C. Beckett et al. (eds), *Belfast: The Making of a City* (Belfast, 1982), 103.
[60] M. Open, *Fading Lights, Silver Screens: A History of Belfast Cinemas* (Antrim, 1985).

to Sunday sports.[61] Instead it was association football that became the preferred entertainment of both Protestant and Catholic working classes, particularly in Belfast, where the founding meeting of the Irish Football Association took place on 18 November 1880. What this meant in practice was that sectarian and political divisions found expression within a shared sporting culture. Already by 1899 the Belfast teams of Celtic and Linfield were recognized as representing opposing political allegiances, while engaging a stranger in a conversation about football quickly emerged as one way of ascertaining his religion.[62] Nor was this the only way in which changing patterns of popular culture had a political as well as a recreational significance. The parading tradition, liberated from restraint by the repeal of the Party Processions Act in 1872, reached a new level of development. Cheap rail travel turned local demonstrations, both Orange and nationalist, into mass rallies. Crude displays of party colours and small assemblages of instruments gave way to elaborately decorated banners and the formation of well-organized bands of skilled performers. The organizations concerned, such as the Orange Order, the Apprentice Boys, and the Ancient Order of Hibernians, offered much the same mixture of sociability, entertainment, and opportunities for display as the brass bands and friendly societies that had by the same period become a staple of working-class culture in the commercialized and industrialized society of late Victorian and Edwardian Britain. But their proceedings also reflected the distinctive features that politics and history had given, in the case of Ulster, to what was recognizably a variant of that culture.

FURTHER READING

S. J. Connolly, *Religion and Society in Nineteenth-Century Ireland* (Dundalk, 1985).
M. Daly and D. Dickson (eds), *The Origins of Popular Literacy in Ireland: Language Change and Educational Development 1700–1920* (Dublin, 1990), 73–96.
J. S. Donnelly and K. A. Miller (eds), *Irish Popular Culture 1650–1850* (Dublin, 1998).
F. Ferguson and A. R. Holmes (eds), *Revising Robert Burns and Ulster: Literature, Religion and Politics, c. 1770–1920* (Dublin, 2009).
N. Garnham, *Association Football and Society in Pre-Partition Ireland* (Belfast, 2004).
A. R. Holmes, *The Shaping of Ulster Presbyterian Belief and Practice, 1770–1840* (Oxford, 2006).
P. Robinson, 'The Scots Language in Seventeenth-Century Ulster', *Ulster Folklife*, 35 (1989), 86–99.

---

[61] D. McAnallen, 'Michael Cusack and the Revival of Gaelic Games in Ulster', *Irish Historical Studies*, 37 (2010), 23–47.
[62] N. Garnham, *Association Football and Society in Pre-Partition Ireland* (Belfast, 2004), 64.

8

Urban Ulster since 1600

R. J. Morris

INTRODUCTION

The urban history of Ulster has an easy periodization. The seventeenth century was one of plantation and the destructive fight for domination; the eighteenth was the age of the merchant and the market town; the nineteenth saw the rise of the industrial urban system; and the twentieth, beginning in 1920, brought fragmentation, contest, de-industrialization, and armed urban conflict, leaving Ulster to puzzle out the meaning of postmodern urbanization. Such an account conceals the many processes and systems embedded in each period as well as basic continuities.

In his purposeful *A Discoverie of the True Causes why Ireland was never entirely subdued, nor brought under Obedience of the Crowne of England until the beginning of his Majesties happie Raigne*,[1] Sir John Davies wrote, 'The natives of Ireland never performed so good a work as to build a city...there were never any corporate towns erected in the Irish Countries.' Sir John's urban theory was clear. English conquest would be a success if they had 'granted them [the Irish] Markets, Fayres, and other Franchises, and erected Corporate Towns among them...assuredly the Irish Countries had long been reduced to Peace, Plenty, and Civility, which are the effect of laws and good government'. Sir John was not being quite fair. Ireland and Ulster entered the seventeenth century with the elements of earlier urban systems. Ulster had been least amenable to English conquest and culture. This was reflected in the minimal indications of urbanism. References to boroughs in pre-1500 Irish records found fifteen for Ulster, all but one in Antrim and Down. Even Connacht scored higher at eighteen, whilst Leinster had 147 and Munster 70.[2]

Ulster started the century with a limited, marginal, and highly specific experience of urbanization. The raths and castles of Gaelic culture provided little stimulus to urban growth. The Anglo-Norman system along the east coast, fortified and fought over, was dominated by Carrickfergus, Downpatrick, and Newry. Armagh was distinctive. The cathedral and other religious establishments generated a sacred economy of educational and devotional activities, food, clothing, and skilled crafts.

---

[1] The first edition was 1612. See pp. 86 and 120 of the 1761 edition.
[2] G. Martin, 'Plantation Boroughs in Medieval Ireland', in D. Harkness and M. O'Dowd (eds), *The Town in Ireland* (Belfast, 1981), 23–54; B. Graham, 'The Evolution of Urbanisation in Medieval Ireland', *Journal of Historical Geography*, 5 (1979), 111–25.

At Downpatrick and Newry, Cathedral and Abbey supplemented the Anglo-Norman fort as the base of an urban economy.[3]

To the distinctive if marginal urban system of 1600 were added the plantation towns of James I. 'Plantation' was an important though not the only factor in the urban development of seventeenth-century Ulster, nor was it always decisive. The plantation towns were seen as a means of destroying the power, culture, and economy of the Gaelic Earls and 'native' society. The initial plans outlined in early 1609 had a comprehensive and coherent rationality. Corporate towns were central to the project of domination, legitimacy, and economic development.

Plantation began with main force domination but the strategy depended upon moving from this to economic development and political integration with England's Dublin-centred government. The eighteen towns of the final 1611 plan were to have a supporting land grant and be allocated to 'undertakers' who would supply capital, settlers, and organization. The target was forty or more houses, preferably built of stone, together with a church, burial ground, school, market place, and streets. The reward for achieving this was corporate status, giving the settlement a legal status to own, buy, and sell property, the right to hold markets and fairs, to create and enforce by-laws, to hold local small debts courts and, importantly, to send MPs to the Dublin parliament.[4] The charter granted to Armagh in 1613 gave details. It established a self-electing Corporation and a small debts court. The Oath of Supremacy, objectionable to Catholics and Presbyterians alike, ensured that the Corporation would send to Dublin MPs loyal to the Episcopalian settlement.[5]

The plantation of 1609–11 was part of a longer-established process of domination by urbanization, reaching back into the Elizabethan period. Warlords like the Bagenals in Newry and Chichester in Belfast established towns independent of the plantation. Sir Thomas Smith's disastrous attempt to establish Elizabetha in the Ards had an intellectual clarity inspired by his classical learning. 'England was as uncivil as Ireland until colonies of Romans brought their laws and orders.'[6] As with the Romans, a 'strong town' would create order and discipline leading to economic development, integrating urban and rural.

PLANTATION AND THEORIES OF URBANIZATION

The processes involved in the urbanization of Ulster can be identified through the theories of Max Weber with his interest in systems of domination and legitimacy. Main force was not an end in itself. Success depended upon a

[3] C. McCulloch and W. H. Crawford, *Armagh,* Irish Historical Towns Atlas, no.18 (Dublin, 2007); T. Canavan, *A Frontier Town. An Illustrated History of Newry* (Belfast, 1989), 32–55; R. H. Buchanan and A. Wilson, *Downpatrick,* Irish Historical Towns Atlas, no.8 (Dublin, 1997); P. S. Robinson, *Carrickfergus,* Irish Historical Towns Atlas, no.2 (Dublin, 1986).

[4] P. Robinson, *The Plantation of Ulster* (Belfast, 1994), 150–64; 'A Project for the Division and Plantation of the Escheated Lands of six several counties of Ulster', as printed in *Hibernica or some ancient pieces relating to Ireland* (Dublin, 1770), 110.

[5] J. Stuart, *Historical Memoirs of the City of Armagh* (Newry, 1819), Appendix 22.

[6] H. Morgan, 'The Colonial Venture of Sir Thomas Smith in Ulster, 1571–1575', *Historical Journal,* 28 (1985), 261–78; M. Dorrian, 'On Some Spatial Aspects of Colonial Discourse on Ireland', *Journal of Architecture,* 6 (Spring 2001), 27–51.

consequent market-led development and legitimation by law and ideology. The urban place was a combination of the fort and the market, of main force, and of the search for profit, to which might be added the 'temple' and the legitimacy of the sacred. The proto-urban economies of the fort and the 'temple' provided a base from which the more complex and varied economy of the urban could develop.

The outcomes of the plantation were uneven. The coherence and rationality of the initial scheme were compromised early on. Ecclesiastical claims on land interfered with the links between urban corporations and supportive land grants. Few were to have 'liberties' on the model of medieval Carrickfergus. Pynaar's Survey of 1619 showed many places were undercapitalized. The Oath of Supremacy required by the initial charters worked to exclude, thus there was little chance of testing theories of integration by urbanization held by the likes of Sir John Davies. Success was greatest when linked with existing urban activity, as in Armagh. Plantation sites were rarely placed in empty space. The selected sites were linked to the existing proto-urban activity of the fort, 'temple', or market. Others exploited positions on strategic and trade routes. A few disappeared leaving little more than a paper record with the occasional remains of a fort. Some became regional administrative and market centres, minor players in the imposition of English systems of law and governance.

The system was tested by the multiple contests which swept across seventeenth-century Ulster. The theory that towns would provide refuge and shelter for the 'civilized' settler population had limited outcomes. In 1641 Armagh and Newry provided little protection for those sheltering from rebellion. Derry had the resources to provide effective refuge. Towns were a significant locus of economic and cultural fixed capital, and targets for any assertion of domination. Avoiding burning and massacre required a mixture of good fortune and skill on the part of urban governors. Belfast proved skilled in this art of survival. The pro-Catholic charter of James II was accepted then rejected depending on whose army was dominant. The Covenant was burnt at the Restoration. The Chichesters were tolerant.[7] They asserted absolute power over urban government, especially in selecting MPs to send to Dublin. In return for their entry fine, the freemen were free of many tolls and taxes, and Chichester did not bother them with awkward oaths. There were no political restrictions on the recruitment of mainly Presbyterian merchants, whose task was to make profits and improve the Chichesters' rent income. The ability to avoid internal and external confrontations served Belfast well, especially in the competition with much-burnt Newry. Once established, the post-plantation urban system proved remarkably robust in the face of seventeenth-century conflict. Many urban centres were variously captured, recaptured, burned, and besieged. Despite this, the major centres maintained their places in the urban hierarchy, suggesting that, with the possible exception of Derry, they had little dependence on fixed capital and that success derived from social capital and reliable trading relationships (see Table 8.1).

---

[7] J. Agnew, *Belfast Merchant Families in the Seventeenth Century* (Dublin, 1996).

Table 8.1. Urban hierarchy of Ulster, 1659

Towns	1659 Poll Tax (number of persons)	Charter	County
Derry	1052	1613	Londonderry
Carrickfergus	962	medieval	Carrickfergus
Coleraine	633	1613	Londonderry
Belfast	589	1613	Antrim
Armagh	409	1613	Armagh
Lisburn	357	1662	Antrim
Downpatrick	308	medieval	Down
Enniskillen	210	1613	Fermanagh
Killyleagh	175	1612	Down
Newry	174	1613	Down

Source: P. Robinson, *The Plantation of Ulster* (Belfast 1994), 225–7.

The 'census' of 1659, probably a count of adult males for poll tax purposes, provided an indicator of the developing urban hierarchy of Ulster. In the seven counties for which records survive, 9 per cent of those counted in the poll tax were urban, although most towns were tiny compared to England and Scotland. This contrasts with studies, albeit with more precise definitions, for England where 14 per cent of the population were in places of more than 5000, as were 9 per cent of Scotland's population.[8]

The most spectacular success was Derry. In part this derived from a position on a sheltered estuary with access to the growing Atlantic trade. In part it was the availability of capital from the Corporation and Companies of London. This provided not only the steady accumulation of an urban infrastructure of stone houses and institutional buildings, but also substantial walls and fortifications. Success was also based upon the thorough manner in which the Corporation and Guilds reorganized the countryside by creating a hierarchy of fortress city, village, and bawn.

Small towns were as crucial to the success of the plantation project as the major centres. In 1600, Cavan inherited a variety of proto-urban assets. There had been various monasteries and at least two castles. There were already regular markets linking the Gaelic economy with Dublin. As part of the plantation and the grant of a charter in 1613, Cavan acquired a church, a school, a session house, and a gaol. Places like Cavan provided the Episcopalian ascendancy with several assets. Church and school provided cultural authority, reinforced by local landowners like Lord Farnham who episodically provided local collective capital. Through the regular holding of courts, petty sessions, assize, and quarter sessions, Cavan ensured the dominance of English common law. Corporation officials like the weighmaster

---

[8] P. Griffiths, J. Landers, M. Pelling, and R. Tyson, 'Population and Disease, Estrangement and Belonging, 1540–1700', in P. Clark (ed.), *The Cambridge Urban History of Britain*, Vol. 2 (Cambridge, 2001), 195 and 384; I. D. Whyte, 'Scottish and Irish Urbanization in the Seventeenth and Eighteenth Centuries', in S. J. Connolly, R. Houston, and R. J. Morris (eds), *Conflict, Identity and Economic Development. Scotland and Ireland, 1600–1939* (Preston, 1995), 24–28.

and petty sessions clerks, ensured a trustworthy environment for the local market economy. For much of the next two hundred years it was a garrison centre which boosted the local economy and provided additional security to the market economy.[9]

The shape of the towns which emerged from this process reflected the variety of ideas and influences which lay behind the plantation and related projects. Some, like the Chichesters in Belfast, adopted the high street with burgage plot and back lanes familiar in English and Scottish market towns. This provided numerous high-prestige, high-value frontages onto the main street and an extensive back of the street for storage, final processing, and accommodation for servants. Others, like Derry, adopted the Roman or colonizing form of a compact town, approximating to a grid with the 'diamond' at the centre for the market and buildings of authority. Armagh was unique with a circular form that responded to topography and the inspiration of the sacred site.[10]

By the mid-eighteenth century, the Ulster town began to reflect the hopes of the idealistic theorists of the sixteenth and seventeenth centuries. The 'fortress' function began to create conditions in which the market prospered. By mid-century, an increasing number of urban places achieved a 'generative' economic function. The towns had partial success in imposing Episcopalian military and political authority and in reducing violence as a means of resolving disputes. Their courts and markets ensured that, at least within the urban context, contract, property rights, and economic exchange were secured under a system of law and profit-seeking. In short, they offered a culture of wealth accumulation and profit-seeking within a framework of capitalist economic opportunities. The towns were key agents in the economic successes of eighteenth-century Ulster.

The Ulster town became the means of organizing the economy of the surrounding countryside and providing links with the wider world in terms of trade, law, and politics. Exports included grain, ham, bacon, butter, and hides. Imports involved luxury and fashion goods. The 1766 local census of Armagh recorded an economy led by merchants, professional people, and tradesmen. Shoemakers and dressmakers provided services to the surrounding countryside.[11] The Corporations managed collective property and appointed officials. In the 1830s, the commons were managed in boroughs with surviving land rights. Belturbet appointed a 'herd' to look after and regulate the cattle on the common. Enniskillen directed the rent from the commons 'to keep in repair the streets' and finance a butter market.[12] Active corporations appointed a clerk of markets and a weighmaster. Regulating weights and measures was crucial to the integrity of the market. A few places like Cavan provided street cleaning. Most earned the criticism of Belturbet where 'it is

---

[9] T. S. Smyth, *Civic History of the Town of Cavan* (Dublin, 1938); R. Gillespie (ed.), *Cavan: Essays on the History of an Irish County* (Dublin, 1995).
[10] G. Camblin, *The Town in Ulster* (Belfast, 1951), 82–3 and 92–3.
[11] L. A. Clarkson, 'Armagh 1770: Portrait of an Urban Community', in D. Harkness and M. O'Dowd (eds), *The Town in Ireland* (Belfast, 1981), 81–102.
[12] *Municipal Corporations, (Ireland). Appendix to the First Report of the Commissioners. Part III. Conclusion of the North-Western Circuit* (B.P.P., 24, 1836), 1066.

considered to be part of the Provost's duty to see to the cleanliness of the town. He does not attend to it.'[13] The major prize was linen. Landlords like Chichester in Belfast (1738) and de Clifford in Lisburn (1755) promoted linen halls. Success with linen was based on the relationships of urban place, landlord, and smallholder weaver/spinner tied together by a network of merchants and bleachers. In Lurgan, the Brownlows used the cashflow of the landed estate to promote the trade. The agents provided finance in return for bills of exchange on London, which provided a means of transmitting rent income to the metropolitan social hub of many landowners. Such a system increased the landowners' potential rents and supplemented the income of farming families. There was little need for the banking functions provided by elite merchants in many English eighteenth-century towns.[14]

There was always a tension between on the one hand, the Corporation with its Charter as a means of imposing Episcopalian and Hanoverian authority, notably in the delivery of MPs to the Dublin parliament, and, on the other hand, as an authority for ensuring orderly profit-seeking activity. The urban power monopoly depended upon exclusions sanctioned by Charter and accompanied by petty restrictions. Most towns excluded Catholics from any status or office. Belturbet refused to allow the purchase of one of the town lots as a site for a Catholic place of worship.[15] The market economy could subvert the sectarian one. In the 1750s, Thomas McCann renounced his Catholic faith in the cathedral in Armagh, paving the way for transforming his economic success into social status as burgess and sovereign of the borough.[16] Catholics tended to gather at the edge of the legal boundaries of urban economy and space, creating suburbs after an established European pattern, accommodating those excluded from the legal status of citizen. In Belfast and Derry, Catholic areas such as Short Strand, the Markets, and Bogside still mark eighteenth-century boundaries.

The patron-landlord borough with its closed corporation and nominated MPs was not unique to Ulster but it was more thorough there in its application and anxiety to resist change. It faced a middle class gaining in wealth and confidence, resentful and impatient with landlord dominance and increasingly seeking ways to break the power monopoly, especially where an extension of local collective action and provisions was wanted. Shrewd patrons organized items of collective capital such as the new butter crane provided by Lord Kilmorey on the canal at Newry.[17] The most important means of circumventing the patron-controlled borough was the development of an associational culture within a growing civil society. At Enniskillen, dissatisfied with the corporation and the Earl, 'the inhabitants themselves associate to prevent or detect fraud, forming a market jury'.[18] The London Hibernian

---

[13] *First Report of the Commissioners appointed to inquire into the Municipal Corporations in Ireland* (B.P.P., 27, 1835), 961.
[14] W. H. Crawford, *The Impact of the Domestic Linen Industry in Ulster* (Belfast, 2005), 69.
[15] *First Report of the Commissioners appointed to inquire into the Municipal Corporations*, 986.
[16] Clarkson, 'Armagh 1770'.
[17] T. Bradshaw, *The General Directory of Newry, Armagh* (Newry, 1820), xix.
[18] *Municipal Corporations, (Ireland). Appendix to the First Report of the Commissioners. Part III* (B.P.P., 24, 1836), 1087.

Society supported schools in Ballymena and Cavan. Dungannon had a dispensary and, like Armagh and Warrenpoint, a Trustee Savings Bank under the 1819 legislation.[19] In Armagh, the Association for the Suppression of Street Begging was based upon 'mutual agreement among the more wealthy part of the citizens'. This culture of the meeting, the subscription, and the committee was inspired by examples in England, Scotland, and Dublin. The open, self-financing committee suited those familiar with the organizational structures of the Presbyterian Church with its self-directing, self-governing congregations. The most distinctive element of Ulster urban culture was the Volunteer movement. The unit raised in Armagh in 1776 was 'unpaid and unbought'. Their self-directing ambitions operated between the power structures of state and patron. They appointed a secretary and elected a committee. State and aristocracy were reluctant in their approval of military units run by committee.[20]

Belfast used the full repertoire of strategies for countering the sterility of patron and closed corporation. The Charitable Society (1752), the Harbour Commissioners (1785), and the Police authorities (1800) all used combinations of subscriber, ratepayer, and representative authority supported by Acts of Parliament.[21] Belfast generated the fullest and most sophisticated list of associations including a Chamber of Commerce (1783), the Belfast Savings Bank (1816), and the General Hospital, supported by subscription and opened in 1817. Among vice presidents of the Hospital were the mayor (a Chichester), two bishops (Catholic and Episcopalian), and two moderators. The Belfast Library and Society for Promoting Knowledge (founded 1788) met in the Linen Hall. The committee and officers were elected annually. Such societies not only generated the opinions and interactions of a public sphere but also provided new urban infrastructure in the form of public walks, race meetings, and assembly rooms. In the 1820s, the Commercial Buildings were added to Belfast's collective resources. Financed by shares of £100 each, the Ionic pillars of the frontage projected an image of taste and authority.[22] Chichester or his nominees were given ex-officio positions in many of these bodies. Sustaining such social and collective capital was a subtle blend of ratepayer politics, subscriber associations, and the power and spending of the patron.

The census of 1831 recorded radical changes in the urban hierarchy since the seventeenth century. Characteristic was the small settlement with a market. Of the 67 places claiming the title 'town', 50 were less than 2000 in population. Antrim, with 25 per cent of the population in places over 1000 in population, was the most heavily urbanized county, followed by Down (14 per cent), and Londonderry (11 per cent). Cavan, Donegal, and Fermanagh had pre-industrial levels of under 5 per cent. The dominance of Belfast was accompanied by the recovery of Newry, with

---

[19] Bradshaw, *The General Directory*, xx, 34, 61, and 131.
[20] Stuart, *Historical Memoirs*, 478–565.
[21] R. W. M. Strain, *Belfast and its Charitable Society. A Story of Urban Social Development* (London, 1961), 46–7; R. Sweetnam, 'The Development of the Port', in J. C. Beckett *et al.*, *Belfast: The Making of the City, 1800–1914* (Belfast, 1983), 58; B. Griffin, *The Bulkies: Police and Crime in Belfast, 1800–1865* (Belfast, 1997), 10.
[22] *The Belfast and Province of Ulster Directory for 1852* (Belfast, 1852), esp. 435–54.

its canal, improved harbour, and position on the road to Dublin. New arrivals included the packet station at Donaghadee and the Belfast industrial suburb of Ballymacarrett. Portadown benefited from linen, agricultural produce, the local distillery, the Tyrone coal mines, and the canal link to Newry. Armagh was still a major religious centre as well as a marketing hub and rentier residence. Belfast leadership was not simply a matter of size and associational culture, but in the quality of the built environment and urban infrastructure. Belfast Corporation spent annually £255 per 1000 population and only 1.4 per cent of the houses were thatched. Elsewhere thatched houses were 14 per cent in Derry, 32 per cent in Lisburn, and 64 per cent in Enniskillen. Ratepayers spent little in local services: £86 per 1000 per year in Derry, £26 in Lisburn, and £7 in Enniskillen.[23]

THE INDUSTRIAL URBAN SYSTEM

During the nineteenth century, the Ulster urban system was transformed by industrialization. By 1901, 31 per cent of Ulster's population lived in places of more than 5000 people. With a 1901 population of 349,180, Belfast dominated Ulster, nine times its nearest rival Derry, and nearly equal to Dublin, where if the suburban municipalities are included, the total was 375,135 (see Table 8.2).

This was a very ordinary European experience. Slowly and decisively, industry came in from the countryside. The density of interaction of the urban place provided easier access to knowledge and new technology, better supervision of production and quality, access to support services and industries, as well as labour supply and infrastructure. Each place gained specializations. Lurgan, where the powerloom weaving factory arrived in 1855, was for hem-stitching and handkerchiefs,

Table 8.2. Urban hierarchy of Ulster, 1901

Town	Population 1901	Rank 1831	Population 1831	Change 1831–1901 (%)	Women per 100 men in 1901
Belfast	349,180	1	53,287	556	116
Derry	39,892	3	10,130	294	118
Newry	12,405	2	13,065	−5	117
Lurgan	11,782	22	2842	315	126
Lisburn	11,461	8	5218	120	120
Ballymena	10,886	13	4067	168	121
Portadown	10,092	15	3794	166	121
Newtownards	9110	12	4442	105	124
Armagh	7588	4	9470	−20	109
Coleraine	6958	7	5752	21	125

Source: Calculated from the Census of Ireland, 1901.

[23] *Parliamentary Representation, Ireland. Further returns...Reports from Commissioners and Plans* (B.P.P., 1831–2, 43).

although many manufacturers continued dealing with country weavers. At least one handloom weaving factory existed in the 1880s, suggesting that supervision was as important as technology for the urbanization of industry. Lisburn was noted for thread, and Newtownards for factory weaving and bed quilts. Like other industrial towns, Ballymena continued as marketplace and supplier to the countryside. John Kane made agricultural machinery at Harryville Bridge. At Lurgan, grass seed, butter, eggs, straw, potatoes, turnips, and pigs were traded.[24]

As in most of Europe, population growth depended upon migration as well as natural increase. Migrants came from the surrounding countryside. In 1881, after a period of rapid growth, 77 per cent of the population of Belfast was born in Antrim, Down, and the Borough of Belfast. Some 14 per cent came from the rest of Ulster, mainly Armagh and Tyrone, and only 3 per cent from Ireland outwith Ulster, 2.7 per cent from England and Wales, and 2.4 per cent from Scotland. As with many textile industry towns, there was a substantial female bias in the population (see Table 8.2). Ulster was perhaps distinct in the extent to which technology and entrepreneurs were imported. For a generation, Belfast led with cotton technology imported from Lancashire before settling on the wet spinning of flax brought from Leeds. Merchants such as Samuel Graeme Fenton, Leeds evangelical Tory and later mayor of Belfast, were key to the transference of such technologies. In Derry, the Glasgow connection was crucial for the shirt industry.

The impact of industry on Ulster towns was very uneven. In 1901 Belfast, 73 per cent of the occupied population was in 'manufacturing'. Amongst women, 43 per cent were in textiles. The male structure was more varied. Initially a support industry for textiles, machine making generated its own external income-earning sector, employing 4.4 per cent of males. By 1891, Combe Barbour Ltd at the Falls Foundry supplied a world market with textile machinery. Firms like Henry Matier had factories in Lurgan and Dromore, and palace-like warehouses and showrooms in Belfast. Benson's in Fountain Street supplied their patent hem-stitching machinery to the factories of Lurgan and beyond.[25] Many skills transferred to the shipbuilding sector, which accounted for 5 per cent of employed males. Equally prominent was the employment offered by the internal economy supplying housing, clothing, and food. Over 10 per cent of males were employed in 'housing, furniture, and decorations'. In Derry, only 63 per cent of the occupied population was in manufacturing; 45 per cent of women were in 'dressmaking', mostly the shirt factories. Males were heavily dependent on the internal and support economy. The limited specialization at the lower end of the labour market was indicated by the 20 per cent of males whose occupation was 'general and unspecified'. Enniskillen lay at another extreme: 27 per cent of occupied males were in 'defence' and almost none in textiles, machine making, or shipbuilding. Amongst women,

---

[24] G. H. Bassett, *The Book of County Armagh. A Manual and Directory* (Dublin, 1880); *The Book of County Down. A Manual and Directory* (Dublin, 1886); *The Book of County Antrim. A Manual and Directory* (Dublin, 1888). All reprinted Belfast, 1988.

[25] *The Industries of Ireland, part one. Belfast and the Towns of the North* (London and Belfast, 1891), 66, 92, and 95, reprinted with introduction by W. H. Crawford (Belfast, 1986).

50 per cent were domestic servants. Comparable figures were 17 per cent in Belfast and 29 per cent in Derry.

The timing and context of Ulster urbanization created a distinctive urban labour market, especially in Belfast. Belfast population growth rates were 43 per cent in the 1860s and 36 per cent in the 1890s, rates not experienced by the likes of Glasgow since the early decades of the century. The wage structure of Belfast was equally distinctive. In 1885, in both engineering and building industries, skilled wages in Belfast were equal if not higher than those in Glasgow, but for unskilled labour the rates were substantially lower. The explanation was partly the shortage of skilled labour in Ireland but also the low-income rural labour market. Inequality and late development accounted for some of the best housing conditions in the industrial United Kingdom, along with pockets of squalid conditions. In 1905, 55 per cent of Glasgow's population lived in one- and two-roomed houses. In Belfast, 59 per cent had five rooms, in brick-built terraced and yarded by-law houses. For a three-roomed house, rents were around 7 shillings in Glasgow and as low as 3 shillings in Belfast.[26]

The increasing scale, density, and complexity of Ulster urbanization was accompanied by fundamental changes in urban governance. This operated within a framework of Westminster legislation, Dublin Castle supervision, and intense localism. For most urban places the key legislation was the *Act to make Provision for the lighting, cleansing and watching of Cities, Towns, Corporate and Market Towns in Ireland* [9 George IV, *c.* 82], 1828, and the *Towns Improvement (Ireland) Act* of 1854. Parallel to these was legislation regulating the election of members to Westminster (1832) and to Municipal Corporations (1840). The thrust of this legislation was to place authority in the hands of bodies elected by property-tax payers rather than borough patrons. Income came from local property taxes (the rates) rather than tolls and rents. Detailed order was imposed on the urban place. There were provisions for sewers, lighting, paving, water and gas supply, for public clocks, the making of maps, the naming of streets, and the numbering of houses. Powers were taken to prevent the sale of unwholesome meat and adulterated food and to control the location of noxious trades like blood boiling and tallow melting. There were clauses against 'furious driving' and powers to 'prevent the obstruction of the streets...in all times of public processions, rejoicings or illumination' as well as powers to arrest 'common prostitutes' found 'loitering'. Under the 1854 Act, settlements needed a population of 1500 to seek the quasi-autonomy of being a 'town' with Commissioners. The fears and prejudices of Dublin Castle were reflected in two sorts of clauses. One excluded 'any Ecclesiastic of any religious Denomination' from being town commissioners. Others gave votes to property holders in towns and boroughs but required them to live within five miles of the town or seven for boroughs.[27]

---

[26] A. C. Hepburn, *A Past Apart: Studies in the History of Catholic Belfast* (Belfast, 1996), 47–136; R. J. Morris, 'Inequality, Social Structure and the Market in Belfast and Glasgow, 1830–1914', in S. J. Connolly, R. A. Houston, and R. J. Morris (eds), *Conflict, Identity and Economic Development. Ireland and Scotland, 1600–1939* (Preston, 1995), 189–203.

[27] Details from the text of the legislation; also M. Potter, *The Municipal Revolution in Ireland. A Handbook of Urban Government in Ireland since 1800* (Dublin, 2011).

When the public servants, attorneys, and administrators of Dublin Castle came to review their handiwork in the 1870s, they were less than satisfied. Ulster had proved especially adept at preserving the inconsistencies, privileges, and exclusions of locality. William Neilson Hancock was a Dublin Castle man who had spent much effort on improving the regulation and audit of Irish local government. He had introduced public health legislation based on English examples. His vision of urban government was based upon the rule of law and clear procedures. Legitimacy was derived from the inclusive representation of citizen property owners. He sought transparency based upon public meetings, audited accounts, and regular record keeping.[28] Ulster gave him little satisfaction. Carrickfergus survived with its medieval boundaries and incomes almost intact by using a transitional procedure of the 1840 Act and doing nothing until the legislation of 1898 forced change. The bulk of their £1162 income was financed from property, land, and houses.[29] Overlapping jurisdictions proved a nightmare for the men from Dublin Castle and local policy ambitions alike. In Lisburn, responsibilities were divided between Town Commissioners, the Court Leet of the Manor of Kilultagh, and the Grand Juries of Counties Antrim and Down. Simple matters like paving for some footpaths proved impossible.[30] In places, urban change defeated policy, such as the Whig ambition of encouraging the responsible leadership of wealthy elites. The five and seven mile limits were designed to exclude absentee property owners, but with the coming of railways, increasing numbers of the elite lived in villas away from the towns where their economic interests lay. Warrenpoint and Newry, like Bangor and Belfast, were tied together by economics and commuting but separated by local governance.

In Belfast, the pressures of urbanization and the tensions and ambitions of Ulster society came together with massive intensity. From the 1840s, Protestant Conservative politicians and municipal officials manipulated the voter registration process with a skill that almost totally excluded Liberal and Catholic representation.[31] The outcome was a tangled culture of accusation. Enquiries of the 1870s were told of the 'timber ring' dominating the Improvement Committee to the benefit of a select group of builders and property developers. There was perpetual mistrust over the location of urban assets. Catholic spokesmen believed that the Ormeau Park was favoured over Falls Park, that the Shankill had a mains sewer whilst the Falls Road did not.[32] In such an atmosphere, opposition took the form of legal action. With the confidence typical of many one-party regimes, the Belfast

---

[28] *Report from the Select Committee on Local Government and Taxation of Towns (Ireland); together with the proceedings of the committee, minutes of evidence, and appendix* (B.P.P., 1876, 10). Evidence of William Neilson Hancock.

[29] *Returns of Local Taxation in Ireland, for the year 1876* (B.P.P., 1877, 71).

[30] *Report from the Select Committee on Local Government and Taxation of Towns*, QQ 881–9.

[31] I. Budge and C. O'Leary, *Belfast Approach to Crisis: A Study of Belfast Politics, 1613–1970* (London, 1973); S. Baker, 'Orange and Green: Belfast, 1832–1912', in H. J. Dyos and M. Wolff (ed.), *The Victorian City* (London, 1973), 789–814.

[32] *Local Government and Taxation of Towns Inquiry Commission (Ireland). Part II. Report and Evidence, Belfast, Trim and Wicklow* (B.P.P., 1877, 40). See in particular the evidence of Bishop Dorrian, QQ. 1629–1644.

administration made a re-allocation of funds from the purchase of gas works to the development of markets in a manner that breached the precise terms of the enabling legislation. The opposition went to the Chancery Court in Dublin which imposed massive financial penalties on the councillors involved. The debilitating row lasted from 1855 to 1864.

In Belfast, as in many places, municipal ambition proceeded through a series of local acts of parliament, but progress was hindered in a variety of ways. The Blackstaff River and its tributary, the Pound Burn, had been recognized as a growing source of pollution and flooding since the 1840s. Plans for intercepting sewers and culverting were continually delayed. Cost was always an issue. The mill owners objected to losing the water supply for their boilers whilst they poured heated sewage back into the river. Excuses and denials were frequent. Montgomery, the Borough Surveyor, claimed the rate of growth of Belfast was so rapid that it was impossible to keep control of building standards and prevent houses being occupied before paving, drainage, and sewerage were complete. Despite its size and wealth, Belfast was never able to generate a tradition of professional independent public servants, men like J. D. Marwick, Town Clerk, who guided Glasgow to its reputation as 'best governed city in the world'. The Medical Officer of Health was downgraded to 'consulting sanitary officer'. The Borough Cashier gained continual salary increases despite or perhaps because of his political services. The greatest failure of all was in policing. There was no equivalent of the local watch committees common across Scotland and England. Dublin Castle took control in 1865. Local aldermen resented paying for police they did not control and claimed a lack of Royal Irish Contabulary (RIC) interest in enforcing local by-laws. Others welcomed the RIC which they saw as impartial and not prone to bribery.[33]

Urban government in Ulster achieved much, despite difficulties, intensified where the jealousies and fears of religion and nationalism met problems familiar in all industrial urban systems. Lurgan was an early taker for the 1854 Act. Industrial culture for Lurgan was not simply a matter of factories, powerlooms, and mechanical stitching. It was part of the infrastructure of pipes and wires, of ceramics and cast iron. Gas lamps and flushing sewers arrived in the 1850s. A new architecture of authority included a town hall, police barracks, workhouse, and court house to challenge Lord Lurgan and Brownlow House.[34] Increased spending from the rates was uneven. In 1901, places like Belfast, Newry, Lurgan, and Derry were spending over £90 per 100 population, whilst Antrim, Downpatrick, and Cookstown were below £15.[35] In Belfast, the infrastructure of an industrial regional metropolis slowly emerged under a triumvirate of Municipal Corporation, Water Commissioners, and Harbour Commissioners. The slow growth of the sewer network included the

---

[33] Ibid. Q. 1944.
[34] Bassett, *County Armagh, A Guide and Directory*; Craigavon Historical Society, <http://www.craigavonhistoricalsociety.org.uk>.
[35] *Returns of local taxation in Ireland for the year 1899–1900* (B.P.P., 1902, 88); 1902 [Cd. 1123] *Census of Ireland, 1901. Part I. Area, houses, and population: also the ages, civil or conjugal condition, occupations, birthplaces, religion, and education of the people. Vol. III. Province of Ulster. No. 1. County of Antrim* (B.P.P., 1902, 126).

culverting of the Blackstaff in the 1880s. The Gas Works were purchased in 1875 and the trams in 1904, taking over initially private enterprise. The Harbour Commissioners and Municipal Corporation used powers of land assembly, demolition, and long-term finance to reform the layout of the city centre and extend the port. From the 1840s, skilful spatial manipulation created new spaces for consumption, commerce, and circulation, blocking areas of social and sanitary disorder. New markets had curbed the expansion of Catholic settlement in the Cromac area in the 1840s, and Royal Avenue destroyed much of Hercules Street in the 1880s. The most spectacular contribution was the new City Hall of 1906.[36] Portland stone was the Edwardian choice for municipal assertion. The commonest municipal spaces were markets. There were twelve in Belfast by the 1870s. Markets were tucked around the centre in Lurgan, Portadown, and Downpatrick. The priority for governance in Ulster towns was still to enable orderly conditions for marketing.

Ulster failed to create any consensus in matters of urban order. Before 1850, places like Belfast experienced levels of disorder quite comparable to other industrial centres like Bristol and Manchester. After 1850, Ulster failed to follow the liberal bargain of the English and Scottish urban. Considered as a system of domination, the triumph of Ulster urbanization was in the manner in which it had incorporated the bulk of the population into a market economy driven by price, private property, and the search for profit and cash income. Less success marked the progress towards cultural and political integration. Civil society was divided and weakened by the attenuated development of Catholic and of working-class labourist institutions, whilst the cautious alliance of Episcopalian and Presbyterian cultures offered only conditional commitment to a civil society based upon consensus, pluralism, and the rejection of non-legitimate main force. In Glasgow, the football clubs were divided by religion but played in the same football league. The Orange Order and Irish nationalist organizations were active there, but Glasgow street demonstrations for the radical reform of parliament raised ten times more support than the Orange walk, and a labour culture incorporating a wide range of Scottish and Irish cultures dominated the 1930s.[37]

THE URBAN IN TWENTIETH-CENTURY ULSTER

The year 1921 was marked by the partition of Ulster and of an urban system which had worked as part of Irish, British, and Atlantic systems. The Orangemen of Cavan like the Nationalists of Derry looked anxiously across a new national border.[38] The census of 1971 reflected the major trends. The majority of the population in

---

[36] Beckett et al., *Belfast*; J. Bardon, *Belfast: An Illustrated History* (Belfast, 1982); S. A. Royle, *Belfast, Part II, 1840–1900*, Irish Historic Towns Atlas, no.17 (Dublin, 2007).
[37] J. Smith, 'Labour Tradition in Glasgow and Liverpool', *History Workshop*, 17 (Spring 1984), 32–56 and 'Class, Skill and Sectarianism in Glasgow and Liverpool, 1880–1914', in R. J. Morris (ed.), *Class, Power and Social Structure in British Nineteenth-Century Towns* (Leicester, 1986), 157–203.
[38] P. Shea, *Voices and the Sound of Drums: An Irish Autobiography* (Belfast, 1981).

the six counties which formed Northern Ireland was urban, with 63 per cent living in places of more than 5000. The Belfast urban area claimed 35 per cent of the province's population. The Borough of Belfast had lost population since 1951, but still held 24 per cent of the Northern Ireland population, more than six times the share of Derry.[39] By 2001, 65 per cent of the Northern Ireland population was classified as 'urban', but the integrity of the town as a distinct unit was dissolving, as was the clear distinction between urban and rural upon which the 1898 local government reforms had been based. This was recognized by the local government reforms of 1973 which created twenty-six regional council areas centred on urban places. The blurring and porosity of urban boundaries was most evident around Belfast. Belfast Local Government District (LGD) lost population between 1971 and 2001, but the Metropolitan area gained to take 34 per cent of the Province's population. The population of Belfast LGD was 47 per cent Catholic but was surrounded by a ring of Protestant LGDs, such as Carrickfergus, 9 per cent Catholic, and Newtonabbey, an amalgamation of new suburbs (19 per cent Catholic). These were all tied together by flows of people, information, and materials. The flows of population each day across LGD boundaries were massive. Belfast had a daytime working population of over 170,000, but only 45 per cent of these were resident in the Borough. Only 37 per cent of Protestants working in Belfast lived within the LGD. The figure for Catholics was 55 per cent.[40]

In England and Scotland, the energies and sense of collective state purpose released by two world wars, were directed towards major changes in health, housing, education, and welfare. In Northern Ireland, such energies were directed towards creating a stable and secure Protestant state.[41] The insecurity of the new statelet was dominated by a contest for space. The urban place, its streets, governance, and infrastructure were key stakes in this contest: a contest carried on by main force, constitutional manipulation, and clientistic politics. The structure of urban governance was much as it had been set by the 1898 reforms, modified only by boundary and voting changes, which ensured Protestant electoral domination, even in places with modest Catholic majorities. The Poor Law survived until 1949, its urban management so insensitive that in 1932 Protestant and Catholic working-class politics were briefly united in protest.[42] Welfare politics, especially in matters of housing, were subordinated to the felt need for political assertion and an ideological reluctance to accept the need for state intervention. As the Westminster government moved in 1924 to promote local authority responsibility for housing, the Northern Ireland state continued to rely on meagre subsidies for private builders. There was little interest in following Westminster legislation on slum clearance and overcrowding, and none of the innovative housing developments of a Liverpool,

---

[39] P. A. Compton, *Northern Ireland: A Census Atlas* (Dublin, 1978), 15; W. E. Vaughan and A. J. Fitzpatrick (eds), *Irish Historical Statistics: Population, 1821–1971* (Dublin, 1978), 47.

[40] *Northern Ireland Census, 2001. Migration, Travel to Work and Workplace Population Report.* Northern Ireland Statistics and Research Agency, <http://www.nisra.gov.uk/Census/>.

[41] P. Bew, P. Gibbon, and H. Patterson, *Northern Ireland, 1921–1994* (London, 1995); M. Farrell, *Northern Ireland: The Orange State* (London, 1980).

[42] P. Devlin, *Yes, We Have No Bananas: Outdoor Relief in Belfast, 1920–39* (Belfast, 1981).

Leeds, or Vienna. Infant mortality rates and the incidence of tuberculosis, a disease which thrived on urban density and crowding, remained significantly above the levels of other industrial cities in the United Kingdom.[43] The inadequate response to German air raids in 1941 was another indicator of a minimalist urban policy.[44]

Like the Northern Ireland statelet, urban government evolved as semi-democratic one-party states. Contested elections declined as each unit identified itself with one ethnic political grouping or another. Maurice Hayes provided a sharp account of the culture of municipal Ulster as it evolved in the Catholic authority of Downpatrick. He became Town Clerk in 1955, a post his father had held before him. He was effectively 'interviewed' by the councillors who attended his father's wake, but still went through the process of canvassing the councilors, which was part of all local authority appointments. By the 1960s, the allocation and management of housing was a major part of the council's work. Hayes, an able and well-liked man, began to apply for jobs in larger authorities. After a failed application to Craigavon New Town, he was told he was 'not strong in Bible studies', a clear code saying that a Protestant authority did not appoint Catholics.[45]

The uneasy sectarian solitudes of the 1950s and 1960s came to a brutal end in 1969. Thirty or more years of conflict and warfare followed. The formation of the Provisional IRA and various Protestant paramilitary groups in the 1970s was the first time that Irish armed resistance to the state had been essentially urban. This time land laws and flying columns were irrelevant.[46] The stakes, strategies, and locations were urban. The spark for the conflict had been the allocation of local authority housing. Ultimately the outcomes were shaped by the urban context of the fighting and violence involved. Some of this was a matter of detail. Soldiers were issued with special padded gloves so they could adopt the firing position on hard urban pavements without damaging their hands. The course of firefights was influenced by the inability to determine the direction of hostile fire as gunshots echoed around densely packed buildings.[47] The conflict was framed by basic features of western European industrial urbanization. The anonymity of the city was mixed with the knowingness of neighbourhood. Whistles and dustbin lids tracked the movement of military patrols. Visitors and strangers were challenged and questioned. Gossip and rumour identified members of different organizations and passed judgement on their activities. The anonymity of the city allowed the transport of arms and bombs but meant it was impossible to avoid the death and injury of the uninvolved and one's 'own side'.[48] The city depended upon density coupled

---

[43] A. Murie, W. D. Birrell, P. A. R. Hillyard, and D. Roche, 'Housing Policy between the Wars: Northern Ireland, England and Wales', *Social Policy and Administration*, 5 (October 1971), 263–97.
[44] B. Barton, *The Blitz. Belfast in the War Years* (Belfast, 1989).
[45] M. Hayes, *Minority Verdict: Experiences of a Catholic Public Servant* (Belfast, 1995), 18–62.
[46] P. Bew, P. Gibbon, and H. Patterson, *The State in Northern Ireland, 1921–72* (Manchester, 1979), 30.
[47] Colonel M. Dewar, *The British Army in Northern Ireland, Arms and Armour* (London, 1996), 88 and 111.
[48] M. O'Doherty, *The Telling Year, Belfast 1972* (Dublin, 2007); C. de Baróid, *Ballymurphy and the Irish War* (London, 1989); Captain R. J. Elliott, 'Countering Urban Terrorism', *British Army Review*, 64 (April 1980), 16–24; A. Edwards, 'Misapplying Lessons Learned? Analysing the Utility of British Counterinsurgency Strategy in Northern Ireland, 1971–76', *Small Wars and Insurgencies*, 21 (2010), 303–30.

with a mixing of varied cultures, classes, and ethnicities, features which made it impossible for any of the major protagonists to achieve their stated aims. It was impossible to sort civilian from military and paramilitary, or Catholic interests from Protestant interests. The city needed a freedom of movement on orderly disciplined streets to achieve the collective aims of profit-seeking, employment provision, consumerism, and service delivery. Thus, the barricade and the checkpoint became major ways of challenging or asserting state authority. The interconnected nature of the city, a city of pipes and wires, provided many targets. Electricity substations, sewage works, and power stations were early targets in a campaign designed to make Northern Ireland ungovernable.[49] There was an intensification of ethnic segregation. The trust of strangers and the benefits of cultural variety were undermined and denied. Within this pattern the market system could operate to subvert sectarianism. Whilst state and social housing could only be allocated with close attention to sectarian identity, the middle classes were using price, amenity, and the market with outcomes that allowed a growing Catholic middle class to enter areas that were more middle class than they were Protestant or Catholic.[50]

Throughout both these periods, Ulster experienced multiple urban processes of twentieth-century western Europe. Suburbanization followed the bus and motor car to places like Glengormley and beyond, the counterpoint to the growth of central business districts where people worked but did not live.[51] The expansion of state-financed and subsidized working-class housing created mass housing estates on the edge of urban areas, often disrupting accepted practices of sectarian space, notably in matters of parades. There was an increased professionalization of much urban governance, especially in matters of health, education, and planning. These processes interacted with Nationalist/Unionist and Catholic/Protestant fears and contests. Before and after 1969, the distortions of sectarianism were evident in the planning processes which became a feature of twentieth-century world urbanization. As with so much else, Northern Ireland came late to the concept of total area planning. Little was achieved until the appointment of Sir Robert Matthew, whose *Belfast Regional Survey and Plan* was published in 1964. He saw Northern Ireland as a planning region dependent on Belfast. 'Unregulated sprawl' was to be limited by a 'stop line' creating a green belt in areas noted for scenic value and quality agricultural land. Growing traffic congestion was to be countered by urban motorway and by-pass provision. He identified the poor housing record of Belfast Corporation, and the need to reduce population density and replace 18,000 unfit houses. The universal contradiction of containing urban sprawl and reducing inner-city density was to be solved by guiding industry and displaced populations towards designated growth centres, including the regional city of Portadown-Lurgan.[52] This had much in

---

[49] T. Craig, 'Sabotage! The Origins, Development and Impact of the IRA's Infrastructural Bombing Campaigns, 1939–1997', *Intelligence and National Security*, 25 (2010), 309–26.

[50] P. Shirlow and B. Murtagh, *Belfast: Segregation, Violence and the City* (London, 2006), esp. 101–23.

[51] J. H. Johnson, 'The Geography of a Belfast Suburb', *Irish Geography*, 3 (1956), 150–61.

[52] R. Matthew, *Belfast Regional Survey and Plan. A Report Prepared for the Government of Northern Ireland* (Belfast, 1964).

common with other regional plans such as that for Clydeside, but the Stormont government was the effective planning authority and, with a mixture of design and insensitivity, added a sectarian dimension. Derry was ignored. Downpatrick was the only Catholic authority amongst the growth centres, whilst the 'new town' was named Craigavon, identifying the whole enterprise with a Protestant hero and architect of the Northern Ireland state.[53] The contest with the ethics of the professional planner took many forms. In Derry, plans to move people from overcrowded and unfit housing met objection where they would disrupt the ethnic population distributions upon which the gerrymandered politics of Derry depended.[54]

As such plans were implemented, they met problems familiar across Europe. Residents of the eastern Belfast commuting settlements organized against the new roads with varied success. The 'Westlink' motorway was driven across inner-city working-class communities with little effective resistance, with the exception of Hamill Street, a survivor of the old Catholic Pound. They avoided being replaced by a motorway interchange by learning to wear 'the suits', namely to gather expertise as well as protest.[55] Residents of the Protestant Shankill found the replacement housing they were being offered was poor in quality and socially dysfunctional. Movement to the growth centres and housing estates on the edge of Belfast threatened long-standing family networks. Meanwhile dispersal met de-industrialization. In West Belfast, industrial closure increased already high rates of unemployment to levels exceeding 60 per cent in specific areas.[56] Sectarianism added to the organized opinion of both areas. Shankill residents felt they were being moved by the ulterior manipulations of the direct rule government, whilst Catholic Belfast, armed with tales of bias in hiring practice and economic policy, became increasingly alienated from the state in all its forms.[57]

The conflict after 1969 deepened the planners' dilemmas. Many detailed decisions were marked by the requirements of security. Trees and bushes were seen as areas of concealment, not a normal aspect of landscaping. Brownfield sites suitable for minor housing developments were left vacant, partly to preserve sightlines and partly to separate various communities. Conflict reduction was a major part of Ulster urban planning as reflected in peace lines or substantial barriers separating nationalist and loyalist communities.[58] In cityside Derry, most Protestants, anxious about safety, moved to the Waterside on the other side of the River Foyle, leaving behind one tiny working-class enclave known as the Fountains. The creation of

[53] L. O'Dowd, 'Craigavon: Locality, Economy and the State in a Failed "New City"', in C. Curtin, H. Donnan, and T.M. Wilson (eds), *Irish Urban Cultures* (Belfast, 1993), 39–62.
[54] G. McSheffrey, *Planning Derry. Planning and Politics in Northern Ireland* (Liverpool, 2000).
[55] T. Blackman, *Planning Belfast: A Case Study of Public Policy and Community Action* (Avebury, 1991), 44–65.
[56] R. Wiener, *The Rape and Plunder of the Shankill. Community Action: The Belfast Experience* (Belfast, 1978); B. Rolston and M. Tomlinson, *Unemployment in West Belfast: The Obair Report* (Belfast, 1988).
[57] These issues were traced in the magazine *Fortnight*: B. Overy, 'Re-development in Belfast', *Fortnight* (11 June 1971), 6–7.
[58] R. Cowan, 'Belfast's Hidden Planners', *Town and Country Planning*, 51 (1982), 163–7; G. M. Dawson, 'Defensive Planning in Belfast', *Irish Geography*, 17 (1984), 27–41; R. Brand, 'Urban Artifacts and Social Practices in a Contested City', *Journal of Urban Technology*, 16 (2009), 35–60.

Poleglass, a public housing scheme on the edge of west Belfast, encapsulated the distortions of planning amidst conflict. Local authority house-building in the 1950s and 1960s had made very modest inroads into the shortages created by the neglect of the 1930s and wartime blitz. The 1971 census indicated that overcrowding was most intense in wards with large Catholic populations. Sectarian intimidation and the movement of families added to the problem. Housing schemes to the north of Belfast lost substantial Catholic minorities to the activities of 'tartan' gangs. Whilst Protestant movers were willing and able to find accommodation in a wide variety of locations, Catholics tended to crowd into west Belfast.[59] In 1974, plans were made to build 4000 homes adjacent to the Catholic areas of Twinbrook and Ballymurphy. In the words of the subsequent enquiry, this was 'a weak scheme in conventional planning terms'. It was a plan which increased segregation and broke into the green belt. The Housing Executive had 2300 families on its waiting list. No amount of removal grants would induce them to move to vacant houses in Craigavon and many other parts of Belfast. Protestant politicians saw such planning as territorial warfare carried on by other means. Professional planners saw it as a sad decision taken on the basis that 'matters of fear and religion had to be accepted as significant issues'. As a result, 2000 houses were built.[60]

One clear outcome of the violence was the creation of a vibrant but divided civil society. At the same time, elements of urban civil society were created which were designed to counter antagonistic and incomplete polarization. Slender, insecure, but fundamentally urban and new, it was evident in the Integrated Schools Movement, the Corrymeela Community, and other varied 'peace' and reconciliation movements. This was accompanied by a redesign of the state with a focus on urban centres. The redesign was not simply a matter of creating bi-sectarian structures but also a revival of professionalism amongst public servants, again evident in planners' ambitions. Urban projects in the new century reflected Ulster as a planning region with commuting patterns that crossed all the six counties. Above all they reflected ambitions to be part of an Irish as well as a British urban system. The arrows crossing borders were new and symbolic.[61] Other policy directions absorbed the postmodern developments of the urban as spectacle and as the creation of the experience of living rather than the accumulation of property and the defence of space. At the opening of the twenty-first century, the Waterfront developments of Belfast and the visit of the Tall Ships competed for attention with the Orange walk, the political murals, and 'recreational' rioting.[62]

---

[59] J. Darby, *Intimidation in Housing* (Coleraine, 1974) <http://cain.ulst.ac.uk/issues/housing/docs/>; M. Melaugh, *Housing and Religion in Northern Ireland* (Coleraine, 1994) <http://cain.ulst.ac.uk/csc/reports/majmin3.htm> accessed February 2011.

[60] F. N. Corr, M. Dennison, and R. S. Hawthorne, *Poleglass Area Public Enquiry. Reports and Recommendations by the Planning Appeals Commission* (Belfast, 1977); D. Singleton, 'Poleglass. A Microcosm of Planning in a Divided Community', *The Planner* (May 1977), 72–5.

[61] *Belfast Urban Area Plan 2001* (Belfast, 1990); *Shaping Our Future. Regional Development Strategy for Northern Ireland, 2025*. Department of Regional Development, Northern Ireland (Belfast, 2001) <http://www.drdni.gov.uk/shapingourfuture>.

[62] M. Smith and K. Alexander, 'Building a Shared Future: The Laganside Initiative in Belfast', in W. J. V. Neill and Hanns-Uve Schedler (eds), *Urban Planning and Cultural Inclusion. Lessons from Belfast and Berlin* (London, 2001), 177–93.

FURTHER READING

S. Baker, 'Orange and Green. Belfast, 1832–1912', in H. J. Dyos and M. Wolff (eds), *The Victorian City* (London, 1973) 789–814.

J. C. Beckett *et al.*, *Belfast: The Making of the City 1800–1914* (Belfast, 1983).

P. Devlin, *Yes, We Have No Bananas: Outdoor Relief in Belfast, 1920–39* (Belfast, 1981).

Capt. R. J. Elliott, 'Countering Urban Terrorism', *British Army Review*, 64 (April 1980) 16–24.

M. Hayes, *Minority Verdict. Experiences of a Catholic Public Servant* (Belfast, 1995).

The Industries of Ireland, part one. Belfast and the Towns of the North (London and Belfast, 1891), reprinted with introduction by W. H. Crawford (Belfast, 1986).

Irish Historical Towns Atlas (Royal Irish Academy Dublin), no.2, Carrickfergus, 1986; no.8 Downpatrick, 1897; no.17, Belfast, part II, 1840–1900, 2007; no.18, Armagh, 2007.

L. O'Dowd, 'Craigavon: Locality, Economy and the State in a Failed "New City", in C. Curtin, H. Donnan, and T. M. Wilson, *Irish Urban Cultures* (Belfast, 1993), 39–62.

M. Potter, *The Municipal Revolution in Ireland. A Handbook of Urban Government in Ireland since 1800* (Dublin, 2011).

I. D. Whyte, 'Scottish and Irish urbanization in the Seventeenth and Eighteenth centuries', in S. J. Connolly, R. Houston, and R. J. Morris (eds), *Conflict, Identity and Economic Development. Scotland and Ireland, 1600–1939* (Preston, 1995), 24–28.

9

Migration and Emigration, 1600–1945

Donald M. MacRaild and Malcolm Smith[1]

INTRODUCTION

The modern history of Ulster is defined by the movement of people and its sometimes calamitous consequences.[2] During the seventeenth century, plantations unleashed a protracted series of events, since the initial migrations and settlements failed to achieve the planners' ambitions and were partially reversed several times by war, social conflict, and violent protest. The depiction of Ulster as a tripartite split between Gaelic Irish, Scots Presbyterians, and English Protestants of various sects is similarly complicated. It took a century, not a decade, to create Ulster's patchwork of Catholic and Protestant communities. Moreover, the plantations buttressed links between Scotland and Ulster—links which were already centuries old, as attested by the migration of Highland soldiers, gallowglasses, and the MacDonnell presence on both sides of the channel. Later on, overseas emigration particularly affected Ulster's Protestants who departed for America earlier and in proportionately greater numbers than southerners and Catholics.[3]

In 1600, Ulster was a region 'beyond the Pale', which eluded England's grasp. Harsh, hostile, and remote, the province was controlled by powerful Gaelic lords whose subjection was the primary objective of the late Elizabethan wars. Less than fifty years later, when Cromwell first set foot on Irish soil, Ulster had become a remarkably different place. The larger Gaelic clan chiefs had been crushed and their lands seized for plantation with Scottish, English, and Welsh incomers. A new county, Londonderry, was shaped from Coleraine and parts of Tyrone and Donegal; a new administrative and legal structure was in place; and the Gaels had been usurped in areas around modern-day Belfast, Lough Neagh, east Tyrone, and

---

[1] The authors gratefully acknowledge the support of the ESRC (Research Methods Programme) for funding the study 'The Isonymic Analysis of Historical Data: Irish Migration in Britain, 1851–1901' (no. H333250057).

[2] Data for Irish emigration and migration are fraught with difficulties, since internal migrations between Ireland and Britain were never systematically counted, and counting of overseas emigrations only began in the early 1850s, and then systematically only from 1876. Cormac Ó Gráda, 'A note on Nineteenth-Century Irish Emigration Statistics', *Population Studies*, 24 (1975), 143–9.

[3] For a useful survey, see P. Fitzgerald and B. Lambkin, *Migration in Irish History, 1607–2007* (Basingstoke, 2009).

within the new county of Londonderry. Although not removed entirely, Gaels were pressed onto poorer, remote lands, including those held by surviving chiefs.[4]

Migrants from Britain brought with them new cultures; indeed, this was a core intention of the plantations. Yet while waves of British immigrants made Ulster different from the rest of Ireland, Ulster also emitted thousands to the colonies and Britain. In the nineteenth century, when Ulster Protestants trumpeted the superiority of their province in terms of entrepreneurship and education, and celebrated its difference from Catholic Ireland elsewhere, Ulster continued to send people abroad. The shipyards of the Clyde, the mining colonies of County Durham, the cities of the USA, and the farmlands of New Zealand and Canada each received waves of Ulstermen and women (see Table 9.1). Contemporaries remarked with surprise that Ulster, the most economically dynamic of the provinces, should see so many people treading emigrant pathways like their poorer, southern counterparts. But in truth, migration and emigration were in the blood of Ulster people. They left for the colonies, America, and Britain at such rates that they drew specific comment in the many commissions and parliamentary investigations. Why did Ulster, a site of such an extraordinary planned migration, which was meant to create a permanent, stable, and happy society, become the source for so prodigious an onward migration thereafter?

SEVENTEENTH-CENTURY ROOTS

In 1600, Ireland was a war-torn land approaching the final phases of the Nine Years War (1594–1603). During these wars, the English, under the Lord Deputy of Ireland, Mountjoy, gradually shifted their attentions northwards from Anglo-Norman and native Irish opponents in Munster to the clan chiefs of Ulster. Mountjoy butchered the Irish and conducted a scorched earth campaign which made Ulster 'a desert'.[5] Downpatrick was 'a ruined town'; Armagh, once 'the metropolitan city of the whole island', was 'altogether ruinated';[6] and vast territories were depopulated. Despoiling lands, burning homes, and clearing towns were features of a struggle which, when it was over, would facilitate one of the most important migrations in Irish history—migrations which would ensure that, over the next century or so, the northern province became the most demographically distinctive, and divided, in Ireland. The defeat of the Gaelic chiefs and their allies in 1603 opened up the prospect of repopulating the island. Nearly a decade of warfare in pursuit of English hegemony over Ireland had, in several senses, been a story of migration itself. A society at war saw armies moving about the country and displaced enemies of the English and refugees shifting to remote parts; whilst some of these same soldiers settled on gifted

---

[4] T. W. Moody, 'The Treatment of the Native Populations Under the Scheme for the Plantation in Ulster', *Irish Historical Studies*, 1 (1938).

[5] R. A. Butlin, 'Land and People, *c*.1600', in T. W. Moody, F. X. Martin, and F. J. Byrne (eds), *A New History of Ireland*, III: *Early Modern Ireland, 1534–1691* (Oxford, 1976), 146–8.

[6] F. Moryson, *The Itinerary of Fynes Morison in Four Volumes*, 4 (1617; Glasgow, 1908), 190; also in Butlin, 'Land and People'.

lands after the cessation of conflicts. The plantations which followed were, however, of an entirely different magnitude and character.[7]

With the most powerful northern lords removed from Ireland by the 'Flight of the Earls' (1607), vast tracts of sequestrated lands were redistributed.[8] Waves of settlers from Scotland and England were encouraged to establish new communities and homes in Ulster.[9] Advisors to King James VI/I, notably Arthur Chichester, Lord Deputy from 1604, and Sir John Davies, the lawyer, favoured the plantation as a definitive response to the challenges of ruling Ireland. Moreover, James, who was the catalyst for a more extensive plantation scheme than had originally been envisaged, knew the value of manipulating populations, since he had, as King of Scotland, utilized smaller-scale systems of exile, expatriation, and planting in the Hebrides and Borders. Moreover, parts of Antrim and Down were already subjected by Crown-supported private plantation. In 1606, James Hamilton and Hugh Montgomery, in partnership with Chichester, had begun to plant Scots Presbyterians there. Scottish interaction with Ulster was a historic phenomenon borne of the close relations between clans which straddled the north-western edge of Europe.[10]

The English plantation, beginning in 1609, was to be financed by the City of London, particularly a cartel of twelve London companies—trade associations, such as the drapers, skinners, and the cutlers—which formed the Right Honourable the Irish Society. Undertakers, servitors, and natives were granted large blocks of land as long as they planted English-speaking Protestants and ensured any native tenants, whom servitors were allowed to plant, adopted English husbandry. These British colonies were meant to 'civilise the rude parts'; or, as Canny put it, to make Ireland British,[11] in what was an inherently colonial policy. The London companies demanded an extension of the original lands surveyed for plantation to include extensive territories west of the Bann and a foothold on the west bank of the River Foyle. In addition to planting Armagh, Cavan, Fermanagh, and Tyrone in this way, there also was a reorganization of County Coleraine, which became County Londonderry, and the fortification of Coleraine town and the refounding of Derry as Londonderry. In 1610 Cavan and Donegal were carved up between Scottish and English undertakers.[12]

---

[7] Perhaps the best and most accessible analysis of the plantation of Ulster is: S. J. Connolly, *Contested Island: Ireland, 1460–1630* (Oxford, 2006), 289–308. But also see A. Clarke with R. Dudley Edwards, 'Pacification, Plantation and the Catholic Question, 1603–23', in Moody *et al.* (eds), *New History of Ireland*, III, 196–204.

[8] C. Ó Scea, 'Irish Emigration to Castile in the Opening Years of the Seventeenth Century', in P. Duffy and G. Moran (eds), *To and from Ireland: Planned Migration Schemes c. 1600–2000* (Dublin, 2004), 17–37. For the most recent statements on the Flight of the Earls, see D. Finnegan, M. C. Harrigan, and É. Ó Ciardha (eds), *Imeacht na n-Iarlaí: The Flight of the Earls* (Derry, 2010).

[9] R. Gillespie, 'Planned Migration to Ireland in the Seventeenth Century', in Duffy and Moran (eds), *To and from Ireland*, 39–57.

[10] See, generally, M. Perceval-Maxwell, *The Scottish Migrations in Ulster in the Reign of James I* (Belfast, 1990); P. Fitzgerald, 'Scottish Migration to Ireland in the Seventeenth Century', in S. Murdoch and A. Grosjean (eds), *Scottish Communities Abroad in the Early Modern Period* (Leiden, 2005), 27–52.

[11] J. Ohlmeyer: '"Civilizing of those Rude Partes": Colonization within Britain and Ireland 1580s–1640s', in N. Canny (ed.), *The Oxford History of the British Empire*, I: *The Origins of Empire*; N. Canny, *Making Ireland British, 1580–1650* (Oxford, 2001).

[12] Connolly, *Contested Island*, 292–3.

The distribution of lands dramatically shifted the ownership of Ulster, and forced migration upon the lowest strata of society.[13] Connolly calculates, from the high turnover of lands in the early years of the plantation, that the high costs of building fortified dwellings, furnishing livestock, and the expense of moving in tenants meant that most of these men, like the poorer London companies themselves, could not meet their obligations easily. Below them were the servitors, who included soldiers 'for whom the happy coincidence of having served in Ireland at just the right time provided a once-in-a-lifetime opportunity to convert the precarious gentility of a military commission into the more solid status of a landowner'. Below them were tenants who, with their offspring, amounted to 6000 persons as captured in surveys in the early 1620s. This figure had climbed to 15,000 adult English and Scottish males accounted for on muster rolls in 1630. Of these, the Scots were a majority, and particularly dominant in Antrim and Down.[14]

Overall, however, the hoped-for transformation of Ulster had not been delivered. Although native Irish may have been replaced as power-brokers and men of influence, they were not removed entirely as landowners. Below the level of the lords who had fled Ireland in 1607, various Gaels retained lands, albeit usually on much reduced holdings. Such was true of the O'Cahans, O'Hanlons, O'Donnells, and numerous branches of the O'Neills. However, ordinary Gaels were pushed onto lands held by native landlords or servitors, and a third of the existing population thus forcibly migrated.[15] Overall, few Gaels were untouched by the plantations.

In the initial phases, however, plantation settlers were few in number. Consequently, resistance could be effective, as was most dramatically demonstrated in the Ulster Rising of 1641. With Charles I showing none of his father's interest in the plantation, the London companies were pursued for failing to clear their lands of the native Irish and, after years of harrying, they formally lost their rights in 1639. The subsequent power vacuum, which was compounded by civil war on both islands from 1641, presented an opportunity for the Irish to shake the structures of plantation and regain their ancestral lands. Anarchy prevailed and the plantation system was not fully restored until the 1650s, following Cromwell's campaign in Ireland. Thereafter, the confiscation of Irish lands which had characterized the period after the Nine Years War, was extended by the Act of Settlement (1652); and with the collapse of the Irish Confederacy, the plantations were restored and extended by further settlements and the awarding of lands in Ulster to both Scottish and English soldiers who had fought against the Confederacy. There were further upheavals and return migrations during the 1680s and 1690s as a consequence of the Williamite wars. However, despite the upheavals of the Confederate and Williamite periods, the fifty years to 1700 witnessed 100,000 settlers, over half

---

[13] M. Caball, 'Responses to Transformation: Gaelic Poets and the Plantation of Ulster', in É. Ó Ciardha and M. Ó Siochrú (eds), *The Plantation of Ulster: Ideology and Practice* (Manchester, 2012), 176–96.
[14] This paragraph and the following one draw substantially on Connolly, *Contested Island*, 294–302 (quotation at 295).
[15] Moody, 'Treatment of the Native'.

of them English, migrating to Ulster.[16] During the two decades following William III's victory of 1690, as many as 50,000 Scots also flowed in to occupy 'farms that were lying waste as a result to the ravages of war'.[17] By the early eighteenth century, Ulster's mixed ethnicity—the foundations of contemporary sectarian conflict—was established, with Protestants outnumbering the Catholics whose lands they had acquired.[18]

EMIGRATION AND MIGRATION IN THE EIGHTEENTH CENTURY

With so much exertion put in to securing parts of Antrim, Down, and Londonderry for Scots settlers, it is interesting that the firm ground they now held acted as a springboard rather than bed, with thousands of their descendants taking part in migrations to the American colonies, in the eighteenth century. Indeed, from the 1720s to the 1770s, Ireland—but particularly Ulster—sent almost as many emigrants to the American colonies than more populous England did.[19] Scholars have noticed that these emigrants included recent immigrants to Ulster as well as those whose families had settled generations earlier. Descendants of English Baptists and Quakers who had first settled Ulster in the seventeenth century, began Ulster migrations to the colonies. These 'were the forerunners of the great movement of Irish Protestants, chiefly Dissenters of Scottish or English descent, who dominated Irish emigration'[20] in the century thereafter. Between 1717 and 1776, more than 100,000 Presbyterians (70 per cent of all leavers) left Ulster ports for Philadelphia and New York, at a time when the entire Presbyterian population of the northern Irish province was perhaps half a million. Ulster continued to send 5000 emigrants per annum in the 1780s and 1790s. The French Wars, the Anglo-American War of 1812, and legislation aimed to prevent the loss of human capital to the former colonies and to protect the Anglican Ascendancy in Ireland, contrived to stem the tide in the period of the late eighteenth and early nineteenth centuries. Yet 100,000 to 150,000 still departed Ulster for America in the thirty years after 1783; indeed, between 1803 and 1805, 70 per cent of all Irish emigrants departed for the United States from the key Ulster ports, notably Derry, providing further evidence of the importance of the Ulster-Scots in this phase of emigration.[21]

---

[16] N. Canny, 'English Migration Into and Across the Atlantic During the Seventeenth and Eighteenth Centuries', in idem (ed.), *Europeans on the Move: Studies in European Migration, 1500–1800* (Oxford, 1994), 39–76.

[17] W. T. Latimer, 'Ulster Emigration to America', *The Journal of the Royal Society of Antiquaries of Ireland*, Fifth Series, 32, (31 December 1902), 385–6.

[18] P. Fitzgerald, ' "Black '97"?: Scottish Migration to Ulster in the 1690s', in W. P. Kelly and J. R. C. Young (eds), *Ulster and Scotland 1600–2000: History, Language and Identity* (Dublin, 2004), 71–84.

[19] 'British Emigration', in J. Powell, *Encyclopaedia of North American Immigration* (New York, 2005), 36–8; A. Murdoch, *British Emigration, 1603–1914* (Basingstoke, 2004).

[20] K. A. Miller, A. Schrier, B. Boling, and D. N. Doyle, *Irish Immigrants in the Land of Canaan* (New York and Oxford, 2002), 13.

[21] R. Gavin, W. P. Kelly, and D. O'Reilly, *Atlantic Gateway: The Port and City of Londonderry since 1700* (Dublin, 2009), esp. 1–44.

All told, perhaps 250,000 Ulster people, mostly though not exclusively Protestants, went to North America in this period.

A variety of forces shaped these emigrations. Terrible weather, poor harvests, and dire famines spurred migrations in the 1720s and 1740s.[22] Legal proscriptions in the early 1700s also spurred the exodus, when the extension of the Test Acts, through which the Privy Council demanded that public office-holders prove they had taken communion in the Anglican Church, affected Presbyterians just as earlier legislation of this type had marginalized Catholics. The magistracy, militia, and other public offices were wrenched from Presbyterians who abjured such an oath, thus adding to the grievances of a people who already suffered from payment of tithes to an alien church and from the fact that legal marriage lay with the sole authority of the Anglican Church. When allied to rising rents, these forces promoted intense migration.

London noted Ulster's growing exodus with real concern. Plantation had been instigated as an exercise in social engineering: the Protestants who had taken up grants of cheap land were supposed to out-match Gaelic power with a loyal Protestant population. Hence, the flight of so many descendants of those who had been introduced to Ulster during the Scottish and English plantations constituted a threat to the power balance which planned settlement had sought to achieve. In 1729, William King, the Archbishop of Dublin, wrote bluntly of the threat to the principles of plantation wrought by the exodus: 'No papists stir [to leave Ireland] ... The papists being already five or six to one, and being a breeding people, you may imagine in what condition we are likely to be in.'[23] As emigration agents, speculators, and ships' captains touted for trade, and with Dissenting ministers preaching the gospel of migration, great numbers left, sometimes *en masse* from single communities. No less than 90 per cent of the 6308 who arrived at Philadelphia in the year of King's strictures were derived from this stock.[24] Such was the pace of migration in this period that Miller has noticed a high degree of 'Hibernicization' in the colonies,[25] as the Irish came to comprise a substantial component of most colonial populations, reaching in 1790 one-quarter of all whites in Pennsylvania, South Carolina, and Georgia.

While these huge colonial flows understandably attract our attentions, the Protestants of Ulster did not look only westwards for salvation. Poorer folk also glanced east. During the early Industrial Revolution, economic transformations reinforced already close links between Scotland and Ulster;[26] while economic competition between the two islands fostered further migrations. From the 1770s, and especially during the 1790s, these forces could be seen at work. Ulster's linen industry was struck by recession, resulting in the displacement of workers, some of whom moved to Scotland and England. Simultaneously, developments in the Scottish textile industry created a demand for skilled weavers and bleachers. Some of the

---

[22] D. Dickson, *Arctic Ireland* (Dublin, 1997).   [23] Cited in R. J. Dickson, *Ulster Emigration to Colonial America, 1718–1775* (1966; Belfast, 1996 edn), 35.
[24] Latimer, 'Ulster Emigration', 387.   [25] Miller *et al.*, *Canaan*, 7.
[26] See E. W. McFarland, *Ireland and Scotland in the Age of Revolution: Planting the Green Bough* (Edinburgh, 1994), Ch. 2.

supply came from Ulster.²⁷ In a series of connected activities which are apparent at all sites of migration, the development of Belfast's textile industry also encouraged a steady inward migration from its hinterland. The pattern of movement from the northern counties into Belfast would be a feature of Ulster life thereafter.

Most of the Ulster workers who arrived in Scotland at this time were from Antrim, Down, Armagh, and Londonderry—the Protestant heartlands of Ulster. When added to the lack of Catholic participation in the better linen trades, we can see why a majority of the vanguard movement to industrial Scotland was Protestant.²⁸ By the mid-1820s, the *Commission on Emigration* was hearing evidence from Scotland detailing the almost exclusively northern roots of the Irish who settled in the central belt, and of their close association with weaving.²⁹ Such Ulster migrations, though concentrated on Scotland, also encompassed northern England's domestic and factory textile centres.

INTERNAL MIGRATION AND THE BRITISH CONNECTION IN THE NINETEENTH CENTURY

Over the course of the century Ulster's population, although it receded severely, did not fall as significantly as in the other three provinces. Declining from 2.3 million (m) in 1831 to 1.4 m in 1891, Ulster's overall loss was 39 per cent compared to an average of 45 per cent for the other provinces. Belfast's rapid growth presented a notable opportunity for the retention of some part of the population of Ulster on the same principle that saw the British population grow so quickly despite high rates of external migration. However, Ulster's overall levels of urbanization, like Ireland's more generally, were not enough to prevent spectacular population loss. Although Belfast grew faster than most British cities, levels of urbanization elsewhere in the province were far lower than in Britain. Without Belfast, Ulster's population would probably have fallen on a par with the rest of Ireland; even with it, the decline was spectacular. This was a century in which the population of England and Wales nearly quadrupled; by contrast, Ireland's halved from its peak in the mid-1840s.

No other towns in Ulster came close to the Belfast population. In 1841, Belfast housed 75,308 persons—greater than any population centre on the island except Dublin. In Ulster in 1851, apart from Belfast, only Newry and Derry topped 10,000.³⁰ By 1911, Belfast had caught up with Dublin, having grown to 386,931 inhabitants. By then, Belfast was one of the UK's major centres, accounting for more than 70 per cent of the part of Ulster's population located in settlements of

---

²⁷ C. Ó Gráda, *Ireland: A New Economic History, 1780–1939* (Oxford, 1994), 283.
²⁸ G. Walker, 'The Protestant Irish in Scotland', in T. M. Devine (ed.), *Irish Immigrants and Scottish Society in the Nineteenth and Twentieth Centuries* (Edinburgh, 1994), 45–6.
²⁹ *Second Report from the Select Committee on Emigration from the United Kingdom, 1827* (B.P.P., 1826–27, 237). Evidence of H. H. Drummond MP, 27–8.
³⁰ *Towns (Ireland). Returns of the names of the several towns in Ireland for which commissioners are now appointed, under the act 9 Geo. 4, c. 82, and present number for each town; numbers of householders registered as qualified to be elected Town Commissioners, and number qualified to vote; number of housholds in each...; and number of inhabitants in each, according to the census of 1851* (B.P.P., 1852–53, 94), 203.

more than 5000 persons. In the same year, there were just six towns beyond Belfast with populations of more than 10,000. The second largest urban centre, Derry, had a population of 40,780, so that Ulster's rates and levels of urbanization were far lower than the industrial counties of central-belt Scotland, the north-east of England, Lancashire, or the Midlands. Belfast and perhaps Derry could be regarded as British-style commercial or industrial towns. Elsewhere, Ulster was decidedly rural. While there were also twenty-two smaller settlements with populations of between 2000 and 5000, spread across the province from Letterkenny to Monaghan and Portrush, all centres of this size together accounted for little more than 50,000 of Ulster's population.[31]

During the period up to the Famine, most Ulster-British movement went to Scotland.[32] Ulster-born workers in Scotland mostly settled in Dumfriesshire, Wigtownshire, Ayrshire, Renfrewshire, and Glasgow and other places where textiles predominated.[33] Indeed, Richard Sinnot, a Catholic priest for Wigtownshire and West Kirkcudbrightshire, told Sir George Cornewall Lewis's parliamentary investigation in 1836 that 'a large number of the Irish in this county are not Catholics', and that 'almost all the Irish in this part of Scotland are from Ulster, a few from Connaught, and scarcely any from the other two provinces'.[34] This pre-Famine connection was continued and strengthened within the context of the integration of a north-British industrial region spanning the great industrial centres from Tyneside in the east to Belfast in the west, Liverpool in the south to Glasgow in the north. Complementary and interconnected pathways of industrial development in the heavy engineering and manufacturing towns and cities of northern England, southern-central Scotland, and Belfast sustained regular and consistent patterns of migration. The same forces which resulted in Belfast having the fourth largest population of Scottish-born people in the United Kingdom beyond Scotland, and an economy heavily reliant on Scots capitalists,[35] also attracted Ulster migrants and Scots to Tyneside and Lancashire (Tables 9.2, 9.3). Whilst Scotland remained the principal centre of settlement of these Ulster migrants, with Protestants accounting for a sizeable minority of Irish settlers,[36] proportions were only a little lower in northern England. Maps 9.1 and 9.2 show how, in 1881, Ulster-born settlers in England were generally more likely to be found in the north of the country.

---

[31] *Census of Ireland, 1911. General Report, with Tables and Appendix*, (B. P. P., 118, 1912–13), 73.

[32] See I. S. Wood (ed.), *Scotland and Ulster* (Edinburgh, 1994) and McFarland, *Ireland and Scotland*.

[33] D. F. Macdonald, *Scotland's Shifting Population, 1770–1850* (Glasgow, 1937), 78; Walker, 'Protestant Irish in Scotland', 48; N. Murray, *The Scottish Handloom Weavers, 1790–1850* (Edinburgh, 1979), 31–2; E. McFarland, *Protestants First: Orangeism in Nineteenth Century Scotland* (Edinburgh, 1990), 104.

[34] *Royal Commission on the Condition of the Poorer Classes in Ireland, Appendix G, Report into the State of the Irish Poor in Great Britain* (B.P.P., 1836, 34), 151–2.

[35] On the Scots in Belfast, see K. Hughes, '"Scots, Stand Firm, and our Empire is Safe": The politicisation of Scottish Clubs and Societies in Belfast during the Home Rule era, *c.* 1885–1914', in T. Bueltmann, A. Hinson, and G. Morton (eds.), *Ties of Bluid, Kin and Countrie: Scottish Associationalism in the Diaspora* (Toronto, 2009), 203–20.

[36] T. Gallagher, *Glasgow, the Uneasy Peace: Religious Tension in Modern Scotland* (Manchester, 1987), 27; Walker, 'Protestant Irish in Scotland', 49.

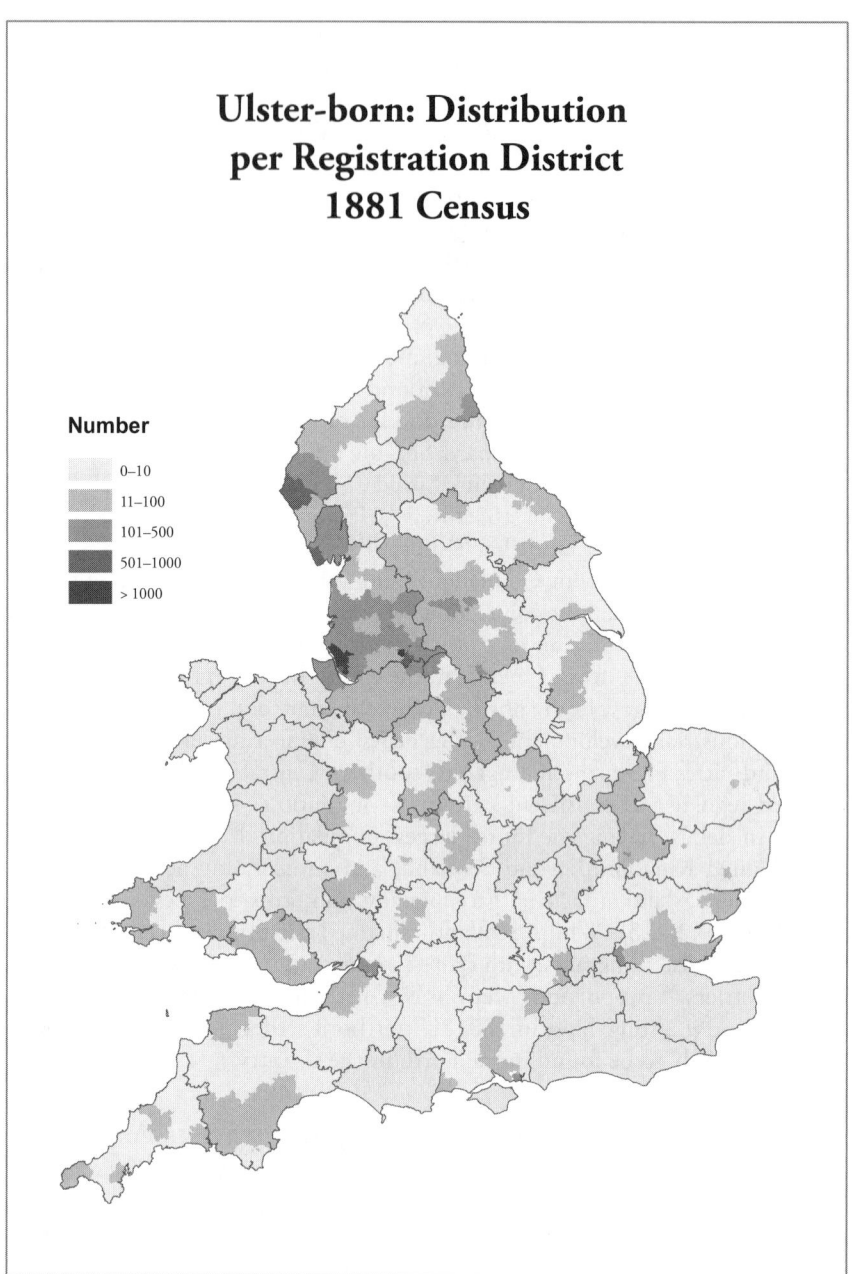

Map 9.1. Migration: Ulster-born people in England and Wales in 1881, shown by Registration District.

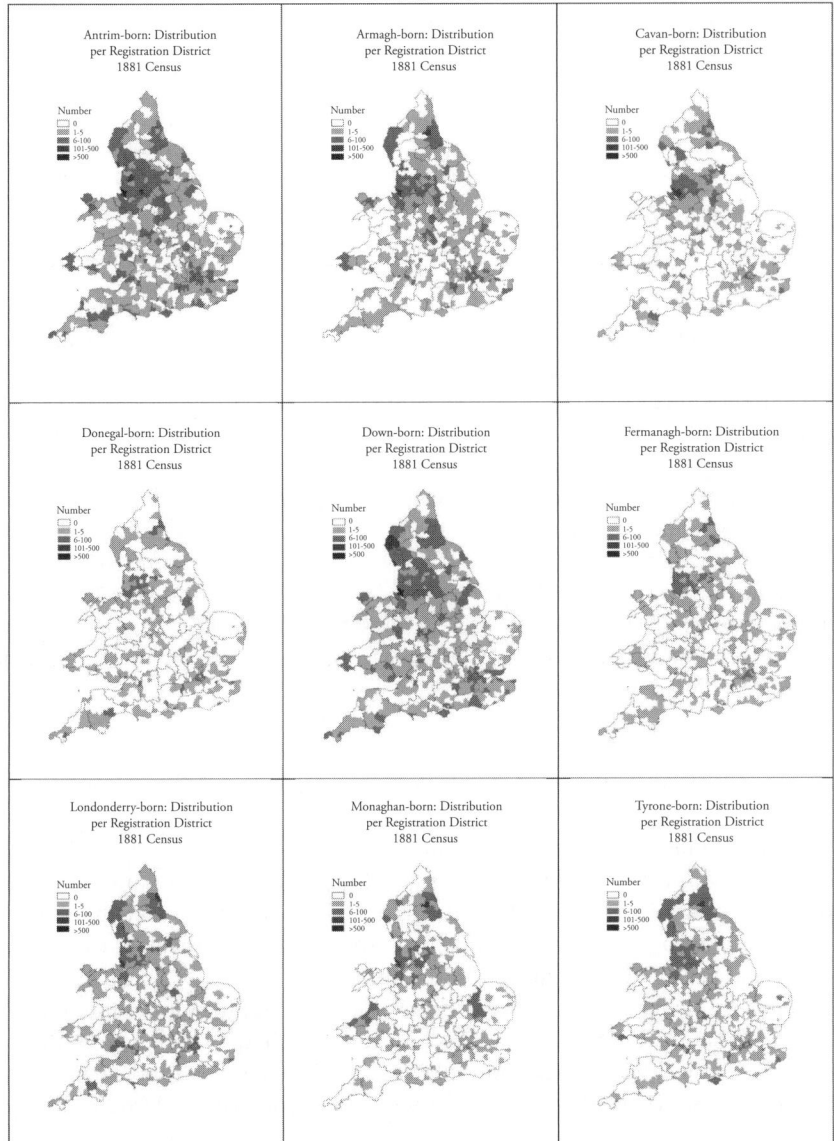

Map 9.2. Migration: Ulster-born people in England and Wales in 1881, shown by Registration District and distinguishing by county of origin.

Although the Irish continued to work in the cotton factories of Scotland and Lancashire, the most noticeable development of this later period was the rapid emergence of iron ore and coal mining, metal manufacture, and shipbuilding. All of these industries seem to have attracted Irish Protestant labour, which in turn perpetuated many noticeable features of earlier Irish Protestantism; for example, the local Orange lodge, a key signature of the presence of Ulstermen. Ulster migration encouraged sectarian tensions in the workplace, for example at Greenock and Port Glasgow, where unskilled work predominated and 'Catholic and Protestant workers from Ireland worked in uneasy proximity in the sugar refineries and quays'.[37] Work opportunities encouraged Ulster migration to Scotland, with heavy engineering, the iron and coal industries, and textiles offering opportunities for both skilled and unskilled workers. The counties of Ayr, Renfrew, Stirling, Dumbarton, and Lanark attracted large numbers of these migrants. In Larkhall, Lanarkshire, Irish Protestants from Ulster exceeded Catholics by about two to one.[38] Even after the Famine, their continued presence was denoted by persistently strong Episcopalian traditions, which they introduced to Paisley, Larkhall, Armadale, Irvine, Girvan, and other places.[39]

The development of large-scale steel shipbuilding also enhanced cross-channel links between Belfast and the Clyde, Tyne and Wear. Indeed, such links were strong enough to ensure Irish Protestant workers entered the Scottish workplace at a higher level than their Catholic countrymen. Many secured skilled or semi-skilled labour in Clydeside towns and, though many Irish Protestants undoubtedly worked as labourers, a significant proportion also entered skilled, apprenticed trades.[40] Barrow and Birkenhead also developed associations which were almost Scottish in scale and intensity. In Barrow, in 1881, for instance, over 50 per cent of the local Irish-born community of around 5000 came from Down and Antrim, 20 per cent from Belfast alone.[41]

EMIGRATIONS IN THE NINETEENTH CENTURY

Until the Famine, Ulster lost a higher proportion of its population to emigration than any other province.[42] Even after that, Ulster was a far more important provider of emigrants than is imagined (see Table 9.1). These rates of emigration from Ulster presented a conundrum to those who trumpeted the province's superiority over the others. 'Tenant right', which protected farmers' leases and granted the legal right to benefit from improvements to land, was meant to sponsor stability.[43] Yet, in one respect, it did not; for a substantial proportion of Ulster emigrants comprised those who sold tenancies and invested the money in land in Canada, New Zealand, and elsewhere. Parliamentary commissions, enquiries, and commentators

---

[37] T. Gallagher, '"A Tale of Two Cities": Communal Strife in Glasgow and Liverpool before 1914', in R. Swift and S. Gilley (eds), *The Irish in the Victorian City* (London, 1985), 110.

[38] A. B. Campbell, *The Lanarkshire Miners: A Social History of their Trade Unions, 1775–1874* (Edinburgh, 1979), 178–81.

[39] I. Meredith, 'Irish Migrants in the Scottish Episcopal Church', in M. J. Mitchell (ed.), *New Perspectives on the Irish in Scotland* (Edinburgh, 2008), 45–6.

[40] S. Pollard and P. Robertson, *The British Shipbuilding Industry, 1870–1914* (Cambridge, Mass., 1979), 163; McFarland, *Protestants First*, 85–8.

[41] D. M. MacRaild, *The Irish Diaspora in Britain, 1815–1939* (Basingstoke, 2010), Ch. 2.

[42] D. Fitzpatrick, 'Emigration, 1801–1870', in W. E. Vanghan (ed.), *New History of Ireland*, v: *Ireland, 1801–1870* (Oxford, 1986), Table 1, 608.

[43] *Report from the Select Committee of the House of Lords on the Tenure (Ireland) Bill [H.L.]; together with the proceedings of the committee, minutes of evidence, and index* (B.P.P., 1867, 14), 235, 290.

Table 9.1. Post-Famine emigration by province

Decade to: Province	1861	1871	1881	1891	1901	Total
Ulster	341,261	201,240	240,110	216,524	86,455	1,085,590
Munster	434,338	304,105	181,370	252,080	177,236	1,349,129
Leinster	235,460	149,838	110,619	138,282	49,552	683,751
Connacht	138,059	113,676	86,551	161,219	117,750	617,255

Source: W. E. Vaughan and A. J. Fitzpatrick, *Irish Historical Statistics: Population, 1821–1971* (Dublin, 1978), 10–13, 311–31.

Table 9.2. Emigration from Ulster by county and as a share of county population, 1851–1911

	1861	1871	1881	1891	1901	1911
Antrim	77,516	54,670	59,431	45,469	14,946	32,804
	30%	22%	25%	21%	8%	17%
Armagh	29,496	17,674	19,603	20,577	7208	8408
	15%	10%	12%	14%	6%	7%
Cavan	36,502	22,348	19,376	21,679	12,033	9353
	24%	16%	15%	19%	12%	10%
Donegal	38,260	11,902	30,085	29,417	12,977	12,622
	16%	6%	15%	16%	8%	8%
Down	47,906	28,270	31,132	23,638	7837	15,709
	16%	10%	13%	11%	4%	8%
Fermanagh	17,372	10,864	10,514	10,158	5403	3562
	16%	12%	12%	14%	8%	6%
Londonderry	27,738	16,841	26,939	23,199	8152	9257
	15%	10%	16%	15%	6%	7%
Monaghan	26,842	14,953	13,356	13,427	5301	4333
	21%	13%	13%	16%	7%	6%
Tyrone	39,629	23,722	26,674	28,960	12,598	10,359
	17%	11%	15%	17%	8%	7%
Average Ulster						
	19%	12%	15%	16%	7%	8%

Note: Emigration as a share of county population is measured as the total number of emigrants per decade for each county relative to the population of that county at census date. Emigration from County Antrim includes Belfast emigrants.
Source: Vaughan and Fitzpatrick, *Irish Historical Statistics*, 10–13, 311–31.

thus regularly asked office-holders why Ulster persistently ranked so high in the provincial league table for emigration (see Map 9.1). One of the members of the Select Committee, the Earl of Kimberley, on hearing evidence prior to the operation of the Landlord and Tenant Act (1870), was told by Mr Hamilton of Sligo, in an explanation which entirely confounded the expected logic of 'tenant-right', that 'the price of his tenant-right enables the tenant to emigrate with his family. The Ulster tenant is more independent in his mind as well as in his circumstances...

Table 9.3. Scots-born and English-born residents of Belfast, 1841–1911

YEAR	Population of Belfast	Born in Scotland	Proportion (%)	Born in England & Wales	Proportion (%)
1841	76,441	890	1.2	888	1.2
1851	100,945	2214	2.2	2216	2.2
1861	121,602	3205	2.6	3047	2.5
1871	174,317	4068	2.3	5017	2.9
1881	184,205	4347	2.4	5120	2.8
1891	212,899	6239	2.9	7574	3.6
1901	349,180	11,074	3.2	12,094	3.5
1911	386,947	12,451	3.2	15,446	4.0

Source: Birthplaces of the people as reported in the Census of Ireland, relevant years.

[T]he Ulster tenant in consequence of his tenant-right can emigrate in a favourable way with his family altogether.'[44]

Hamilton reckoned these people, supported by the sale of the improvements to their tenancies, usually headed for Canada. These emigrations to Canada initially focused on the Maritime Provinces and Ontario.[45] Until the Famine, migrants directly from Ulster more commonly went to British North America rather than the United States because Liverpool dominated the direct America trade. In 1836, for example, 85 per cent of the 4457 who left on vessels crossing the Atlantic headed for Canada.[46] Emigrants on board these ships for Canada were drawn from all classes of people with the means to contemplate the expense of travelling to North America and establishing a new life; in both Armagh and Down, as well as farmers, tradesmen, and mechanics, shoemakers, carpenters, and masons departed.[47]

In the pre-Famine years, Ulster's ports accounted for more emigrants than those of the other three provinces and 36 per cent of the total emigrant traffic captured in 1841 by the census commissioners.[48] A snapshot from 1846–47 shows that Ulster (611) and Munster (618) sent far more emigrants than Leinster (347) and Connacht (207) to Australia.[49] As late as the 1860s, although Munster, with 38,322, had forged ahead, Ulster, at 14,512, was still sending more emigrants than either Connacht (12,617) or Leinster (9521).[50] Ulster's important position was

[44] *Report from the Select Committee of the House of Lords on the Landlord and Tenant (Ireland) Act, 1870; together with the proceedings of the committee, minutes of evidence, appendix, and index* (B.P.P., 1872, 11), 46.
[45] T. P. Power (ed.), *The Irish in Atlantic Canada* (Fredericton, New Brunswick, 1991), 7–9.
[46] *Poor Inquiry (Ireland). Appendix (C), Part I* (B.P.P., 1836, 30), 17.
[47] *Third Report of the Commissioners for Inquiring into the Condition of the Poorer Classes in Ireland* (B.P.P., 1836, 30), 15, 16.
[48] *Report of the Commissioners appointed to take the Census of Ireland, for the year 1841* (B.P.P., 1843, 24), xxviii.
[49] *Emigration. Papers relative to emigration to the Australian colonies* (B.P.P., 1850, 40), 57.
[50] Evidence of William Donnelly, Head of the Department of Agricultural Statistics, Ireland, *Index to the Report from the Select Committee on Taxation of Ireland* (B.P.P., 1864, 15), 139.

maintained long after the Famine. Although the three southern provinces generally supplied more emigrants than Ulster, the latter provided a significant flow of emigrants throughout the nineteenth century: to Britain for the poorer, landless, or urban classes; or to the Dominions and America for capitalized farmers and artisans. Throughout the century, no other province remotely matched Ulster emigration to Canada. As late as 1880, Ulster was providing three-quarters of the relatively small number (3052) heading there.[51] Ulster and Munster dominated the flows of Irish people to Australia and New Zealand; but only Leinster had a weaker connection with the United States than Ulster.

During the 1860s, the overall balance of Irish emigration began to shift away from Ulster and towards the poorer south and west. Whereas in the decade to 1871 Ulster accounted for 222,378 emigrants, 26 per cent of Ireland's total, Munster registered 336,965 (40 per cent).[52] Thereafter, Connacht's share increased dramatically and along with Munster became dominant; and by 1880 both provinces had outstripped Ulster's rates of emigration. In that year, the northernmost province provided 23.5 per cent of the total of 74,636. When these figures are weighted to account for relative population size, only Cavan and Monaghan rank in Ireland's top-ten counties for emigration in 1880, with Antrim and Down placed thirteenth and twenty-third out of thirty-two counties. By contrast, Munster occupied six of the top-ten positions.[53] When we account for Connacht's smaller size, we can see that, by 1899, the province sent proportionally four times more emigrants overseas than Ulster.[54]

Overall, the picture of emigration from Ulster is one of persistence and importance. Although the southern and western provinces outstripped Ulster's migrations in the later nineteenth century, outward movement remained important, affecting all classes in Ulster. Whilst the province's most southerly counties, Monaghan and Cavan, sent higher proportions of their populations overseas, the most remote county, Donegal, was only twenty-ninth in Ireland's rankings in 1880. Even the more urban and industrial counties, Down and Antrim, were not immune from migration. Urban growth, specifically in the industrial entrepôt of Belfast, was not enough to prevent Ulster providing around one-fifth of all Irish emigrants around 1880. When some allowance is made for the uncounted migrations (internal to the UK) to Scotland and northern England, Ulster's position is further strengthened and probably underestimated in a literature which stresses the southern and Catholic nature of emigrations in the post-Famine period.

Dickson once lamented how the great colonial migrations from eighteenth-century Ulster had been overlooked in comparison to the Famine exodus.[55]

---

[51] 1882 *Census of Ireland 1881, Part II, General Report* (B.P.P., 1882, 76).
[52] *Census of Ireland 1871, Part III, General Report* (B.P.P., 1876, 76), 10,193. See also Table 38: 'Emigration from each county in Ireland', 434.
[53] *Census of Ireland 1881: General Report*, Table 75.
[54] *Reports and Tables..... of the Emigrants from each County and Province in Ireland, during the year 1899* (B.P.P., 1900, 102), 3.
[55] Dickson, *Ulster Emigration*, xix.

This situation is now largely rectified; however, nineteenth-century Ulster emigration remains under-examined. Seemingly, Protestants, small farmers, industrial workers, and landless agriculturalists who converted to industrial labour in Britain, have lacked the appeal of the ragged waves fleeing the turbulent disjuncture of the Famine. Yet both Protestant migration in particular, and Ulster emigration in general, continued to be important in the nineteenth century. Moreover, Ulster's poorest peripheral regions were hardly immune from the worst effects of the 'potato blight' and hunger; indeed, south Ulster was one of the areas of heaviest emigration in the 1840s.[56]

Assisted passages became more common in the post-Famine period, enabling persons from the poorer districts to emigrate overseas. Indeed, the migration of independent farmers was probably outmatched by the movement of lower classes of people in the 1870s and 1880s. Canadian support for the poor of Ulster resulted in steady flows in the 1880s to the prairie states, as Charles Pringle told official enquirers.[57] Though emigration to Canada subsided after the 1860s, even in 1871, 850,000 (25 per cent) of the population was Irish-born. In the provinces of Ontario and New Brunswick the figure was even higher at some 30–40 per cent. In Newfoundland, the Irish comprised one-half of the population as early as the 1830s.[58] Furthermore, it has been estimated that some 55 per cent of the Irish who went to Canada were Protestants, mostly from Ulster.[59] In Canada, rural locations and pursuits were far more important for the Irish than in any other country of settlement. Yet big cities were also important, with Toronto, for example, noted for Irish political activity, ethnic associationism, and sectarian violence.

Particularly after the Famine, migrations to Australia and New Zealand became important. Until the spread of assisted passage after 1850, few, except the convicts, were poor; and some, like Henry Osborne of Ulster, who took money and goods with him and made a fortune in farming, were comfortably off before they left. When he died, in 1857, his estate included nearly a million acres of prime New South Wales dairy pasture.[60] Ulster settlement in Australia became especially marked in the later decades of the century, so that in 1911, one-quarter of them were Protestants.[61] In New Zealand, around one-fifth of all United Kingdom settlers hailed from Ireland, with more than half of these being Protestants, mostly from Ulster.[62] Horn's work on the Ulster-New Zealand flows demonstrates

---

[56] J. S. Donnelly, Jr, 'Excess Mortality and Emigration', in W. E. Vaughan (ed.), *New History of Ireland, V: Ireland Under the Union, I. 1801–1870* (Oxford, 1989), 352, 354. Cavan, Monaghan, and Fermanagh were in the top ten counties for mortality.

[57] *Land Acts (Ireland). Report of the Royal Commission on the Land Law (Ireland) Act, 1881, and the Purchase of Land (Ireland) Act, 1885* (B.P.P., 1887, 26), 212.

[58] Power (ed.), *Atlantic Canada*, 8.

[59] W. J. Houston and C. J. Smyth, *Irish Emigration and Canadian Settlement* (Belfast, 1990), 8, 188–9.

[60] T. Parkhill, 'Convicts, Orphans, Settlers: Patterns of Emigration from Ulster to Australia, 1790–1860', in J. O'Brien and P. Travers (eds), *The Irish Emigrant Experience in Australia* (Dublin, 1991), 12–13.

[61] D. Fitzpatrick, *Oceans of Consolation: Personal Accounts of Irish Migration to Australia* (Dublin, 1994), 14.

[62] B. Patterson, 'Introduction', in idem (ed.), *Ulster-New Zealand Migration and Cultural Transfer* (Dublin, 2006), 9; J. Phillips and T. Hearn, *Settlers: New Zealand Immigrants from England, Ireland and Scotland, 1800–1945* (Auckland, 2008); Alasdair Galbraith, '"The Invisible Irish?" Re-discovering the Irish Protestant Tradition in Colonial New Zealand', in L. Fraser (ed.), *A Distant Shore: Irish Immigration and New Zealand Settlement* (Dunedin, 2000), 36–54.

the class issues affecting migrants' choices of destinations. Many of these Ulster Protestants in New Zealand came from similar places as those who travelled to northern England: the mid-Ulster portions of Londonderry and Tyrone or the east Ulster towns of Ballymena and Ballymoney. However, the New Zealand emigrations comprised small farmers with capital and prospects, whereas those who went to England were landless workers who moved into industrial occupations.[63]

Migrants to New Zealand and northern England shared a cultural affinity with the Orange Order.[64] Indeed, the Order was the province's cultural export par excellence.[65] For our purposes, the most fascinating feature of the Order is its maintenance of connections between Ulster and the outposts of Empire, particularly after 1865 when the Grand Lodge of Ireland inaugurated an international Triennial Council, the first of which was held at Downpatrick, County Down.[66] Occasional flashes in the press point to transnational connections among lesser individuals: this was the case in 1874 when J. J. Bond, a prominent Orangeman of Brooklyn, New York, received a gold medal from the Earl of Enniskillen as a memento of his trip to Ireland in the previous year and in recognition of 'the prominent part he took in the celebration of the July anniversary in the United Kingdom'.[67] Such connections persisted in 1900 when the 210th anniversary of the Battle of the Boyne was celebrated with a triennial council meeting in New York, overseen by the veteran Ulster Orangeman and MP, William Johnstone of Ballykilbeg.[68] Still later, during the 1930s, the 'kinship between the people of the overseas Dominions and those of the Motherland' was demonstrated when Sir William Allen, County Grand Master of Armagh, received a certificate from the Sons of William Lodge, Toronto, 'the majority of whom are Co. Armagh men'.[69]

MIGRATION IN THE AGE OF PARTITION, DEPRESSION, AND WAR

Loss of population through emigration to the colonies and migration to Britain also were characteristics of life in the infant state of Northern Ireland, formed in 1921 from six of Ulster's nine counties. As a consequence of depressed economic

---

[63] Compare, G. E. Horn, '"A Loyal, United, and Happy People". Irish Protestant Migrants in Wellington 1840–1930: Aspects of Migration, Settlement and Community', Ph.D., Victoria University of Wellington, 2010, Ch. 4 with D. M. MacRaild, *Culture, Conflict and Migration: The Irish in Victorian Cumbria* (Liverpool, 1998), Ch. 3.

[64] B. Patterson, 'New Zealand's "Ulster Plantation": Katikati Revisited', in idem (ed.), *Ulster-New Zealand*, 85–102; 154–64.

[65] J. Harland-Jacobs, '"Maintaining the Connexion": Orangeism in the British North Atlantic World', *Atlantic Studies*, 5 (April, 2008), 27–49.

[66] *Report of the Proceedings of the Grand Orange Conference… 1866* (Downpatrick, 1866), 1, 2.

[67] *New York Times,* 21 January 1874.

[68] Ibid., 24 July 1900.

[69] *The Scotsman*, 16 July 1937. See also P. Ollerenshaw, 'Northern Ireland and the British Empire-Commonwealth, 1923–61', *Irish Historical Studies*, 36 (2008), 227–42.

conditions in Northern Ireland in the inter-war years, the population of the new state fell until the mid-1930s, with continued movement to Australasia, North America, and Britain ingrained in Ulster life. In one respect, these movements of people were fuelled by the social and cultural life of the province. Just as injustice fuelled migrations in the eighteenth century, so too, bitter sectarian cleavage prompted a steady flow of migration from Northern Ireland to Britain after 1922, following partition, boundary disputes, and the final settlement, in 1925, on the six-county border of Northern Ireland.

Ulster people with specific reasons to migrate were many in number: victims of general sectarian attacks; those driven from their homes and farms, particularly urban Belfast during the 'Pogroms' of 1920, or in the general border disputes of the early 1920s; parents who simply wanted better lives for their children; and even young lovers of different religions seeking the freedom to marry regardless of their faith. For those departing Ireland's shores, Britain remained a major destination. Yet the 1920s were also a propitious moment for travelling further afield. Emigration to the Dominions was encouraged by the general tenor of discussions at the Imperial Conferences between the wars, notably in 1923 when the New Zealand Prime Minister, W. F. Massey encouraged emigration by reference to the surplus populations of Ulster, Scotland, and Wales.[70]

The issue of migration in Ulster is complicated by partition, the splitting of Ulster into the six counties of Northern Ireland, the consequent exclusion of Monaghan, Cavan, and Donegal, and the creation of a border with the Irish Free State. This created sites of intimidation, violence, boycotting of shops and other businesses, and resulted in consternation and fear on the part of Protestants in the three abandoned Ulster counties.[71] Territorial changes also shifted the realities of potential migrants. Persons from Donegal, traditionally a major supplier of labour to Scotland, now had to negotiate cross-border migration since Derry was their historic port of embarkation. While the border was uncertain until finally agreed in 1925, and cross-border movements were restricted during wartime to prevent IRA movements,[72] the reality was that people from Éire could move relatively easily to the north and then on to Britain. Moreover, there was no direct counting of migrants from the South who travelled to England or Scotland via the North, with the result that data on the migration is hazy. Even in wartime, according to the Home Office, there was no border control established between Éire and the North, although the Irish Sea routes were closely monitored.[73]

---

[70] *The Times*, 30 November 1923. These migrations fell markedly in 1927–28, according to reports in the *Board of Trade Journal*, quoted in *The Times*, 12 May 1928.

[71] P. Ollerenshaw, 'Business Boycotts and the Partition of Ireland', in B. Collins, P. Ollerenshaw, and T. Parkhill (eds), *Industry, Trade and People in Ireland, 1650–1950* (Belfast, 2005), 205–27; D. Fitzpatrick, 'The Orange Order and the Border', *Irish Historical Studies*, 33, 129 (May, 2002), 52–67.

[72] P. Ollerenshaw, 'War, industrial mobilisation and society in Northern Ireland 1939–1945', *Contemporary European History*, 16 (2007), 176.

[73] *Statistics of Foreigners Entering and Leaving the United Kingdom, 1939–1951* (B.P.P., 1952–53, Cmd. 8967), 3; E. Delaney, *Demography, State and Society: Irish Migration to Britain, 1921–1971* (Liverpool, 2000), 117.

Though the political machinations of creating two Irelands undoubtedly played a part, the primary cause of emigration remained economic. Reliant on traditional industries, notably textiles and shipbuilding, Northern Ireland suffered from economic hardship during the 1920s and 1930s. In this respect, Northern Ireland was simply one region of the United Kingdom and its people acted little differently from their counterparts in other depressed areas. Its position was, however, worsened by politics. Having used Ulster's industrial prowess as an argument in favour of its partition from the rest of Ireland, the government felt compelled to reject the Special Area status for fear of a consequent blow to prestige. As economic conditions hardened, this factor undoubtedly presaged migrations. After the disruptions of the War of Independence, the British Army began to report an upturn in recruitment from Ulster, a source of soldiers whose health and attitude drew approval.[74] Ministry of Labour calculations based on the movement of unemployed workers in 1937 noted that aside from a heavy migration of 1460 Northern Irish workers in that year, there was a generalized drift towards the south of England from outlying and depressed industrial regions across the whole UK.[75]

Wartime migrations were stimulated by persistent economic problems and targeted recruitment of Northern Irish workers by British firms. In 1939, there were complaints in Northern Ireland about the general economic relationship with Britain. Inward investment and industrial relocation had few positive effects for Northern Ireland. Labour continued to migrate to Britain at a time when Northern Ireland's heavy industry might reasonably expect to benefit from re-armament. However, Admiralty orders for Harland and Wolff were more modest than might be expected and a combination of logistics, transport, and the risk of IRA attack meant there was no place for Northern Ireland in the government's plans for Royal Ordnance Factories, which emerged in the immediate pre-war years.[76] Moreover, the structure of businesses in Northern Ireland, most of which were small or medium in size, and restrictive practices by both firms and unions, ensured the province fell short of the efficiencies found elsewhere in the UK. Whilst most migration was general and uncontrolled, there were also claims of poaching, particularly of skilled industrial workers.[77] Poaching was not simply confined to skilled machinists or shipwrights; it also swept up unskilled labour for the munitions factories. Whilst Northern Ireland politicians bitterly opposed this haemorrhaging of labour, the reception of these same migrations was met with warm approval in the north-west of England.[78] Northern Irish workers did not suffer the same level of suspicion and prejudice which led government to segregate wartime workers from Eire.[79] The loss of skilled workers to Britain attested to the value of

---

[74] *The Times*, 25 October 1924.   [75] Ibid., 21 September 1938.
[76] Ollerenshaw, 'War, Industrial Mobilisation and Society', 177–8.
[77] Ibid., 173, 177, 182 ff.
[78] *The Times*, 30 April 1941, which noted Northern Irish labour recruited alongside Poles, Belgians, French, and 'some aliens from the enemy territories who have passed the test of reliability'.
[79] A. V. Judges, 'Irish Labour in Great Britain, 1939–45', unpublished official history, TNA, LAB 8/1528, a shortened version of which is published in E. Delaney, 'Irish Migration to Britain, 1939–1945', *Irish Economic and Social History*, 28 (2001), 47–71.

Northern Irish labour. But at home it had a disproportionately negative effect on productivity in an economy in which 51 per cent of all insured labour was restricted to two desirable trades: shipbuilding and linen.[80]

At first sight it is perhaps ironic, given the rates of migration and emigration in Irish society that, during the Second World War, '[T]he potential supply of women workers *within* Northern Ireland seems to have been characterized by a very high degree of immobility'.[81] A local study around Antrim Town in 1943 suggested that widows with children and single women with family responsibilities comprised three-quarters of more than 2200 persons in this position. By a process of sifting and sorting those who could work from those who could not, only 3–4 per cent were genuinely available for migration to work.[82] A closer investigation suggests that these women were, in essence, the remainder of a much larger group: those who had moved of their own volition to find work in other parts of Northern Ireland, but who went unrecorded as such, and the more than 4500 who had been shipped to Britain to work in Royal Ordnance Factories.[83] From the outset of war to 1942, over 30,000 people from Northern Ireland, 10 per cent of them women, transferred to Britain for war work. In the three years following that a further 40,000 were recruited from Éire. All told, there was significant strategic movement from both Irelands to Britain.

CONCLUSIONS

Although it is hard to look beyond overseas emigration as the main driving force of population movement in Irish life during the period covered here, Ulster's situation was somewhat different. The cultural map of the province was redrawn in the seventeenth century, not because of the 'Flight of the Earls' and the launching of a tradition of overseas emigration, important though this was. More significant change was wrought by incomers, and, although their new environs were not entirely secured until after the Williamite wars, they nevertheless changed Ulster forever. Overseas emigration became important for English planters in Ulster in the later seventeenth century, but not until the eighteenth did the Presbyterians of Scottish extraction begin to follow them to the Americas. Thereupon began Ireland's first genuine mass emigration. However, Ulster's contribution to the story of population movement did not end there. The province remained the source of the largest migrations from Ireland until the famine of the 1840s, and it regained pre-eminence again in the 1870s. Only during the Famine, and again in the 1880s, did Munster and then Connacht become the main providers of emigrants. Ulster's share of the emigrant traffic overseas fell at that point so that the poorer western counties of Munster and especially Connacht became pre-eminent. Throughout the entire period, migration to Britain remained a key feature of Ulster life. While

---

[80] Figures on insured trades from 1926: *The Times*, 26 February 1926.
[81] Ollerenshaw, 'War, Industrial Mobilisation and Society', 190.
[82] Ministry of Labour for Northern Ireland, Availability of Unemployed Women Registered at Employment Exchanges, July/August 1943, PRONI COM 61/958.
[83] Ollerenshaw, 'War, Industrial Mobilisation and Society', 190–1.

most of these migrants went to Scotland, a significant minority also went to northern England. Even after partition, Northern Ireland provided steady flows of labour to Britain. Although we finish this survey at the end of the Second World War, the same connections between Ulster and the Clyde, Barrow and Tyneside, meant that Northern Irish labour—skilled men from Harland and Wolff, university-educated elites, professionals, mill-workers, and aspirant agriculturalists—continued to follow the path trodden by their forebears.

FURTHER READING

D. H. Akenson, *Ireland, Sweden and the Great European Migration, 1815–1914* (Liverpool, 2011).
R. J. Dickson, *Ulster Emigration to Colonial America, 1718–1775* (1966; Belfast, 1996 edn).
P. Fitzgerald and B. Lambkin, *Migration in Irish History, 1607–2007* (Basingstoke, 2009).
D. Fitzpatrick, *Oceans of Consolation: Personal Accounts of Irish Migration to Australia* (Dublin, 1994).
D. M. MacRaild, *The Irish Diaspora in Britain, 1815–1939* (Basingstoke, 2010).
K. A. Miller, A. Schrier, B. Boling, and D. N. Doyle, *Irish Immigrants in the Land of Canaan* (New York and Oxford, 2002).

10

The Rural Economy, 1780–1914

Liam Kennedy and Peter M. Solar

INTRODUCTION

The rural economy of Ulster was different from that of the rest of the island, the distinctions being particularly marked in relation to eastern or inner Ulster.[1] Observers in the late eighteenth century commented variously on the neatness of its farmyards and farmsteads, its commercial and market orientation, and the symbiotic relationship between farming and rural industry. Some attributed this progressiveness to ethnic factors: to the potent admixture of New English, New Scots, and native Irish to be found in the north-eastern part of the island. Be that as it may, the English agricultural expert, Arthur Young, had the severest reservations about farming practices in the province. Downplaying the economic significance of rural industry—primarily growing flax and manufacturing linen cloth—Young complained that industry in the countryside was impeding the adoption of larger-scale, technically efficient farming.[2] 'Change the scene, and view the North of Ireland', he remonstrated: 'you there behold a whole province peopled by weavers; it is they who cultivate, or rather beggar the soil, as well as work the looms; agriculture is there in ruins...all the crops you see are contemptible, are nothing but filth and weeds.'[3] Less fundamentalist 'agricultural improvers', however, recognized that the mixed or dual system of small-scale agriculture and rural industry was well adapted to the economic and demographic realities of life in Ulster in the later eighteenth century.

By the eve of the First World War, the rural economy of the region had been transformed, not only economically but socially as well. Small-scale, family farming still predominated but the tenant farmers, as they once were, were now owners and masters of the soil they tilled. Their landlords had been forced back, in economic terms at least, behind their great demesne walls, though the Big Houses dotted round the countryside still exercised a disproportionate influence within local and regional unionist politics. Further altering the social structure, cottiers and agricultural labourers had largely disappeared, though child and adolescent

---

[1] Inner Ulster is taken to comprise counties Antrim, Down, Armagh, and Londonderry.
[2] *Arthur Young's Tour in Ireland (1776–1779)*, edited with an introduction and notes by A. W. Hutton (Vol. 2, London, 1892), 214–15.
[3] Ibid., 214.

migratory labour still mattered in the better-off farming districts. Land-use patterns also changed as pastoral farming advanced at the expense of tillage crops, in line with comparative advantage. Partly as a consequence, the numbers of people in the countryside had diminished greatly from the mid-nineteenth century peak. Labour flowed off the land into the towns or overseas. But the biggest change of all was the narrowing of the economic base of rural society, as the once numerous rural handicraft enterprises contracted and eventually withered away. This was the 'agriculturalization', as it were, of the mixed or dual economy of eighteenth-century rural Ulster. Arthur Young's vision had been finally realized.

THE ENVIRONMENT

This chapter traces the course of that socio-economic change, but first it is worth identifying certain fundamental features of the Ulster rural economy that persisted over the entire period and that distinguish Ulster from the rest of Ireland. Some of these have their roots in the province's climate and in the nature of its soils. Like the rest of Ireland, Ulster has cool summers and mild winters by continental standards. But its northern situation makes it even cooler. Wheat is a precarious crop in these conditions and even during the boom in wheat cultivation before the Famine, relatively little was grown in Ulster. Some barley was cultivated, particularly in County Down until mid-century, but oats, a hardier cereal, was always the predominant grain crop in the province. In the year 1854, for example, oats accounted for 55 per cent of the cultivated land in Ulster, with only six per cent devoted to wheat and barley. In the rest of Ireland less than half (43 per cent) was under oats, but a considerably larger proportion (20 per cent) was under wheat and barley.[4]

Ulster, like the rest of Ireland, is noted for its rainfall, a condition made all the worse in the northern counties by the poor natural drainage of most of the soils. Sheep, which are prone to disease under wet conditions, were thus rare except in marginal upland areas. During the second half of the nineteenth century the highland county of Donegal accounted for over a third of the sheep in the province. Wet, poorly drained soils also required more human intervention if they were to remain productive. Unlike the limestone-based central plain just south of Ulster, extensive grazing was not an option. Ulster land needed mixed farming, with enough cultivation to prevent pastures from becoming waterlogged and enough pasture to restore soil fertility. Liming and marling, both quite labour-intensive activities associated with cultivation, could also improve the quality of Ulster soils. The Ordnance Survey Memoirs of the 1830s are replete with references to lime kilns and fertilizing practices.[5]

---

[4] *Returns of Agricultural Produce in Ireland in the year 1854* (British Parliamentary Papers, 1856, 53).

[5] See A. Day and P. McWilliams (eds), *Ordnance Survey Memoirs of Ireland* (40 vols, Belfast, 1990–9).

MIXED FARMING AND ULSTER'S DISTINCTIVENESS

Mixed farming on holdings of from five to fifty acres was thus the norm in Ulster agriculture throughout this period. This contrasts with the midlands and southern Ireland where much of the land was held in farms of fifty acres and upward, and where mixed farming was largely abandoned in many areas in the post-Famine decades. It is worth emphasizing that although in Ulster there were also many holdings of five acres or less, they occupied very little land, as can be seen in Table 10.1. After the Famine they accounted for less than 2 per cent of the land area. Just before the Famine it could have been no higher than 6 to 7 per cent.[6] By contrast, the five-to-fifty acre category of farms accounted for almost 60 per cent of the land in Ulster, but less than a third of that outside Ulster. This indicates a more egalitarian distribution of landholdings in the North. The product mix of Ulster agriculture remained remarkably stable over the century. Although Ulster farmers adapted to changing market conditions, their staple commodities remained as potatoes, oats, flax, butter, and pork throughout.

Climate and the needs of small family farms seem to have led to a distinct Ulster livestock system. Cattle, mainly dairy cows, in the north seem to have been smaller than those in the more fertile southern dairying areas and to have had correspondingly lower butter yields and smaller calves. The trade in cattle, therefore, was largely confined to Ulster (and some neighbouring areas in Connaught), with calves from the dairying districts being sold to upland areas, where they were reared and then sold back to dairymen. In some places dry cows and bullocks were also fattened for sale as meat. Pigs also seem to have been of a different breed to those

Table 10.1. Occupation of the land, by holding size (cumulative percentages) for the years 1854 and 1873

Holding	Ulster		Rest of Ireland	
Size (acres)	1854	1873	1854	1874
<1	0.1	0.1	0.1	0.1
1–5	2.0	1.7	1.4	1.3
5–15	18.0	16.1	8.1	8.0
15–30	42.6	40.3	20.0	20.1
30–50	60.4	58.7	32.9	33.2
50–100	77.5	76.7	52.9	53.8
100–200	86.3	86.1	71.3	72.3
200–500	92.8	92.6	88.3	88.7
>500	100.0	100.0	100.0	100.0

Source: *Returns of Agricultural Produce in Ireland, in the year 1854* (B.P.P., 1856, 53); *Agricultural Statistics of Ireland for the year 1874* (B.P.P., 1876, 78).

[6] P. M. A. Bourke, 'The Agricultural Statistics of the 1841 Census of Ireland: A Critical Review', *Economic History Review*, 18 (1965), 380. Bourke's figures for the numbers of holdings in various size classes in 1845 for Ireland as a whole have been converted into areas using figures for average holding sizes in various ranges from the Irish agricultural statistics, which were published annually from 1847. The share for farms of five acres or less is 4 per cent, as against 1.5 per cent for all of Ireland in 1854.

in the south. By the end of the century crosses of native pigs with various English breeds eventually produced the White Ulster pig.

This depiction of the continuities in the Ulster rural economy and of its distinctiveness within Ireland needs qualification in two respects. First, provincial boundaries were not necessarily economic boundaries. Some northern parts of counties Louth and Meath were also characterized by small-scale, mixed farming.[7] Further west, parts of Leitrim, Sligo, and even Mayo were also similar in certain respects and there were connections with these counties through the livestock trade and in the development of rural industry. In the eighteenth century, Ulster had also drawn supplies of oats and potatoes from these areas in times of dearth.[8] The second qualification is that there were important differences among regions within Ulster. The upland areas of Antrim and west Donegal had different crop mixes and social structures. So, too, did the Ards peninsula in eastern County Down. Fermanagh was unusual in many respects, not least in being prone to flooding.

SOCIAL STRUCTURE

By the 1780s the Ulster countryside had become thoroughly permeated with industrial activity, most of it associated with the spinning of flax and the weaving of linen cloth. During the eighteenth century the linen industry had grown spectacularly, coming to dominate Ireland's manufactured exports. Whilst there was some production of coarse linens in County Cork and in north Leinster, the bulk of output, including all of the more valuable fine linens, was made in Ulster. The heartland of the industry was in counties Antrim, Armagh, and Down where the finest linens were woven and where bleaching was concentrated. Further west, in counties Tyrone, Londonderry, Monaghan, Cavan, and eastern Donegal, coarser cloths were woven and yarn was spun to supply both local weavers and those in eastern Ulster. Although the industry never seems to have become firmly established in much of County Fermanagh, its tentacles were starting to reach even further west, into counties Sligo and Mayo. The industry is often characterized as one pursued by more or less self-sufficient rural households, in which the flax was cultivated and prepared on the farm to be spun into yarn by the women of the household, and the yarn woven into cloth by the men.[9] Whilst this was sometimes the case, the dominant pattern was one of extensive trade in flax and yarn, both between and within regions.[10]

The social structure of rural Ulster might be conceptualized along the lines of a steep, multi-layered pyramid. At the apex were the relatively small number of aristocratic families and institutions such as Trinity College and the London

---

[7] P. Connell, *The Land and People of County Meath, 1750–1850* (Dublin, 2004), Ch. 7.
[8] J. M'Parlan, *A Statistical Survey of the County of Sligo* (Dublin, 1802), 14.
[9] L. Kennedy, 'The Rural Economy, 1820–1914', in L. Kennedy and P. Ollerenshaw (eds), *An Economic History of Ulster, 1820–1939* (Manchester, 1985), 2.
[10] W. H. Crawford, *Domestic Industry in Ireland* (Dublin, 1972), 39; W. H. Crawford, *The Impact of the Domestic Linen Industry in Ulster* (Belfast, 2005), 138.

companies that owned most of the land, but farmed very little of it. The great proprietors, like the Marquis of Downshire, the Earl of Antrim, or the Earl of Gosford, had tens of thousands of acres. Some constructed magnificent houses and parks within the demesne lands, and lived at least part of the year on their estates. Some lived in England or in the south of Ireland, and left the management of their estates in the hands of agents. In some cases, such as much of the London companies' property in County Londonderry and the Trinity College estates in counties Armagh and Donegal, the proprietors had effectively ceded control of their estates to large tenants by granting very long leases.[11] More typically though, landlords exercised not only economic power over their tenants but social and political power as well. Landlords or their representatives dominated the rudimentary local government afforded by the system of county Grand Juries. They were dominant also on the early boards of poor-law unions, although tenant representation (and sometimes hostility) increased in the later nineteenth century. Some landlords had parliamentary ambitions as well, sometimes expending vast sums of money to ensure election to Westminster.

Below the great proprietors was a stratum of tenant farmers. Some in areas like north Antrim and the Foyle Valley had large holdings, but the bulk of Ulster farmers were small scale, living on holdings ranging in size from ten to fifty acres. By the late eighteenth century many farmers held their land by lease from the head landlord rather than middlemen. These leases were generally for three lives, an indeterminate term that could often run for decades. The tenants of some of the smaller farms, those with five to ten acres or so, may have also been engaged in textile production, but tenants with more land, certainly those with twenty acres or more, were primarily farmers.

Farmer-weavers and cottier-weavers usually held five acres or less, just enough to sustain a family on a fairly meagre diet of potatoes, oatmeal, and perhaps some buttermilk. Sometimes these holdings were sublet from farmers, but increasingly landlords had become willing to grant leases for such small plots. A fairly rosy picture of this class was given by one of the assistant handloom weavers' commissioners in 1840:

> The weavers are small farmers and cotters, cultivating land; the loom occupies one corner of a cabin, and a pig another. In fine weather, the weaver is in the field looking after his crop of oats or potatoes; when the weather is unfavourable, he returns to the loom; or perhaps the wife, or some junior member of the family, is kept at the loom, while the husband attends to the field work. Thus when the loom pays the rent, and the farm supplies provisions, a family may live in much more favourable circumstances than one earning three times the amount in money wages, but having to buy everything.[12]

At the bottom of the social heap were the journeymen weavers and agricultural labourers ('unbound labourers') who were without secure access to land. They often had to settle for the right to cultivate potatoes on a farmer's field in exchange for their labour on the loom or on the farmer's cereal crops. Less easy to classify are

---

[11] R. B. MacCarthy, *The Trinity College Estates, 1800–1923* (Dublin, 1992), Ch. 5.
[12] *Report from the Assistant Handloom Weavers' Commissioners* (B.P.P., 24, 1840), 651.

the farm servants. These might be the sons and daughters of small farmers, committed to farm servanthood for only the early years of their lives, or they might be the children of labouring households destined for a life of servitude. Farm servants were both male and female, living-in with their employers, and were often children or young adolescents. They were usually hired by the half year. Hiring fairs were held twice yearly, usually around the 12 May and the 12 November, in the main towns. In Donegal the big hiring fairs were at Letterkenny, Milford, and Ballybofey, while farther east, Strabane, Coleraine, and Newry were important 'open-air, labour exchanges'.[13] Typically the movement of child and adolescent labour was from west to east, or from upland to lowland; that is, from areas of high population density and impoverished smallholdings to the more fertile, commercial farming areas. This sometimes meant crossing from one cultural zone into another: from Irish or Gaelic-speaking to English-speaking districts and from Catholic to Protestant households. Thus the child migrants who travelled from west Donegal to the Foyle Valley in the east of the county crossed social as well as geographical boundaries. A period of farm servanthood, in turn, could be an apprenticeship for seasonal migration to England and Scotland or for more permanent emigration at a later age.

TRADE AND FLUCTUATIONS BEFORE THE GREAT FAMINE

While farming dominated the Ulster landscape at the end of the eighteenth century, as is evident from contemporary sketches of the small enclosed fields and the scattered farm dwellings, it is perhaps surprising that little agricultural produce was exported. Ulster's comparative advantage lay in linen production, and it was linen textiles that accounted for the bulk of exports from the Ulster ports. Thus, as Table 10.2 shows, Ulster accounted for less than 10 per cent of Irish agricultural exports in the 1780s. The exceptions were the irregular, but often large, flows of live cattle and lesser movements of live pigs shipped from Donaghadee and other east Ulster ports, but many of these animals had been driven from the grazing areas in the south of Ireland to take advantage of the short sea crossing to Scotland. The low level of agricultural exports suggests that Ulster was largely self-sufficient in food and raw materials, although it imported grain from elsewhere in Ireland in some years.

The period from the 1780s to the end of the French wars in 1815 has been called the 'golden age of the handloom weaver'.[14] Irish linen exports grew rapidly until the 1790s, then levelled off. That exports did not fall in the face of increased competition from Lancashire cotton goods owed much to the specialization of the Ulster industry in medium and fine qualities of cloth. The mechanization of cotton

---

[13] J. Bell, 'Hiring Fairs in Ulster', *Ulster Folklife*, 25 (1979), 67–78; J. Campbell, 'Are ye fer Hiring?', *Journal of the Poyntzpass and District Historical Society*, 9 (2003), 15–23.

[14] W. A. Crawford, *Domestic Industry in Ireland: The Experience of the Linen Industry* (Dublin, 1972), 26–8, 37.

Table 10.2. Ulster's share (%) of Irish agricultural exports: selected commodities, 1783–87

Wheat	
Barley	7
Oats	14
Live cattle	96
Live pigs	98
Bacon	0
Salt beef	5
Butter	9
Salt pork	8
All agricultural exports	12

Source: National Library of Ireland, MSS 357–359, Irish customs accounts.

spinning, and the steep fall in the price of cotton yarn from the 1780s, increased the demand for cotton weavers and some of this spilled over to Ireland, and the Belfast region in particular. Weavers round Belfast were enticed by higher wages to switch from linen to cotton, drawing their supplies of yarn from the nascent Ulster cotton-spinning industry and from British manufacturers.[15] This, in turn, sustained the demand for linen weavers in more peripheral areas. The demand for textiles maintained rural household incomes, even in the face of very rapid population growth. Weavers' earnings remained high until the end of the French wars. There was little emigration during this period, although recruitment for the military during the wars had the same effect in removing significant numbers of young men from the labour force, sometimes permanently.

The period from the 1780s to the end of the wars might also be termed a golden age for Ulster farmers. The wars increased demand for agricultural products, as did the prosperity of the textile sector. Whilst prices rose dramatically during the wars, farmers' costs lagged well behind. In general, rents on new lettings rose along with prices, although they lagged behind a bit in the 1790s. But farmers who had long leases dating from the eighteenth century were able to capture all of the increase in the return to land, either by cultivating it themselves or by subletting it to weavers eager to have smallholdings. Only when leases came due were the landlords able to extract higher rents. For those farmers who hired labourers, and they were less common in Ulster than in Leinster or Munster, the wages for agricultural labourers tended to lag behind prices, thereby reducing the real cost of labour.[16] Whatever growth there was in agricultural output, most of it was consumed in Ulster. Exports grew only modestly until the mid-1800s, about doubling since the mid-1780s.

---

[15] E. R. R. Green, *The Lagan Valley* (London, 1949), 97–9; A. Bielenberg and P. M. Solar, 'The Irish Cotton Industry from the Industrial Revolution to Partition', *Irish Economic and Social History*, 34 (2007), 1–28.

[16] F. Geary and T. Stark, 'Trends in Real Wages during the Industrial Revolution: A View from across the Irish Sea', *Economic History Review*, 57, 2 (2004), 376–8.

The years up to 1815 were not ones of unbroken prosperity. Even in normal years there were the hungry or 'meal' months of early summer, when the old potato crop was rotting and the new potato crop had yet to come on stream. This was less of a problem in Ulster, where the consumption of oatmeal as well as potatoes was an established part of the people's diet, than in the poorer south-western counties where dependence on the potato was more extreme. But crop failures certainly brought misery to the poor, as the necessities of life became much more expensive.[17] This bore heavily on the rural and town labourers, and it could be even worse for their dependents. Many labourers were paid in kind as well as in cash, and clearly meals received at a place of work could not be shared with other family members. The effects on farmers' incomes, however, depended on the size of the surpluses they had to sell at the high prices that characterized such crises.[18] Those needing to enter the market place to secure provisions clearly lost out. Marginal surplus producers, such as those with holdings of less than five acres, could be forced back into self-subsistence and might well feel the debilitating effects of scarcity. Farmers producing a sizeable surplus in normal years, by contrast, would find that reduced yields were more than compensated for by the high prices they now received. Thus social class differences need to be borne firmly in mind when assessing the distributional impact of years of dearth. Moreover, even for those close to the margin of subsistence, earnings from rural industry could help cushion Ulster's dual producers; that is, unless a downturn in demand for linen yarn or cloth happened to coincide with a poor harvest. Not all of the rural poor, it should be added, were dual producers.

The series of poor harvests in 1782–85 led to one of the few bursts of transatlantic emigration in this period. 1795 was also a bad year, but the worst years of all were in 1799–1801.[19] Crop failures in these years resulted in potato and oatmeal prices that were even higher than those that would prevail during the Great Famine of the late 1840s.[20] Exports of agricultural produce largely stopped. There were imports of cereals and even maize from North America, though they were not sufficiently prompt as to prevent spasmodic food riots.

The years from the end of the French wars to the Great Famine were difficult ones for the Ulster rural economy. There was very little growth in exports of linen cloth and prices were depressed by the competition from cotton fabrics.[21] The handloom weaving of cotton cloth in east Ulster largely disappeared as the powerloom was adopted in Lancashire from the 1810s and in the Belfast cotton industry from the

---

[17] On short- and long-run changes in the cost of living see L. Kennedy, 'The Cost of Living in Ireland, 1698–1998', in D. Dickson and C. Ó Gráda (eds), *Refiguring Ireland* (Dublin, 2003), 249–76.

[18] For some theoretical reflections on social structure and scarcity see J. D. Gould, 'Agricultural Fluctuations and the English Economy in the Eighteenth Century', *Journal of Economic History*, 22, 3 (1962), 313–33.

[19] R. Wells, 'The Irish Famine of 1799–1801: Market Culture, Moral Economies and Social Protest', in A. Randall and A. Charlesworth (eds), *Markets, Market Culture and Popular Protest in Eighteenth-Century Britain and Ireland* (Liverpool, 1996), 163–93.

[20] L. Kennedy and P. M. Solar, *Irish Agriculture: A Price History* (Dublin, 2007), 142, 150. Using harvest or production years, the price of potatoes on the Belfast market in 1800 was five times that of 1798, the year of revolution in the North.

[21] P. M. Solar, 'The Irish Linen Trade, 1820–1852', *Textile History*, 21 (1990), 57–85.

1820s. Weavers' real earnings fell markedly between the 1810s and the 1830s.[22] Households also saw women's earnings fall away as the mechanization of flax spinning began in earnest at the end of the 1820s, although in east Ulster the development of a putting-out trade in muslin embroidery from around 1830 provided employment for many women.[23] The advent of cheaper machine-spun yarn also put weavers far from the spinning mills at a disadvantage. The difficulties in the textile industry led many individuals and families, particularly from the southern and western parts, to leave Ulster either to work in the textiles mills of Britain or to try their luck in North America.[24] Those who stayed often resorted to seasonal migration to sustain a shrinking household income. In the hinterland of Derry some former spinners found employment in the shirt-making trade that took off from the 1830s.

Falling earnings from textile production made rural households more dependent on agriculture. There was a marked increase in agricultural exports from around 1810 to about 1830, but there was little subsequent growth in the 1830s and early 1840s. This burst in exports might have been the result of a significant increase in output, but it is not clear what could have caused it to happen at this particular time. There do not appear to have been any major technological changes in Ulster agriculture from the late eighteenth century to the Famine.[25] Crop yields remained more or less constant from the time of Arthur Young's tour of Ireland in the 1780s until the early 1840s.[26] There is no convincing evidence of significant increases in butter yields or livestock weights. The agricultural system described by Young, involving rotations of potatoes, flax, oats, and grass, and the use of spade husbandry, was still in place in the early 1840s.

It is likely that Ulster farmers were having to work harder to keep in the same place. One can get an idea of the productivity of the resources being employed in agriculture by comparing the prices of the outputs with the prices of the inputs. If input prices are rising faster than output prices, then in order to be able to pay more to the factors of production there have to have been increases in the efficiency with which they are used. A rough calculation for Ulster, based on agricultural prices at Belfast, rents in County Armagh, and various observations on the wages of rural labourers, shows that prices and rents rose by about the same amount from the 1780s to the 1830s, but that wages lagged well behind.[27] What this suggests is that the efficiency with which resources were used was declining. It is likely that more and more labour had to be applied in order to maintain existing yields. If so,

---

[22] Geary and Stark, 'Trends', 378–80.

[23] B. Collins, 'Sewing and Social Structure: The Flowerers of Scotland and Ireland', in R. Mitchison and P. Roebuck (eds), *Economy and Society in Scotland and Ireland, 1500–1939* (Edinburgh, 1988), 242–53.

[24] B. Collins, 'Proto-Industrialisation and Pre-Famine Emigration', *Social History*, 7 (1982), 127–46.

[25] On the gradual adoption of improved English and Scottish farm tools and techniques see J. Bell, 'Scottish Influences on Irish Farming Techniques', in R. J. Morris and L. Kennedy (eds), *Ireland and Scotland: Order and Disorder, 1600–2000* (Edinburgh, 2005), 45–57.

[26] R. C. Allen and C. Ó Gráda, 'On the Road Again with Arthur Young: English, Irish and French Agriculture during the Industrial Revolution', *Journal of Economic History*, 48 (1988), 93–116.

[27] For prices see Kennedy and Solar, *Irish Agriculture*, 131–53; for rents see P. M. Solar and L. Hens, 'Land under Pressure: The Value of Irish Land in a Period of Rapid Population Growth, 1730–1844', forthcoming in *Agricultural History Review*, 2012; and for wage rates see L. Kennedy and M. Dowling, 'Prices and Wages in Ireland, 1700–1850', *Irish Economic & Social History*, 24 (1997), 62–104.

this suggests greater industriousness on the part of farmers and labourers, mirroring what was claimed for handloom weavers in Ulster: longer working hours and possibly increased work intensity.

It is tempting then to read the burst of exports after the French wars as due, at least in part, to a diversion of goods from domestic consumption, as well as a reduction in leisure, in the face of pressures on rural incomes. There is no doubt the post-war deflation in agricultural prices redistributed income toward landlords, as the real value of the rents paid on long leases increased. In addition, as time went on eighteenth-century leases fell in and land could be re-let at higher rents. This redistribution of income did not proceed smoothly. The downward trend in prices was made difficult to discern by the bad crop yields and accompanying epidemics of 1816–18. During the late 1810s and early 1820s arrears of rent tended to accumulate on some estates and landlords offered temporary abatements of rent. Eventually tenants who had taken leases at high wartime rates were often able to renegotiate their rents downward. Yet by around 1830 the total rents due to Ulster landlords were almost always higher than they had been *c.*1810 and, insofar as one can tell, they were being paid. Largely as the result of more eighteenth-century leases falling in, rents would continue to creep upwards until the Famine, but not sufficiently to squeeze out more exports from the farming sector.

An important development in the twenty years before the Famine was the beginning of egg exports to Britain. The introduction of steam ships on the Irish Sea in the 1820s, by making the crossing quicker and, above all, more reliable, started a trade that would grow to account for 10 per cent of Irish agricultural exports on the eve of the First World War. The production of eggs took hold in a big way on the small farms in Ulster, particularly those in the south and west. Collectors in these areas assembled crates of eggs to be shipped by steamer from the ports of Belfast, Derry, Newry, and Dundalk.

The effects of the wartime inflation and the post-war deflation were factors in pushing landlords to tighten up the management of their estates. During the wars they started granting shorter leases, although one life and twenty-one years was still a fairly long term. Such leases were still being granted in the 1830s and 1840s, but other landlords were moving toward yearly tenancies or tenancies at will. The decline of rural textile production brought into question the viability of very small holdings, and wariness about poor tenants was reinforced by the introduction of the Irish Poor Law in the late 1830s.

The *raison d'être* of the poor law was to stretch an institutional safety net, financed by local rates, under the very poorest in Irish society. Workhouses in each locality— there were initially 130 of these—formed the centrepiece of the system, offering food and shelter but only under the most stringent conditions, to those incapable of earning a living. This elaborate system was funded from taxes on landed property, something that was less than popular with landlords and their more substantial tenant farmers who paid rates. Landlords were responsible, however, for payments for their poorer tenants, the cut-off point being holdings valued at under £4. So, when the occasion presented itself, some landlords tried to rid themselves of small tenants and encourage the consolidation of holdings.

The massive Poor Enquiry of 1836 took evidence on the extent to which holdings were being amalgamated, and by implication smallholders squeezed out, in the decades after 1815.[28] While the evidence is mixed, it appears that the tendency had achieved little momentum by the 1830s, thereby indicating the clear limits to landlord power. In Ulster the tradition of Ulster Custom, and the right of the outgoing tenant to sell the value of his or her interest in the holding, meant that there was an incentive for distressed tenants to sell up, moving the whole family to another district or to Britain or North America.[29] This practice was held to account for the more quiescent relationship between landlords and tenants in Ulster, as compared to counties notorious for agrarian violence and agrarian secret societies, such as Tipperary and Limerick in the far south.[30]

THE GREAT FAMINE AND AFTER

The crisis of the late 1840s did not spare Ulster, but its effects were less severe than they were elsewhere in Ireland. The advent of blight led to repeated deficiencies in the potato crop. The potato crop failures in 1845 and 1846 were exacerbated by poor cereal crops over much of northern Europe in 1846, leading to the peak in distress in the first eight months of 1847. Even the burgeoning industrial town of Belfast was not immune. The average price of oatmeal rose by 27 per cent between 1845 and 1846 while potato prices more than doubled in the same period.[31] Soaring inflation for the necessities of life plunged households into dire poverty. Downward pressure on wages and under-employment in the textiles industry in late 1846 added to the misery. In Belfast and the Lagan Valley this meant that thousands of weavers and town labourers were thrown out of work or onto greatly reduced incomes. The problems were sufficiently acute for the Mayor of Belfast, John Kane, to summon a public meeting in the Town Hall on the 17 November 1846. A motion moved by the Rev. Dr Edgar urged: 'That, in seasons like the present, when, by the visitation of a mysterious Providence, the working classes have been deprived of their staple article of food, and when the calamity is accompanied by diminished employment and wages, it becomes the duty of the opulent to make more than ordinary efforts to contribute to the comforts of their suffering neighbours.'[32] The seriousness of the crisis was underlined by a food riot in Belfast in the following month. Seemingly unimpressed either by theodicy or the prospect of charity, hundreds of labourers took their fate into their own hands, assembling outside the main bakeries and demanding bread. Hughes Bakery in the town centre and the Church Street Bakery felt obliged to offer bread to the demonstrators, although some of the leaders were apprehended and later imprisoned.[33] With rising

---

[28] *Poor Inquiry (Ireland): Appenidix F* (B.P.P., 1836, 33).
[29] T. W. Guinnane and R. I. Miller, 'Bonds without Bondsmen: Tenant-Right in Nineteenth-Century Ireland', *Journal of Economic History*, 56, 1 (1996), 114.
[30] J. S. Donnelly Jr, *Landlord and Tenant in Nineteenth-Century Ireland* (Dublin, 1973).
[31] Kennedy and Solar, *Irish Agriculture*, 144, 152.
[32] *Belfast News Letter*, 20 November 1846.   [33] *Northern Whig*, December 1846.

food imports, particularly American maize, the price of provisions wound downwards and was on a lower plane by the start of 1848. In the autumn of that year, however, Ulster was caught up in the sharp but short-lived trade depression of 1847–48 which affected the industrial regions of the United Kingdom more generally. A healthy but tiny potato crop in 1847 and the return of the potato blight in 1848, and to a lesser extent in 1849, meant that the period was one of prolonged back-to-back famines, with varying regional and social effects.

Because of its comparative prosperity, Belfast was a magnet for refugees from other parts of Ulster. With refugees came disease, in particular the deadly famine disease typhus. By the spring of 1847—Black '47 as it is known in the Irish folk memory—Belfast was in the grip of famine fever. One sympathetic clergyman, the Rev. Richard Oulton, spoke of how his feelings 'had been harrowed by the dreadful sights he had seen in graveyards, of late, when attending at the graves of the departed. Coffins were heaped upon coffins, until the last one very often was not more than two inches under ground; and in finding room for others, bodies that had not been long buried were often exhumed.'[34] He feared the terrible Famine scenes of Skibbereen in West Cork might soon be brought to their own doors.

Fortunately this proved not to be the case, despite the trade depression of 1847–48. Because of its more diversified economic base, Belfast and other industrializing towns of east Ulster did not experience the most terrifying effects of malnutrition, disease, and death. Particular districts of rural Ulster, however, experienced the most severe effects of the crisis.[35] Small farming, potato-dependent households in south Ulster—Cavan, Monaghan, and south Armagh—were especially vulnerable to semi-starvation and the death-dealing effects of famine-related diseases.[36] In parts of Ulster, landlords were active in 1848 and 1849 in clearing their estates of pauper tenants, destroying their habitations, and throwing the unfortunate people onto the roadside. The parish priest of Drung in County Cavan accused some landlords of 'wanting in common humanity', as they 'exterminate [evict] right and left'. In his parish, he wrote, 'at present there are fifty farms vacant, 200 human beings sent adrift in an inclement season to beg or die; many of them have since died'.[37] The misery of a natural disaster was thus compounded by callous policies of disregard for the sufferings of the rural poor. Thousands died, while many thousands more migrated to the industrializing towns of east Ulster. Still larger numbers emigrated.

It was the case, nonetheless, that famine mortality was lower in Ulster than in Ireland generally. This was for several reasons. First, many of Ulster's poor had already emigrated. Second, the persistence of handloom weaving of linens and the introduction of some other rural by-employments, such as the embroidery of muslins, meant that many households in Ulster did not depend solely on agriculture. Third, those who had leases on smallholdings had an asset to sell, either to feed

[34] *Belfast News Letter*, 16 July 1847.
[35] C. Kinealy and T. Parkhill (eds), *The Famine in Ulster: The Regional Impact* (Belfast, 1997).
[36] For a view of the denominational impact see D. W. Miller, 'Irish Presbyterians and the Great Famine', in J. Hill and C. Lennon (eds), *Luxury and Austerity* (Dublin, 1999), 165–81.
[37] Quoted in D. Gallogly, 'The Famine in County Cavan', in Kinealy and Parkhill, *Famine in Ulster*, 72.

themselves or to finance emigration. Fourth, the prevalence of small farms in Ulster probably meant that the distribution of income was less unequal, leaving a lower share of the population at risk. Fifth, the widespread cultivation of oats on Ulster's farms provided an alternative source of food.

The introduction of the blight had longer-term consequences for the Ulster rural economy. Average potato yields fell by about half and the potato became a much less reliable crop. For farmers this meant that the real cost of labourers fed primarily on potatoes had increased significantly. Even labourers fed on cereals were becoming more expensive, as wages rose because of the massive loss of population in Ireland and because British wages had started to rise more rapidly from mid-century. Within a few decades the unattached farm labourer would largely disappear, and farmers would have to depend on family resources.[38]

The fallibility of the potato also encouraged some reorientation of Ulster agriculture toward pasture. More importantly, the trend in relative prices favoured livestock production, a movement in relative prices whose origins pre-dated the Famine. Still, tillage remained important, more important than in other parts of Ireland but cattle numbers increased markedly over the Famine and post-Famine decades. Butter and livestock exports showed a strong upward movement.

Another casualty of increased wages after the Famine was the rural handloom weaver. It had been possible to use powerlooms to make coarse linens since the 1820s, but it took some technical advances in mid-century to weave fine linens using steam power. Higher wages after the Famine encouraged manufacturers to adopt powerlooms, which began the slow, but inexorable, decline of handloom production. Weaving had largely moved into the factories by the 1860s, but handloom weavers clung on in some districts, such as north Antrim, until around 1900.[39]

The two decades after the Famine were largely favourable for Ulster's farmers, although the outlook did not look immediately promising. The repeal of the corn laws and other agricultural protection in 1846 constituted a potentially dangerous development for rural interests, though of course benefiting Ulster's urban dwellers. The threat to rural incomes seemed to be confirmed by the very low food prices in 1849–51. These were among the lowest of the century, and served to stimulate the formation of Presbyterian-dominated tenant right clubs. Yet in the 1850s agricultural prices had more than recovered, and Ulster farmers could sell their oats, pork, and butter in the industrial towns of England and increasingly in the rapidly expanding Belfast market.

In Ulster, cereal and potato cultivation, whilst less than before the Famine, proved more resilient than in the rest of Ireland. This happened in the face of a strong movement in relative prices in favour of pasture products that was especially evident from the late 1840s until the mid-1880s.[40] The persistence of tillage in

---

[38] D. Fitzpatrick, 'The Disappearance of the Irish Agricultural Labourer', *Irish Economic and Social History*, 7 (1980), 66–92.

[39] K. J. James, *Handloom Weavers in Ulster's Linen Industry, 1815–1914* (Dublin, 2007).

[40] Kennedy and Solar, *Irish Agriculture*, 98.

Ulster may be attributed to the prevalence of small farms and the need for mixed farming. Within Ulster the decline in tillage was concentrated in the south Ulster counties of Fermanagh, Cavan, and Monaghan.

In the early 1860s, the American Civil War caused shortages of raw cotton, which created a boom in the linen industry and a greatly increased demand not only for food, but for flax as well. Ulster farmers responded by increasing the amount of land under the crop from around 100,000 acres in the 1850s to over 200,000 acres in the mid-1860s, but this was far from enough. Even before the Famine, the industry's demand for flax had started to exceed local supplies. First the Royal Society for the Promotion and Improvement in the Growth of Flax in Ireland, founded in early 1840s, then the Flax Supply Association, founded in 1867, sought to encourage cultivation, not only in Ulster but in the rest of Ireland, but their efforts outside Ulster largely came to nought. Even Ulster supplies were to prove inadequate, and by the late nineteenth century the industry had come to rely increasingly on imported flax. The acreage under flax in 1914 was less than that in 1851. An important reason why Ulster farmers were reluctant to increase flax cultivation is that it was a very labour-intensive crop and labour was becoming more expensive as the Ulster countryside thinned out due to migration and emigration.

The Famine led to rising rent arrears on many Ulster estates. Some already heavily indebted estates, such as those of the Donegall family, were pushed over into insolvency and ended up in the Encumbered Estates Court. As leases fell in, landlords raised rents during the 1850s and 1860s. Thus, on most estates rents due in the late 1850s were well above those in the early 1840s, and they were in general being paid.

TRIUMPH OF THE TENANT FARMER

The early to mid-1870s marked a turning point for European and Ulster agriculture. Agricultural prices stopped rising, and in Britain and Ireland fell by about 25 per cent between the early 1870s and the late 1880s. There was a modest upward movement from the late 1890s, but on the eve of the First World War agricultural prices were still about 10 per cent below their peak. The volatility of food prices had, however, diminished over the century, which was of benefit both to farmers and consumers. An outline impression of long-run changes in the price level for agricultural goods can be gleaned from Table 10.3.

Trends in the relative prices of different farm commodities also mattered. Broadly speaking, from the early 1790s to the early 1880s, relative price change had favoured pastoral products at the expense of tillage products, though the swing to pastoral production was less pronounced in the northern province. This long-run trend was reversed, but only mildly, in the quarter century before the First World War, and was not sufficient to arrest the tendency away from tillage production.

The abrupt reversal in farming fortunes in the later nineteenth century brought landlord-tenant relations into sharp relief. By the autumn of 1879 the west of

Table 10.3. An agricultural price index, based on Belfast market prices, selected years 1785–1913 (1856–60 = 100)

1785	1813	1840	1846	1850	1876	1896	1913
51	108	88	118	76	114	83	97

Source: Kennedy and Solar, *Irish Agriculture*, 188–91.

Ireland was ablaze with agrarian agitation. The Land War had begun, and Land League clubs spread rapidly in the south and west of the island. What of Ulster? Traditionally, Ulster tenants had enjoyed rather loosely defined rights or privileges that were summed up in the phrase 'Ulster tenant right'. These customary claims supplemented, indeed sometimes contradicted, the more narrowly contractual relationships binding landlord and tenant. These extra-legal rights varied from estate to estate, but often carried the presumption that a sitting tenant could expect renewal of a lease, once it had expired; that rents would be 'fair', meaning essentially lower than the competitive or rack-rent; and that on vacating a holding he or she had the right to sell the value of the unexpired lease to the incoming tenant. The last could be valuable, amounting on some farms to ten times or more the annual rent paid to the landlord, suggesting that *actual* rents were well below the *competitive* rent level.

Some of the larger social benefits claimed for the Ulster Custom may be questioned, but it does help explain the relatively quiescent state of relations between landlords and their tenantry in eighteenth- and nineteenth-century Ulster.[41] However, falling prices and incomes severely strained these relations. By 1880 Protestant as well as Catholic tenants were demanding rent reductions. In Fermanagh some tenant farmers who were members of the Orange Order actually joined the militant Land League.[42] Thus the Land War sent shock waves through Ulster society, opening up divisions between landlords and tenants, intensifying conflict between Tories and Liberals, and dividing Catholic voters between liberalism and Home Rule politics.[43] Agrarian militancy was less marked in the North as compared to the South, not because Protestant tenants were 'free-riding' on the sacrifices of their southern counterparts, but because over time Protestant farmers were repelled by the nationalist trappings of the Irish National Land League. Presbyterian radicalism, linked to political liberalism, concentrated on alternative strategies of collective representation, negotiation and use of the land courts, and was focused more narrowly on rent reductions and land reform. Home Rule was simply a turn-off.

In response to widespread agitation in Ireland, Gladstone's Liberal government introduced a Land Act in 1881 that was to have momentous consequences. It established land courts which adjudicated between landlords and tenants. To the dismay of landlords, the typical decisions of the land courts were in one direction

---

[41] Kennedy, 'Rural Economy', 38–9.
[42] P. Bew and F. Wright, 'The Agrarian Opposition in Ulster Politics, 1848–87', in S. Clark and J. S. Donnelly Jr, (eds), *Irish Peasants: Violence and Political Unrest, 1780–1914* (Dublin, 1983), 218.
[43] Ibid., 213–19.

only, that of rent reductions. Still, against a backdrop of depressed prices, market conditions would have exerted downward pressure on rents in any case. A further Land Act in 1882 abolished rent arrears for smallholders. This was particularly important for farms in the hill country of south Armagh, Cavan, and west Donegal.

In the longer term, one of the most important features of Gladstone's 1881 Land Act was the provision for tenants to buy out their landlords. Peasant proprietorship was in the air, though only a few short years earlier Charles Stewart Parnell, the president of the Land League, had deemed this an unrealistic goal.[44] A series of land acts from the 1880s onwards extended these initial, tentative movements in the direction of owner occupancy. The key land act was promoted by George Wyndham, Chief Secretary for Ireland. The Wyndham Land Act of 1903, extended in 1909, provided the financial means for most Irish tenants to buy out their landlords. This was 'social revolution from above'. Whether viewed as 'killing Home Rule with kindness'—the major land purchase acts were originated by Tory administrations—or as attempts at 'justice for Ireland', there is no doubt that a social revolution was in train.

By the eve of the First World War, the rural social structure was very different from that at the time of Waterloo, at the end of the Napoleonic era. Textile industries in the countryside had been extinguished by competition, and with them went the world of the hand spinner and the handloom weaver. The rural labourer had not quite disappeared but the Famine, migration, and emigration had greatly diminished their numbers. The representative figure in the rural landscape was now a property holder, a small- or middling-sized farmer, employing family labour in the main. Admittedly small-scale farming, with its associated low productivity and low incomes, harboured structural problems for the region in the twentieth century, as is apparent in Chapter 17 by Greer. (Had the United Kingdom adopted agricultural protectionism in reaction to the 'great agricultural depression' of 1876–96, as did many of its European neighbours, the stored-up problems of rural poverty would have been all the greater. Certainly rural Ulster exemplified the structural deficiencies of West European agriculture—a proliferation of smallholdings with low family incomes—but it was by no means an extreme case.) Meanwhile the landed ascendancy had surrendered most of its lands to its former tenants; in effect, the one-time landowners of Ulster had become peripheral to the economic if not the political concerns of rural society. But the rural economy itself had shrunk heavily relative to the industrial and service sectors of the Ulster economy, in part because economic activities that once characterized the countryside had shifted to urban, industrial locations, mainly in the east of the province. But industrialization had developed its own momentum, achieving huge productivity, employment, and wealth gains. So, rural Ulster, while still a significant employer of male labour, was increasingly an adjunct to the urban, industrial economy of the Lagan Valley and the wider international economy.

---

[44] L. Kennedy, 'The Economic Thought of the Nation's Lost Leader: Charles Stewart Parnell', in G. Boyce and A. O' Day (eds), *Parnell in Perspective* (London, 1991), 171–200.

FURTHER READING

W. H. Crawford, *The Impact of the Domestic Linen Industry in Ulster* (Belfast, 2005).
C. Ó Gráda, *Ireland before and after the Famine: Explorations in Economic History, 1800–1925* (Manchester, 1988).
L. Kennedy, 'The Rural Economy, 1820–1914', in L. Kennedy and P. Ollerenshaw (eds), *An Economic History of Ulster, 1820–1939* (Manchester, 1985), 1–61.
L. Kennedy and P. M. Solar, *Irish Agriculture: A Price History* (Dublin, 2007).
D. W. Miller, 'Irish Presbyterians and the Great Famine', in J. Hill and C. Lennon (eds), *Luxury and Austerity* (Dublin, 1999), 165–81.

11

Business and Finance, 1780–1945

Philip Ollerenshaw

In eighteenth-century Europe, rural manufacture of goods by men, women, and children for national and international markets was a feature of many regions, including Ulster, and that manufacture was typically undertaken alongside agricultural activity. Some regions successfully made the transition to factory-based industry while others experienced declines in industry. In searching for explanations of the wide diversity of regional experience, studies of proto-industrialization sought to explain relationships between an ambitious number of factors, including the productivity of the soil, seasonal agricultural and industrial production, patterns of landholding and inheritance, credit networks and the accumulation of capital and skills, the family, household, and everyday life.[1] Proto-industrialization led to a resurgence of interest in regional studies, and such a regional focus can also be seen as a response to macro-economic research which has increasingly stressed the gradualism of British economic growth in the eighteenth and early nineteenth centuries. Some writers see the emphasis on slow economic growth as neglecting the discontinuities in economy and society during the classic industrial revolution period and have sought to rehabilitate these discontinuities through regional research.[2]

TEXTILES BEFORE THE FIRST WORLD WAR

The prominence of rural textile manufacture in studies of proto-industrialization led to renewed interest in the Ulster linen industry.[3] Most of the flax produced for the Irish linen industry in the late eighteenth and early nineteenth centuries was grown on farms in Ulster. Having been prepared, the flax was spun and wound onto bobbins by women and children, then woven into cloth by the farmer-weaver and perhaps older children who would then take it to market.[4] Although the farmer-weaver predominated, by the later eighteenth century the journeyman-weaver

---

[1] S. Ogilvie and M. Cerman (eds), *European Proto-Industrialisation* (Cambridge, 1993).
[2] P. Hudson (ed.), *Regions and Industries* (Cambridge, 1989).
[3] See especially, M. Cohen (ed.), *The Warp of Ulster's Past: Interdisciplinary Perspectives on the Irish Linen Industry, 1700–1920* (New York, 1997).
[4] Part of this account draws directly on P. Ollerenshaw, 'Industrialisation' and 'Banking' in J. S. Donnelly Jr (ed.), *Encyclopedia of Irish History and Culture* (New York, 2004).

working for a variety of middlemen was increasingly in evidence. One important consequence of the growth of the linen industry, often under landlord patronage, was that it stimulated competition for land, drove up rent levels, encouraged subdivision of holdings and rising population pressure. This has been observed particularly in the 'linen triangle' on the south side of Lough Neagh between Lisburn, Dungannon, and Armagh, where the finest linen was woven. In this area the rising numbers and status of leaseholding Catholic and Protestant farmer-weavers, who were able to outbid farmers for leases, were important ingredients in the communal strife which worsened in the volatile atmosphere of the later eighteenth century, especially in those districts where Catholic/Protestant numbers were finely balanced. Social and economic forces were thus significant in the development of the Defenders, Peep O'Day Boys, United Irishmen and Orange Order, in this part of Ulster.[5]

Drapers played a key role in organizing and merchanting the cloth, but it was the bleachers who were responsible for initiating profound long-term changes in the industry. Technological changes in bleaching in the 1780s led to an increase in the scale and function of bleachers which had fundamental long-term significance since bleachers turned drapers and linen merchants provided some of the earliest machine spinners and weavers.

During the eighteenth century, access to the English market provided the main stimulus to Irish linen, especially following the abolition of duties on flax, yarn, and cloth into England from Ireland in 1696. Further encouragement for Irish linen came with the formation in 1711 of the Trustees of the Hempen and Flaxen Manufactures of Ireland: the 'Linen Board'. The Board continued to function until 1828 but it lacked the expertise to ensure that its grants were used in the most cost-effective way. Even so, the most balanced assessments of the Board's activities have judged them to have been mildly positive.[6] A number of related developments contributed to the subsequent transition to factory production. These included changes in bleaching and finishing technology and the emergence of the large-scale bleachers and drapers; the move away from Dublin as the main entrepôt in the Anglo-Irish trade and the associated switch to direct exports from Ulster; and the impact of the short-lived factory-based cotton industry whose appearance coincided with the final phase of domestic spinning in the linen industry. These developments were crucial in the acquisition of skill, the accumulation of capital, the refinement of credit and banking networks, and the introduction of factory techniques. Ultimately they contributed enormously to an increasing concentration of the linen industry in north-east Ulster in general and the Belfast area in particular.[7]

The role of Belfast as a centre of textile production was transformed in the later eighteenth and early nineteenth centuries by the cotton spinning industry.

---

[5] W. H. Crawford, *The Impact of the Domestic Linen Industry in Ulster* (Belfast, 2005), 106–15.

[6] H. D. Gribbon, 'The Irish Linen Board, 1711–1828', in L. M. Cullen and T. C. Smout (eds), *Comparative Aspects of Scottish and Irish Economic and Social History* (Edinburgh, 1977), 77–87.

[7] W. H. Crawford, 'The Evolution of the Linen Trade in Ulster Before Industrialization', *Irish Economic and Social History*, 15 (1988), 32–53.

The need to import raw cotton, coal, and machinery meant that the Ulster cotton industry tended to be concentrated in coastal towns such as Belfast, Bangor, Larne, and Carrickfergus, although it also spread inland. In origin, the region's cotton manufacturers were from a range of backgrounds, including haberdashery, and significantly, linen bleaching and drapery. The industry was stimulated by the wars with France and by grants from the Linen Board. The principal type of cotton produced in Belfast was muslin, a finer and lighter product than calico, although the latter was also made. Long experience with the manufacture of fine linens in the area provided a ready supply of skilled labour that could easily move into muslin production.[8]

The Irish cotton industry has been described as 'one of the great "might have beens" of Irish economic history'.[9] In east Ulster the cotton industry expanded in the late eighteenth and early nineteenth centuries, making important technical and other connections with industrializing British regions. At the same time, cotton handloom weaving became of significance in Ulster, with perhaps 10,000 engaged in this activity, the same number as in Leinster and Munster combined. Expansion continued at a slower rate in the 1810s with capital investment concentrated in spinning and some in calico printing. Powerloom weaving began in the 1820s but handweaving especially of muslin continued for decades afterwards. Further, bleaching, printing, and finishing cottons, including muslin, continued to be of some significance in east Ulster with some firms handling both cottons and linen for British and Irish firms, not least the growing shirt industry centred on Derry. Cotton spinning was the first example of factory-based textile production in Ireland and it provided essential skills and infrastructure, including credit networks, on which mechanized flax spinning could draw in the decades from the 1820s and 1830s.[10]

In the 1820s, the advent of the wet-spinning process for flax created new opportunities for cotton spinners to switch to flax spinning by power. Provincial production of linen was responsible for the growth of industrial villages in many parts of Ulster. Provision of housing for workers by employers began in the second half of the eighteenth century, and damask weavers Coulsons of Lisburn were an early example of this in 1764, as was John Barbour at his thread manufacturing firm at 'the Plantation' near Lisburn twenty years later. Many of the industrial villages in Ulster date from the period 1830–70 and they were mainly to be found in the east of the province, with a smaller number (including Sion Mills in County Tyrone) in the west.[11]

The mechanization of flax spinning was of fundamental importance in extending the industrialization process in north-east Ulster. The pressure to refine powerloom

---

[8] D. Dickson, 'Aspects of the Rise and Fall of the Irish Cotton Industry', in Cullen and Smout (eds), *Comparative Aspects of Scottish and Irish Economic and Social History*, 100–15.

[9] A. Bielenberg and P. M. Solar, 'The Irish Cotton Industry from the Industrial Revolution to Partition', *Irish Economic and Social History*, 34 (2007), 1–28.

[10] Ibid. See in general A. Bielenberg, *Ireland and the Industrial Revolution* (Abingdon, 2009) esp. Ch. 2 which provides the best account.

[11] D. S. Macneice, 'Industrial Villages of Ulster, 1800–1900', in P. Roebuck (ed.), *Plantation to Partition: Essays in Honour of J. L. McCracken* (Belfast, 1981), 172–90.

technology intensified during the 1850s, not least because of the post-Famine rise in labour costs, and the necessary improvements had in fact been made just in time for Ulster to reap huge, if brief, benefits from the unprecedented demand for linen occasioned by the 'cotton famine' during the American Civil War, 1861–65.[12] However, handweaving, increasingly undertaken by women and usually on a putting-out basis, remained a part of the family economy in a number of parts of rural Ulster into the twentieth century.[13]

In many ways the American Civil War period was a crucial one for the linen industry, with much new investment, predicated on a view of the future which proved to be far too optimistic. A number of spinning and bleaching firms integrated weaving into their operations, but there were now more opportunities for specialist, single process, weaving enterprises to develop. At the same time, a relatively small number of large, fully integrated firms developed and became the giants of the industry between the 1860s and 1914. This process was accelerated by the decision, first taken by the York Street Flax Spinning Company in 1864, and soon after by many others including the Ulster Spinning Company (both these firms had nominal capitals of £500,000), to adopt a joint-stock form with limited liability. This development contributed considerably to the extension of the stockmarket in Belfast.[14] It was also aided by an immense expansion of bank credit, the availability of flax increasingly imported from Europe, and by the development of a textile engineering sector which, by mid-century, also competed successfully in American and European markets. The largest linen firms developed international, sometimes even global, connections.

Ulster emerged by 1870 as the world's leading linen-producing area, specializing in the medium- and fine-end of the market, and by 1914 accounted for some three-quarters of UK linen output. Within Europe as a whole the industry stagnated or declined in most regions before the war. Relatively low labour costs, low unionization, dependence on cheap imported flax (80 per cent of which came from Russia and the Low Countries), together with an internationally stable economic environment and growing demand in certain relatively affluent markets, especially the USA, all helped to sustain linen production in Ulster. Increasingly protected overseas markets and relentless competition from other textiles were problems well before 1914 and led directly to a substantial increase in protectionist sentiment in the Ulster linen industry. Nationalist Ireland tended to see protection in purely Irish terms, but in the predominantly unionist north-east protectionism tended to be seen in UK-wide or in imperial perspective. One of the linen industry's leaders, R. H. Reade, Chairman of the York Street Flax Spinning Company, was also a member of the pre-war Tariff Commission which lobbied for abandonment of the established UK free-trade policy. Another leading Ulster businessman, tobacco manufacturer

---

[12] O. M. Greeves, 'The Impact of the American Civil War on the UK Textile Industries' (unpublished Ph.D. thesis, University of Bristol, 1968–9).
[13] B. Collins 'The Loom, the Land and the Marketplace: Women Weavers and the Family Economy in Late Nineteenth and Early Twentieth-Century Ireland', in Cohen (ed.), *Warp of Ulster's Past*, 241, 247.
[14] W. A. Thomas, *The Stock Exchanges of Ireland* (Liverpool, 1986), 148.

Thomas Gallaher, was also a member of the Tariff Commission, and Vice-Chairman of the Tariff Reform League.[15]

Despite the evidence of growing challenges before 1914, it was the First World War which decisively exposed the vulnerability of the Ulster linen industry. Much of the industry entered the war working short time, and in general the process of wartime mobilization in the regional economy was relatively slow. By June 1915 only one of the Belfast shipyards, and none of the engineering companies, had significant government orders, but in that month the establishment of the Belfast Munitions of War Committee was designed to serve as a link between government and industry. Chaired by Samuel Davidson of Sirocco Engineering, the linen industry had six members from a total of twenty. However, the traditionally weak links between most firms and government, the preponderance of small firms, the physical distance from London, and the disruption to and expense of cross-channel shipping, militated against the award of contracts in the First World War and also in the Second.[16]

Imports of Belgian flax all but ceased from an early stage of the war while those from Russia held up reasonably well until the 1917 revolution. A temporary increase in Irish flax acreage helped very partially to offset the shortfall from Europe but after 1914 the supply conditions for raw material were problematic, causing most spinning mills to experience extensive short-time working and leading to price inflation, in absolute terms and in relation to competitor textiles, which would adversely affect demand in the post-war years.[17]

THE EVOLUTION OF BUSINESS AND FINANCE

The transition to factory production in the linen industry was the most significant feature of industrialization in nineteenth-century Ireland. The majority of workers in the linen industry as a whole were women, but the diversification of the economic base in nineteenth-century Belfast meant that men increasingly found work, and relatively high wages, in engineering, shipbuilding, food, drink and tobacco. By the 1820s, the diversity of business activity was reflected in the membership of the Chamber of Commerce. Although textile interests—cotton, linen, and wool—were dominant there were also representatives from shipbuilding and engineering, tanning, distilling, printing, and, among many from the service sector, members drawn from accountancy, banking, and insurance. From the 1820s, the Chamber lent support to the promotion of railways in Britain and Ireland as well as improvements in mail services between Belfast and the west of Ireland. It attached great importance to free trade across the Irish Sea and would later become a militantly unionist body, playing a key role in anti-Home Rule politics from the 1880s.

---

[15] A. Marrison, 'Businessmen, Industries and Tariff Reform in Great Britain, 1903–30', *Business History*, 25 (1983). Both Reade and Gallaher had multiple business interests.
[16] The Ministry of Supply and Ireland, 1918, TNA MUN 4/6724.
[17] *Textile Recorder*, 15 May 1918, 31.

The growth and role of the Belfast Chamber, which became the most important mouthpiece for business interests in Ulster, was just one of many examples of an organization which facilitated the development of business networks. As a growing urban area with a distinctive, Protestant-dominated, business sector, Belfast combined manufacturing, finance, and other services within a compact geographical area. While business networks can have a social, cultural, ethnic, religious, or political basis, or a combination of these, they serve to reduce information and transaction costs and enable network members to reduce business risk and to develop new business opportunities. They can also be defensive and anti-competitive.[18] The Belfast Chamber provided a focal point for business interests and, along with a significant number of trade associations especially in textiles, gave broad institutional expression to regional business networks.

The largest enterprises in Belfast before 1914 were the two shipyards. Belfast gained much from the concentration of UK shipbuilding between the mid-nineteenth century and 1913. UK shipyards established their competitive advantage in the 1860s and 1870s and sustained it through to the First World War for three main reasons: access to the largest market for merchant ships and the opportunities this afforded for mass production, specialization, and external economies; reliable supplies of cheap raw materials and components; management capacity, and the supply of mobile skilled and unskilled labour.[19] From being centred on the south of England in the 1840s, on the eve of the First World War the industry had relocated to Clydeside, the north-east of England, Belfast, and a few other centres such as Barrow-in-Furness and Birkenhead. Harland and Wolff, established in the late 1850s, and Workman Clark in 1879, grew on trend in internationally favourable economic conditions, so that from the 1880s to the First World War, they came to epitomize the success and self-confidence of industrial Belfast. Shipbuilding in Belfast owed much to entrepreneurs and to skilled labour from Britain, but design flair, technical progress, reputation for quality, and lower wage rates for unskilled labour were critical too.

In the case of Harland and Wolff, personal and family contacts were crucial in winning initial orders with Bibby Line and especially White Star Line. The latter was by far the most important single customer before 1914. The close relationship between Harland and Wolff and the Bibby and White Star Lines enabled contracts to operate on a cost-plus basis, where certified cost plus a fixed percentage allowed for alterations during construction—something which was typical in very large ships where building might take over a year. Such arrangements had to be based upon trust, but had the significant advantage of avoiding the need for wrangling over price between customer and builder as specifications were modified during construction. The development and organization of the Queen's Island yard, which reached 80 acres in size by 1912, was led by William James (later Lord) Pirrie who had joined the firm as an apprentice in 1862 and who became a partner twelve years later. Both Sir Edward Harland and Gustav Wolff became MPs, in 1887 and

---

[18] M. C. Casson, 'An Economic Approach to Business Networks', in J. Wilson and A. Popp (eds), *Industrial Clusters and Business Networks in England, 1750–1970* (Aldershot, 2003), 19–43.
[19] S. Pollard and P. Robertson, *The British Shipbuilding Industry, 1870–1914* (Cambridge, Mass., 1979), 48–69.

1892 respectively, and after this, Pirrie's control over the direction of the enterprise became even clearer. The period from the 1880s to the First World War saw Belfast grow faster than any other major shipbuilding location (see Table 11.1) and in the early twentieth century, the two big Belfast shipyards were amongst the UK's largest manufacturing employers. Since, like Barrow-in-Furness, Belfast was located away from the main centres of shipbuilding, both Harland and Wolff and Workman Clark tended to make more of their own components. While this made sense from the point of view of business organization, it did mean that links between the firm and its hinterland were not as strong as in some other shipbuilding centres. This was especially important in wartime when poorly developed connections to subcontractors became most obvious. By the Second World War, for example, the firm had long regarded itself as 'an isolated unit' and was not inclined to cooperate easily with other firms or government officials or trade unions.[20] In addition to their Belfast operation, after 1907 the firm expanded their operations on the Clyde and developed repair facilities at Southampton, Liverpool, and Woolwich in addition to the acquisition of rights to produce Burmeister and Wain diesel engines which facilitated the move from steam power.[21] On the eve of the First World War, Harland and Wolff continued to concentrate on merchant ships, although they did have some Admiralty work, including the supply of boilers and engines for large navy vessels.[22] Pirrie himself became associated with a very wide range of businesses in many parts of the UK; by the end of the First World War, he was chairman of six companies and director of twenty-seven others.[23]

Belfast was exceptional in Ulster terms, but like other large UK cities, its wholesale, retail, construction, and manufacturing sectors included a wide range of enterprises including mineral waters, brewing, and distilling.[24] Derry, the province's second

Table 11.1. Percentage of gross UK tonnage launched in selected shipbuilding regions, 1880–1938

Years	Belfast	Clyde	Newcastle	Sunderland
1880–9	3.9	33.0	19.2	15.0
1890–9	8.6	32.7	17.2	16.5
1900–9	9.8	35.6	19.2	16.7
1910–4	10.4	36.2	19.5	16.3
1921–9	8.8	38.4	20.6	11.9
1930–8	11.4	36.5	15.6	11.7

Source: F. Geary and W. Johnson, 'Shipbuilding at Belfast, 1861–1986', *Irish Economic and Social History*, 16 (1989), 46, 55.

[20] W. D. Scott to Vice-Admiral Sir Harold Brown, 31 May 1941, PRONI COM 61/541.
[21] D. S. Johnson, 'William James Pirrie', in D. Jeremy (ed.), *Dictionary of Business Biography*, 4 (London, 1984), 702–9.
[22] *Engineering*, 94, 5 July 1912, 4–5.
[23] A. Slaven, 'A Shipyard in Depression: John Browns of Clydebank, 1919–38', *Business History*, 19 (1977), 195.
[24] S. Gribbon, 'An Irish City: Belfast, 1911', in D. Harkness and M. O'Dowd (eds), *The Town in Ireland* (Belfast, 1981), 210.

city, had no comparably dynamic industrial base; rather it developed a specialization in shirt and collar making and embroidery, mostly using female labour.[25] The rapid development of shirt manufacture in Derry dates from the early 1850s with the adoption of factory-based sewing machine production, first at Tillie and Henderson's and then in other firms. Productivity gains led to the expansion of factory-based shirt workers in Derry city to about 3000 in the mid-1860s, and a very much larger number of outworkers in the north-west counties of Donegal, Tyrone, and Londonderry. By the early twentieth century, there were perhaps 18,000 indoor workers and more than 60,000 in surrounding rural areas. Hand sewing could take place within factories, and sewing-machines could be used outside them. This combination of hand and mechanized production remained viable for decades. Moreover, in the north-west, sewing and hand embroidery for the market, organized on an outwork basis, had developed with the cotton industry in Ulster and the west of Scotland. In the later nineteenth century, however, the embroidery and 'making up' of fine linen goods for national and international markets became much more important for the women in north-west Ulster.[26]

The evolution of business in Ulster and Ireland more widely involved not only manufacturing but transport and a range of financial services such as banking, accountancy, and stockbroking. The virtual absence of coal and iron was not only a profound influence on the growth and location of modern industry but an equally strong influence on the development and performance of canals and railways. In Britain, many canals and railways were both cause and effect of the exploitation of coal deposits. The modern railway system in Ireland grew from slow beginnings in the 1830s, through mania in the mid-1840s to extensive and more solid growth from mid-century. Maps 11.1 and 11.2 summarize the growth of canals and railways. In Ulster by 1860, only County Donegal was outside the railway system. The standard gauge system was supplemented from the 1880s by 'light' or narrow gauge lines mainly in the west, and the total railway mileage reached about 3000 by the time of partition.[27]

The emergence of formal banking institutions was preceded by the development of credit facilities in internal and cross-channel trade. The shortage of banks in the mid-eighteenth century was to some extent offset by the fact that some important areas of economic activity, linen markets for example, functioned mainly on a cash basis, while much of the credit for cross-channel trade was provided by London merchants. In Belfast the formation of three new banking partnerships, the Belfast Bank (1808), the Commercial Bank (1809), and the Northern Bank (1809) indicated the extent to which religion and finance combined to produce a set of durable banking houses firmly rooted in Ulster's industrial and commercial development. Within a few years the banks established agencies in country towns and villages, the principal function of which was to increase note circulation through the discount

---

[25] See the fine account of the economic development of Derry in R. Gavin, W. P. Kelly, and D. O'Reilly, *Atlantic Gateway: The Port and City of Londonderry since 1700* (Dublin, 2009).

[26] B. Collins, 'The Organisation of Sewing Outwork in Late Nineteenth Century Ulster', in M. Berg (ed.), *Markets and Manufacture in Early Industrial Europe* (London, 1991), 139–56.

[27] M. Ó Riain, *On the Move* (Dublin, 1995), Ch. 1.

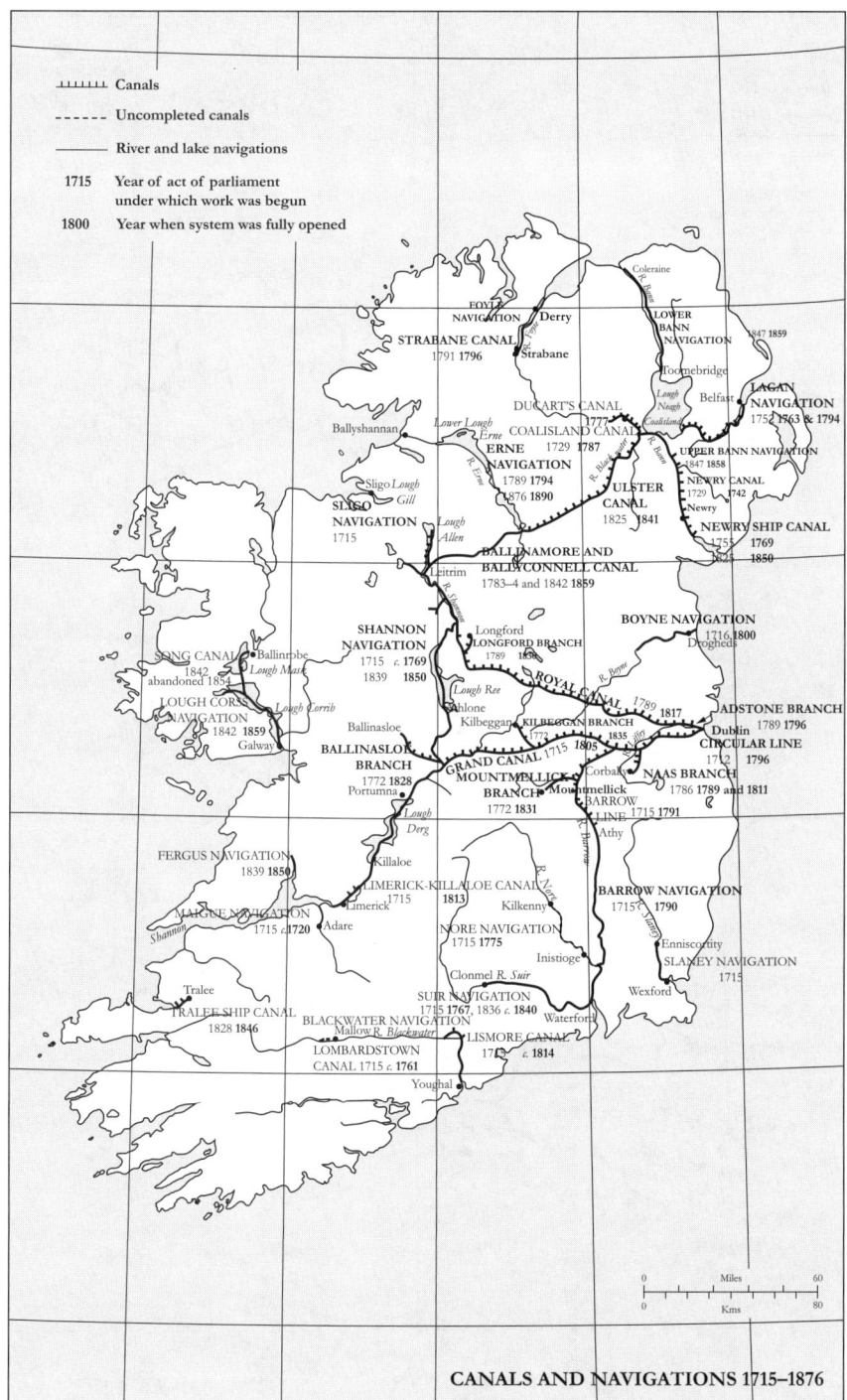

Map 11.1: Canals and navigations in Ireland, 1715–1876. From T. W. Moody, F. X. Martin, and F. J. Byrne (eds), *A New History of Ireland*, Volume IX: *Maps, Genealogies, Lists: A Companion to Irish History, Part II* (Oxford, 1989), 53.

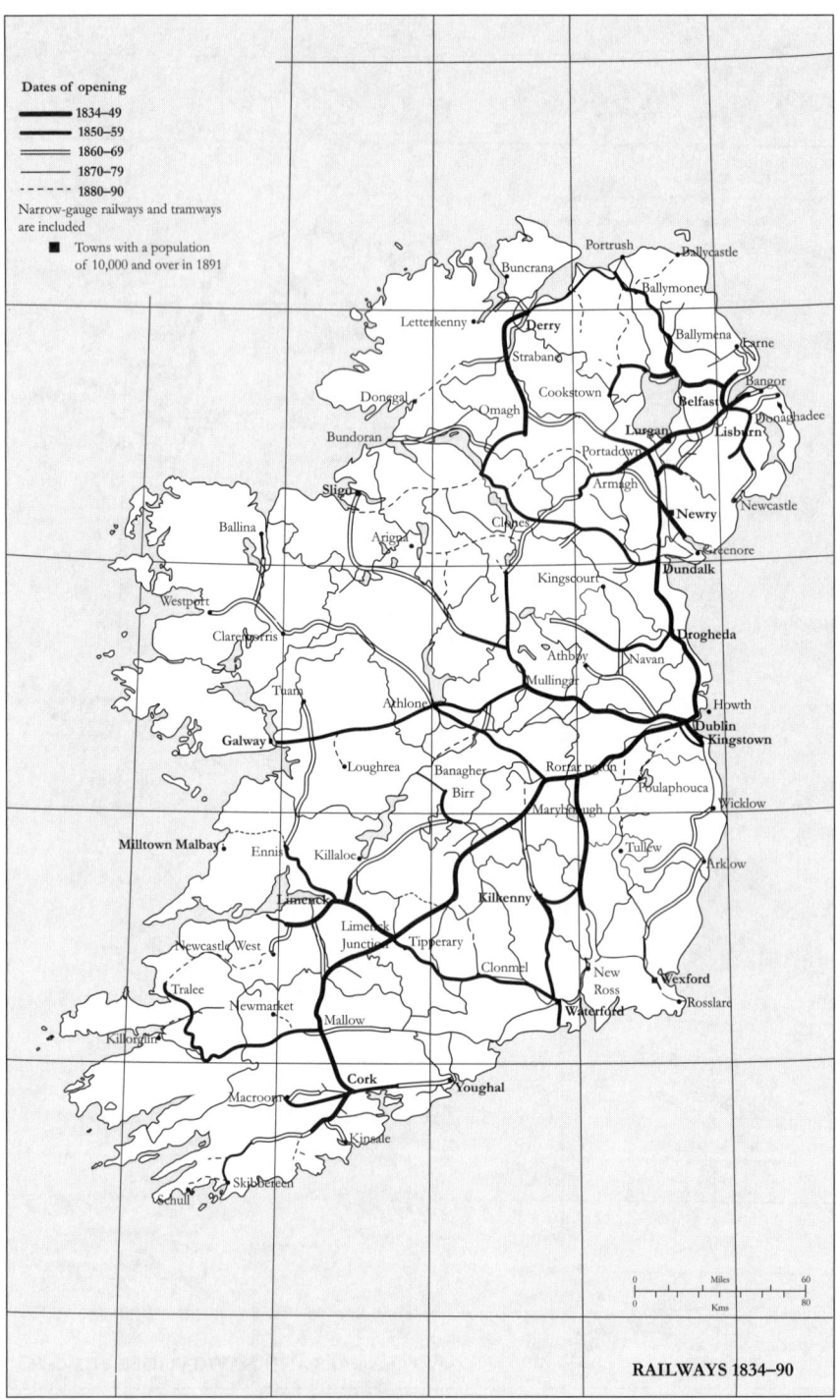

Map 11.2: Railways in Ireland, 1834–1890. From T. W. Moody, F. X. Martin, and F. J. Byrne (eds), *A New History of Ireland*, Volume IX: *Maps, Genealogies, Lists: A Companion to Irish History, Part II* (Oxford, 1989), 63.

of bills of exchange, thereby facilitating industrial and commercial development. Bank agents were the forerunners of branch managers, and an agency brought considerable income and social prestige to the incumbent.

Economic instability in the decade following the end of the Napoleonic Wars, causing bank failures, was the most important factor leading to legislation in the mid-1820s which permitted the formation of banks with more than six partners, the first of which was the Northern Bank in Belfast in 1824. The banking network in Ulster was strengthened by the arrival of branches of Dublin and London-based Irish banks. Tested severely during a number of severe commercial and credit crises, such as 1847–48 and 1857–58, the banks survived and trust in them rarely wavered. Between 1850 and 1913 the Irish banking system continued to expand, from less than 200 offices to around 850. Of the many reasons driving this expansion, the main one was the need to maximize deposits which was a key determinant of lending capacity and of profitability. Branch expansion brought banking facilities within reach of most of the Ulster population and some towns attracted several different banks. On the eve of the First World War, some 320 offices in Ireland were open only on specified days of the week, particularly market or fair days, to cater for local need. In Ulster, much of the business was seasonal and tied to agriculture or agriculture-related activity. A substantial proportion of the deposits came from rural areas and branch networks enabled banks to utilize them to fund industrial and commercial development, as well as to spread their risks in a diversified economy of agriculture, industry, and trade. The First World War brought great prosperity for much of Irish agriculture and led to a huge increase in deposits which helped to provide financial stability for the country and its banking system after partition.[28]

In addition to banking, the development of stockbroking and the opening of a stock exchange in Belfast in 1897 was an indication of higher levels of financial intermediation. In 1843, Josias Cunningham, a merchant, became the town's first share-dealer. As in Dublin, the mania in railway shares in the mid-1840s did much to popularize share ownership and greatly increased the scope for specialist brokers, even if not all the projected railway schemes were successful. A necessary part of business development was the provision of services such as bookkeeping and accountancy. The teaching of bookkeeping was seen as an important part of the curriculum from the eighteenth-century hedge schools, through to National Schools after 1831 and a range of other schools, colleges, and universities in the later nineteenth and twentieth centuries. Book-keeping skills were essential for a range of private businesses and increasingly for public-sector employment. They might contribute to upward social mobility not only for those within the country but also for those emigrating overseas.[29] A further important development in the later nineteenth century was the formation of the Institute of Chartered Accountants in Ireland (ICAI) in 1888. Of the small founding membership numbering thirty-one, twenty-seven of whom were Protestant, thirteen were based in Dublin, twelve

---

[28] P. Ollerenshaw, 'The Business and Politics of Banking in Ireland, 1900–43', in P. L. Cottrell, A. Teichova, and T. Yuzawa, (eds), *Finance in the Age of the Corporate Economy* (Aldershot, 1997), 52–78.

[29] P. Clarke, 'The Teaching of Bookkeeping in Nineteenth Century Ireland', *Accounting, Business and Financial History*, 18 (2008), 21–33.

in Belfast, and six in Cork. The aims of ICAI were to raise the professional status of accountants, strengthen connections with barristers, solicitors, bankers, and merchants, and to act as an influential business lobby. The relative decline of industry in much of Ireland, and the business expansion of the north-east before 1914 was reflected in the growing importance of Belfast in the ICAI. By 1909, Belfast accountants represented 53 per cent of the membership, while articled clerks from the city registered with the Institute represented 71 per cent of the total. The Belfast membership was almost entirely Protestant.[30]

AFTER THE FIRST WORLD WAR

Although it is undeniable that much of the industry of the Belfast region depended upon imported raw materials and export markets, it is also true that the region's links with the rest of Ireland never disappeared and indeed remained significant for a range of manufacturing and service businesses, including many in retailing, wholesaling, and distribution. However, as is so often the case in inland trade, much of this was unrecorded and has often been overlooked. The nature of links between the north-east and the rest of Ireland became more visible in the early 1920s during the period of the 'Belfast boycott'. Boycotting had a long history before 1920, even before the invention of the term during the Land War of the 1880s. The post-war boycott started in 1920 and was triggered by a mixture of anti-partitionism and, more importantly, by the high-profile expulsion of thousands of mainly Catholic employees from their workplaces and homes during the summer of that year. Businesses including banks, distillers, drapers, candle manufacturers, confectioners, tobacco manufacturers, and many others suffered a substantial drop in turnover and profits. The boycott was wide-ranging, sometimes violent, involved men and women, and had far-reaching consequences at local level. It also led to a loyalist boycott of goods from outside the north-east. It involved large and small businesses, local government bodies, the Royal Irish Constabulary as well as pro-Treaty and anti-Treaty IRA forces. Boycotting as an economic and political weapon would continue sporadically throughout the twentieth century.[31]

European linen producers recovered unexpectedly rapidly from war and posed a much more serious threat to Northern Ireland where an average of more than 40 per cent of spindles and looms were idle between 1921 and 1928, with many others working short time. Many linen firms in this period passed their dividends and shares usually traded at a discount. Rather better performance came from the shares of more resilient firms such as Gallaher's tobacco.[32] The chronic excess capacity which epitomized the inter-war years was one reason why contemporary

---

[30] P. O'Regan, '"Elevating the Profession": The Institute of Chartered Accountants in Ireland and the Implementation of Social Closure Strategies 1888–1909', *Accounting, Business and Financial History*, 18 (2008), 35–59.
[31] P. Ollerenshaw, 'Business Boycotts and the Partition of Ireland', in B. Collins, P. Ollerenshaw, and T. Parkhill (eds), *Industry, Trade and People in Ireland, 1650–1950: Essays in Honour of W. H. Crawford* (Belfast, 2005), 205–27.
[32] Thomas, *The Stock Exchanges of Ireland*, 51, 219–47.

observers began to reflect seriously on the range of problems facing the industry. Amongst the more important initiatives were the Linen Industry Research Association in 1919 and the Irish Linen Guild in 1928. The latter concentrated its efforts on improving the marketing of trademarked and standardized goods, especially in the United States, where during the later 1920s the Guild heard much about the deficiencies in design as well as the excessive competition amongst firms, not least in marketing.[33] Serious structural change in the industry, however, did not take place.

In Northern Ireland, the weakness of the traditional staple industries became increasingly obvious from the time of partition. Several members of the new Belfast government had business interests and there is no doubt that businessmen had easy access to ministers, including the prime minister, to an extent unknown in Britain.[34] Moreover, representatives of the staple industries of textiles and shipbuilding were potentially effective lobby groups and clearly had an advantage in seeking assistance. An early initiative designed to reduce the risks faced by private firms in a period of heightened market uncertainty was the Loans Guarantee Acts, introduced in 1922 and extended on a number of occasions until 1946. Loans made by financial institutions to businesses could be guaranteed by the government so that the preferred private enterprise framework of both business and government could be maintained. The principal beneficiaries of this legislation were the shipyards and it is no coincidence that there were detailed discussions between the region's premier industrialist, Viscount Pirrie of Harland and Wolff, and members of the government, during the framing of the legislation.

By 1925 about a quarter of Northern Ireland's insured population was unemployed, compared to 11 per cent in Britain, and in the general election of April, the Unionist Party lost seven seats in Belfast, four to the Independent Unionists, and three to the Labour Party, both of which were highly critical of the government's responses to the emerging unemployment problem. This provided the fundamental motivation for supporting manufacturing industry and particularly the shipyards so as to maintain the support of the male Protestant working class. In Norton's phrase, the government was 'creating jobs, manufacturing unity'.[35] The problem of global excess capacity in shipbuilding hit both of Belfast's shipyards in the 1920s, and Workman Clark, after a very difficult period, closed in 1935. Harland and Wolff in peacetime would never again achieve its pre-1914 position. The problems of UK shipbuilders between the wars are well known, and from 1922 Harland and Wolff began to build vessels for fixed prices which were virtually at cost.[36] The Loans Guarantees Acts were supplemented by further

---

[33] *Textile Recorder*, 15 February 1919, 366; 15 August 1919, 146. Some of the criticisms dated from before 1914. See for example *Irish Textile Journal*, 9 July 1904, 15 December 1904 and 15 January 1907.
[34] P. Buckland, *The Factory of Grievances: Devolved Government in Northern Ireland, 1921–39* (Dublin, 1979), Ch. 1.
[35] C. Norton, 'Creating Jobs, Manufacturing Unity: Ulster Unionism and Mass Unemployment, 1922–34', *Contemporary British History*, 15 (2001), 1–14.
[36] F. Geary and W. Johnson, 'Wages and Employment in Northern Ireland and Scotland Between the Wars: The Case of Shipbuilding', in S. J. Connolly, R. A. Houston, and R. J. Morris (eds), *Conflict, Identity and Economic Development: Scotland and Ireland, 1600–1939* (Preston, 1995), 245.

initiatives to reduce the problem of unemployment. These included the Ulster Industries Development Association, established in 1929, which focused on the encouragement of local industries with its slogan 'Push Ulster Goods'. Then in 1932 the New Industries (Development) Act (Northern Ireland) provided grants and also, from 1937, loans for a variety of purposes to new industrial undertakings. Local authorities could also provide rate relief to enterprises which qualified for support under this legislation.[37]

On the eve of rearmament, between 1930 and 1934, the UK shipbuilding industry experienced an exceptionally severe depression, with the consequence that massive excess capacity characterized the industry, although as Table 11.1 shows, in terms of market share, Belfast performed relatively well during the 1930s.[38] In all UK regions specializing in traditional staple industries, rearmament after 1935 offered the hope of government contracts and a decline in unemployment. Northern Ireland was not a 'Special Area', as some of the most depressed British regions had been labelled after 1934, and it was these regions which often received priority in contracts. In the years before the war, and well into the conflict, a recurrent criticism of the Belfast government was that it failed to secure adequate government contracts for Northern Ireland under the rearmament programme. In fact the Belfast government did lobby for contracts from the earliest stages of rearmament in 1935 and continued to do so.[39] Northern Ireland's claim for more government work was formally made to British Prime Minister Stanley Baldwin at a meeting between himself and Northern Ireland's Westminster MPs in the spring of 1937.[40] The MPs argued that geography favoured shipbuilding and aircraft production in the region, as it did the import of those raw materials which had to come from North America. The region could also make a major contribution to clothing (including uniforms), shirts, blankets, and canvas. Moreover, the number and severity of industrial disputes was proportionately much lower than in Britain.

The need for government contracts to bear fruit increased sharply with the Northern Ireland general election of 1938, the last one to be held before 1945. By this time it had become apparent that government contracts were making inroads into high unemployment in several of the Special Areas in Britain, and that Northern Ireland was not sharing in this welcome development to anything like the same extent. In the Scottish Special Areas, for example, a 28.7 per cent unemployment rate on the Live Register in December 1934 had fallen to 15.6 per cent by September 1937. The corresponding figures for Northern Ireland were 24.2 per cent and 21.7 per cent.[41] The most obvious potential beneficiary of rearmament in the region was Harland and Wolff, at once the largest firm in Northern Ireland and the most potent symbol of industrial Belfast. However, not only did the firm fail to secure Admiralty orders commensurate with its capacity, relations between

---

[37] *Ulster Year Book, 1938* (Belfast, 1938), 87–8, 263–4.
[38] See especially Slaven, 'A Shipyard in Depression', which has much of value on Harland and Wolff.
[39] J. Milne Barbour to Viscount Hailsham, 5 February 1935, PRONI FIN30/AC/8.
[40] Inter-Departmental Committee on Unemployment, Second Interim Report, Schedule A, 1 November 1937, ibid.
[41] 'Course of Unemployment in the Scottish Special Areas, December 1934–September 1937', ibid.

the firm, the government, and the Admiralty proved to be problematic on a number of occasions before and during the war.

Unlike the Clydeside firms of John Brown or Fairfield, or Swan Hunter of Tyneside, Harland and Wolff had no long tradition of building for the Admiralty. The chairman Frederick Rebbeck, however, argued that both the available labour supply and the distance of Belfast from 'enemy contact' favoured the city as a location for more Admiralty work. Moreover, although the firm were not on the Admiralty list for some categories of vessel, most notably destroyers and submarines (the latter being a 'very paying proposition' for shipbuilders) their claims to construct both were strengthened by their expertise in diesel engine construction.[42] The problem facing Harland and Wolff was outlined by Rebbeck at the launch of the *Pretoria Castle* in October 1938. By that time it was almost eighteen months since an Admiralty order had been received, and Rebbeck warned that by January 1939 only five of the slipways, amounting to one third of capacity, would be occupied. All five berths in the South Yard, three in the East Yard, and one in the North Yard would be empty. Although yards in all UK shipbuilding regions suffered from the shortage of merchant shipping orders, the *Belfast Telegraph* emphasized the differences between Belfast and the others: 'On the Tyne, Mersey, and Clyde, where merchant tonnage has been even more scarce than in Belfast, the big shipbuilders are busy with contracts issued by the Admiralty for the rebuilding of the Royal Navy.'[43]

While some important Belfast manufacturers, such as James Mackie and Sons in engineering, were based exclusively in the city, others such as Combe Barbour (and Harland and Wolff) were part of enterprises which had operations in several British locations. Combe Barbour were part of a substantial engineering concern, Fairbairn, Lawson Combe Barbour Ltd (FLCB) formed in 1900 with the amalgamation of three firms. The new firm had its head office in Leeds. Like many UK engineering enterprises, it had experienced some extremely adverse trading conditions in the 1920s and 1930s. During this period it leaned heavily on its bankers, Westminster Bank and its subsidiary Ulster Bank in Belfast, and it is doubtful whether the firm could have survived without such assistance.[44] Had firms like this been forced into bankruptcy, the subsequent rearmament programme and wartime munitions production would have been very much more difficult. Corporate memory of the First World War was a powerful influence on the firm's behaviour in the period just before and during the Second. In Combe Barbour's case there was a legacy of missed opportunity in not having become involved in armaments production as much as they could have done, or as much as their major competitor (Mackies) had done between 1914 and 1918, with significant negative results. In the words of James Anderson, Chairman of FLCB, Combe Barbour during the Great War had 'a glorious opportunity to make good in Belfast but declined it with the result that the bulk of the work went to our present day competitors, and they had new

---

[42] Notes of a Conversation at Harland and Wolff, 8 December 1937, Prefatory Note by Sir Charles Blackmore, Secretary to the Cabinet, ibid.

[43] *Belfast Telegraph*, 1 November 1938.

[44] Fairbairn Lawson Combe Barbour Ltd, Balance Sheets for the Years Ending 31 December 1932 and 31 December 1933, West Yorkshire Archives Service, WYL 365, Box 50.

Shops and new equipment supplied by the government which have stood them in good stead ever since'.⁴⁵ Anderson made strenuous efforts to ensure that his firm was well placed to lobby for re armament contracts after 1935.

The British government, in the person of Home Secretary Sir Samuel Hoare, reassured the Northern Ireland Minister of Finance, J. M. Andrews, in 1938 that the region would 'receive full and fair consideration', and that it was open to any firm to be put on the list for tendering for government contracts. He also revealed that, *ceteris paribus*, towns in Northern Ireland with high levels of unemployment would be given the same preference in tendering as the Special Areas or Distressed Areas in Britain.⁴⁶ This met Craigavon's wish that Northern Ireland would have similar benefits to Britain's Special Areas 'without being stigmatised as a distressed area, which...would prejudice those actively engaged in industries which had a world-wide reputation'.⁴⁷ However positive such a development seemed, the fact was that it did not translate into the orders that the Belfast government felt it had a right to expect. The expansion of Short and Harland, an aircraft manufacturer established in 1936, and the announcement of a new army barracks at Ballymena did not compensate for the shortfall in Admiralty orders.

Another indicator of political pressure on the Belfast government was a deputation from the Orange Order's County Grand Lodge which urged Craigavon and three ministers to seek more rearmament work for the city.⁴⁸ Further, in the spring of 1939, some members of Belfast City Council declared in favour of designating Northern Ireland as a distressed area and the Council itself passed a strong resolution supporting both public works and re armament contracts as weapons against unemployment.⁴⁹ In the summer of 1939, Northern Ireland had the highest unemployment rate (20.2 per cent) of any UK region, almost a third higher than the next worst, Wales (14.2 per cent), and twice the level of Scotland (10.2 per cent). While the Belfast government did lobby for orders, the British government's priority clearly lay with British regions.

Continuing economic hardship in manufacturing during the later 1930s was also reflected in the business of banking. In May 1939, the National Bank of Ireland manager in Belfast pointed out that advances were at a five year low, which were 'indicative of depressed conditions in industry since mid-1937'.⁵⁰ In Derry, the manager judged that trade depression had been characteristic of the years since partition. He also noted a decline in deposits and current accounts and a rise in advances. The latter were largely to existing customers and, although 'soundly secured', reflected the problems in farming and in the large shirt and collar industry. 'Very great difficulty' was experienced in keeping customers to their agreed credit limits and this manager thought that unless cross-border restrictions to trade

---

⁴⁵ Fairbairn Lawson Combe Barbour Ltd Correspondence, J. Anderson to Sir F. Cleaver, 5 March 1936, PRONI D/769/4/5/1.
⁴⁶ Hoare to Andrews, 2 February 1938, FIN 30/AC/8.
⁴⁷ *Northern Whig*, 5 February 1938.
⁴⁸ *Belfast News Letter*, 30 November 1938.   ⁴⁹ Ibid., 4 April 1939.
⁵⁰ Manager's Report on the National Bank Branch in Belfast, 5 May 1939, Royal Bank of Scotland Archives.

were relaxed it would be extremely difficult to expand business.⁵¹ The challenging conditions for livestock farmers and those involved in producing most of the principal crops were also noted at the Magherafelt branch, together with its subbranches at Bellaghy, Draperstown, Kilrea, and Toomebridge. The consequence was both a decline in deposits and a rise in borrowing.⁵² The evidence suggests that bank lending to both industry and agriculture during the inter-war period was often characterized by a good deal of informality and convention. In the Belfast Bank, with some fifty branches in Northern Ireland, a locally based board of directors, Board of Superintendence, and other officials had the necessary knowledge to keep business under close scrutiny. Informal arrangement and the absence of agreed credit limits seem to have been common, even for larger overdrafts of more than £5000. Although most loans were fully secured by shares, property, or guarantees, controlling borrowing could be problematic. This way of conducting banking business could only work where there was detailed local knowledge of economic circumstances and it was a world away from the much more formalized procedures of the Belfast Bank's parent company, the London-based Midland Bank.⁵³

The limited impact of rearmament and continuing problems in the staple industries in Northern Ireland translated into an economy which had substantial unemployment and surplus capacity in the early war years.⁵⁴ Linen, one of the industries in the UK most dependent on raw material from Europe, lost much of its flax supply in 1939 and 1940. This had very serious consequences for employment in the region's most important manufacturing industry, especially for women, and throughout the war the industry would continue to suffer from excess capacity. Politicians such as Sir Basil Brooke, Minister of Commerce from 1941 and Prime Minister from 1943, continued to argue that war contracts should be awarded to Northern Ireland rather than men and women being sent to Britain to work. Transport costs between Northern Ireland and Britain were a handicap to firms submitting competitive tenders for war contracts, but distance from decision making in London and lack of integration into the British war economy was perhaps the biggest problem. Nevertheless, the war economy developed especially in engineering and shipbuilding and aircraft manufacture. Some of the most spectacular expansion was in textile machine makers James Mackie, which demonstrated a quite extraordinary capacity to manufacture high quality shells, aircraft parts, and other products in very large numbers. At the end of the war in 1945 it had 12,000 employees, more than half of whom were women.

Employment at Short and Harland exceeded 15,000 by 1942, many of them women in 'dispersal' factories away from the main Belfast works. Concentration on the problematic Stirling heavy bomber did not help the firm but, despite hopes to the contrary, production of the much more successful Lancaster never

---

⁵¹ Manager's Report on the National Bank Branch in Derry, 12 May 1939, ibid.
⁵² Manager's Report on the National Bank Branch in Magherafelt, 11 August 19380, ibid.
⁵³ Report on the Procedure of the Belfast Banking Co. Ltd in Relation to Advances, with Comments and Criticisms, October 1938, HSBC Archives, 30/308.
⁵⁴ This paragraph draws on the much more detailed discussion in P. Ollerenshaw, 'War, Industrial Mobilisation and Society in Northern Ireland, 1939–45', *Contemporary European History*, 16 (2007), 169–97.

came to Belfast.[55] Harland and Wolff, which in addition to shipbuilding diversified into other areas such as tank production, had more than 30,000 employees by 1944, though it sometimes had a difficult relationship with the Admiralty and it also needed very large credit facilities: from a credit of £129,000 in 1939, the firm's overdraft with Midland Bank grew to £3.26 million in 1942.[56] Northern Ireland faced considerable criticism from wartime Prime Minister Winston Churchill and his Minister of Labour and National Service, Ernest Bevin, for its slow rate of mobilization, its resurgent strike activity, and its inability to mobilize fully. The war economy peaked well before the end of the conflict and unemployment, especially among men, started to rise again. At the end of the war, none of the Northern Ireland's staple industries faced a confident future, and the region would find it impossible to share in the high levels of employment which characterized most British regions after 1945.

FURTHER READING

A. Bielenberg, *Ireland and the Industrial Revolution* (Abingdon, 2009).

M. Cohen (ed.), *The Warp of Ulster's Past* (New York, 1997).

B. Collins, P. Ollerenshaw, and T. Parkhill, (eds), *Industry, Trade and People in Ireland, 1650–1950: Essays in Honour of W. H. Crawford* (Belfast, 2005).

W. H. Crawford, 'The Evolution of the Linen Trade in Ulster before Industrialization', *Irish Economic and Social History*, 15 (1988), 32–53.

M. Moss and J. R. Hume, *Shipbuilders to the World: 125 Years of Harland and Wolff, Belfast, 1861–1986* (Belfast, 1986).

P. Ollerenshaw, 'War, Industrial Mobilisation and Society in Northern Ireland, 1939–45', *Contemporary European History*, 16 (2007), 169–97.

---

[55] E. Devons, *Planning in Practice: Essays in Aircraft Planning in Wartime* (Cambridge, 1950), 209.

[56] M. Moss and J. R. Hume, *Shipbuilders to the World: 125 Years of Harland and Wolff, Belfast, 1861–1986* (Belfast, 1986), 346.

12

Labour and Society, 1780–1945

John Lynch

INTRODUCTION

This chapter engages with the history of labour in Ulster, as experienced by tens of thousands of households within the context of an urban, industrializing society. It is worth remarking at the outset that the history of labour in Ulster, as elsewhere, is not reducible to the history of organized labour, be it in the form of trade unions, socialist groupings, or labour parties. Men and women who might be considered as belonging to the working classes were not typically members of labour organizations, although some of course were. Working-class identity and consciousness were, above all, complex and found diverse forms of expression.

We have few glimpses of the rich texture of working people's lives in the distant past but we do know that the origins of organized labour in Ulster stretch back into the eighteenth century. As in pre-industrial Britain, these combinations tended to be short-lived and locally based. In the 'turn-out' of 1762, handloom weavers in east Ulster came out in their thousands to demand higher remuneration and repeal of the Combinations Acts of the preceding decade.[1] In that year, also in Lisburn, weavers rioted over new regulations governing brown linen markets, then proceeded to ransack a draper's premises until they were finally dispersed by the military.[2] Outbreaks of militancy of this kind, however, seem to have been relatively uncommon, though in the nature of things workmen leave few marks in the written record and there may well be other episodes that are now hidden from history. Prosperous if unstable conditions in the textile industry in the closing decades of the eighteenth century may have served to reduce the scope for labour conflict.[3] Moreover, most craftspeople in textiles and in other branches of handicraft industry were still independent producers. Major differences of interest between employers and workers only crystallized with the development of industrialization in the nineteenth century.

---

[1] B. Black, 'Reassessing Irish Industrial Relations and Labour History: The North East of Ireland up to 1921', *Historical Studies in Industrial Relations*, 14 (2002), 63–4.
[2] W. H. Crawford, *Domestic Industry in Ireland* (Dublin, 1972), 16.
[3] Economic change may, however, have enlarged the possibilities for other forms of conflict, in particular communal and sectarian conflict within the Linen Triangle. See D. W. Miller, 'The Armagh Troubles, 1784–1795', in S. Clark and J. S. Donnelly Jr (eds), *Irish Peasants: Violence and Political Unrest, 1780–1914* (Madison, 1983), 155–91.

The precocious development of a cotton industry in Belfast around 1800 introduced modern industry to the Lagan Valley. The new industrial order was characterized by large-scale production, with hundreds of cotton spinners concentrated in newly built factory buildings. In addition, the putting-out system, whereby weavers worked increasingly for merchant-entrepreneurs rather than as independent producers, enmeshed thousands of workers in wage relationships.[4] In response to these new relations of production, the Belfast Muslin Weavers Society was formed in 1802. Depressed conditions at the end of the Napoleonic Wars sparked labour demonstrations. In 1815, weavers marched the ten miles from Lisburn to Belfast to protest at wage cuts. A year later the home of an employer, Francis Johnson, was destroyed by what Kerby Miller has dubbed 'Belfast's first bomb'.[5] Johnson was an employer of several hundred weavers (on the putting-out system) and a vigorous opponent of 'combinations'. These combinations were shadowy unions, illegal under existing laws, that artisans had set up to regulate wages and working conditions in the different trades. Two members of the Muslin Weavers Society were subsequently hanged for the bomb outrage. In a further sign of murderous conflict, in late 1816 John McCann, a manufacturer in Lisburn, was acquitted of killing one of his employees, Gordon Maxwell, the leader of the muslin weavers' union, in a shooting on Belfast's Malone Road.[6] These are extreme examples but they point towards undercurrents of tension surrounding wage bargaining, the cost of living, and work conditions, even under conditions of proto-industrial production. Such tensions could be especially acute in periods of economic dislocation and unemployment which followed the end of the French Wars in 1815.

The first factory-based unions were to be found in the cotton industry. However, these tended to be weak and much of the history of trade unionism in the first half of the nineteenth century was of short-lived organization, episodic acts of violence, occasional strikes, and defeats.[7] The mechanization of the linen industry, from the 1830s onwards, was largely on the basis of female labour and this also seems to have militated against effective union organization. In 1910, union density in the linen industry was only 10 per cent of a workforce of 80,000, of whom 80 per cent were women, young people, and children.[8]

The shipbuilding and engineering industries that burgeoned in the second half of the century offered a more fertile ground for labour organization. The 'new model' unions that emerged after mid-century in Britain spread to Ireland.[9] These catered for male craftworkers in the main, of the kind to be found in shipbuilding, engineering, and the building trades. By 1881, it was possible to form the Belfast Trades Council as a forum for representatives of the different trade unions. Derry followed a few years later, being a secondary outpost of trade union

---

[4] L. Kennedy, 'The Rural Economy', in L. Kennedy and P. Ollerenshaw (eds), *An Economic History of Ulster, 1820–1939* (Manchester, 1985), 1–61.

[5] K. A. Miller, 'Belfast's First Bomb, 28 February 1816: Class Conflict and the Origins of Ulster Unionist Hegemony', *Éire-Ireland*, 39 (2004), 262–80.

[6] Ibid.   [7] Black, 'Industrial Relations', 62–4.

[8] E. Boyle, 'The Economic Development of the Irish Linen Industry' (Ph.D., Queen's University, Belfast, 1979), 148, 154–5, quoted in Black, 'Industrial Relations', 68.

[9] A. Boyd, *The Rise of the Irish Trade Unions, 1729–1970* (Tralee, 1972).

organization in Ulster.¹⁰ From the 1890s onwards, strenuous efforts were made to organize unskilled workers, with varying degrees of success. Jim Larkin, the charismatic union organizer sent over from Liverpool, succeeded in reviving the dockers' union in Belfast in 1907 and also recruited dockers in Derry into the National Union of Dock Labourers.¹¹ On the eve of the First World War, the major centres of industry in Ireland, and of trade unionism, were to be found in the north-east.

LABOUR AND INDUSTRIAL TRANSFORMATION

All this suggests unprecedented degrees of economic and social change in Ulster society and economy, and in particular a massive contraction of rural-based industry in favour of modern industry in the east of the province. This in turn meant major demographic adjustments. In 1831, according to the census of that year, the province of Ulster contained half of Ireland's weavers. These were spread widely if unevenly across the province. The three southern counties of Ulster, those of Cavan, Monaghan, and Fermanagh, contained only 11 per cent of Ulster's weavers, though the hand-spinning of yarn was extensive over much of this area. The share of the western and mid-western counties of Donegal, Tyrone, and Londonderry was much higher at 32 per cent, but the heartland was in east Ulster, in Antrim, Armagh, and Down, although not in Belfast itself which held comparatively few weaving households. The rural districts were the site of linen textile manufacturing, in terms of both spinning and weaving, but, as Ollerenshaw shows in Chapter 11, technical and organizational changes were just beginning to transform the industry.

By 1911 the social and economic landscape had been transformed. Ulster now contained over 48 per cent of Ireland's industrial workers, including almost 83 per cent of all textile workers on the island. The regional variations within Ulster that were apparent in 1831 had become much more pronounced. In the southern counties of Ulster, industrial workers comprised less than 17 per cent of the working population, while less than 2 per cent of Ulster's textile workers were in this region. In the western and mid-western counties, industrial occupations accounted for 28 per cent of the labour force, including 10 per cent of Ulster's textile workers. The eastern counties and Belfast contained 58 per cent of Ulster's employed population and a remarkable 57 per cent of these were engaged in industrial activity. Almost 73 per cent of Ireland's textile workers were to be found in eastern Ulster, as were more than 90 per cent of those engaged in ship and boat building. Belfast had become the industrial capital of Ireland and one of the principal industrial cities of the United Kingdom.

It is against this background of change that we can speak of an urban working class coming into existence. This was most obviously so during the second half of the nineteenth century. But what do we mean by 'the working class'? One answer is to say that society was divided into distinct and self-aware groups or strata,

¹⁰ E. O'Connor, *A Labour History of Ireland 1824–1960* (Dublin, 1992), 55.
¹¹ A full account of Larkin's activities in Belfast can be found in J. Gray, *City in Revolt: James Larkin & the Belfast Dock Strike of 1907* (Belfast, 1985).

distinguishable from each other and often antagonistic or even confrontational in their interactions. However, within the 'working class', widening economic and social differentials between the skilled and unskilled tended to undermine both unity and perceptions of shared identity. Can it be said that urban workers overcame sufficiently the inherent divisions and antagonisms consequent on an elaborate division of labour, so as to fit snugly under an umbrella term such as 'labour' or 'the working class'? British industrial society in the late nineteenth and early twentieth centuries was too complex to be explained in terms of a simple, though admittedly attractive, upper-/middle-/lower-class social model. An internal division of the working class, based on occupation and earning power is also appealing but again is inadequate in bringing out the complexity of the 'labouring classes' in this era. The different experience of men and women within the labour market was a further complication: a female occupation might be 'genteel' or even 'skilled' but remain poorly paid. Even amongst men, as Hunt has shown, wages could differ widely between industries and between regions.[12] Less easily quantifiable aspects of working-class behaviour such as religious beliefs or political attitudes are even less amenable to generalization. The conclusion must be that the 'working-class' experience in Ulster, as elsewhere in the United Kingdom, was one of very great diversity.

THE POLITICS OF LABOUR

Trade union organization in Ulster, and in Ireland more generally, owed much to developments across the Irish Sea in Britain. The forging of a labour politics based on an emerging urban working class—one of the concomitants of industrialization in England and Scotland—proved to be a more difficult matter in Ulster. The prospects of labour representation at local and national level looked promising enough at first. The trade unionist, Alexander Bowman, stood as a Liberal candidate in North Belfast in 1885 and came within a few hundred votes of winning a parliamentary seat. He was the first trade unionist in Ulster to stand for election to Westminster, but when Gladstone introduced a bill for Home Rule for Ireland, the following year Liberal labourism was destroyed. The city witnessed fierce communal and sectarian rioting, mainly involving working-class neighbourhoods in north and west Belfast.

Conflicting national claims were the crux of the matter. Protestant workers, by and large, supported the union of Britain and Ireland, seeing their economic interests as bound up with the Union and with export-oriented industry that might be damaged by a protectionist-minded Irish parliament. At a visceral level, they also feared the power of the Catholic Church and clergy within a self-governing Ireland. In terms of social identity, their primary identification was with the monarchy, the constitution, the empire, and British traditions more generally. By contrast, Catholic workers, staunchly Irish nationalist and religious with few exceptions, welcomed the idea of a parliament in Dublin, controlled by Irish nationalists, and willing to relieve them of the burden of social and economic discrimination which they felt they expe-

---

[12] E. H. Hunt, *Regional Wage Variations in Britain 1850–1914* (Oxford, 1973).

rienced in Belfast and elsewhere. While job discrimination in the industrial districts of Ulster is hardly in doubt, its scale and significance are subject to sharp debate.[13]

In recognition of these difficulties, the Belfast Trades Council banned discussion of politics and religion at its meetings, though individual members were free to pursue political roles outside of the Council. Belfast's first working class MP, T. H. Sloan, was elected for South Belfast in 1905. Sloan occupied a curious position on the ideological spectrum. He had earlier founded the breakaway Independent Orange Order, which took a militantly anti-Catholic line.[14] His election signified the dislike felt by Protestant workers at being patronized by upper-class unionists: they wanted independent working-class Protestant representation, sometimes with a sectarian tinge.

With the benefit of hindsight it is clear that the 'national question', interwoven with communal and sectarian passions, would always take precedence over mundane issues such as wages, working conditions, and union recognition. Labour concerns formed a weak cross-current in the torrent of nationalist and unionist politics. Nonetheless, when Home Rule was on the back-burner, a space for labour politics could open up. The labour historian, Emmet O'Connor, sees 1907 as the high point in the fortunes of political labour. The British Labour Party held its annual conference in Belfast for the first time, and three branches of the Independent Labour Party were formed. This was also the year in which Larkin led a dockers' and carters' strike in Belfast, to enforce the principle of the closed shop. Catholic and Protestant workers stood side-by-side against the employers but after several months of industrial and street action, the strike was resolved in the employers' favour. With a Liberal government in power, and progress towards a third Home Rule bill, the prospects of Catholic-Protestant working-class solidarity in favour of labour representation receded. The unionist threat to oppose Home Rule legislation with force, and the Irish Revolution of 1916–22 further marginalized labour politics and labour political representation. The Catholic Church warned of dangerous socialist and communist influences and promoted the Ancient Order of Hibernians (closely linked to Catholic nationalist politics) as an alternative to labour politics. It is revealing also that Sir Edward Carson, and other leaders of the Ulster Unionist Party, were acutely aware of the importance of seeming to accommodate the interests of Protestant workers within a pan-class Unionist alliance. Speakers from a trade union background were given prominent positions on anti-Home Rule platforms. A more formal expression of this was the creation of the Ulster Unionist Labour Association (UULA) in 1918, whose base was among Protestant trade unionists in the Belfast shipyards. Three of its members were put forward in the 1918 General Election but with the formation of the state of Northern Ireland, the significance of the UULA declined.[15] For the next few decades politics circled, predictably enough, round the obsessions of Ulster unionism and Irish nationalism, the newly created 'border' being a particular focus. Controversies over Irish-based unions as against British-based unions did not help, the holy grail of

---

[13] For a discussion, see Black, 'Industrial Relations', 50–61.
[14] E. O'Connor, *A Labour History of Ireland, 1824–1960* (Dublin, 1992), 65.
[15] A. Morgan, *Labour and Partition: The Belfast Working Class 1905–23* (London, 1991); H. Patterson, 'The Decline of the Collaborators: The Ulster Unionist Labour Association and Post-War Unionist Politics', in F. Devine, F. Lane and N. Puirseil (eds), *Essays in Irish Labour History* (Dublin, 2008), 238–56.

worker solidarity proving more apparent than real. The Northern Ireland Labour Party (NILP), founded in 1924, was initially neutral on the 'national question', and indeed won three seats in the Northern Ireland general election of the following year.[16] This was testament to the continuing significance of a Labour constituency in Northern Ireland, most notably in Belfast and with pockets of support in Larne, Newtownabbey, Newry, and Derry as well. It is true also that social class, religion, and locality intersected with nationalism and unionism in complicated ways. But the fluctuating vote for the NILP also signified the vulnerability of class-based politics to the passionate but conservative aspirations of Irish nationalism and Ulster unionism.

CONDITIONS OF LABOUR: SHIPBUILDING

Trade unionism and labour politics are only one aspect of the experience of labour, so we now turn to the structure and working conditions of the labour force, focusing on Belfast in particular. In the early nineteenth century, the town of Belfast did not appear as a particularly promising site for a modern shipbuilding industry, yet by 1880 the industry employed 5000 men, and by 1911, about 20,000. The other port towns of Derry and Newry had by then lost any significant shipbuilding facilities as the logic of industrialism dictated concentration and specialization. The construction of large ships and their engines was a highly complex industrial process and consequently British shipyards in this era were characterized by a diverse labour force. Shipyard workers formed a highly stratified social grouping in which relationships between workers and employers and between different groups of workers were complex.

Skilled workers formed the core of a shipyard's labour force. As a group they were united by shared status and social origins; their fathers had usually been skilled workers; and all had undergone the experience of apprenticeship. The lists of 'hands employed' by Harland and Wolff show twenty-three trades in which apprentices were employed, but other sources suggest up to ninety trades in a shipyard.[17] In August 1919, skilled men represented 8733 out of the 20,057 employed in the yard (44 per cent), and in May that year 1,739 out of the 6245 in the engine works (28 per cent).[18] In the early twentieth century, the wages paid to skilled workers in Belfast were amongst the highest in the British shipbuilding industry, suggesting that their skills were in short supply (see Table 12.1).[19] This meant they were difficult to replace easily, and so employers were obliged to recognize and cooperate with the unions. These workers formed a self-reproducing elite within Belfast's labour force as it was their sons, or other close male relatives, who entered 'trades' through an apprenticeship.

Demarcation disputes were common as craftsmen sought to safeguard their employment in a rapidly changing industry. Certain trades declined and their

---

[16] G. Walker, 'The Northern Ireland Labour Party, 1924–45', in F. Lane and D. Ó Drisceóil (eds), *Politics and the Irish Working Class, 1830–1945* (London, 2005), 229–45.

[17] S. Pollard and P. Robertson, *The British Shipbuilding Industry* (Cambridge, Mass., 1979), 154.

[18] List of hands employed, 28 June 1919 (engine works) and 27 August 1919 (shipyard); Harland and Wolff Papers, (H&WP), PRONI, D2805, Box 41.

[19] *Report of an Inquiry by the Board of Trade into Working Class Rents, Housing, Retail Prices, and Standard Rate of Wages in the United Kingdom* (B.P.P., 1908, 107).

Table 12.1. Weekly wages of engineering workers, October 1905

	Belfast	Range in ten other shipbuilding areas	Average of other areas
Fitter	37s	35 to 36s	35s-1d
Turner	38s	35 to 36s	35s-2d
Smith	37s	34 to 38s	35s-6d
Pattern Maker	39s	37 to 39s-6d	38s
Labourer	15s to 18s	18s to 23s-6d	c.20s

Source: *Working Class Rents, Housing Retail Prices* (B.P.P., 1908, 107). The 'other areas' were Barrow, Birkenhead, Glasgow, Greenock, Jarrow, Middlesbrough, Newcastle, South Shields, Stockton-on-Tees, and Sunderland.

members were forced to fight to retain employment in the yards while, conversely, other crafts aggressively tried to create monopolies at the expense of their less powerful 'brothers'. The shipwrights, for example, who dominated shipbuilding when wood was the main material, had refused to adapt to working in iron. In 1850, 90 per cent of new UK-produced tonnage was built in wood, but by 1880 this had declined to only 4 per cent.[20] Within a generation the shipwrights were reduced from being the dominant trade to fighting a desperate rearguard action to protect what remained of their work from encroachment by joiners and carpenters. Demarcation disputes led to major strikes in Belfast in 1890, 1891, 1911, and 1913 with, in each case, the joiners gaining work at the expense of the shipwrights.[21]

Although skilled workers in the yards enjoyed good wages and were seldom affected by seasonal unemployment, their working conditions remained harsh and dangerous. They faced, as did all shipyard workers, high rates of industrial injury. In 1907, forty-eight foundry workers in every thousand were subject to industrial injury and their average life expectancy was about fifty-nine years.[22] The average life expectancy of engineers was under thirty-eight years in the 1860s, and only forty-eight years by the end of the 1880s.[23] In many of the shipyard trades, physical injury and disablement were common and accepted features of working life.

> It may be taken as a fact, based upon experience, that artisans who are exposed to such loud noises as are made in hammering rivets suffer from deafness. Boilermakers and riveters become deaf at an early age, while their comrades engaged in other kinds of work in the shipyard do not suffer.[24]

In 1912 in the yards at Belfast, the Clyde, and the Tyne, 1448 workers were injured and sixty-two killed in falls, while another 1400 were injured and fifteen killed by objects falling on them.[25]

---

[20] J. B. Jefferys, *The Story of the Engineers* (London, 1946), 45.
[21] *Report on the Strikes and Lockouts of 1890, by the Labour Correspondent to the Board of Trade* (B.P.P., 1890–91, 78); *Report on Strikes and Lockouts...* (B.P.P., 1893–94, 83; 1914–16, 36).
[22] H. J. Fyrth and H. Collins, *The Foundry Workers* (Manchester, 1959), 114–15.
[23] Jefferys, *Story of the Engineers*, 66–7.
[24] T. Oliver, *Dangerous Trades* (London, 1902), 752.
[25] *Report of the Secretary of State for the Home Department on Accidents Occurring In Shipbuilding Yard* (B.P.P, 1913, 60).

Apprentices can be seen as part of the skilled working class. An apprenticeship usually began at the age of 16 and in most cases lasted for five years, although carpenters, joiners and painters served six and plumbers seven years in Belfast.[26] Compared to the Clyde, where opportunities for training were more plentiful, apprenticeships in Belfast lasted longer and rates of pay were lower. Parents also had to pay a deposit, of between £2 and £5, to ensure the good behaviour of their sons. This practice had been abandoned on the Clyde. In addition, parents had to purchase a boy's toolkit, which amounted to a considerable outlay. A shipwright's tools lost in transit in 1915 were valued by the owner at £6 11s 4d, the equivalent of almost three weeks' wages.[27] At the end of August 1919, there were 1780 apprentices employed in Belfast by Harland and Wolff, representing just under 9 per cent of the labour force.[28] Their status was ambiguous: subordinated to skilled workers, legally bound to their employer, yet anticipating skilled status in the future. They could, and indeed were expected, to join the trade unions representing their respective skills but they were invariably treated as second-class members. There were occasional revolts against such treatment, notably a strike in 1913 that involved 1300 apprentices from Harland and Wolff and Workman Clark,[29] but in the main, the control exercised by employer and craftsman ensured rigid discipline.

Throughout industry in the United Kingdom there were workers who did not undergo a formal apprenticeship but acquired skills that made them difficult to replace; for example, railway men, miners, and dockers. In the shipyards there existed a range of workers who were classified as semi-skilled. A letter to the City Clerk of Belfast in 1919 identified groups of workers who were counted as semi-skilled.[30] There were 2122 men employed in semi-skilled jobs in Harland and Wolff in June 1919 (11 per cent of the firm's labour force). The proportion was higher still, at 15 per cent, in the boiler shop.[31] Overall, in the Belfast shipyards it is probable that about one worker in eight was semi-skilled.

What was the status of such workers compared with the skilled workers? There is evidence that some categories of semi-skilled workers were in short supply in the Belfast yards. In 1911, holders-up (those members of a riveter's 'gang' who held the plate in position during the riveting process) in Belfast were the best paid in the UK, at 31s a week. Conversely, a smith's striker (a worker who swung a hammer while the smith worked the metal) in the city received the worst wages in the industry, 19s a week, much the same as an unskilled labourer.[32] By late 1918 a semi-skilled rigger, the best paid of the semi-skilled workers, earned as much as a sail-maker, which was a

---

[26] Letter from Govan Shipyard to Harland and Wolff Belfast, 17 August 1912; H&WP, PRONI, D2805, Box 31.

[27] Ibid., early 1915.   [28] Ibid., Box 41, List of Hands Employed, 27 August 1919; ibid, Box 41.

[29] *Report on Strikes And Lock-Outs and on Conciliation and Arbitration Boards in the United Kingdom in 1913* (B.P.P., 1913, 36).

[30] Letter from Harland and Wolff to the Town Clerk, Belfast, 19 April 1920; H&WP, PRONI, D2805, Box 41.

[31] List of Hands Employed in the engineering works, 20 and 28 June 1919; ibid., Box 41.

[32] The weekly wages were: smith's strikers—Clyde, 20s 6d–22s; Tyne, 24s 6d; Wear, n/a; Barrow, 23s 6d–24s; Belfast 19s; holders-up—Clyde, 21s. 4d–27s 1d; Tyne, 28s 6d; Wear, 28s 6d; Barrow, 29s; Belfast, 31s; ibid., Box 30.

declining skilled trade. It is apparent that semi-skilled workers constituted a diverse category whose status varied from those seen, and paid, as little better than labourers, to others such as stagers and iron-dressers whose wages approached those of skilled workers. The intermediate status of semi-skilled men can be judged by examining their trade union affiliations. Some groups were admitted by craft unions: boilermakers, for example, recruited holders-up whose work was critical to the riveting process, while the electricians organized temporary lightmen.[33] Other groups formed local unions such as the Belfast Ship Riggers' Protective Society. But, by the early twentieth century, there was a tendency for these groups to amalgamate into national bodies or be absorbed by craft unions.[34]

By the First World War, the main union representing semi-skilled labour in Belfast was the National Amalgamated Union of Labour (NAUL), established in the Tyneside shipyards in 1889 to protect platers' helpers and others who were directly employed by craftsmen rather than by the shipyard.[35] Tensions between skilled craftsmen and their semi-skilled helpers were a feature of industrial relations. In the year the NAUL was established, over 200 platers' helpers and rivet heaters struck in Belfast against the platers, with the strikers insisting that they had no grievance against the employers.[36] There were similar outbreaks of industrial unrest between craftsmen and helpers in 1892, 1893, 1894, 1897, 1900, and 1911.[37] Given the *raison d'être* of the NAUL and its record of confrontation with craft bodies, it was hardly surprising that the latter were rather slow and begrudging in accepting that the semi-skilled had the right to unionize. However, the NAUL successfully unionized a large proportion of the labour force and had to be treated with respect, albeit begrudging at times, by the employers. In 1911, the union wrote to the management of Harland and Wolff enclosing a copy of a resolution that had been passed by their members, threatening not to work with anyone who was not a member of the union.[38]

The response of the company to this uncompromising demand for the imposition of a closed shop was both moderate and conciliatory.

> As you are aware, the firm have always fully recognised the various trade and labour unions, and have endeavoured to work amicably with them, and we are somewhat surprised that your members should take this step. We hope, however, that on further consideration they will see some other way out of the difficulty.[39]

Harland and Wolff clearly distinguished between 'trade' and 'labour' unions but emphasized that they tried to work with both groups, an indication perhaps that the NAUL was strong enough in the yard to present a threat.

---

[33] W. C. Stevens, *The Story of the E.T.U* (London 1952), 60; J. E. Mortimer, *History of the Boilermakers* (London 1973), 122.
[34] S. Ward-Perkins, *Select Guide To Trade Union Records in Dublin* (Dublin, 1996), 24.
[35] H. A. Clegg and A. F. Thompson, *History of British Trade Unions since 1889* (Oxford, 1964), 66.
[36] *Report on Strikes and Lock-Outs* (B.P.P., 1889, 68).   [37] Ibid.
[38] Letter from the National Amalgamated Union of Labour to Harland and Wolff, 2 December 1911, PRONI D2805, Box 30.
[39] Letter from Harland and Wolff to the National Amalgamated Union of Labour 3 December 1911, ibid.

Over a third of those working in the Belfast shipyards were classified as unskilled. Many of them were casually employed and, unlike the semi-skilled for instance, they could be easily, and cheaply, replaced. Belfast employers always enjoyed a surplus of unskilled labour with the result that the wages of shipyard labourers were amongst the lowest in the industry.[40] On the morning of 28 March 1911, a member of the office staff of Harland and Wolff passed a note to William Pirrie, the firm's managing director, explaining that he had received a phone call from the Company Secretary of Workman Clark. The neighbouring yard was proposing 'if we have no objection' to give their unskilled workers a 6d a week pay rise.[41] Pirrie simply wrote his reply on the bottom of the original note: 'If Messrs Workman Clark & Co grant an advance of 6d per week I am disposed to advocate our doing the same rather than that there should be any feeling of discontent on the part of our men.'[42] Further correspondence indicated that Harland and Wolff had just over 1700 unskilled labourers on their books.

Status as well as pay differences separated skilled workers from the unskilled. This division was often marked by ill-feeling, as Bob Getgood, a union official recalled in an interview with Sam Hanna Bell in the 1950s:

> There was no association. The labourers herded together, went off together. But an odd one would have curried favour with a foreman but much more likely to be currying favour with his skilled employee or his fellow employee.... He felt that if he could be on good terms with the craftsmen then his value to the craftsmen was seen and if a choice had to be made he was likely to be retained in preference to the fellow who was probably a better man but harder to work with.[43]

If timekeepers, pay-office staff, the drawing office, foremen and such staff as messengers and porters are included, the 'office' at Harland and Wolff in late 1919 contained about 5% of the total workforce.[44] Many of these workers came from the middle class or upper-working class and were highly trained supervisors and technicians. It was considered a step-up if an apprentice, on completing his training, was taken 'upstairs' into the office. In terms of status, office staff perceived themselves as being superior to those employed in the yards and works. There was a hierarchy within the office as well, the top echelon being formed by the managers who actually ran the yard. In Harland and Wolff, this group numbered fifty-four in late 1919. Below them came the supervisory grades, head and assistant foremen, and storekeepers, highly trained and experienced individuals who effectively ran the yards on a day-to-day basis. In late 1919, Harland and Wolff employed 136 in these grades. The drawing office and pay office were critical to the shipbuilding process, and in late 1919 Harland and Wolff had 330 in the drawing office and 161 in the pay office. Clerical support was also necessary and in 1919 the company employed

---

[40] Letter from the Clyde Shipbuilders' Association, 29 August 1911, ibid., Box 30. Labourers' wages were 20s 6d to 21s 6d in Tyne and Wear, 19s in Barrow, 18s to 20s in Clyde, and 19s a week in Belfast.
[41] Note of a telephone call from Workman Clark to Harland and Wolff, 11 March 1911, ibid.
[42] S. Bartlett to G. Payne, 15 March 1911, ibid.
[43] Interview with Bob Getgood, Sam Hanna Bell Papers, PRONI, D3358/1.
[44] Return of Administrative Staff of Harland and Wolff working in Belfast, Greenock and Govan, 22 December 1919, PRONI D2805, Box 41.

453 individuals in this grade (including typists), a modest 1.6% of the total labour force. To such a compact administrative organization may be added the twenty-two staff in the dining room, six hall porters, and 101 porters and messengers.[45]

As a group, office workers were slow to unionize. Comparatively good conditions combined with vulnerability to victimization made union membership less attractive than for others. However, by late 1918 the employers were discussing war bonus payments with the National Union of Clerks (NUC) and meetings continued to be held with this body after the war.[46] The Association of Shipbuilding and Engineering Draughtsmen (AESD) was also active in Belfast from late 1916.[47] Various unions were formed to represent foremen and other supervisory staff during the war years, but none of these was ever recognized by the Shipbuilders' Federation.[48]

Female workers within the shipbuilding industry are frequently overlooked. Yet within what was a predominantly male labour force, there were always some female employees. As military conscription was never introduced in Ireland there was no need to introduce female labour in Belfast on a comparable scale to Britain in either the First or the Second World Wars. A report dated July 1916 shows that 163 women were working in the yard (1.7 per cent of the labour force). The only groups for which details are given in this report are waitresses (nineteen) and charwomen (twenty-two), working in the offices rather than the yard.[49] In the drawing offices, tracers were often women, while typists were increasingly, but by no means exclusively, female. Moss and Hume note that the last workers in Harland and Wolff to be driven out during the politico-sectarian 'expulsions' of August 1920 were female, four waitresses in the staff dining room.[50] These attacks on Catholic workers, and others, were in part a reaction to political violence in southern Ireland, where the Irish Republican Army was intensifying its military campaign to create an Irish Republic.[51]

CONDITIONS OF LABOUR: TEXTILES, TRANSPORT, AND RETAILING

Belfast's other major industry, textiles, employed far more people than the shipyards. Most workers, however, were semi-skilled and poorly paid by comparison. Average female earnings in 1908 were 10s-10d a week (girls 6s-5d); men, who tended to form the more skilled element in the textile workforce, averaged 26s-2d (boys 7s-8d).[52]

---

[45] Ibid.
[46] Notes of a meeting between Harland and Wolff and the National Union of Clerks, undated but late 1918, ibid., Box 38; Letter from Harland and Wolff to the National Union of Clerks, 15 October 1921, bid., Box 45.
[47] J. E. Mortimer, *A History of the Association of Shipbuilding and Engineering Draughtsmen* (London, 1960), 28, 39.
[48] A. Marsh and J. Ryan, *Historical Directory of Trade Unions*, Vol. 1 (Aldershot, 1980), 4–5, 40–1, 151.
[49] Note on wartime dilution at Harland and Wolff, 31 July 1916, PRONI D2805, Box 35.
[50] M. Moss and J. R. Hume, *Shipbuilders to the World* (Belfast 1986), 225.
[51] H. Patterson, *Class Conflict and Sectarianism: The Protestant Working Class and the Belfast Labour Movement, 1868–1920* (Belfast, 1980); A. Morgan, *Labour and Partition: The Belfast Working Class, 1905–1923* (London, 1991).
[52] *Report of Board of Trade Enquiry into the Earnings and Hours of Labour of Work People* (B.P.P., 1909, 80).

In 1911 some 53,000 persons were employed in textiles and clothing, most of these in the city's linen mills and factories. The gender composition was also very different to shipbuilding and engineering: three out of every four workers were female.

In Derry, textiles were also to the fore in employment terms. From modest beginnings in the 1840s, Derry developed a strong specialism in shirt making, using labour concentrated in large factories but also employing thousands of dispersed outworkers in the country districts radiating out from the town. By 1896 the town boasted twenty factories, employing 10,000 people in town and countryside.[53] In the city of Derry itself, according to the 1911 census, almost 4500 were employed in textiles and dress, three-quarters of them female. Derry was the province's second industrial city, while the other significant but smaller industrial towns of Lisburn, Lurgan, and Portadown were in the hinterland of Belfast. There are, however, no close comparisons between the growth trajectories of Belfast and Derry. Between 1821 and 1911, the population of Belfast increased tenfold; that of Derry increased only fourfold.[54] Belfast had 129,000 persons classified as engaged in industry in 1911; Derry had 11,000, less than ten per cent of the Belfast figure. The striking implication is one of scale; the extent to which Belfast dominated the industrial and demographic landscape of Ulster.

Conditions of work in linen manufacture, the principal sector of the textile industry in Ulster, could be extremely severe. In the spinning rooms the steam used to lubricate the flax produced temperatures of over 27 degrees centigrade. Combined with high humidity, this gave rise to serious health problems amongst the largely female workforce. In areas of Belfast city where mill workers predominated, the tuberculosis rate was 50 per cent higher than for the city as a whole, while the death rate was a third higher.[55] The mill operatives were difficult to unionize, as they were vulnerable to victimization. There was limited alternative employment and their wages were too low to risk undertaking industrial action. The Women's Trade Union League, with some support from the Belfast Trades Council, tried to organize textile workers in 1890, but the three unions they established all collapsed within a year. In 1893 the Trades Council itself established the Textile Operatives Union of Ireland.[56] However, only a small proportion of linen workers were unionized. One union veteran later recalled how she contacted a girl in the spinning room to see about organizing the workers there. 'She was too frightened—said she was too frightened. She wouldn't take it on.' She added, 'I hadn't enough sense to be frightened.'[57]

Most of Belfast's manufacturing industries were heavily dependent on imported raw materials and fuel, so in many ways the city's growth and economic success was dependent on the transport sector. By 1911, 11,704 were employed in road-, rail-, or sea-related transport activities (10 per cent of the male labour force) and they

---

[53] E. McLaughlin, 'Women and Work in Derry City: A Survey', *Saothar*, 14 (1989), 35–46.
[54] Calculated from W. Vaughan and A. J. Fitzpatrick (eds), *Irish Historical Statistics, 1821–1971* (Dublin, 1978), 36–9.
[55] *Report of the Departmental Committee on Humidity and Ventilation in Flax Mills and Linen Factories* (B.P.P., 1914, 36).
[56] A. McKee, *Belfast Trades Council* (Belfast 1983),13–14.
[57] B. Messenger, *Picking up the Linen Threads* (Belfast 1980), 207–8.

represented a very diverse group of workers who experienced widely differing conditions. The best-paid and most unionized were the 1273 railway workers. Some of them, notably drivers, were earning as much as, if not more than, skilled craftsmen. In contrast, the dock workers were hardly unionized at all until 1907 and were amongst the most deprived workers in the city.[58] Most dockers, the more than 2000 'spellsmen', were employed on a casual basis. They were taken on daily or not, as determined by the stevedores, and often took home less than 10 shillings a week. As John Gray describes it: 'Work when found was brutally hard; it was common for a man to shift 170 tons a day in two and a half hundredweight sacks, all taken from the ships on narrow planks.'[59]

As cities grow, the structures for feeding their populations have to become more complex and sophisticated. In 1901 there were 1473 persons engaged in food-processing industries and 15,293 employed in retail and wholesale activities. Those employed in shops considered themselves socially superior to those who earned their living by dirtying their hands but they too were open to abuse and exploitation. In 1901, a government committee, looking into the question of shop opening-hours, received evidence on the normal practice in Belfast: 'In the centre of the city amongst the better class of shops they run from eight in the morning till seven at night—five nights a week—and eleven on Saturday, altogether about 70 hours a week. In middle class shops they run 80 hours a week and in the smaller shops still up to 100 hours a week.'[60] Although efforts were made to organize retail workers the nature of their employment—the sharp divisions within the sector, the fear of intimidation and, above all, the threat of refusal of a reference if dismissed—made effective organization difficult.

Another important, but often forgotten, category of workers in the history of Belfast's industrial development was the tens of thousands of women working in the 'making-up' trades, who perhaps constituted the classic exploited proletarian class in Belfast. Their most important product in Belfast was handkerchiefs, which were produced in such huge numbers that from the mid-1880s onwards they were a separately listed item in Ireland's export statistics.

In order to compete with cotton, linen employers had to pare costs to the bone, with the result that the wages of the workers were cut to a bare minimum. In September 1910, J. J. Mallon, secretary of the National Anti-Sweating League, visited Belfast and addressed the Trades Council: 'Since he arrived in the city he had seen on hoardings an announcement that "the wages of sin is death" but when he took up the papers he saw the wages of virtue were three farthings per hour. He thought there was hardly sufficient distinction.'[61]

Two years later, the Factory Inspector reported that conditions for outworkers in Belfast were actually getting worse as a result of technical innovation in the industry,

> ... owing to the high speed of the power driven machines [in factories], the output has materially increased, while the rates of pay have been lowered to meet the altered

---

[58] J. Gray, *City in Revolt* (Belfast 1985), 6.   [59] Ibid., 6.
[60] *Report of the House of Lords Select Committee on Early Closing of Shops* (B.P.P., 1901, 6).
[61] *Belfast News Letter*, 2 September 1910.

conditions. One worker told me she had stitched 32 dozen handkerchiefs in a day, whereas about eight years ago 16 dozen was considered a hard day's work...work that is fairly paid in the factory becomes terribly sweated as outwork if it takes twice or even three times as long to do it on a treadle machine.[62]

Outside of Belfast, in the provincial towns of Ulster, the problem of organizing labour unions was greater still. The shirt-making industry, Derry's principal manufacturing activity, is a case in point. Scottish capital and entrepreneurs had helped reorganize the industry, partly on a factory basis but still relying heavily on outworkers as we have seen. Thus the Scottish firm of Tillie and Henderson had a workforce of 4000 by the late 1850s but most of its workers were dispersed around the north-west of Ulster.[63] This hybrid organizational form hindered the effective organization of labour in pursuit of higher wages or improved working conditions. In the mill villages of Ulster, at Sion Mills, Darkley, Drumaness, and elsewhere, the mill owner was the major single employer. This geographical monopoly, reinforced sometimes by control of housing as well, tilted the balance of power heavily in favour of the employer. Still, the key determinant of wages was the large reservoirs of unskilled labour to be found in Ulster, as elsewhere in Ireland. And what ultimately constrained wages were the fierce competitive pressures which characterized the market position of Ulster clothing producers generally in the late nineteenth and twentieth centuries.

STABILITY AND CHANGE

The inter-war period witnessed momentous political and economic changes but it is striking how many of the pre-war patterns of work and occupations persisted within the newly formed statelet of Northern Ireland. Table 12.2 shows the numbers of insured workers at various points in time from the mid-1920s to the late 1930s. It also shows the proportion of the insured labour force in each sector—7 per cent of insured workers were in the building sector in 1925 for example—as well as the male to female ratio.

Although the problem of unemployment affected all parts of the UK, its severity varied by region and Northern Ireland was amongst the hardest hit.[64] In 1932 British unemployment peaked at 22 per cent of the insured labour force, whereas in Northern Ireland the figure was 27 per cent. Other older industrialized regions suffered badly also, the comparable figures for Scotland and Wales being higher still at 28 per cent and 36 per cent respectively. Some sectors were especially badly affected: shipbuilding and engineering in Northern Ireland experienced a massive 57 per cent unemployment rate in 1932.[65]

---

[62] *Report of Inspector of Factories and Workshops* (B.P.P., 1913, 23).
[63] P. Ollerenshaw, 'Industry', in Kennedy and Ollerenshaw (eds), *Economic History of Ulster*, 84–5.
[64] W. R. Garside, *British Unemployment 1919–1939* (Cambridge 1990), 10.
[65] See especially K. S. Isles and N. Cuthbert, *An Economic Survey of Northern Ireland* (Belfast, 1957), 29, 582.

Table 12.2. Distribution of the insured workforce in inter-war Northern Ireland

	1925	1928	1931	1934	1937
Insured Workers	266,000	251,000	270,000	268,000	294,500
(Male/Female)		*(60/40)*	*(62/38)*	*(62/38)*	*(63/37)*
Unemployment rate	24%	17%	28%	24%	24%
Building Trades	7%	8%	10%	10%	10%
(Male/Female)		*(98/2)*	*(99/1)*	*(99/1)*	*(99/1)*
Unemployment rate	25%	22%	35%	37%	42%
Distributive Trades	9%	13%	14%	14%	15%
(Male/Female)		*(66/34)*	*(67/33)*	*(67/33)*	*(67/33)*
Unemployment rate	16%	11%	20%	19%	21%
Clothing, Shoes	10%	10%	9%	9%	8%
(Male/Female)		*(7/93)*	*(12/88)*	*(12/88)*	*(11/89)*
Unemployment rate	14%	14%	29%	26%	24%
Linen & Related	27%	30%	24%	23%	22%
(Male/Female)		*(31/69)*	*(31/69)*	*(31/69)*	*(30/70)*
Unemployment rate	33%	21%	29%	17%	19%
Food & Drink	5%	5%	4%	5%	5%
(Male/Female)		*(75/25)*	*(73/27)*	*(71/29)*	*(68/32)*
Unemployment rate	18%	12%	17%	16%	15%
Shipbuilding & Engineering	12%	10%	9%	8%	8%
(Male/Female)		*(98/2)*	*(98/2)*	*(98/2)*	*(93/7)*
Unemployment rate	33%	28%	45%	37%	19%

Source: *Ulster Year Books* (Belfast, 1926, 1929, 1932, 1935, and 1938).

The attitude of the authorities towards the unemployed was often less than sympathetic. The views of William Strachan, company secretary of Workman Clark, were typical of many: 'Not until more factory gates are closed and no money is forthcoming with which to pay rates out of which sheltered men and dole lifters receive their demands, will authorities and men believe that there is a limit to what employers can stand.'[66]

In a similar vein a Poor Law Guardian in Belfast in August 1928 railed against 'sloth, fecklessness and iniquity', stating it was the Guardians' duty to penalize idleness and instil a spirit of independence. He knew, he said, 'of three betting shops in one street which did a roaring business amongst the poor... These people would make an effort to find work if they found that they could not get relief.'[67]

In January 1927, the Belfast Guardians had been making payments to 6446 claimants but, motivated by sentiments such as these, they had slashed the number in receipt to 997 by refusing assistance to all able-bodied unemployed.[68] In the circumstances, it is not surprising that there were outbreaks of protest against the

[66] J. Bardon, *A History of Ulster* (Belfast 1992), 523.
[67] P. Devlin, *Yes, We Have No Bananas: Outdoor Relief in Belfast, 1920–39* (Belfast, 1981), 81.
[68] Ibid., 84.

system, the most serious of which was the 'Outdoor Relief Strike' in Belfast in 1932. Catholic and Protestant workers displayed a solidarity that briefly seemed to threaten the status quo. However, such militancy was short lived and, like many workers elsewhere in the United Kingdom, the workers of Ulster continued to vote for conservative, unionist, or nationalist parties rather than labour or socialist alternatives. In times of constitutional crisis the differing political and communal identities invariably trumped a sense of class solidarity.[69] This is not to say, however, that workers, whether organized or not, were incapable of pressing distinctly labour claims when the occasion or the opportunity arose. In various formal and informal ways they did so—sometimes successfully, sometimes suffering setbacks—throughout the long period surveyed here.

The experience of the Second World War, in some respects, is a case in point. In the 1930s, the very high unemployment rates were one factor which contributed to Northern Ireland's position as the least strike-prone region in the United Kingdom. Labour market conditions changed with the outbreak of war in 1939 but the relatively slow rate of economic mobilization meant that unemployment declined much more slowly than in other major UK industrial regions. Even so, as labour markets became tighter, industrial relations in Northern Ireland deteriorated not only compared to the 1930s but also compared to Britain. Amongst the most serious confrontations with employers was that of 1944 which involved more than 20,000 workers in the shipyards and elsewhere. Trade union membership in Northern Ireland, it may be noted, rose from 114,000 to 147,000 during the war years.

Still, the chronic uncertainty of the 1930s returned even before the war ended and the pre-war pattern of relatively high male unemployment reasserted itself.[70] So, although post-war unemployment turned out to be lower than during the 1930s, the prospects for both union and non-union labour, were distinctly uncertain as the war economy wound down and the troops returned home.

FURTHER READING

J. C. Beckett, et al. *Belfast: The Making of the City* (Belfast, 1983).
J. C. Beckett, and R. E. Glasscock, *Belfast: Origins and Growth of an Industrial City* (Belfast, 1967).
F. W. Boal, and S. A. Royle, (eds) *Enduring City: Belfast in the Twentieth Century* (Belfast, 2006).
D. Nevin, (ed.) *Trade Union Century* (Dublin, 1994).
E. O'Connor, *A Labour History of Ireland*, 1824–1960 (Dublin, 1992).
S. A. Royle, *Portrait of an Industrial City: 'Clanging Belfast', 1750–1914* (Belfast, 2011).

[69] Patterson, *Class Conflict and Sectarianism*.
[70] O'Connor, *Labour History*, 187.

13

Education since the Late Eighteenth Century

N. C. Fleming

INTRODUCTION

The present system of education in Ulster is the product of two centuries of inter-denominational antagonism and tension between interest groups and the state. These features are not unique to the province, but its peculiar religious demography has ensured the denominational segregation of generations of schoolchildren. On two occasions, in the 1830s and again in the 1920s, the state attempted to curtail segregated schooling by inhibiting denominational control. It failed each time because resistance to its reforms undermined the main objective of education policy: the maintenance of an efficient system of mass education which regulates and controls rapidly changing social structures. The propensity of vested interests to resist state-directed reform has since moved beyond denominationalism. Legislation in the 1940s to promote technical education was largely ignored, especially in rural Ulster, as local authorities preferred instead to create new grammar and secondary schools. And in the 1970s and early 2000s, the Northern Ireland education ministry struggled to end academic selection in the face of determined opposition from grammar schools. The most significant challenge to vested interests has not, therefore, been the state, but the emergence in the 1970s of campaigns for integrated education and Irish-medium schools.

Until the late-nineteenth century, education policymakers throughout Europe regarded their established churches as the obvious instrument for developing education systems which distinguished young people by class and gender, and trained them for particular roles in a society pre-ordained by birth.[1] It was the state's responsibility to ensure the charge was properly executed.[2] In late-eighteenth century Ireland, the British-appointed administration at Dublin Castle reluctantly recognized that the Established Church of Ireland could not fulfil this duty. Its monopoly of formal education had not only exacerbated inter-denominational tension, but also encouraged poorly resourced informal schooling for non-Episcopalians. The Castle

---

[1] R. Lowe, 'Schooling as an Impediment to Social Mobility in Nineteenth and Twentieth-Century Britain', in C. Majorek, E. V. Johanningmeier, and F. Simon (eds), *Schooling in Changing Societies: Historical and Comparative Perspectives*, 4 (1998), 57–67.

[2] N. Morris, 'State Paternalism and *Laissez-Faire* in the 1860s', in History of Education Society (ed.), *Studies in the Government and Control of Education since 1860* (London, 1970), 13–25.

therefore devised a scheme which expanded state-supported education through a system of non-denominational schools that facilitated access to all clerics. After several decades of delay this new system was launched in the early 1830s, but it quickly succumbed to denominationalization as clerics constituted the bulk of newly appointed school managers. The denominational influence this established proved resilient despite increasing lay participation. Ireland's expanding middle classes regarded church loyalty as an integral part of their civic identity.[3] Denominational schools were increasingly the focus of middle-class investment and consumption. This entrenched class and sectarian interests and ensured it was these, and not the interests of reformers in government, which continued to control the pace and degree of modernization.[4]

ORIGINS OF MASS EDUCATION

From the plantation of Ulster in the early seventeenth century, the Church of Ireland possessed a near monopoly of formal education. Their privileged entitlement, was, however, never fully realized given the contrary confessional allegiances of the majority of Irish people, and as a consequence episcopalian schools depended on state support. The Established Church's most conspicuous successes, Ulster's five 'royal schools'—Armagh, Cavan, Dungannon, Enniskillen, and Raphoe—were founded by royal charter in 1608, but further government intervention was necessary in the years that followed to ensure their long-term viability. Beyond the Ulster plantation and the administrative centre of Dublin, episcopalian schools met with little success, so that by the eighteenth century the government preferred instead to give grants to voluntary charitable societies. The proselytizing function of these societies appealed to Irish parliamentarians, not least because it directly addressed the numerical weakness of episcopalians. The societies achieved modest success in educating Protestant and Catholic children together, especially in Ulster, and in some instances they developed working relationships with Catholic schoolmasters; around eight hundred in Ulster accepted financial aid in 1826.[5]

It was clear by the late-eighteenth century that proselytizing societies were unable to provide an education acceptable to the majority of Catholics, let alone secure their conversion to Protestantism.[6] The middle ranks of Catholic society relied instead on so-called 'hedge schools', a system of itinerant schoolmasters dependent on the ability of individual families to pay for their children's tutelage. The hedge school system suffered considerably from pedagogic and structural failings, and experienced only marginal improvement following relaxation of the

[3] P. O'Mahony and G. Delanty, *Rethinking Irish History: Nationalism, Identity and Ideology* (Basingstoke, 1998), 54.
[4] R. Aldrich, *An Introduction to the History of Education* (London, 1982), 16–18; J. MacLaughlin, *Reimagining the Nation-State: The Contested Terrains of Nation-Building* (London, 2001), 103.
[5] J. J. Campbell, 'Primary and Secondary Education', in T. W. Moody and J. C. Beckett (eds), *Ulster since 1800: Second Series: A Social Survey* (London, 1957), 183; F. Wright, *Two Lands on One Soil: Ulster Politics before Home Rule* (Dublin, 1996), 61–2.
[6] K. Milne, *The Irish Charter Schools 1730–1830* (Dublin, 1996).

penal laws in the late-eighteenth century. The repeal in 1782, 1792, and 1793 of the most pernicious penal laws relating to education allowed Catholic schoolmasters to practice their profession openly and to convene classes in buildings more easily, but their teaching was limited to the three Rs, and the Dublin Parliament failed to repeal legislation preventing the endowment of Catholic schools.[7] Despite this, Catholics demonstrated a remarkable determination to remain independent of the state and its charitable stooges. In 1826 the Irish Education Inquiry found 3449 such schools listed in Ulster, with 141,882 pupils, and a clear majority of schoolmasters completely dependent on pupils' fees.[8]

Dublin Castle realized its aspiration for a mass system of education had to acknowledge rather than oppose or ignore Catholic concerns. A report presented to the Irish parliament in 1791 proposed a break with the past. It recommended a new island-wide system of non-denominational parish schools, centrally funded, supervised nationally by a board of control, and locally by bodies consisting of laymen. Religious instruction was catered for outside the shared curriculum through a right of entry for all clergy.[9] The report met with opposition from existing bodies in receipt of state support and quickly disappeared from the parliamentary agenda. The need to address Ireland's educational deficiencies remained nevertheless. Several years after the Union of parliaments, the report's ideas helped inform a specially convened parliamentary commission (1806–12). It fared slightly better than its predecessor, creating a national board to oversee endowed schools, and established in principle the need for a system which did not unduly prejudice any one denomination.

Dublin Castle cast about for a suitable and readily available means of implementing this principle and found it in the Kildare Place Society. Established in 1811, the society's schools were religiously neutral by the standards of the time and therefore more acceptable to Catholics. In 1816 the government initiated an annual grant to the society of £6000, rising every year to a peak of £30,000 in 1831.[10] Catholic cooperation was significant locally and nationally. Yet it remained a Protestant-dominated body, and within several years of achieving its new status began to act with increasing disregard for Catholic sensitivities. Tensions boiled over in 1820 when Daniel O'Connell resigned from its national board and joined Catholic bishops to campaign against the Society. The resulting official inquiry (1824–27) drew the same conclusions as the parliamentary reports of 1791 and 1806–12.

THE NATIONAL SCHOOL SYSTEM

Catholic support for the latest parliamentary report paved the way for a significant departure in government policy. In 1832 the Chief Secretary for Ireland, Edward Stanley, later fourteenth Earl of Derby, successfully steered his Irish Education Bill

[7] M. E. Daly, *Social and Economic History of Ireland since 1800* (Dublin, 1981), 112–13.
[8] Campbell, 'Education', 183.
[9] D. H. Akenson, 'Pre-University Education, 1782–1870', in W. E. Vaughan (ed.), *New History of Ireland, Vol. 5: Ireland under the Union: I: 1801–1870* (Oxford, 1989), 527.
[10] Akenson, 'Education, 1782–1870', 528–9.

through parliament. The resulting National School system was overseen by a central board of commissioners and was intended to foster lay participation locally. It was given the substantial grant previously awarded to the Kildare Place Society. Its unpaid commissioners were charged with making grants towards school construction, contributing substantially to teachers' salaries, issuing approved texts, and publishing textbooks. Catholic influence on the board was at first limited—although regularly increased—but this was more than compensated by the Church's influence locally. Each school manager was permitted to exercise extensive powers, including the appointment and dismissal of teachers, the selection of approved textbooks, and arrangement of the timetable. Catholic priests quickly assumed this role in many National Schools.

It was Stanley's intention that a truly national education system should be non-denominational, and that this could be achieved through lay control, a positive effort to educate all denominations together, and separation of moral and religious education, with the latter provided for through a right of entry for clergy. Important practical considerations undermined Stanley's idealism.[11] The commissioners' eagerness to quickly establish the system by appointing school managers trumped their desire for joint applications from Catholics and Protestants. Aid was granted to anyone of good character and sound social standing, which in many instances meant applications from individual local clergy, particularly Catholic priests. There was no tradition of local government in Ireland at parish level to check this development, and it was unintentionally encouraged by the Protestant denominations' initial hostility to the new system, effectively handing state-subsidized schools to Catholic interests without the risk of Protestant interference. In 1852, only 175 schools, less than 4 per cent of the total, were under the joint management of Protestants and Catholics.

School managers overwhelmingly tended to use their powers to appoint teachers of a similar denomination. In 1867 only 10.7 per cent of National Schools had managers who appointed teachers not of the same faith, and in most of these it was the manager of one Protestant denomination appointing a teacher of another. In only 6.8 per cent of schools did a Protestant manager appoint a Catholic teacher or a Catholic manager a Protestant teacher.[12] The commissioners' belated attempts to enforce non-denominationalism in such circumstances largely failed. Indeed, their reliance on the cooperation of school managers meant rules on denominational instruction became gradually more flexible. The most significant pressure to amend these regulations, especially concerning the right of all clergy to enter a National School, came not from Catholic managers but Ulster's Presbyterians. In large swathes of south and west Ireland, there were few Presbyterians and even fewer Presbyterian clergy to visit National Schools. In contrast, the concentration of Presbyterian schools in Ulster was potentially accessible to the province's largest denomination, the Catholic Church.

---

[11] A. Hawkins, *The Forgotten Prime Minister: The 14th Earl of Derby, Vol. 1: Ascent: 1799–1851* (Oxford, 2007), 108.

[12] Akenson, 'Education, 1782–1870', 533–4.

A vocal section of Presbyterian opinion in the late 1830s agitated against the new system on the basis that National Schools part-funded by Presbyterian subscriptions could not facilitate Catholic instruction. Some Presbyterian ministers went further and actively intimidated teachers, destroying several schoolhouses, and defacing others with anti-Catholic slogans. Negotiations between the commissioners and leading Presbyterians duly followed. The resulting compromise of 1840 redefined and considerably expanded the category defined as 'non-vested schools'. Built solely from local funds, the commissioners' financial liability was restricted to books and teachers' salaries. School managers were thereby allowed to operate a policy of giving children of different denominations the right to leave the schoolroom during hours of religious instruction.[13] Presbyterians utilized the non-vested category with enthusiasm, and reached a further compromise in 1847 allowing them to refuse the withdrawal of children in their schools from religious instruction.[14] Concessions granted to Presbyterian schools, intended to deter the attendance of Catholics, were enthusiastically taken up by other denominations, further polarizing the National School system. In 1850, 68 per cent were classed as non-vested, rising to 74 per cent by 1870.

This denouement served as a bridge for episcopalians to enter the new system. Thinly spread across the island, with a substantial presence in Ulster and Dublin, episcopalians were reluctant to surrender their traditional duty to educate all children and therefore attempted to perpetuate the old system with the creation in 1839 of the Church Education Society. Initially successful, recruiting half its 120,000 pupils from other denominations, the society from the late 1850s ran into financial difficulties and reluctantly came in from the cold. Church of Ireland participation in the National School system soon distinguished itself from other denominations through significant lay leadership; two-thirds of its school managers, in contrast to one-third for Presbyterians, and an almost negligible figure for Catholic schools.

Denominational control did not mean the segregation of children in every instance. A number of non-denominational factory schools were established by mill owners in the late nineteenth century for the children of employees, such as Herdman's, Sion Mills, County Tyrone, and Barbour's, Hilden, County Antrim. And in parts of rural Ulster, the practical consideration of convenience meant many schools had a handful of pupils who attended the school of another denomination through having no other reachable alternative. It is instances of the latter which largely account for the official recorded instances of 'mixed' schooling, 82.6 per cent of National Schools in Ulster in 1870, a figure which declined in subsequent years. Dublin Castle had failed to realize the non-denominational ideal of Stanley's reforms, but it drew satisfaction instead from the creation of a nationwide network of elementary schools and the consequent improvement of literacy rates: from 47 per cent of persons of ages five years and above in 1841 to 67 per cent in 1871.[15]

[13] Wright, *Two Lands*, 68, 156.   [14] Campbell, 'Education', 186.
[15] Akenson, 'Education, 1782–1870', 533–6.

INTERMEDIATE EDUCATION

Concentrating their resources on elementary education, the National Schools commissioners left the major denominations to their own devices in the provision of intermediate education. This tended to favour episcopalians, especially in Ulster, where, in addition to the royal schools, they had direct or indirect influence over the voluntary boards of several diocesan schools, classical schools, and academies in Belfast and other urban centres.[16] Other denominations were obliged to utilize their clerical training colleges. Belfast boasted several such schools: Royal Academical Institution, St Malachy's College and Methodist College; Presbyterian, Catholic, and Methodist respectively. The inherent flaws of this system were disproportionately felt by Catholics, who made up only half the pupils recorded in 1871 attending Ireland's 'superior' schools. Beyond this there was, of course, a much larger injustice, for in comparison to the 998,999 pupils attending National Schools that year, only 24,170 had the privilege of attending intermediate schools.[17]

The Catholic hierarchy lobbied William Gladstone's first government for state funding, but anti-papal unrest in Liberal ranks meant it was his Conservative successor, Benjamin Disraeli, who eventually responded. The 1878 Intermediate Education Act utilized money recently obtained from disestablishing the Church of Ireland to increase school funding. In order to dampen ultra-Protestant feeling in parliament, the Act also included a conscience clause allowing children of a minority to absent themselves from the religious instruction of the majority.[18] The funds made available by the Act were limited and as a result were devoted largely to helping existing schools through exam performance-related payments. Epitomizing the late-Victorian preoccupation with 'efficiency', the atmosphere of competition this fostered between intermediate schools came to possess a sectarian tinge, as nationalists and unionists vied with each other in newspapers to demonstrate the prowess of Catholic and Protestant schools.[19]

Such behaviour increased anxiety among education policymakers about the lack of regulation for intermediate schools. Exam-directed teaching, as in England and Wales, inevitably meant post-elementary schools were little more than crammers. Supporters of the status quo, including the Catholic hierarchy, pointed to improving results: in 1879 only 3954 candidates took the first intermediate school examinations that year, but by 1896, this figure had risen to 8711.[20] Increased oversight of intermediate schools came nevertheless with legislation in 1885 establishing a permanent board of commissioners. Within a decade these commissioners sought to replace exam performance with inspections as the means of determining school funding. Facing opposition from the Catholic hierarchy, which viewed inspection as an infringement of Church

---

[16] Campbell, 'Education', 187.
[17] D. H. Akenson, 'Pre-University Education, 1870–1921', in W. E. Vaughan (ed.), *A New History of Ireland, Vol. 6: Ireland Under the Union: II: 1870–1921* (Oxford, 1996), 523.
[18] Campbell, 'Education', 188.
[19] S. Pašeta, *Before the Revolution: Nationalism, Social Change and Ireland's Catholic Elite, 1879–1922* (Cork, 1999), 31.
[20] Akenson, 'Education, 1870–1921', 525.

responsibility, and considerable procrastination on the part of Dublin Castle, the commissioners achieved only modest success, in 1913, when they were able to apply the principle to classes for 12 and 13- year-olds.[21]

LIMITED MODERNIZATION

Increased efforts at regulating elementary schools also met with opposition from denominational interests, but the scale of state investment in elementary schools served to strengthen the government's hand in treating with school managers, and also led to a succession of parliamentary reports and various calls for reform. The Powis Commission, appointed in 1868, recommended a more explicit acknowledgment of denominational schooling, but sought a return to Stanley's emphasis on lay involvement through the collection of local rates. Dublin Castle was reluctant to acknowledge the failure of non-denominationalism, and wary also of clerical opposition to local control, so it declined to assent to either of these proposals. The Castle also delayed until 1892 Powis's demand for compulsory attendance as the Catholic hierarchy regarded this as an infringement of parents' rights. However, the administration did implement Powis's recommendation that a portion of teachers' salaries be calculated based on their pupils' exam performance.

Increasing concern in the 1890s about payments by results in elementary schools prompted the Belmore Report (1897–98) which, in contrast to the failure of the intermediate education commissioners, succeeded in replacing it with funding based on school inspection. This in turn helped broaden the curricula with a new emphasis on practical education and greater freedom of organization. Belmore's success, however, was limited. Catholic hostility—heightened by government refusal to aid Christian Brothers' schools—saw off proposals for compulsory attendance and the merging of small schools. The hierarchy's wariness of the former has already been noted; it opposed the latter because it undermined gender separation, and was seen as an attempt to rescue Protestant National Schools.[22] The proliferation of small schools was especially marked in Belfast. The city experienced rapid growth in the late-nineteenth century and a range of sects sought to establish their own National Schools.[23] The 1841 census recorded 256 people in Belfast 'Ministering to Education'; by 1901 the number had increased eightfold to nearly 2000, exceeding the almost fivefold growth in its population during the same period.[24] Rather than succumb to any compulsion to merge, Protestant educationalists in Ulster hoped the dire state of their schools might be addressed through local rates. Catholic opposition to any extension of lay interference, especially if it

---

[21] Campaigners in Belfast sought to ameliorate the low standard of education among workers by establishing in 1910 a local branch of the Workers' Educational Association, founded in England seven years previously.
[22] M. Harris, *The Catholic Church and the Foundation of the Northern Irish State* (Cork, 1993), Ch. 6.
[23] Campbell, 'Education', 186.
[24] L. A. Clarkson, 'The City and the Country', in J. C. Beckett *et al.*, *Belfast: The Making of the City 1800–1914* (Belfast, 1983), 163.

effectively subsidized Protestant denominations, led Irish nationalist MPs to successfully oppose attempts at Westminster during and after the First World War to introduce local government involvement.[25]

NORTHERN IRELAND'S NEW SYSTEM

Ulster played a conspicuous role in the early development of Irish education, only to be overshadowed in the late-nineteenth century by the marked growth of Catholic temporal power. The latter convinced some Ulster Protestants to argue for a return to the founding ideal of the National School system. This was most pronounced in Belfast as it offered a rationale for levying local rates. In the outlying Ulster counties, however, Protestants regarded their denominational schools as bulwarks against the Catholic majority. This attitude entrenched further after partition in 1921. Protestant schools in Monaghan, Cavan, and Donegal jealously guarded denominational control as a means of insulating their dwindling communities from Dublin's promotion of gaelicization and catholicization.

The Belfast government, established in June 1921, regarded denominational control as invidious to the interests of Protestant schools in particular and education in general. Northern Ireland's first Prime Minister, James Craig, immediately determined that schools would be funded by local authorities and justified ignoring the inevitable Catholic backlash by citing Section 5 of the Government of Ireland Act 1920, the *de facto* constitution of Northern Ireland.[26] This prohibited the Belfast parliament from passing any law which directly or indirectly endowed, preferred, or prejudiced any religion or religious group. Intended to prevent the unionists favouring Protestant interests, it supplied an opportunity to resuscitate the original intention of the 1832 Act and revitalize Belfast's impoverished schools.

Craig handed the education portfolio to the seventh Marquess of Londonderry, whose father, the sixth Marquess, had overseen the creation of local education authorities in England and Wales.[27] Londonderry did not regard his brief as an assault on Catholic power, but as an intrinsic part of his self-declared 'mission' to create an inclusive Northern Ireland. Addressing the Belfast parliament shortly after his appointment, he declared 'There are naturally difficulties... but I do feel that with co-operation and with sympathy we will be able to evolve a system which will be the admiration of all other countries.'[28] Such idealism encountered setbacks from the outset. The work of the new Ministry of Education was initially hampered by delays in transferring staff and powers from Dublin and London, and by the political violence and uncertainty which accompanied the creation of Northern Ireland.[29] Communal violence undermined the ministry's ability to engage the

---

[25] Akenson, 'Education, 1870–1921', 538.
[26] St John Ervine, *Craigavon: Ulsterman* (London, 1949), 119.
[27] N. C. Fleming, *The Marquess of Londonderry: Aristocracy, Power and Politics in Britain and Ireland* (London, 2005), Ch. 4; Aldrich, *History*, 42–3.
[28] Hansard N. I. (Senate), Vol. 1, col. 24 (23 June 1921).
[29] B. A. Follis, *A State Under Siege: The Establishment of Northern Ireland, 1920–1925* (Oxford, 1995), 33.

Catholic hierarchy, despite reassurances from Londonderry and the appointment of a Catholic senior civil servant, A. N. Bonaparte-Wyse.

The committee established by the ministry to examine education reform was regarded by Cardinal Logue as the pretext for an attack on Catholic schools.[30] Its chairman, Robert Lynn, editor of the unionist *Northern Whig*, was an unlikely figure to encourage Catholic confidence, but the hierarchy's reluctance ultimately rested in the belief that a boycott could help bring down Northern Ireland, and when this proved erroneous, that Catholic schools must not submit to the influence of unionist-dominated local authorities. The steadfastness of this position prevented the hierarchy from accepting Londonderry's assurances about the legislation he laid before the Belfast parliament in 1923, especially its rejection of Lynn's recommendation of scriptural instruction. The bill provided the means by which elementary schools could be fully or partially transferred to state control. All teachers would be paid by the ministry so the question of control rested on the appointment of school managers. In schools fully transferred, the local education authority would appoint school managers and the school receive full funding. Schools wishing to remain independent would receive teachers' salaries, minimal funding for buildings and maintenance, and retain their own managers. A third class of school would act as a bridge for those hesitant about full transfer. Known as four-and-two schools, the education authorities would appoint two managers and the school retain power of appointment over the remaining four.

Londonderry's 1923 Education Act revived the 1832 right of entry for all clergy, outside school hours, in those schools fully transferred to local education authorities, and forbade denominational tests for teacher appointments. Catholic schools quickly signalled their determination to remain independent. The hierarchy's willingness to rely on its flock to make up the shortfall in structural funding was not matched by Protestant church leaders. The poor state of Belfast schools made most Protestant clerics enthusiasts for the creation of local education authorities, but the conditions attached to this—no Bible instruction within school hours and the prohibition of denominational teacher appointments—proved too much for some. Reliant on state support but unwilling to divest themselves of their influence, these critics grew in number as the provisions of the 1923 Act were gradually implemented. They became particularly agitated by the fifty or so Catholics who ignored the ban imposed by their hierarchy on attending Stranmillis teacher training college. The presence of these Catholics at the state's training college fuelled alarmist suggestions that Protestant schools were to be staffed by Catholics and 'communists'.[31]

Londonderry was unsympathetic and unresponsive to Protestant discontent. The Prime Minister, however, expressed alarm about its consequences for unionist solidarity. In cabinet and in public, the Education Minister assured critics their case was unfounded, and believed teachers and parents would support him regardless

---

[30] Londonderry to Logue, 29 August 1921, PRONI, CAB/4/18/1; Logue to Londonderry, 2 September 1921, PRONI, D/3099/2/7/61.

[31] Hansard N. I. (Commons), Vol. 3, col. 356 (17 April 1923).

of what agitators suggested.[32] In December 1924, Protestant critics of Londonderry sought to mobilize public opinion through the United Education Committee (UEC). Ostensibly a pan-Protestant coalition, this predominantly Presbyterian organization campaigned for an amendment bill to allow Bible instruction and denominational teacher appointments. It organized a show of strength on 5 March 1925 at Belfast's Presbyterian Assembly Hall, prompting a meeting with Craig at which the Premier—conscious of the general election he scheduled for April—agreed to pass an amendment bill along the lines requested.[33]

Londonderry took a different line. He continued to insist his ministry was constitutionally prohibited from endowing religion, and informed a visiting UEC delegation the day before the general election 'that circumstances had radically changed with self-government in Ulster, that the decentralisation in education under the Education Act was a necessary corollary to the new position, and that the Churches must be prepared to surrender their privileged position in education'.[34] The UEC indicated it would agree to such a surrender if teachers were compelled to give religious instruction. On 17 April, the Education Minister addressed a teachers' union on their freedom not to give religious instruction, and the right of teachers to work in any state school regardless of their denomination.[35] The UEC reacted by mounting a legal challenge to the government's interpretation of section five of the 1920 Government of Ireland Act. On 12 June, the Presbyterian General Assembly passed a resolution demanding amendments and calling on local councillors to withdraw levies to the Education Ministry. Craig quickly bowed to the agitation and successfully pressed Londonderry to concede 'non-denominational' Bible instruction.

DEEPENING DIVISIONS

The outcome of this crisis was the state endowment of *de facto* Protestant schools and the relative underfunding of voluntary schools, most of which were Catholic. Protestant agitators nevertheless remained unhappy with outstanding restrictions on denominationalism, and the Catholic hierarchy, now reluctantly reconciled to Northern Ireland, demanded increased funding for voluntary schools. Wary of raising the issue of non-denominationalism, neither Catholic nor Protestant spokesmen sought a fundamental revision of the system that might square these aims. It was left to the government to pass another Education Act in 1930 which answered their grievances separately. Voluntary schools were given a 50 per cent increase in structural funding, and it was established in law that state schools had a right to provide denominational education. On both counts the 1930 Act breached Northern

---

[32] N. C. Fleming, 'The First Government of Northern Ireland, Education Reform, and the Failure of Anti-Populist Unionism, 1921–1925', *Twentieth-Century British History*, 18 (2007), 146–69.
[33] Cabinet conclusions, 7 March 1925, PRONI, CAB/4/137/10.
[34] Minutes of meeting of Protestant church leaders and the Minister of Education, 2 April 1925, PRONI, Londonderry Papers, D/3099/5/9.
[35] *The Times*, 18 April 1925.

Ireland's 'constitution'. But the 1930 measure was consistent with Irish education policy for almost a century and, together with the 1923 Act, succeeded in improving pupil attendance, rehabilitating Belfast's elementary schools, and constructing 230 new elementary schools over the next two decades.[36]

The demarcation and differentiation between controlled (Protestant) and voluntary (Catholic) schools satisfied short-term demands at the cost of long-term political and social stability. This was not fully apparent in the inter-war years when most people received only elementary education. In the aftermath of the Second World War, however, with intermediate education provided to all children, the extension of the segregation principle to this sector meant most Catholic and Protestant children, from the 1950s to the present, would spend at least a decade of their lives schooled apart. In framing its post-1945 education reforms, the Northern Ireland government had no intention of revisiting the crisis sparked by the 1923 Act and came under no outside pressure to do so. Only the Attorney-General, John MacDermott, sounded a note of caution, warning government colleagues that any scheme for universal intermediate education must not replicate the unconstitutionality of the 1930 Act.[37]

Ostensibly, the Northern Ireland government intended to follow the example of Rab Butler's 1944 Education Act for England and Wales. This meant constructing new intermediate schools to meet the demands of universal access, but in Northern Ireland this fell foul of the unresolved Catholic and Protestant grievances relating to earlier education acts. The Education Minister, Samuel Hall-Thompson, faced demands from the UEC to extend the 1930 Act's provisions on religious instruction to controlled intermediate schools, and calls from the Catholic hierarchy for full funding to facilitate its control of new Catholic intermediate schools. Hall-Thompson's Education Bill partially met the latter demand, increasing maintenance funding for voluntary schools from 50 to 65 per cent, but he angered the UEC by refusing its demand for Bible instruction in controlled intermediate schools.

The 1947 Act reclassified all schools as either county (local education authority) or voluntary, and created a tripartite system of intermediate education. Secondary schools were free of charge and provided non-academic education. Grammar schools continued to be selective and fee paying and provided academic education. Technical intermediate schools were free but did not normally take pupils until aged 13. This last provision aggrieved proponents of technical education and was typical of the low regard for technical schools among educators and parents. Originating at the turn of the century, technical elementary and intermediate schools in Ireland came under the supervision of local authorities and were funded on the basis of reports rather than exam performance. These features made them especially successful in industrial Ulster where forty-five existed in 1921. Their

---

[36] D. H. Akenson, *Education and Enmity: The Control of Schooling in Northern Ireland 1920–50* (Newton Abbot, 1973), 89; R. H. Semple, 'Education and Social Services', in British Association for the Advancement of Science (ed.), *Belfast in its Regional Setting: A Scientific Survey* (Belfast, 1952), 179–84.

[37] Akenson, *Education and Enmity*, 165.

importance to civic pride was clearly demonstrated in 1906–7 with the opening of Belfast's magnificent Municipal Technical Institute.[38]

Initially, the concerns of advocates of technical education appeared unwarranted. The 1947 Act extended resources to twenty-eight technical intermediate schools which in 1948–49 educated around half of those not attending grammar school. Within a few years, however, attendance at technical schools declined relative to secondary and grammar schools.[39] This outcome was partly a consequence of delays implementing the 1947 Act, especially in rural districts. Counties Armagh, Tyrone, and Fermanagh took up to eight years to open their first intermediate school, delaying also the raising of the school leaving-age to 15. By the time construction increased, from two in 1947 to 129 in 1964, especially in new suburban developments, the overwhelming preference of parents, councils, and the Catholic hierarchy was for grammar and secondary schools (county and voluntary). This inclination sealed the fate of technical education and exacerbated both the shortage of technical skills in west Ulster and the unpreparedness of the industrial east to tackle the decline of traditional industries.

As in England and Wales, demand for grammar school places outstripped supply.[40] The desire of the expanding middle classes to safeguard their family's social and economic status meant calls for the problem to be addressed took the form of requests for more grammar school scholarships rather than the removal of academic selection. Whereas increasing prosperity and social mobility in England and Wales encouraged a shift in the 1960s towards comprehensive schooling, the relative underperformance of Northern Ireland's economy served to strengthen the role of academic selection as a means of guaranteeing future economic success for those who passed. The 1947 Act, therefore, was no more successful in establishing its underlying ethos than the 1832 and 1923 Acts, but like them it was successful in inaugurating massive structural changes which increased access to education. From an estimated 13,800 students attending sixty-six fee-paying grammar schools before the Second World War, by 1956 almost 200,000 more pupils attended the new tripartite network of intermediate schools.[41]

The modernization of education in Northern Ireland encouraged rather than challenged denominational segregation. Those at the forefront of the violent upheaval which engulfed the province from 1969 were the first generation to benefit from universal education. Few had any sustained experience of mixing with children from the 'other side', and by the early 1970s growing numbers of politicians and parents regarded segregation as a destabilizing force which perpetuated sectarianism and anachronism. The Prime Minister, Terence O'Neill, declared on Good Friday 1966 that Catholic and Protestant children should eventually be educated together, and in the meantime they could 'at least be united in working

---

[38] S. Farren, *The Politics of Irish Education 1921–65* (Belfast, 1995), 38; W. E. Coe, *The Engineering Industry of the North of Ireland* (Newton Abbot, 1969), 176–7.

[39] Akenson, *Enmity*, 215.

[40] M. Sanderson, 'Education and Social Mobility', in P. Johnson (ed.), *Twentieth Century Britain: Economic, Social and Cultural Change* (London, 1994), 378.

[41] Campbell, 'Education', 189.

together in a Christian spirit'.[42] His 1967 White Paper, which became the Education Act 1968, seized the initiative by obliging voluntary schools to become 'maintained': sharing management with the state. Catholic clerics would appoint four managers and local education authorities two in return for increased government support for maintenance costs. Bishop William Philbin declared the measure 'an invasion of the established system of school management'.[43] O'Neill regarded this attitude as 'a textbook definition of apartheid', but his recent well-publicized charm offensive directed at Catholic schools, and the lack of a Protestant backlash, ensured most nationalist MPs and northern bishops adopted a less critical stance than Philbin.[44]

UNIVERSITY EDUCATION

O'Neill's other significant educational achievement was the opening in 1968 of the New University of Ulster. Like the expansion of universities throughout the rest of the United Kingdom, the New University was intended to address greater demand for university places—a product of increased enrolment at grammar schools—and expansion of middle-class occupations. A similar rationale had underpinned the creation in 1845 of Ulster's first university, Queen's College, Belfast, as part of the Queen's (later, Royal) University of Ireland. The failure to realize a 1781 proposal for a university for Ulster, presented to the Irish parliament, led Belfast's merchant class to create its own Academical Institution in 1814.[45] Comprising a school and collegiate department, the latter included from 1835 a faculty of medicine. Its non-sectarian policy attracted professors and students from a range of backgrounds, but 'Inst' struggled financially and was the subject of acrimony amongst rival Presbyterian factions. Following the establishment of Queen's College, Presbyterians who disapproved of the new college's non-denominational character founded their own institution in 1865 at Derry, Magee College. Those Presbyterians prepared to work with Queen's created in 1853 a parallel institution, the Assembly's College, providing the theology prohibited in the former.[46]

Queen's left the Royal University to become a university in its own right in 1908–9. This moment also heralded the end of the hierarchy's ban on Catholic students attending the 'godless college'. The Northern Ireland government provided much needed capital from the 1920s. Teacher training was catered for by St Mary's College, for Catholic women, and Stranmillis College for men and women. The financial restraints on constructing another college meant Catholic men were directed to Strawberry Hill, near London, until the 1950s when St Joseph's opened in Belfast (St Mary's and St Joseph's merged in 1985).

---

[42] Quoted in J. Bardon, *A History of Ulster* (Belfast, 1992), 633.
[43] M. McGrath, *The Catholic Church and Catholic Schools in Northern Ireland: The Price of Faith* (Dublin, 2000), 167.
[44] Cabinet Conclusions, 23 November 1967, PRONI, CAB/4/1377.
[45] Akenson, 'Education, 1782–1870', 527.
[46] T. W. Moody, 'Higher Education', in T. W. Moody and J. C. Beckett (eds), *Ulster since 1800: Second Series: A Social Survey* (London, 1957), 192–203.

Increasing demand for university education across the United Kingdom necessitated the foundation of new 'green field' universities in the 1960s, and the creation in 1969 of the Open University. Unexpectedly high demand in Northern Ireland for the Open University's distance-learning degree programmes led to the establishment of a regional office at Belfast in 1970. The 1965 report of the Lockwood Commission paved the way for Northern Ireland's two green-field institutions: the New University of Ulster in 1968 and the Ulster Polytechnic in 1971 (merged in 1984). The absence of calls for a specifically Catholic institution did not prevent the Lockwood Report causing considerable offence to nationalists. Contrary to expectation, it recommended situating the New University outside the Protestant market town of Coleraine rather than the predominantly Catholic city of Derry which was already home to Magee College.[47] Lockwood had rational if controversial arguments for its recommendation, but the government's decision to implement it convinced even moderate nationalists they could not expect fair treatment from unionists.[48]

THE LIMITS OF RESISTANCE

At the outset of the 'Troubles', non-denominational education was the preserve of the two universities and a small number of technical colleges and factory schools. Political polarization and sectarian violence increased calls for its extension to all elementary and intermediate schools. No longer confined to Protestant opponents of Catholic power, integrated education had since the mid-1960s attracted the support of Northern Ireland's Liberal and Labour parties, and even sections of radical nationalism. The Church of Ireland Synod in 1970, and the General Assembly of the Presbyterian Church in 1971, expressed their cautious support. The following year Bernadette Devlin informed fellow MPs at Westminster that segregated education was 'a prejudicial factor in Northern Ireland and we must legislate to remove it'.[49] This enthusiasm did not extend to nationalist MPs at Stormont; although most were outwardly committed to socialist ideals, none wanted to publicly challenge the unequivocal opposition to integration adopted by Cardinal Conway.[50]

The prorogation of Stormont in 1972 heralded almost four decades of direct rule from London. The succession of British ministers appointed to govern Northern Ireland conspicuously avoided integration although related issues were addressed. In 1972, discredited local education authorities lost their oversight of education to five new education and library boards appointed by Whitehall. In the case of several boards, Catholic majorities decided policy for controlled (Protestant) schools.[51] Northern Ireland Office circulars were issued in 1982, 1987, and

---

[47] G. O'Brien, '"Our Magee Problem": Stormont and the Second University', in G. O'Brien (ed.), *Derry and Londonderry: History and Society: Interdisciplinary Essays on the History of an Irish County* (Dublin, 1999), 647–96. A cross-community 'University for Derry' campaign emerged in the 2000s.
[48] T. Wilson, *Ulster: Conflict and Consent* (Oxford, 1989), 147.
[49] Hansard, HC (series 5) vol. 840, col. 2064 (14 July 1972).
[50] McGrath, *Catholic Schools*, 182.   [51] Wilson, *Ulster*, 141.

1989 encouraging controlled and maintained (Catholic) schools to engage in shared activities.[52] And in 1993 the Northern Ireland Education Order granted voluntary schools full state funding.

Direct rule policy accepted denominationalism but implicitly acknowledged its potential to worsen community relations. The reticence of Conservative Secretaries of State (1979–97) to take on the Catholic Church was guided in part by a policy of shoring up moderate nationalism. It also reflected the Conservative government's early exposure to the power wielded by vested interests. The Chilver Commission, established in 1979 by the outgoing Labour government, was charged with investigating an end to the costly separate provision of teacher training for controlled and maintained schools. Chilver was perceived by the Catholic hierarchy as a threat to be resisted at every step. Even the Presbyterian General Assembly, in marked contrast to its acceptance of non-denominationalism a decade before, came out against Chilver in January 1982.[53]

The inability of direct rule government to face down opposition to education reform was not confined to integration. The Labour government (1974–79) hoped to bring Northern Ireland into line with the rest of the United Kingdom by abolishing academic selection. The Northern Ireland government ruled it out in 1964 on the basis that grammar schools would declare themselves independent and become unaffordable to many parents.[54] In 1976, Labour's junior minister for Northern Ireland, Lord Melchett, again raised the prospect of abolition, but opposition from grammar schools forced him the following year to moderate this to transfer based on teachers' reports and parental choice.[55] Allowed to drift, the policy was swiftly extinguished in 1979 by the election of a Conservative government. In marked contrast to bringing academic selection into line with the rest of the United Kingdom, there was no significant dissent in Northern Ireland to the introduction of revised methods of examination for 16- and 18-year-olds already pertaining in England and Wales—GCSEs and GCEs.

Lacking government backing, the movement for integration was fuelled by the determination of ordinary parents, supported to some extent by a stream of reports from the two universities, on the detrimental effects of segregated schooling. A catalyst was supplied in 1974 by Basil McIvor, Ulster Unionist Education Minister in the brief power-sharing Executive of that year. His statement favouring 'shared education' was followed by the formation of a parents' campaign group, All Children Together. Not unexpectedly, Cardinal Conway criticized McIvor's recommendation, but it found unlikely support from the youth wing of the Official Irish

---

[52] Department of Education (NI) circular no. 1982/21 (1982); Cross Community Contact Scheme, circular no. 87/47 (1987); Education Reform (NI) Order 1989.

[53] R. McMinn and É. Phoenix, 'The Chilver Report: Unity and Diversity', *Irish Educational Studies*, 24 (2005), 5–19.

[54] M. Wallace, *Northern Ireland: 50 Years of Self-Government* (Newton Abbot, 1971), 152–3.

[55] M. Wallace, *British Government in Northern Ireland: From Devolution to Direct Rule* (Newton Abbot, 1982), 169–70.

Republican Army, a demonstration, if nothing else, of the growing gulf between the Catholic hierarchy and radical nationalists.[56]

Progress thereafter came slowly. In 1977, the Alliance Party's Lord Dunleath successfully persuaded the Labour government not to block his private member's bill for the creation of a new category of 'integrated' state school. Another major breakthrough appeared in January 1979, when Catholic student teachers representing St Joseph's proposed an integrationist motion at the Union of Students in Ireland conference, although student representatives pressed for the opposite in subsequent years following strenuous efforts by the authorities at St Joseph's to encourage support for denominationalism.[57] All Children Together opened its first school, Lagan College, in 1981, in a Scout hut on the outskirts of Belfast, and opened a further three by 1985. This set a pattern of one to three integrated schools established each year, under the auspices of the Northern Ireland Council for Integrated Education, reaching a total of sixty-one in 2010.[58]

Until Peter Robinson's unexpected declaration of support for integrated education in October 2010—in which the Democratic Unionist Party First Minister echoed O'Neill by referring to the status quo as 'benign apartheid'—the integrationist cause was not markedly affected by the peace process and return of self-government in 1998. The two successive Sinn Fein ministers for education, Martin McGuinness and Caitríona Ruane, directed their reforming energies instead to the encouragement of Irish-medium education and the abolition of academic selection. Republican support for the former was in stark contrast to the relative indifference, up to the 1980s, of nationalist MPs and Catholic schools.[59] Almost extinct in Ulster—the 1851 census recorded only 6.8 per cent as Irish speakers—the Belfast government reluctantly facilitated its teaching from the 1920s. Irish achieved greater significance amongst constitutional nationalists and Catholic school managers from the 1970s, but it was the effort of grassroots activists, supported by Sinn Fein, which led to the opening of the first Irish-medium elementary school in the 1970s, Bunscoil Phobal Feirste, the achievement of grant-maintained status in 1984, and subsequent expansion to twenty-three schools by 2010.[60]

Unionists were ill-disposed to this development, but a less traditional division of opinion emerged over Sinn Fein's abolition (after 2008) of the 11-plus examination. Almost all unionist assembly members opposed the end of academic selection, although many Protestant secondary school principals welcomed it. The Catholic hierarchy and Social Democratic and Labour Party supported abolition, but individual members and a number of Catholic grammar schools came out

---

[56] B. Murphy, October 1975, cited in Multitext Project in Irish History <http://multitext.ucc.ie/d/INTEGRATED_EDUCATION_NOW_OCTOBER_1975>, accessed 1 December 2010; O. Rafferty, 'The Catholic Church and the Nationalist Community in Northern Ireland since 1960', Eire-Ireland, 43 (2008), 99–125.
[57] McGrath, Catholic Schools, 194.
[58] J. Bardon, The Struggle for Shared Schools in Northern Ireland: The History of All Children Together (Belfast, 2010), passim.
[59] McGrath, Catholic Schools, 184.
[60] D. H. Akenson, S. Farren, and J. Coolahan, 'Pre-University Education, 1921–84', in J. R. Hill (ed.), A New History of Ireland, Vol. 7: Ireland, 1921–84 (Oxford, 2003), 711–56.

against. Ruane, like her predecessors, Stanley, Londonderry, Hall-Thompson, and Melchett—came up against the middle-classes' considerable investment in Irish education policy. In the poorest constituent part of the United Kingdom, lacking the resources for a private school sector matching the scale of grammar school provision, many of Northern Ireland's middle classes could not, like their British and southern-Irish counterparts, look to private education as a means of avoiding the perceived defects of comprehensive schools. Historically high levels of university attendance from the 1990s and a shrinking population might have lessened the cachet of grammar schools, but public debate about academic selection was no less passionate for it, and, more remarkably, was almost unique in the history of education in Ulster for creating a division of opinion which in many instances ignored the traditional cleavage between Catholic and Protestant.

FURTHER READING

D. H. Akenson, *Education and Enmity: The Control of Schooling in Northern Ireland 1920–50* (Newton Abbot, 1973).
J. Bardon, *The Struggle for Shared Schools in Northern Ireland: The History of All Children Together* (Belfast, 2010).
S. Farren, *The Politics of Irish Education 1921–65* (Belfast, 1995).
N. C. Fleming, *The Marquess of Londonderry: Aristocracy, Power and Politics in Britain and Ireland* (London, 2005).
M. Harris, *The Catholic Church and the Foundation of the Northern Irish State* (Cork, 1993).
M. McGrath, *The Catholic Church and Catholic Schools in Northern Ireland: The Price of Faith* (Dublin, 2000).
D. Murray, *Worlds Apart: Segregating Schools in Northern Ireland* (Belfast, 1985).

14

Politics and Society, 1800–1960

James Loughlin

At once the most important political and constitutional landmark of the nineteenth century, the Act of Union of 1801 not only framed Irish politics for the next 120 years but profoundly influenced its development. The inclusion of predominantly Catholic Ireland in the Protestant British state created a dysfunctional dynamic that would endure to the end of the original Union in 1922 and beyond. It found expression in the triangular relationship between Westminster administrations and the Protestant and Catholic communities. This chapter will take that relationship as its central theme, but with a particular focus on Ulster.

ULSTER AFTER THE ACT OF UNION

Ulster entered the nineteenth century in the shadow of the 1798 rebellion: the massacre of Protestants at Scullabogue, County Wexford, together with the brutality and violence that attended the rebellion's suppression—especially by a Yeomanry strongly influenced by Orangeism—had a 'lasting effect on the political landscape'.[1] Scullabogue energized ancestral Protestant fears originating in the Ulster Rising of 1641, fears which would find a generational carrier in the Orange Order. By 1835 Ireland had 1500 Orange lodges, the great majority located in Ulster,[2] 32 of which were in Belfast.[3] The fact that most Ulster Catholics were not involved in the 1798 rebellion, and their clergy were loyal, would be lost on Protestant propagandists.[4] Furthermore, former Presbyterian rebels, anxious to integrate into the loyalist community, seemed only too ready to frame the rebellion through the lens of 1641 as a vast Popish conspiracy from which they had been delivered.[5] In fact, not only were northern Catholics largely uninvolved in rebellious activities, but a clerical policy of cultural accommodation was pursued, especially the adoption of English language and habits to enhance Catholic economic prospects, while in Belfast it went so far as the copying of Presbyterian church practice, with clergy and laity seeking to assert

---

[1] J. Bew, *The Glory of Being Britons: Civic Unionism in Nineteenth Century Belfast* (Dublin, 2009), 64.
[2] R. B. McDowell, *Public Opinion and Government Policy in Ireland 1801–1846* (London, 1953), 114.
[3] Bew, *Glory of Being Britons*, 11.
[4] M. Elliott, *The Catholics of Ulster: A History* (London, 2000), 259, 261.
[5] A. Blackstock, *Loyalism in Ireland, 1789–1829* (Woodbridge, 2007), 111.

control over clerical appointments; something, that with other features, set the North apart from the rest of the country.[6]

The heightening of inter-ethnic tensions that followed the rebellion, however, screened out cultural accommodation in favour of ethnic stereotyping and aggression. The violence attending the foundation of the Orange Order in County Armagh in 1795, and a subsequent wave of ethnic cleansing of Catholics in the county, set a pattern of violent activity for the future: 1802, 1813, 1829–30, and the mid-1840s registered Orange-inspired sectarian conflict across the region,[7] often facilitated by a local magistracy which ensured that culprits went unpunished. Recurrent sectarian conflict, however, was but one—if very serious—element of a quite complex pattern of inter-community relations, the other side of which was significant Anglican and Presbyterian financial and other support for Catholic church-building. The most noteworthy single example of this was the donation of a site by Lord Cremore for a Catholic cathedral at Armagh in 1839. Politically, moreover, there was considerable Anglican, and especially Presbyterian, support for the removal of the remaining penal restrictions on Catholics, and which found expression in the new Presbyterian print, the *Northern Whig*.[8]

A range of factors have been suggested for these instances of inter-denominational cooperation: the legacy of Presbyterian radicalism in the 1790s: intermarriage in some areas; congenial relations between parish priests and ministers in individual localities; the minority status of Catholics in much of the North, together with their demonstrable constitutional loyalty. Indeed, this loyalty seems to have been the predominant or overarching consideration which subsumed the others. So long as Catholicism appeared non-threatening, liberal Presbyterians remained supportive, but in 'frontier' counties, where the two communities were more evenly balanced, ethnic perspectives tended to be more solidly communal, with great inter-community tension.[9] Insofar as the Catholic community was influenced by nationalist or proto-nationalist ideas, it was manifest in relation to Ribbonism, which tended to be strong in areas where the influence of the Church was weak.[10] At the same time, it is difficult to make a meaningful distinction between Catholic and nationalist/Ribbon worldviews in this context, given the sectarian dimension to Ribbonism. Catholic mentalities seemed to have remained largely framed within sectarian terms of reference and lagging behind the politicization of Catholics evident elsewhere in Ireland.[11]

Certainly the chief concern of the Church in the context of O'Connell's ill-judged attempts to carry his campaigns into Ulster, and the populist Protestant response they tended to provoke, was discouragement of political activity so as to deter violence.[12] Thus, though the ethnic border zones of west and south Ulster

---

[6] O. P. Rafferty, *Catholicism in Ulster 1603–1983* (London, 1984), 107–8.
[7] Ibid., 117.
[8] F. Heatley, 'Community Relations and the Religious Demography 1800–86', in J. C. Beckett *et al.*, *Belfast: The Making of the City 1800–1914* (Belfast, 1983), 129–34 Rafferty, *Catholicism in Ulster*, 112.
[9] Rafferty, *Catholicism in Ulster*, 112–14.   [10] Ibid., 104.
[11] S. J. Connolly, 'Catholicism in Ulster', 1800–50', in P. Roebuck (ed.). *Plantation to Partition: Essays in Honour of J. L. McCracken* (Belfast, 1981), 168–71.
[12] Rafferty, *Catholicism in Ulster*, 132; D. Murphy, *Derry, Donegal and Modern Ulster 1790–1921* (Derry, 1981), 90.

evidenced significant pro-O'Connellite activity, the record of Ulster Catholics in the emancipation and Repeal campaigns in general, was, compared to other provinces, unimpressive. Active political engagement seems to have remained the concern of 'an articulate minority'.[13]

Ulster was heavily influenced by 'the Second Reformation'. This largely evangelical movement, of which the demagogic Reverend Henry Cooke was a leading light, was directed at thwarting Catholic emancipation through conversion.[14] O'Connellism had raised the shade of Scullabogue and Cooke exploited it to the full to forge a Presbyterian-Anglican alliance in defence of the Protestant ascendancy.[15] Within the Protestant, and particularly Presbyterian, community, the 'reformation' established a strong reaction against liberal New Light principles that rejected the doctrine of the Trinity and favoured toleration, especially Catholic relief.[16] Cooke's success in marginalizing New Light Presbyterianism was evident from 1830, the year following Catholic emancipation, when the Non-Subscribing Presbyterian Church was established to give it expression, while in 1840 Cooke united the great majority of Presbyterians in the formation of the General Assembly of the Presbyterian Church in Ireland.[17] It was a victory, however, reflecting societal division. The second reformation had provoked Catholics to seek an educational context free of conversionist intent, something delivered by the National Education system, and which initially attracted Protestant criticism as a papist concession.[18]

More importantly, Cooke's triumph reflected defensiveness in a decade when a Whig government, dependent on O'Connellite support, delivered a succession of Irish reforms accompanied by a crackdown on Orangeism that induced the voluntary dissolution of the Grand Orange Lodge of Ireland in 1836. Undoubtedly one of the period's most important developments,[19] it signalled the failure of Ulster Conservatism to thwart the Whig government's intention to free police and judicial functions from local control, thereby substantially improving Catholic security. In a wider British context, moreover, suppression both closed a period when Orangeism exerted great influence[20] and registered the state's gradual transition from its ethno-Protestant foundations, something that had allowed Ulster Orangeism and British identity an easy synergy. The Order was reconstituted in 1846,[21] but following a serious sectarian riot at Dolly's Brae, County Down, in 1849, at which up to twenty Catholics may have lost their lives, its processions were banned in 1850 under the Party Processions Act (PPA).[22]

---

[13] Connolly, 'Catholicism in Ulster', 167–8; Rafferty, *Catholicism in Ulster*, 130.
[14] 'Second Reformation', in S. J. Connolly (ed.), *The Oxford Companion to Irish History* (2nd edn), Oxford, 2002), 532–3.
[15] F. O'Ferrall, *Daniel O'Connell* (Dublin, 1981), 48, 83–4.
[16] J. Bardon, *A History of Ulster* (Belfast, 1992), 249–52.   [17] Ibid., 250.
[18] F. Wright, *Two Lands on One Soil: Ulster Politics before Home Rule* (Dublin, 1996), 19.
[19] Ibid., 55–6.
[20] Ibid., 150–1.
[21] H. Senior, 'The Early Orange Order, 1795–1870', in T. D. Williams (ed.), *Secret Societies in Ireland* (Dublin, 1973), 43.
[22] Ibid., 42–5; J. Lee, *The Modernisation of Irish Society 1848–1918* (Dublin, 1973), 49–50.

The reputation of Orangeism for disorder and lawlessness, the impact of policing reforms and enactments directed at suppressing Orange demonstrations, together with the dismissal of magistrates sympathetic to Orangeism, functioned to effect a virtual abandonment of upper-class involvement in the Order's activities.[23] Its influence among lower-class Protestants, however, remained strong, especially in the ethnic frontier zones west of the Bann River.[24] The Order would constitute the most influential institution in the North opposed to Irish autonomy, but by mid-century there were other influential reasons for Ulster Protestant opposition. In rejecting Repeal, the Reverend Henry Cooke added to his usual anti-Catholic diatribes the further argument that the greatly expanding wealth of Belfast and north-east Ulster was due to the Union with Britain.[25]

Growth in the cotton industry and a revolution in linen production were concentrated in the north-east, and accompanied the expansion of Belfast from a town of less than 20,000 people in 1803 to one of over 100,000 in 1851. It was by then the second largest town in Ireland with its growth stimulated by an expanding textile industry and engineering works.[26] Also, the development of its port, which in the years up to 1850 increased the tonnage of ships entering the harbour fivefold, and the reorientation of the North's transport routes to facilitate its economic integration, served, by mid-century, to make Belfast an outpost of industrial Britain, thereby doing much to separate 'Ulster middle-class liberalism from Irish nationalism'.[27] In this context it might be noted that addresses of loyalty from Ulster to Queen Victoria on the occasion of her first visit to Ireland in 1849 exhibited a tendency to assert a binary opposition between loyal Ulster and the supposedly disloyal south of Ireland.[28] Belfast, however, was not only the home of economic and political hubris, but also of Presbyterian Whiggism and a theory of civic identity that sought to define the state as a realm within which all of Ireland's grievances could be satisfactorily resolved.

The central figure in this development was William Drennan. Influenced by the French Revolution, he had been one of the creators of the United Irishmen. Drennan, however, became disillusioned with revolutionary violence and Napoleonic dictatorship, and encouraged by progressive developments in British politics from 1806—especially ambitions for Catholic emancipation—he pressed radical Ulster politics in the direction of re-engagement with 'mainstream British political (and cultural) debate'.[29] Drennan did not regard this change of political direction as a deviation from the discourse of the 1790s; rather, that a modernizing British state offered the best opportunities for their radical ambitions: civic West Britonism offered a far more attractive future than that suggested by the Protestant ethnicity of Ulster Orangeism or the Catholic nationalism of the O'Connellite movement.[30]

---

[23] J. C. Beckett, *The Making of Modern Ireland 1603–1923* (London, 1966), 316–17; McDowell, *Public Opinion and British Government*, 114–15; Bardon, *History of Ulster*, 254.
[24] Bew, *Glory of Being Britons*, 65.   [25] O'Ferrall, *O'Connell*, 86.
[26] E. R. R. Green, 'The Beginnings of Industrial Revolution', in T. W. Moody and J. C. Beckett (eds), *Ulster since 1800: A Political and Economic Survey* (London, 1955), 34.
[27] Ibid., 35–7.
[28] J. Loughlin, *The British Monarchy and Ireland: 1800 to the Present* (Cambridge, 2007), 70.
[29] Bew, *Glory of Being Britons*, 61–2.   [30] Ibid., 64–72.

Nevertheless, the shallow communal underpinning of West Britonism should be noted. Both Protestant ethnicity and Catholic nationalism were informed by an emotive engagement with influential sectarian histories that served to energize politics. West Britonism's success was predicated on a departure by both communities from divisive sectarian traditions together with the assumption of the Protestant community's constitutional security. Political developments in the later nineteenth century would undermine both these assumptions.

MID-CENTURY DEVELOPMENTS

The mid-nineteenth century in Ireland (1850 to mid-1870s) is generally accepted as a period in which localism predominated in the absence of hegemonic nationalist movements,[31] but as we have seen, Ulster's development since 1800 had been quite singular, and this continued to be the case. While it had been affected by the Great Famine, it was to a lesser extent than other Irish provinces, and with effects not evident elsewhere.

In the period 1841–51, Ulster's population dropped from 2,400,000 to 2,000,000, with the Catholic community worst affected,[32] but the famine also accelerated a drift from the land, with the result that the Catholic population of Belfast increased significantly. By 1850 it had reached 35 per cent, a proportion 'alarming even to Liberal-minded Protestants'.[33] Moreover, as it was concentrated in west Belfast, in close proximity to the working-class Protestant area of the Shankill, the latter responded aggressively. Thus the riots of 1857 initiated a phase of urban sectarian conflict that culminated in the widespread destruction and killings of June to September 1886, the worst of the century. Growing sectarian conflict, moreover, indexed general pan-Protestant anxieties about a more confident, if not strident, public persona of the Catholic community in the post-famine era.

It was driven by Archbishop Paul Cullen, aggressively anti-English and with an intense dislike of Protestants and the Established Church. Appointed to the See of Armagh in 1850, Cullen, at the Synod of Thurles of that year, set out a programme of reforms that included a discouragement of mixed marriage and mixed education, together with a condemnation of the 'godless' Queen's Colleges.[34] A more strident Catholic presence in the public arena was also evident, in 'a veritable craze for church building.... indicative of the refusal of Ulster Catholicism to be seen as second best'.[35] But it was advanced at the expense of an 'older, milder, less partisan catholicism', more attuned to the sensitivities of a volatile inter-ethnic environment. Its last hierarchical representative in Ulster was Cornelius Denvir, Bishop of Down and Connor, and whose resignation Cullen, affronted at his apparent failure to 'stand up to the hostile onslaughts of Presbyterian Belfast', energetically sought and eventually secured in 1865.[36]

---

[31] See K. T. Hoppen, *Elections, Politics and Society in Ireland, 1832–1885* (Oxford, 1984).
[32] T. P. O'Neill, 'The Famine and its Consequences', in T. W. Moody and J. C. Beckett (eds), *Ulster since 1800: A Social Survey* (London, 1957), 40–1.
[33] Emrys Jones, 'Belfast', in Moody and Beckett (eds), *Ulster since 1800: A Social Survey*, 97.
[34] Rafferty, *Catholicism in Ulster*, 139–40, 147.
[35] Ibid., 150.   [36] Ibid., 153–5.

Publicly assertive Catholicism inevitably met with a hardening of attitude from an apprehensive Protestant majority whose anxieties often found expression in the sectarian diatribes—and associated violence—of demagogues such as Reverend Hugh Hanna, William 'Ballykilbeg' Johnston, and Wesley de Cobain;[37] and more generally in the Ulster Orange press.[38] Until the Liberal conversion to Home Rule in 1886, a corrective to Orange extremism was provided by the *Northern Whig*, but even the liberal Protestantism it represented was discomfited by Catholic assertiveness and the concomitant disappearance of the deference and gratitude that formerly was accorded a Whig leadership. The latter had a smaller space for manoeuvre as the conflictual environment of the North was increasingly informed by the antagonistic historical memories of the Protestant and Catholic communities, with 1641, 1689, and Scullabogue in 1798 being countered by the history of Catholic persecution, all the more relevant given the continuation of persecution in the present.[39] In this context the prospects for success of any movement transcending sectarian, communal identities were bleak, as the agrarian League of North and South demonstrated.

An alliance of the northern and southern tenant-farmer interest in pursuit of broad agrarian interests, but especially the legalization of the 'Ulster custom'—fair rent, fixity of tenure, and free sale of the interest a tenant had invested in his holding—had been stimulated by the agricultural crisis of the late 1840s, and especially landlord exploitation of tenant weakness to effect evictions.[40] For the chief strategist of the movement, Charles Gavan Duffy, a former Young Ireland leader, common agrarian interests would facilitate the growth of a common nationalist sentiment: in Ulster 'Nationality could only appear under some decent disguise'.[41] But while North and South could make common cause on the agrarian question, the former firmly resisted any attempt to extend the platform to nationalism. That the formation of the League was coincident with the nativist British response to 'papal aggression'—the papacy's establishment of Catholic ecclesiastical jurisdictions in Britain for the first time since the Reformation—was unfortunate. The historically conditioned anxieties of northern Protestants could easily be integrated with those of British Protestantism,[42] and though the British anti-papist frenzy soon dissipated, in the run-up to the general election of 1852 the sectarian card was played against the League for all it was worth.[43] The result was telling. While forty members associated with the League were elected in southern Ireland, in Ulster only one success was recorded. Thereafter, sectarian division arising out of the disputatious affairs of the Independent Opposition in parliament—the Irish Catholic electoral response to the papal aggression controversy—proved detrimental

---

[37] Ibid., 155–7. [38] Ibid., 158.
[39] Ibid., 171. [40] Wright, *Two Lands on One Soil*, 166–7.
[41] Quoted in Bew, *Glory of Being Britons*, 114; D. Kennedy, 'Ulster and the Antecedents of Home Rule', in Moody and Beckett (eds), *Ulster since 1800: A Political and Economic Survey*, 81.
[42] Loughlin, *British Monarchy and Ireland*, 83.
[43] B. Kennedy, 'Tenant Right before 1870', in Moody and Beckett (eds), *Ulster since 1800: A Political and Economic Survey*, 45.

to the League's interests,[44] together with the developing prosperity of the Irish economy in the 1850s. By 1858 the League was effectively defunct.[45]

By then the flaws in the Whig civic state prospectus of the 1830s were clear. Instead of acting as an agency of common British identity for both communities in the North, the state's policy of community equidistance—especially the disabling of local Orange control of law and order—may have offered greater security for an increasingly self-confident Catholic community, but for Protestants it invoked a zero-sum scenario that posited Catholic gain *only* at Protestant expense. Moreover, the anxiety engendered among Protestants by government policy, together with an empowered Catholicism asserting its own sectional reform agenda, inevitably diminished the Whig reformist impulse. Certainly the direction of political influence within the Belfast Protestant community was clear by the 1860s.

The formation of the League of North and South may have gone ahead despite the opposition of the Reverend Henry Cooke, but the Anglican-Presbyterian compact he had engineered was influential. Thus while the political leadership of the city was Liberal, its two parliamentary representatives were Tories, one from each church.[46] Also, the revival of both militant and constitutional nationalism stimulated the growth of a nearly moribund Orange Order.[47] Fenianism, in particular, was highly important in this respect, while enhanced strength lent weight to William Johnston of Ballykilbeg's campaign for repeal of the Party Processions Act (PPA). But it was a constitutional nationalist initiative that allowed Johnston to establish his presence on the processions issue.

Legal mass demonstrations attending the inauguration of the O'Connell monument in Dublin in 1864 provoked Johnston to undertake a populist Orange campaign against the PPA. Pursued through illegal mass demonstrations which incurred prosecution and imprisonment, Johnston became a self-constructed Orange hero whose following, against the background of the franchise reform of 1868, was large enough to see him elected for one of the two Belfast seats, in alliance with a Liberal, at the general election of that year.[48]

Liberals thought an alliance with Johnston would allow the spread of political enlightenment and liberal values among the Orange population. But Ulster elected only four Liberals to twenty-five Tories, while the price of the alliance with Johnston was Liberal support for his campaign for repeal of the PPA. Thus in reality, the alliance 'had more to do with accommodating ultraism than defeating it by progress, prosperity and shared values'.[49] Johnston's election was a portent for a future characterized by autonomous lower-class Orangeism acting in defiance of the Protestant establishment and influenced by 'a long-term narrative of siege and

---

[44] The League had entered into an alliance with the Independents in 1851 on the basis of common interests: R. V. Comerford, 'Independent Opposition Party', in Connolly (ed.), *Oxford Companion to Irish History*, 268–9.

[45] Comerford, 'Tenant League', in Connolly (ed.), *Oxford Companion to Irish History*, 568; Kennedy, 'Antecedents of Home Rule', 83.

[46] Rafferty, *Catholicism in Ulster*, 165.

[47] Senior, 'Early Orange Order', 44.

[48] A. McClelland, 'The Later Orange Order', in Williams (ed.), *Secret Societies in Ireland*, 126–8.

[49] Bew, *Glory of Being Britons*, 182.

struggle'.⁵⁰ It found an immediate provocation in the programme of the Gladstone government of 1868–74, especially its first major legislative measure, the disestablishment of the Irish Anglican Church in 1869.

The measure delighted Cardinal Cullen and encouraged Ulster Liberals,⁵¹ but it provoked Orange fury and ill-considered threats against the government and the Crown.⁵² As the ending of a subsidy paid to the Presbyterian clergy went together with the Disestablishment Act, the way was opened for a substantial Presbyterian influx to the Orange Order.⁵³ This was further stimulated by the abolition of the PPA in 1872. Supported by Ulster Liberals as an illustration of equality of governance between the Catholic and Protestant communities, it no less facilitated communal confrontation. By the early 1870s the Order had established an effective basis for growth and would pursue aggressive agitation against the Catholic and nationalist presence in the public arena throughout the decade.⁵⁴

POLITICAL UPHEAVAL AND REORGANIZATION

The outbreak of the land war in 1879 and subsequent nationalist agitation in Ulster stimulated the growth of an already expanding Orange Order.⁵⁵ Meeting nationalist meetings with counter-meetings supported by a sympathetic local magistracy that often attempted to disable legal proceedings arising from its—usually armed—activities, a modus operandi was established to meet nationalist challenges. Thus the 'Invasion of Ulster' in 1883, a voter registration campaign undertaken with the great seat redistribution and franchise reforms of 1884–85 in mind,⁵⁶ occasioned widespread violence in the counties of Cavan, Londonderry, Down, Fermanagh, Armagh, and Tyrone. It posed problems for the state, both in terms of maintaining public order and impartiality of governance. Moreover, the fact that Orange aggression failed to deter the registration campaign—nationalists won a majority of Ulster seats (17–16) at the 1885 general election—acted as a stimulant for the much more serious violence in Belfast the following year.

Gladstone's Home Rule initiative of 1886, prompted by Parnellite success at the general election and a variety of personal and political motives,⁵⁷ was constructed primarily to conciliate nationalists and protect the landlord minority. No specific provisions were included to address Ulster Protestant concerns. Indeed the Home Rule Bill might have seemed intentionally designed to heighten their anxieties.

⁵⁰ Ibid., 218.   ⁵¹ Ibid., 179–80.   ⁵² McClelland, 'Later Orange Order', 128–9.
⁵³ Senior, 'Early Orange Order', 44–5.
⁵⁴ *Return... of all Party Processions... specifying those which did not suffer Molestation... since the Repeal of the Party Processions Act 1872* (B.P.P., 1880, 60), 435–47; *Return in Continuation... up to 30th Day of August 1880*, (B.P.P., 1880, 60), 395–432.
⁵⁵ P. Bew and F. Wright, 'The Agrarian Opposition in Ulster Politics,1848–87', in S. Clark and J. S. Donnelly Jr (eds), *Irish Peasants: Violence and Political Unrest 1780–1914* (Dublin, 1983), 212–23; R. W. Kirkpatrick, 'Origins and Development of the Land War in Mid-Ulster, 1879–85', in F. S. L. Lyons and R. A. J. Hawkins (eds), *Ireland Under the Union: Varieties of Tension: Essays in Honour of T. W. Moody* (Oxford, 1980), 203.
⁵⁶ J. Loughlin, 'Parades and Politics: Liberal Governments and the Orange Order 1880–86', in T. G. Fraser (ed.), *The Irish Parading Tradition: Following the Drum* (Basingstoke, 2000), 27–43.
⁵⁷ See J. Loughlin, *Gladstone, Home Rule and the Ulster Question, 1882–93* (Dublin, 1986), Ch. 2.

A nationalist-controlled parliament threatened complete separation and Ulster's access to imperial markets; Protestant victimization, if not worse, was deemed inevitable given the precedents of 1641 and 1798; while inadequate financial underpinning would ensure that prosperous north-east Ulster would be overtaxed to pay for poorer parts of the country.[58] Nor was compromise likely as nationalist absolutism on the North was matched by the Ulster Unionist conviction that they could defeat Home Rule for any part of Ireland.

The Home Rule crisis of 1886 was a watershed in British and Irish politics. It split the Liberal Party into pro-and anti-Home Rule factions, with the great majority following Gladstone into an alliance with Parnellites, and a smaller, but significant, section led by Joseph Chamberlain joining the Tory Party in a Unionist alliance. It also had a profound effect on the political landscape of Ulster. By forcing almost the whole Protestant community into the one political camp, the fragile unity between Catholics and Presbyterians on which Ulster Liberalism was based, was destroyed, while Orangeism received a boost which was sustained for the next century. In the 1880s alone, the six years from 1881 to 1887 saw the number of Orange halls in Ulster increase from 134 to 167, while in the three years from 1887 to 1890, it rose from 167 to 218.[59]

The political configuration established in 1886 would endure through to 1914, partly because the first Home Rule Bill set the template for those that followed, in 1893 and 1912, with the same failure to address Ulster loyalist interests. Moreover, the Ulster Unionist response to Home Rule in 1886—united community opposition together with a stated willingness to resist Home Rule to the point of armed conflict if necessary—also set a precedent for the future.

The parliamentary defeat of the first and second Home Rule bills rendered these threats hypothetical, but when the Home Rule threat became serious in 1912–14, so too did the mobilization against it in the North, in terms of leadership, mobilization, and arms. Similarly, the rhetorical support of the Tory leadership for Ulster resistance in 1886 was translated, in 1912–14, into practical support for the militant designs of the Ulster Volunteer Force (UVF). The period 1886–1914, moreover, was to see the Ulster Unionist movement becoming more united, as dissentient Liberal Unionism was suppressed. The Ulster Unionist Council, established in 1905, provided a coherent voice for the whole Unionist family, and the social composition of Ulster Unionist parliamentary representation changed to give a stronger voice to constituency opinion.[60] At the same time, Ulster Unionism greatly enhanced its influence in the wider Unionist movement in this period, especially in setting limits to constructive unionism in the years 1886–1905, with particular reference to the issues of a university for Ireland acceptable to Catholics and also to devolution.

---

[58] Table 9, on Ulster Unionist fears of Home Rule in ibid., 296; D. Hempton and M. Hill, *Evangelical Protestantism and Ulster Society 1740–1890* (London, 1992), 180–6; also P. Ollerenshaw, 'Businessmen and the Development of Ulster Unionism 1886–1921', *The Journal of Imperial and Commonwealth History*, 28 (2000), 35–64.
[59] Loughlin, 'Parades and Politics', 32.
[60] A. Jackson, *The Ulster Party 1884–1911* (Oxford, 1989).

However, while Ulster Unionism steadily increased its political influence and significance in this period, this should not be read as entailing a corresponding influence with British popular opinion, at least in terms of how north-east Ulster was presented in influential press organs. Orange aggression may have been directed against perceived enemies of the Union, but from a British perspective the demonstrations and processions which were the occasions for it merely served to illustrate an increasingly alien and dysfunctional mindset. In this period analogous celebrations in Britain to those of Ulster Orangeism, such as 5 November, were losing their overt anti-Catholic dimensions while public processions and demonstrations in general were becoming more controlled, disciplined, and free from disorder.[61] When Belfast descended into a three-month long orgy of violence following the *defeat* of the first Home Rule Bill in early June 1886, the town was seen as having failed the test of respectability set by cities in Britain.[62] By the Edwardian period it was increasingly identified as characteristically Irish—that is, violent—rather than British,[63] and when the crisis of 1912–14 came, there was relatively little British support for Ulster loyalist paramilitary resistance to Home Rule.[64]

An important element in sustaining loyalist aggression, of course, was nationalist absolutism on the North. The hopes for a new approach to the region through a conciliation initiative promoted by the Ulster Liberal Unionist MP, T. W. Russell, and the leading nationalist, William O'Brien, in the early Edwardian period disappeared when John Redmond, from considerations of party unity, felt unable to support it.[65] Again, although the Irish Parliamentary Party gained a local Ulster manager in Joe Devlin in this period, no new thinking emerged. Devlin was committed to the party position on Ulster, while his attempt to allay Protestant fears of Catholic clerical dominance under Home Rule by challenging, through a lay organization, the political power of the hierarchy in Ulster—a consequence of the Parnellite split of 1890–91—was less than successful. To forestall accusations of anti-clericalism, he was compelled to adopt an explicitly Catholic stance. Thus his leadership of the Ancient Order of Hibernians impressed, rather unfairly, a sectarian cast on his politics.[66]

The period 1885–1914 stands out, not only as one of the most crucial in the modern history of Ulster, but also in its historiography. The apparent conundrum of a loyal community defying the authority of the government of the state to which it

---

[61] R. D. Storch, '"Please to Remember the Fifth of November": Conflict, Solidarity and Public Order in Southern England 1815–1900', in R. D. Storch (ed.), *Popular Culture and Custom in Nineteenth Century England* (London, 1982), 71–99.

[62] *Annual Register, 1886* (1887), 308–9; *Illustrated London News*, 11 June, 14, 21 August 1886.

[63] S. Gribbon, 'An Irish City: Belfast 1911', in D. Harkness and M. O'Dowd (eds), *The Town in Ireland* (Belfast, 1911), 203–20.

[64] See, for example, J. Smith, 'Class, Skill and Sectarianism in Glasgow and Liverpool 1880–1914', in R. J. Morris (ed.), *Class, Politics and Social Structure in British Nineteenth-Century Towns* (Leicester, 1986), 202–2; J. Loughlin, *Ulster Unionism and British National Identity since 1885* (London, 1995), Ch. 3.

[65] A. Jackson, *Home Rule: An Irish History 1800–2000* (London, 2003), 92–6; also P. Bew, 'Politics and the Rise of the Skilled Working Man', in Beckett, *et al.*, *Belfast*, 146–50.

[66] A. C. Hepburn, 'Irish Nationalism in Ulster 1885–1921', in D. G. Boyce and A. O'Day (eds), *The Ulster Crisis 1885–1921* (Basingstoke, 2006), 105–15; A. C. Hepburn, *Catholic Belfast and Nationalist Ireland in the Era of Joe Devlin 1871–1934* (Oxford, 2008).

pledged allegiance directed academic attention to the nature of Unionist identity. The debate on this subject, however, has lacked a unifying theme other than Unionist alienation from Britain. It has been approached from a variety of perspectives.

'Contractarianism' defined the Unionist-British relationship in terms of a 'bargain' between the Protestant community and the state that underpinned the original plantation, and has endured as a crucial element of the loyalist mindset.[67] A sense of self-reliance by a community 'in a clear territorial area informed by allegiance to the Crown' has provided another explanatory approach to alienation,[68] while territoriality has also been the basis for more nationality-oriented explanations, such as the suggestion that territorial identity and the construction of a regional being, the 'Ulsterman', in the later nineteenth century, denoted 'a form of nationalism'.[69] Ulster nationalism, moreover, has found more definite expression in the suggestion of a separate 'Ulster nation'; namely, 'a cohesive Protestant and particularist community' in the north-east, concerned chiefly with the pursuit of narrow selfish interests disguised by a rhetoric of British and imperial loyalty, and which no less disguised a preference for complete independence as opposed to Home Rule.[70]

While these assessments of Unionist identity have merit to varying degrees, they are open to the criticism that alienation offers too narrow a focus of explanation; that Ulster Unionism's relationship with Britain can only be accurately understood by taking a more in-depth account of the nature of Britishness, and of Britain itself as the home of a myriad and complex range of communities and regions. In this context, for instance, contractarianism as applied to the Unionist-British relationship appears much less singular than has been argued, and can be identified as having a much wider application, not least in the contract between Scotland and England on which the Union of 1707 was based.[71] In the same vein, interpretations of Ulster Unionism based on proto- or emergent nationality and nationalism are challenged by the extent to which community particularity in Britain approximated that of Ulster. Further, a closer engagement with the literature on nationalism specifying the distinction between an ethnic group and an ethnic nationality, cautions against reading national*ism* into the cultural specificity of the Ulster Protestant community. The drive for national expression in the form of independent statehood that is characteristic of ethno-nationalism has never defined the Unionist community. In this context the unity of opinion between Ulster Unionist and British Tory commentaries on imperial and foreign issues might be noted.[72] The most recent work on Unionist identity has tended to focus on its Britishness in this period, rather than alienation.[73]

---

[67] D. W. Miller, *Queen's Rebels: Ulster Loyalism in Historical Perspective* (Dublin, 1978).
[68] D. G. Boyce, 'The Marginal Britons: The Irish', in R. Colls and P. Dodd (eds), *Englishness: Politics and Culture 1880–1920* (London, 1986), 232–3.
[69] P. Gibbon, *The Origins of Ulster Unionism* (Manchester, 1976), 136–7.
[70] Jackson, *The Ulster Party*, 10–13, 122–3.   [71] Loughlin, *Gladstone*, Ch. 6.
[72] See J. Loughlin, *Ulster Unionism and British National Identity since 1885* (London, 1995), 33–5.
[73] See Bew, *Glory of Being Britons*, 223–9; E. Biagini, *British Democracy and Irish Nationalism 1876–1906* (Cambridge, 2007), 260.

CONSTITUTIONAL CRISIS, WAR, AND PARTITION

The trajectory of the third Home Rule crisis is well established: elections in 1910 returned the Liberals to office but dependent on nationalist support, the price for which was the introduction of a Home Rule bill. Thus a British crisis focused on the powers of the House of Lords came to have an Irish context with an Ulster focal point. By the summer of 1914 Ulster Unionism had made great progress in achieving exclusion from the remit of a Dublin parliament. This was due to a number of interrelated factors: their own determination to achieve it—demonstrated in paramilitary mobilization and the acquisition of arms; an effective leadership that correctly judged the mettle of a Prime Minister, H. H. Asquith, whose crisis management was characterized by irresolution; cabinet disunity reflected in a mishandling of the army, thereby casting doubt on government ability to effect its will; the trenchant support of a Tory leader with Ulster family connections—Andrew Bonar Law—and a party leadership that, it seems, might well have actually assisted in arming the UVF.[74] The upshot was that Ulster frontier extremism prevailed in rejecting Home Rule for six of the nine Ulster counties, over Redmondite trust in parliamentary methods to achieve it.[75]

The outbreak of war saw Home Rule formally enacted, together with an accompanying bill intended finally to resolve the issue of Ulster—now geographically defined in terms of the counties of Antrim, Armagh, Down, Fermanagh, Londonderry, and Tyrone. The implementation of both bills was suspended until the end of what was initially expected to be a short conflict. The war, however, proved to be much longer than anyone expected, and in the process transformed the Irish question, not least in that it widened the difference between the north-east and the rest of Ireland.

The split in the Irish National Volunteers (INV) that followed John Redmond's commitment of that force to the British war effort was less severe in the North, where one-third of the force was present, than in the rest of the country. In six-county 'Ulster', the breakaway Irish Volunteers constituted only 4.5 per cent of the INV compared to 9.9 per cent in the rest of Ireland, while Belfast Catholics provided proportionately more recruits for service in the Great War than did Protestants.[76] In the same vein, the controversy over Lloyd George's duplicitous attempt to implement Home Rule following the 1916 Rising[77] had a less damaging effect on Redmond's reputation in Ulster than in the rest of the country, while Ulster managed to withstand the Sinn Fein landslide at the general election of November 1918—in part at least because Ulster nationalists believed that Sinn Fein 'knew little of the problems of the North':[78] the Irish Parliamentary Party polled more votes than Sinn Fein and Devlin trounced de Valera in West Belfast.

---

[74] Jackson, *Home Rule*, 133.
[75] M. Laffan, *The Partition of Ireland 1911–1925* (Dublin, 1983).
[76] Hepburn, 'Irish Nationalism in Ulster', 119–22.
[77] Redmond was promised the temporary exclusion of the six counties from Home Rule, Carson was promised permanent exclusion.
[78] D. Kennedy, 'Catholics in Northern Ireland 1926–39', in F. McManus (ed.), *The Years of the Great Test 1926–39* (Dublin, 1967), 139.

Nevertheless, Sinn Fein's overall electoral success, its boycott of Westminster, and the War of Independence thereafter functioned to assist the Unionist campaign to retain their membership of the United Kingdom. Unionists effectively exploited their wartime sacrifices for Britain, especially that of the 36th (Ulster) Division on the first day of the Battle of the Somme, to make the moral case against constitutional 'betrayal'.[79] In this context not only was the Ulster Catholic case difficult to assert, but the decision of the Irish Republican Army (IRA) to resolve the Irish question by violent means left northern Catholics its primary victims; taking the brunt of loyalist retaliation, especially in Belfast; abandoned by a republican leadership unwilling to become involved in 'sectarian' activities; while at the same time willing to exploit the plight of 'our people in the North' for propaganda purposes.[80]

Further, the Anglo-Irish Treaty of 1921—which left Catholics a disgruntled one-third of the North's population—did not improve their position, as constitutional uncertainty endured until the Boundary Commission, allowed for by the treaty finally to determine the boundary between Northern Ireland and the Irish Free State, ended its deliberations without substantive effect in late 1925. The influence of historically conditioned anxieties and their contemporary reification functioned to ensure that the governance of Northern Ireland would primarily serve the interests of the Protestant community.

UNIONIST RULE AND ITS CONSEQUENCES

By the end of the 1920s, and aided in the early years by a northern nationalist boycott of state institutions, the Unionist regime had assumed the characteristics that would, in the 1960s, be the focus of attack by the civil rights movement. Proportional representation in local elections was abolished in 1922 for the purpose of reducing Catholic and nationalist power,[81] an objective furthered, especially in Derry city, by rigged local electoral boundaries and voting inequalities. The Catholic community also suffered in education provision, while Unionist control was further enhanced by discrimination in public appointments, draconian security legislation, and a Westminster policy of non-intervention in Northern Ireland's affairs.

The constitutional and ethnic anxieties that underlay Unionist dominance were exacerbated in the early 1930s, when, for a community accustomed to viewing southern events through the most lurid of lenses,[82] Eamonn de Valera acceded to

---

[79] See J. Loughlin, 'Mobilising the Sacred Dead: Ulster Unionists, the Great War and the Politics of Remembrance', in A. Gregory and S. Paseta (eds), *Ireland and the Great War: 'A War to Unite Us All'?* (Manchester, 2002), 140.

[80] Hepburn, *Catholic Belfast and Nationalist Ireland*, Ch. 8.

[81] Abolition of PR for elections to the northern parliament in 1929 was aimed more at splinter groups within the Unionist community.

[82] D. Kennedy, *The Widening Gulf: Northern Ireland and the Independent Irish State 1919–49* (Belfast, 1988).

power on a republican, anti-partitionist programme designed to break the Irish Free State's constitutional links with the British crown. North-South antagonism inevitably served to sharpen inter-community hostility within Northern Ireland. With Lord Craigavon (raised to the peerage in 1927) and Sir Basil Brooke giving—against a background of severe economic depression—a public imprimatur to Protestant privilege and sectarian discrimination, the early to mid-1930s was to witness a new phase of violence.

Relatively minor outbreaks of conflict occurred variously in Armagh, Lisburn, Portadown, Ballymena, Belfast, and Larne between 1931 and 1934;[83] however, the violence of the Belfast pogrom of 1935, during which 430 Catholic homes were burned and 514 families intimidated and forced out of Protestant areas[84]—95 per cent of compensation payments went to Catholics[85]—was on a scale not seen again until 1969. By the late 1930s a form of internal apartheid was established in the North, with a demoralized Catholic community, whose political representatives, constitutional and republican, had failed to make any significant impact either in, or against, the northern parliament, cohering around its church and the range of services the church provided.[86]

The political partiality of government practice, characterized in its law and order policy by leniency towards Protestant offenders as against the stringent application of the law in the case of Catholics,[87] reflected constitutional anxieties, not only about the internal Catholic enemy and developments in the South, but also to an extent Northern Ireland's relationship with Britain. These anxieties were not entirely unfounded. Westminster rejected Unionist attempts to construct a more psychologically secure imaginative identity for Northern Ireland by refusing proposals to have the name 'Northern Ireland' changed to 'Ulster'; and while in the 1930s several prominent Tory politicians guaranteed Northern Ireland's constitutional position—together with the confirmatory presence of George VI in 1937—as war approached, that position appeared uncertain when the Chamberlain government sought Eire's support.[88] The outbreak of hostilities, however, brought constitutional uncertainty to an end.

WAR AND ITS REWARDS

Eire's declaration of neutrality at the beginning of the Second World War, and assumed collusion with the Axis powers, threw into sharp relief the loyalty of the northern regime, expressed in Lord Craigavon's pithy declaration during a BBC radio broadcast of 5 February 1940 to the British people: Unionists were 'King's

---

[83] Kennedy, 'Catholics in Northern Ireland', 145–6.
[84] A. C. Hepburn, *A Place Apart: Studies in the History of Catholic Belfast, 1850–1950* (Belfast, 1996), 185.
[85] R. Munck and B. Rolston, *Belfast in the 1930s: An Oral History* (Belfast, 1987), 54–5.
[86] Kennedy, 'Catholics in Northern Ireland', 148–9.
[87] P. Buckland, *The Factory of Grievances: Devolved Government in Northern Ireland 1921–39* (Dublin, 1979), 219–20.
[88] Loughlin, *Ulster Unionism and British National Identity*, 95–100, 114–15.

men and we shall be with you till the end'.⁸⁹ That there were limits to the North's wartime contribution was evident in Westminster's failure to extend conscription to the area; nevertheless, the regime's loyalty and its practical war contribution were appreciated in London, and by Princess Elizabeth, who would reaffirm Northern Ireland's place in the British state and nation in the post-war years.⁹⁰ Initial complications were evident in the Unionist relationship with the 'socialist' Labour government of Clement Attlee, but the reality of Northern Ireland's constitutional dependence on Britain dictated accommodation. Thereafter, the North was a major beneficiary of the welfare state and the great increase in socio-economic benefits it entailed. Within a decade it had passed 'from an exceptionally backward area to full membership of the welfare state'.⁹¹ For Unionists, however, it was not an unmixed blessing.

While expanded state provision increased the socio-economic difference between North and South, it also lessened the pressure on Catholics to emigrate. This was unsettling to Unionists for whom demographic superiority was deemed essential to state security. There was also the constitutional threat posed by the IRA campaign of 1956–62, though cross-border internment and weak Catholic support meant it was effectively over well before 1962. Against this background, and as local authorities became the recipients of funds unthinkable in the inter-war years, so discrimination intensified—especially in the constitutionally 'vulnerable' area west of the Bann River—in public decisions and appointments, public housing, and regional policy. In fact, all the accusations of gerrymandering, virtually all complaints about housing and regional policy, and a disproportionate number of complaints about public and private employment would come from this area, with Derry city as a synecdoche.⁹² In this climate tentative attempts at cross-community cooperation, including a suggestion that the Unionist Party open itself to Catholic membership, foundered due to Orange opposition.⁹³

However, if the IRA campaign served to sustain Unionism's constitutional anxieties, it no less functioned to evidence the closeness of the Stormont-Westminster relationship. Premier Harold Macmillan and other leading government ministers came to Northern Ireland to offer enthusiastic support for the regime, while Britain's most popular magazine, *Picture Post*, tellingly carried a cover legend marking the outbreak of the IRA campaign: 'Terrorists on Britain's Borders'.⁹⁴ For border Unionists, however, Westminster support, however enthusiastic, did not really address local demographic anxieties,⁹⁵ and the past

---

⁸⁹ St J. Ervine, *Craigavon: Ulsterman* (London, 1949), 551.
⁹⁰ Loughlin, *British Monarchy and Ireland*, 350–2.
⁹¹ P. Buckland, *A History of Northern Ireland* (Dublin, 1989), 89.
⁹² J. Whyte, 'How Much Discrimination Was There Under the Unionist Regime 1921–68?', in T. Gallagher and J. O'Connell (eds), *Contemporary Irish Studies* (Manchester, 1983), 1–35.
⁹³ H. Patterson and E. Kaufmann, *Unionism and Orangeism since 1945: The Decline of the Loyal Family* (Manchester, 2007), 53–4. For overall coverage of the Ulster Unionist Party, see G. Walker, *A History of the Ulster Unionist Party: Protest, Pragmatism and Pessimism* (Manchester, 2004).
⁹⁴ Loughlin, *Ulster Unionism and British National Identity*, 171–2; *Picture Post*, 31 December 1956.
⁹⁵ Patterson and Kaufmann, *Unionism and Orangeism since 1945*, Ch. 1.

might well have cautioned against placing too much reliance on it anyway. An IRA threat might clarify Stormont-Westminster solidarity, but the harmony of that relationship was based substantially on the British convention of non-interference in Northern Ireland's affairs, and that would not survive the outbreak of civil disorder in 1969.

The greatly improved educational opportunities of the post-war era extended to university level; and university education facilitated the emergence of highly articulate spokesmen voicing Catholic grievances. They would ground their demands, not on the traditional terrain of Irish nationalism, but on British civic values, thereby exposing the failure of the Stormont regime to live up to the standards of the identity it so vociferously asserted.

CONCLUSION

The triangular relationship between the British state and the nationalist and Unionist communities that shaped developments in the period 1800–1960 was marked by significant turning points. Catholic emancipation in 1829 not only compelled the state gradually to abandon the Protestant ascendancy and pursue more independent, if not actually pro-Catholic, policies in Ireland, but also to accelerate its own disengagement from the Protestant ethnicity in which it was born. Nevertheless, modernization had some distinctly retrograde consequences in Ulster. As Catholic advances and community self-confidence made themselves felt, popular Protestantism, which counted the cost of the suppression of the Orange Order in 1836 and the legal proscription of Orange processions in 1850, reacted aggressively in the public arena, while liberal Protestant champions of reform saw their primacy undermined. However, if political modernization induced a Protestant and loyalist sense of loss, it would also, through franchise reform, allow their passions to find parliamentary expression, and thus to have effect, as the party processions and Home Rule controversies evidenced. The emotional scene-setting for the latter controversy was provided by Anglican disestablishment, after which the Home Rule Bill of 1886 appeared the culmination of constitutional betrayal. This substantially, if not completely, explains the violence of the loyalist reaction to its defeat, and its political consequences in Ulster: the region's sectarian and political divisions were crystallized, leaving little room for compromise, while a geographic template for partition was established that would successfully come to fruition in the period 1912–21.

The Ulster crisis had much in common with that over Catholic emancipation: both had a long gestation and were only resolved when the constituencies concerned pressed their case to the point of putting the stability of the state at risk. Each crisis illustrated Westminster's unwillingness or inability to resolve serious problems in a timely fashion. That characteristic would be no less evident during the civil rights struggle of the late 1960s.

FURTHER READING

J. Bew, *The Glory of Being Britons: Civic Unionism in Nineteenth-Century Belfast* (Dublin, 2009).
J. Bowman, *De Valera and the Ulster Question 1917–73* (Oxford, 1982).
J. Brewer, *Anti-Catholicism in Northern Ireland 1600–1998* (Basingstoke, 1998).
I. Budge and C. O'Leary, *Belfast: Approach to Crisis: A Study of Belfast Politics 1613–1970* (London and Basingstoke, 1973).
G. Hall, *Ulster Liberalism 1778–1876* (Dublin, 2011).
E. Phoenix, *Northern Nationalism: Nationalist Politics, Partition and the Catholic Minority in Northern Ireland 1890–1940* (Belfast, 1994).
H. Senior, *Orangeism in Ireland and Britain 1795–1836* (London, 1966).
E. Staunton, *The Nationalists of Northern Ireland 1918–1973* (Dublin, 2001).

15

Gender, Family, and Sexuality, 1800–2000

Diane Urquhart

Family and sexuality are two defining aspects of women's lives but they remain under-researched in an Irish context. Family was, however, central to most decisions in a woman's life. In the nineteenth and early twentieth centuries, placing in a family affected the chance of marriage as well as migration prospects; fathers exercised control over the choice of a spouse, and on a father's death this passed to the inheriting son. Social class and geographical location also shaped opportunity and experience. In addition, the centrality of family in women's lives was apparent in constructions of the female ideal as wives and mothers which crossed both centuries and religious divides.[1] Yet this ideal and the significance of the mother figure within families did not automatically equate to power; women 'generally do not have power relative to men' within families.[2] Female sexuality was also tightly controlled and again, strictures 'transcended religious and other cultural boundaries' to shape attitudes toward illegitimacy, birth control, abortion, and prostitution.[3] Breaking the moral code could cause familial and social ostracization, and leave women stigmatized and outcast.

Some of Ulster's gendered demographic history is distinct. A female majority, in evidence during the nineteenth century, continued into the twentieth century: in 1971, for example, 51 per cent of Ulster's population was female. The lure of employment in urban Ulster produced high levels of inward migration which helps to explain this pattern but there were regional disparities, especially in less economically diverse areas. Cavan, for instance, only maintained a female majority to 1881; Fermanagh to 1891 and Tyrone, Monaghan, and Donegal to 1901.[4]

---

[1] See, for example, A. Brozyna, *Labour, Love and Prayer: Female Piety in Ulster Religious Literature, 1850–1914* (Belfast, 1999).

[2] E. McLaughlin, 'Women and the Family in Northern Ireland: A Review', *Women's Studies International Forum*, 16, 6 (1993), 564.

[3] Cited in M. Hill, *Women in Ireland: A Century of Change* (Belfast, 2003), 106.

[4] W. E. Vaughan and A. J. Fitzpatrick (eds), *Irish Historical Statistics: Population, 1821–1971* (Dublin, 1978), 4, 10–16, and 25–6. The Ulster figures include counties Cavan, Donegal, and Monaghan until partition in 1921.

MARRIAGE, FERTILITY, AND BREAKING THE MORAL CODE

Marriage rates are difficult to determine with any degree of accuracy for much of the nineteenth century, but the proportion of married women in Ireland aged 15–45 fell from 43 per cent in 1871 to 36 per cent in 1911, with the average female age at marriage increasing from 24–25 years in 1841 to 28 years in 1911.[5] In Ulster, however, although the marriage age increased, the average age at marriage in the province was the lowest in the country: 30.3 years for men and 27.8 years for women in 1861. The rate of permanent celibacy in the province, measured for those unmarried in the 45 to 54 age group, increased during the nineteenth century from 14 per cent for women and 10 per cent for men in 1841, to 27 per cent and 25 per cent respectively by 1911. Whilst Ulster's male celibacy rate was below the national average, the female rate was above it.[6] The sustained female majority in Ulster's population again explains this pattern, and regional marital distinctions continued. Twentieth-century marriage rates were higher in Northern Ireland than in the rest of Ireland. In 1921, 8121 marriages (6.46 per 1000 population) were registered in Northern Ireland, a figure which had increased by mid century, and particularly during the Second World War, and continued to rise: in 1971, 12,152 marriages were recorded, representing 7.9 per 1000 population.[7] The female average age at marriage also fell, declining from 26.4 years in 1937 to 22.6 in 1971, and a decline in marriage rates was only apparent in the closing decades of the twentieth century.[8]

Although 'fertility trends in Ireland during the nineteenth century and earlier are almost a blank',[9] the Rev. Anthony McIntyre, working for the Unitarian Mission to the Poor of Belfast, recorded families with as many as nineteen children in the 1850s.[10] Births were in decline in Ulster from the start of the twentieth century, but by the 1960s, birth and infant mortality rates were the highest in the UK, the Republic of Ireland, and Europe. Births in Northern Ireland numbered 29,710 (23.4 per 1000 population) in 1921 and peaked at 34,345 births (23.6 per 1000 population) in 1964, the highest number recorded since the establishment of the Northern Irish state. Although the rates levelled thereafter, they still amounted to 31,756 births (20.7 per 1000 population) in 1971.[11] This was partly due to the lower average age at marriage in Northern Ireland which lengthened women's reproductive lives.

---

[5] M. E. Daly, *A Social and Economic History of Ireland since 1800* (Dublin, 1981), 92. The average male age at marriage increased over the same period.

[6] D. Fitzpatrick, 'Marriage in Post-Famine Ireland', in A. Cosgrove (ed.), *Marriage in Ireland* (Dublin, 1985), 129–30.

[7] Vaughan and Fitzpatrick, *Irish Historical Statistics*, 256.

[8] G. Jones, 'Marie Stopes in Ireland: The Mothers' Clinic in Belfast, 1936–47', *Social History of Medicine*, 5 (1992), 247. By comparison, marriage rates in the Republic of Ireland averaged 4.76 per 1000 population between 1921 and 1930; 5.59 between 1941 and 1950, and 6.0 between 1961 and 1970 (Daly, *A Social and Economic History*, 204).

[9] C. Ó Gráda, 'Did Ulster Catholics always have Larger Families', *Irish Economic and Social History*, 12 (1985), 80.

[10] Diary of Rev. Anthony McIntyre, 1853–56, 82, PRONI, D/1558/2/3.

[11] Vaughan and Fitzpatrick, *Irish Historical Statistics*, 254.

The difference in family size between Catholics and Protestants was also apparent by the early twentieth century and this continued. Catholic fertility across the classes was two-thirds higher than that of Protestants in 1971, although the gap lessened from the 1980s.[12]

Generic fertility rates mask the number of illegitimate births and here Ulster's history again appears to be distinct. Mid nineteenth-century illegitimacy levels were highest in Ulster.[13] By 1913, with a rate of 35 illegitimate births per 1000 in the province, this figure was considerably higher than that in the rest of Ireland, and had more in common with English and Welsh rates. Dr O'Brien, medical inspector to the Local Government Board, suggested that this could be explained by Ulster's manufacturing base and the associated inward migration of female workers.[14] Internal migration to Belfast certainly left some young women vulnerable to pregnancy outside of marriage. One 'country girl of respectable parents', coming to work in a Belfast shop in the mid 1920s was believed to have 'fallen through ignorance'. Taken into the Church of Ireland Rescue League in Belfast, her 'distress' was described as 'very great, and she entreated us not to tell her mother. She was nursed back to health, and a good home found for the baby.'[15] For other women, pregnancy outside marriage could lead to a quick marriage with the resulting child being labelled premature or cause the mother to be sent, or come voluntarily to, a city like Belfast and the anonymity and relief it could afford. Some were certainly sent further away, often to England, to give birth, their children then adopted either formally or informally: reared by a grandmother or other married family member, often without the child's knowledge.[16]

There was a plethora of maternity and rescue homes in Belfast to help the 'fallen' as well as women deemed uncontainable or at risk of a 'first fall'. The Midnight Mission Rescue and Maternity Home, established in the early 1860s conducted ante-natal visits and arranged the boarding out and adoption of babies. Although the mission saw private patients, much of its work focused on young and unmarried women: by 1946, 55 per cent of its patients were unmarried.[17] These women were often referred to as 'girls' and sometimes as 'girl mother' and many were from 'country districts', with one 15-year-old reportedly walking twenty-four miles from Lurgan.[18] Others were made vulnerable by mental illness, needed help for a short

[12] Ó Gráda, 'Did Ulster Catholics always have Larger Families', 79–80. Higher levels of poverty and rural dwelling as well as cultural factors are posited as explanations.
[13] L. M. Ballard, *Forgetting Frolic: Marriage Traditions in Ireland* (Belfast, 1998), 138.
[14] L. McCormick, *Regulating Sexuality: Women in Twentieth-Century Northern Ireland* (Manchester, 2009), 115.
[15] 13th Annual Report of the Church of Ireland Rescue League, Belfast, 1924–5, PRONI, D1326/26/18. She later donated £1 saved from her wages to the league 'in gratitude for the help she had received' (ibid.). The League also worked with women prisoners and workhouse inmates.
[16] McCormick, *Regulating Sexuality*, 69 and Hill, *Women in Ireland*, 29.
[17] Belfast Midnight Mission Minutes, 13 March 1946, PRONI, D/2072/1. Lack of financial support from the local authority caused the mission's closure in 1949.
[18] Ibid., 10 October 1934 and 5 May 1937.

time whilst seeking employment or were referred by the police. Two such cases were a 14-year-old found in a field and 'beyond' her widowed father's control, and a 23-year-old unmarried mother of two 'without friends or relatives'.[19]

Northern Ireland's illegitimacy rate increased throughout the twentieth century, rising to 16 per cent in 1988 and 21 per cent in 1995.[20] Higher instances of illegitimacy did not lessen the stigmatization of birth outside marriage which caused familial ostracization into and beyond the 1950s. The continued establishment of homes for single mothers, such as the Legion of Mary's Mater Dei Hostel on Belfast's Antrim Road in 1942, illustrates the moral climate determining that these women needed external assistance and the tendency for single mothers to give birth outside of the familial home. The sense of moral panic that accompanied the Second World War may also have impacted on the perceived need for another refuge in Belfast.[21]

A close association between single motherhood and prostitution was also apparent. From 1812 special voluntary constables were appointed to patrol Belfast's streets from 10 p.m. to 3 a.m., an initiative which was later revived with female patrols in the city during both world wars.[22] Legislation like the 1845 Belfast Improvement Act, which levied a 40-shilling fine and imprisonment in default of payment for solicitation in a public place, was extended to smaller urban centres by the Towns Improvement (Ireland) Act of 1854. The operation of the latter in Dundalk from 1859 to 1860, for example, saw large numbers of prostitutes being re-arrested as well as discharged.[23] By 1926 plainclothes police were employed to distinguish between 'a frivolous girl' and 'the common prostitute', identifying the latter by her association with 'known and convicted prostitutes', and speaking 'to men who are obviously strangers to her', although a woman who had not previously been convicted of prostitution was usually cautioned before being taken into custody.[24]

As the 1845 Act indicated, Belfast was identified as the main site for prostitution in Ulster. The Rev. Dr John Edgar's 1840 investigations into prostitution in the city, conducted in the company of two policemen, recorded fifty-nine brothels housing 236 prostitutes. The Rev. McIntyre also questioned some women in Suffern's Entry, 'a very bad place', on the 'life they were leading' in the 1850s: 'Some asked me what I would have them do... asked me for money... talked the language of their profession.'[25] The high level of re-arrests for prostitution and the peaks in moral policing which occurred during both world wars, mean that convictions are a poor gauge of the extent of the profession, but between 1902 and 1946, 90 per cent of all prosecutions for prostitution in the six counties were made in Belfast,

[19] Ibid., 8 December 1937 and 11 May 1938.
[20] McLaughlin, 'Women and the Family', 556; Hill, *Women in Ireland*, 146.
[21] See L. McCormick, '"Filthy Little Girls": Controlling Women in Public Spaces in Northern Ireland during the Second World War', in G. McIntosh and D. Urquhart (eds), *Irish Women at War: The Twentieth Century* (Dublin, 2010), 103–18.
[22] See special police reports, 1812–16 (2 Vols., PRONI, D46). See also M. Luddy, *Prostitution and Irish Society, 1800–1940* (Cambridge, 2007), 172–8.
[23] Offences in Dundalk regarding contraventions of the Town Improvement (Ireland) Act, 1859–60, PRONI, D/2458/3.
[24] Memoranda on measures to combat Venereal Disease in Northern Ireland, 1926, PRONI, CAB/9B/23/1.
[25] McIntyre Diary, 64.

and over 10,000 women were arrested in Northern Ireland for prostitution from 1924 to 1940.[26] Although Belfast's association with prostitution is clear, rescue homes were established in smaller urban centres like Derry, Lisburn, and Castlereagh in County Down during the nineteenth century whilst brothels were reported in Fermanagh, Armagh, and Derry in 1912.[27] Thus, although Belfast's industrial profile was marked by higher levels of diversification and investment and consequently by higher levels of employment, particularly for women, this was insufficient to counter prostitution. This, and a strong philanthropic tradition, led to the establishment of an array of rescue asylums, both religious and lay.

Opened in 1816, the Presbyterian Ulster Female Penitentiary was under Rev. Dr Edgar's control from 1839, adopting his name in 1892. Between 1900 and its closure in 1926, it helped 2786 women.[28] The Church of Ireland-run Ulster Magdalen asylum in the city took in over 3000 women from 1849 until its closure in 1916. Belfast Midnight Mission was also active in trying to remove women from the streets from the early 1860s, employing a male agent to work at night; over 300 women passed through its rescue home in the period 1874–75. The mission's focus shifted to single mothers from the 1900s, but it still employed a female visitor to frequent areas where 'dishonoured sisters congregate'.[29] A second Magdalen asylum was originally Mercy Sister-run in the 1840s but its work was taken over by the Good Shepherd Sisters in 1867, marking the beginning of some of the longest-lived rescue work in Ulster. The Good Shepherd laundry and home for single mothers on the Ormeau Road were operative until 1977 and 1990 respectively. Between 1851 and 1899, 894 entrants were recorded, with a third entering voluntarily.[30] High levels of asylum inmates were also listed as orphans with Belfast Salvation Army registers, for instance, recording 36 per cent of all female entrants between 1905 and 1917 as without parents.[31] Although this could be a tactic used to hide an illegitimate pregnancy, prostitution, or identity from family, the relationship between breaking the moral code, familial dislocation, and philanthropic dependency remains striking.

The correlation between illegitimacy, infanticide, and child abandonment is also strong. Cases of infanticide and child abandonment, even with an estimated one case in fifty being prosecuted, feature regularly in court records and the press, revealing the very real cost of an unwanted pregnancy or pregnancy outside of marriage.[32] Infanticide was perceived as a female crime applying solely to a woman 'who wilfully causes the death of her newly born child', and was punishable by death. That sentence

[26] Luddy, *Prostitution*, 246–8.   [27] Ibid., 22 and 80–2.
[28] McCormick, *Regulating Sexuality*, 24, 64. Of this sample, 16 per cent were placed in service, 5 per cent went into employment, and 7 per cent returned to family.
[29] Luddy, *Prostitution*, 84–5 and 111. The Ulster Female Penitentiary closed for a period in the 1820s but re-opened c.1831 (ibid., 79). The Midnight Mission became Malone Place Maternity and Rescue Home in 1944.
[30] Ibid., 79–82 and 98–9.
[31] McCormick, *Regulating Sexuality*, 54–6. Poor parenting or mental deficiencies could also put girls at risk.
[32] A. Guilbride, 'Infanticide: The Crime of Motherhood', in P. Kennedy (ed.), *Motherhood in Ireland* (Cork, 2004), 173.

was, however, frequently commuted: 'if the jury are satisfied that her balance of mind was disturbed and not fully recovered from the effects of childbirth [they] may find her guilty of… "Infanticide" which may be punished as manslaughter'.[33]

In 1900, Bessie C. was found guilty in Belfast of the infanticide of her son after being witnessed dropping a parcel into a sewer pipe which 'contained the body of a newly born male child still alive'. Despite a neighbour tying the naval cord and bathing and rubbing the child with brandy, it died in the workhouse infirmary. A post-mortem recorded the cause of death as acute jaundice as a result of liver congestion 'brought on by exposure shortly after birth'; so shortly that the mother's afterbirth was still intact when she was examined. Bessie C. claimed that she left the child 'to get some food. I had it on the road side.'[34] Marion C. was found guilty of the infanticide of her 16–18-month-old daughter in 1903. Although witnesses confirmed that she gave up laundry work to care for her child when it became ill and had it admitted to Belfast Children's Hospital, the cause of death was recorded as 'tuberculosis and exhaustion… accelerated by gross neglect'. Her testimony, however, alluded less to negligence than to the realities of life for a single mother: 'I am not a married woman. The child is illegitimate. I do not know the father' and added that she paid childminders 6d per night to care for her daughter whilst she worked.[35]

Other cases reveal the close association between poverty, pregnancy outside marriage, and infanticide. Infants born in Irish workhouses were often 'killed shortly after they left the institution'[36] as was the case of Ellen B. found guilty of 'feloniously, wilfully and of her malice aforethought' killing her daughter on Belfast's Ravenhill Road in 1904 after giving birth in the workhouse. The child died aged two and a half weeks on the day it left the workhouse, its body found in a parcel 'lying in a bed of nettles at the side of a partly made street… its head partially covered with a dress'. Post-mortem results found the child to be well nourished and recorded the cause of death as suffocation: 'There were no marks of strangulation or violence… the child was alive when placed in the spot where it was found.' When questioned by police, the mother claimed the child was 'sick and vomiting' when she left the workhouse, and she 'left it down' before taking the train to Bangor in County Down to resume work as a domestic servant.[37] It is unclear whether economic need, post-natal depression, or a desire to escape the shame of illegitimacy led Ellen B. to infanticide, but hers was not an isolated case: prosecutions for infanticide continued in Northern Ireland until the 1970s.[38]

---

[33] Northern Ireland Ministry of Home Affairs—Infanticide now Child Destruction Bill, 1928, PRONI, HA/5/1449.

[34] Bessie C. infanticide case, 1900, PRONI, BELF/1/1/2/3/5. Surnames are abbreviated to protect anonymity.

[35] Marion C. infanticide case, 1902–3, PRONI, BELF/1/1/2/10/6.

[36] C. Rattigan, '"Dark Spots" in Irish Society: Unmarried Mothers and Infanticide in Ireland from 1926–38', in M. C. Ramblado-Minero and A. Pérez-Vides (eds.), *Single Motherhood in Twentieth-Century Ireland* (Lampeter, 2006), 99.

[37] Ellen B. infanticide case, 1904, PRONI, BELF/1/1/2/15/18.

[38] See, for example, the 1975 infanticide case in Tyrone, PRONI, TYR/1/3/B/2/58, and that of 1978 in Belfast, PRONI, BELF/1/1/2/279/25.

MATERNAL AND CHILD MORTALITY

Many more infants died of natural causes and whilst it is difficult accurately to gauge the level of infant mortality in the nineteenth century, an estimated 154 infants from every 1000 live births in Ireland died in the 1820s and 1830s, with higher rates occurring in urban areas into the twentieth century. In 1915, a countrywide infant death rate of 69.9 per 1000 live births was recorded, with an urban rate of 134.4 and that was increasingly out of step with the decline in infant mortality in Britain.[39] Child mortality in Belfast was described in 1852 as 'absolutely excessive—the average age at death being as low as nine years'.[40] Given this, and the state's shift in emphasis towards child welfare which emerged from the late nineteenth century, it is unsurprising to see a heightened level of government and voluntary involvement. By 1931, Dr Grace Pollock was appointed medical officer to Belfast's Maternity and Child Welfare Scheme and the need for intervention was clear: 127 infants under the age of 1 died in Belfast over a six-week period ending on 10 January 1931. The city corporation's Maternity and Child Welfare Committee identified 'mothercraft' as the cure: 'The physical condition of the mother during the ante-natal period is most important. Housing has some responsibility, but it is secondary to maternal knowledge... our needs are great.'[41] Although more women attended ante-natal clinics and child welfare centres, and expectant mothers experiencing poverty received milk towards the end of the 1930s, infant mortality rates remained high, particularly in urban areas, and Northern Ireland lagged behind falling levels of infant deaths elsewhere. On average, seventy-seven infants died from every 1000 live births in Northern Ireland (compared to an English and Welsh average of fifty-seven) between 1934 and 1938; of these 38 per cent were born to single mothers.[42] Belfast's Maternity and Child Welfare Committee could only conclude that the rates were 'abnormally high'.[43] A survey carried out by the Temperance and Social Welfare Committee of the Irish Methodist Church into infant mortality from 1937 to 1938 also hints at the widespread level of concern.[44]

Pioneering Lurgan doctor, James Deeny, connected child-feeding practices to infant mortality amongst Belfast linen workers as early as the 1930s, identifying the class dimension to infant death: 'it is usually the poor who are the victims'. Deeny also acknowledged that family size impacted on the quality and quantity of nutrition, the likelihood of disease or infection and the time spent on childcare.

---

[39] L. Kennedy and L. A. Clarkson, 'Birth, Death and Exile: Irish Population History, 1700–1921', in B. J. Graham and L. J. Proudfoot (eds), *An Historical Geography of Ireland* (London, 1993), 170–1.
[40] A. G. Malcolm, 'The Sanitary State of Belfast, with Suggestions for its Improvement: A paper read before the Statistical Section of the British Association, 1852' (Linen Hall Library, Belfast).
[41] Belfast Corporation Maternity and Child Welfare Committee Minutes, 21 January 1931 and 11 January 1933, PRONI, LA/10/9/AD. I am grateful to Alyson Lattimer of the Ulster Hospital for advice regarding the causes of infant mortality.
[42] Report of Maternity Services Committee on Maternal Mortality and Morbidity in Northern Ireland, 1939, PRONI, SO/1A/219, 31.
[43] Belfast Corporation Maternity and Child Welfare Committee Minutes, 7 December 1942, PRONI, LA/7/9/AD/3.
[44] See papers in the Mercer Library of the Royal College of Surgeons, Dublin.

In 1943 an estimated one child in eight still died during its first year of life in Belfast.[45] Northern Ireland government inquiries tried, with limited success, to salve the situation from the 1950s to the 1970s. Although the level of infant deaths fell from twenty-three in every 1000 live births in Northern Ireland in 1971 to seventeen in 1977, the rate remained higher than the UK average of fourteen.[46] A government committee, assessing the 708 neonatal deaths in Northern Ireland in 1974, found the main causes of death as congenital malformation (such as spina bifida and anencephaly), prematurity, and respiratory distress syndrome constituting 30 per cent, 21 per cent, and 20 per cent of deaths respectively, with the highest rates of death now recorded in the southern and western areas of the province.[47] Another report in the late 1970s suggested a multiplicity of factors, some of which had been earlier identified by Deeny, and many 'determined before the time of conception': poor housing, large family size, and inadequate nutrition which contributed significantly to the level of low-birthweight babies 'who form a major component of deaths during the early period of life'. Limited use of family planning techniques were still contributing to poorly spaced pregnancies and larger families: 'A mother able to space her children is likely to be healthier during pregnancy' and thus less likely to develop conditions like anaemia and deliver a low-birthweight baby. The average family size in Northern Ireland was recorded at 3.4 compared to 2.9 for Britain in 1971.[48] Questions asked by Lord Plant, chair of the Standing Committee on Human Rights, in the House of Lords in 1979 underscored the uniquely high levels of Northern Irish infant mortality in a UK, industrialized Western European, and North American context, and identified the same causal factors: high levels of poverty with deprivation in a mother's early childhood heightening the risk of infant death. Women in the lowest category of 'social class V' were, therefore, considered twice as likely to experience infant mortality as those in the highest 'social class I', while 'unsupported' mothers were also considered at high risk of losing a child, again highlighting the continued import of familial support.[49]

Improvements in ante-natal care were clearly still required, particularly in encouraging women to seek medical advice in the early stages of pregnancy. Practical moves were being made in this direction: a health centre programme, established in 1965, set up sixty-four centres within fourteen years, and a health committee 'to prepare young women for motherhood and discourage pregnant women from smoking and drinking', increase screening, vaccinate against rubella, and provide counselling and family planning advice, was operative from 1978. However, the impact of community segregation and relatively low levels of intermarriage between the Protestant and Catholic communities on infant

---

[45] J. Deeny, *To Cure and to Care: Memoirs of a Chief Medical Officer* (Dun Laoghaire, 1989), 26 and 53.

[46] Community Health, Infant Mortality, Northern Ireland Department of Health and Social Services, 1978–9, PRONI, HSS/13/35/46.

[47] Northern Ireland Committee on Infant Mortality and Handicap, 1979, PRONI, HSS/13/36/10. Anencephaly is the congenital absence or minimal development of the brain.

[48] Community Health, Infant Mortality, Northern Ireland Department of Health and Social Services, 1978–9, PRONI, HSS/13/35/46. An estimated 25 per cent of Northern Ireland's housing stock required renewal or improvement, compared to the English and Welsh figure of 17 per cent in the 1970s.

[49] *Belfast News Letter*, 10 April 1979.

mortality rates in Northern Ireland has yet to be fully explored.⁵⁰ Smaller families, improved maternal health and housing all gradually produced a long-term decline in infant death in Northern Ireland: infant mortality was 7 per cent in 1993 and fell to 5 per cent, with half of all deaths occurring in the first week of life, by 2000.⁵¹

The level of maternal mortality, the death of a woman while pregnant, during labour or puerperium (the two to four week period immediately following childbirth), was another cause for grave concern in Northern Ireland. In 1939 this spurred the establishment of a Committee on Maternity Services, reporting to the Northern Ireland Ministry of Home Affairs: between 1927 and 1936, 1377 women died in childbirth, with an additional 342 dying from non-puerperal diseases associated with childbirth. These figures were regarded as 'deplorably high'. The 1936 maternal death rate constituted 7.3 per 1000 births when diseases associated with childbirth were included which compared very unfavourably to the English and Welsh figure of 4.91. Although the committee noted maternal death 'black spots' in Wales and parts of Yorkshire and Lancashire, in many other areas of the UK the maternal death rate was 2 per 1000 births or less. Heart or kidney disease, tuberculosis as well as insanitary conditions, malnutrition, overwork, or abnormalities during pregnancy, labour, and the puerperium, and a lack of 'adequate skilled assistance' all impacted on Northern Ireland's high rate of maternal deaths.⁵²

From 1924 it was illegal habitually to assist women in labour for remuneration unless registered as a midwife or under the direction of a medical practitioner. The long tradition of the 'handywoman' was, therefore, on the wane and the experience of newly appointed Ballymoney GP, Dr James Nevin, assisting a birth in the 1880s where 'the women in attendance were inclined to dictate rather too much ... owing to me being a stranger to all of them' became less common.⁵³ But poorer women continued to use cheaper, unqualified 'midwives', some of whom Deeny described as 'shockers', and maternal deaths were not easy to counter.⁵⁴ In tandem with the reforms suggested to curb infant mortality, education, and the improvement and coordination of services from the ante- to post-natal period were key. Many women, particularly outside Belfast, were not in receipt of any ante-natal care in the 1930s. Other suggested reforms included reorganizing services on a county basis, supplementing the diet of 'necessitous pregnant women', changing midwives' remuneration so that it was not solely dependent on the number of patients they attended, separating maternity services from the poor law 'in order that there may be no reluctance on the part of any pregnant woman to avail herself of them', offering free services where required, and reviewing arrangements for emergencies which occurred during home births.

---

⁵⁰ Fewer than 10 per cent of marriages were interreligious in Northern Ireland in 2003.
⁵¹ Hill, *Women in Ireland*, 197.
⁵² Report of Maternity Services Committee on Maternal Mortality and Morbidity in Northern Ireland, Northern Ireland Ministry of Home Affairs, 1943, 7, PRONI, SO/1A/219. The Northern Ireland Ministry of Home Affairs included health in its remit until the late 1940s.
⁵³ Autobiography of Dr James Nevin, 1902–36, Vol. 2 (Ballymena Branch Library, IR-920NEV).
⁵⁴ Deeny, *To Cure and to Care*, 26.

With 119 midwives registered in the 152 dispensary districts outside Belfast in 1939, there were obviously serious gaps in provision which were only partially filled by hospitals. However, finance was in short supply, with Belfast Corporation, for example, reducing funding for maternity and child welfare services from £12,000 in 1937 to £11,250 in 1938. Given this situation, it is not surprising that a 1939 Northern Ireland committee concluded that half of all maternal deaths were preventable. It appealed for help with 'the one human function which is vital to the continued existence of the Province… The problem is a national one and is the direct responsibility and concern of every man and woman.'[55]

This problem tried the Northern Ireland government for decades, spurring confidential inquiries and reports from 1955. A report, reviewing deaths between 1964 and 1967, noted 'a gradual and significant change', with deaths from haemorrhage and sepsis in decline, and thirty-seven 'true maternal deaths' from a total of 137,360 births. However, when deaths linked to pregnancy and associated causes were considered, the figure increased to 140 with the highest levels recorded in Antrim (thirty), Belfast (twenty-nine), and Down (twenty-nine).[56] Even with the creation of a Ministry of Health and Local Government in Northern Ireland in 1944, the introduction of the National Health Service in 1948, increasing medical intervention, hospitalization of births, and the wider use of drugs, particularly penicillin in the 1950s, it took at least a generation to affect the rate of maternal and infant deaths whilst the age of mothers, lower parity, and improving socio-economic conditions were all causal factors.[57]

FERTILITY CONTROL

As the date of the decline in family size in Northern Ireland indicates, contraceptives were not widely used until the 1970s. However, artificial methods of controlling and spacing births were certainly entering the public domain by the later nineteenth century. American doctor, Robert Swift Bruce, advertising his 'entirely harmless and infallible little appliance', the Pessarie Preventive in 1872, used testimony from a Belfast millworker to highlight the human cost of large families. Writing from the Crumlin Road, the anonymous mother of seven asked Bruce for pessaries, a medical almanac, and a book on overpopulation: 'i have been savin up this money ever since i was tolde about these things'. With her children, 'very Sickley [with measles] and… very weak, for they wante plenty to ete… i have always ben very bad in my confinements and i do dread to have any more children for i am very weak, my husbin was a Soljer' but now rheumatic, he could only

---

[55] *Report of Maternity Services Committee on Maternal Mortality and Morbidity in Northern Ireland* (Belfast, 1939), PRONI, SO/1A/219, *passim*. The committee cited the success of Rochdale where publicity and coordinating services led the maternal mortality rate to fall from 9 to 2 per 1000 births.
[56] *A Report on an Enquiry into Maternal Deaths in Northern Ireland, 1964–7* (Belfast, 1968), PRONI, SO/2/J/3/2. According to the report, pulmonary embolism and toxaemia accounted for over half of all maternal deaths in Northern Ireland.
[57] Kennedy, 'Childbirth in Ireland', in Kennedy (ed.), *Motherhood*, 79.

work sporadically in a factory earning 12 shillings per week. With 'non of the children...able to worke and i cant worke mulch to ern for the childern...it is not esy to find anuf for 9 people [sic].' For Bruce's help, she pledged to secure 'some more custim among the mil workers for poor women do not like to sea their poore children die for whant of food so they will be plesed when they have no childern [sic]'.[58] Bruce claimed to have sent her contraceptives and books free of charge, and whilst there is no way to test the veracity of this statement, even if fictional, it highlights the notion that urban working-class women wanted to control family size not only for financial considerations but for their own health and that of their children. This was later reinforced by Belfast's chief medical superintendent, who noted 'few mothers, indeed can be expected to bring sturdy children forth year after year'.[59]

The origins of institutional family planning in Northern Ireland lie with birth-control pioneer Marie Stopes's Mothers' Clinic at The Mount in East Belfast which opened in 1936. Although a Northern Ireland Society for Constructive Birth Control was in existence from 1930, Stopes's venture faced both internal strife and external opposition from the Catholic Church.[60] The clinic's limited success was apparent in its continual financial deficit and its unsuccessful 1937 approach to the city corporation for £100 towards its work. The clinic closed in 1947 after advising approximately 3000–4000 women.[61] Stopes's work needs to be assessed alongside that of Dr Olive Anderson, medical officer for a new family planning clinic at the Royal Maternity Hospital in Belfast from 1940. This clinic gave advice to medically referred patients although Anderson admitted that she 'smuggled in one or two patients from local GPs'. In 1951, Anderson and Dr Charlotte Arnold founded the Belfast Women's Welfare Clinic at Malone Place in the south of the city which moved to Belfast City Hospital in 1959. By 1960, 44 per cent of its patients were from outside Belfast, with some travelling seventy miles to access its services, which suggests a demand to plan and space births. Yet like Stopes, Anderson found religion 'the stumbling block' in popularizing family planning.[62]

The Northern Ireland Family Planning Association (NIFPA) was founded in 1965 and aimed to augment services, heighten publicity, and help to finance the training of medical staff. Like Stopes's earlier venture, much of the work at NIFPA clinics continued on a volunteer basis until the 1960s. NIFPA chair, Dr Joyce Neill, addressing an audience of seventy-five at its first public meeting in Belfast in 1965, acknowledged the specific regional challenges: 'Northern Ireland family planning clinics must be prepared to advise Roman Catholic patients on methods

---

[58] Pamphlet advertising Robert Swift Bruce's contraceptives, 1872 (PRONI, D/1128/2/17). Bruce claimed the consequences of overpopulation included infanticide, pauperism, and crime.
[59] Cited in Jones, 'Marie Stopes in Ireland', 267.
[60] Ibid., 261 and 263.
[61] Belfast Corporation Maternity and Child Welfare Committee Minutes, 22 October 1937, PRONI, LA/28/9/AD/2. Figure from Jones, 'Marie Stopes', 268.
[62] Cited in L. McCormick, '"The Scarlet Woman in Person." The Establishment of a Family Planning Service in Northern Ireland, 1950–74', *Social History of Medicine*, 21 (2008), 346, 348, 353.

of family planning acceptable to their beliefs'.[63] Although by this time the Church of Ireland and the Presbyterian Church approved of the use of contraception within marriage, Neill also noted the 'strong Calvinist' (Presbyterian) tradition in Northern Ireland which they had to contend with.[64] The rhythm method, as well as artificial methods such as caps, pessaries, oral contraceptives, and condoms, were therefore prescribed by NIFPA.

This inclusive approach worked: between 1963 and 1964, 2996 patients 'from all denominations' with a 'proportion of Catholics who come to be instructed in their Church's approved rhythm method; and also some ask about mechanical forms of contraception' attended NIFPA clinics.[65] Patients paid for contraceptive devices with 15s 1d estimated as the cost of a first visit, but fees would be waived for medical referrals or for those 'whose husbands are unemployed or who have large families and cannot afford to pay'.[66] Following the ruling of the Family Planning Association in London, women who were soon to marry would also be seen, with two visits prior to nuptials being advised. However, as Dr Mary Adams, a NIFPA director, noted: 'there might be individual circumstances where advice could be given' to unmarried women.[67] The number of new patients and those re-attending the clinics continued to rise: 2600 new patients and over 6000 attendances were recorded in 1966 with an increased interest noted in 'the pill' and intra-uterine devices (IUDs).[68] NIFPA's services also included a non-profit postal contraceptive service for those without a local clinic, routine cervical smears for women aged over 40, counselling for those with psychological or sexual problems, and patients were encouraged:

> to discuss any marital family problems and often feel more free to ask for help or advice from a woman doctor who does not attend them or their family outside the clinic. Many patients do not wish to approach their general practitioners with problems such as these.[69]

By 1967 there were NIFPA clinics at Belfast's City Hospital and Newtownards Road, Bangor Hospital, Rathcoole, Portadown, Coleraine, and Dungannon with new clinics planned for Derry, Ballymena, Omagh, and Belfast's Ormeau Road, and the Association believed that attitudes towards birth control were 'changing...rapidly'. Buoyed by this they placed an advertisement over sixteen nights in the *Belfast Telegraph*. Family planning, however, remained controversial and NIFPA 'were still very concerned about making the addresses of clinics widely known'.[70]

Family planning legislation, like so many areas in Northern Ireland, followed Westminster initiatives. An act of 1967, for example, placed the onus on local health authorities in Northern Ireland to provide family planning services, a move which

[63] *Belfast Telegraph*, 12 November 1965.
[64] Cited in McCormick, 'The Scarlet Woman', 351.
[65] *Belfast Telegraph*, 22 March 1965. NIFPA board members were disappointed by the level of publicity generated by this meeting with the BBC refusing to advertise 'a controversial cause'. See NIFPA Minutes, 22 November 1965, PRONI, D/3543/2/2.
[66] NIFPA Minutes, 1965, PRONI, D/3543/2/1.
[67] *Belfast Telegraph*, 22 March 1965.
[68] NIFPA Annual Report, 1966, PRONI, D/3543/2/2.
[69] NIPFA Minutes, undated notes [1965], PRONI, D/3543/2/1. The attendance figure includes return patients.
[70] NIFPA Minutes, 1 March and 6 December 1966, PRONI, D/3543/2/2.

led to 'great battles in some cases' and the need for continued 'dialogue between different points of view especially acceptance of the R. C. standpoint'.[71] The act also allowed local authorities to help finance the work of existing NIFPA clinics; a move which the association hoped would 'greatly ease' their 'financial burden'. This legislation also arguably helped to lessen the stigma attached to family planning: an annual increase of 800 new patients and 3000 attendances was recorded at NIFPA clinics in 1967 and figures continued to rise.[72] This was, however, interrupted by the outbreak of civil strife in 1968. The following year saw NIFPA annual returns record a significant increase in the number of patients, from 5300 to 17,900, but numbers attending Belfast clinics declined for the first time. The establishment of new clinics in areas like Lisburn reduced the number of commuter patients coming to Belfast but 'The "troubles" of the year resulted in noticeably low attendance during certain months.'[73] The Derry City clinic also recorded an estimated 20 per cent drop in attendance in 1970 'believed to be due to the riots in the city', while in Omagh the requirement to travel to Belfast to have IUDs fitted increased the popularity of alternative contraceptive methods. The disruption was so severe in Belfast that a clinic was opened in the Suffolk estate in the west of the city to assist women who could not travel to other clinics, but even it was forced to cancel sessions in mid 1970 due to the disturbances, and by 1971 'clinic attendances to some extent fluctuated according to the degree of disturbance in particular areas'.[74]

A wholesale acceptance of sex outside of marriage was also still far from assured and in 1969 NIFPA's Executive Committee ruled that 'large numbers of unmarried girls could not and should not be coped with'. Premarital patients and those who needed advice for 'social reasons' were the only categories of unmarried women that could be assisted in clinics on local health authority premises or those in receipt of health authority grants. Independent clinics like that on east Belfast's Newtownards Road or those which were self-supporting could, however, dictate their own policy. This hinted at a growing liberalization which was furthered by both the Northern Ireland National Health Service Amendment (Family Planning) Act of 1969, granting local authorities the right to provide contraceptives to unmarried women and without age restrictions, and a Ministry of Health circular promoting family planning regardless of marital status. NIFPA therefore decided 'to give advice to the increasing numbers of unmarried persons who seek it', which they presented as crucial to their work 'if we really wish every child to be a wanted child'.[75] Family planning subsequently became more integrated into the National Health Service with hospitals and GPs becoming increasingly involved. Local authorities took over all former NIFPA clinics by 1974 and provided free contraceptives by the following year. NIFPA's focus thus shifted to didactic work before ceasing operations in 1977

---

[71] Ibid., undated handwritten notes, 1964–65, PRONI, D/3543/2/1. McCormick charts the difficulties faced in establishing family planning clinics in Derry: 'The Scarlet Woman', 354–5.
[72] Forty new NIFPA members were also recorded. NIFPA Annual Report, 1967, PRONI, D3543/2/2.
[73] NIFPA Annual Report, 1969, ibid.
[74] Cited in McCormick, 'The Scarlet Woman', 355–6. See also NIFPA Annual Report, 1971, PRONI, D/3543/2/3.
[75] NIFPA Minutes, 12 June 1969 and Annual Report, 1970, PRONI, D/3543/2/2.

but with thirty-eight family planning clinics in Northern Ireland by the early 1970s there can be no doubt of the efficacy of its work.

MORAL CONSERVATISM AND CENSURE

Despite significant changes in patterns of birth control and illegitimacy, much of Northern Ireland remains morally conservative. The decriminalization of homosexuality and sex education were contested,[76] and abortion is still illegal with the 1861 Offences Against the Person Act applicable in the province alongside section 25 (1) of the 1945 Northern Ireland Criminal Justice Act under which the 'crime' of 'procuring a miscarriage' is punishable by a maximum sentence of life imprisonment.[77] Attempts to reform abortion law increased in the 1980s with the establishment of the Northern Ireland Abortion Campaign whose shock tactics included 600 wire coat hangers sent to Westminster, each with a copy of a flight ticket attached and the words, 'These are the two ways in which NI women get abortions'.[78] Another attempt at reform failed to garner support in the Northern Ireland Assembly in June 2000 and opposition again crossed denominational boundaries.[79]

In spite of its criminalization, abortion was a reality for some Northern Irish women. Twelve abortion cases were tried in Belfast between 1925 and 1950;[80] abortion caused the deaths of nine known women in 1935 and Belfast Midnight Mission reported two cases of abortion to the Medical Officer for Health in 1941. Abortions caused five maternal deaths in Northern Ireland in the period from 1964 to 1967 and five further deaths from 1967 to 1981. Recent estimates also suggest that 2000 women per year travel from Northern Ireland to England to procure abortions.[81] There are also concerns that the 2004 Appeal Court Judicial Review brought by the Family Planning Association of Northern Ireland further complicated the legal situation by allowing abortion if a woman's life is believed to be at risk, either due to physical or mental considerations, but not for foetal abnormality: 99 such abortions were carried out at Northern Ireland hospitals in

---

[76] Note, for example, the Rev. Ian Paisley's 'Save Ulster from Sodomy' campaign in the late 1970s which, coupled with protests from at least seven of Northern Ireland's twenty-six district councils, delayed reform. Following a successful European Court of Human Rights challenge in 1981, homosexual acts between consenting adults in Northern Ireland were decriminalized in 1982.

[77] L. Smyth, 'The Cultural Politics of Sexuality and Production in Northern Ireland', *Sociology*, 40 (2006), 666.

[78] Hill, *Women in Ireland*, 199.   [79] McCormick, 'The Scarlet Woman', 345–6.

[80] Clíona Rattigan, '"Crimes of Passion of the Worst Character": Abortion Cases and Gender in Ireland, 1925–50', in M. Valiulis (ed.), *Gender and Power in Irish History* (Dublin, 2009), 116.

[81] Jones, 'Marie Stopes', 267; Belfast Midnight Mission minutes, 10 September 1941, PRONI, D/2072/1 and McCormick, *Regulating Sexuality*, 199. Northern Ireland Department of Health figures recorded 6400 abortions carried out in England and Wales on women giving Northern Irish addresses between 2003 and 2007. The 2007 annual figure of 1343 was an increase of 48 on the previous year. Numbers are likely to be higher as women may not give Northern Irish addresses and abortions procured in Scotland or further afield are not included in these figures (*Belfast Telegraph*, 2 January 2009).

2007.[82] Specifying foetal abnormality as outside of the law is believed by some 'to have reduced abortion availability' and prompted demands for clearer legal guidelines for medical practitioners.[83] The latter was addressed with the Department of Health's 2010 'Guidance on the termination of pregnancy: the law and clinical practice in Northern Ireland' but even this admits a 'grey area' in regulating abortion.[84] Ongoing protests outside Belfast's Brook clinic, which provides contraceptive advice to the under 25s, from both Catholics and Protestants, act as another reminder of moral conservatism where 'placard-carrying men taunted and belittled young women seeking admission to its twice weekly sessions'.[85]

Thus, although state involvement in some of the most private aspects of life increased during the twentieth century, acceptance of moral nonconformity was often lacking. The censure exercised by some for those deviating from the moral code also denied many of emotional and financial support and cast them aside at a time when they were most vulnerable.

FURTHER READING

D. Ferriter, *Occasions of Sin: Sex and Society in Modern Ireland* (London, 2009).
M. Hill, *Women in Ireland: A Century of Change* (Belfast, 2003).
F. Kennedy, *Cottage to Crèche: Family Change in Ireland* (Dublin, 2001).
P. Kennedy (ed.), *Motherhood in Ireland* (Cork, 2004).
M. Luddy, *Prostitution and Irish society, 1800–1940* (Cambridge, 2007).
L. McCormick, *Regulating Sexuality. Women in Twentieth-Century Northern Ireland* (Manchester, 2009).
E. McLaughlin, 'Women and the Family in Northern Ireland: A Review', *Women's Studies International Forum*, 16 (1993), 553–68.
M. C. Ramblado-Minero and A. Pérez-Vides (eds.), *Single Motherhood in Twentieth-Century Ireland* (Lampeter, 2006).
C. Rattigan, *'What else could I do?' Single Mothers and Infanticide, Ireland 1900–1950* (Dublin, 2012).

---

[82] *Belfast Telegraph*, 2 January 2009.
[83] Smyth, 'The Cultural Politics', 665 and 671–5.
[84] See <http://www.dhsspsni.gov.uk/guidance-termination-pregnancy-jul-2010.pdf>, 18. Accessed 1 December 2010.
[85] Hill, *Women in Ireland*, 193. Attempts to establish a Brook clinic in Derry city also met with opposition.

16

Sport in the Nineteenth and Twentieth Centuries

Alan Bairner

INTRODUCTION

On 11 November 2009, an Ulster Sports Exhibition opened in Belfast's City Hall. Its aim was to celebrate the achievements of, amongst others, sporting luminaries such as footballer George Best, Olympic gold medal-winning athlete Mary Peters, boxer Barry McGuigan, and cyclist Wendy Houvenghel. The exhibition was organized by the Ulster Sports Museum Association, the ultimate objective of which was the establishment of a permanent museum dedicated to Ulster sport.[1] According to the Association's honorary secretary, Brian Morrison, the event was about 'celebrating the past and inspiring the future'.[2] The questions that immediately arise are: whose past and whose future?

The history of sport in Ireland is in many ways a microcosm of the island's political and cultural history.[3] As Mike Cronin noted, 'until there is only one idea of Irish nationalism, and a singular and commonly shared expression of identity, then sport will continue to reflect the multifaceted and ever-changing nature of Irishness'.[4] In this respect, the nine-county province of Ulster has played a pivotal role, standing as it now does with one foot in the Republic of Ireland and the other in the United Kingdom of Great Britain and Northern Ireland, with all of the political and sporting implications which that divide involves. The story of sport in Ireland is a significant element in the history of three different Irelands—pre-partition Ireland, the Irish Free State (subsequently the Republic of Ireland), and Northern Ireland. It also embraces the distinct but dialectically interwoven narratives of Catholic and Protestant Ireland, urban and rural Ireland, post-imperial and post-colonial Ireland, and traditional, modern, and even post-modern Ireland.[5]

Sport in modern Ulster has functioned variously as a means by which to escape from political and social hardship, and as an important influence on the construction

---

[1] <http://www.nisf.net/proposals-to-create-an-ulster-sports-museum-485.asp>. Accessed 12 January 2011.
[2] <http://www.belfastforum.co.uk/index.php?topic=26506.0>. Aaccessed 12 January 2011.
[3] See A. Bairner, 'Irish Sport', in J. Cleary and C. Connolly (eds.), *The Cambridge Companion to Modern Irish Culture* (Cambridge, 2005), 190–205.
[4] M. Cronin, *Sport and Nationalism in Ireland: Gaelic Games, Soccer and Irish Identity since 1884* (Dublin, 1999), 190.
[5] Bairner, 'Irish Sport', 190–1, 203–5.

and reproduction of competing identities.⁶ Not only has sport been influenced by and implicated in the political struggles that have taken place within urban areas, it has also been a major signifier of cultural affiliation and a conduit for community cohesion in rural areas as well.⁷ In that sense, the chapter engages with broader debates about sport, space, and identity. The focus is primarily on association football, cricket, rugby union, and hockey—the so-called 'foreign games' denounced by some Irish nationalists—and on the Gaelic Athletic Association (GAA). Limited reference will be made to some other sports. All in all, sport has played a colourful and socially significant part in the life of Ulster, with highlights including the rise and fall of Belfast Celtic Football Club, the historic rivalry between Cavan and Monaghan in Gaelic football, the astonishing triumph of Ireland's cricketers over the West Indies at Sion Mills, the glittering prizes won by Clones-born Barry McGuigan, and Ulster's triumph in the 1998–99 European Rugby Cup.

ORIGINS OF MODERN SPORT IN IRELAND

Modern sport followed a similar evolutionary path in Ireland to that traced out in Britain during the nineteenth century, albeit with a degree of noteworthy local divergence. Urbanization played its part; so too did schools. In Ireland, however, rural society was a more forceful influence on the development of sport than was the case elsewhere, and the military played a more significant role than in Britain in relation to the emergence of modern sport forms. A lasting reminder of the latter is to be found in the name of the interprovincial trophy for men's hockey—the Leinster Regiment Cup.⁸

Prior to the middle of the nineteenth century, the idea of sport had a very different meaning from the one that we associate it with today. A good day's sport for an Irish country gentleman involved hunting. Meanwhile the agricultural labouring classes took their intermittent pleasures, as did their counterparts in England and elsewhere in Europe, from rough and tumble ball games—specifically in Ireland the game of *caid* or Cad—and differing forms of stick and ball games. Livestock fairs and other public gatherings were further occasions for sociability, and could result in the kind of chaotic behaviour now immortalized in the case of one such fair, that of Donnybrook Fair, near Dublin.⁹ Whereas Cad and earlier forms of hurling would evolve into the major sports of the GAA, members of the leisured classes became increasingly attracted to cricket, that most quintessentially English of games, during the first half of the nineteenth century.

The first cricket match to be played in Ireland took place as early as 1792 on grounds adjacent to the home of the Viceroy, Lord Westmoreland, and featured on

---

⁶ See J. Sugden and A. Bairner, *Sport, Sectarianism and Society in a Divided Ireland* (Leicester, 1993).
⁷ See A. Bairner, 'The GAA in a Global Sporting Context', in D. McAnallen, D. Hassan, and R. Hegarty (eds.), *The Evolution of the GAA. Ulaidh, Éire agus Eile* (Belfast, 2009), 220–9.
⁸ T. Wynne and C. Glennon, *Ninety Years of the Irish Hockey Union* (Naas, 1985), 177.
⁹ See Bairner, 'Irish Sport', 192–3.

one side members of the British Army and, on the other, a number of Anglo-Irish gentlemen, including, almost certainly, the future Duke of Wellington.[10] So embedded in Anglo-Irish life did cricket become that one might easily assume that only Protestants and those with a strong attachment to the union of Ireland and Britain would have favoured this English pastime. It is certainly true that, until relatively recently with the emergence of Ed Joyce (Middlesex), Eoin Morgan (Middlesex), and Niall O'Brien (Northamptonshire), those few Irishmen who have played county cricket in England have tended to be from what might loosely be described as an Anglo-Irish background. Even Samuel Beckett, celebrated Irish writer and the only Nobel Prize winner to feature in the pages of cricket's 'bible', *Wisden*, was a Protestant, educated at Portora Royal School in Enniskillen, County Fermanagh.[11]

It is too simplistic, however, to associate cricket with only one section of the Irish population or with one part of the country, the province of Ulster with its sizeable Protestant population. In terms of schools' cricket, for example, although St Columba's College, a Church of Ireland establishment, was prominent in the development of the game, so too was Clongowes Wood College, a Jesuit institution and the *alma mater* of James Joyce.[12] More significantly, as Hunt reveals, cricket was commonly the chosen summer sport of Gaelic footballers despite subsequent attempts by the Gaelic Athletic Association to proscribe participation in 'foreign' games.[13] Although de Bùrca suggests that 'the rapid growth of the GAA also brought to a halt the spread of cricket in rural areas where the game had gained a foothold',[14] in Westmeath at least, according to Hunt, 'newspaper analysis reveals that cricket experienced a period of steady growth, both geographic and demographic, throughout the 1880s and 1890s'.[15] Hunt's research shows that cricket was particularly popular amongst the farm labourer and general labouring classes, 'a finding that challenges the traditional perception of Irish cricket as an elitist activity'. Hunt argues that 'playing cricket presented members of this group with an opportunity to earn respectability, display skill, and win prestige in their own locality'.[16]

Two other studies have revealed the strength of cricket among the nineteenth-century Irish in the counties of Tipperary and Kilkenny, both strongholds of Gaelic games in subsequent years. Patrick Bracken reveals that there were as many as forty-three cricket teams in Tipperary in 1876.[17] Michael O'Dwyer shows that, in the nineteenth century, cricket in Kilkenny had spread far beyond the Big House to be played in every town and village, by labourers and peasantry alike.[18] At its

---

[10] See Sugden and Bairner, *Sport, Sectarianism and Society*, 48.
[11] J. L. Knowlson, *Damned to Fame: The Life of Samuel Beckett* (London, 1996).
[12] W. P. Hone, *Cricket in Ireland* (Tralee, County Kerry, 1955).
[13] T. Hunt, *Sport and Society in Victorian Ireland: The Case of Westmeath* (Cork, 2007).
[14] M. de Bùrca, *The GAA: A History*, 2nd edn (Dublin, 2000), 16–17.
[15] T. Hunt, 'The Early Years of Gaelic Football and the Role of Cricket in County Westmeath', in A. Bairner (ed.), *Sport and the Irish. Histories, Identities, Issues* (Dublin, 2005), 39.
[16] Hunt, 'The Early Years of Gaelic Football', 41.
[17] P. Bracken, '*Foreign and Fantastic Field Sports'. Cricket in County Tipperary* (Thurles, 2004).
[18] M. O'Dwyer, *The History of Cricket in County Kilkenny: The Forgotten Game* (Kilkenny, 2007).

peak in 1896, twelve years after the founding of the GAA, there were fifty teams in the county. If further evidence is needed, 'the great Parnell...inherited his father's taste for the English game...and he captained the Wicklow team for many years before entering nationalist politics'.[19] Moreover, other luminaries of the Irish nationalist movement such as John Redmond and his brother, Willie, both educated at Clongowes, were also enthusiastic cricketers, whilst Tom Kettle, another old Clongownian, retained a great affection for the game throughout a life cut short by the Great War.[20]

Cricket, perhaps surprisingly, was much slower to establish a foothold in Ulster than in other parts of the island. Although regarded by some to be just as 'foreign' as association football or hockey, the development of cricket in Ulster differs to some extent from that of these other sports. Ulster clubs competed in two separate senior leagues—the North West Cricket Union which administers the game in counties Londonderry, Donegal, Fermanagh, and Tyrone and the Northern Cricket Union. Although the game appears to have developed more slowly in the north of Ireland than in the south, the Lisburn club in County Down was founded as early as 1836.[21] Other pioneers included North Down (founded in 1857) and the North of Ireland Cricket Club (founded in 1859). Donegal has been the only one of the three Ulster counties now located in the Republic of Ireland that has continued to make a significant contribution to cricket in post-independence Ireland, with the St Johnston club very much to the fore. In Northern Ireland the game has come to be regarded as a predominantly, although not exclusively, Protestant and unionist affair and by implication a non-Irish pastime.[22]

THE DEVELOPMENT OF 'FOREIGN' GAMES IN ULSTER

Although claims have been made that golf enjoyed an early Celtic existence in Ireland[23] and despite the fact that the game has certainly been traced back to 1606 and the Hamilton and Montgomery Plantation of Ulster,[24] golf, together with numerous other sports, has tended to be ignored in most of the literature on sport in the province. The primary focus has been on association football and Gaelic games.

Viewed in a United Kingdom context, 'the game of association football came late to Ireland'.[25] The Football Association had been formed in England in 1863. Yet it was not until 24 October 1878 that the Caledonians and Queen's Park, both Scottish clubs, played a demonstration football match at the Ulster Cricket Club's

---

[19] Hone, *Cricket in Ireland*, 11.
[20] See A. Bairner, 'Ireland, Sport and Empire', in K. Jeffery (ed.), *'An Irish Empire'? Aspects of Ireland and the British Empire* (Manchester, 1996), 57–76.
[21] See Hone, *Cricket in Ireland*, 38.
[22] See Sugden and Bairner, *Sport, Sectarianism and Society*, 50–2.
[23] See R. Browning, *A History of Golf: the Royal and Ancient Game* (London, 1955), 7.
[24] See W. H. Gibson, *Early Irish Golf: the First Courses, Clubs and Pioneers* (Naas, 1988), 1–7.
[25] N. Garnham, *Association Football and Society in Pre-Partition Ireland* (Belfast, 2004), 4.

ground in Belfast. By the summer of 1880, at least four Ulster clubs—Cliftonville, Knock, Moyola, and Banbridge Academy—were playing regular games and later that year, at the instigation of the Cliftonville club, the Irish Football Association was established.[26]

Particularly striking in terms of the geographical reach of the game has been the dominance of Belfast clubs in Irish (subsequently Northern Irish) competitions in the late nineteenth century and during the first half of the twentieth century. Cliftonville won the Irish Challenge Cup (Irish Cup) in 1883 and 1888, Distillery in 1884, 1885, 1886, and 1889, and Linfield in 1891, 1892, and 1893. The Irish League Championship was won by Linfield in 1891, with subsequent early winners being Distillery, Glentoran, Belfast Celtic, and Cliftonville. Early winners of the Irish Cup also included in 1890, the Gordon Highlanders, based at the time in Belfast, once again reflecting the influence of the British Army in the development of sport in Ireland. Beaten finalists included the Black Watch (1892) and the Sherwood Foresters (1897). Ironically, given the subsequent division of Ireland, and of football in Ireland, the next winners of the competition not located in the greater Belfast area were Shelbourne (1906) and Bohemians (1908), both from Dublin. Shelbourne repeated the feat in 1911 and 1920 and both they and Bohemians were beaten finalists on numerous occasions. The first Ulster winners of the Irish Cup from outside Belfast were Ards (Newtownards) who won the competition in 1927. No clubs from the outer Ulster counties of Cavan, Monaghan, or Donegal have ever won the cup. As regards the Irish League Championship, an even starker picture emerges. This competition was not won by a club from outside Belfast until 1952 when Glenavon, from Lurgan in County Armagh, broke the city's monopoly.

This Belfast hegemony in association football is in marked contrast with the situation in hockey, another of the sports stigmatized by Gaelic revivalists as a 'foreign' or 'garrison' game. Yet hockey has consistently proved at least as popular in smaller towns as in Belfast. Prominent early hockey clubs in Ulster included North Down (based in Comber) and Banbridge, also in County Down. Other centres of the game in its formative years were Portrush, Newry, Newtownards, and Killyleagh, with school hockey being quickly established in Bushmills, Ballycastle, Strabane, Cookstown, and Kilkeel. The Irish Senior Cup was won by an Ulster team (Banbridge) for the first time in 1907. The club repeated this achievement in 1923, 1924, and 1926 with Lisnagarvey (from Lisburn, County Down) emulating the feat in 1925 and 1927 and Cliftonville (from Belfast) winning in 1932.

The Ulster Branch of the Irish Rugby Football Union was formed in 1879. The grassroots of the game are to be found in the state grammar schools, with a highly competitive Schools' Cup competition being contested fiercely each year. Three Belfast schools—Methodist College with thirty-two victories, the Royal Belfast Academical Institution with twenty-nine, and Campbell College with twenty-two—have dominated the competition. In terms of senior club rugby, however, the pattern has been rather different with clubs from rural or small town Ulster coming to the fore in the modern era. This is reflected in the location of leading Ulster clubs in

---

[26] See Garnham, *Association Football*, 5.

the 2009–10 Allied Irish Bank League. Ballymena (County Antrim), Dungannon (County Tyrone), and Ballynahinch (County Down) played in Division 1A whilst the highest placed Belfast clubs—Belfast Harlequins and Malone—were in Division 1B. A majority of Ulster clubs were to be found in Division 3. These were Ards (County Down), Banbridge (County Down), Queen's (Belfast), Portadown (County Armagh), Rainey Old Boys (County Londonderry), and Instonians (Belfast).

This means that all but one of the counties of Northern Ireland was operating in the upper echelons of senior rugby in Ireland. Monaghan Rugby Club, meanwhile, was arguably the most successful team from Ulster's remaining counties, competing in the Foster Cup, a competition for junior clubs and minor teams from senior clubs. On a more positive note, the Ulster Branch is clearly trying to promote the game beyond its Northern Ireland base with its Donegal Project.[27] Given the increasingly high profile of rugby in the Republic of Ireland, this may yet prove to be a more productive task than attempting to develop the game in Northern Ireland's Catholic grammar schools where Gaelic football is dominant and rugby is still frequently prohibited.

Today Ulster rugby is primarily identified with the Ulster professional team which, in 1998–99, following the introduction of professionalism, became the first Irish province to win the Heineken Cup. Ulster had also established an impressive record in interprovincial competition during the amateur era. In recent years, however, both Leinster and Munster have been more successful on the European stage and also in terms of providing players for the Irish national side. That said, many of Ireland's rugby greats have been Ulstermen. These include Jackie Kyle (forty-six caps), Mike Gibson (sixty-nine caps), and Willie John McBride (sixty-three caps). So, using evidence drawn from the examples of football, hockey, and rugby, Ulster emerges as very much a six-county sporting entity. In other sports, however, the nine-county province is not only the formal organizing principle but also a highly visible reality.

THE GAA AND SHIFTING IDENTITIES

One major sporting organization which undeniably takes the idea of a nine-county Ulster seriously, both in theory and in practice, is the GAA. To take hurling first, as Seamus King notes, there were two forms of the traditional game of hurling— 'commons' or *camánacht*, also known as 'shinny' in County Antrim, and *iomáin* or *báire*, a summer game played largely in the south of Ireland and generally regarded as an aristocratic activity.[28] With reference to the former, it is possible, according to Ó Maolfabhail, 'the game spread southward from the north-east with the rise of northern influence which took place between the fourth and seventh centuries'.[29]

---

[27] <http://www.irishrugby.ie/22_96.php>. Accessed 12 January 2011.
[28] See S. J. King, *A History of Hurling* (Dublin, 1998).
[29] A. Ó Maolfabhail, *Camán: Two Thousand Years of Hurling in Ireland* (Dundalk, 1973), 9.

The northern version—*camánacht*—was well remembered throughout most of Ireland in the nineteenth century—but was closely linked to the fate of the Gaelic language. Summer hurling, on the other hand, was transformed into an activity more commonly associated with opposition to British culture and, by extension, British rule. Curiously, *camánacht* was kept alive in no small measure by the students and graduates of Trinity College Dublin.[30] Despite such efforts, however, 'there is no doubt that hurling was in a precarious state when Michael Cusack turned his attention to it' following the formation of the GAA.[31] The task of drafting the agreed rules of hurling was assigned to Maurice Davin who, whilst adopting elements of both traditional forms, drew largely upon *iomáin*.[32] Ulster, by way of Trinity College, had played its part in the reinvention of hurling but its contribution to the modern sport was, and has remained, relatively small.

The early connections of Ulster to the GAA are few. Although Michael Cusack, the driving force behind the Gaelic games movement, had taught at St Colman's College in Newry from 1871 to 1874, John McKay from Belfast was the only Ulsterman to attend the GAA's inaugural meeting in Thurles in 1884. The limited support in the early days that emerged in Ulster for the GAA was surprisingly ecumenical, with prominent supporters of Gaelic games including the Reverend Samuel Holmes from County Down, Dr Larry Slevin from Armagh, and the Patterson brothers from Newry.[33] That said, this characteristic of the early years of the GAA in Ulster should not be exaggerated. Indeed, more important arguably was the fact that many northern nationalists, particularly in Belfast, had already been drawn to association football. This helps to explain why the province's major city was not fertile soil for the development of Gaelic games, with the major areas of growth occurring in the more rural counties of Cavan, Monaghan, and Fermanagh.

By 1888, however, Gaelic football was being played throughout the nine counties and hurling matches had taken place in counties Antrim, Donegal, and Londonderry.[34] There was then a steady decline in the fortunes of Gaelic games in Ulster until the end of the century which continued even after the formation of the Ulster Council of the GAA on 22 March 1903. In the period after 1916, the Association was subject to constant surveillance from the British state, specifically through the activities of the Royal Irish Constabulary. This policing of the Gaelic games movement persisted after partition and the formation of *An Garda Síochána*, in the Irish Free State, and the Royal Ulster Constabulary (RUC) in Northern Ireland. Nevertheless, 'in spite of obvious difficulties the GAA in Ulster enjoyed something of a revival in the second decade of the twentieth century'.[35] The year 1923 witnessed the opening in Cavan of Breffni Park which was to become so closely identified with Ulster football. Indeed, Cavan, and to a lesser extent Monaghan, dominated

---

[30] Ó Maolfabhail, *Camán, 9*.   [31] King, *A History of Hurling*, 237.
[32] Ibid., 237.
[33] See D. Hassan, 'The GAA in Ulster', in M. Cronin, W. Murphy, and P. Rouse (eds), *The Gaelic Athletic Association 1884–2009* (Dublin, 2009).
[34] See Hassan, 'The GAA in Ulster', 80.   [35] Ibid., 84.

Ulster football until the 1950s. Cavan went on to become the first Ulster team to win an all-Ireland senior title. That was in 1930 and Armagh had won the junior title three years earlier. Antrim's pre-eminence in hurling within the province had already become apparent, though the standard was generally low by comparison with the powerhouses of hurling in the southern counties.

One might be forgiven for thinking that partition and its consequences would have been less likely to affect Gaelic games than the so-called garrison or foreign games where representation of Ireland became a matter of contestation. For example, whilst the MacRory Cup in Gaelic football is contested by Ulster schools on both sides of the border (although it was last won by a team from outside Northern Ireland—St Patrick's, Cavan—back in 1972), the Schools' Cup in rugby union is very much the preserve of Northern Ireland's state grammar schools. It is important to recognize, however, that this has little to do with partition and is essentially a reflection of the ways in which these different sporting activities evolved in the context of the nine counties of Ulster. In fact, the reality was and remains considerably more complex than one might at first imagine. Whilst some of the 'garrison' games, notably rugby union and hockey, continued to be centrally governed from Dublin and remained representative of Ireland as a whole, the experiences of Gaelic games and association football are comparable to the extent that partition had an undeniable impact on both.

As an all-Ireland organization with provincial councils, the GAA was unaffected constitutionally by partition, at least in any formal sense. In addition, the Association was unequivocally committed to Irish nationalism, albeit with all of the internecine rivalry that this implied. It thus differed markedly from those other Dublin-based governing bodies which were obliged not only to operate in two separate jurisdictions but also to accommodate members with radically opposed political viewpoints. One might still hypothesize that the new political dispensation led to the emergence of two very different mindsets within the GAA. It has been suggested, for instance, that the GAA in Northern Ireland attained a *de facto* semi-autonomous status.[36] Even within the province of Ulster most Gaelic football rivalries tend to follow the contours established by partition—Tyrone versus Derry and Down versus Armagh in the North, for example, and Cavan versus Monaghan on the other side of the border. But the potential divide goes deeper than this.

Whilst the GAA in the Irish Free State (subsequently the Republic of Ireland) was able to play an important role in providing cultural and sporting ballast to the newly independent state and thereby to become part of the establishment, in Northern Ireland the Association continued to play its traditional oppositional role in the face of ongoing state surveillance (which included the occupation by the British Army of some Gaelic grounds, most notably that of Crossmaglen Rangers in south Armagh during the more recent Troubles) and increasingly violent attacks by loyalist paramilitary organizations. Ulster's border regions together with parts of greater Belfast were particularly vulnerable in this regard.[37] It is difficult to gauge

---

[36] See D. Hassan, 'Sport, Identity and Irish Nationalism in Northern Ireland', in Bairner (ed.), *Sport and the Irish*, 123–39.
[37] See D. Fahy, *How the GAA Survived the Troubles* (Dublin, 2001).

precisely what impact these differing circumstances had on individual members of the GAA, North and South. It seems that the GAA in the North, where there was some overlap in membership between Sinn Fein and the GAA, was more seriously affected by controversy surrounding the 1981 republican hunger strikes, with some Ulster clubs declaring their support for the hunger strikers and the Ulster Council fighting hard to maintain unity.

Similar tensions came to a head in the debate about temporarily rescinding the GAA's Rule 42 to allow Croke Park in Dublin to be used for rugby union and soccer international matches and, to an even greater extent, during earlier discussions in 2001 about allowing members of the British security forces (including the RUC and subsequently the Police Service of Northern Ireland (PNSI)) to have membership of the GAA.[38] Thus in 2005, 'Northern Irish' delegates, as they had done in 2001 when Rule 21 was repealed, voted in overwhelming numbers not to amend the rulebook. As was the case in 2001, their vote was widely interpreted as an expression of a hard-line, traditional nationalism, one increasingly confined to nationalists in Northern Ireland. The day after Congress voted to amend Rule 42 the editorial in the *Sunday Times* commended the Association and encouraged it to take the next step and repeal the rule altogether. 'The GAA's mono-culturalism', it stated, 'belongs in the early years of the 20th century, not the 21st, and that is where yesterday's vote has consigned it.'[39] It also bemoaned the votes of the northern counties:

> Unfortunately, the vote also revealed the traditional faultlines that run through the GAA. It is deeply disappointing that, after a decade of peace in Northern Ireland, the northern counties should vote in favour of the status quo. Their refusal to countenance change demonstrates how far the peace process has still to travel if it is to decommission mindsets as well as illegal arms.

Insofar as the editorial presented the political developments of the peace process in a singularly positive manner, it misrepresented the social and political context within which Northern Irish GAA delegates cast their votes. There is little appreciation of the ways in which the peace process, in its attempts to manage conflict and celebrate difference, has contributed to positive political change *and* simultaneously served to 'institutionalize sectarianism'. An alternative implication to be drawn from the geography of the vote might be: northern Gaels were more traditional, less globally aware, and less modern, than their southern counterparts.[40]

---

[38] It is worth noting that Ronan Kerr, a young police constable killed by dissident republicans in April 2011, was a GAA member. Indeed, fellow club members joined with PSNI officers in forming guards of honour at his funeral. See <http://www.tyronegaa.ie/category/club-news/>. Accessed 29 June 2011.

[39] *Sunday Times*, Comment: 'GAA Back to the Future', 17 April 2005.

[40] The exception here was Cork, the only southern county that voted not to amend Rule 42. Cork delegates were criticized for being 'out of touch' with their county membership who were said to favour changes to the rule. In recent years, divisions between northern and southern Gaels have not only been expressed in relation to GAA policy, such as Rules 21 and 42. The recent success of northern counties in the All-Ireland Gaelic football championship has given rise to debates concerning different styles of play. Further, it has been suggested by some northern GAA officials that the clamping of illegally parked cars outside Croke Park on match day unfairly targets vehicles from Northern Ireland! See *Irish News*, 28 November 2005, 11.

In addition to these constitutional differences of opinion, there has also developed a significant rivalry between the Ulster counties (particularly those within Northern Ireland) and the rest. This was especially true of Gaelic football (though not of course of hurling where Ulster teams were only weakly competitive). In no small measure, this has been fuelled by the relative success of northern counties since the early 1990s, with the focus shifting, it should be stressed, from Cavan to Down, Tyrone, Armagh, and Londonderry. During this period, the All-Ireland football championship has been won by Down (1991 and 1994), Donegal (1992), Derry (1993), Armagh (2002), and Tyrone (2003, 2005, and 2008). Of these, only Donegal is situated outside Northern Ireland. Thus, although it has long been recognized that the Ulster football championship is arguably the most competitive of the four provincial competitions, the extent to which counties in Northern Ireland may also have benefitted from financial support from the British government, not least in the form of lottery funding, is a matter worthy of debate.[41]

QUESTIONS OF IDENTITY

It was perhaps inevitable that 'British' or 'foreign' games would become embroiled in politics, not least if they happened to be relatively inclusive in their reach. As Garnham reports with reference to the pre-partition era, it seems that association football 'was both influenced by and affected by the politics of the day, and in some areas by allied sectarian considerations'.[42] Thus, 'its identity was eventually to be defined by some in terms of the national and political'.[43] Certainly, the influence of partition was immediate, direct, and persistent. Even before then, however, the sport had been affected by the various political crises that had occurred. For example, during the period that appeared to herald 'the inexorable approach of Home Rule',[44] Belfast's football grounds became embroiled in the political unrest. Glentoran's ground in the east of the city was used for unionist demonstrations, and Celtic Park in the west was used for Home Rule rallies and for the drilling of Nationalist Irish Volunteers.

Garnham further suggests that 'as early as 1893 footballers in Dublin voiced their belief that they were being excluded from international honours by an IFA dominated by the representatives of the larger northern clubs'.[45] However, it was not only Dubliners who were concerned with what were perceived to be pro-Belfast biases; similar complaints were being voiced in counties Armagh, Londonderry, and Tyrone.[46] What was undeniable was that football games in Ireland were becoming more and more contentious both on and off the field of play, creating a sense that even had Ireland not been divided, Irish football almost certainly would have been. In October, 1919 during a match in Dublin between representative teams from Leinster and Ulster, members of the crowd attacked one of the Ulster players.[47] Similar incidents

---

[41] See J. McKeever, 'The Coming of Age of Gaelic Games in Ulster', in McAnallen *et al.* (eds), *The Evolution of the GAA*, 30–41.
[42] Garnham, *Association Football*, 148.   [43] Ibid., 134.
[44] Ibid., 149.   [45] Ibid., 162.   [46] Ibid., 164.   [47] Ibid., 176.

occurred elsewhere such that, by 1920, most competitions had been suspended so that 'only the Irish Cup remained as a functioning all-Ireland tournament'.[48]

Following partition, soccer in Ireland had two national governing bodies, two sets of domestic competitions, and two national teams. Until the 1950s the northern Irish Football Association (IFA) continued to select players for international duty from throughout Ireland and, until the early 1970s, reference was still being made to Ireland rather than Northern Ireland when the 'national' team was discussed.[49] As the Troubles deepened, however, the IFA's team became increasingly identified with Ulster Unionism even though Catholics from Northern Ireland—Pat Jennings, Martin O'Neill, Mal Donaghy, and Gerry Armstrong, among others—were amongst its more prominent players. The fact that most northern nationalists supported the Irish Republic's team meant that at the level of the fans, at least the existence of two 'national' soccer teams reflected the sectarian conflict in the North rather than the constitutional status quo.[50] Moreover, in Northern Ireland itself, because the game is so popular with members of both political traditions, it has frequently provided a sporting space in which surrogate inter-community (and intra-community) rivalries can be fought out.[51] For example, matches between Belfast Celtic, a club with predominantly nationalist supporters and their city rivals, Linfield and Glentoran, who drew on mainly unionist support, were often disrupted by violence. Indeed, the threat of sectarian conflict was one of the factors which led Celtic to withdraw from the Irish League in 1949.[52] In the early years of the recent Troubles, Derry City was also obliged to leave the League for similar reasons.[53] For many years—with security issues again being cited as the reason—Cliftonville from the north of the city was forced to play its 'home' games against Linfield at the latter's Windsor Park in south Belfast. Even junior games and matches involving schoolchildren have fallen prey to sectarian tensions. Indeed, some leagues are virtually exclusive to one tradition or the other.[54] In sum, although association football may well be the national sport of Ireland according to some criteria, it appears to have done very little to unite the peoples of the island. This distinction it shares with the GAA.

In more recent years, the chasm between the IFA and its southern counterpart, the Football Association of Ireland (FAI) has widened, not least as a consequence of young northern nationalists opting to play for the Republic of Ireland rather than Northern Ireland. Just as partition divided Ireland, it also divided Irish football with the three counties of Ulster that remain outside Northern Ireland producing players—including goalkeepers Pat Bonnar and Shay Given, both from Donegal—for

---

[48] Ibid., 176.
[49] See match programmes for international fixtures during this period published by the Irish Football Association, Belfast.
[50] See Hassan, 'Sport, Identity and Irish Nationalism in Northern Ireland'.
[51] See A. Bairner and P. Shirlow, 'Loyalism, Linfield and the Territorial Politics of Soccer Fandom in Northern Ireland', *Space and Polity*, 2 (1998), 163–77, and J. Magee, 'Football Supporters, Rivalry and Protestant Fragmentation in Northern Ireland', in Bairner (ed.), *Sport and the Irish*, 172–88.
[52] See P. Coyle, *Paradise Lost and Found: The Story of Belfast Celtic* (Edinburgh, 1999).
[53] See V. Duke and L. Crolley, *Football, Nationality and the State* (Harlow, Essex, 1996), 70–6.
[54] See Price Waterhouse Coopers, *Creating a Soccer Strategy for Northern Ireland: Views of the Stakeholders* (Belfast, 2001).

the Republic of Ireland team. Despite episodic attempts to surmount divisions, Ireland, and with it Ulster, have remained divided in sport as in much else.[55]

In a variation on a common theme, historians of Irish hockey note recurring problems in relation to representative selections, anthems, and flags. Commenting on the period from 1916 through to the 1920s, Wynne and Glennon write, 'while the troubles in Ireland had little effect on hockey, nevertheless there were signs of the times. On the setting up of the Irish Free State (1922) the Royal Hibernian Military School was closed', thereby depriving the country of one of its most famous clubs.[56] More significant, though, hockey was now being played in two different political jurisdictions, hence the emergence of problems connected with representation.

The Olympic Games have created perennial problems for sports people in Northern Ireland and Ireland, as each is associated with a separate National Olympic Committee.[57] For many years, personal choice was often the decisive factor, with athletes choosing to represent Ireland or the UK in accordance with their political persuasions, or, just as often opting for one or the other (but usually Ireland) on the basis of pragmatism: the greater likelihood of selection in the smaller country. Many of these issues have now been resolved with the governing bodies of specific sports being formally affiliated to specific Olympic committees. That said, the related issues of flags and emblems have never been far away. In rugby union, matters came to a head in 1954 on the eve of Ireland's match with Scotland at Ravenhill in Belfast.[58] The unwillingness of southern rugby players to stand for the British national anthem prior to the game was an influential factor in the decision to move all future major international matches from Belfast to Dublin. Conversely, the agreement by the Irish Rugby Football Union in 1995 to add the specially commissioned 'Ireland's Call' to *Amhrán na bhFiann* (the Irish national anthem) before games in Dublin was an acknowledgement of the political and cultural sensitivities of Ulster unionists. The fact that the Ulster rugby team, with its home stadium at Ravenhill in Belfast, has to all intents and purposes been seen to represent Northern Ireland rather than the historic province adds further piquancy to this quasi-political mix.[59]

SPORT AND SECTARIANISM

Considerable academic attention focuses on the relationship between sport and sectarianism.[60] A survey of public attitudes conducted in 2003 provided information about the attitudes and experiences of people in Northern Ireland who play

---

[55] See Sugden and Bairner, *Sport, Sectarianism and Society*.
[56] Wynne and Glennon, *Ninety Years of the Irish Hockey Union*, 75.
[57] See Sugden and Bairner, *Sport, Sectarianism and Society*, 129–31.
[58] See S. Diffley, *The Men in Green: The Story of Irish Rugby* (London, 1973).
[59] B. McKendry, *Champions: The Players' Story* (Irish Rugby Football Union, Ulster Branch, Belfast, 1999).
[60] See Sugden and Bairner, *Sport, Sectarianism and Society*; A. Bairner, '*Sport, Sectarianism and Society in a Divided Ireland Revisited*', in J. Sugden and A. Tomlinson (eds), *Power Games; Towards a Critical Sociology of Sport* (London, 2004), 181–95; Bairner (ed.), *Sport and the Irish*; A. Bairner, 'Still Taking Sides: Sport, Leisure and Identity in Northern Ireland', in C. Coulter and M. Murray (eds), *Northern Ireland After the Troubles: A Society in Transition* (Manchester, 2008), 215–31.

sport as well as of members of the wider public.⁶¹ It was clear from these surveys that people in Northern Ireland, particularly males, exhibit high levels of interest in sport. In addition, there is an accepted belief that sport is, or at least certain sports are, implicated in those processes whereby cultural identities are constructed and reproduced. However, it is not surprising to find that opinions differ as to which sports actually perform this type of role. Most respondents, including many Catholics, believe that the GAA is an exclusive organization. Reference is often made to the use of the Irish national anthem, the flying of the Irish tricolour, and the overall symbolism that surrounds Gaelic games. However, when attention turns to association football, there is confusion as to whether it should be described as Protestant or neutral. There is no doubt the game is played and watched by members of both communities. On the other hand, the ambiguous responses may reflect the perception that this particular sport was controlled by Protestants, operating in the interests of their co-religionists, regardless of who actually played or spectated.

The divided education system in Northern Ireland appears as a major influence in relation to the sports that people play and watch. Curiously this was felt to be of more significance than religion, although it would be difficult to disaggregate the education system from religious belief in Northern Ireland. Few recognized, however, that sport may have contributed, albeit indirectly, to political instability by helping to reproduce sectarian identities and attitudes. On a more inclusive note, many people felt that a wider range of sports should be made available in all schools.⁶²

Most research has concentrated on male experiences and those only in relation to a relatively small selection of activities. Little attention has been paid to women's sporting activities or to individual, as opposed to team sports. In addition, for fairly obvious reasons, it is Northern Ireland rather than the province of Ulster as a whole that has constituted the unit of analysis for most scholars. The border areas merit more detailed attention. According to Hassan, 'Among the border people of Northern Ireland—mostly members of the minority Catholic community—the most popular cultural pastime is sport, specifically Gaelic football, hurling, and camogie.'⁶³ This is a large claim when one considers the rival attractions of alcohol and television, and Hassan provides no supporting evidence. More detailed explorations might well lead to more nuanced understandings of the meaning of 'Ulster' within the context of sport.

History and sport cannot be separated. As Connerton comments, 'concerning social memory in particular, we may note that images of the past commonly legitimate a present social order'.⁶⁴ The alternative, of course, is that they may destabilize an already fragile present. This was certainly the case in relation to debates about a proposed 'national' sports stadium for Northern Ireland. The British government

---

[61] S. Megaw, A. Bairner, and G. Fulton, *Sport and Sectarianism in Northern Ireland* (Office of the First Minister and Deputy First Minister, Belfast, 2003).

[62] See Megaw *et al.*, *Sport and Sectarianism*.

[63] D. Hassan, 'Sport, Identity, and the People of the Irish Border Lands', *New Hibernia Review*, 10 (2006), 26.

[64] P. Connerton, *How Societies Remember* (Cambridge, 1989), 3.

decided that the most appropriate location for a new 42,500-seater stadium was the site of the former Maze Prison (which housed generations of loyalist and republican prisoners from the 1970s until 2000).[65] All of the relevant parties initially agreed to support the proposal in principle. Subsequent controversy, however, shed light on the intimate relationship between sport and politics in Northern Ireland. A major complication was that the Maze prison was the site of the republican hunger strike in 1981 which led to the deaths of Bobby Sands and nine other prisoners. More generally, the very idea that the project should be referred to as a 'national' stadium for Northern Ireland was contentious.

Part of the unionist critique was also clearly political. According to the Amalgamation of Official Northern Ireland Supporters' Clubs, 'although the SIB (Strategic Investment Board) assured us that the site would be a neutral space, it is hard to believe that the site will not be honoured as a place of martyrdom turning into a ghoulish tourist attraction. This is unlikely to endear the site to an average sports fan who is not interested in such controversial and divisive symbolism.'[66] In the end, the project was aborted, dashed in no small measure by divided opinions about how and where historical events should be remembered.

Sports museums are relatively common features of the cultural landscape of North America and of many parts of Europe. This is hardly surprising. Museums are places in which memories are given meaning and few human activities are more enticing than sport in terms of imbuing specific memories with meaning. The Alabama Sports Hall of Fame (ASHOF) in Birmingham, Alabama, reminds state residents and visitors alike that 'the ASHOF is a magnificent state treasure, dedicated to the celebration and preservation of Alabama's exceptional sports heritage'.[67] What makes matters relatively easy for the museum staff, however, is the fact that the boundaries of Alabama are clearly delineated. The people and teams which the museum celebrates represent Alabama as a spatially identifiable entity. The word 'Ulster' on the other hand means different things to different people, not least in the context of sport. Representing Ulster poses problems that representing Alabama does not.[68]

Representation is an important concept in the world of sport. Athletes 'represent' their school, their club, their county, their province, their country, and so on. However, in this regard as in many others, representation has wider connotations which are bound up with the equally problematic process constituted by acts of naming. Acts of naming are of massive political and social importance because they are central to what Chang and Holt describe as 'the intricate intertwining of language, ideology, and identity construction'.[69] That which athletes represent has a specific name. This may be relatively uncontroversial—the name of a club, for

---

[65] See A. Bairner, 'From Sands to Sanchez: The Making of a "*National*" Sports Stadium for Northern Ireland', *Entertainment and Sports Law Journal*, 5 (2007) <http://go.warwick.ac.uk/eslj/issues/volume5/number1/bairner> (accessed 12 February 2011).
[66] Amalgamation of Official Northern Ireland Supporters' Clubs, *The Future*, 25.
[67] See <http://www.ashof.org/>. Accessed 12 February 2011.
[68] See A. Bairner 'Representing the North: Reflections on the Life Stories of Northern Ireland's Catholic Footballers', in P. Dine and S. Crosson (eds), *Sport, Representation and Evolving Identities* (Oxford, 2010), 217–38.
[69] H.-C. Chang and R. Holt, 'Taiwan and ROC: A Critical Analysis of President Chen Shui-bien's Construction of Taiwan Identity in National Speeches', *National Identities*, 11, 3 (2009), 301–30, 303.

example, or the name of a school—although even here the very act of naming can be fraught with difficulties. Sports people, more than most, are engaged in the act of representing specific geopolitical entities. In doing so, they confirm the identity of such entities. But sometimes these places and identities are contested, Ulster being a case in point. It seems that sport is a particularly good prism through which to begin to glimpse the complexities involved in discussions of place, identity, ethnicity, and nationality.

FURTHER READING

A. Bairner (ed.), *Sport and the Irish: Histories, Identities, Issues* (Dublin, 2005).
P. Coyle, *Paradise Lost and Found: The Story of Belfast Celtic* (Edinburgh, 1999).
D. Fahy, *How the GAA Survived the Troubles* (Dublin, 2001).
N. Garnham, *Association Football and Society in Pre-Partition Ireland* (Belfast, 2004).
S. J. King, *A History of Hurling* (Dublin, 1998).
D. McAnallen, D. Hassan, and R. Hegarty (eds), *The Evolution of the GAA: Ulaidh, Éire agus Eile* (Ard Mhacha, 2009).
J. Sugden and A. Bairner, *Sport, Sectarianism and Society in a Divided Ireland* (Leicester, 1993).

17

Agriculture and Rural Policy since 1914

Alan Greer

INTRODUCTION

This chapter considers agriculture and rural policy in the six counties of Ulster that formed Northern Ireland after 1921. First, trends in the socio-economic structure of the rural world are examined, considering changes in farm size, production patterns, and employment. Political developments and their influence, especially on prices and marketing, are discussed in two main periods: 1914–72, and 1972 to the present. This is interleaved with reflections about the political relationships between administrations in Belfast, London, and Dublin, and between government and farmers.

TRENDS IN ECONOMY AND SOCIETY

Before the First World War, rural Ulster looked very different from today, with the countryside dominated by farming and the horse and cart. Over the next century, particularly after 1945, the nature of rural society changed. While the importance of traditional farming has waned, rural areas—especially those accessible to urban centres—are still socially important as the countryside becomes a dormitory for workers in other industries. In 2009 agricultural land took up around one million hectares, 75 per cent of total area but a decline from nearly 90 per cent in 1918. This is reflected in development and urban sprawl, and although there are variations in remoteness, one estimate puts those living in rural areas at 35 per cent of the population.[1]

The basic influences on rural economic development were geographic remoteness, lack of natural resources, and the close trading relationships with Britain. While the Northern Ireland share of UK agricultural output has always been small (around 4 per cent of gross value added—GVA—in 2009), it has been an important export-oriented sector because production substantially outstrips local demand. Although profitable markets in other countries were opened up from the 1970s,

---

[1] Northern Ireland Department of Agriculture and Rural Development, *Rural Strategy 2007–13* (Belfast, 2006), para. 8.

Britain has been the main trading partner, the destination for the two-thirds of total agricultural output sent out of Northern Ireland and the chief source of raw materials. The contribution of agriculture to the total value of production in the regional economy peaked at around 20 per cent of gross domestic product (GDP) in 1948, but was just above 1 per cent (GVA) in 2009. This reflected the steep decline in the importance of farming although the official view emphasizes that the agri-food sector still made 'a very important contribution to the manufacturing and production base'.[2] Indeed, food and drinks processing (also utilizing imported raw materials) made the largest contribution to the sales, exports, and employment of the Northern Ireland manufacturing sector in 2009.[3]

TRENDS IN AGRICULTURAL STRUCTURE AND PRODUCTION

Major changes have taken place in agriculture since 1914, especially in the size and composition of the workforce, the nature of production, and in farm structures.[4] First, for many years agriculture, forestry, and fishing provided the largest source of civil employment but there was a long-term decline from the mid-nineteenth century. This was particularly rapid after 1945. Numbers working in primary agriculture totalled 48,000 in 2009—just 4 per cent of total employment and a steep fall from over 200,000 in 1923. Partly this indicates increased efficiency through mechanization but at the outbreak of the Second World War agriculture still accounted for around one-fifth of total employment. Family working has traditionally been important because of the owner-occupied nature of farms. In 2009, 70 per cent of land area and over half of all farm businesses were owner-occupied, although rented land using the traditional Ulster system of 'conacre' was crucial for efficiency (indeed a cultural attachment to the land made it difficult to increase the size of holdings through amalgamation). Farmers, spouses, and partners numbered around 35,000 in 2009 compared to over 70,000 in the mid-1930s, but conversely the proportion of owners in the total farm workforce had increased from 40 per cent to three-quarters. The vast majority of these worked on businesses 'unlikely to provide full time employment or an adequate income solely from farming activities'.[5] As a result, the survival of many farms depends on off-farm work, diversification into enterprises such as leisure and tourism, and on subsidies, mainly via the Common Agricultural Policy

---

[2] Northern Ireland Department of Agriculture, *Fifty Second General Report, 1992–93*, (Belfast, 1993), 13.
[3] Northern Ireland Department of Agriculture and Rural Development, *Statistical Review of Northern Ireland Agriculture 2009* (Belfast, 2010); Northern Ireland Department of Agriculture and Rural Development, *Size and Performance of the Northern Ireland Food and Drinks Processing Sector, Subsector Statistics 2008, with Provisional Estimates for 2009* (Belfast, 2010).
[4] See A. Greer, *Rural Politics in Northern Ireland: Policy Networks and Agricultural Development since Partition* (Aldershot, 1996), Ch. 1.
[5] *Statistical Review of Northern Ireland Agriculture 2009*, 41.

(CAP). Part-time working became more prevalent over the period, covering nearly half of all farmers and partners in 2009.

Although family farms predominate, hired labour has always been essential, notwithstanding claims that the period between 1841 and 1912 witnessed 'the virtual disappearance of the hired labourer from Irish agriculture'.[6] Hired labourers totalled around 11,000 in 2009 when they comprised around a quarter of the agricultural workforce, an increase of 20 per cent on 1923. Three-quarters were part-time and casual/seasonal workers—many drawn from countries in eastern and southern Europe—concentrated in the horticulture, mushroom, and meat processing industries. Indeed by the early 2000s, shortages of local labour had made migrant workers 'an increasingly visible social group within Northern Irish society'.[7]

Second, partly because the mild and wet climate favours livestock enterprises, the most obvious change in the face of the countryside has been the virtual disappearance of crop and cereal growing, which are unsuited to local topography and soil types.[8] Only 6 per cent of land was used for crops in 2009 (grown on 17 per cent of farms) compared with 26 per cent in 1923 and over 40 per cent in the mid-nineteenth century. Once-important field crops such as flax and oats almost completely vanished, the former reflecting the decline of the linen industry, the latter mechanization (oats was primarily used as horse feed in the last century). Potato production fell to around 5000 hectares in 2009 from over 65,000 hectares in 1923 but barley growing (now the main cereal crop) and horticulture (especially mushrooms) have become more important.

Conversely, with the exception of the Second World War a trend to grassland-based animal husbandry characterized the twentieth century. As Symons noted in 1963, the 'outstanding fact' of the agricultural economy was that 'the climate favours grassland farming and that Ulster's specialization in livestock and their products is a logical consequence'.[9] Grassland (including rough grazing) increased to 93 per cent in 2009 from 74 per cent in 1923, and livestock and livestock products accounted for around 80 per cent of estimated gross output. Cattle numbers doubled between 1923 and 2009 when they were reared on over 80 per cent of farms, peaking at 1.7 million in 2005. Income from cattle production provided the largest source of revenue for farmers, with milk historically the most valuable enterprise. The intensive livestock sector (pigs, poultry, and eggs) was an integral part of the agricultural economy, reaching its heyday in the 1950s when it accounted for over half of the value of agricultural output. It then declined from the 1970s, and in 2009 poultry meat accounted for 14 per cent of gross output, pigs 7 per cent, and eggs 4 per cent.

---

[6] D. Fitzpatrick, 'The Disappearance of the Irish Agricultural Labourer, 1841–1912', *Irish Economic and Social History*, 7 (1980), 66.
[7] K. Bell, N. Jarman, and T. Lefebvre, *Migrant Workers in Northern Ireland* (Belfast, 2004), 3.
[8] J. G. Cruickshank and D. N. Wilcock (eds), *Northern Ireland: Environment and Natural Resources* (Belfast and Coleraine, 1982).
[9] L. Symons (ed.), *Land Use in Northern Ireland* (London, 1963), 22.

Third, there have been changes in farm structures. A consequence of the land purchase acts from the late nineteenth century (culminating in the Northern Ireland Land Act of 1925) was that a political response to the Irish question fostered an industry based on small family-owned farms. Economic pressures worked in the opposite direction, however, and there was a remorseless reduction in the number of farms. A crucial political question was whether the state should attempt to slow down—or quicken—the 'drift from the land'. In 1939 for example, the Northern Ireland Cabinet considered action to speed up rural electrification and mechanization to help tackle the problems of the agricultural sector. Yet while there were many advocates of modernization, a senior official in the Ministry of Finance argued that promoting larger enterprises would lead to the destruction of traditional family farms, the maintenance of which he believed should be a government priority.[10] In the 1950s and 1960s, government-funded Small Farmer Schemes were introduced to hasten farm amalgamation. This was linked to an economic development strategy (crystallized in the 1964 Wilson Report) that aimed to create jobs in new industries to provide work for those leaving the land. While this approach was enthusiastically embraced by the Northern Ireland government, hostile rural voices still regarded state sponsored farm amalgamation as an attempt to 'crush the small farmer out of existence'.[11]

By 2009 the number of farm businesses (taking account of labour requirements, rented land, and production intensity) was just over 25,000 whereas the 1923 agricultural census enumerated over 100,000 holdings above one acre—although many were not agriculturally productive. Farms also became larger. In 2009, 20 per cent were above 125 acres, with average area per holding around 100 acres; 20 per cent were below 25 acres, compared with 70 per cent of 'significant' holdings of less than 30 acres in 1923. (These figures involve conversions between hectares and acres.) Nonetheless, in 2009 over three-quarters of farm businesses were still classified as 'very small', with just over 10 per cent 'medium' or 'large'. Of the 1500 large businesses, over 80 per cent had more than 125 acres, but nearly 15 per cent had less than 75 acres, indicating intensive production in sectors such as poultry.[12] The trend to fewer and larger farms also was accompanied by increasing specialization at the expense of traditional mixed farming.

AGRICULTURE DURING THE STORMONT PERIOD

Control over agriculture was transferred to the Northern Ireland parliament under the Government of Ireland Act 1920, and the constant presence since then has been the Ministry of Agriculture (later 'Department'), which succeeded the all-Ireland

---

[10] Greer, *Rural Politics*, 11–12; PRONI CAB/4/401, Agriculture Policy, 15 September 1938; PRONI CAB/9E/134/1, Mechanisation of Farming, September 1939.
[11] Greer, *Rural Politics*, 71–4.
[12] *Statistical Review of Northern Ireland Agriculture 2009*.

Department for Agriculture and Technical Instruction (DATI).[13] As noted by Lloyd-George, the intention was that the Irish parliaments would 'deal exclusively with the problems of agriculture and agricultural development in all its forms, legislatively as well as administratively'.[14] He also suggested that it was a mistake to divide responsibility for such a crucial sector, and partition was especially disliked by influential voices in British agriculture because it would undermine effective action against animal diseases. Indeed agriculture was a prime candidate for transfer to the proposed Council of Ireland, and animal disease administration remained a reserved matter until 1926.

Early problems resulted from the obstructionist approach taken by the provisional government in Dublin, which withheld records, blocked the transfer of personnel, refused a request from Edward Archdale, the first Minister of Agriculture, for a meeting to discuss the transfer of agricultural services, and tried to operate its own animal disease machinery in the North.[15] Yet once the regional administration had been successfully consolidated, its capacity for action was limited by the 1920 Act and by the dominant ideology of economic liberalism. Before partition, DATI saw its role as 'removing the obstacles which at present hinder in Ireland the due exercise of initiative in industrial matters, and to creating a state of things in which private enterprise can act with confidence and freedom'.[16] Economic orthodoxy post-partition was dictated partly by the reversion to laissez-faire in the UK after the end of the First World War but also by elements within unionism. Ultimately a struggle over the basic approach of the government was settled in favour of the 'populists' such as Craig and Andrews, who advocated a step-by-step policy with Britain. But there was also an influential 'anti-populist' strand, centred on Finance Minister Hugh Pollock and Head of the Civil Service Wilfrid Spender, that stressed strict financial autonomy and housekeeping, even if this meant lower living standards. Its practical impact on early agricultural policy was summed up by Pollock, who noted in his 1927 budget speech that distributing large sums of money among lots of farmers 'has no good effects whatever and is simply squander-mania... the agricultural industry will never be brought into a state of prosperity by a system of pauperization'.[17] So in the 1920s the Northern Ireland government rejected farmers' demands for subsidies and reduced land annuities, partly because they could not afford them but also because they were ideologically unacceptable and would place an unjustifiable burden on taxpayers.

Politically there was an elite level overlap between senior figures in the administration, in the high echelons of the Unionist Party (and government), and the leadership of the main agricultural organization, the Ulster Farmers' Union (UFU), formed in 1917. Key figures including Prime Ministers Basil Brooke and

[13] This section draws to a considerable extent on Greer, *Rural Politics*.
[14] HC Deb., Vol. 127, col. 1326, 31 March 1920.
[15] J. McColgan, *British Policy and Irish Administration 1920–22* (London, 1983), Ch. 6.
[16] Department of Agriculture and Technical Instruction for Ireland, *First Annual General Report*, Cd. 838 (Dublin, 1901), 21.
[17] NIHC Deb., Vol. 8, cols 1321–2, 11 May 1927; also P. Bew, P. Gibbon, and H. Patterson, *The State in Northern Ireland 1921–72* (Manchester, 1979).

James Chichester-Clark, and all seven ministers of agriculture, had landowning and farming backgrounds; Brooke, Robert Moore, and Harry West also were past presidents of the UFU.[18] These strands were unified by a consensus around unionism and the 'populist' principle of parity with Britain, which became institutionalized after 1945 as a sort of reward for the part played by Ulster farmers in the war effort. Parity however was always strongly resisted by the British Treasury, and also co-existed uneasily with a unionist demand that devolution should be utilized to vary programmes to suit regional conditions. Within this political context, the two central elements in the agricultural policy followed by the Northern Ireland government up to 1972 were marketing, and parity in prices and subsidies, with the former most important before 1939 and the latter from the Second World War.

EDUCATION AND MARKETING

For most of the inter-war period, the government used supply-side mechanisms to modernize farming and improve quality, prompted by concerns about the poor reputation of Northern Ireland produce in Britain. From the outset, policy aimed to develop the grassland sector and the first piece of farming legislation passed by the new parliament was the Livestock Breeding Act 1922. The other main elements of policy were improved research/education, organized marketing, facilitating agricultural credit, and preventing animal and plant disease.[19] Agricultural education was paramount because farmers had to be persuaded of the value of modern methods, and initially the government 'largely confined itself to the policy of educational activity' which DATI 'had been carrying out for all Ireland'.[20] This was linked to better science because it was a central conviction that lasting improvement lay not in subsidies but in the wider dissemination of 'knowledge of those principles of farming practice which scientific research makes available'.[21] Innovations in this area included the collaboration with Queen's University in the foundation in 1924 of the Faculty of Agriculture, and the establishment on the initiative of the UFU of an Agricultural Research Station at Hillsborough in 1928.

Attempts to improve marketing were hindered by the Government of Ireland Act, which prevented interference with trade out of Northern Ireland. However an amendment passed at Westminster in 1928 facilitated a suite of measures that introduced compulsory grading and inspection regimes for agricultural 'exports', notably potatoes, eggs, fruit, and livestock products.[22] Farmers, however, blamed depressed prices on subsidized foreign imports rather than poor

---

[18] A. Greer, 'Policy Networks and State-Farmer Relations in Northern Ireland, 1921–72', *Political Studies*, 42 (1994), 396–412.
[19] Greer, *Rural Politics*, Ch.2; P. Buckland, *The Factory of Grievances: Devolved Government in Northern Ireland 1921–39* (Dublin, 1979), Ch. 6.
[20] D. A. E. Harkness, 'The Evolution of Agricultural Policy', *Ulster Year Book, 1935* (Belfast, 1935), xiv.
[21] Northern Ireland Ministry of Agriculture, *Ninth General Report*, Cmd. 129 (Belfast, 1930), 5.
[22] Greer, *Rural Politics*, 35–7; Buckland, *Factory of Grievances*, Ch. 6.

marketing. For them the solution was comprehensive import control, a belief shared by key figures in government. In 1930 for example, Craig expressed hope that 'it might be possible by some form of protection—and I have always been madly keen in favour of keeping out the foreign stuff—to give the farmers of Ulster a fair crack of the whip'.[23] Such a policy was not in his gift but the situation changed following the rejection of economic orthodoxy in 1931. Still, the political unacceptability of increased food prices, and the need to maintain 'imperial preference' (favourable treatment for Empire produce agreed at the 1932 Ottawa Conference), meant that the most important agricultural products were exempted from general tariffs. Instead different combinations of quotas, subsidies, levies, and marketing schemes were developed for individual products such as wheat and bacon.

Protection was central to the effort of the British state 'to bring about the reorganization and rationalization of home industry and agriculture'.[24] In agriculture the main instrument was commodity marketing boards, facilitated by Westminster legislation in 1931 and 1933, the latter paralleled by the Northern Ireland Agricultural Marketing Act. Schemes were introduced in an incremental fashion, sometimes involving the creation of producer-controlled boards with trading and price-fixing powers—including those for pigs (1933), milk (1934), and potatoes (1938). After 1945 marketing policy was even more directly linked to the British approach and the regional Ministry became incorporated into Whitehall administrative arrangements. While the UFU preferred national schemes to producer-controlled regional boards, because they were the best way to maintain parity of prices throughout the UK, the Ministry always had serious reservations. The result was a hotchpotch of post-war programmes. Those for beef (the Livestock Marketing Commission was set up in 1967), potatoes, poultry, and flax operated directly under Stormont legislation; producer-controlled boards were created for products including pigs (1953), milk (1955), seed potatoes (1961), and herbage seeds (1964); while the schemes for wool (1950), and eggs (1957) included Northern Ireland in UK-wide marketing boards.[25]

From the beginning, the policy of the Ministry of Agriculture was highly controversial and was criticized by MPs and farmers alike. This transcended political divisions. Nationalist George Leeke hated 'throwing money away on senseless policies of research', while for Unionist Rowley Elliott 'all the available money that can be conserved for agriculture should not go so much for research as in the alleviation of the unbearable burden of rates'.[26] This highlighted the basic problem for the Ministry which was convinced that the conservatism of Ulster farmers bred a resistance to new methods, scepticism about the benefits of research and education, and a hostility to state intervention (although not to subsidies or import controls!). In an effort to assuage concerns about state control the Ministry always

---

[23] *Northern Whig*, 15 July 1930.
[24] S. H. Beer, *Modern British Politics* (London, 1969), 279.
[25] Greer, *Rural Politics*, Ch. 3.
[26] NIHC Deb., vol. 8, col. 2390, 27 October 1927; vol. 8, col. 216, 21 March 1927.

emphasized that its approach was based on consultation. A core value was that it was essential 'to work in complete understanding with the agricultural community, so as to provide that combination of effort which is essential if administrative measures for the development of agriculture are to attain the fullest success'.[27] Agricultural progress would be 'greatly accelerated if farmers were better organised', and the Ministry thought that its work could 'be done more efficiently and economically through organised bodies of farmers than through private individuals'.[28] So although the UFU represented only a small proportion of farmers (barely 15 per cent in the 1930s and only around half by the 1960s), it was given exclusive consultation rights over agricultural policy.[29] The Ministry believed that the cooperation of the UFU—composed of what the Union itself described as the 'most intelligent and far seeing of our men' who consequently 'carry more weight than their numbers might lead one to expect'[30]— was necessary to help convince sceptical farmers of the benefits of improved methods.

Nonetheless, the Ministry also argued that the individualism and lack of expertise of the Ulster farmer required 'a greater degree of state intervention in and control of agriculture than in the rest of the United Kingdom'.[31] This led to tensions in the relationship with farmers, and especially with the UFU, over marketing schemes in the late 1930s. In broader political terms, while representatives of the working class wanted democratic accountability of marketing boards to protect the interests of consumers, libertarian conservatives such as R. J. Lynn, the editor of the *Northern Whig*, complained about 'socialistic' interference with private enterprise. For one vocal critic of the Ministry, Independent Unionist George Henderson, the marketing legislation of the 1930s was 'Hitlerism run mad. The Potato Marketing Board, the pig board, the dog board and the hen board—there is no board under the sun which Northern Ireland has not secured, and they are retarding the progress of the farming community.'[32]

THE SECOND WORLD WAR

During the Second World War the British government controlled agricultural policy for the United Kingdom as a whole. The war effort was influenced by memories of 1914–18, when initially it had been assumed that 'business as usual' could be relied upon to secure food supplies—DATI for example limited its early action to a publicity campaign using posters, leaflets, and lectures. As food shortages and price inflation took hold, a state-directed Food Production Campaign was launched in late 1916 that combined guaranteed prices for cereals (never paid because market

---

[27] Northern Ireland Ministry of Agriculture, *Second General Report, 1922–23* (Belfast, 1924), 1.
[28] NIHC Deb., vol. 7, col. 605, 20 April 1926.
[29] Greer, 'Policy Networks' 404–6.   [30] *Farmers' Journal* (May 1937), 1019.
[31] Buckland, *Factory of Grievances*, 131.
[32] NIHC Deb., vol. 21, col. 1901, 26 October 1938.

prices remained high), decentralized administration, and the ultimate sanction of the dispossession of the land of inefficient farmers and landowners. Controversially, in the wake of the Easter Rising and the refusal to introduce conscription, this campaign extended to Ireland, where DATI exercised statutory powers with the assistance of the County Committees of Agriculture. In 1917, under the Defence of the Realm Act, every occupier of more than 10 acres of arable land was required to plough an additional 10 per cent on top of that cultivated in 1916, subject to the proviso that no one should have to plough more than half of their total land.

According to the official historian of UK Agriculture in the Second World War, memories of how close the country had come to running out of food in 1917 were 'too vivid to allow any illusions' that what would be required could be 'merely a continuation of peace-time practices or even at most an intensification of them'.[33] There was general acceptance that the tilling of grassland and comprehensive state control would be necessary, allied to financial incentives and campaigns such as 'Dig For Victory'. Between 1939 and 1945, the Ministry of Agriculture was stripped of its autonomy (formal responsibility lay with the British Home Secretary) and became an agent of Whitehall in implementing the food production programme. The Permanent Secretary, James Scott Robertson, spent most of the war based in London where he kept in constant touch with relevant departments and attended meetings of the Food Policy Committee.[34]

The main problem for Northern Ireland was that production had to be reoriented back to crops. In this the government cleverly linked its livestock strategy to the tillage programme by arguing that every farmer had to realize that 'he was not growing corn crops which will go directly to feed the population, he is growing crops to preserve his own existence by producing stock and stock products'.[35] Tillage orders required farmers to cultivate a portion of their total arable area, although this varied according to soil conditions (see Table 17.1). At the peak of the war effort in 1943, 851,000 acres of land were cropped, an increase of over 80 per cent on 1939 and only a little short of the peak attained during the First World War.[36]

The scope to fit schemes to regional conditions was limited by constitutional formality and by the need for 'equality of sacrifice' throughout the UK. Nonetheless, unlike in Britain, farmers were not given specific directions about which crops to grow in which fields; rather within the overall quota it was 'left to the good sense of farmers to decide the type of crops to be sown or planted and to choose what new land would be broken up'.[37] Voluntary compliance was generally forthcoming and during the ten years of compulsory tillage, only 320 farmers were prosecuted for evasion and just four had their land taken over.

---

[33] K. A. H. Murray, *Agriculture* (London, 1955), 40.
[34] J. W. Blake, *Northern Ireland in the Second World War* (Belfast, 1956), 26–33.
[35] PRONI CAB/3A/116, 'Speeches by Craig, Brooke etc', Ministry of Agriculture Letter to Farmers, January 1940.
[36] Murray, *Agriculture*, Chs. 11 and 12.
[37] Northern Ireland Ministry of Agriculture, *Twelfth General Report*, Cmd. 295 (Belfast, 1951), 3.

Table 17.1. Minimum tillage quotas 1940–49 (%)

County	1940	1941	1942	1943	1944	1945	1946	1947	1948	1949
Armagh, Down, Londonderry, Tyrone and North Antrim	20	33.3	40	45	45	45	35	30	35	30
Fermanagh	20	33.3	40	45	30	30	25	20	20	20
South Antrim	20	33.3	40	40	40	30	25	20	20	20

Source: Northern Ireland Ministry of Agriculture, *Twelfth General Report*, Cmd. 295 (Belfast, 1951), 2.

The wartime food production programme facilitated the modernization of Ulster farming and changed the face of the countryside. As the Ministry of Agriculture noted, the 'outbreak of hostilities found Northern Ireland farms very deficient in the mechanical power necessary for the fulfilment of the formidable tasks created by the urgent need for greatly intensified food production'.[38] Strikingly, by 1945 there were 7300 tractors in the province compared to less than a thousand in 1939, eventually peaking at 32,000 in 1961.[39]

PRICES AND THE PARITY PRINCIPLE

Except for potatoes and milk, during the war Northern Ireland farmers received the same fixed price for their produce as those in the rest of the UK, that is, prices negotiated at the national level. Discontent among farmers early in the war led to 'the pledge' given by the British government in late 1940 that fixed prices and assured markets would be guaranteed for the duration of hostilities and at least one year thereafter.[40] As the war progressed farmers saw decisions about prices as an indication of what they could expect when it ended, informed by still fresh memories of the 'great betrayal' after the First World War when guaranteed prices were abruptly withdrawn.[41] So for the UFU the refusal to increase prices in 1944 not only destroyed 'confidence' but was a sign that with the 'great improvement in our military position throughout the world the history of the last war is repeating itself and that the country's pledges and obligations to its farmers are once again to be dishonoured'.[42]

As in the UK generally, post-war reconstruction had a high political priority. In 1943 the government set up the Babington Committee to report upon 'the future of Agriculture in Northern Ireland and to advise upon the steps necessary

---

[38] Ibid., 17.   [39] Greer, *Rural Politics*, 11–12.
[40] M. J. Smith, *The Politics of Agricultural Support in Britain: The Development of the Agricultural Policy Community* (Aldershot, 1990); P. Self and H. J. Storing, *The State and the Farmer* (London, 1962).
[41] E. Whetham, 'The Agriculture Act, 1920 and its Repeal—The "Great Betrayal"', *Agricultural History Review*, 22 (1974), 36–49.
[42] *Farmers' Journal* (January 1944), 116.

to effect its maximum development and improvement'.[43] Its scope was limited by two factors. First, recommendations needed to be consistent with the core elements of UK post-war agricultural policy, especially on prices; indeed on wartime reconstruction generally the lead came from the British government with varying degrees of input from the local administration.[44] Second, as Brooke noted, there could 'be no deviation' from the policy of maintaining 'parity' with Britain and that 'our working classes should not suffer by the grant of self-government to Northern Ireland'.[45]

In agriculture, 'parity' meant ensuring as far as possible that farmers received the same subsidies as those in Britain, which because of Northern Ireland's parlous financial state, depended on help from London. During the inter-war period, the government had tried unsuccessfully to persuade a hostile Treasury to accept the principle that 'whatever Exchequer assistance is given to an agricultural product in Great Britain shall be given on an equal basis by the United Kingdom Exchequer in respect of that product produced in Northern Ireland'.[46] Nonetheless in the late 1930s it did succeed in getting some British subsidies extended to Northern Ireland, for example on milk and fertilizers. The war changed everything and the most important milestone in agricultural policy during the twentieth century was the inclusion of Northern Ireland in Part I of the 1947 Agriculture Act (complementary efficiency measures in Part II were introduced under the local 1949 Agriculture Act). Based on the wartime system of guaranteed prices, this effectively instituted a price and production policy for the United Kingdom as a whole. It also marked the high point of the parity strategy. Typically the Treasury financed 95 per cent of the subsidies and grants paid to Northern Ireland agriculture after 1945 and farmers benefitted to a degree far beyond the capacities of the local exchequer. In 1961–62 for example, they received around £40 million in subsidies, five times the total budget of the Ministry of Agriculture.[47]

What the parity approach meant was encapsulated by Brooke when he tried to counter 'an impression in some quarters that Northern Ireland is in danger of losing its independence in regard to agricultural policy' by asserting that the aim of the government was 'to preserve our freedom to make, within the framework of the United Kingdom system, our own arrangements to meet local conditions'.[48] This was criticized by both unionists and nationalists, mainly because the price of inclusion in UK programmes was increased Treasury oversight and the requirement that Ulster farmers be subject to the same rules as those in Britain. On the unionist side, the chief criticism was that while parity in subsidies was imperative, this made it difficult to adjust policies, especially to allow lighter regulation. Nationalists, unsurprisingly, also had objections. As noted by one Stormont MP, Malachy Conlon, 'we in Ireland live under different conditions, our

---

[43] *Reports of the Agricultural Enquiry Committee* [The Babington Committee], Cmd. 249 (Belfast, 1947), 7.
[44] J. Ditch, *Social Policy in Northern Ireland between 1939–1950* (Aldershot, 1988), 88.
[45] PRONI CAB/4/735, Cabinet Conclusions, November 1947.
[46] PRONI CAB/4/397, Cabinet Conclusions March 1938.
[47] See Greer, *Rural Politics*.   [48] NIHC Deb., vol. 38, col. 38, 10 November 1953.

climate is different, our stock is different, our mode of living is different, our standards are different and everything else is different. There is no sense in legislating for us in the same way as for the people in England.'[49]

Nonetheless after 1945 Northern Ireland was integrated into a UK-wide agricultural policy, within which the government aimed to adapt programmes to local conditions. Unlike during the war however, 'parity' did not mean equal prices. As markets were decontrolled in the early 1950s, a deficiency payments system was introduced that made up the gap between market and guaranteed prices. Because this was calculated as a national average, it disadvantaged Northern Ireland producers whose distance from their main markets meant higher transport costs and consequently the government lobbied strongly for a compensatory arrangement. This led to the introduction in 1954 of the so-called 'remoteness grant', paid until 1977.[50] Despite initial enthusiasm, both government and farmers protested that the level of the payment (initially £1 million per annum) was nowhere near enough to offset the disparity in prices. Nonetheless the grant did give the Ministry greater flexibility to develop schemes to meet specific local problems in some areas, such as improving marketing and competitiveness (for example, funding the Agricultural Trust set up in 1965).

AGRICULTURE AFTER 1972

When Stormont collapsed in 1972, agricultural policy for Northern Ireland had been assimilated into one for the United Kingdom as a whole to an extent unthinkable in 1920. Indeed by the mid-1960s, some MPs such as John Taylor admitted that despite the importance of the agricultural industry

> the major decisions lie not here but at Westminster. Here we have the Ministry doing a great job but its actual power affects only how the remoteness grant is paid out, how it educates people and what kind of drainage is carried out. These are the only things in which we have essential power. Most of the other aspects lie at the door of Westminster.[51]

Two factors set the political context within which agriculture and rural areas developed: 'direct rule' from London and entry into the Common Market (hereafter the European Union, EU). First, direct rule changed the institutional framework. All ministers in charge of agriculture between 1972 and 1998, apart from the brief tenure of the Unionist Leslie Morrell during the power-sharing Executive in early 1974, had their political base outside Northern Ireland. They often were members of the House of Lords, shared portfolios were common, and they were criticized for being ignorant of regional conditions.[52] Yet the Ministry—renamed Department in 1973—still dominated the politico-administrative system, with the same locally based officials trying to maintain

---

[49] NIHC Deb., vol. 31, col. 579, 21 May 1947. [50] Greer, *Rural Politics*, 64–71.
[51] NIHC Deb., vol. 63, cols 317–18, 26 April 1966. [52] Greer, *Rural Politics*, 133–6.

the parity principle while ensuring that national and EU policies were adapted to regional circumstances.

Second, EU membership meant that crucial decisions, for example about Common Agricultural Policy (CAP) reform and price support, were formally taken in Brussels after negotiations involving British ministers. This added another layer to existing bilateral contacts, and one estimate put the number of meetings attended by Department officials at about 100 each year in both Brussels and London.[53] It also led to disputes about whether the British government was willing or able to protect Northern Ireland interests at EU level, especially over the introduction of milk quotas in the 1980. Nevertheless agriculture was still subsidized to a substantial extent by the Treasury and the EU. Payments for Less Favoured Areas, beef and milk production, for example, remained a core part of farm incomes, and the 'single farm payment' subsidy to farmers in 2009 totalled £339 million.[54]

In policy terms, after 1972 much continued as before, and the first Secretary of State, William Whitelaw, gave an assurance that the work of the Department would continue along established lines. Traditional concerns with prices and marketing were joined by newer issues including environmental sustainability and broad rural development. Efficient marketing remained central to the strategy for improving the competitiveness of the agri-food industry. However, the system of marketing boards developed from the 1930s was undermined by a combination of local and national developments, and EU requirements. In the 1960s controversial changes to some marketing schemes, including weakening producer representation, had been introduced after huge losses were incurred by the Herbage Seeds Marketing Board and by a subsidiary of the Pigs Marketing Board (Belfast Food Products Ltd), both of which collapsed in late 1966. At UK level the move away from producer-controlled marketing was highlighted by the abolition of the British Egg Marketing Board in 1968. More emphasis was placed on free market approaches, especially after the election of the Thatcher government in 1979. The local Seed Potato Marketing Board was wound up in 1982, then—in the case Pigs Marketing Board v Redmond—the European Court of Justice adjudged powers of compulsory purchase to be incompatible with the Treaty of Rome. Finally in December 1991, the Milk Marketing Board moved to a voluntary cooperative structure because it was time to return to 'a totally free and open market.... Choice and free markets will be the buzzwords of the dairy industry in the future.'[55]

From the mid-1980s the Department of Agriculture emphasized its wider role in matters such as environmental sustainability, food quality and safety, and rural development. In 1988 it created a division for conservation, land use, and diversification. A strategy published in 1990 aimed to make countryside management integral to all farming activity, and specific schemes included those for Farm Woodland and Environmentally Sensitive Areas. In 1991 the Department assumed responsibility for rural development, formally adding this to its title in 1998.

[53] *Farmweek*, 2 May 1981.
[54] *Statistical Review of Northern Ireland Agriculture 2009*.
[55] *Belfast Telegraph*, 7 October 1992.

Recognition that rural economic development involved the encouragement of non-agricultural activities as well as diversification of traditional farm businesses was embodied in EU-funded programmes such as LEADER.[56] Nevertheless, the core conviction of the Department remained that the agri-food industry played the key role in 'sustaining the Province's rural communities, contributing social as well as economic benefits and keeping the countryside inhabited, active and cared for'.[57] Generally, however, the approach to the 'rural' in Northern Ireland has always been focused on agriculture, relegating 'other dimensions of the wider rural economy to the sidelines of inquiry and policy formation'.[58] Rural development programmes (2000–6 and 2007–13) were funded from the CAP, as was funding farmers for less-favoured area status and agri-environment actions.[59] In 2009, 70 per cent of utilized agricultural area was designated as 'less favoured' (compared with EU and UK averages of 57 and 47 per cent respectively) and nearly 40 per cent of farmland in Northern Ireland was registered in an agri-environmental scheme.[60]

THE 'BELFAST AGREEMENT' AND AGRICULTURE

Despite the divergent political trajectories of north and south after 1921, commentators often note that 'in many respects the island of Ireland still functions like a single economy to-day despite partition'.[61] Even so, there was little cross-border cooperation between jurisdictions, except for low-level administrative contacts on issues such as animal disease and a few meetings in the 1960s between agriculture ministers Harry West and Charles Haughey. Direct rule and EU membership gave impetus to greater cross-border cooperation after 1972, and the British and Irish governments developed joint approaches on important issues, and relations generally were good at ministerial and senior official level.

At civil society level, links developed between the UFU and its southern equivalent—the Irish Farmers' Association (IFA)—especially at commodity committee level, facilitated by common membership of COPA, the EU-wide farmers' body. Nonetheless rural society in Northern Ireland had a political edge that resulted from an approximate correlation between Catholics and small farms located on poorer marginal land west of the River Bann and concentrating on extensive beef production, and between Protestants and larger, more specialized farms east of the Bann specializing in dairying, pigs, and poultry. The strength of the UFU was in the latter area, whereas the

---

[56] See M. Scott, 'Building Institutional Capacity in Rural Northern Ireland: The Role of Partnership Governance in the LEADER II Programme', *Journal of Rural Studies*, 20 (2004), 49–59.
[57] Northern Ireland Department of Agriculture, *Fiftieth General Report 1990–91* (Belfast, 1991), 49.
[58] J. Greer and M. Murray, 'Rural Ireland—Personality and Policy Context', in M. Murray and J. Greer (eds), *Rural Development in Ireland* (Aldershot, 1993), 3–4.
[59] A. Greer, *Agricultural Policy in Europe* (Manchester, 2005), 153–61; Northern Ireland Department of Agriculture and Rural Development, *Rural Strategy 2007–13* (Belfast, 2006).
[60] *Statistical Review of Northern Ireland Agriculture 2009*.
[61] S. J. Sheehy, J. T. O'Brien, and S. D. McClelland, *Agriculture in the Republic of Ireland and Northern Ireland* (Dublin and Belfast, 1981), 68.

Northern Ireland Agricultural Producers' Association (NIAPA), which emerged in 1975, drew its support from marginal western areas. Reflecting the political preferences of its members, it focused on developing contacts with nationalist elements including the SDLP, the Irish government, and key Irish individuals in Brussels such as Ray MacSharry.[62]

With the better performance of southern agriculture under EU membership, coupled with the more farmer-friendly policies of Irish governments compared to the UK, nationalists such as SDLP leader John Hume campaigned for 'a common agricultural regime for farmers in Ireland within the overall framework of European agricultural policy'.[63] While unionists accepted that 'friendly neighbours' should cooperate for mutual benefit, they wanted a more sympathetic agricultural policy at UK level, with proper consideration of the needs of Northern Ireland. Ulster Unionist MEP Jim Nicholson, for example, called the EU 'no friend of Northern Ireland' and claimed that the only solution to farmers' problems was to press the British government to ensure that the region's agriculture received special recognition.[64]

In the early 1980s Adam Butler, speaking for the British government, rejected an all-Ireland agricultural policy, because it 'would not be acceptable to the people of Northern Ireland, let alone to the Government'.[65] However, the political context was changed by the 1985 Anglo-Irish Agreement and the 1998 Belfast Agreement, culminating in the restoration of devolution in 1999 (although direct rule was reintroduced on several occasions). DARD retained responsibility for farming and rural matters, but under local democratic control several of its ministers were drawn from the nationalist parties. These included Brid Rogers (SDLP) between 1999 and 2002, during whose tenure DUP leader Ian Paisley chaired the Assembly's Agriculture and Rural Development Committee, and Michelle O'Neill of Sinn Fein chaired the committee after 2011. Agriculture also was a designated area of cross-border cooperation in the Belfast Agreement, with collaboration on issues such as CAP reform and animal health developed under the auspices of the North/South Ministerial Council (NSMC). The NSMC coordinated a response for Ireland as a whole during the foot-and-mouth disease outbreak in 2000–1, and in 2010 it formally agreed an All-Island Animal Health and Welfare Strategy. Nonetheless the overall approach changed little under the pressures of devolution after 1998, not least because Northern Ireland still had to work within a national and EU framework. Policy and strategy documents continued to reflect the main concerns around improving the competitiveness of the agri-food sector, environmental sustainability, animal health, and strengthening the socio-economic infrastructure of rural areas.[66]

---

[62] Greer, *Rural Politics*, 125–9, 160–5; N. Collins, 'Agricultural Policy Networks in the Republic of Ireland and Northern Ireland', *Political Studies*, 43 (1995), 664–82.
[63] *Belfast Telegraph*, 3 April 1984.   [64] Ibid., 24 April 1984.
[65] HC Deb., vol. 58, col. 876, 26 April 1984.
[66] Northern Ireland Department of Agriculture and Rural Development, *Strategic Plan 2006–11* (Belfast, 2006).

The period after 1914 witnessed great changes in the social, economic, and political structures of agriculture and rural areas in Northern Ireland. There was a dramatic fall in the importance of farming, and in the numbers of farmers and farm businesses. Increasing specialization in livestock virtually saw the end of extensive crop growing and of traditional mixed enterprises. In policy terms the regional government pursued a modernization strategy in areas such as marketing, and integrated this into a policy for the UK as a whole that emphasized parity in subsidies, especially from 1939. Despite the changed political context after 1972, the main lines of this approach were continued, even in the period when devolved government was resumed, albeit with greater emphasis on cooperation between north and south.

FURTHER READING

D. A. Gillmor, 'The Political Factor in Agricultural History: Trends in Irish Agriculture, 1922–85', *Agricultural History Review*, 37 (1989), 166–79.

A. Greer, 'Policy Networks and State-Farmer Relations in Northern Ireland, 1921–72', *Political Studies*, 42 (1994), 396–412.

A. Greer, *Rural Politics in Northern Ireland: Policy Networks and Agricultural Development since Partition* (Aldershot, 1996).

D. A. E. Harkness, 'The Evolution of Agricultural Policy', *Ulster Year Book, 1935*, (Belfast, 1935).

J. M. Mogey, *Rural Life in Northern Ireland: Five Regional Studies* (Oxford, 1947).

T. F. Stainer, *An Analysis of Economic Trends in Northern Ireland Agriculture since 1970* (Belfast, 1985).

18

Business and Labour since 1945

Graham Brownlow

INTRODUCTION

The era between the end of the Second World War and the first oil crisis in 1973–74 has come to be termed the Golden Age of Economic Growth.[1] This is evident from a range of European economic indicators, including growth in real GDP and in real GDP per capita. Table 18.1 takes a long-range view, setting the period 1950–73 in the context of the century since 1890. The UK economy grew more slowly than its international competitors did. Consequently, it fell from second place in real income per person in Europe in 1950 to tenth by 1979.[2] Within the United Kingdom, Northern Ireland performed particularly badly during this period; indeed, it has been suggested that it missed out on the Golden Age.[3] Table 18.2 shows there has been little convergence between GDP per capita, compared with the UK average, since the Second World War.

The headline unemployment figures for Northern Ireland and the UK for the period 1950–2009, shown in Table 18.3, support this view.[4] Moreover, as Tables 18.4 and 18.5 demonstrate, measured in terms of manufacturing output growth and unemployment rates, the region performed worse than Scotland and Wales.

There are a number of reasons why this might have been so. These include problems associated with geographical remoteness, which are often termed 'hard peripherality' in the literature. Isles and Cuthbert, in their pioneering *Economic Survey of Northern Ireland*, considered some of the 'hard' factors associated with remoteness, placing particular emphasis on the direct and indirect costs of transport.[5]

---

[1] N. Crafts and G. Toniolo, *European Economic Growth, 1950–2005: An Overview* (London, 2008).
[2] A. Maddison, *Dynamic Forces in Capitalist Development* (Oxford, 1991), 6–7.
[3] N. Crafts, 'The Golden Age of Economic Growth in Postwar Europe: Why did Northern Ireland Miss Out?', *Irish Economic and Social History*, 22 (1995), 5–25.
[4] By way of further illustration, Northern Ireland for the period 1950–73 had 'a negative residual of 0.53 per cent per year, indicating a weaker performance than would be expected simply from sharing in UK disadvantages'. Ibid., 11.
[5] K. Isles and N. Cuthbert, *An Economic Survey of Northern Ireland* (Belfast, 1957). Isles and Cuthbert also considered that remoteness tended to impede the efficient operation of the capital and goods markets in Northern Ireland relative to 'producers in the corresponding industries in good industrial centres in Great Britain'. Ibid., 48.

Table 18.1. European growth, 1890–1992: average annual growth rates

Period	Real GDP	Population	Real GDP per capita	Real GDP per person-hour
1890–1992	2.5	0.6	1.9	2.6*
1890–1913	2.6	0.8	1.7	1.6
1913–50	1.4	0.5	1.0	1.9
1950–73	4.6	0.7	3.8	4.7
1973–92	2.0	0.3	1.7	2.7**

* 1890–1987; ** 1973–87

Note: GDP and population are aggregates for 12 countries (Austria, Belgium, Denmark, Finland, France, Germany, Italy, Netherlands, Norway, Sweden, Switzerland, United Kingdom, all adjusted for boundary changes). The data for real GDP per person-hour are only available for a subset of these countries.

Source: 1870–1989, A. Maddison, *Dynamic Forces in Capitalist Development* (Oxford, 1991). See also N. Crafts and G. Toniolo, *Economic Growth in Europe since 1945* (Cambridge, 1996), 2.

Table 18.2. GDP per capita in Northern Ireland compared to the UK average, 1926–2000

	NI/UK
1926	62%
1947	71%
1960	63%
1973	73%
1986	80%
1991	75%
2000	76%
2009	79%

Source: Adapted from E. Birnie and D. Hitchens, 'Chasing the Wind? Half a Century of Economic Strategy Documents in Northern Ireland', *Irish Political Studies*, 16 (2001), 1–27. 3. The 2009 figure for Northern Ireland is for regional gross value added (see website of the Northern Ireland Statistics and Research Agency).

Table 18.3. Comparative unemployment rates for Northern Ireland and the UK, 1950–2009

Year	UK	NI
1950	1.4	5.5
1960	1.5	6.1
1970	2.4	6.1
1980	6.9	12.1
2009 (April–June)	7.8	6.9

Source: For the period 1950–1980 see L. McClements, 'Economic Constraints', in D. Watt (ed.), *The Constitution of Northern Ireland: Problems and Prospects* (London, 1981), 101. For 2009 see the website of the Office for National Statistics.

Table 18.4. Annual average percentage growth of net manufacturing output, 1948–70

Region	1948–51	1951–54	1954–58	1948–58	1958–70
N. Ireland	6.0	0.6	1.7	2.3	4.9
Scotland	3.4	1.2	3.1	2.6	3.8
Wales	9.1	6.3	3.0	5.8	4.6
UK	4.4	2.6	3.2	3.4	3.6

Sources: Calculated from Census of Production, and R. Harris, *Regional Economic Policy in Northern Ireland 1945–1988* (Aldershot, 1991), 16 and 52.

Table 18.5. Unemployment as a proportion of the civil labour force (expressed as a multiple of the average UK ratio), 1947–75

	Northern Ireland	Scotland	Wales
1947	3.9	2.0	3.2
1950	3.4	2.1	2.2
1955	5.3	2.1	1.4
1960	3.6	2.2	1.4
1965	3.7	2.0	1.6
1970	2.5	1.6	1.3
1975	1.9	1.3	1.3
Average 1947–75	3.47	1.80	1.77

Source: Derived from British Labour Statistics, 1886–1968 and later editions of the *Department of Employment Gazette*.

This 'hard peripherality' argument does not seem plausible. As Birnie and Hitchens observed, differences in transport cost were modest compared to other UK regions.[6] They noted that as a proportion of total gross output, the differences were minor. In any case, the lower wages in the region relative to Britain reduced any competitive disadvantage associated with remoteness.[7] Neither does historical evidence support a 'hard peripherality' interpretation, as is evidenced by Ulster's industrialization in the late nineteenth and early twentieth centuries. Moreover, international evidence provides examples of how technical and organizational changes can allow geographically remote economies to achieve high levels of living standards.[8]

More plausible are 'softer' arguments that focus on the links between remoteness, competitiveness, and economic performance.[9] While Ulster was a participant in the 'first industrial revolution' and developed industries such as shipbuilding, linen, textile machinery, rope-making, and tobacco, Birnie and Hitchens observe that even in 1914, weaknesses existed in the region's ability to adapt to structural change.[10]

---

[6] E. Birnie and D. Hitchens, *Northern Ireland Economy: Performance, Prospects, Policy* (Aldershot, 1999), 81.
[7] Ibid., 84.
[8] See G. Wood, 'Preface' to D. Brash, *New Zealand's Remarkable Reforms* (London, 1996), 7.
[9] For more details see Birnie and Hitchens, *Northern Ireland Economy*, 82–3.   [10] Ibid., 4.

Electrical engineering and chemicals, the basis of 'the second industrial revolution' of the 1880s and the succeeding decades, largely passed Ulster by, as did industries such as automobiles and consumer goods that emerged elsewhere in the 1930s.[11] Thus by 1945, opportunities for economic development had been missed,[12] although in this Northern Ireland was far from being alone among the UK regions.

MISSED OPPORTUNITIES

While the decline of traditional industries such as shipbuilding and linen was undoubtedly an important part of the explanation of missed opportunities, it is not the full story. There are at least three reasons why the composition of industries may not have been as great an impediment to prosperity as has previously been supposed. First, over time, declining industries became increasingly less important as a source of productivity gaps.[13] Second, Northern Ireland did not have a reliance on industries such as coal, steel, and automobiles that elsewhere in the UK were responsible for industrial decline.[14] Third, while other regions in Britain (and indeed elsewhere in the OECD) experienced de-industrialization, they managed to outperform Northern Ireland.[15] A clue to the ultimate sources of weak performance by Northern Ireland is that even when it did benefit from the arrival of new industries, as in the case of synthetic fibres, the opportunities associated with these sectors proved to be short-lived.[16]

Nicholas Crafts acknowledged that the efficiency failures had to be connected to a 'political economy context', but he did not explain why the incentives facing politicians and policy agencies were so perverse.[17] The economist, Charles Carter, suggested in the 1950s that devolved government in Northern Ireland had a positive impact on the region's economy.

> Things which would take months to settle within Whitehall can be settled in a day by driving out to Stormont and talking to the people concerned. Some industrialists are believed to have been glad to escape from the tiresome complexity of getting things done in Britain to a land where enterprise is made officially welcome.[18]

[11] Ibid., 4.
[12] The Wilson Report (1965) identified an over-representation of declining sectors (e.g. agriculture, textiles, and shipbuilding) as an explanation of poor regional employment growth. See E. Birnie and D. Hitchens, 'Chasing the Wind? Half a Century of Economic Strategy Documents in Northern Ireland', *Irish Political Studies*, 16 (2001), 6–7.
[13] On the sources of the gap and its relationship to structure see D. Hitchens and E. Birnie, *The Competitiveness of Industry in Ireland* (Aldershot, 1994), 92–3.
[14] In contrast, the Republic of Ireland's relatively 'late start' meant that by skipping, more or less, the Industrial Revolution it was not burdened with declining staple industries. See P. Sweeney, *Ireland's Economic Success* (Dublin, 2008), 21.
[15] Successful regions elsewhere continued to enjoy high levels of employment and output growth because these economies were flexible enough to create jobs in new ventures to more than offset the effects of the decline of older industries. Northern Ireland Economic Council, *Successful European Regions: Northern Ireland Learning From Others*, Research Monograph 3 (Belfast, 1996).
[16] The rise and fall of Cyril Lord's carpet businesses provides another clue on the sources of corporate failure in the region. See P. Ollerenshaw, 'Innovation and Corporate Failure: Cyril Lord in UK. Textiles, 1945–1968', *Enterprise & Society*, 7 (2006), 777–811.
[17] Crafts, 'Golden Age', 24.
[18] C. Carter, 'A Chance of Prosperity', *The Statist*, (November 1954), 3.

It may be, however, that the form of devolution practised in Northern Ireland gave rise to institutional structures that impeded adjustment to economic change.[19] Indeed, as Isles and Cuthbert observed, an 'attitude of mind which prefers safety through restriction' could produce adverse effects on industrial development.[20] Still, such a business culture could not have been so important without the existence of a political framework that supported vested business interests.[21]

Looking at the governing Unionist Party, a tension existed among politicians between the allocation of resources that would maximize the region's wealth by promoting creative destruction and the allocation that would maximize their own wealth and/or political support.[22] In Schumpeterian terms, it is the entrepreneur who is the innovator and prime-mover of progress. Economic progress is the product of 'creative destruction', whereby new products and processes are introduced and older forms of production discontinued.[23] Any convincing explanation of missed opportunities during the Golden Age, it is argued here, should centre on institutions, entrepreneurship, and creative destruction.

In contrast to Britain, there was minimal oversight of the disbursement of industrial grants in Northern Ireland until the rules were changed in 1963. This was to the advantage of local business leaders in traditional or declining industries seeking government finance to subsidize their own firms. This had the effect of inhibiting structural change.[24] After 1963 conflicts of ministerial interest were reduced as Northern Ireland was brought into line with British practice. The evidence indicates that this change (combined with an increase in the region's industrial policy budget) was associated with an increase in the quantity and quality of inward investment.[25] This improvement in the investment climate boosted efficiency.[26]

DECADES OF DECLINE

Political instability after 1969 did have negative economic repercussions, although precise measurement of these losses is very difficult.[27] As the conflict coincided with the onset of stagflation, it is difficult to disentangle empirically the effects of violence from the role of recession. One undoubted implication was that the conflict negated the main thrust of economic strategy since the 1960s; namely, the

---

[19] G. Brownlow, 'The Causes and Consequences of Rent-Seeking in Northern Ireland', *Economic History Review*, 60 (2007), 70–96; Brownlow, 'A "Tiresome Complexity"? Rent-Seeking, Devolution and Economic Performance in Northern Ireland, 1945–1972', in W. Garside (ed.), *Institutions and Market Economies: The Political Economy of Growth and Development* (Basingstoke, 2007), 39–65.

[20] Isles and Cuthbert, *Economic Survey*, 349.   [21] Brownlow, 'Causes and Consequences', 75.

[22] Brownlow, 'A Tiresome Complexity?'.

[23] The term 'creative destruction' was coined by Schumpeter. His economic vision was that any successful capitalism was characterized by a churn of old economic forms being replaced by new economic forms. A. Heertje, 'Schumpeter, Joseph Alois (1883–1950)', in S. N. Durlauf and L. E. Blume (eds), *New Palgrave Dictionary of Economics* (2nd edn, Basingstoke, 2008), 319–24.

[24] Brownlow, 'Causes and Consequences', 74.

[25] Ibid., 88–94.

[26] Ibid., 87–95.   [27] For an attempt see Birnie and Hitchens, *Northern Ireland Economy*, 149–51.

promotion of development by means of attracting inward investment.[28] This had been a particular feature of policy under Terence O'Neill, Prime Minister since 1963, and his energetic Minister for Commerce, Brian Faulkner. Moreover, violence tended to impede the promotion of tourism across the island.[29]

It is, however, implausible to attribute the economic failures after 1969 largely or exclusively to conflict.[30] As the Cairncross and Quigley Reports made clear, the pursuit of political stability rather than the promotion of market flexibility was the primary concern of policymakers.[31] The Cairncross Report argued that in the conditions of the early 1970s Northern Ireland was a special case, requiring public funds to support ailing firms. Likewise, the Quigley Report even posited the creation of public enterprises to act as an 'employer of last resort' in response to the violence.[32] The focus on employment stability thus implied costly interventions. After the introduction of Direct Rule in 1972, British governments ploughed increasing amounts of money into Northern Ireland. Public spending as a share of regional GDP grew from 21 per cent in 1950 to 52 per cent by 1977, peaking at 61 per cent in 1984 in a surge stimulated by de-industrialization and recession in the early 1980s.[33] The notion that the region's public revenue and spending should be in some kind of balance was a victim of civil unrest.[34] In effect, the economy was now characterized by 'soft' budget constraints.[35] Birnie and Hitchens concluded that if intervention was aimed at attaining British productivity levels then it must be judged a failure. However, the evidence suggests that the policymakers were trying to balance a range of economic and non-economic considerations rather than merely maximizing productivity.[36]

DE-INDUSTRIALIZATION

The 1970s represented the nadir of Northern Ireland's economic performance, for three reasons in particular. The old staple industries were in severe decline, as was the case in other old industrialized regions of Britain, Western Europe, and North

---

[28] D. S. Johnson and L. Kennedy, 'The Two Economies in Ireland in the Twentieth Century', in J. R. Hill (ed.), *A New History of Ireland, 3: Ireland, 1921–1984* (Oxford, 2003), 479.

[29] Ibid., 484–5.

[30] C. Ó Gráda, *A Rocky Road: The Irish Economy since the 1920s* (Manchester, 1997), 136; J. Bradley, 'The History of Economic Development in Ireland, North and South', in A. Heath, R. Breen, and C. Whelan (eds), *Ireland North and South: Perspectives from Social Science* (Oxford, 1999), 46–50.

[31] A. Cairncross, *Review of Economic and Social Developments in Northern Ireland*, Cd. 564 (1971); G. Quigley, *Economic and Industrial Strategy for Northern Ireland: Report by the Review Team* (Belfast, 1976).

[32] Birnie and Hitchens, 'Chasing the Wind?', 17–18.

[33] Johnson and Kennedy, 'The Two Economies', 468–9.

[34] The result was that the subvention by the early 1980s was equivalent to a quarter of regional GDP. Ibid., 469.

[35] M. Smyth, 'The Public Sector and the Economy', in P. Teague (ed.), *The Economy of Northern Ireland: Perspectives for Structural Change* (London, 1993), 136–7.

[36] For a more detailed analysis of the issues involved see G. Brownlow, 'Towards an Acceptable Level of Violence: Institutional Lessons from Northern Ireland', *Terrorism and Political Violence* (forthcoming).

America, and for much the same reasons. Dis-investment by externally owned firms was also marked. Worst of all, it was virtually impossible to attract new inward investment against a background of bombs, bullets, and communal strife. De-industrialization was the order of the day, or the decade. Plant closures meant a shrinking industrial labour force and rising unemployment.

Manufacturing output contracted by a remarkable 5 per cent per annum during the period 1973–79, and suffered further falls during the downswing of 1979–82. The fate of synthetic fibre manufacture, an industry new to the province at the end of the 1950s, is an extreme example of the widespread decline of industry. Rising oil prices (petroleum being a major raw material), excess capacity in synthetic fibre production in Europe, as well as increased competition from low-wage developing countries, ensured that Northern Irish industry was largely devastated by the early 1980s.

The contrast with the Republic of Ireland could not have been more marked. Entry into the (then) European Economic Community, aided by a hugely attractive corporate tax regime, made the Republic a magnet for internationally mobile capital. American enterprise in particular found Ireland a convenient base from which to penetrate European markets. Employment, incomes, manufacturing output, and exports surged forward in what were the early stages of a long awaited Irish 'industrial revolution'.

The Northern Ireland economy languished by comparison. Indeed it was during the 1970s, for the first time in Irish history, that the industrial centre of gravity of the island shifted southwards, in what was a remarkable reversal of long-standing economic patterns.[37] The challenge facing Northern Ireland at the end of the 1970s was twofold: first, to create a stable societal environment in which business could invest with confidence (almost certainly implying a political settlement of some kind); second, to refresh and restructure the Northern Ireland economy.

CONTINUITIES OF A KIND

The second oil crisis of 1979–81, and the accompanying economic recession, hit Northern Ireland severely. De-industrialization continued into the 1980s, though at a decelerating pace. The once great shipbuilding firm of Harland and Wolff lingered on but only on the basis of massive public subsidy. Most linen firms had long since withered away, the industry having been in secular decline since the international textiles recession of 1951.

The 1970s and the 1980s constituted a grim episode in the industrial history of Ulster. Still, it is only fair to add, while job losses in industry were steeper than in other parts of the United Kingdom, they were not wholly out of line with job losses in the older industrialized regions of the UK. In other words, de-industrialization

---

[37] L. Kennedy, *The Modern Industrialization of Ireland, 1940–1988* (Dublin, 1989).

was a feature of similar type regions of Western Europe and North America during the 1970s and 1980s.[38]

The policy response to the problems of the Northern Ireland economy, one beset by political as well as economic turmoil, was interesting. By 1979 an inter-related strategy had been codified in policy-making documents. The strategy was encapsulated in the guidelines on the aims, objectives, and special considerations that needed to be followed in modifying formal British institutions in the light of Northern Irish circumstances.[39] Such deviations covered a wide range of areas including the legal system, labour market legislation, and privatization.[40] Legal scholars have made much of the lessons that might be drawn from this divergence.[41] The economic implications were perhaps less evident.

The dilution of Thatcherite economic reforms, such as privatization and trade union reform, during the 1980s is one important example of the ramifications that could follow from this inter-related strategy. The need for the UK government to keep trade unions on board in the implementation of anti-discrimination legislation was a crucial consideration that explains why the province was not opened up to the full rigours of market forces.[42] The sequel to the moderation and delay in implementing Thatcherite policies was that the recession of 1991–93 was not as severe in Northern Ireland as elsewhere in the UK.[43] That the region escaped full-blown Thatcherism proved to be a mixed blessing, however. Sure enough, the economy was partly insulated from the recession of the early 1990s. But in the preceding decade it had not benefited from market-orientated reforms that would have raised potential economic performance over the longer term.[44] Again political and communal circumstances conspired to ensure that yet another opportunity was missed.

1998 ONWARDS: MIRACLE OR MIRAGE?

Unemployment fell sharply in the decade after the signing of the Good Friday Agreement. The unemployment rate went from the highest regional rate in the UK to nearly the lowest.[45] By the time of the publication of the second Varney Report

---

[38] For the classic survey of the issues surrounding the topic the interested reader should consult N. Crafts, *Can De-Industrialization Seriously Damage Your Wealth?* (London, 1993); more recent analysis can be found in C. Kollmeyer, 'Explaining Deindustrialization: How Affluence, Productivity Growth and Globalization Diminish Manufacturing Employment', *American Journal of Sociology*, 114 (2009), 1644–74.

[39] G. Brownlow, 'Institutional Change and the Two Irelands 1945–1990: An application of North's Institutional Economics' (unpublished PhD thesis, Queen's University, Belfast, 2002), 214–57.

[40] Ibid.

[41] J. Hayes and P. O'Higgins (eds), *Lessons from Northern Ireland* (Belfast, 1990).

[42] Brownlow, 'Institutional Change', 214–57.

[43] Johnson and Kennedy, 'The Two Economies', 479.

[44] N. Gibson, 'The Quigley Report and Prospects for the Northern Ireland Economy', *Irish Banking Review* (December 1977), 12–19.

[45] J. Simpson, 'Ten Years of NI's Economic Growth', 18 March 2008. Downloaded from <www.bbc.co.uk> 19 March 2008.

in 2008 regional unemployment (at 4.2 per cent) was lower than the UK average of 5.2 per cent and the EU average of 6.8 per cent.[46] Employment during the same period, buoyed by job creation in specialist call centres and information technology businesses, increased by 100,000. Moreover, this increase in employment was 40,000 more than would have been expected if the region had merely grown in line with the overall UK performance.[47] In a related change, Northern Ireland swapped its persistent pattern of net emigration for net immigration.[48] The composition of employment changed as well as its level: in particular, employment in manufacturing declined by 18,000 between 1997 and 2007. This decline of 18 per cent to 88,000 was less dramatic than the 28 per cent fall experienced across the UK during the same period.[49] Shorter dole queues and more people in work were accompanied by an improvement in productivity. This process of productivity catch-up began in the early 1990s and continued thereafter.[50] It is tempting to attribute this economic transformation to the Good Friday Agreement and resulting political stability, but this is to oversimplify.

The boost to immigration into Northern Ireland, for example, was the result of the eastward expansion of the European Union rather than being merely a vote of confidence in any economic and political settlement. Employment growth began in the early 1990s, so it preceded the Agreement.[51] Likewise, the persistence of internal weaknesses in the economic sphere, despite the attainment of political progress, needs to be recognized. By 2008, despite the decline in the rate of unemployment to well below the UK average, the proportion of the long-term unemployed was nearly twice the UK average.[52] As nearly a quarter of working age adults in the region still had no qualifications in 2008, it seems plausible to link the persistent problem of long-term unemployment to inequities in the schooling system.

Economic improvement, while undoubtedly in part the result of a boost to investment caused by greater political stability, was at least to an equal extent the result of macroeconomic policies pursued after 1997. Growth in the first decade of New Labour owed more to Keynesian than Schumpeterian economics. Economic activity was stimulated by a buoyant demand-side, which began with the UK's involuntary exit from the Exchange Rate Mechanism (ERM) in 1992, rather than any supply-side 'miracle'.[53] Gordon Brown, after a few years in which he stuck to the Conservatives' spending plans, inaugurated a public sector spending spree. Ultimately, it was this abandonment of fiscal prudence that is crucial to understanding the economy after 1998. The increase in public expenditure undoubtedly

---

[46] D. Varney, *Review of the Competitiveness of Northern Ireland* (London, 2008), 30.
[47] Simpson, 'Ten Years of NI's Economic Growth'. [48] Ibid. [49] Ibid.
[50] Per capita gross value added (GVA) in NI relative to the UK average increased from 74 per cent to 79 per cent during 1990–2002. NI's real total GVA growth between 1990 and 2002 exceeded the UK average in nine out of the thirteen years. See T. Morahan, 'Progress in the Northern Ireland Economy: A UK Regional Comparison', *Labour Market Bulletin*, No. 18 (Belfast, 2004) 29–37.
[51] Varney, *Review*, 30. [52] Ibid., 33–4.
[53] M. Kitson and F. Wilkinson, 'The Economics of New Labour: Policy and Performance', *Cambridge Journal of Economics*, 31 (2007), 813.

boosted output and employment. Health and education were major beneficiaries of this increase. Total UK public spending in the financial year 1997/98 was £320 billion. By 2007/8, it had risen by over 80 per cent to nearly £590 billion.[54] Between 2003/4 and 2008/9 UK public spending as a proportion of GDP grew from 45 per cent to 48 per cent. In Northern Ireland the increase over the same period was from 70 per cent to 73 per cent.[55]

This return to Keynesian deficit financing was felt especially in Northern Ireland because of the region's greater dependence on public sector employment.[56] The average public sector wage in Northern Ireland was 19 per cent higher than the average private sector wage.[57] Data from 2004, moreover, indicate that while full-time public sector staff earned more than their counterparts in Britain, to a larger extent the reverse was true in the private sector.[58] Against this backdrop of increasing government spending, consumers across the UK who were fuelled by easier credit and rising house prices, went on a spending spree of their own. Between June 1993 and June 2007 real personal debt in the UK increased by 137 per cent.[59] The £400 million Victoria Square shopping development in the centre of Belfast, which was opened in 2008, may be the region's most emblematic manifestation of the conspicuous consumption that characterized the boom.

Owners of bricks and mortar, as in the UK economic boom of the later 1980s and the Celtic Tiger phenomenon of the 1990s, were notable beneficiaries of this irrational exuberance. UK house prices doubled in real terms in the decade and a half following withdrawal from the ERM.[60] A variety of factors including tight planning restrictions, demographic expansion, and low real interest rates were responsible for the change in the UK housing market. Northern Ireland shared in this overheating of the housing market, and local supply and demand conditions made the situation worse. House price inflation in just a few years saw average prices in the region move from one of the lowest levels to one of the highest in the UK. House prices at the peak of the boom grew by an unprecedented 51 per cent between the second quarters of 2006 and 2007.[61] In addition to the drivers of demand found in the rest of the UK, one must add the impact of the neighbouring Celtic Tiger economy—also experiencing massive house price inflation, with spillover effects in Northern Ireland—as well as the region's relatively young demographic structure. On the supply side, the local planning system and the shortage

---

[54] R. Lea, 'Our Economy in His Hands…A Golden Legacy That Was Wasted', *Yorkshire Post*, 21 January 2008.

[55] Northern Ireland Economic Reform Group, *The Case for a Reduced Rate of Corporation Tax in Northern Ireland* (Belfast, 2010), 13.

[56] The public sector still as late as 2008 accounted for 67 per cent of GVA compared with 45 per cent for the UK as a whole. Varney, *Review*, 18.

[57] Ibid., 18.

[58] DETI, *The Northern Ireland Economic Bulletin 2005* (Belfast, June 2005), 150.

[59] O. Hartwich, B. Lipson, and H. Schmieding, 'More Mirage than Miracle: Assessing the UK's Economic Performance', *Policy Exchange: Research Notes* No. 3, (October 2007).

[60] Ibid.

[61] Average house prices in Northern Ireland peaked at £249,264 in August 2007. One indicator of just how unsustainable this situation was can be seen by comparing house prices with wages. Average earnings in 2007 (April) were at £17,225, the lowest of all UK regions. DETI, *Quarterly Economic Review* (Spring 2008), 11.

of social housing provision must also be considered important determinants. If there is a link between house prices and aggregate demand in the UK economy, as is generally held to be the case, then rapid house price inflation in Northern Ireland added a further demand-side stimulus to the region's economy.

LABOUR AND UNEMPLOYMENT

With regard to industrial relations after 1945, Northern Ireland remained part of a broader UK system although given its particular history, especially the continued existence of devolved government and the problems arising from sectarianism in recruitment and promotion, it is not surprising that the region at the end of the twentieth century had 'a more developed institutional architecture for industrial relations' than any other part of the UK.[62] In an important sense, pre-partition institutional structures continued to have an impact on trade unionism in Northern Ireland after 1945. Because the Dublin-based Irish Trade Union Congress (ITUC), established in 1894, remained the focus for trade union organization after partition, there were bound to be difficulties not simply with the new Northern Ireland government but also with how unions would fit into a UK framework as well as an all-Ireland one. The Northern Ireland Committee (NIC) of the ITUC emerged at the end of the Second World War from a series of complex discussions within the trade union movement and the Northern Ireland Labour Party. One of the problems it faced, however, was non-recognition by a Northern Ireland government profoundly suspicious of any links with Dublin. By the late 1950s it had become clear that non-recognition was an obstacle not only to constructive industrial relations but also to an initiative such as the new Productivity Council. In 1958 a Northern Ireland branch of the British Productivity Council could not be established since the Stormont government refused to accept members of the NIC on it. Only in 1964 following the election of O'Neill's government and pressure from some business and other groups was the NIC ITUC recognized.[63]

While much of the framework of industrial relations in Northern Ireland mirrored that in Britain, there were some significant differences in the legislation. The 1927 Trade Disputes and Trade Unions Act, passed in the aftermath of the General Strike, was repealed in Britain by the Labour Government in 1946, but the equivalent legislation for Northern Ireland was not modified until 1958 and even then left trade unions in the region with more constraints than in Britain.[64] After the introduction of Direct Rule in 1972, initiatives to improve equality and labour relations included the Labour Relations Agency (1976) and the Advisory, Conciliation and Arbitration Service (ACAS) in Britain. In the same year, the Fair

---

[62] P. Teague and J. McCartney, 'Industrial Relations in the Two Irish Economies', in Heath *et al.* (eds), *Ireland North and South*, 360.
[63] D. Birrell and A. Murie, *Policy and Government in Northern Ireland: Lessons of Devolution* (Dublin, 1980), 121–2.
[64] Ibid., 119–20.

Employment (Northern Ireland) Act led to the establishment of the Fair Employment Agency (FEA) to tackle the problem of discrimination in the workplace.[65] There was significant considerable opposition to the FEA from some quarters and considerable scepticism about its effectiveness in the short term.[66] However, at the end of the twentieth century a more positive view began to emerge, following a strengthening of the legislation and its incorporation within a broader equality agenda which sometimes went beyond that in Britain.[67] In 1989, for the first time, affirmative action was given statutory support with statutory duties on both employers and on the Fair Employment Commission (FEC). Later still, in 1998, the Northern Ireland Act established the Equality Commission whose declared mission was 'to advance equality, promote equality of opportunity, encourage good relations and challenge discrimination through promotion, advice and enforcement'. How much the fair employment legislation achieved is debatable, but an examination of evidence from the 1990s 'tentatively' indicates that the FEC 'enjoyed some success in its attempts to achieve fair participation through the negotiation and maintenance of affirmative action agreements with private sector firms and public sector concerns'.[68]

In addition to the institutional framework, two features of trade unionism and industrial relations in Northern Ireland during and just after the Second World War stand out. First, the dominance of British-based trade unions in accounting for the great majority of trade union members and, second, the increase in the incidence and duration of industrial disputes in Northern Ireland compared to the UK as a whole. The context for organized labour in Northern Ireland after 1945 was an unemployment rate generally much higher than other UK regions. Within the region, unemployment was generally higher in the west than in the east, higher amongst men than amongst women, and higher for Catholics than for Protestants. During the 1980s and early 1990s, unemployment rates for Catholic men were usually at least twice the rates for Protestant men, while the unemployment rates for Catholic women were also higher than for Protestant women but not by the same margin as men. Within Protestant denominations, members of the Church of Ireland had higher rates of unemployment than Presbyterians.[69] One of the most striking features of unemployment in Northern Ireland at this time was the significance of the long-term unemployed, defined as those out of work for more than twelve months. Between 1979 and 1997 the long-term unemployment rate in Northern Ireland was always much higher than for the UK as a whole, and indeed for any other UK region, and this problem was much greater for men than for

---

[65] B. Black, 'Industrial Relations in Northern Ireland: A Survey', *Industrial Relations Journal*, 15 (1984), 30.
[66] B. Rolston, 'Reformism and Sectarianism: The State of the Union after Civil Rights', in J. Darby (ed.), *Northern Ireland: The Background to the Conflict* (Belfast, 1983), esp. 221–4.
[67] C. McCrudden, R. Ford, and A. Heath, 'Legal Regulation of Affirmative Action in Northern Ireland: An Empirical Assessment', *Oxford Journal of Legal Studies*, 24 (2004), 363–415.
[68] Ibid., 415.
[69] G. Gudgin, 'The Northern Ireland Labour Market', in Heath *et al.* (eds), *Ireland North and South*, 269–70.

women. The reasons for this are unclear.[70] In general terms, however, a key factor in explaining relatively high levels of unemployment in Northern Ireland in the long run was the high birth rate. In Gudgin's words, at the end of the twentieth century, 'With the highest birth rate of any European region, Northern Ireland will always have a large potential surplus of labour unless employment expands at a rate much above the UK and European averages.'[71]

In 1950, the membership of the 68 British-based unions operating in Northern Ireland totalled 166,000. By contrast, the fifteen unions based in Northern Ireland had only 15,000 members.[72] British-based unions have retained their dominance down to the present day. Between 1953 and 1983 the Amalgamated Transport and General Workers Union (ATGWU) remained by far the largest union in Northern Ireland, although with the contraction in manufacturing it declined in both relative and absolute terms. By the same token, public sector unions became far more important within total trade union membership. Virtually all of these were British-based, with the important exception of the Northern Ireland Public Service Alliance (NIPSA) which became the largest public sector union in the region.[73] The marked dominance of British-based unions, together with the trade union density (actual trade union membership divided by the total potential union membership) between 1953 and 1983 declined only slightly for men (56.3 per cent to 52.9 per cent) but almost doubled for women (23.4 per cent to 43.6 per cent), again reflecting the growth in public sector employment.[74] Moreover, for most of the second half of the twentieth century and beyond, Northern Ireland had a relatively high trade union density compared to the UK as a whole. Thus in 2006, union density in the region (39.7 per cent) exceeded that in Wales (35.9), Scotland (34.6), and England (27.0). Further, in Northern Ireland, union density was higher amongst women (42.7) than amongst men (36.4), and markedly higher amongst workers over the age of 35 than those aged 16–34.[75]

On the question of how strike-prone Northern Ireland was compared to other UK regions, adjustment has to be made for the fact that the region has no coal or iron and steel manufacture, two of the industries which figured so largely in post-war British strike activity. Excluding those industries enables more meaningful comparisons to be made between Northern Ireland and the UK as a whole. The evidence suggests that between 1926 and 1937 Northern Ireland was comparable to the UK average in strike activity, but between 1941 (when labour markets tightened appreciably under war-time pressure) and 1952 the region became much more strike-prone than the UK average and that this position was retained through to the mid-1980s. Detailed data on the 1980–84 period indicate that in this period of economic recession some 62 per cent of all strikes occurred in the private sector, accounting for 44 per cent of working days lost.

---

[70] Ibid., 258–60.   [71] Ibid., 280.
[72] Isles and Cuthbert, *Economic Survey of Northern Ireland*, 212.
[73] B. Black, 'Against the Trend: Trade Union Growth in Northern Ireland', *Industrial Relations Journal*, 17 (1986), 72–5.
[74] Ibid., 77.
[75] H. Grainger and M. Crowther, *Trade Union Membership, 2006* (London, 2007), 1, 16, 24.

So, a majority of working days lost during this period resulted from public sector strike activity, which was notably higher than in the 1970s.[76]

STRENGTHS AND WEAKNESSES

An overview of the Northern Ireland economy in the early twenty-first century can identify a number of strengths and weaknesses. Educational standards, operating costs, improvements in infrastructure, and incentives could all be seen as strengths, even if the corporation tax regime could not.[77] As the two Varney Reports and the Independent Review of Economic Policy (IREP) made clear, a number of weaknesses still remained. There was the region's long-standing dependence on public expenditure, a situation copper-fastened by the inter-related strategy identified earlier in the chapter. While public sector employment in health, education, and administration accounted for a disproportionately high share of the region's employment relative to other UK regions, it is also the case that private sector employment in business services, finance, and communications were under-represented relative to the UK average.

The consequent over-reliance on the public sector illustrated below in Table 18.6 has recently been identified by the second Varney Report as one of the region's major challenges.[78] The second Varney Report stressed the need to 'rebalance' the public and private sector. The rationale behind this prescription was that the excessive reliance on the UK taxpayer for the prosperity of NI was not 'sustainable' for at least three reasons. First, it created a net fiscal deficit, in the form of a subvention of £7 billion per annum, equal to about 30 per cent of GVA. Second, there was a danger that the private sector would be 'crowded out'. For example, the relatively high levels of public sector wages, benefit levels, and public sector assets all appear to have distorted the operation of markets. Third, the regional composition of public

Table 18.6. Index of identifiable public expenditure per head in the UK, minus social protection and agriculture (UK = 100) 2002–8

	2002–03	2003–04	2004–05	2005–06	2006–07	2007–08
England	96	96	97	97	96	97
Scotland	121	120	115	119	122	121
Wales	113	110	109	109	110	108
N. Ireland	138	130	127	125	123	121
UK	100	100	100	100	100	100

Source: I. McLean, G. Lodge, and K. Schmuecker, *Fair Shares? Barnett and the Politics of Public Expenditure* (London, 2008), 39.

---

[76] B. Black, 'Collaboration or Conflict? Strike Activity in Northern Ireland', *Industrial Relations Journal*, 18 (1987), esp. 21.
[77] J. Fitch, 'Is Northern Ireland a Persuasive and Successful FDI Proposition?', *First Trust Bank Economic Outlook and Business Review*, 23, (2 May 2008), 1–4.
[78] Varney, *Review*, 18.

expenditure was skewed towards 'general public services, law and order, agricultural subsidies, housing and culture' rather than to outlets that directly increased competitiveness.[79]

Any assessment of the economic performance of the UK economy under New Labour needs to take account of the supply-side impediments that continued to restrain growth after 1997. Despite nearly two decades of economic reform, research and development and human capital levels in the UK were still inadequate.[80] These kinds of obstacles were arguably magnified in the Northern Ireland context. Inward investors often chose not to bring R&D functions despite political stability, nor did indigenous firms always buy into this aspect of the innovation process.[81] By the early twenty-first century, Northern Ireland still had one of lowest rates of R&D spending in the developed world; figures for R&D expenditure for 2005 indicate that at 1.2 per cent of GVA, Northern Ireland compares unfavourably with the UK average of 2 per cent. Moreover, Northern Ireland was the only UK region in which expenditure by universities on R&D persistently exceeded expenditures by businesses.[82] The innovation record, nearly a decade after the Good Friday Agreement, thus remained far from the Schumpeterian ideal.

The combination of a bloated public sector and weak R&D was linked to a more general shortage of entrepreneurship. A study for instance showed that of the 324,000 entrepreneurs on the island of Ireland only 71,000 were located in Northern Ireland.[83] Moreover, business start-ups were lower than the UK average, and the rate of 'churn' (at its simplest, the exit and entry of firms from an economy) was low.[84] The shortage of 'productive' entrepreneurship is perhaps the starkest example of the skill shortage. It is important to recognize that educational and training attainment remains very unequally distributed. This human capital deficiency was studied by the authors of the Independent Review in 2009, who found significant evidence of weakness relative to other UK regions, especially in terms of lower level skills.[85]

In terms of opportunities and threats, the future performance of the economy will in large part rest on the extent to which its entrepreneurs (both indigenous and foreign) innovate in an era of globalization. The fostering of strong links between Northern Ireland and the so-called BRIC (Brazilian, Russian, Indian, and Chinese) economies may be a particularly important determinant of how much the region will benefit from globalization in the decades to come. Inward investment from the BRIC economies may eventually provide the potential to increase the innovation and entrepreneurial performance of exporters. These links are getting stronger,

---

[79] Varney, *Review*, 18.
[80] N. Crafts, *Britain's Relative Economic Performance 1870–1999* (London, 2002).
[81] IREP, *Independent Review of Economic Policy (DETI and Invest NI)* (September 2009).
[82] DETI, *The Northern Ireland Economic Bulletin 2007* (Belfast, June 2007), 56.
[83] H. McGrath, 'Globalisation and its Impact on Northern Ireland', *First Trust Bank Economic Outlook and Business Review*, 22 (March 2007), 4.
[84] Varney, *Review*, 19.
[85] The region's working age population was characterized by a large proportion without qualifications (22 per cent compared to the UK average of 12 per cent). This was the highest proportion of any UK region. IREP, *Independent Review of Economic Policy*.

but there is still scope for further growth.[86] Just as Irish economic development in the nineteenth century was stimulated by the mobility of entrepreneurs across the Irish Sea, so Northern Ireland may in the future develop by attracting entrepreneurial firms from around the world.

CONCLUSIONS

Isles and Cuthbert observed that it was Northern Ireland's level of wealth rather than the lack of it that was the puzzle *circa* 1957. They wrote: '... in some respects the most interesting and important question relating to the economy of Northern Ireland is not why industrial growth has not been greater—why the growth in income and employment has tended to lag behind that in Great Britain—but why it has been as great as it has'.[87] By 2008 a large part of the answer to the question could be traced back to the subvention. Gaps in competitiveness remained a problem. The second Varney Report acknowledged, in an unusual and perhaps questionable choice of metaphor, that there were still no 'silver bullets' that policymakers could use to solve the competitiveness problem.[88] The publication of IREP in 2009 confirmed that despite decades of interventions, living standards remained substantially below the UK level. The Report viewed these lower living standards as being primarily due to a productivity gap.[89]

The fragility of the economy was further exposed by the recession that started in the second quarter of 2008. Some 33,000 jobs were lost between March 2008 and June 2010, taking the figure back to just above the September 2005 levels.[90] Furthermore in the two years before the start of the downturn, the region's manufacturing sector had grown by 8.3 per cent compared with the national decline of 0.2 per cent; but the recession had a particularly severe impact on the region.[91] Between 2008 and 2010 Northern Ireland's manufacturing output fell by 15 per cent, worse than the national decrease of 12 per cent. Output in 2010 was forced back down to its 2003 levels.[92]

The long-run development of Northern Ireland since 1945 indicates that the conjunction between factors such as institutional change, innovation, entrepreneurship, and productivity should form the basis of any informed explanation of its long-run economic backwardness. It is these aspects of supply-side competitiveness, rather than partition, peripherality, or political violence, which provide a more convincing explanation of its observed economic fragility.

---

[86] Indian firms in 2006/7 accounted for 24 per cent of inward investment in NI. As late as 2006/7, 80 per cent of external sales by Northern Ireland firms still went to EU member states. DETI, *Quarterly Economic Review* (Spring 2008), 14–15.
[87] Isles and Cuthbert, *Economic Survey*, 4. [88] Varney, *Review*, 1.
[89] IREP, *Independent Review of Economic Policy*.
[90] DETI, *DETI Economic Commentary*, June 2010. [91] Ibid., 7. [92] Ibid., 7.

FURTHER READING

E. Birnie and D. Hitchens, 'Chasing the Wind? Half a Century of Economic Strategy Documents in Northern Ireland', *Irish Political Studies*, 16 (2001), 1–27.

G. Brownlow, 'The Causes and Consequences of Rent-Seeking in Northern Ireland', *Economic History Review*, 60, 1 (2007), 70–96.

N. Crafts, 'The Golden Age of Economic Growth in Postwar Europe: Why Did Northern Ireland Miss Out?', *Irish Economic and Social History*, 22 (1995), 5–25.

IREP, *Independent Review of Economic Policy (DETI and Invest NI)*, September 2009.

K. Isles and N. Cuthbert, *An Economic Survey of Northern Ireland* (Belfast, 1957).

D. S. Johnson and L. Kennedy, 'The Two Economies in Ireland in the Twentieth Century', in J. R. Hill (ed.), *A New History of Ireland, 3: Ireland, 1921–1984* (Oxford, 2003), 452–86).

Northern Ireland Economic Reform Group, *The Case for a Reduced Rate of Corporation Tax in Northern Ireland* (Belfast, 2010).

19

Social Policy and Social Change since 1914

Peter Martin

INTRODUCTION

While much is known about how governments attempted to deal with Northern Ireland's problems, a modern social history of the region is only beginning to emerge. The Troubles have set historians' agendas until very recently with the effect that ordinary life was studied more for its contribution to the conflict than as a historical subject in its own right. As a part of the island of Ireland, Northern Ireland offers a useful contrast with Southern Ireland and helps historians to detect common themes despite the very different ideological and constitutional situations in the two jurisdictions. It was the longest running experiment in devolved government attempted in the UK and many of the problems it experienced are still relevant such as financing, regional underdevelopment, and pressure to maintain British standards of living.

This chapter has two objectives: to introduce the main changes in Northern Irish social life, as measured in the vast array of statistics produced by the government, and to examine how state policy changed in response. During the twentieth century, the Northern Irish state operated under three systems of government. From 1914 to 1921 there was no Northern Ireland—it was merely the six north-eastern counties of Ireland, ruled by Britain and administered by Dublin Castle. From 1921 to 1972 Northern Ireland became the first devolved government in the UK, exercising power over domestic matters through a locally elected parliament and government. This arrangement collapsed amid the violence of the Troubles. From 1972 to 1998, and sporadically thereafter, it was ruled by a British Secretary of State based in the Northern Ireland Office. It is particularly useful to examine the role of devolved government in the light of the new experiment in devolution now underway, not only in Northern Ireland but also in Scotland and Wales.

THE GREAT WAR AND THE INTERWAR PERIOD

Despite its reputation as the most industrialized part of Ireland, large parts of Ulster, including the six counties that would become Northern Ireland, were decidedly rural in 1914. In 1911, 53.1 per cent of the population lived outside towns and this would not reverse itself until the 1920s. In 1926, 50.8 per cent of the population was urban, and nearly two-thirds of this crammed into the Belfast area. There were therefore not two but three communities. The rural, agricultural community to the west had much in common with the border counties of the Irish Free State, whereas the industrial, urban society around the capital resembled the industrial cities of Britain. Finally there was a significant group of people living in small or large towns throughout the region. This clash of cultures was perhaps best expressed in the writings of Michael McLaverty whose novels *Call My Brother Back* (1939) and *Lost Fields* (1941) dealt with the dislocation of rural families in Belfast. Farms were small on average and relied on the labour of families, neighbours, and occasional workers to make them viable. The towns and cities offered a greater variety of work and a higher standard of living to those with skills but also reduced people's dependence on one another and made sectarian segregation more likely.[1]

Partition gave the incoming Unionist government a curious legacy. Although the new region was somewhat more advanced than the rest of the island, it compared less favourably to the rest of the United Kingdom. Industrialization was centred on Belfast and the promise of employment had been an irresistible pull for decades, resulting in some 415,000 of the population living in the new capital or its hinterland.[2] No other town compared; Derry had only 45,159 people, and no other urban area had more than 14,000.[3] Belfast became a densely populated industrial city; its 18,300 people per square mile in 1937 was comparable to Hull or Manchester, and this put pressure on housing and other civic resources.

As the wartime and post-war booms came to an end, the gap between incomes in Northern Ireland and Britain widened. In 1924, the average income per head was 61 per cent of the UK average; by 1937 it was only 57 per cent. This was caused by a combination of high unemployment and slow growth in wages. By British standards of deprivation, Northern Ireland fared badly.[4]

The new government was ostensibly in charge of a wide range of social policies. Education is examined in Chapter 13 of this volume, so the focus of this chapter is on health, housing, and social welfare. Traditionally the Unionist government's policy has been described as following 'step by step' with Britain in an effort to guarantee its people the same benefits as their compatriots to the east. Although that policy extended mostly to social services which could be compared in direct cash terms to Britain, it meant that a great deal of the region's expenditure was spoken for in advance. As the money for this was largely provided by reserved taxes, collected by the British exchequer and paid back after the costs of reserved services and the Imperial contribution had been deducted, there was in fact little flexibility. The government wished to bring services up to British standards, but from the British point of view this was unreasonable as Northern Ireland was comparatively lightly taxed. In 1923 the Colwyn Committee was set up to reorganize

---

[1] *Ulster Year Book, 1938* (Belfast, 1938), 38.
[2] W. A. Maguire, *Belfast: A History* (Lancaster, 2009), 191.
[3] W. E. Vaughan and A. J. Fitzpatrick (eds), *Irish Historical Statistics: Population 1821–1971* (Dublin, 1978), 48.
[4] R. J. Lawrence, *The Government of Northern Ireland* (Oxford, 1965), 32.

the system. The main effects of its report in 1925 were a reduction in the Imperial contribution and a decision that 'per capita expenditure in Northern Ireland should increase at the same rate as that in Britain'.[5]

This evolving relationship also affected the balance of power within the Northern Irish government. The broad church of unionism combined what have been described as 'populist' and 'anti-populist' factions.[6] The populists, Prime Minister James Craig, Minister of Labour John Andrews, and Minister of Home Affairs Sir Richard Dawson Bates, sought to maintain high levels of social expenditure. This would allow them to retain Protestant working class support, to implement some necessary social reforms and to maintain Northern Ireland's status within the UK. By contrast, the anti-populists, Minister for Finance Hugh Pollock—who was succeeded by John Milne Barbour—and the head of the civil service, Sir Wilfrid Spender emphasized following British budgetary policy and opposed what they saw as extravagant public spending. It is hard to separate the ideological elements of these differences from the demands of political expediency but both played their part. To some extent the two policies reflected the fact that unionism had been formed as a nineteenth-century alliance between Liberals and Conservatives who had very different ideas as to the proper role of the state.

The Northern Irish government was so limited financially that it had little freedom to make policy. As the British welfare system evolved, Northern Ireland moved to match it. Contributory widows' and orphans' pensions were introduced in 1925 and the system was liberalized in 1929 and 1931. This pushed the cost of pensions up from £1.1m in 1924 to £1.7m in 1931.[7] The higher rates of unemployment in the region (Table 19.7) also added to the costs of social welfare. The unemployment funds designed to pay those out of work were overwhelmed and required the government to bridge the deficit. For political reasons it was considered impossible to ask the Northern Irish people to accept inferior services, and Craig threatened to resign rather than let this happen.[8] The unemployment fund was £3.6m in deficit by 1925.[9] Increasing numbers of unemployed were being denied benefit as the state tightened its criteria. Furthermore, the Poor Law system in Northern Ireland provided only limited outdoor relief or other benefits.[10] The solution lay in partially merging the British and Northern Irish unemployment funds. This gave the region financial relief but increased British control over policy. It covered the cracks until 1932 when the effects of depression threw the whole burden back on the Northern Irish exchequer. The result was an even tighter budgetary policy than usual which further limited the government's scope for social reform. In 1936 an insurance agreement with the British exchequer helped the government deal with unemployment.[11]

---

[5] P. Buckland, *The Factory of Grievances: Devolved Government in Northern Ireland 1921–39* (Dublin, 1979), 92.

[6] P. Bew, P. Gibbon, and H. Patterson, *Northern Ireland 1921/2001: Political Forces and Social Classes* (London, 2002), 48.

[7] Lawrence, *Government of Northern Ireland*, 50.

[8] PRONI CAB/4/144, Cabinet Minutes, 26 May 1925.

[9] Lawrence, *Government of Northern Ireland*, 50.

[10] PRONI CAB/4/165, Cabinet Minutes, 20 April 1926.

[11] Buckland, *Factory of Grievances*, 93.

Between 1921 and 1927 there was a hint of reformist spirit in the Northern Irish government, and changes to the welfare system were contemplated. The Poor Law had remained more influential in the region than elsewhere in the UK and provided the bulk of free health care, emergency accommodation, and aid to the destitute and, in some cases, relief to the unemployed. In 1923 it catered for some 9896 recipients of relief and cost some £391,642.[12] It suffered from several problems, however. It was controlled by local boards of guardians and paid for by local rates, so standards of provision varied widely. It required those seeking help to apply to the guardians, thus creating a strong 'pauper taint' and the potential for corruption and patronage. One dispensary doctor under the system complained that tickets 'are issued by wardens and guardians who are, in many cases, grocers or publicans, and who dispense them as bonuses with quarter bottles of tea or bottles of stout, irrespective of the medical needs or financial circumstances of the applicant'.[13]

In 1927 a Government Commission recommended that the workhouses be closed and a clear distinction drawn between medical services and the relief of destitution. Financial difficulties and government inertia delayed any action on the report and, despite some detailed discussions by the cabinet, reform was delayed until after the war.[14] The failure to reform the welfare system was a serious mistake which badly hindered the state's ability to cope with the subsequent social crisis sparked by the Great Depression. As unemployment rose it challenged not only the state's ability to pay relief but many of the established social divisions and mores which contributed to the outdoor relief protests of 1932.[15]

Some lesser reforms were implemented. Medical benefit, the provision of free medical care to insured workers, was introduced in 1930, but Northern Ireland usually lagged behind the UK average in both health provision and outcomes. Death rates tended to be higher than the rest of the UK until about 1950 (see Table 19.1). Despite relatively good infant mortality figures at the turn of the century and a notable improvement between 1918 and 1923, Northern Ireland lost ground afterwards. It was not so much that conditions in Northern Ireland deteriorated as that they did not match the rate of improvement in Britain.[16] (See Table 19.2.)[17] Likewise there was a fall in the death rates from tuberculosis, and the proportion of total deaths it accounted for, but these remained among the highest figures in the UK, although sometimes exceeded by Scotland (Table 19.3).[18] Throughout the 1920s, 8–10 per cent of all deaths were caused by tuberculosis. Along with heart disease,

---

[12] Government of Northern Ireland Ministry of Home Affairs, *Report on the Administration of Local Government Services for the Period 1 April 1923 to 31 March 1924* (Belfast, 1925), 26–30.

[13] W. B. Lyle, 'The Dispensary Doctor', *Ulster Medical Journal*, 6 (October 1937), 301–3.

[14] PRONI CAB/4/267, Minister for Home Affairs, 'Poor Law and Medical Services Reformation', 21 August 1930.

[15] T. Hennessey, *A History of Northern Ireland, 1920–1996* (Basingstoke, 1997), 59–61.

[16] B. M. Browne and D. S. Johnson, 'Infant Mortality in Inter-War Northern Ireland', in R. Mitchison and P. Roebuck (eds), *Economy and Society in Scotland and Ireland 1500–1939* (Edinburgh, 1988), 277.

[17] Maguire, *Belfast*, 195.

[18] *Report on the Administration of Local Government Services 1 April 1923 to 31 March 1924*, 37–8.

respiratory illnesses and cancer it remained one of the region's most common causes of death (Tables 19.4 and 19.5).[19] The hospital system was complicated by the existence of local authority and voluntary hospitals which meant that there were sixty-five bodies administering the health services.[20]

One of the reasons for the poor health of Northern Ireland's people was the conditions in which many of them lived. Although there was no systematic study until 1943, it was obvious that an ageing housing stock needed replacement but

Table 19.1. Death rates per 1000 population in Northern Ireland, England and Wales, Scotland, and Southern Ireland, 1922–99

	NI	England & Wales	Scotland	IFS/Eire
1926	15.0	11.6	13.1	14.1
1937	15.1	12.4	13.9	15.3
1941*	15.2	13.5	14.7	14.6
1951	12.8	12.5	12.9	14.3
1961	11.3	12.0	12.3	12.3
1971	10.6	11.6	11.8	10.6
1980	10.9	12.1	12.3	9.7
1990	9.7	11.1	12.1	9.0
1999	9.3	10.6	11.9	8.7

* Civilian death rates.
Source: Ulster Year Books, 1926–1985; <http://www.gro-scotland.gov.uk/files/02t1-1.pdf> accessed 10 January 2011; <http://www.statistics.gov.uk/STATBASE/xsdataset.asp?vlnk=5805&More=Y> accessed 10 January 2011; <http://www.cso.ie/statistics/bthsdthsmarriages.htm> accessed 10 January 2011.

Table 19.2. Infant mortality per 1000 live births in Northern Ireland, England and Wales, Scotland, and Southern Ireland, 1922–80

	NI	England & Wales	Scotland	IFS/Eire
1922	77	77	101	69
1926	85	70	83	74
1931	73	66	82	69
1936	77	59	82	74
1941	77	59	83	74
1945	68	46	56	71
1950	40	30	39	46
1955	32	25	30	37
1960	27	22	26	29
1965	25	19	23	25
1970	23	18	20	20
1975	20	16	17	18
1980	13	12	12	11

Source: As for Table 19.1.

[19] *Ulster Year Book, 1933* (Belfast, 1933).
[20] J. Ditch, *Social Policy in Northern Ireland between 1939–50* (Aldershot, 1988), 48.

Table 19.3. Death rates (per 1000 of population) from tuberculosis in Northern Ireland, England and Wales, Scotland, and Southern Ireland, 1926–60

	NI	England & Wales	Scotland	IFS/Eire
1926	1.47	0.96	1.0	1.47
1937	0.98	0.68	0.74	1.23
1941	1.04	0.73	0.85	1.24
1945	0.8	0.62	0.79	1.24
1950	0.48	0.36	0.64	0.8
1955	0.15	0.15	0.19	0.31
1960	0.08	0.08	0.10	0.17

Source: As for Table 19.1.

Table 19.4. Deaths from heart disease per 1000 of population in Northern Ireland, England and Wales, Scotland, and Southern Ireland, 1926–80

	NI	England & Wales	Scotland	IFS/Eire
1926	2.14	1.65	1.51	1.57
1937	2.89	3.14	2.89	2.65
1951	4.01	4.06	4.22	3.93
1961	4.14	3.89	4.25	4.16
1971	3.77	3.8	4	3.4
1980	3.98	4.08	4.2	3.3

Source: As for Table 19.1.

Table 19.5. Deaths from cancer per 1000 population in Northern Ireland, England and Wales, Scotland, and Southern Ireland, 1926–80

	NI	England & Wales	Scotland	IFS/Eire
1926	1.12	1.36	1.37	1.02
1937	1.3	1.58	1.57	1.26
1951	1.48	1.9	1.86	1.44
1961	1.53	2.09	2.09	1.6
1971	1.08	2.3	2.4	1.8
1980	1.86	2.53	2.65	1.8

Source: As for Table 19.1.

neither local nor national government was willing to bridge the divide. Only 50,000 dwellings were built between the wars, proportionately fewer than in the UK and there was a heavy dependence on private suppliers rather than local government stocks.[21] This affected both urban and rural dwellers, whether workers or small farmers. Without an adequate supply of new dwellings there was no prospect

[21] Buckland, *Factory of Grievances*, 174.

Table 19.6. Life expectancy in Northern Ireland by selected ages and gender, 1910–99

	From birth		Expectation of life at age 1		Expectation of life at age 65	
	Male	Female	Male	Female	Male	Female
1910–12	50.7	51			12.1	12.8
1925–27	55.4	56.1	59.9	59.5	11.9	12.7
1936–38	57.8	59.2			11.6	12.4
1950–52	65.5	68.8	67.5	70.3	12.1	13.5
1960–62	67.6	72.4	68.7	73.2	12.2	14.4
1970–72	67.6	73.7	68.3	74.1	12	15.2
1980–82	69.2	75.6	69.2	75.5	12.5	16.4
1990–92	72.6	78.5	72.1	78	14	18
1997–99	74.3	79.6	73.8	79	14.9	18.4

Source: *Northern Ireland Annual Abstract of Statistics: 2000* (London, 2001), 12.

Table 19.7. Twelve-monthly average unemployment of insured workers in all industries in Great Britain and Northern Ireland, 1923–80

Year	Great Britain (%)	Northern Ireland (%)
1923	11.6	18.2
1925	11.0	23.9
1930	15.8	23.8
1935	15.3	24.8
1940	5.8	19.4
1945	1.0	5.5
1950	1.5	5.8
1955	1.1	6.8
1960	1.6	6.7
1965	1.4	6.1
1970	2.5	6.8
1975	4.1	7.9
1980	7.3	13.7

Source: K. S. Isles and N. Cuthbert, *An Economic Survey of Northern Ireland* (Belfast, 1957), 566; B. R. Mitchell, *British Historical Statistics* (Cambridge, 1988), 126.

of clearing slums or controlling rents, although overcrowding in Belfast was reduced. The government's policy was to offer incentives to private builders and local authorities through a series of thirteen Housing Acts between 1923 and 1936. In this respect they notably ignored the path taken by the British government in giving funds to local authorities. The Unionist Party's deeply conservative instincts and the Ministry of Finance's parsimony inhibited state intervention.

Real improvements in social conditions were hindered by serious financial problems, a lack of agreement within government as to what the aims of social policy should be, and the severity of the social problems faced by the region. The Second World War would alter this context considerably, but at a political cost.

THE SECOND WORLD WAR AND THE WELFARE STATE 1939-51

The war challenged many of the political and social certainties in Northern Ireland. Although no one in positions of authority had any illusions about the problems of health, welfare, and housing, these became matters of public debate. In the aftermath of the Belfast Blitz, the Davidge Report exposed the problems of the urban poor and the need for reform of the slums.[22] The war also offered a new opportunity to reform the system as British politicians began to prepare for post-war change. Both political will and money were suddenly available, the former from new ministers and the latter from the Treasury.

Serious discussions within the government about post-war reform of social policy began in May 1942 leading to the formation of the Post-War Planning Committee that June. John Andrews, the Prime Minister, argued for radical post-war welfare reforms. In doing so he angered both the Treasury and anti-populists in the Unionist Party. His successor, Basil Brooke, pursued the full inclusion of Northern Ireland in the post-war reconstruction more diplomatically. There was an inevitable tension between the Northern Irish desire to match British standards of public services and the British need to keep control of spending. It became clear that Northern Ireland would have to trade a great deal of independence for the generous welfare system it needed. This was, however, based on the assumption that the changes would be along the lines envisaged by the Conservative Party rather than the more radical plans that were eventually implemented by Labour. The actual welfare state brought into being was a significant ideological challenge for many unionists but by then it was too late.

The central pillar of the new dispensation was the National Health Service. William Grant, the first Minister for Health and Local Government, managed to bring together the medical professionals, his own party, and the majority of the vested interests such as boards of guardians and voluntary hospitals with little controversy. His gratuitous refusal to give the Catholic Mater Infirmorum hospital in Belfast the same status offered to similar institutions in Britain did much to alienate minority opinion, however. The result was that the Mater stayed outside the NHS until 1972. In other respects, Grant showed a genuine passion for reform stemming from his own working class background. He had the advantage that the structure and underlying principles of the system had been established by Aneurin Bevan, the British Minister of Health, and Grant had merely to apply it to Northern Ireland. He also benefited from a supportive medical profession which was happy to work with a Unionist government rather than the more radical Labour regime in Westminster.[23]

The Northern Irish health service was if anything more centralized than that of Britain. The new Northern Ireland Hospital Authority took control of a wide range of services from poor law boards (which were abolished), district councils, voluntary

---

[22] Ditch, *Social Policy in Northern Ireland*, 72.
[23] For a detailed account of the implementation of the welfare state see Ditch, *Social Policy in Northern Ireland*.

hospitals, and county and borough councils. Hospitals, specialist treatment, ambulance services, laboratory testing, and blood transfusion services were all centralized. The Health Services Board contracted general practitioners, dentists, pharmacists, and opticians. A separate Tuberculosis Authority was retained and local authorities were left in charge of public and environmental health matters.

The NHS was probably the most successful element of the welfare state in Northern Ireland. It delivered better health outcomes than its predecessors, and was largely lacking in sectarian controversy. Apart from the Mater Hospital, the health service would feature very little in the complaints of either nationalist politicians or later civil rights campaigners. Even the Catholic Church, which vociferously opposed any similar reforms in the Republic of Ireland, accepted most of the system with only token complaints. Why this service should have avoided so much sectarian controversy is not entirely clear but some reasons might be considered. The health service broke the financial link between doctor and patient so discrimination in care offered no advantage to either side. It was rationed on the basis of judgements by the medical professionals themselves, based usually on need, and thus not subject to a great deal of political interference. Finally it was popular with both communities and was kept out of the political fray.

The changes to welfare were just as radical. The new system offered a chance for Northern Ireland to escape the perpetual financial crisis in which it had been caught since its creation. The old ad hoc methods of relief were replaced by a comprehensive and universal system. This offered sudden improvements in the rates and methods of relief. Again these were centralized under the Ministry of Health and Local Government. Between 1946 and 1948, an interim agreement with Britain covered unemployment insurance, unemployment assistance, and family allowances. This was followed by the introduction of the National Insurance Acts (UK and Northern Ireland) on 5 July 1948. There was also a Social Services Agreement covering National Assistance, Old Age, and Blind pensions, non-contributory pensions, temporary unemployment benefit, family allowances, and the health services. This was a reciprocal agreement: to transfer funds from Britain to Northern Ireland and to maintain the new levels of social spending.[24]

The new social welfare system offered enormous improvements. In return for fixed contributions, claimants became entitled to cash benefits in cases of unemployment, sickness, retirement, maternity, widowhood, orphanhood, and funerals. The National Insurance (Industrial Injuries) Act (Northern Ireland) 1946 replaced the Workmen's Compensation Acts (Northern Ireland) 1927 to 1943 which offered compensation for loss of earning capacity, but the employer liability often led to disputes in the courts. Under the 1946 Act, there were fixed rates of benefits depending on the degree of injury. Payment came from a national fund of contributions by workers and employers and disputes were settled by insurance officers. The National Assistance system replaced outdoor relief and other allowances for the poor and family allowances were paid to almost all children.[25]

[24] *Ulster Year Book 1950*, (Belfast, 1950), xxxi. [25] Ibid., 203–24.

Northern Ireland faced a serious crisis in the provision of quality housing to its people. In 1943 the government was advised that 200,000 new dwellings were required and up to 323,000 were in need of repair if slums and overcrowding were to be dealt with fully.[26] Despite this, its instinct was to avoid radical action. The rural landed elite within the Unionist Party had little interest in the issue, and their representatives in local government showed little urgency in implementing reforms. There were also shortages of suitable sites and raw materials during war time. The Northern Ireland Housing Trust (NIHT) was set up in 1945 to bypass the local authorities and centralize the planning and construction process. Therefore there were now two bodies responsible for housing and this division of responsibility was to have significant political effects. Substantial transfers of funds from the UK exchequer allowed the rate of construction to be greatly increased. More troublesome was the allocation of new housing by local authorities which was done in a partisan fashion and led to deep resentment by the Catholic community. There were also significant failures in planning and regional development which held back the social modernization of the region.

While there were ideological objections to the welfare state from the most conservative elements of unionism and nationalism, it is striking how much of the cabinet discussions of these measures concerned bureaucratic practicalities rather than the principles behind them. The Northern Irish welfare state was an exercise in transplantation rather than re-imagination.[27]

THE MODERNIZATION OF NORTHERN IRELAND 1952–72

It would be a mistake to credit the welfare state with all of the social changes that took place in the post-war period. Life expectancy at birth had risen impressively even before the welfare state arrived (Table 19.6). Infant mortality, however, remained almost unchanged (Table 19.2). The NHS, housing reforms, and other improvements began to have their effects in the 1950s and infant mortality fell considerably by the 1970s.

Other signs of modernization began to appear. In 1925 there had been 10,252 private cars in Northern Ireland. After the war there were 33,542, and ownership rose to 83,542 ten years later. State regulation soon followed in the form of driving tests and more widespread speed limits under the Road Traffic Act (Northern Ireland) 1956. Air travel was a rare luxury in 1945, when only 13,695 passengers left Belfast airport. In 1972 1,186,540 flew to a much wider variety of destinations, reducing the isolation of the region but also opening new opportunities for emigration. The 1950s was the golden age of the radio and telegram in Northern Ireland.

---

[26] D. Birrell and A. Murie, *Policy and Government in Northern Ireland—Lessons in Devolution* (Dublin, 1980), 212.
[27] G. Walker, *A History of the Ulster Unionist Party: Protest, Pragmatism and Pessimism* (Manchester, 2004), 106–7.

Both were superseded by television and the telephone respectively which became well established by the 1970s. In rural parts the change to mechanized farming accelerated. The number of tractors finally overtook that of horses in the 1950s, and about a third of farms were connected to the electricity grid by 1960. Farms themselves remained small and farmers were heavily dependent on the help of neighbours and family. Amidst all this change, Northern Irish society remained traditional in many ways. Possession of consumer goods such as telephones, washing machines, refrigerators, and televisions remained lower than in the rest of the UK. Rates of marriage increased from 5.8 per 1000 in 1926, to 7.9 in 1971, suggesting that increased prosperity fuelled a desire for stability and respectability rather than establishing new social norms.[28]

Northern Ireland also remained comparatively poor. Peter Townshend recalled that in Belfast in 1968, 'I was struck not only by the evident poverty of Catholics and Protestants alike but also by scenes which seemed to belong more to the 1930s'.[29] In January 1951, Northern Irish unemployment was 7 per cent. This may have been stubbornly high by British standards (1.6 per cent) but it seemed miraculous compared to the 20 per cent recorded before the start of the war. The number of agricultural workers declined after the war, pushed off the land by mechanization and pulled to the urban centres by new employment.

Government policy under Brookeborough was to expand the welfare state without any unseemly exertion. As a result, its policy was often at odds with the more politically cynical and inept actions of local interests in housing. This was despite legal changes relaxing rent controls and making it incumbent on local authorities to deal with unfit dwellings. House building was heavily subsidized at a rate more than double the equivalent subsidy in England and council house rents were low. By 1963, 112,383 houses had been constructed; approximately a third came from local authorities, a third from private builders and a quarter from the NIHT.[30] The problems lay more in the allocation and location of housing than in supply. Planning remained limited to central government with little effort and few resources available at local level. The social effect of this was to prevent the tackling of poverty and sectarian division in existing developments.

The social security system remained essentially the same as that of 1948. The Social Services Agreement of 1949 obliged Northern Ireland to maintain general parity with Britain but not to stay in lock-step. This was highlighted in 1956 when a general increase in family allowances in Britain was considered 'highly unsuitable' for Northern Ireland, in part because Catholics would have benefited more from it as they had on average larger families, but also because of a fear that a growing population would add to unemployment. The Minister of Finance, George Hanna, suggested weighting increases in favour of smaller families.[31] The government backed down, however, when confronted with accusations of anti-Catholic

---

[28] Statistics collated from the *Ulster Year Books*, 1926–1983.
[29] P. Townshend, *Poverty in the United Kingdom* (London, 1979), 558.
[30] Lawrence, *Government of Northern Ireland*, 153–4.
[31] PRONI CAB/4/1006, Cabinet Minutes, 26 April 1956.

discrimination and pressure from Unionists to maintain parity with the rest of the UK.[32] The incident demonstrated that while the region had considerable freedom of action, there were real political limits on its ability to exercise it. In 1961, graduated contributions and pensions were introduced and earnings related supplements to the flat-rate benefits were introduced for the first six months of sickness, unemployment, or widowhood.

By 1954 it was clear that whatever the popularity of the NHS, there were questions to be asked about its bureaucracy and efficiency leading to an official committee on the subject. Its recommendation that the Hospitals Authority be placed more clearly under ministerial control was not implemented by the minister, Dehra Parker, but she did reform the board somewhat. A proposal that the Mater Hospital be offered a contractual arrangement involving state remuneration for its services was ignored for fear of the reaction of Unionist backbenchers. The Hospitals Authority was publicly attacked in 1964 by Dr Robert Nixon, MP for North Down and Ian McClure, a gynaecologist and the MP for Queen's University, who accused it of mismanaging the Royal Maternity Hospital and demanded it be put under greater ministerial control. There was a curious diffidence about the government's response—although they recognized the problem, they were reluctant to take on more responsibility for it.[33]

The health of the population had improved considerably for both medical and environmental reasons. Infant deaths per 1000 live births fell 34 per cent between 1951 and 1971. Deaths resulting from pregnancy and childbirth continued to fall. Death rates in general fell steadily for both men and women. Tuberculosis all but ceased to be a serious problem and heart disease became the most common killer, accounting for 35.7 per cent of all deaths and 38 per cent in men. Deaths from cancer were also increasing with the most notable being the prevalence of lung cancer among men. Although it was increasingly clear that this was linked to smoking, the state was reluctant to act, preferring to leave health education on the subject to local authorities. This was partly motivated by a belief in personal choice but the biggest factor was the fact that the tobacco industry was one of the few growing sources of employment in Northern Ireland. Their inaction was to have serious consequences. By 1981, the generation who had been school children in Northern Ireland during the 1950s were among the most likely to smoke of any UK region.[34]

The extent to which the state's social policies had become intertwined with everyday life is partly illustrated by the fact that these issues dominated much of the discourse of the civil rights campaigns of the 1960s. Housing was notoriously the biggest complaint, but at a deeper level the government's reluctance to rein in local authorities, to rectify regional imbalances, or to tackle discrimination in state and private employment was at the heart of the debate. Universal services such as national insurance or the NHS were notably absent. The government's record in

---

[32] PRONI CAB/4/1011, Cabinet Minutes, 31 May 1956.
[33] PRONI CAB/4/1278, Cabinet Minutes, 18 November 1964.
[34] K. D. Brown, 'Smoking in Northern Ireland: A Case Study in Local Health Education 1950–1973', *Social History of Medicine* 17 (2004), 285–99.

social policy from 1945 to 1972 was certainly more progressive than that of its interwar predecessor, but it remained heavily dependent on the competence of individual ministers and the willingness of local authorities to do their jobs fairly. That would change utterly after 1972 when direct rule returned.

MODERNIZATION FROM ABOVE: 1973–98

Successive Secretaries of State for Northern Ireland inherited a society that was still substantially poorer than Britain in many areas but was ahead of the Republic of Ireland. Security interests as much as charity required them to address this. The tendency of the Stormont governments to invest in growth centres had resulted in the poorer areas drifting further behind. Over a quarter of the labour force was certified incapable or qualified for sickness benefit. Only Wales had higher rates.

Reforms were introduced quickly to strip local authorities of their housing powers and centralize authority in the Northern Ireland Housing Executive (NIHE) which took charge of 155,000 dwellings almost overnight. It took over a rapidly deteriorating housing stock. Between 1968 and 1972, 14,922 dwellings had been closed or demolished as unfit. In 1974, 89,370 houses, 19.6 per cent of the total stock, was still unfit and 26.2 per cent of houses lacked one or more basic amenity (Table 19.8).[35] Poor quality housing was most apparent in rural areas.

These problems were exacerbated by the intense violence of the period. The effects of the Troubles are almost impossible to quantify exactly, but it is clear that segregation was made stronger and the economic plight of the poorest regions intensified. Paramilitary 'defenders' attracted violence into their communities while deterring investment and thus increasing segregation.[36] A highly developed culture of separation evolved which fascinates anthropologists today. The urban milieu became the most segregated as the size of the populations made co-existence less necessary, residential areas were already well divided, and there were fewer

Table 19.8. Unfit dwellings in Northern Ireland, 1974–97

	Unfit dwellings		Lacking one or more basic amenity	
	Number	Percentage	Number	Percentage
1974	89,370	19.6	119,510	26.6
1979	66,208	14.1	84,132	17.9
1984	51,330	10.4	45,133	9.2
1987	42,900	8.4	28,330	5.5
1991*	50,336	8.8	19,100	3.3
1997*	43,970	7.3	17,600	2.9

* Not directly comparable due to changes in methodology.
Source: *Northern Ireland Housing Statistics* 1979–1999 (Belfast).

[35] *Northern Ireland Housing Statistics* 1979–1999 (Belfast).
[36] R. Alonso, *The IRA and Armed Struggle* (Abingdon, 2003), 38–66.

opportunities for activities which crossed ethnic lines. Towns and cities were easy to mark into territories with flags, murals, and other symbols or more blatantly with peace walls. Where there were no physical clues, violence created a mental map for the public, rendering certain routes home or places of recreation as off limits. These developments were largely impervious to government policies which in any case were often more focused on security rather than social improvement.

There were serious attempts to reform the religious balance in employment. The 1976 Fair Employment (Northern Ireland) Act established the Fair Employment Agency (FEA). This proved ineffective as the code of practice it prescribed was largely voluntary and the charge of discrimination was almost impossible to prove. Of 409 complaints between 1977 and 1985, only twenty-nine were upheld. The provision allowing the Secretary of State to set the law aside on the grounds of protecting public order or national security diminished Catholic confidence in it. Inequality was also deeply rooted in the economic geography and class structure of Northern Ireland. It was not enough to simply treat actual cases of negative discrimination. Many industries were so socially associated with Protestant areas and populations that it was almost unthinkable for Catholics to apply. Also, the general decline of many major industries made reform even harder. One effect of this was that change took place more quickly in the public sector—one of the few parts of the economy that was growing—and Catholics became increasingly numerous, if not always prominent, in the state machine. The law was reformed in 1989 and the FEA was replaced with the Fair Employment Commission (FEC). This transferred the burden of ending discrimination to the employer and allowed the FEC to monitor the religious make-up of workplaces and demand reforms in businesses with more than ten workers.[37]

The violence claimed 3717 lives between 1969 and 2000 and left an unknown number physically or mentally injured. The typical fatality was a young, male, non-belligerent from Belfast, Derry, or South Armagh, who had been killed by paramilitaries—a crude generalization, it is true, but one which reflects the fact that the Troubles did not have a uniform effect throughout the region. More generally felt throughout Northern Ireland were the economic and social impacts of low private investment and the wanton destruction of property and resources. In 1977, 10.5 per cent unemployment was recorded. In 1982, it was up to 18.7 per cent.[38]

As noted above, Northern Ireland was already a relatively poor part of the UK. By the late 1970s, Northern Irish people were in most cases more likely to be poor or marginally poor than others in Britain and in some wards of Belfast half of all children received free school meals. Throughout the city, the average was one in eight. Townshend found high levels of social deprivation and disability and the region contained relatively high numbers of elderly or poorly skilled people.[39]

---

[37] F. Gibson, G. Michael, and D. Wilson, 'Discrimination and Employment' from 'Perspectives on Discrimination and Social Work in Northern Ireland', <http://cain.ulst.ac.uk/issues/discrimination/gibson2.htm> accessed 24 August 2010.
[38] *Ulster Year Book* (Belfast, 1983).
[39] Townshend, *Poverty in the United Kingdom,* 953.

During the 1970s, the majority of Northern Irish households were considered to be on low income; this was the result of large families and low wages. This combined with the ongoing violence did have the effect of deterring governments from any experiments in tightening the purse strings. Between 1984 and 1989 public spending in Northern Ireland rose 1.3 per cent compared to 0.5 per cent in the UK overall. This still left spending at a lower level than in the mid-1970s and areas such as agriculture, industry, transport, and housing suffered severe cuts. It should also be remembered that social services in Northern Ireland are comparatively expensive to deliver as the region has a low population density.

By contrast, Northern Ireland remained ahead of the Republic of Ireland in several areas until the 'Celtic Tiger' of the late 1990s, perhaps temporarily, revolutionized living standards in the South. Northern standards of living were 40 per cent higher, per capita government expenditure was 66 per cent higher, while taxes were lower and consumer spending was 35 per cent more. This was often hailed with triumph but was more a reflection of the depths to which the southern economy had sunk in the 1980s than success on the part of the North. The major Northern Irish industries continued their decline. With a depressed economy, public services became the largest source of employment, especially for women. Their employment patterns had changed radically. Although in 1981 the number of economically active women was 17 per cent higher than it had been in 1926, they worked in fewer sectors of the economy. Women had all but ceased to work in agriculture and the numbers in industry had fallen 58 per cent. Instead, 76.7 per cent worked in services, up from 38.3 per cent in 1926. Only 51 per cent of men worked in this sector, and many men still worked in industry (27 per cent), and some still remained in agriculture (8.4 per cent) or construction (11.6 per cent).[40] There were some attempts to extend Thatcherite social policies into Northern Ireland. The 1983 Housing Order encouraged tenants to buy their homes, and the NIHE sold 35,546 dwellings between 1979 and 1987. There was an increase in the proportion of people who owned homes from 45 per cent in 1966 to 60 per cent in 1986 but this was matched by a fall in private rentals rather than those from local authorities.[41]

The direct rule administration radically restructured the NHS in 1973. Under the Health and Personal Social Services (Northern Ireland) Order 1972, the service was integrated. Four Health and Social Services Boards took charge of planning, managing, and delivering services in the north, south, east, and west of the region. Common services were provided by the Northern Ireland Central Services Agency for Health and the Northern Ireland Staff Council for the Health and Social Services. A range of committees represented the interests of the public and health professionals. Health outcomes began to come into line with British norms by the late 1980s (see Tables 19.1 and 19.6). The NHS was, despite complaints to the contrary, relatively well resourced with 15 per cent greater expenditure per capita

---

[40] A. M. Gallagher, 'Majority Minority Review 2: Employment, Unemployment and Religion in Northern Ireland', <http://cain.ulst.ac.uk/csc/reports/mm22.htm> accessed 24 August 2010.
[41] F. Gaffikin and M. Morrissey, *Northern Ireland: The Thatcher Years* (London, 1990), 155–61.

than in Britain, more hospital beds, and lower occupancy rates. Obviously the effects of the Troubles on the medical system undid some of the benefits from this.[42]

How did these changes affect the average household in comparison with Britain? In 1980 Northern Irish people were more likely to live in rented dwellings, and were far less likely to have a mortgage—although retired people were more likely to own their property outright. Housing was cheaper but the cost of living, particularly fuel, power, and lighting, was greater. They had larger families than their neighbours to the east. By 1999, the gap in the price of fuel had narrowed somewhat but food was still significantly more expensive. One result of this was that Northern Irish people spent less on leisure than their British counterparts. The other was that the high prices of food and energy affected the poor particularly severely.

Northern Ireland also took time to catch up with Britain in the development of a consumer society between 1972 and 2000. Car ownership was quite closely matched, reflecting the Ulster obsession with automobiles; in 1977, 51.7 per cent of households had a car while only 30 per cent had central heating. Not until the 1990s would Northern Ireland match Britain in the possession of heating, washing machines, refrigerators, televisions, or telephones. In most of these cases, this was due to very low levels of ownership in 1972 followed by a rapid increase over the subsequent thirty years. By the early twenty-first century, Northern Irish consumers matched British levels of ownership of new products such as computers, microwaves, and satellite or cable television.[43]

CONCLUSION

Northern Ireland saw radical shifts in its society in the twentieth century. Although successive governments hoped to manage rather than to direct these changes, it was impossible for the state to be a neutral party. Despite the innate conservatism of the Unionist Party, the state intervened in agriculture, welfare, industrial safety, and health to a greater degree than in the south of Ireland. The welfare state revolutionized government's relationship with its citizens to the extent that it helped provoke radical demands for political reform. It also made life better for most of the population and many of the systemic problems of poor health and poverty were addressed.

The Troubles did inhibit the development of Northern Irish society. The conflict depressed the economy, intensifying poverty and worsening the plight of the poor of both communities. It also heightened sectarian segregation and inequality. The introduction of direct rule and its single-minded, albeit often inefficient and undemocratic, focus on containing the conflict led to significant attempts to reform employment practices and other social services.

Northern Ireland has spent most of the twentieth century poised between being a British region, a part of Ireland, and having an independent identity. In its

[42] Ibid., 188.   [43] *Northern Ireland Abstract of Statistics* (Belfast, 1973–2001).

small-scale agriculture, urban-rural divide, and problems of underdevelopment, it appears recognizably Irish. Belfast and its hinterland are comparable to many Victorian industrial cities in Britain. However, its ethnic make-up, religious variety, and devolved status mean that characteristically British patterns of development have expressed themselves in distinctive ways.

FURTHER READING

P. Bew, P. Gibbon, and H. Patterson, *Northern Ireland 1921/2001: Political Forces and Social Classes* (London, 2002).

D. Birrell and A. Murie, *Policy and Government in Northern Ireland: Lessons in Devolution* (Dublin, 1980).

B. M. Browne and D. S. Johnson, 'Infant Mortality in Inter-War Northern Ireland', in R. Mitchison and P. Roebuck (eds), *Economy and Society in Scotland and Ireland 1500–1939* (Edinburgh, 1988), 277–87.

J. Ditch, *Social Policy in Northern Ireland between 1939–50* (Aldershot, 1988).

F. Gaffikin and M. Morrissey, *Northern Ireland: The Thatcher Years* (London, 1990).

20

Politics since 1960

Graham Walker

At the end of the 1960s, Northern Ireland began to command international attention as a site of violent political conflict. Before long it would become one of the most studied parts of the world, with academics and journalists producing a steady flow of literature. The history of community divisions, displayed in the geography and physical appearance of Northern Ireland's urban and rural landscapes, fascinated and attracted anthropologists, artists, and novelists, as well as merely curious outsiders. The political crisis engaged national governments and international institutions. As violence became a way of life, the people of Northern Ireland demonstrated a remarkable capacity to adapt to it and continue their lives. By the twenty-first century there was an uneasy peace, yet the legacy of the conflict brought its own problems, dilemmas, and dangers. This chapter charts and explains the development of the conflict and the politics of finding a settlement.

COUNTDOWN TO CONFLICT

Northern Ireland entered the 1960s poised between increased prosperity and gathering instability. The region had shared in the British post-war experience of the welfare state, rising living standards, new educational opportunities, consumerism, and economic expansion.[1] On the other hand, much of Northern Ireland's staple industry, particularly shipbuilding and engineering, was in decline and faced an uncertain future, while the unemployment rate was significantly higher than the UK average.[2] More fundamentally, divisions between the majority Protestant community and the Catholic minority, a mirror of the Ulster unionist–Irish nationalist political polarization, remained deep-rooted. It was clear that communal consensus around the central question of the legitimacy of Northern Ireland as a political entity had still to be built.[3]

---

[1] T. Wilson, *Ulster: Conflict and Consent* (Oxford, 1989), 151–4.
[2] The problems were well signposted in K. S. Isles and N. Cuthbert, *An Economic Survey of Northern Ireland* (Belfast, 1957).
[3] A key text in relation to this question, produced as Northern Ireland was entering its long period of crisis, is R. Rose, *Governing without Consensus* (London, 1971). The census figures for 1961 put the Catholic population at 34.9 per cent and the combined Protestant population at 61.5 per cent.

The man to whom this task fell was Terence O'Neill, who succeeded to the premiership and to the leadership of the Ulster Unionist Party (UUP) in 1963. O'Neill wished to break with the caution of his predecessors and use Northern Ireland's devolved powers to the full. He identified the potential for regional innovations in commercial and industrial development, planning, and social policy. It was, indeed, a rhetoric of 'self-help' which Whitehall, long used to demands simply to prop up Northern Ireland's traditional industries, was pleased to hear. Nevertheless, it was also about obtaining largesse from the Treasury in London to underwrite O'Neill's ambitions.[4] O'Neill simply grasped the changing priorities of the era, and recast Northern Ireland government policy according to the fashionable new tenets of planning, regional development, and modernization. Unfortunately for O'Neill, Northern Ireland was not to be given a proper chance to test the potential of devolution. The new schemes and dreams were overtaken by the growing political crisis from the mid-1960s, a crisis whose roots lay deep in the circumstances of the Irish question in British politics, and in the varieties of neglect on the part of both British and Belfast governments over the course of Northern Ireland's history as a political unit. Moreover, O'Neill's vision required the modernization of the Unionist Party and of the state's political culture as well as his new plans and the more dynamic approach to devolution. With hindsight it appears that O'Neill was naive to believe that the economic improvement he sought would of itself assuage the minority's historically rooted resentments and reconcile them to the state.[5] O'Neill can be credited with introducing a new tone into Northern Ireland politics, and with making symbolic gestures of reconciliation. However, when such developments were not matched with tangible reforms, and when vaunted schemes such as the location of the new university caused offence to the minority community, the increased expectations of that minority were left to find expression in protest politics, most notably through the Northern Ireland Civil Rights Association (NICRA) from 1967.[6] The civil rights agitation was led largely by Catholics who had benefited from the expansion of educational opportunities put in place after the Second World War, and the youthful leadership of such figures as John Hume, Austin Currie, Bernadette Devlin, and Eamonn McCann, whatever their own political differences, was to serve the most serious challenge to the unionist state since its foundation. It proved to be a challenge to which there was no effective, or sufficiently rapid, response.[7]

The civil rights movement deftly focused its campaign on the issue of the ratepayers' and property-based local government franchise which had been discarded in favour of universal adult suffrage in the rest of the UK in 1946. In Northern Ireland its advantage to the unionists, particularly in areas west of the Bann where

---

[4] See M. Mulholland, *Northern Ireland at the Crossroads* (Basingstoke, 2000); J. Mitchell, *Devolution in the UK* (Manchester, 2009), Ch. 4.

[5] See M. Elliott, *The Catholics of Ulster* (London, 2000), Chs 11 and 12.

[6] The latest scholarly treatment of the civil rights movement, its precursors, and the era is S. Prince, *Northern Ireland's '68* (Dublin, 2008).

[7] See C. Farrington, 'Mobilisation, State Crisis and Counter-Mobilisation: Ulster Unionist Politics and the Outbreak of the Troubles', *Irish Political Studies*, 23 (2008), 513–32.

the population balance was roughly even or, indeed, Catholic by a small majority, was the decisive factor in its retention. Although the property franchise did not discriminate against Catholics per se—many Protestants were also disenfranchised—it was widely viewed, along with instances of the gerrymandering of local government boundaries, as an instrument of sectarian domination. Unionist fears that reform would upset local power bases acted as a brake upon the leadership.[8] It was, of course, within the competencies of Stormont to intervene and reform local government, and a widespread 'reorganization' was promised by O'Neill; however, the risks of the government coming into conflict with its own supporters were very clear. When O'Neill came under pressure for reform from the Westminster Labour government led by Harold Wilson elected in 1964, and re-elected in 1966, he could not afford to admit to the local dynamics of the problem. In contrast, NICRA took the opportunity to pitch its demands within the impeccable context of 'British rights for British citizens'; the organization astutely limited its objectives to bringing northern Ireland into line with British democratic standards. This made it difficult for O'Neill to counter the campaign with the time-worn justification of a nationalist threat to the state, notwithstanding the republican presence in the civil rights movement and the sense in which many pragmatically regarded the campaign as the most effective way of attacking unionism and perhaps destabilizing Northern Ireland.[9]

The view that civil rights was merely another nationalist-republican plot was firmly held by unionists both moderate and extreme, but it was the manner in which the issue could be exploited by the Reverend Ian Paisley, the new limelight-stealing demagogue of militant loyalism, that proved particularly devastating for O'Neill and the government. Paisley was the latest in a long line of 'Independent' Unionists whose stock-in-trade was a populist appeal around an aggressive defence of the constitutional position and agitation over the conditions of the less well-off in the Protestant community.[10] Paisley took to new political territory the ability to exploit the distance between the comfortably off image of the Unionist Party and the grievances, fears, and uncertainties of the Protestant masses. In addition, as an evangelical preacher, he sought to anchor unionism even more assuredly in ethnic 'Protestant Ulster' interests. Indeed, he combined attacks on religious ecumenism with what he saw as its political counterpart of 'O'Neillism'. The intervention of Paisley in the 1960s added to the perennial problem of separating issues of social justice from the 'national question'.

Following clashes between the police and civil rights demonstrators in Derry in October 1968, images of which were beamed around the world, O'Neill was pressured

---

[8] See J. Whyte, 'How Much Discrimination Was There Under the Unionist Regime, 1921–68?', in T. Gallagher and J. O'Connell (eds), *Contemporary Irish Studies* (Manchester, 1983); G. Walker, *A History of the Ulster Unionist Party* (Manchester, 2004), 98–9, 107–8, 165–70; H. Patterson and E. Kaufmann, *Unionism and Orangeism since 1945* (Manchester, 2007), Ch. 1.

[9] Such issues are discussed at length in Prince, *Northern Ireland's '68*; B. Purdie, *Politics in the Streets* (Belfast, 1990); N. Ó Dochartaigh, *From Civil Rights to Armalites* (Basingstoke, 2005).

[10] The most recent study is S. Bruce, *Paisley* (Oxford, 2007) which builds on his earlier *God Save Ulster!* (Oxford, 1986).

by London into announcing a package of reforms the following month.[11] The reforms stopped short of altering the local government franchise, so nervous was the Prime Minister of losing the support of his own party. While the package bought O'Neill time, there was nonetheless a real sense of the genie escaping the bottle. Crucially, the myth of a Unionist Party in control of Northern Ireland's destiny was exploded. The government's troubles with its own members and supporters stemmed from the notion that it had more power than it in fact did. It came as a profound shock to many unionist voters that their government was subject to control from Westminster, such had the impression of Stormont's supreme status been fostered over the years.[12] The Unionist Party was now a victim of its own propaganda, that unionists had the right to run their own show to the end of securing their position. It benefited the Unionist Party to be seen as the controllers of a people's destiny and the party with the greatest entitlement to Protestant and pro-Union votes. The revelation of O'Neill's government as vulnerable to outside pressure delivered a blow to communal self-esteem which subsequent developments were only to compound with serious political consequences.

As O'Neill was seen to bend to pressure so, at this juncture, a left-wing faction of the civil rights movement, the People's Democracy (PD), wrote itself into the history books. The PD, in contrast to NICRA, refused to permit the Prime Minister political breathing space, and organized a protest march from Belfast to Derry through areas where antagonism was assured. At Burntollet the infamous ambush of the march reinforced Catholic alienation when O'Neill most needed cooperation; the brutal attacks on the demonstrators were alleged to have been carried out by some off-duty 'B' Specials, the auxiliary police force historically despised by the minority.[13] The measure of Catholic support O'Neill needed for a genuine reform programme did not materialize at the Stormont election of February 1969, called by O'Neill in a bid to shore up his position. Notwithstanding a heavy vote for his version of liberal unionism, the election did not remove O'Neill's unionist opponents and indeed provided a boost for Paisley.[14] Following a series of bomb attacks on electricity installations, which were later found to be the work of disgruntled loyalists, and after forcing through a divided parliamentary party the reform of the local government franchise in April, O'Neill resigned and was succeeded by the equally moderate yet politically more circumspect James Chichester-Clark. The new Prime Minister, however, floundered as communal tensions soared.

The outbreaks of sectarian rioting in August 1969 are widely viewed as the beginnings of what became colloquially known as 'the Troubles', although, as has been indicated, they were long in the making.[15] The British Army was deployed on

---

[11] The reforms were as follows: a points system for the allocation of public authority housing; the appointment of an ombudsman; the abolition of the company vote; a Development Corporation to replace the corporation in Derry city; and a phased withdrawal of the Special Powers Act.

[12] The 1949 Ireland Act fed this notion with the stipulation that the constitutional status of Northern Ireland could only be altered by the Stormont parliament.

[13] M. Farrell, *Arming the Protestants* (London, 1983).

[14] Paisley stood against O'Neill in the Bannside constituency and came close to unseating him.

[15] See special issue of *History Ireland* 17 (2009).

14 August in Derry and the following day in Belfast. Its subsequent role in the Troubles has been surrounded by controversies over covert and undercover operations and alleged collusion with loyalists. Later in 1969, the Report of the (Cameron) Commission established by O'Neill to investigate the background of the October 1968 disturbances, laid stress on a history of discrimination and on the crisis in the relationship between the minority and the police, both the regular Royal Ulster Constabulary (RUC) and the 'B' Specials.[16] Before the end of 1969 the Special Constabulary had been disbanded, fuelling loyalist and Orange denunciations of the Unionist government as a 'puppet' regime, and adding to the sense of crisis over security in the new context of the British Army presence which had been occasioned by the summer's riots.

In retrospect, the case for winding up the Stormont regime at the time when troops had to be deployed seems compelling.[17] Yet this reckons without the long-established desire on the part of the British political classes to keep Northern Ireland at a distance. Indeed, the flawed nature of the inter-governmental relationship between London and Belfast was long part of the problem. The Westminster governments, both Labour and, after June 1970, Conservative, craved an internal settlement on the basis of the reforms which were implemented in 1969–70. This proved to be wishful thinking. The new factor in the equation by the time the Conservative government came to power was the Provisional IRA (PIRA) which emerged out of a split in the IRA in December 1969,[18] and the transformation of Catholic perceptions of the British Army from protectors to oppressors. The upsurge in PIRA attacks on the security forces was met by a rise in loyalist paramilitarism on the part of the Ulster Volunteer Force (UVF) whose activities from 1966 had played an important role in the deterioration of the situation, and through the foundation in 1971 of the Ulster Defence Association (UDA).

The campaign of political violence led Chichester-Clark to stand down in March 1971 and prompted his successor, Brian Faulkner, to introduce internment without trial in August. Again with hindsight, this takes on the appearance of Stormont's epitaph. At a stroke the measure killed off any hope of Faulkner reaching a political 'modus vivendi' with the non-violent nationalist party, the Social and Democratic Labour Party (SDLP), which had taken over as the minority's main political representative. The one-sided nature of the application of internment against the Catholic community, combined with the measure's failure to hit the PIRA effectively, only created conditions for the republican 'armed struggle' to intensify and shift the conflict more perceptibly on to the ground of competing nationalisms.[19] Stormont was already on borrowed time when the events of 'Bloody Sunday' on 30 January 1972 brought international opprobrium down upon the head of the British government. Unwilling to go on taking the blame for a situation

---

[16] Northern Ireland Parliament *Disturbances in Northern Ireland* [Cameron Report] (Belfast, 1969, (Cmnd. 532); also Elliott, *Catholics*, 415–16.
[17] See P. Bew, *Ireland: The Politics of Enmity* (Oxford, 2007), 496.
[18] For an authoritative account see R. English, *Armed Struggle* (Basingstoke, 2003), Part 2, Ch. 3.
[19] J. Todd, 'Northern Ireland: From Multiphased Conflict to Multilevelled Settlement', *Nationalism and Ethnic Politics* 15 (2009).

over which it had not yet assumed full political responsibility, the Conservative government led by Edward Heath took away Northern Ireland's law and order powers in March 1972, prompting the resignation of Faulkner's government, the prorogation of the Stormont parliament, and the instigation of the system which came to be known as Direct Rule.

DIRECT RULE, INITIATIVES, AND STRIKES

Direct rule was designed to be temporary but it became 'the default option' after 1972.[20] At Westminster a bipartisan approach to the restoration of devolution on a cross-community basis quickly took root, and there were to be notable efforts made along these lines in the 1970s and 1980s. Northern Ireland continued to send twelve MPs to Westminster—in 1972 all but one a unionist of some description—but their influence was slight; the position looked even more threadbare when the UUP's traditional parliamentary alliance with the Conservatives disintegrated over the question of the power-sharing Executive which emerged out of the Sunningdale accord late in 1973.

In the context of the PIRA campaign of terrorism[21] and the lingering bitterness over the suspension of Stormont, it is perhaps unsurprising that unionists should be reluctant to endorse London's attempt to win the consent of the minority. Moreover, Sunningdale provided for a Council of Ireland to permit Dublin a role in the North's affairs, the 'Irish Dimension' pushed for by the SDLP with the backing of both the London and Dublin governments. Faulkner appears to have been browbeaten into acquiescence, although it was clear that he would have serious problems in persuading the broad unionist community to comply.[22] Faulkner duly had to resign as UUP leader shortly after leading the power-sharing Executive into office in January 1974.[23] Anti-agreement unionists banded together into a 'United Ulster Unionist Council' (UUUC) and dealt a severe blow to the initiative by scooping eleven of the twelve Northern Ireland seats at the Westminster election of February 1974. The election saw the defeat of Heath's Conservatives and the restoration of Wilson's Labour Party to office. Gone, abruptly, was the Anglo-Irish harmony of objectives around Northern Ireland within the new context of membership of the European Economic Community (EEC) so prized by Heath, and any sense of proprietorial concern on the part of Labour for the fledgling Executive. In May, a paramilitary-bolstered strike called by the Ulster Workers' Council (UWC) put it out of its misery, at the further cost of Catholic anger over the security forces'

---

[20] Mitchell, *Devolution*, 170.
[21] This involved atrocities such as the multiple bombing of Belfast city centre on 'Bloody Friday' in July 1972.
[22] K. Bloomfield, *Stormont in Crisis* (Belfast, 1994), 182–3.
[23] The make-up of the Assembly which was established along with the Executive was determined by the outcome of the elections held in June 1973 under the Single Transferable Vote (STV) form of Proportional Representation. For full details see W. D. Flackes, *Northern Ireland: A Political Directory* (London, 1980), 267–73.

failure to counter intimidation, and Protestant indignation over Wilson's scathing reference to them as 'spongers'.[24] Faulkner's career in effect ended—he died three years later—and it proved also to be a premature political plateau for his deputy, the SDLP's Gerry Fitt.

The direct rule arrangements gave considerable power to the Secretary of State for Northern Ireland, and the local parties wasted no time in describing the position as akin to a 'colonial governor'. The various Secretaries of State from 1972 have not been answerable through the ballot box to the people of Northern Ireland, a state of affairs which reflected its exclusion from the British party system. In the crucible of the crisis of 1969–73, the local party political landscape was reshaped with the emergence of the SDLP and the small cross-community Alliance, the establishment by Paisley of the Democratic Unionist Party (DUP) to rival the UUP, and, briefly, the appearance of the Vanguard Unionist Progressive Party (VUPP) led by former Unionist cabinet minister and leadership contender William Craig.

The democratic deficit was deepened by the conduct of Northern Ireland business at Westminster through an Orders-in-Council system by which the region's legislation could not be amended in parliament, only debated. In addition, many of the powers once exercised by local councils, having been transferred to Stormont in 1970, were then, upon Stormont's removal, assumed by a number of unelected public bodies. Much power also passed to unelected civil servants in the Northern Ireland Office (NIO) which came into existence with direct rule. On a more positive note, some scholars have pointed to the virtues of 'neutral government' in the sense of non-sectarian and modernizing policies, assistance for conflict-resolution, and greater fairness for the whole community.[25] It might be added that the British government continued to pay the bills for the escalating security costs and to keep Northern Ireland on a par with the rest of the UK in the field of social services. Indeed it has been suggested that the British state's willingness to provide such a 'cushion' reduced the incentives for the two sides to make hard compromises and reach agreement. As violence disrupted local business and deterred private investors so did the public sector grow in importance regarding the provision of employment. Gradually, the Catholic community's overall social profile began to improve, although they still remained twice as likely to be unemployed.[26]

A further attempt was made by Labour to fashion a cross-community form of devolved government through the Constitutional Convention of 1975–76. The UUUC was elected to forty-seven out of the seventy-eight seats at the Convention. It rejected the idea of imposed power-sharing and of an institutionalized Irish dimension, and thus ensured that there would be no breakthrough for Secretary of State Merlyn Rees. The Convention episode was, however, notable for the surprising

---

[24] G. Gillespie, *Years of Darkness* (Dublin, 2008), 97.
[25] See D. Birrell, *Direct Rule and the Governance of Northern Ireland* (Manchester, 2009).
[26] J. Whyte, 'Dynamics of Social and Political Change in Northern Ireland', in D. Keogh and M. H. Haltzel (eds), *Northern Ireland and the Politics of Reconciliation* (Cambridge, 1993).

breaking of UUUC ranks by William Craig who declared in favour of a 'voluntary' power-sharing deal with the SDLP only to be disowned by most of his own Vanguard colleagues and denounced vehemently by Paisley. It has been well observed that Craig's initiative has to be evaluated in the febrile context of apocalyptic speculation at this juncture concerning possible British withdrawal, the promotion of Ulster independence as a solution to the problem, the prospects of a no-holds-barred civil war, and the panicky political reactions in Dublin.[27] A patchily observed PIRA truce which had led to speculation about a deal being reached between the 'Provos' and the British government, broke down amidst republican feuding and a sectarian killing spree.[28] During the truce the British government decided to end internment but also the practice of granting political status to convicted paramilitary prisoners, a move which would have far-reaching ramifications.[29]

The resignation of Harold Wilson and his replacement by James Callaghan as Prime Minister in March 1976 led soon after to Rees being succeeded as Secretary of State by Roy Mason. The latter's approach was blunt and down to earth. He prioritized the security situation and the amelioration of the employment problem. He also presided over the development of the process of 'Ulsterization', the scaling down of the British Army presence and their replacement by the RUC and the Ulster Defence Regiment (UDR). The latter had emerged in 1970 following the disbandment of the 'B' Specials. While this went down well with metropolitan opinion, it had the effect of deepening sectarian divisions in Northern Ireland where the overwhelmingly Protestant security forces were the main targets of a renewed IRA campaign.[30] While Mason claimed security successes, the IRA repositioned itself for a 'Long War'. The emergence of the 'Peace People' movement, which seemed to hold out real hope of uniting Protestant and Catholic grassroots against the gunmen, proved evanescent.[31]

The turn taken by Mason has been viewed as congenial to the 'integrationist' variety of unionism, represented most obviously at Westminster by James Molyneaux and Enoch Powell, the latter having joined the UUP in 1974. As such it discomfited the SDLP, increasingly directed by John Hume whose antagonism towards the British government, insistence on the Irish dimension to any settlement, and impatience with unionism, saw the party undergo a 'greening' process which eclipsed the social democratic strand in its make-up. Paddy Devlin (the most left-wing member of the Sunningdale Executive) departed as a result, as did Fitt shortly after Hume replaced him as leader in 1979. Unionism in fact was torn between the integrationist approach and the hankering after a return to Stormont, more or less on a pre-1972 majority-rule basis, and there were serious tensions between the UUP leader in Northern Ireland, Harry West, and the Westminster contingent. Meanwhile, Paisley's robust style ensured that he continued to be

---

[27] See Bew, *Ireland*, 516–23.
[28] The feud between the Official and Provisional IRA claimed ten lives, and on a single day in October in 1975, UVF attacks claimed twelve lives.
[29] Mention should also be made of the non-jury 'Diplock' courts in which many paramilitaries were convicted. See H. Patterson, *Ireland since 1939* (Dublin, 2006), 247.
[30] Ibid., 247–8.   [31] See Gillespie, *Years of Darkness*, 126–30.

regarded by most outsiders as the main voice of Unionism, although his stock suffered a fall at home with the failure of his attempt to recreate the UWC strike in 1977. This proved a fillip for Mason in his quest to gain greater cross-community acceptance for direct rule.

Mason's period indeed saw a concerted attempt to represent direct rule in a 'purposive and positive' light, and to counter the impression of government indifference to Northern Ireland. A NIO memo at the beginning of 1977 proclaimed 'a commonsense approach' which kept Northern Ireland legislatively and administratively broadly in line with Britain, but which allowed latitude to adapt or supplement cross-channel measures to meet its particular problems and needs.[32] Mason's attempts to provide more employment opportunities involved tempting the American car manufacturer John DeLorean to west Belfast, but this short-lived and expensive gamble would end in the courts. The economic stringency of the late 1970s was not conducive to any easing of the unemployment problem; in fact, Northern Ireland's predicament worsened against the UK trend, and Catholic areas remained the worst affected.[33] Northern Ireland's dependence on the public sector was reinforced.

In 1978 Mason informed Callaghan that he would continue to work for a 'partnership administration' but that he was worried about the prospect of the government legislating for the extra parliamentary seats to which Northern Ireland was entitled at Westminster. This, he pointed out, would bring satisfaction to the unionists and further alienate the SDLP and Dublin. He also drew attention to the PIRA protest over the denial of political status to paramilitary prisoners although he took the view that it was not making the impact republicans wished.[34] It would not be long before Mason's fear over the matter of extra seats was given practical force: the Labour government, fighting for survival, duly passed the legislation (bringing Northern Ireland up to seventeen MPs), and the SDLP was predictably hostile. In the end it led to Gerry Fitt withdrawing support from Labour in the vital House of Commons vote which brought the government down at the end of March 1979 and paved the way for the subsequent election which resulted in victory for Margaret Thatcher's Conservatives. The first major challenge her government would face in Northern Ireland would be the PIRA's campaign for political status and the republican hunger strikes of 1980–81.[35]

It is difficult to exaggerate the impact of the hunger strikes whether in relation to the sympathetic mobilization of the nationalist community, the deepening of the sectarian divide in Northern Ireland, the international attention paid to the ordeal of Bobby Sands in particular, and the strengthening of the republican movement's political wing, Sinn Fein. It was in effect a collision of absolutist mentalities and postures. Thatcher's refusal to concede to the strikers' demands—something which needs to be put in the context of her other political difficulties of

[32] PRONI, FIN/30/R/1/11, Administrative Devolution, January 1977.
[33] PRONI, CENT/1/7/24, memo by R. H. Kidd to Secretary of State, 13 September 1978.
[34] PRONI, CENT/1/7/24, memo by Mason to Callaghan, 13 September 1978.
[35] See English, *Armed Struggle*, Pt 3, Ch. 5; also P. O'Malley, *Biting at the Grave* (Belfast, 1990).

the time—earned her the undying hatred of a generation of nationalists and almost resulted in her murder by an IRA bomb at the 1984 Conservative Party conference in Brighton. The hunger strikes at once reinforced the political radicalism of Irish republicanism and the traditional Catholic piety of the broader community context in which it moved. They conjured up the sacrificial republicanism of Pearse and Easter 1916 and fed the expectation that such sacrifices would produce a dramatically transformed political and cultural context. While Sinn Fein duly reaped electoral benefits in Westminster elections—Gerry Adams defeated Fitt in West Belfast in the 1983 General Election—and in the elections for a new Northern Ireland Assembly in 1982, there was no weakening of the PIRA's military campaign. The leading republican Danny Morrison put it into words for his fellow believers in 1981: '... will anyone here object if, with a ballot paper in one hand and the Armalite in the other, we take power in Ireland?'[36]

The Assembly set up in 1982 by the then Secretary of State James Prior envisaged a process of 'rolling devolution'—the more the local parties agreed between themselves the more powers would be devolved. In the event the SDLP boycotted it, the Molyneaux-led UUP in effect disengaged, and only the DUP and Alliance continued to work its limited scrutinizing functions until it was superseded by events in 1985 and wound up in 1986.[37] In the early 1980s there was little significant dialogue between the parties, and the Thatcher government was distrusted on all sides. Clearly there was a strong argument for a different approach to be adopted.

In 1980 soon after taking office, Thatcher had met with the Irish Taoiseach Charles Haughey. It was the beginning of an Anglo-Irish process which was to culminate in the Agreement of November 1985. The initial meeting produced an intergovernmental council and studies were then undertaken of what was called 'the totality of relationships in these islands'. Progress was slow and almost scuppered by the crisis created by the hunger strikes, but there was a bureaucratic momentum which survived the political turbulence. Additionally, there were important developments within constitutional Irish nationalism in response to the rise of Sinn Fein. In 1983 a new Fine Gael-Labour coalition government in the South launched 'The New Ireland Forum', chiefly as a means of re-energizing the SDLP and restating the case for peaceful change. Although the Forum reiterated the traditional demand for Irish unity, it also floated the notion of some kind of joint authority over Northern Ireland on the part of both the British and Irish governments. The latter idea could be said to have informed the thinking behind the 1985 Agreement.[38]

The 'Anglo-Irish Agreement' placed the Northern Ireland problem squarely within the context of British-Irish relations. The future course of solution-seeking was clearly marked out as a joint venture; there was recognition that the two

---

[36] Quoted in P. Bew and G. Gillespie, *Northern Ireland: A Chronology of the Troubles* (Dublin, 1993), 157.

[37] For an appraisal see C. O'Leary, S. Elliott, and R. A. Wilford, *The Northern Ireland Assembly 1982–1986* (London, 1988).

[38] A. Kenny, *The Road to Hillsborough* (Oxford, 1986).

governments had a mutual interest in building political stability in Northern Ireland. Moreover, the Agreement signalled the internationalization of the conflict: besides the supportive structure of the European Union (EU) there was the crucial factor of American pressure. For Thatcher, emboldened by her greater political security at home after the Falklands War in 1982, the main motivation in signing up was the expectation of greater cooperation from the South over security; while for Dublin, there was the prize of a role in the North's affairs through the intergovernmental conference which was at the heart of the deal. This role was to be consultative, and the Agreement stopped clearly short of joint authority; nevertheless, the text spoke of 'determined efforts' being made to meet any concerns the Irish government might have in its concern for the Catholic minority. The SDLP had secured an apparently meaningful 'Irish dimension'. The governments tried to reassure unionists that no constitutional change would be made without their consent, but the unionist opposition was total and uncompromising. It united the UUP and DUP in defiance, although their subsequent 'Ulster Says No' joint campaign of protest achieved mixed results.[39]

The Agreement was in many respects ambiguous, not least in relation to whether or not it was really designed indirectly to lead to the power-sharing internal settlement long favoured by London.[40] Moreover, it did not initially give republicans pause for any reflection on the wisdom of their campaign, or even significantly impede Sinn Fein's electoral march. By the end of the 1980s there were serious question marks over how effective the Agreement had been, and matters seemed to have settled back into the confines of direct rule, albeit with a 'green tinge'.[41]

Meanwhile, there was increasing evidence of an improvement in the minority's economic situation with 'Fair Employment' legislation and institutional pressures helping to boost the Catholic presence in areas such as the civil service as well as other non-manual and skilled manual occupations.[42] The extent to which those from a nationalist background viewed such matters as diluting traditional political goals is unclear, although they could not but be aware of the reluctance of the political establishment in the Republic of Ireland to encourage any thoughts of Irish unity. In the 1991 census, the Catholic population figure stood at 38.4 per cent with the combined Protestant figure coming out at roughly 45 per cent.[43] Clearly many people were now unable, or unwilling, to identify themselves in religious terms.

THE PEACE PROCESS

It was in the context of the continuing political deadlock that important talks between Gerry Adams of Sinn Fein and John Hume began towards the end of the decade. It was not only Hume who was in touch with the Republican movement:

---

[39] See F. Cochrane, *Unionist Politics and the Politics of Unionism* (Cork, 1997), Ch. 4; D. Trimble, 'A Unionist Perspective', in C. Townshend (ed.), *Consensus in Ireland* (Oxford, 1988).
[40] D. Goodall, 'Hillsborough to Belfast: Is it the Final Lap?', in M. Elliott (ed.), *The Long Road to Peace in Northern Ireland* (Liverpool, 2002).
[41] Patterson, *Ireland*, Ch. 10.   [42] Whyte, 'Dynamics'.   [43] Northern Ireland Census 1991.

there were contacts with the Irish government, the Catholic Church, and indeed the British government, but such dealings were shrouded in secrecy and carried substantial political risks. Hume knew he too was taking a big risk: his main objective was to end the violence, but he also set out to convince republicans that they should pursue their aims by exclusively political means. This in turn implied that Sinn Fein would pose an even greater electoral threat to the SDLP. Hume strove to get the British government to state that it had no particular interest in remaining in Northern Ireland, and to impress upon Sinn Fein that the real task for them was to reach an internal accommodation with the unionists.

In 1990 the then Secretary of State, Peter Brooke, made such a statement which, while not unambiguous, had the desired effect of strengthening Hume's hand. Brooke's successor, Patrick Mayhew, made similar declarations. All of this perturbed unionists, but did not prevent Brooke and Mayhew bringing the political parties (excepting Sinn Fein) together for talks organized around a three-strand framework. The first strand was concerned with an internal political settlement in Northern Ireland; the second with North-South relations; and the third with British-Irish relations. While these rounds of talks yielded no definite outcome they could be said to have laid the ground for what became known as the peace process. They provided a clear route map for future negotiations.

The political climate was also shaped significantly by the joint 'Downing Street Declaration' drawn up by the British and Irish governments in 1993. This declaration was notable for its reference to 'the right to national self-determination based on consent freely given, north and south'.[44] This appeared to be an attempt to make compatible—or at least allow to coexist—the nationalist and republican belief that the unit of self-determination should be the whole island of Ireland; and the unionist stress on the principle of consent as applied to Northern Ireland and the majority's wish to remain part of the UK. The Declaration was the forerunner of the Framework Document of 1995 which was produced in the circumstances of the cessation of violence brought about by the republican and loyalist paramilitary ceasefires of the previous year.

In August 1994 the IRA ordered a cessation of the armed campaign which had claimed the bulk of the 3000 and more lost lives of the Troubles.[45] Behind the decision there was at least an element of war weariness and a pragmatic acceptance that outright military victory was unlikely. However, the notion of the 'tactical use' of violence had clearly not been dispensed with. There was in fact a brief return to violence in 1996–97 as political progress appeared, from a Republican perspective, to have again stalled. Indeed, the issue of the decommissioning of weapons as a condition of Sinn Fein entering all-party talks provided a taste of problems and crises to come.[46] On the other hand, there was no doubting the sway exerted by the

---

[44] The text of the declaration is in Cochrane, *Unionist Politics*, Appendix 2.
[45] D. McKittrick *et al.*, *Lost Lives* (Edinburgh, 2004).
[46] Sinn Fein—and the SDLP—were also in disagreement with the British government's decision to set up an elected 'Forum for Dialogue' in 1996.

Adams's leadership, and he and others had clearly concluded that their struggle could best be advanced in the political arena, however gradually.

Unionists were deeply divided over the peace process,[47] and the coincidental eruption of the bitter dispute over the Orange Order's march at Drumcree in Portadown, destabilized the Protestant community more widely. Drumcree in fact was to prove helpful to David Trimble's ascent to the UUP leadership in 1995; that summer he had been prominent in his support for the marchers. However, Trimble was a modernist political figure keen to ensure that there were no more British-Irish agreements reached over unionist heads and drawn up without suitable unionist input.[48] At this stage Paisley and the DUP were the main symbols of the traditional 'not an inch' approach, in stark contrast to the political representatives of the loyalist paramilitaries. The 'Combined Loyalist Military Command' involving both the UDA and UVF and their respective offshoots indeed called off their campaign in October 1994.

The key development in the process bearing fruit came in the election of the Labour government led by Tony Blair in May 1997. Blair made Northern Ireland a priority from the start.[49] Indeed, the personal roles played by Blair, Taoiseach Bertie Ahern, and US Senator George Mitchell proved instrumental. Mitchell[50] had been installed as Chair of an international commission on the subject of decommissioning of paramilitary weapons back in 1995, and the commission's report of January 1996 outlined six principles (thereafter referred to as the Mitchell principles) to which all parties had to subscribe if they wished to enter talks on Northern Ireland's future. In signing up to these principles in September 1997, Sinn Fein committed itself to exclusively peaceful means of resolving political issues. They joined the talks, chaired by Mitchell but boycotted by the DUP and other fringe unionists not persuaded that the process was in unionist interests.

The Good Friday Agreement (GFA) of April 1998[51] represents the most successful attempt to resolve the political conflict in Northern Ireland since the outbreak of the Troubles. It received a substantial endorsement—71 per cent in favour—by the electorate in a referendum in May 1998, and an overwhelmingly positive verdict on a much smaller poll in the South.[52] This allowed for the 108-member Assembly to be set up at Stormont, although continuing political difficulties, particularly over the vexed topic of decommissioning, delayed the transfer of powers till late 1999, and indeed caused suspensions in both 2000 and 2001. After sitting for almost a year the Assembly was again suspended in October 2002 over alleged Republican intelligence-gathering. When devolution was restored in 2007, following

---

[47] See C. Farrington, *Ulster Unionism and the Peace Process* (Basingstoke, 2006).
[48] D. Godson, *Himself Alone* (London, 2004); F. Millar, *David Trimble: The Price of Peace* (Dublin, 2004).
[49] See F. Millar, *A Triumph of Politics* (Dublin, 2008), Ch. 6.
[50] See his memoir: G. Mitchell, *Making Peace* (London, 1999).
[51] It has also been commonly labelled 'The Belfast Agreement'. For examples of scholarly treatments see R. Wilford (ed.), *Aspects of the Belfast Agreement* (Oxford, 2001); and J. Ruane and J. Todd (eds), *After the Good Friday Agreement* (Dublin, 1999). The latter includes the text of the Agreement.
[52] A simultaneous referendum in the South resulted in the removal of Articles 2 and 3 (which had claimed the territory of Northern Ireland) from the Irish Constitution.

modifications to the GFA agreed at St Andrews in 2006, the DUP and Sinn Fein had emerged as the leading parties of the respective unionist and nationalist voting blocs.[53] With Sinn Fein committing itself to support the new Police Service of Northern Ireland (PSNI)[54] and the IRA having decommissioned, the way was cleared for the improbable spectacle of the four-party Executive being headed by Paisley and Martin McGuinness. In 2008 Paisley's retirement saw his long-standing deputy Peter Robinson assume the position of First Minister and the leadership of the DUP.

Devolved government—within the context of a constitutionally reformed and restructured UK[55]—was only one strand of the Agreement. The second strand involved North-South bodies directed by a North-South Ministerial Council; while the third addressed East-West relations primarily through the creation of the British-Irish Council (BIC). The spirit of the Agreement was pluralist and open-ended: equal recognition was given to British and Irish identities, and the validity of both unionist and nationalist aspirations confirmed.

Among most political scientists the Agreement is considered eminently consociationalist, although there has been significant debate about whether this model is a help or a hindrance to a lasting settlement.[56] The consociational features include cross-community power-sharing in the Executive; proportionality; equality and parity of esteem for both traditions; and veto rights for minorities. For some, the stipulation that Members of the Assembly designate themselves 'Unionist', 'Nationalist', or 'Other' for the purposes of ensuring cross-community support or parallel consent for key legislation, has had the effect of reinforcing or institutionalizing sectarian divisions and producing political inertia. However, advocates of the consociationalist approach contend that progress can only be made on the basis of a realistic management of long-established divisions. What is less disputed is that the Executive has struggled to lay down a coherent policy course and that the Assembly is weakened by the lack of a credible opposition.[57]

The peace process has been distinctive from what had gone before by virtue primarily of its all-inclusive character. This time the extremes were involved, notwithstanding the 'in and out' conduct of the DUP for a period of time and the initial hopes of both British and Irish governments for the 'centre ground' of the UUP and the SDLP to hold the arrangements together. The main victim of the process to date has been the UUP, for so long the dominant political party in Northern Ireland. From the signing of the Agreement until his departure as leader of the UUP in 2005, David Trimble fought an increasingly uphill battle to

---

[53] See Millar, *Triumph*, Chs 7–14 for the period 1998–2007. Sinn Fein emerged as the top nationalist party at the Assembly elections of 2003; the DUP eclipsed the UUP in the same elections and in the 2005 British election, and absorbed several UUP defectors.

[54] The new force replaced the RUC as a result of the recommendation of the Report of the Commission chaired by Chris Patten, the setting up of which was a result of the GFA.

[55] Mitchell, *Devolution*; R. Hazell (ed.), *Constitutional Futures* (Oxford, 1999).

[56] The best guide to the debate is R. Taylor (ed.), *Consociational Theory* (London, 2009).

[57] See R. Wilford and R. Wilson, 'Northern Ireland: Polarisation or Normalisation?', in R. Hazell (ed.), *Constitutional Futures Revisited* (Basingstoke, 2008).

prevent a unionist retreat to old certainties. In taking power with Sinn Fein, the DUP have put at risk much of the support which came their way on account of their depiction of Trimble and the UUP as 'pushovers'. The nationalist community's support for the Agreement was always far more emphatic,[58] and Sinn Fein appear to be holding their position. Nevertheless, the violent emergence on the scene of 'dissident' republican groups revives old uncertainties and fears.

CONCLUSION

As a society Northern Ireland has progressed hesitantly and tentatively beyond ethnic polarization. The decline of religious identity, or at least the hold exercised by the Churches, is mirrored—as in the South—by the growth of a more secular culture and a loosening of sexual taboos.[59] Northern Ireland now possesses little to put it at odds with the mainstream British or Irish experience in relation to leisure pursuits or consumption. The impact of the internet and the electronic media could be said to have connected Northern Ireland to wider trends and discourses, both high and low. Impressive work has been done by conflict resolution organizations and community workers, some of them former paramilitaries, to help those areas worst affected by the Troubles.[60]

Nevertheless, the endurance of 'peace walls' in working-class Belfast and elsewhere, and the still limited scale of social interaction between Protestant and Catholic communities, is a reminder that much of the old survives into the new. Indeed, studies by social geographers of Belfast and Derry in the years since the GFA stress the extent to which residential segregation, and a continuing fixation on controlling territory, contributes to the reproduction of sectarianism and hinders the formulation of policies aimed at increasing employment opportunities and building social inclusion.[61] All of this militates against the fashioning of a common civic identity and the credibility of ideas of a shared future.

The legacy of the Troubles is manifest in the difficulties of creating trust across the ethno-national or ethno-religious divide, and the task of reconciliation is deeply complicated by the different ways in which the Troubles are remembered and interpreted. The sensitive issue of making reparations to the victims of the conflict has recently demonstrated that there is little agreement over fundamental questions such as who is to be categorized as victims.[62] Emotions still run high over

---

[58] It was in the region of 90 per cent at the time of the referendum whereas unionist support never topped 55 per cent.
[59] The legalization of homosexuality took place in 1982 after a legal challenge taken to the European Court of Human Rights. However, it took until the new century for the gay community to become more visible and to intervene effectively in political discourse.
[60] See F. Cochrane, 'Unsung Heroes? The Role of Peace and Conflict Resolution Organisations in the Northern Ireland Conflict', in J. McGarry (ed.), *Northern Ireland and the Divided World* (Oxford, 2001).
[61] See P. Shirlow and B. Murtagh, *Belfast. Segregation, Violence and the City* (London, 2006); P. Shirlow et al., *Population Change and Social Inclusion Study: Derry/Londonderry September 2005* (University of Ulster, 2005).
[62] *Report of the Consultative Group on the Past* [Eames-Bradley Report] (Belfast, 2009).

events such as 'Bloody Sunday', as developments surrounding the Saville Inquiry indicate.[63] Politics in Northern Ireland are still conducted on the basis of competing unionist and nationalist blocs, and the 'national question' still constricts the political space for less ethnically divisive issues. Although the GFA provided a context for the coexistence of identities, it left both sides with the option of striving to put its aspirations on an advantageous footing. For Republicans and most nationalists, a sense of 'unfinished business' remains and this reinforces a continuing unionist desire to tie Northern Ireland closer to the rest of the UK.

As anniversaries bearing ancestral voices beckon in 2012 and 2016, Northern Ireland stands poised between signs of creeping normalization and potential political upheaval.

FURTHER READING

P. Bew, P. Gibbon, and H. Patterson, *Northern Ireland: Political Forces and Social Classes* (London, 2002).
C. Coulter and M. Murray (eds), *Northern Ireland After the Troubles* (Manchester, 2008).
D. McKittrick *et al.*, *Lost Lives* (Edinburgh, 2004).
F. Millar, *Northern Ireland: A Triumph of Politics* (Dublin, 2009).
J. Tonge, *Northern Ireland* (Cambridge, 2006).
J. H. Whyte, *Interpreting Northern Ireland* (Oxford, 1990).

---

[63] See P. Bew, 'The Role of the Historical Adviser and the Bloody Sunday Tribunal', *Historical Research*, 78 (2005).

Index

Bold entries denote figures

Abercorn, Earl of 20
abortion 258, 259
Academical Institution, *see* Royal Belfast Academical Institution
academic selection 225, 226
Act of Settlement 1652 143
Act of Union 4, 8, 41, 84
    Ulster after 228–32
Adair, John George 97
Adams, Gerry 334, 335
Adams, Mary 256
Advisory, Conciliation and Arbitration Service (ACAS) 301
agrarian conflicts 103
agricultural labourers 164
agricultural land 275
agricultural price index, 1785–1913 174 *table*
agriculture 6–7, 9–10
    after 1972 286–8
    Belfast Agreement and 288–90
    education and marketing 280–2
    employment in 276
    mechanized farming 318
    Ministry of 283
    mixed farming 162–3
    occupation of the land by holding size in 1854 and 1873 162 *table*
    prices and the parity principle 284–6
    and rural policy since 1914 275–90
    and the Second World War 282–4
    during the Stormont period 278–80
    see also farming
Agriculture Act 1947 285
Ahern, Bertie 337
air travel 317
Akenson, Donald H. 8, 51
Alabama Sports Hall of Fame (ASHOF), Birmingham, Alabama 273
alcohol consumption 110, 111, 115, 117
Alhambra Theatre 119
All Children Together 225, 226
Allen, Sir William 155
Allied Irish Bank League 265
All-Ireland football championship 269
All-Island Animal Health and Welfare Strategy 289
Amalgamated Transport and General Workers Union (ATGWU) 303

American Civil War 173, 180
Ancient Order of Hibernians 87, 120, 199, 237
Anderson, James 191
Anderson, Olive 255
Andrews, John 310, 315
An Gárda Síochána 266
Anglo-Irish Agreement 1985 289, 334–5
Anglo-Irish Treaty 1921 240
Anglo-Normans 121
animal health 289
ante-natal care 252
Antrim, County 127, 153, 267
    Antrim-born people in England and Wales in 1881 **149**
    emigration 1851–1911 151 *table*
    permanent celibacy among females and males in 1841 and 1911 68 *table*
    rates of prosecution in 1884–90 99 *table*
    weavers in 197
Apprentice Boys 120
apprenticeships 202
Archdale, Edward 279
Ards (Newtownards), County Down 264
Armagh (city) 25, 123, 128, 141
    1613 charter 122
    1766 local census 125
    Association for the Suppression of Street Begging 127
    urban hierarchy in 1659 124 *table*
    urban hierarchy in 1901 128 *table*
Armagh, County 267
    Armagh-born people in England and Wales in 1881 **149**
    emigration 1851–1911 151 *table*
    numbers of settlers and native Irish population 15
    percentage of land held by native Irish 16
    permanent celibacy among females and males in 1841 and 1911 68 *table*
    rates of prosecution in 1884–90 99 *table*
    weavers in 197
Armstrong, Gerry 270
Arnold, Charlotte 255
Articlave, County Londonderry 117
Asquith, H. H. 239
assisted passages 154
assize courts 90
association football 263, 264, 269, 272

342 Index

Association of Shipbuilding and Engineering
    Draughtsmen (AESD) 205
Attlee, Clement 242
Australia 152, 153, 154
Ayr, Scotland 150

Babington, Brutus 74
Babington Committee 284
bacon 166 *table*
Baldwin, Stanley 190
Ballybofey, County Donegal 165
Ballymena, County Antrim 127, 128 *table*, 129, 265
Ballynahinch, County Down 265
Banbridge Academy 264
Bangor, County Down 131
banking 184, 187, 192–3
baptisms 75
Barbour, John 179
Barbour, John Milne 310
barley 161, 166 *table*, 277
Bartlet, Daniel 34
Bateson, Thomas 97
Bates, Sir Richard Dawson 310
Beckett, J. C. 27
Beckett, Samuel 262
beef 20, 166 *table*, 281, 287, 288
Belfast 2, 3, 6, 18, 127, 183, 309
    association football 264
    associations 127
    Catholicism in 86–7
    Catholic population in mid-19th century 232
    charity schools and societies 53
    child mortality in 251
    famine fever 171
    freemen admitted 17
    gatherings at Cave Hill on Easter
        Monday 118
    growth of 132
    Harbour Commissioners 132, 133
    import trade 19
    industrialization in 7, 309
    Local Government District (LGD) 134
    Maternity and Child Welfare
        Committee 251
    migrant population in 1881 129
    Municipal Corporation 132
    permanent celibacy among females
        and males in 1841 and 1911 68 *table*
    Poleglass 138
    population growth from 1663 to 1725 19
    population in 19th century 129, 130, 146–7
    pressures of urbanization in 131
    prostitution in 248
    religious practice and the development of 85
    Scots-born and English-born residents
        1841–1911 152 *table*
    sectarian conflict 94
    shipbuilding labour conditions 200–5
    urban hierarchy in 1659 124 *table*
    urban hierarchy in 1901 128 *table*
    urban planning 137
    Water Commissioners 132
Belfast Agreement, and agriculture 288–90
Belfast Bank 184, 193
'Belfast Boycott' 188
Belfast Celtic 270
Belfast Celtic Football Club 120
Belfast Chamber of Commerce 7, 127, 181, 182
Belfast Charitable Society 23
Belfast Corporation 128
    funding for maternity and child welfare
        services 254
Belfast General Hospital 127
Belfast Improvement Act 1845 248
Belfast Library 127
Belfast Lying-in Hospital 53
Belfast Midnight Mission 249
Belfast Munitions of War Committee 181
Belfast Muslin Weavers society 196
Belfast Police District, rates of prosecution
    1884–90 99 *table*
Belfast Poor Law Guardians 209
Belfast Regional Survey and Plan 136
Belfast Savings Bank 127
Belfast Trades Council 196, 199, 206
Belfast Women's Welfare Clinic 255
Bell, Sam Hanna 204
Belmore Report 217
Belturbet, County Cavan 125, 126
Bennett, Judith 50
Bevan, Aneurin 315
Bevin, Ernest 194
Bibby Line 182
birth rates 62, 246, 303
'Black Oath' 17
Black Watch 264
Blair, Tony 337
Blake, Anthony 81
Blake, Michael 82
bleachers 24, 25, 126, 145, 178
blood sports 118
'Bloody Sunday' 329, 340
Bohemians 264
Bond, J. J. 155
Bonnar, Pat 270
book clubs 116
book-keeping 187
books 54
Boulter, Hugh 79
Boundary Commission 240
Bovevagh, County Londonderry 112
Bowman, Alexander 198
boycotting 188
Bracken, Patrick 262
Bramhall, John 76
Breffni Park, Cavan 266
Britain, *see* Great Britain
British Army 328–9, 332
British Egg Marketing Board 287
British-Irish Council (BIC) 338

British Labour Party 199
British Productivity Council 301
Brook Clinic 259
Brooke, Peter 336
Brooke, Sir Basil 193, 241, 279, 280, 315
brothels 249
Brown, Gordon 299
Brownlow, Arthur 20
Bruce, Robert Swift 254
'B' Specials 328, 329
bubonic plague 59
Bunscoil Phobal Feirste 226
Burke, Peter 107
Burns, Robert 107
business and finance
 1780–1945 177–94
 evolution of 181–8
 after the first world war 188–94
business and labour since 1945 291–307
Butler, Adam 289
Butler, Rab 221
butter 20, 125, 129, 162, 166 *table*, 172

caid/Cad 261
Cairncross Report 296
Callaghan, James 332, 333
camánacht 266
Cambridge, Alice 52
Campbell College 264
Canada 152, 153, 154
canals and navigations in Ireland 1715–1876 **185**
cancer 312, 313 *table*, 319
car ownership 317, 323
Carrickfergus, County Antrim 38, 99 *table*, 124 *table*, 131
Carson, Sir Edward 199
Carter, Charles 294
Catholic clergy 115–16
Catholic Defender movement 41, 96
Catholic emancipation 8, 243
Catholicism 5, 51, 82
 in Belfast 86
Catholics 8, 39, 199
 at the beginning of the 20th century 87
 exclusion from status or office 126
 family size 247
 financial support for clergy 81
 funerals 112
 growth in County Fermanagh 70 n.46
 population growth 70
 repression of 80
 and the Test Acts 145
 wakes 112
cattle 20, 21, 125, 162, 165, 166 *table*, 172, 277
Cattle Acts 1663 and 1665 20
Cavan (town) 124, 125
Cavan and Heron, provision merchants 113
Cavan, County 127, 142, 153, 266–7
 Cavan-born people in England and Wales in 1881 **149**

emigration 1851–1911 151 *table*
 female majority in 245
 percentage of land held by native Irish 16
 permanent celibacy among females and males in 1841 and 1911 68 *table*
 rates of prosecution in 1884–90 99 *table*
 weavers in 197
celibacy 67, 68 *table*, 246
Celtic Park 269
Celtic Tiger economy 300
Cennick, John 80
census
 of 1659 124
 of 1831 127
 of 1971 133
Chamberlain, Joseph 236
Chamber of Commerce (Belfast) 7, 127, 181, 182
Charitable Society 127
Charles I 30, 31, 32, 35, 36, 143
Charles II 19, 37
Chichester-Clark, James 280, 329
Chichester, Sir Arthur, Lord Deputy 15, 45, 142
child abandonment 249
child mortality 251
Chilver Commission 225
Christ Church 85
church attendance 88
Church Education Society 215
Churchill, Winston 194
Church of Ireland 39, 75, 78, 85, 87–8
 in 18th century 79
 education and 212
 participation in the National School system 215
 Synod 1970 224
 wakes 112
Church Temporalities Act 1833 84
civil rights movement 326–7
clergy 81, 114–15
Cliftonville Football Club 264, 270
climate 161
Clongowes Wood College 262, 263
Clotworthy, Sir John 30, 31
Coach, Lady 46
Coach, Sir Thomas 46
cock-fighting 115
Coleraine, County 142
Coleraine, County Londonderry 165
 urban hierarchy in 1659 124 *table*
 urban hierarchy in 1901 128 *table*
Cole, Sir William 32
Colwyn Committee 309–10
Combe Barbour 191
Combinations Acts 195
Combined Loyalist Military Command 337
Commercial Bank 184
Commercial Buildings 127

344 Index

Commission on Emigration, 1827 146
Committee on Maternity Services 253
commodity marketing boards 281
Common Agricultural Policy (CAP) 276–7, 287, 288, 289
common law 90, 103
Common Market (later European Union, EU) 286–7
communion 78
conflict 135–6
   in the 18th century 39–41
   see also sectarian conflict
Conlon, Malachy 285
Connacht/Connaught 31, 98, 121, 147, 151, 158
   emigration in the late 1800s 153
   indictable offences before the courts 99 *table*
   policing in 1832–52 94 *table*
   post-Famine emigration in 151 *table*
   reported homicides 1866–92 98 *table*
Connell, K. H. 62
Constitutional Convention 1976–76 331
contractarianism 238
Conway, Cardinal 224, 225
Cooke, Henry, Reverend 115, 230, 231, 234
Coote, Sir Charles 35
COPA 288
Cork, County, GAA Rule 42 vote 268 n.40
Cornewall Lewis, Sir George 147
Corrymeela Community 138
cost of living 323
cottier-weavers 164
cotton 7, 165–6
cotton industry 178–9, 196, 231
Council of Trent 75
Counter-Reformation 77
County Infirmary Bill 1765–66 61
courts 91, 103
court system 5
Covenanters 79
Crafts, Nicholas 294
Craigavon, County Armagh 137
Craigavon, Lord 241
Craig, James 218, 220, 310
Craig, William 331, 332
cricket 261–3
crime 95–100, 104
   indictable offences 98, 99 *table*
Cromwell, Oliver 35
Cronin, Mike 260
crop and cereal growing 277
crop failures 167
   potato 170–3
Crown Solicitors in Ireland 102
Cullen, Paul 81, 232, 235
Cunningham, Josias 187
Currie, Austin 326
Cusack, Michael 266

dairy cows 162
DARD (Department of Agriculture and Rural Development) 289
DATI (Department of Agriculture and Technical Instruction) 279, 280, 282, 283
Davey, J. E. 83
Davidge Report 315
Davidson, Samuel 181
Davies, Sir John 101, 121, 142
Davin, Maurice 266
death rates 311, 312 *table*, 319
   from cancer 313 *table*
   from heart disease 313 *table*
   from tuberculosis 313 *table*
Deeny, James 251
Defence of the Realm Act 283
deficiency payments system 286
de-industrialization 296–7
Delap, James 54
Democratic Unionist Party (DUP) 11, 331, 337, 338, 339
denominational schools 211, 212
Denvir, Cornelius, Bishop of Down and Connor 86, 232
Department of Agriculture and Technical Instruction (DATI) 279, 280, 282, 283
Derry (city) 3, 123, 124, 137, 183–4, 200, 309
   freemen admitted during the 1640s 18
   labour market in 129
   Magee College 223
   population growth 19
   population in 1911 147
   ratepayers 128
   refounding as Londonderry 142
   sectarian conflict 94
   shirt manufacturing in 184, 208
   textile industry 206
   thatched houses 128
   trade depression in 192
   urban hierarchy in 1659 6, 124 *table*
   urban hierarchy in 1901 128 *table*
   vessels using port in 1700s 22
   see also Londonderry (county)
Derry City Football Club 270
Desertlyn, County Londonderry 115
de Valera, Eamon 240
Devenish island, County Fermanagh 115
Devlin, Bernadette 224, 326
Devlin, Joseph (Joe) 87, 237, 239
Devlin, Paddy 332
Direct Rule from London 10, 11, 286
direct rule from London 330
Disraeli, Benjamin 216
Distillery Football Club 264
dock workers 207
domestic service 49
Donaghmoyne, County Monaghan 111
Donaghy, Mal 270
Donegal, County 127, 142, 153, 156
   Donegal-born people in England and Wales in 1881 **149**
   emigration 1851–1911 151 *table*

female majority in 245
  permanent celibacy among females and males
    1841 and 1911 68 *table*
  rates of prosecution in 1884–90 99 *table*
  sheep in 161
  weavers in 197
Donnybrook Fair, Dublin 261
Dorrian, Patrick 86
Down, County 127, 153
  Down-born people in England and Wales in
    1881 **149**
  emigration 1851–1911 151 *table*
  permanent celibacy among females and males
    in 1841 and 1911 68 *table*
  rates of prosecution in 1884–90 99 *table*
  weavers in 197
Downing Street Declaration 336
Downpatrick, County Down 124 *table*, 133,
  135, 137, 141, 155
dowries 45–6
drapers 24, 25, 178
Drennan, William 231
Drew, Thomas 85, 88
Drumcree march 337
Dublin Castle 130, 131
Duffy, Charles Gavan 233
Dumbarton 150
Dundrum, County Down 14
Dungannon, County Tyrone 127, 265
DUP (Democratic Unionist Party) 11, 331,
  337, 338, 339

Easter 109
Easter Monday 118–19
economic growth
  between 1890 and 1992 292 *table*
  between 1950 and 1973 291
  after 1969 295–6
Economic Survey of Northern Ireland 291
Edgar, John 114
Edgar, Rev. Dr 170, 249
education 8, 53–5
  academic selection 225, 226
  denominational segregation in 222
  integrated education 224
  intermediate education 216–17
  mass education 212–13
  modernization of 217–18
  national school system 8, 213–15
  in Northern Ireland 218–20
  payment by results in elementary
    schools 217
  since the late 18th century 211–27
  state funding 225
  university education 223–4
  see also schools
Education Act 1923 219
Education Act 1930 220
Education Act 1947 222
Education Act 1968 223

Education Act for England and Wales
  1944 221
education and library boards 224
eggs 277
  exports to Britain 169
Eire, *see* Republic of Ireland
Elizabeth II, Queen 11n., 242
Elliott, Rowley 281
emigration
  in the 19th century 150–5
  and migration 1600–1945 140–59
  and migration in the
    18th century 144–6
  post-Famine emigration
    by province 151 *table*
  from Ulster 1851–1911 151 *table*
employment 333
  religious balance in 321
  see also unemployment
England 2
  death rates, 1922–99 312 *table*
  death rates from cancer 313 *table*
  death rates from heart disease 313 *table*
  death rates from tuberculosis between 1926
    and 1960 313 *table*
  English-born Belfast residents
    1841–1911 152 *table*
  infant mortality rates 312 *table*
  migration of Ulster-born people in 1881
    to **148, 149**
Enniskillen, County Fermanagh 124 *table*, 125,
  126, 129
  ratepayers 128
  thatched houses 128
environment 6, 161
Equality Commission 302
European Economic Community (EEC)
  297, 330
European Union (EU) 335; *see also* Common
  Market
Evans, Estyn 1
Exchange Rate Mechanism (ERM) 299
expenditure, public expenditure per head in the
  UK 304 *table*
exports 165

Fairbairn, Lawson Combe Barbour Ltd (FLCB) 191
Fair Employment Agency (FEA) 302, 321
Fair Employment Commission (FEC) 321
Fair Employment (Northern Ireland) Act
  301–2, 321
fairs 110, 261
family 8, 245
family planning 255
Family Planning Association 256
Family Planning Association of Northern
  Ireland 258
family planning legislation 256
family size 246, 247, 252, 254
famine fever 171

farm businesses 278
farmer-weavers 164
farming, *see* agriculture
farm servants 165
farm sizes 278, 309
farm structures 278
Faulkner, Brian 296, 329, 330, 331
Fenianism 234
Fenton, Samuel Graeme 129
Fermanagh, County 127
   Catholic and Protestant growth in 70 n.46
   emigration 1851–1911 151 *table*
   female majority in 245
   Fermanagh-born people in England and
      Wales in 1881 **149**
   permanent celibacy among females and males
      in 1841 and 1911 68 *table*
   rates of prosecution in 1884–90 99 *table*
   weavers in 197
fertility 8, 65 n.29, 72–3, 246, 247, 254–8
Fielding, Sarah 54
First World War 181, 187
   and the interwar period 308–17
fishing 276
Fitt, Gerry 331, 333, 334
Fitzgerald, Bridget 45, 47
flax 173, 277
Flight of the Earls 13, 27, 43–7, 142
food and drinks processing 276
food-processing industries 207
Food Production Campaign 282
Football Association 263
Football Association of Ireland (FAI) 270
forestry 276
Foster Cup 265
Framework Document 1995 336
France 41
French Wars 64
funerals 75
   Catholic 112

Gaelic Athletic Association 119, 262, 265–9, 272
   partition and 267
   Rule 21, 268
   Rule 42, 268
   Ulster Council 9
Gaelic Football 266, 269
Gallaher, Thomas 181
Garda Síochána 266
Garnham, Neal 118
gender ratios 9
General Assembly of the Presbyterian
   Church 224, 230
Getgood, Bob 204
Gibson, Mike 265
Gillespie, Raymond 90
Given, Shay 270
Gladstone, William 216, 235
Glasgow 130, 133
Glentoran Football Club 269, 270

Golden Age of Economic Growth 291
golf 263
Good Friday Agreement 1998 6, 11, 298,
   337, 340
Good Shepherd laundry 249
Gordon Highlanders 264
Gore, Sir Ralph 32
government contracts 190
Government of Ireland Act 1920 220, 278, 280
grain production 64
grammar schools 221, 222
Grand Orange Lodge of Ireland 230
Grant, William 315
grassland 277
Gray, John 207
Gray, Paul 51
Great Britain
   export of eggs to 169
   support for Ulster loyalist resistance to Home
      Rule 237
   unemployment 1923–1980 314 *table*
Great Famine 59, 66, 71, 96, 170–3, 232
Great War, *see* First World War

hallow-e'en 110
Hall-Thompson, Samuel 221
Hamilton, Sir James 28, 142
Hancock, William Neilson 131
handkerchiefs 207
handloom weavers 172
Hanna, George 318
Harbour Commissioners 127
Harland and Wolff 182, 183, 189, 194,
   200, 297
   Admiralty orders 190–1
   apprentices employed in 1919 202
   office staff 204–5
   unskilled labourers 204
Harland, Sir Edward 182
harvest time 110
Haughey, Charles 288, 334
Hayes, Maurice 135
health 319
Health and Local Government, Ministry of
   10, 254
Health and Personal Social Services (Northern
   Ireland) Order 1972 322
Health and Social Services Boards 322
health services 312
Health Services Board 316
heart disease 313 *table*, 319
hearth tax 20
Heath, Edward 330
hedge schools 212
Heineken Cup 265
Henderson, George 282
Henry, Henry 86, 87
Henry VIII 74
Herbage Seeds Marketing Board 287
high-days and holidays 109

hired labourers 277
hiring fairs 165
Hoare, Sir Samuel 192
hockey 264, 267, 271
Holmes, Samuel 266
Holy Eve 110
home for single mothers 249
home ownership 322
Home Rule 236
Home Rule Bill 87, 235, 239, 243
homicides 97, 98 *table*
homosexuality 258
horticulture 277
house prices 300
housing 312–14, 317, 318, 323
   unfit dwellings 320 *table*
Housing Acts 314
Housing Executive 138
housing market 300
Housing Order 1983 322
housing schemes, in Belfast 138
Howard, Charles 45
Hume, John 289, 326, 332, 335, 336
hunger strikes 333, 334
hunting 261
hurling 261, 265–6
Hutchinson, Francis 79

illegitimate births 247, 248
income 322
Independent Labour Party 199
Independent Orange Order 199
Independent Review of Economic Policy
   (IREP) 304
industrial disputes 302
industrialization 2, 6, 72, 128–33
industrial relations 301, 302
industrial workers 197
infanticide 249–50
infant mortality rates 246, 251, 311, 312 *table*, 319
inheritance of land 45–6
Institute of Chartered Accountants in Ireland
   (ICAI) 187–8
Insurrection Act 1796 100
integrated education 225, 226
Integrated Schools Movement 138
inter-denominational cooperation 229
intermediate education 221
Intermediate Education Act 1878 216
Invasion of Ulster, 1883 235
IRA (Irish Republican Army) 240, 242, 243, 338
Ireland
   indictable offences before the courts 99 *table*
   reported homicides 1866–92 98 *table*
Irish Challenge Cup 264
Irish Constabulary 93
Irish Cup 264
Irish Education Bill 213
Irish Farmers' Association 288

Irish Football Association 120, 264, 270
Irish language 108
Irish League Championship 264
Irish Linen Guild 189
Irish-medium education 226, 227
Irish National Volunteers (INV) 239
Irish Parliamentary Party 237
Irish Poor Law 169
Irish Republican Army (IRA) 240, 242, 243, 338
Irish Rogues and Raparees (Cosgrove) 113
Irish Rugby Football Union 264
   Ulster Branch 9
Irish Senior Cup 264
Irish Trade Union Congress (ITUC) 301
   Northern Ireland Committee (NIC) 301
Irish Volunteers 239

James II 21, 37, 39, 80, 91
James Mackie 193
James VI and I, King 27, 28, 122, 142
Jennings, Pat 270
Johnson, Francis 196
Johnston, William 104, 155, 234
journeymen weavers 164
Joyce, Edmund 262

Kane, John 129, 170
Kerr, Ronan 268 n.38
Kettle, Tom 263
Kildare Place Society 213
Kilkenny, County 262
Killyleagh, County Down 124 *table*
King, Seamus 265
King, William 79, 145
kirk session 52
Knock club 264
Kyle, Jackie 265

labour
   and industrial transformation 197–8
   politics of 198–200
   in retail 207
   shipbuilding structure and working
      conditions 200–5
   and society, 1780–1945 195–210
   textile industry structure and working
      conditions 205–8
   in transport 206–7
   and unemployment 301–4
Labour Relations Agency 301
labour unions 208
Lagan College 226
Laggan army 32, 36
Lanark 150
Land Act 1881 174, 175
Land Act 1882 175
Land Act 1903 175
land courts 174
Land League 174
Landlord and Tenant Act 1870 151

landlords 26, 164, 171
land, organization of 12
land purchase acts 278
Land War 97, 104, 174, 235
Larkin, Jim 197, 199
Laud, William, Archbishop of Canterbury 30
law 5, 100–1
   attitudes to crime and 101–3
Law, Andrew Bonar 239
League of North and South 234
Leeke, George 281
Leinster
   indictable offences before the courts
      99 *table*
   policing in 1832–52 94 *table*
   post-Famine emigration in 151 *table*
   reported homicides 1866–92 98 *table*
Leinster Regiment Cup 261
leisure, work and 109–13
Leitrim, County 40, 163
Leslie, Henry 51
Letterkenny, County Donegal 165
Liberals 235
life expectancy 314 *table*
   of shipbuilding workers 201
Linen Board 178
linen exports 165
linen industry 6, 7, 20, 145, 177–8, 180–1
   and the American Civil War 173
   and cotton industry 207, 231
   after the First World War 188, 193
   growth in the 18th century 24–5, 163
   success of 40, 126
Linen Industry Research Association 189
Linfield Football Club 120, 264, 270
linguistic diversity 117
Lisburn 20, 124 *table*, 129, 131, 206
   ratepayers 128
   thatched houses 128
   urban hierarchy in 1901 128 *table*
Lisburn Club (cricket) 263
literacy 54–5, 113
Livestock Breeding Act 1922 280
livestock farming 64, 162, 172, 277
Lloyd George, David 239
Loans Guarantee Acts 189
local authority housing 10
local government, reforms in 1973 134
Lockwood Commission 1965 report 224
London companies 142, 143
Londonderry, County 127, 140, 142
   emigration 1851–1911 151 *table*
   Londonderry-born people in England and
      Wales in 1881 **149**
   numbers of settlers and native Irish
      population 15
   permanent celibacy among females and males
      in 1841 and 1911 68 *table*
   rates of prosecution in 1884–90 99 *table*
   weavers in 197

London Hibernian Society 126–7
Lough Derg 116
Lurgan, County Armagh 126, 128–9, 132,
   133, 136, 206
   linen market 20
   population in 1901 128 *table*
luxury goods, purchased in the 1670s and
   1680s 19
Lynn, Robert J. 219, 282

McBride, Willie John 265
McCann, Eamonn 326
McCann, John 196
McCann, Thomas 126
McClure, Ian 319
MacCooey, Art 107, 108
McCracken, Margaret 50
McCracken, Mary Ann 50, 56
MacDermott, John 221
MacDonnell, Fiona 46
McGuinness, Catherine 43, 44
McGuinness, Martin 11 n.226, 338
McIntyre, Rev. Anthony 246, 248
McIvor, Basil 225
McKay, John 266
McKenna, John 101
MacMahon, Heber 35
Macmillan, Harold 242
MacRory Cup 267
McSharry, Ray 289
McTier, Martha 53, 54, 56
McTier, Tom 54
Magee College, Derry 223
Maguire, Alice 52
Makee, John 52
Mallon, J. J. 207
Manson, David 54
Mant, Richard 83
manufacturing, growth in 293 *table*
marketing boards 287
markets 14, 110, 133
marriage 74, 75
marriage age 64–6
marriage ceremonies 112
marriage dowry 45–6
marriage rates 62, 246, 318
martial law 96
Mary of Modena 37
Mason, Roy 332, 333
Massey, W. F. 156
Mater Hospital 319
maternal and child mortality
   251–4
Matthew, Sir Robert 136
Maxwell, Gordon 196
May Day 109
May Eve 109, 110
Mayhew, Patrick 336
Mayo, County 163
Maze Prison 273

meat 166 *table*; *see also* bacon; beef; pork
medical benefit 311
Memoir of Ballymartin 114
men
　celibacy rate 246
　employment of 322
Methodist College, Belfast 216, 264
Methodists 51, 52, 80
Midnight Mission Rescue and Maternity Home 247
midwives 254
migration 6
　during the inter-war depression 155–8
　and emigration 1600–1945 140–59
　and emigration in the 18th century 144–6
　during partition 155–8
　Ulster-born people in England and Wales in 1881 **148, 149**
　during World Wars 155–8
Milford, County Donegal 165
Milk Marketing Board 287
Ministry of Agriculture 283
Ministry of Health and Local Government 10, 254
Mitchell, George 337
mixed farming 162–3
modern sport, origins of 261–3
Molyneaux, James 332
Monaghan, County 153, 266
　celibacy in 67
　emigration 1851–1911 151 *table*
　female majority in 245
　Monaghan-born people in England and Wales in 1881 **149**
　permanent celibacy among females and males in 1841 and 1911 68 *table*
　rates of prosecution in 1884–90 99 *table*
　weavers in 197
Monaghan Rugby Club 265
Monro, Henry 41
Monro, Robert 33, 34, 35, 36
Montgomery, Elizabeth 46–7
Montgomery, Sir Hugh 28, 142
Moore, Acheson 48
Moore, Robert 280
moral conservatism 258–9
Moravians 80
Morgan, Eoin 262
Morrison, Brian 260
Morrison, Danny 334
mortality 61
　maternal and child mortality 251–4
mortality rates 246
Moryson, Fynes 101
Mountjoy, Lord Deputy of Ireland 141
Moyola Football Club 264
Municipal Technical Institute, Belfast 222
Munster
　emigration in the 19th century 153
　indictable offences before the courts 99 *table*

policing in 1832–52 94 *table*
post-Famine emigration in 151 *table*
reported homicides 1866–92 98 *table*
Murphy, James 82
Murray, James 97
music halls 119

National Amalgamated Union of Labour (NAUL) 203
National Anti-Sweating League 207
National Assistance system 316
National Health Service Amendment (Family Planning) Act 1969 257
National Health Service (NHS) 10, 254, 315, 319, 322
　and family planning 257
　success of 316
National Insurance Acts (UK and Northern Ireland) 316
National Insurance (Industrial Injuries) Act (Northern Ireland) 316
national school system 8, 213–15
national sports stadium, proposed sites for 272–3
National Union of Clerks (NUC) 205
Neill, Joyce 255
neutrality of Eire during the Second World War 241
Nevin, James 253
New Industries (Development) Act (Northern Ireland) 190
New Ireland Forum 334
New Light Presbyterianism 230
'New Lights' 40
New Magazine 54
New Model Army 35
Newry 123, 124 *table*, 128, 131, 165, 200
　urban hierarchy in 1901 128 *table*
Newry canal 24
Newtownards, County Down 128 *table*, 129
New University of Ulster 223, 224
New Zealand 141, 150, 153, 154, 155, 156
Nicholson, Jim 289
Nicolson, William 79
NIHE (Northern Ireland Housing Executive) 320, 322
Nine Years War 141
Nixon, Robert 319
non-denominational schools 212
non-marriage 67
North Down Cricket Club 263
Northern Bank 184, 187
Northern Cricket Union 263
Northern Ireland
　cricket in 263
　death rates, 1922–99 312 *table*
　death rates from cancer 313 *table*
　death rates from heart disease 313 *table*
　death rates from tuberculosis between 1926 and 1960 313 *table*

Northern Ireland (*cont.*)
  GDP per capita 292 *table*
  infant mortality rates 312 *table*
  insured workforce from 1920s to 1930s 208, 209 *table*
  life expectancy 314 *table*
  links with BRIC (Brazil, Russia, India and China) 305
  missed opportunities for new industries 294–5
  modernization 1952–72 317–20
  modernization 1973–98 320–3
  strengths and weaknesses of the economy in the early 21st century 304–6
  unemployment 1923–1980 314 *table*
  see also Ulster
Northern Ireland Abortion Campaign 258
Northern Ireland Agricultural Marketing Act 281
Northern Ireland Agricultural Producers' Association (NIAPA) 289
Northern Ireland Assembly 334
Northern Ireland Central Services Agency for Health 322
Northern Ireland Civil Rights Association (NICRA) 326, 327
Northern Ireland Education Order 1993 225
Northern Ireland Family Planning Association (NIFPA) 255, 256, 257
Northern Ireland Hospital Authority 315
Northern Ireland Housing Executive (NIHE) 320, 322
Northern Ireland Housing Trust (NIHT) 317
Northern Ireland Labour Party (NILP) 200
Northern Ireland Parliament 11
Northern Ireland Public Service Alliance (NIPSA) 303
Northern Ireland Society for Constructive Birth Control 255
Northern Ireland Staff Council for the Health and Social Services 322
North of Ireland Cricket Club 263
North/South Ministerial Council 338
North/South Ministerial Council (NSMC) 289
North West Cricket Union 263

Oakboy disturbances 100
Oath of Supremacy 122, 123
oatmeal 62, 167
oats 62, 64, 161, 166 *table*, 172, 277
O'Brien, Niall 262
O'Brien, William 237
O'Cahan, Donal Ballagh 44
O'Connell, Daniel 213
O'Connell, Peter 87
O'Connor, Emmet 199
O'Doherty, Rosa 43, 44–5, 55
O'Donnell, Hugh 46
O'Donnell, Hugh Roe 44, 46

O'Donnell, Mary 44
O'Donnell, Nuala 43
O'Donnell, Rory 43
O'Donnells of west Ulster 13
O'Dowd, Mary 4
O'Dwyer, Michael 262
Offences Against the Person Act 1861 258
oil crises 297
'Old Lights' 40
Olympic Games 271
O'Neill, Catherine 46
O'Neill family 13
O'Neill, Hugh 27, 43
O'Neill, Martin 270
O'Neill, Michelle 289
O'Neill, Molly 49
O'Neill, Owen Roe 33, 34, 35, 55
O'Neill, Róise 44
O'Neill, Sir Phelim 29, 32, 33, 35, 46
O'Neill, Terence 222, 296, 326, 328, 329
Open University 224
Orange Order 4, 41, 120, 155, 234
  growth in 1879 235
  suppression in 1836 243
Orange processions 243
Ordnance Survey Memoirs 1830s 161
O'Reilly, Sir Philip MacHugh 35
Osborne, Henry 154
Oulton, Rev. Richard 171
'Outdoor Relief Strike' 210

Paisley, Reverend Ian 258 n.76, 289, 327, 331, 332–3, 337, 338
Parker, Dehra 319
Parnell, Charles Stewart 175
Parsons, William 14
partition 156
  effect on Gaelic games 267
Party Emblems Act 100
Party Processions Act 1850 100, 104, 230, 234, 235
patriarchy 47–50
peace and reconciliation movements 138
Peace Preservation Force 93
peace process 335–9
peace walls 339
Peep O'Day Boys 96
Penal Laws 39, 213
penance 74
pensions 310
People's Democracy (PD) 328
Philbin, Bishop William 223
Phillips, Sir Thomas 101
Picture Post 242
pigs 162–3, 166 *table*, 277
Pigs Marketing Board 287
Pirrie, William James 182, 183, 204
plantation 142
  problems of 13–16

and theories of urbanization 122–8
  of Ulster 3
plantation towns 122
Plunkett, Oliver 13, 77
poets in south Armagh 107
Police authorities 127
Police Service of Northern Ireland (PSNI)
  268, 338
policing 92–4
  density of policing in Ulster, Munster,
    Connaught and Leinster 94 table
politics and society, 1800–1960 228–44
politics, since 1960 325–40
Pollard, Sidney 2
Pollock, Grace 251
Pollock, Hugh 279, 310
Poor Inquiry 1836 170
poor house 23
Poor Law 134, 169, 311
Popery Acts 1704 and 1708 80
popular culture 5, 106–20
  continuities and change in 118–20
Popular Culture in Early Modern Europe
  (Burke) 107
population
  in 1841–1851 232
  in 1911 308–9
  population change between 1600 and
    1914 58
  population loss between 1831 and 1891 146
  of Ulster in the early 1800s 93, 94 table
population decline 72
population density 64
population growth 61
population movements, *see* migration
pork 166 table
Portadown, County Armagh 128, 128 table, 133,
  136, 206
Post-War Planning Committee 315
potato 62–3, 65 n.29, 277
potato blight 172
potato crop failures 170–3
poverty 318
Powell, Enoch 332
Powis Commission 217
prayer meetings 85
pregnancy outside marriage 247
premarital sex 51, 52
Presbyterian General Assembly 225
Presbyterianism, pastoral and moral reform 83
Presbyterians 5, 22, 39, 51, 77–8, 230
  at the beginning of the 20th century 87
  Common Sense philosophy 83
  national schools 214–15
  planting of Scots Presbyterians in Antrim and
    Down 142
  population of 71
  and the Test Acts 145
  wakes 112, 115
Presbyterian Ulster Female Penitentiary 249

primogeniture 48
Pringle, Charles 154
Prior, James 334
privatization 298
Privy Council 145
Productivity Council 301
proportional representation 240
prostitution 248, 249
Protestantism 51
Protestants 5, 8, 78
  family size 247
  population in County Fermanagh 70 n.46
  population of 70
  share of the Ulster population between 1630
    and 1911 71 table
  support of union of Britain and Ireland 198
  wakes 112
Provisional IRA (PIRA) 329, 333
public houses 119
public sector employment 300, 322
Pym, John 30–1
Pynaar's Survey of 1619 123

Quakers 51, 52
Queen's College, Belfast 223
Queen's University, Belfast 223
  Faculty of Agriculture 280
Queen v McKenna case 101
Quigley Report 296

R&D expenditure 305
railway system 184, **186**
railway workers 207
rainfall 161
rates 128, 132
Reade, R. H. 180
reading 113
reading societies 116–17
re-armament 190, 192, 193
Rebbeck, Frederick 191
rebellions
  1641 3, 5, 17, 29–32
  1798 4, 41
Redmond, John 237, 239, 263
Redmond, Willie 263
Rees, Merlyn 331, 332
Reformation 4, 74
Reformed Presbyterians 79
regional council areas 134
religion 50–3
  religious balance in employment 321
  religious structure at the beginning of the
    20th century 87
  and society, 1600–1914 74–89
religious conversions 69
religious persecution 5
religious practice 74
remoteness grant 286
Renfrew, Scotland 150
Report of the (Cameron) Commission 329

Index

Republic of Ireland 297
   death rates, 1922–99 312 *table*
   death rates from cancer 313 *table*
   death rates from heart disease 313 *table*
   death rates from tuberculosis between 1926 and 1960 313 *table*
   infant mortality rates 312 *table*
resident magistrates (RMs) 102
Restoration land settlement 20
retail industry 207
Robinson, Peter 226, 338
Rodgers, Brid 289
Rowan, Andrew 19
Royal Belfast Academical Institution 216, 223, 264
Royal Hibernian Military School 271
Royal Irish Constabulary (RIC) 132, 266
royal schools 212
Royal Ulster Constabulary (RUC) 266, 268, 329, 332
Ruane, Caitríona 226, 227
rugby 264–5
rugby union 267
rural development programmes 288
rural economic development 275
rural economy 7, 160–76
rural industry 160
Russell, T. W. 237

sacramental test 78
St Columba's College 262
St John's Eve 110
St Johnston cricket club 263
St Mary's College 223
saints feast days 111
salt beef 166 *table*
salt pork 166 *table*
Saville Inquiry 340
Schomberg, Duke de 38
school books 54
schools 53–5, 221–2
   Gaelic Football 267
   hockey in 264
   rugby 264
   see also education
Schools's Cup 264, 267
Scotland 1
   death rates, 1922–99 312 *table*
   death rates from cancer 313 *table*
   death rates from heart disease 313 *table*
   death rates from tuberculosis between 1926 and 1960 313 *table*
   infant mortality rates 312 *table*
   migration from Ulster to 146, 147
   Scots-born Belfast residents 1841–1911 152 *table*
Scots language 107
Scots, religious culture of 75–6
Scott Robertson, James 283
SDLP (Social Democratic and Labour Party) 329, 333, 335

Seceders 79, 80
secondary schools 221
Second Reformation 88, 230
Second World War 241–3, 282–4
   neutrality of Eire during the 241
   and the welfare state 1939–51 315–17
sectarian conflict 5, 93–4, 96, 103, 135–6, 233
   economic growth and 295–6
   sport and 271–4
   and urban planning 137
   see also conflict; Troubles
Seed Potato Marketing Board 287
servitors 143
sex education 258
sex outside marriage 257
sexuality 245
Shankill 137
sheep 161
Shelbourne 264
sheriffs 92
Sherwood Foresters 264
Shipboy, Elizabeth 49, 50
Shipboy, James 49–50
Shipboy, Robert 49
shipbuilding 129, 150, 182–3, 189, 191, 294
   female workers in 205
   labour conditions 200–5
   wages of engineering workers 201 *table*
shirt manufacturing 168, 206, 208
Short and Harland 192
single mothers 248
Sinn Féin 226, 240, 333, 334, 338, 339
   and the 1918 general election 239
   and the peace process 336, 337
   sharing government with the DUP 11
Sinnott, Richard 147
Slevin, Larry 266
Sligo, County 25, 40, 163
Sloan, T. H. 199
Smith, Sir Thomas 122
smoking 319
soccer 268, 270
Social Democratic and Labour Party (SDLP) 329, 333, 335
social policy, and social change since 1914 10, 308–24
social security system 318
Social Services Agreement 316, 318
social structure 163–5
social welfare 310
Society for Promoting Knowledge 127
Society of Friends/Quakers 51, 52
Society of United Irishmen 41
Southern Ireland, *see* Republic of Ireland
spectator sports 119
Spender, Sir Wilfrid 279, 310
sport 9
   in the 19th and 20th centuries 260–74
   development of foreign games 263–5

and identity 269–71
and sectarianism 271–4
sports museums 273
standards of living 322
Stanley, Edward 213, 214
Stewart, A. T. Q. 1
Stewart, Sir Robert 32, 33, 34, 35
Stewart, Sir William 32, 34
stipendiary magistrates 102
Stirling, Scotland 150
stockbroking 187
stock exchange 187
Strabane, County Tyrone 20, 165
Strachan, William 209
Stranmillis College 223
strike activity 303–4
Struel Wells, County Down 116
Sunday services 111
Synod of Ulster 82, 83

Talbot, Richard 37
Taylor, John 286
teacher training 223
technical intermediate schools 221–2
telephones 318
televisions 318
temperance movement 117
tenant farmers 164, 173–5, 233
tenant right 150, 151
tenants 26
Tennent, Anne 55
Tennent, Eliza 55
Tennent, John 55
Tennent, William 55
Test Acts 145
textile industry 129, 168, 197
before the first world war 177–81
labour conditions in 205–8
textile machine makers 193
Textile Operatives Union of Ireland 206
thatched houses 128
Thatcher, Margaret 333–4, 335
tillage farming 64, 172–3, 284 *table*
Tillie and Henderson 208
Tipperary, County 262
tobacco industry 319
towns
refuge and shelter provision 123
shape of 125
Townshend, Peter 318
Towns Improvement (Ireland) Act 1854 130, 248
tractors 318
trade
before the Great Famine 165–70
Restoration Ulster trade boom 20
Trade Disputes and Trade Unions Act 1927 301
trade unions 7, 196–7, 210, 298
organization in Ulster 198

during and after the Second World War 302, 303
transport industry, labour in 206–7
Trimble, David 337, 338
Trinity College Dublin 266
Troubles 11n, 321, 323, 328, 339
Trustee Savings Bank 127
Trustees of the Hempen and Flaxen Manufacturers of Ireland (Linen Board) 178
tuberculosis 206, 311, 313 *table*, 319
Tyrone, County
emigration 1851–1911 151 *table*
female majority in 245
numbers of settlers and native Irish population 15
permanent celibacy among females and males in 1841 and 1911 68 *table*
rates of prosecution in 1884–90 99 *table*
Tyrone-born people in England and Wales in 1881 **149**
weavers in 197

Ulster
1600–1780 12–26
in the 1690s 21
in 17th century 141–4
in the 1960s 10, 325–40
after the Act of Union 228–32
adult male settler population in 1659 18
age at marriage for females and males 1841 and 1911 60 *table*
clerical residence in the 1800s 84
conflict in the 18th century 39–41
economy 2
indictable offences before the courts 99 *table*
internal migration in the 19th century 146–50
links with the rest of Ireland 188
in the mid-19th century (1850 to mid-1870s) 232–5
mortality during the Great Famine 171–2
as a patriarchial society 47–50
policing in 1832–52 94 *table*
population 1600–1911 **59**
population between 1600 and 1914 58–67
population in the early 1800s 93
post-Famine emigration in 151 *table*
rates of prosecution in 99 *table*
recovery in the 1750s 24–5
reported homicides 1866–92 98 *table*
share of Irish agricultural exports 1783–87 166 *table*
ties with Scotland 1
urban hierarchy in 1659 124 *table*
war in the 1640s and its aftermath 32–6
and the Williamite war 36–8
see also Northern Ireland
Ulster: An Illustrated History (Beckett) 27
Ulster army 32–3

Ulster Custom 174, 233
Ulster Defence Association (UDA) 329
Ulster Defence Regiment (UDR) 332
Ulster Farmers' Union (UFU) 279, 282, 288
Ulster Industries Development Association 190
Ulster Liberal Unionist 237
Ulster Magdalen asylum 249
Ulster nationalism 238
Ulster Plantation 6, 27–9
  native Irish under 28
  settlers 15
Ulster plantation, conditions of 14
Ulster Polytechnic 224
Ulster Rising 1641 143
Ulster rugby team 265
Ulster Sports Exhibition 260
Ulster Sports Museum Association 260
Ulster Tenant League 96
Ulster Unionism 238
Ulster Unionist Council 236
Ulster Unionist Labour Association (UULA) 199–200
Ulster Unionist Party (UUP) 199, 326, 330, 337, 338
Ulster Unionists, response to Home Rule in 1886 236
Ulster Volunteer Force (UVF) 236, 329
Ulster Workers' Council (UWC) 330
unemployment 192, 194, 208–9, 302, 310, 321
  between 1923 and 1980 314 *table*
  in 1925 189
  in the 1930s 190, 210
  between 1950 and 2009 291, 292 *table*
  in 1951 318
  after 1998 298–9
  de-industrialization and 137
  as a proportion of the civil labour force 293 *table*
  see also employment
Unionist rule, and its consequences 240–1
Unionists, peace process and 337
unions, factory-based unions 196
United Education Committee (UEC) 220
United Irish League 87
United Irishmen 4, 55, 231
United Irishwomen 55–6
United Ulster Unionist Council (UUUC) 330, 331, 332
university education 223–4
urban governance 130, 132
urbanization in Ulster 6, 72, 121–39
  in 20th century 133–8
  industrialization 128–33
  plantation and theories of 122–8
  urban hierarchy in 1901 128 *table*
urban planning 138
UUP (Ulster Unionist Party) 199, 326, 330, 337, 338
UUUC (United Ulster Unionist Council) 330, 331, 332

Vanguard Unionist Progressive Party (VUPP) 331
Varney Reports 304, 306
Volunteer movement 127

wages
  in 1885 130
  of engineering workers 201 *table*
  public sector 300
  of unskilled workers 204
wakes 112, 115
Wales
  death rates, 1922–99 312 *table*
  death rates from cancer 313 *table*
  death rates from heart disease 313 *table*
  death rates from tuberculosis between 1926 and 1960 313 *table*
  infant mortality rates 312 *table*
  migration of Ulster-born people in 1881 in **148, 149**
Warrenpoint, County Down 127, 131
Watson, Peggy 49
weavers 196, 197
Weber, Max 122
welfare state 318
  Second World War and 315–17
Wentworth, Thomas 30, 31, 76
Wesley, John 52–3, 80
West Belfast 137
West Britonism 232
West, Harry 280, 288, 332
'Westlink' motorway 137
Westmeath, County 262
wheat 161
Whiteboy Act 1766 100
Whitelaw, William 287
White Star Line 182
widows' and orphans' pensions 310
William III 144
Williamite wars 3, 21, 36–8, 91, 143
William of Orange 37, 38, 39, 78
Wilson, Harold 327, 332
Wilson Report 294 n.12
Wolff, Gustav 182
Wollstonecraft, Mary 56
women 8–9, 129–30
  celibacy rate 246
  employment of 322
  family and sexuality 245
  in 'making-up' trades 207
  in politics 55–6
  population 245
  in religion 52–3
  right to control property under Gaelic and English common law 45
  role on a planter estate 46–7
  in shirt manufacturing 184
  status of 4, 56
  supply of women workers during the Second World War 158

in Ulster, 1600–1800 43–57
  working in shipbuilding industry 205
Women's Trade Union League 206
Wooden Bridge, Magilligan, County
  Londonderry 110
work, and leisure 109–13
workhouses 169
working class 119, 195, 197–8

Workman Clark
  182, 189, 209
Workmen's Compensation Acts (Northern
  Ireland) 316
Wyndham, George 175
Wyndham Land Act 1903 175

Young, Arthur 160, 168